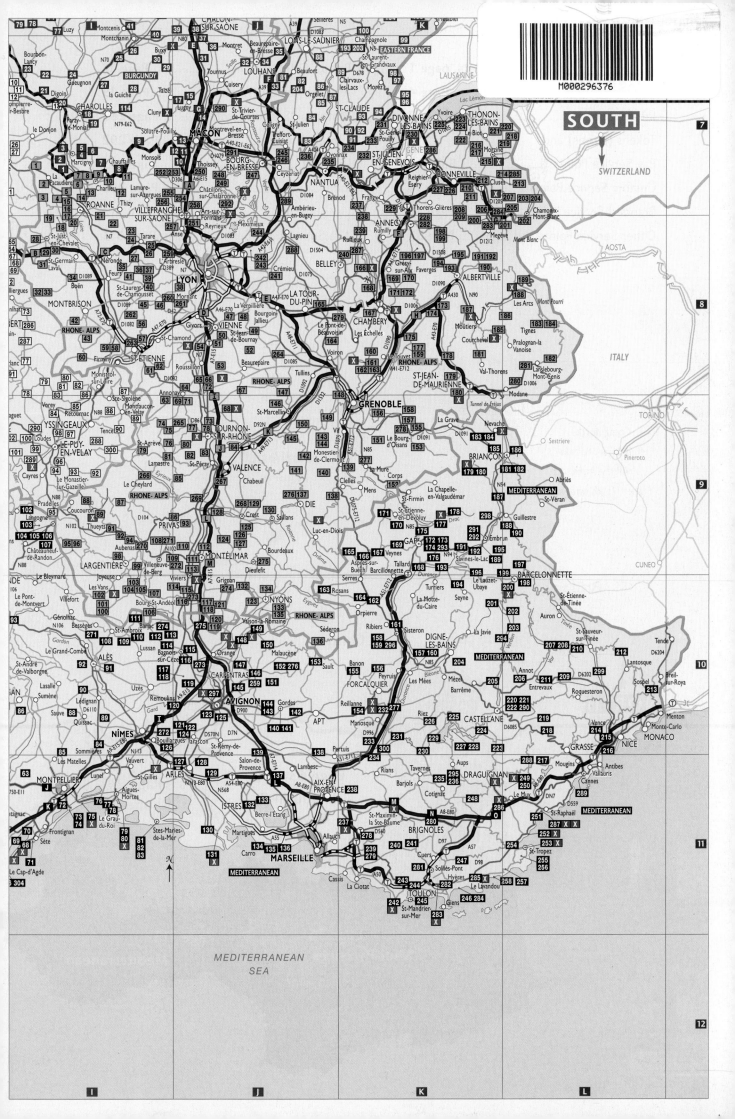

CONTENTS

Going north?
Remember to take
All the Aires
France North with you

Northern France

Normandy

Brittany

Champagne

Eastern France

Pays de Loire

Centre

Burgundy

NORTH

SOUTH

Page 203
Poitou

Page 63
Limousin &
Auvergne

Page 241
Rhone-Alps

Page 19
Atlantic

Page 161
Midi-Pyrenees

Page 113
Mediterranean

Experience the Freedom of France

French Aires enable you to make the most of your adventures because you can travel all over France, all year around, day or night, and never go through the rigmarole of booking in. This carefree travel is enjoyed by hundreds of thousands of motorhomers from all over the world, so it pays to have the best information available.

This definitive guide of French Aires shows and tells you about all of the best and most popular motorhome stopovers. We also reveal undiscovered gems, as well as places to avoid. Our inspectors are the most experienced in the world. Their professional photos and reviews provide you with a personal insight that you cannot find anywhere else; you may feel that you have had a vicarious visit before you arrive.

Every Aire, Everywhere

These unparalleled guidebooks are the most comprehensive, accurate and data-rich in any language.

Half of the Aires featured in the second edition volumes were inspected by the editors, Meli and Chris, from April 2016 to February 2017. They scrutinised 1,760 in total. John and Janet Watts inspected an additional 358 between editions, for which we are extremely grateful. In total, 2,118 Aires were professionally inspected including 619 new Aires for you to discover for yourself. Customer submissions updated hundreds more Aires.

First published in Great Britain by Vicarious Books LLP, 2007. This edition published April 2017.
© Vicarious Media Ltd 2017.
Copyright © text Vicarious Media Ltd. All rights reserved.
Copyright © photographs Vicarious Media Ltd unless otherwise stated.
ISBN: 978-1-910664-09-4

Editorial Team, Vicarious Media, Unit 1, North Close Business Centre, Folkestone, CT20 3UH. Tel: 0131 2083333
Chief Editor: Meli George
Associate Editor: Chris Doree
Managing Editor: Pami Hoggatt
Editorial Assistant: Sam Hogbin
Design and Artwork: Chris Gladman Design

Page 12. Useful information.

Before you depart read the introduction.

Avant votre départ, lisez l'introduction.

Lesen Sie die Einführung, bevor Sie abfahren.

Prima di partire leggi l'introduzione.

Antes de partir, lea la introducción.

Outer cover flaps.
Key to symbols.
l'explication des symbols.
Erklärung der Symbole.
Spiegazione dei simboli.
Explicación de los símbolos.

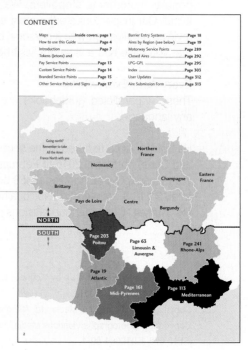

CONTENTS

Page 2. Colour-coded regional overview map with page numbers.

Seite 2. Carte avec couleurs codées régions et numéros de page.

Seite 2. Karte mit farbcodierten Regionen und Seitenzahlen.

Pagina 2. Mappa con colori codificati regioni e numeri di pagina.

Página 2. Mapa con códigos de color de las regiones y números de página.

Step by step

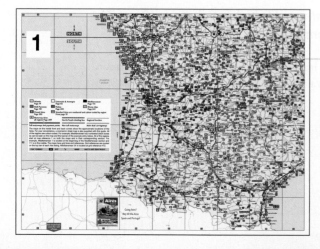

Inside covers. Maps colour-coded by region. All Aires numbered 1-2-3... in each region.

Cartes codées par couleur selon la région. Toutes les aire de service numérotées 1-2-3... dans chaque région.

Karten farblich nach Regionen codiert. Alle stellplätze nummeriert 1-2-3... in jeder Region.

Mappe a colori di un codice regionale. Tutti le aree di sosta numerati 1-2-3... in ciascuna regione.

Mapas codificados por color según la región. Todos área de servicio numerados 1-2-3... en cada región.

Page 19-288. Colour coded chapters by region.
All regions use map numbers 1-2-3… Service Points
only at end of chapter.

Code couleur chapitres par région. Toutes les
régions utilisent des numéros de carte 1-2-3…

Farbcodierte Kapiteln nach Region. Alle Regionen
verwenden Zahlen auf der karte 1-2-3…

Codice colore capitoli per regione. Tutte le regioni
usare i numeri 1-2-3…

Código de colores capítulos según la región. Todas
las regiones utilizar los números del mapa 1-2-3…

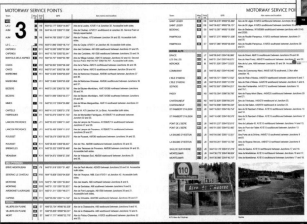

**Page 289-291. Autoroute Aires with motorhome
Service Points. Identified with letters on the maps.**

**Autoroute aires de services avec borne camping car
identifié avec lettres sur les cartes.**

**Autoroute Service-Bereich mit Wohnmobil
Abwasserentsorgung auf der Karte identifiziert mit
Buchstaben.**

**Autoroute area diservizio con servizi igienico-sanitari
per camper identificato con lettere sulle mappe.**

**Autoroute área de servicio con saneamiento de
autocaravanas identificado con letras en los mapas.**

Page 292-294. Closed Aires [X] on maps.
Aires de services fermé [X] sur les cartes.
Wohnmobilstellplätze geschlossen [X] auf der Karte.
Aree di sosta chiuso [X] sulle mappe.
Area para autocaravan cerrado [X] en los mapas.

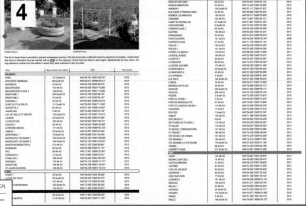

Page 295-302. Fuel stations with LPG by region.
Stations d'essence au GPL par region.
Tankstellen mit Flüssiggas nach Region.
Stazioni di servizio con GPL per regione.
Estaciones de combustible con GLP por región.

Page 303-311. Alphabetical index by town name.
Index alphabétique par nom de ville.
Alphabetischer Index nach Ort Name.
Indice alfabetico per nome paese.
Indice alfabético por nombre de ciudad.

Explanation of an entry

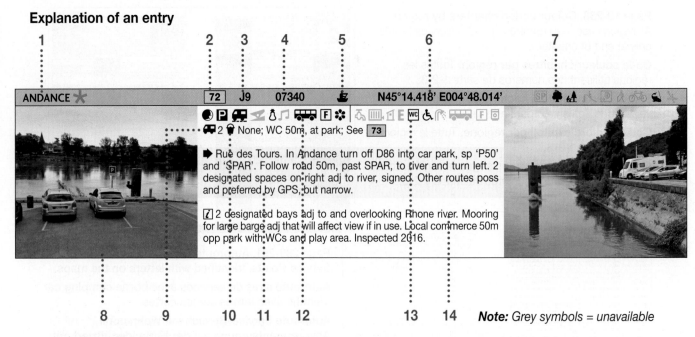

Note: *Grey symbols = unavailable*

1 Town Name.

✳ The inspectors rate the Aire or location to be better than most. Often the view or surrounding area is of interest.

2 Map number.

3 Map grid reference.

4 Postcode. Further information on page 9.

5 Surroundings. Key on cover flaps.

6 GPS coordinates. Further information on page 9.

7 Local amenities, see cover flaps for key.

8 Photographs of Aire.

9 🚐 Number of parking spaces; Cost per night; Time limit.

10 🛠 Service Point type; Payment type if not cash; Cost.

11 Directions. Further information on page 9.

12 Parking details, see cover flaps for key.

13 Service Point details. Key on cover flaps.

14 Description of Aire and surrounding area.

Abbreviations and Glossary of Terms

Adj	Adjacent.
Alt	Altitude in metres, if over 800m.
Beau Village	Designated as one of the most beautiful. villages in France www.les-plus-beaux-villages-de-france.org/en.
CC	Credit card.
CL style	Small grass parking area.
Commerce	
Local commerce	One or more: bar, baker, restaurant, convenience store, hair dresser.
Resort commerce	Big winter skiing and/or summer beach or walking commerce.
Small town commerce	As above plus a mini market and bank.
Tourist commerce	Seasonal restaurants, activities and commerce.
Town commerce	Big enough to have a wedding dress shop.
Commercial Aire	Set up for profit, often pay at barrier or Service Point.
Dead quiet	Peaceful location adj to cemetery.
Grand Site	Landscapes protected because of their artistic, historic, legendary or picturesque character.
Grass parking	Will not be marked as open all year, but can be used whenever conditions allow.
Hell's bells	Especially noisy church bells that chime all night or go like the clappers at 6am.
HGV	Heavy goods vehicle.
Inc	Included in price.

Inside barrier	Service Point behind barrier at pay Aire. Access may be free or reduced cost for short duration.
May feel isolated if alone	Normally locations without habitation nearby, but don't lose sleep over it.
Open access	No fence or barrier.
Opp	Opposite.
Oversubscribed	Aire unlikely to have space.
Popular	Aire likely to be busy.
Poss	Possible.
pp	Per person.
Private Aire	Run by an individual, often at home or business.
Signed	Aire signed with symbol or text.
Sp	Signposted 'Town name'.
Space likely	Aires always likely to have space.
'text'	Extracts from signs.
TO	Tourist Office.
Tolerated	Unofficial motorhome parking.
Trucking hell	Noisy HGV's hurtling past day and night.
Inspected	Inspected by Vicarious Media staff.
Visited	Customer submission.
Submitted	Owner supplied information.
Updated	Previously inspected but updated by customer.

Every Aire, Everywhere
This definitive guidebook is the most comprehensive, accurate and data rich in any language. All of the Aires featured in this guide have been inspected and 64 percent have been inspected specifically for this edition; in figures it reads 1,801 total Aires, of which 834 were reinspected and 321 new Aires were discovered.

Easy come, easy go
Aires provide motorhome travellers with the freedom to come and go as they please. Aires do not have a reception, so you cannot reserve a space and there is no booking in. Most Aires should be considered a convenient en-route stopover rather than a holiday destination. This does not mean to say that you cannot have a motorhome holiday when stopping at Aires, just that you should be motorhoming from place to place.

What are Aires and what does Aire mean?
The English translation of 'Aire' is 'area', and many French facilities have 'Aire' in their name. The full title for French motorhome Aires is 'Aire de service/stationnement pour Camping Car', which translates to 'Service area/parking for motorhomes' and are referred to as Aires in this publication. Aires are frequently signed with the motorhome service point symbol, and it is common for these signs to also refer to parking. A maximum of 48 hours parking is the national standard at Aires and this is assumed unless local signs or the articles in Mairie regulations state otherwise. Facilities differ significantly, but normally include a Service Point for water collection and disposal of waste fluids.

Motorway Aires. Do no park overnight at motorway service stations and rest areas!
French motorway services are also named "Aire 'something or other'". Motorhomes, HGVs and cars are frequently broken into at motorway rest areas. Often the occupants of motorhomes are asleep during the burglary; surely a situation you would not want to be in. For completeness, a list of motorway services with Service Points has been provided at the back of the guide.

Who can use Aires?
French traffic law forbids caravans and tents from using the Aires in this guide. The law permits motorhome users to park and to cook, eat and sleep within the confines of their vehicle. This law actually enabled Aires to develop in the first place. French law does not permit camping activities at Aires, such as winding out awnings or putting out tables and chairs. We see countless examples of the rules being broken and often by French nationals, many of whom seem completely unaware of the written rules and unwritten etiquette. Thus, following their example may be unwise. Camping is permitted at all 9,200 French campsites.

Operation evasion

Over the past 12 years there has been a rapid increase in the number of motorhomes on French roads, and 95 per cent of them are local camping cars. We have observed that, like birds of a feather, motorhomers flock together. For example, French motorhomers rarely venture off the main trunking routes. Consequently, overcrowding can occur at any Aire which is a short distance from a main road and is likely at those that are also in a quiet or pleasant location. Motorhomers from all nations appear compelled to drive to the coast and the sheer number of motorhomes has forced coastal authorities to put measures in place to manage parking. Motorhome parking is often controlled at well-known tourist attractions, lakes, rivers and canals. With control comes cost, so expect to pay if you want to stopover in popular areas. Freedom seekers should plan to end their day off the beaten track. We recommend that you travel with regional guidebooks, such as the Michelin green guides, in order to make the most of your visits to the lesser-known tourist attractions and villages.

Offsite parking

Some of the Aires in this guide are Service Points only without any parking. These are provided so that motorhomers can discharge waste responsibly. Motorhoming changed in France during 2012; this was not due to a change in the law but a change in attitude. As explained above, French law permits offsite parking and French motorhomers embraced this freedom. However, we have noticed that most French motorhomers were parking overnight at official places. Presumably they realised that because they congregate en masse they were spoiling it for themselves. We believe that you should continue to enjoy offsite parking, but make sure you are away from the popular motorhome destinations.

Vicarious Media champions responsible tourism

Motorhoming is booming in France and more than 600 new Aires have opened in the past two years. Some act as control measures, but many more were paid for by the local community in the hope that extra tourism would help to keep the local shops, restaurants or fuel stations open. Over the past ten years motorhomes have become much bigger, typically occupying 50 per cent more space. Bear this in mind when you park during siesta in a sleepy town square or in an empty Aire, because you are unlikely to remain alone. When parking somewhere for free you should at least try to spend what you are saving in camping fees. We would all like to see the Aires network continue to grow and this will happen if motorhomers are perceived as valuable visitors.

We can all be valued visitors if we are RESPONSIBLE and:

R espect the environment
E lect to use un-crowded Aires
S pend locally
P ark sensibly
O rganise your recycling
N o camping
S ave water
I mpeccable behaviour
B e quiet
L eave before you outstay your welcome
E valuate your impact

Finding Aires

Forward planning is advised, especially if you intend to drive late into the night. Select an area where there are two or more Aires nearby because Aires can be full, occupied by the funfair, or simply closed for maintenance. Vicarious Media is not responsible for any Aires. This book is a guide only and was correct at the time of going to press. Should you have any complaints about an Aire or wish to know why an Aire has closed, please speak to the local Mairie and remember to let us know about any changes.

Directions: The directions are written to assist you with map navigation. As far as is practical, the simplest route, that is free of height and weight restrictions, has been selected. Where possible, you should follow signs and be aware of any obstacles or diversions.

GPS navigation: The GPS coordinates provided in this guide were taken on site and it should be possible to drive to the spot where they were taken. However, this does not mean to say that your navigator will get you there. Check the directions against your printed map and look at the suggested route on your navigator. Should you not be able to use the coordinates, be aware that French postcodes cover at least a 10km radius; therefore you will need to input the town and street, too.

Signs: When provided, it is advisable to follow the motorhome symbols to the Aire. Signs and symbols differ widely, so you will need to look carefully. Unfortunately, campsites have taken to displaying motorhome Aire symbols on their direction and advertising signs. Often there is no indication that the signs are referring to campsite facilities. It is safe to assume that all campsites have sanitary facilities and this deception is unwelcome. Please do not submit campsite details to us unless the Service Point is in an accessible location outside of the campsite.

Parking

Aires operate on a first come, first served basis. Generally they are unsupervised, thus it is not possible to reserve a space. The available parking may be impractical for many reasons and parking your motorhome may make the situation worse, so always consider others first. Use bays when provided. In unmarked parking areas it is normal to park close to your neighbour when necessary, so try to leave enough space for another motorhome to slot in if the need arises. Everybody enjoys a view, so share them as much as possible. Never park overnight on the Service Point or obstruct roadways.

Large motorhomes (RVs) >7.5m: Many Aires have been designed to accommodate motorhomes up to 7m long. The highlighted coach symbols 🚌 identify Aires where the inspectors believe it should be possible for motorhomes over 7.5m to access the parking. In many cases, parking large motorhomes is only possible when there are few or no other motorhomes. Remember to put your responsible tourist hat on when you are making parking decisions. During busy periods Service Point access may not be possible. There are very few Service Points suitable for emptying fixed tank toilet systems. We strongly recommend you have a macerator fitted and travel with a long length of pipe.

Using Aires all year: Aires make suitable night stops all year round and, unlike campsites, few close for the winter. Most Aires have a hard surface. Grass covered parking areas often have compacted gravel underneath. The open all year ❁ symbol is not highlighted on grass parking, but it can usually be accessed as long as weather conditions allow. Drinking water is frequently turned off during the winter to prevent frost damage; 'Hors Gel' signs indicate this, whereas 'Hors Service' indicates out of order. Flot Bleu Euro and Pacific Service Points normally stay in service all year because they are heated and insulated. Many of the Aires in this guide have been inspected during winter and the water was found to be on, unless otherwise stated. However, there is no guarantee that water will be on, so plan to visit several Service Points.

Time limits: Known time restrictions are provided in the listings. Many Aires restrict use to 48hrs, which is logical because it should be enough time to visit the local attractions. Aires not displaying time limits should be assumed to be 48hrs.

Service Points

There are several professionally manufactured Service Point brands. The most common are Euro Relais (Raclet) and Aire Services followed by Urba Flux, see page 15. Approximately half the Service Points in France are custom made, see page 14. Service Points normally facilitate three vital functions:

Drinking water: French tap water is very palatable, and consistent countrywide. Thoughtless users are known to contaminate taps when rinsing toilet cassettes. Using disinfectant wipes or spray before drawing water will improve hygiene. Taps are normally threaded to assist connection of hoses. Flot Bleu Euro and Pacific Service Points have all the facilities located in one enclosed space increasing the risk of cross contamination. In addition, we have found the drinking water hose down the toilet emptying point on several occasions, so consider disinfection essential.

Waste water: Drive over drains differ widely in construction. Typically a metal grid is set in concrete near to the Service Point. Some drains are so badly designed or located that it is necessary to use a length of flexible pipe to direct waste water accurately. Some Service Points do not have a drain, but it is often possible to direct a pipe to the toilet emptying point. Flot Bleu Euro and Pacific Service Points often have a short flexible pipe instead of a drive over drain.

Toilet cassette emptying: Cassette emptying points differ so widely you may have to think about it before you work out the correct place. It may be necessary to remove a grid. Some drains are too small, notably Aire Services, so do not rush this operation as spillage will occur. Often two taps are provided; as a general rule toilet rinsing taps are unthreaded. Euro Relais Service Points often have a toilet rinsing tap that will flow even if tokens are required for other services. We often see small amounts of toilet contents on grids. This is not deliberate but as a result of rinsing and assuming that the cassette has liquids only. Flot Bleu Euro and Pacific Service Points have to be unlocked before the toilet emptying point is accessible.

Left: Maintain a hygiene gap.

Who turned out the lights?

The illumination symbol ☪ is highlighted when the inspectors have seen light fittings. There is no guarantee that lights work and it has become common practice to turn the lights off during the middle of the night to save electricity.

Flot Bleu Electric

Electricity

Approximately half of the Service Points in France provide electricity, but unlimited (unmetered) electricity is uncommon at Aires. We have highlighted the electricity symbol **E** for every Aire that has an electricity supply, regardless of cost or duration. No further information is provided if the electricity supply is less than one hour. Aires that offer unlimited or practical electricity supplies have the details written in the further information of either the Service Point or the Parking.

Branded Service Points that charge for use, such as Aire Services or Euro Relais, normally have one or two electricity points. 55-60 minutes of electricity and 100 litres or 10 minutes of water is distributed upon payment, typically charging €2-€3.

Flot Bleu Service Points normally provide 20 minutes of 'environ', access to water and electricity. The least we have seen is 12 minutes supply. In addition, some brands produce electricity distribution bollards. Flot Bleu electricity bollards normally provide four hours of electricity per token and up to 12 hours of electricity can be paid for in one go. Token costs differ from Aire to Aire.

Should you be lucky enough to stay at an Aire with free electricity, you will be expected to share it with several motorhomes.

In recent years, there has been a growth in what we have named 'commercial Aires'. These Aires often include electricity in their nightly charge. Be aware that there may not be enough electricity points for the number of motorhomes staying. Approximately half the plug sockets we have tested have reverse polarity and an alarming amount had no earth. Our recommendation is if you must have electricity, then you should book into a campsite.

Tokens are called 'jetons' in French. Payment by jeton is dwindling, whereas payment by bank card is increasing. Typically Service Points requiring tokens, coins or credit cards dispense 10 minutes or about 100 litres of drinking water. When provided, electricity is normally available for one hour. Tokens are normally available from local commerce, especially boulangeries (bakers), bar tabacs, tourist offices, the Mairie (town hall) and campsites if adjacent. Tokens may be free, but typically cost €2-€3. Information panels or signs fixed to the Service Point normally indicate where tokens are available.

The main types of token are:

 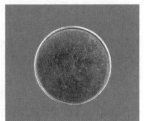

The front of the Flot Bleu token is branded. It is the size of the old £1 coin, but not as thick.

The Aire Services 3/3 token is the same both sides with 3 grooves on each. It is the same size as a 10p piece.

The front of the Euro Relais (ER) token is branded. It is slightly bigger than a 10p piece.

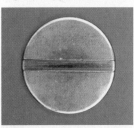 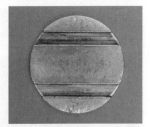

The 2/1 token has one groove on the front and 2 on the back. It is the size of a 2p piece.

Techno Money (TM) has a distinctive pattern on the front. It is the same size as a 10p piece.

Unusually expensive card payment.

CUSTOM SERVICE POINTS

Half of the Service Points in France have been custom-built by local craftsmen with inevitable differences in design and construction. Most are simple but durable and electricity is rarely provided. This has several benefits; they are rarely broken, they normally have a ground level drain, they don't require tokens and are normally free to use all year round. Sometimes the layout of a Service Point is confusing or a facility is a little way from where you expect it to be. Occasionally instructions state that cassettes should be emptied in the adjacent public toilet. However, we have seen more signs stating that cassettes must not be emptied in public toilets.

Push down hard on top of red tap.

Euro Relais and Raclet: Euro Relais and Raclet are the same. All Raclet units are at least 12 years old. Euro Relais has manufactured various sizes, but they are all basically the same. In general they are easy to use, but are often in a bad state of repair. Intentional damage is common on unsupervised units that take tokens or coins. Often there are two water taps. The one for toilet rinsing normally works without payment. The toilet tap is usually marked 'Eau non potable' for hygiene reasons, but it is in fact plumbed to the same supply. When tokens or payment is required, 100 litres of water and one hour of electricity is dispensed. A lift up cover at the base enables access to the toilet emptying chamber. The hole is big enough to lose the cap from your Thetford cassette.

Mini

Junior stainless steel

Maxi

Box

Aire Services 3000

Aire Services Plastic

Aire Services: The Aire Services brand of Service Point functions in much the same way as Euro Relais units, but is a little more confusing due to the press button operation. The robust stainless steel units are common and normally charge a fee. Credit card payment is the norm for new units. The plastic units are generally free, and thus are less likely to be damaged. Pay units generally have one or two CEE electricity points and all have fresh water and toilet rinsing taps. A small WC disposal drain is located at the front. Water is normally distributed for 10 minutes and electricity for 55 minutes. Waste water is usually disposed of in a separate drain.

Aire Services 7005

Aire Services 7010

BRANDED SERVICE POINTS

Urba Flux: Urba Flux Tall are becoming more common each year, especially for barrier entry or parking ticket payment. The Service Points are simple and robust units that distribute water and electricity. Toilet and waste water is usually disposed of in drains at the base. You will need a male adapter as seen in the photos.

Urba Flux

Tall

Barrier

Photo: John Watts

Male hozelock connector required

Photo: Ian & Janet Wallace

Inspection cover

Flot Bleu inside

Flot Bleu: There are several models in the range but only two designs. Mostly they are blue, but they can also be green, white or burgundy. Fontaine, Océane and Marine units have all the services fitted to the outside of the casing. Fontaine units are free, the others take payment by coin or token.

Euro, Pacific and Station Sanitaire have services located behind a narrow door on the left-hand side of the cabinet. These units are rarely free but are very robust and are likely to be in service during winter. Euro units always take bank card payment, the others will be coin or token. Sewage inspection covers are often located at the foot of the Euro/Pacific units, which is useful if you do not need water. These cabinets are also used to distribute tokens and operate barrier systems.

Electricity

Fontaine, Océane, Marine

Point Belle Eau

SOS

Bollard. These are old.

Signs

There are numerous signs which apply to motorhomes and should be adhered to.

Motorhomes are not allowed.

Designated parking, no unpacking.

Clearway except motorhomes.

Barrier entry systems

As previously discussed, it has become necessary to control motorhome parking at popular destinations. Local authorities have taken to installing barriered entries and, to a lesser extent, rising bollards at both existing and new Aires. We have frequently observed that entering and exiting is often slow or impossible. Our greatest concern is that there is no emergency override should a fire break out. We have also observed that controlled entry systems are often broken, left in the open position or removed within a year or two.

Flot Bleu sentries

Oh bollards

Credit card-operated barrier

PARKNIGHT barrier

Caumont sur Garonne

ATLANTIC

Soustons Plage

BUSSEROLLES

| 1 | F8 | 24360 | | N45°40.620' E000°38.577' | SP |

🚐 5 🛒 Euro Relais Junior; Token (2/1)

➡ D90. Just off D90 in centre of village adj to bar, signed.

ℹ Bar adj. Numerous walking trails from 5km. Pleasant spot away from the madding crowd. Reinspected 2013.

ST ESTEPHE

| 2 | F8 | 24360 | | N45°35.684' E000°40.447' | SP |

🚐 7; €5/night; Max 48hrs; Must depart by 8pm 🛒 Custom; By lake

➡ C201. In St Estèphe turn off D88 onto C201, sp 'Augignac' and 'Le Grand Étang'. Follow road to lake. Service Point on right adj to lake: N45°35.587' E000°40.340'. Parking further down road on right, past campsite, signed.

ℹ Pleasant designated parking amongst trees adj to large leisure lake. Motorhomes banned 8pm-8am at lake. Service Point has been relocated. Now adj to road and partially obstructed by boulders, access may be difficult for users of large motorhomes. Reinspected 2015.

ST FRONT LA RIVIERE

| 3 | F8 | 24300 | | N45°27.983' E000°43.450' | SP |

🚐 10; Max 72hrs; Apr-Oct 🛒 Euro Relais Junior; 2 unmetered CEE elec points

➡ D83. From south on D83 Aire is on left at picnic area approximately 500m past Le Caneau going towards Saint Front la Rivière, signed.

ℹ Pleasant Aire overlooking grassy picnic area. Nightingales can be heard at night. Local commerce 650m. Updated 2015.

ST JEAN DE COLE

| 4 | F8 | 24800 | | N45°25.185' E000°50.433' | SP |

🚐 5 🛒 Euro Relais Junior; Token (ER); €3

➡ Le Bourg. Turn off D707 south of village by Mairie, sp 'St Martin de Fs'. Turn left in 20m, just past tennis courts, signed.

ℹ Aire in small car park with pleasant rural views. Pretty Beau Village with tourist commerce 250m. Reinspected 2016.

LA COQUILLE

| 5 | F8 | 24450 | | N45°32.562' E000°58.689' | SP |

🚐 4; Very sloping 🛒 Euro Relais Mini; Landscaped; Risk of grounding

➡ Place St Jacques de Compostelle. From south on N21 turn 1st right after traffic lights into Place St Jacques de Compostelle. Drive past front of church and Service Point on right-hand side at bottom of car park.

ℹ Village with local commerce 100m. Very little level parking. Bells signal every quarter hour throughout day. Reinspected 2013.

JUMILHAC LE GRAND

| 6 | F8 | 24630 | | N45°29.525' E001°03.665' | SP |

🚐 2 at Service Point; Poss near château 🛒 Custom

➡ D78. From château in village take D78, sp 'Thiviers'. Service Point on the right in 100m.

ℹ Large château, cafés and TO in village. Limited parking at Service Point; poss to park near château, but this is very sloping. Reinspected 2016.

LANOUAILLE — 7 · F8 · 24270 · N45°23.533' E001°08.417'

🚐 5; Max 48hrs 🚰 Euro Relais Junior; 2 unmetered CEE elec points; 2 drive over drains

➡ D75. Exit village to east on D75, sp 'Pompadour' and signed. Aire 150m on left, signed.

ℹ Service Point in car park on edge of village; suitable for any unit configuration. A notice requests that only 3 motorhomes use elec at one time. Local commerce and TO 150m. Reinspected 2016.

SAVIGNAC LEDRIER — 8 · F8 · 24270 · (A) N45°21.849' E001°13.242'

🚐 (A) 15; (B) 7; Max 24hrs 🚰 (A) Euro Relais Junior; Token (ER); (B) None

➡ (A) Rue Simone Degreze. Turn off D75 onto D75e sp 'Savignac-Ledrier'. Follow sp 'Savignac Ledrier' into village and turn left, sp 'Pôle touristique' and signed. Aire on right. (B) N45°22.084' E001°12.831': D75e. As approach village turn left into lay-by on D75e before river bridge, sp 'Le Forge'. Parking allowed in lay-by, signed on info board.

ℹ (A) Large parking area with rural views. Suitable for any unit configuration; space likely. Tokens free from Restaurant des Forges, 100m. Just off village centre; local commerce 100m. (B) Lay-by parking under deciduous trees adj to forge, which is the local historical attraction. No view of river or forge, 300m. Inspected 2016.

Le Forge

HAUTEFORT — 9 · F8 · 24390 · ☼ · N45°15.607' E001°08.937'

🚐 5 🚰 Flot Bleu Océane

➡ Allées du Avril 1944, off D72. Drive into Hautefort on D62. Turn onto D72 just past château at square with TO, sp 'Flot Bleu'. Aire on left.

ℹ Service Point in small car park with WC and recycling. Town square with TO, small town commerce and old hospital adj. Views of Château de Hautefort from parking. Reinspected 2016.

EXCIDEUIL — 10 · F8 · 24160 · N45°20.157' E001°03.157'

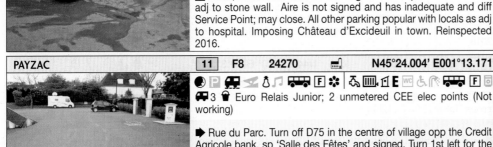

🚐 4; €3/night; Collected 🚰 Urba Flux; No drive over drain; 4 unmetered CEE elec points

➡ Allée André Maurois, off D705. Approach from Périgueux on D705. At the roundabout take 1st exit onto D705, sp 'Dussac'. Turn 1st right at statue of man. Aire in car park immediately on right.

ℹ Small, oversubscribed Aire backing onto small park. Service Point adj to stone wall. Aire is not signed and has inadequate and diff Service Point; may close. All other parking popular with locals as adj to hospital. Imposing Château d'Excideuil in town. Reinspected 2016.

PAYZAC — 11 · F8 · 24270 · N45°24.004' E001°13.171'

🚐 3 🚰 Euro Relais Junior; 2 unmetered CEE elec points (Not working)

➡ Rue du Parc. Turn off D75 in the centre of village opp the Credit Agricole bank, sp 'Salle des Fêtes' and signed. Turn 1st left for the Service Point which is located behind the Hôtel de Ville, signed.

ℹ Local commerce 100m. Children's play area and boules court on opp side of Salles des Fêtes. Large leisure lake with swimming and water sports 5km. www.payzac24.fr Reinspected 2015.

ANGOISSE — 12 · F8 · 24270 · N45°24.778' E001°10.072'

🚐 20; Max 48hrs 🚰 Custom

➡ D80e1. From either Angoisse or Payzac follow D80, sp 'Base de Loisirs de Roufflac'. Turn off D80 onto D80e1, sp 'Base de Loisirs de Roufflac'. Take 1st turning on left, signed. Service Point in far corner (looks like a bin), signed.

ℹ At leisure lake, 400m downhill, with swimming, drag water skiing and restaurant. May feel isolated out of season. Reinspected 2015.

AZERAT

| 13 | F9 | 24210 | | N45°08.970' E001°07.512' | SP |

🚐 10; €3/day inc service; Honesty box at Mairie 🛒 Custom; €3 inc overnight stay

➡ Turn off D6089 in Azerat towards the church, sp 'Mairie' and signed. Follow road to left around church and turn left past Mairie, sp 'Parking' and signed. Aire in car park beside/behind Mairie.

ℹ Aire located in a small, pleasant village away from main road noise. Views over tennis courts and swimming pool. Honesty box on Mairie wall. Reinspected 2016.

TERRASSON-LAVILLEDIEU

| 14 | F9 | 24120 | | N45°08.037' E001°18.429' | SP |

🚐 30; €6/night; Collected 🛒 Euro Relais Mini (In barn); €2; Elec €3

➡ Rue Alphonse Daudet. Turn off D6089 in town onto 7.5t weight restricted road, sp 'Maison de la Petite Enfance' and signed. Turn right, signed. Follow road to right, signed. Aire on left, signed. Service Point inside barn.

ℹ Pleasant and peaceful private Aire with rural views and barn adj. Vézère river adj, no views. Town commerce 600m with large popular market Thurs am. Inspected 2016.

PEYZAC LE MOUSTIER/TURSAC

| 15 | F9 | 24620 | T | (A) N44°59.258' E001°04.260' | SP |

🚐 (A) 30; (B) 10; Grass parking 🛒 (A) None; WCs by café; (B) None

➡ (A) Peyzac: D66. Follow D706 from St Leon sur Vezere sp 'Les Eyzies'. Cross river and turn left onto D66, sp 'Peyzac' and 'Cité Troglodytique de la Roque St Christophe'. Follow road through rocks and up slope into rear car park, signed. (B) Tursac N44°58.805' E001°03.263': D706. Continue on D706 after bridge for 2km and turn off opp Troglodyte castle into visitor parking. Motorhome parking at rear, signed.

ℹ (A) Pleasant, shaded parking in wooded dell. La Roque St Christophe Troglodyte city 200m up slope, worth a visit; €8.50pp. (B) Designated, open grass parking at Maison Forte de Reignac, a castle built into the rock, enter up steps; €8.20pp. Pre-history museum 250m. Inspected 2016.

(A)

ST LEON SUR VEZERE

| 16 | F9 | 24290 | | N45°00.730' E001°05.369' | SP |

🚐 10; €6/8pm-8am Apr-Nov; Collected; Free 8am-8pm 🛒 Euro Relais Mini; Token (ER); €2; WCs, showers (€1.50) and washing up sinks all adj to TO

➡ C201. From D706 take D66 into St Léon sur Vézère. Turn 1st right past cemetery, signed. Follow lane for 300m and Aire on left, signed.

ℹ Pleasant grass and hardstanding parking on outskirts of Beau Village with TO, 150m along river. Tourist commerce inc seasonal canoe hire. Small municipal riverside campsite opp TO. Reinspected 2016.

LEMBRAS

| 17 | E/F9 | 24100 | R | N44°53.003' E000°31.510' | SP |

🚐 10; Max 11m 🛒 Custom; Free; Aire Services Elec x2; 8 CEE elec points; Token (3/3); €4/12hrs

➡ Aire du Caudeau. In Lembras turn off N21 by bus stop, signed. Aire 100m on left, signed.

ℹ Landscaped Aire just far enough away from main road noise. Local commerce 100m on N21. Inspected 2016.

BEYNAC ET CAZENAC

| 18 | F9 | 24220 | T | N44°50.702' E001°08.727' | SP |

🚐 20; Gravel parking 🛒 None

➡ Turn left off D703, sp 'Mairie' and signed. Follow road uphill and designated parking on right in gravel car park past all the pay car parks, not signed.

ℹ Popular parking on edge of Beau Village with imposing château, 600m downhill towards banks of Dordogne river. Do not drive to Château de Beynac as motorhomes are excluded from parking and the surrounding roads. Inspected 2016.

MONTIGNAC — 19 — F9 — 24290 — N45°04.067' E001°09.883'

🚐 40; €5/8pm-8am inc elec; CC; Pay at machine; Must not park widthways 🔧 Urba Flux Tall; 40 16amp CEE elec points throughout parking

➡ Rue des Sanges. At D46/D67/D704 roundabout take D704, sp 'Montignac'. At next roundabout go straight over onto D704, sp 'Centre Ville', 'Les Eyzies' and signed. Enter one-way road, then in 200m turn left, sp 'P Vieux Quartiers' and signed. Parking to left in gravel area at end of road.

ℹ Popular parking only 150m from small town commerce; market Wed. Some road noise. Signs indicated motorhomes should be parked diagonally, therefore it is no longer suitable for motorhomes with trailers. Canoe hire by river, 400m. Reinspected 2016.

SALIGNAC EYVIGUES — 20 — F9 — 24590 — N44°58.361' E001°19.238'

🚐 10; Max 2 nights 🔧 Custom; Waste water and WC emptying marked on ground

➡ Rue des Écoles. Exit village on D61, sp 'Simeyrols'. Take the 1st turning on the right, sp 'P Groupe Scolaire'. Aire in car park on right.

ℹ Aire adj to school so can be very busy and noisy. Far field used for school sports and football. Town centre with small town commerce 300m. Circular walk detailed outside TO. Reinspected 2016.

CARSAC AILLAC — 21 — F9 — 24200 — N44°50.420' E001°16.448'

🚐 30; Grass parking 🔧 Aire Services 7005; Token (3/3); €2

➡ D703. From Montfort follow D703, sp 'Carsac Aillac'. As enter Carsac Aillac turn right into car park, sp 'Parking'. Aire past WCs.

ℹ Pleasant Aire offering grass parking between deciduous trees on edge of village backing onto large, open picnic field. Cont elec points by laverie not intended for motorhome use. Small town commerce 150m inc Souffleur de Verre, a glass factory; watch some glass blowing Tue-Sat. Inspected 2016.

STE ALVERE — 22 — F9 — 24510 — N44°56.705' E000°48.301'

🚐 5 🔧 Euro Relais Box; Token (ER); €2.50

➡ Route de Périgueux. In village turn off D32 onto D2, sp 'Cendrieux' and signed. Turn left after bridge, signed. Aire in parking on left.

ℹ Pleasant location adj to sports facilities on edge of village. Local commerce 400m. Reinspected 2016.

LES EYZIES DE TAYAC — 23 — F9 — 24620 — T — N44°56.325' E001°00.552'

🚐 25; €5/24hrs; Collected 🔧 Raclet; €2

➡ Promenade de la Vézère, off D47. Turn off D47 in village, sp 'Pde la Vézère'. Follow road to right and under railway bridge. Aire at end of car park on right, signed.

ℹ Popular Aire in peaceful, pleasantly landscaped parking. Notices request diagonal parking. Tourist commerce 150m. Motorhomes banned from all other car parks at night. Grotte de Font de Gaume, caves with prehistoric paintings, 2km; €7.50pp, open 9.30am-5.30pm, except 12.30-2pm mid Sept-mid May; advanced booking recommended. Reinspected 2016.

LE BUGUE — 24 — F9 — 24260 — N44°54.980' E000°55.577'

🚐 100; €7/night; CC; Pay at machine; Max 72hrs 🔧 Custom

➡ Place Léopold Salme, off D31e1. Exit town on D31e1, sp 'Fumel'. Cross river bridge, then turn left behind Crédit Agricole building, signed; GPS taken here. Follow road to Aire. Follow road to left and around parking for Service Point: N44°54.976' E000°55.706'.

ℹ Popular parking on open grass or under trees when dry, limited hardstanding parking. River with water access 50m, no view; take your chairs for a walk. Town commerce 150m; older part of town across river. Reinspected 2016.

TREMOLAT	25	F9	24510		N44°52.433' E000°49.853'	

🚐 10 Flot Bleu Océane; Token (FB); €2

➡ D30. Turn off D30 in village into central car park, signed

ℹ Aire just 150m from pretty village with tourist facilities and local commerce. Suitable for any unit configuration and space likely. Dordogne river nearby. Rubbish collection 7.30am Mon and 7.30-9am Wed. Reinspected 2016.

QUEYSSAC	26	F9	24140		N44°54.319' E000°32.899'	

🚐 7 Custom

➡ In village turn off D21e1 down narrow road, sp 'Le Bourg'. At church follow road to right over cobbles, then to left past covered market. Cross bridge over stream and turn immediately right into large car park. Access difficult for drivers of large motorhomes.

ℹ Aire in open car park adj to green space and covered market. The only commerce is a very popular restaurant opp church, customers park in Aire. Local walks depart from Aire. Visited 2016.

Info/photos: Alistair MacFadyen

BADEFOLS SUR DORDOGNE	27	F9	24150		N44°50.560' E000°47.488'	

🚐 10 Raclet; Token; Tap in WC

➡ D29. Turn off D29 in village, sp 'P' and 'Boulangerie'. Service Point immediately on left against building: N44°50.591' E000°47.485'. Follow road to parking at rear.

ℹ Pleasant but slightly sloping gravel parking to rear of local shops; even suitable for large motorhomes. Far enough away to limit road noise. Walking/cycling path and green space adj. Reinspected 2016.

MERCULOT	28	E10	24220		N44°50.579' E001°02.019'	

🚐 6; €5/night inc service; +€0.22pp tax Custom; 6 16amp Cont elec points; Elec €2.50

➡ Lieu dit Merculot. Turn off D703 onto D48, sp 'Berbiguières'. Turn off D48, sp 'Merculot'. Follow road for 400m uphill, then turn left into farm. Follow drive and Service Point to left of barn. Designated parking adj.

ℹ Private Aire on working farm with lovely views across pastured valleys. Owners speak limited English, but very friendly. Small café in barn. Local produce sold on site. Inspected 2016.

LIMEUIL	29	F9	24510		N44°53.135' E000°53.479'	

🚐 20; Grass parking None

➡ D31. Exit village on D31, sp 'Le Bugue' and signed. Turn left up slope into parking area adj to D31 at village boundary sign. Steep access with 90° turn at the top. Not recommended for large motorhomes.

ℹ Zigzag woodland path up hill behind Aire leads to garden, panoramic viewpoint and Beau Village. Circular walk: Up footpath, through village and down other side to river; walk along river to left, through bridge arch, then left past boules courts and seasonal WCs to Aire. Tourist commerce, seasonal canoe hire and river 300m on level. Reinspected 2016.

BELVES	30	F9	24170	T	N44°46.633' E000°59.822'	

🚐 20 Custom

➡ Rue de l'Aérodrome. Turn off D710 onto D52, sp 'Belvès'. Turn right at roundabout, sp 'Urval' and signed. Follow road, sp 'Aérodrome' and signed. Turn right, sp 'Cadouin' and signed. Aire on left opp cemetery.

ℹ Dead quiet. Large, level, open Aire on edge of town with rural view. Centre of Beau Village 1km with local and tourist commerce and a market Sat am. Reinspected 2016.

ST CYPRIEN
31 | F9 | 24220 | N44°52.102' E001°02.663'

🚐 10; Max 24hrs 🚰 Euro Relais Mini; Token (ER); 8 elec points; 1 Token/12hrs elec; €3.50

▶ Rue du Priolat. Turn off D703 onto D49, sp 'Siorac'. At the roundabout turn right onto C201, sp 'Meyrals'. Aire on left in 300m, signed.

ℹ️ Popular, designated parking in a section of car park. Motorhomes banned from all other parts of car park at night. Small town commerce 100m via alley. Reinspected 2016.

VEZAC
32 | F9 | 24220 | N44°49.438' E001°10.180'

🚐 17; €9.60/24hrs Sept-Jun; €12/24hrs Jul-Aug; +€1.50 tax; Inc elec; CC; Grass parking 🚰 Euro Relais Junior; Inside barrier; 24 6amp CEE elec points; WiFi code at campsite reception

▶ D703. Follow sp 'La Roque-Gageac' onto D703. Aire on right 1km west of La Roque-Gageac, visible from road. Enter through PARKNIGHT barrier.

ℹ️ Commercial Aire with grass parking adj to main route, some road noise. Camping la Plage adj; open Mar-Oct. Dordogne river nearby, access through adj campsite. La Roque-Gageac 1km. Inspected 2016.

LA ROQUE GAGEAC
33 | F9 | 24250 | T | N44°49.500' E001°11.017'

🚐 20; €5 day parking; €8/7pm-noon; Pay at machine; Max 10m 🚰 Raclet; €2

▶ Parking Place Publique, off D703. Aire in large car park at eastern end of village centre, adj to river, signed. Park in parking furthest from road, closest to Service Point. Large motorhomes will have difficulty accessing car park if full.

ℹ️ Popular Aire in busy tourist car park adj to Dordogne river with boat trips and kayak hire. Views of cliffs with troglodyte fort. Beau Village adj with tourist commerce/restaurants. Reinspected 2016.

MONTFORT (VITRAC)
34 | F9 | 24200 | N44°50.125' E001°14.912'

🚐 20; Max 12hrs 🚰 Euro Relais Junior; Token (ER); €3

▶ D703. Turn off D703 on west side of village, sp 'Village de Montfort' and signed. Follow road for 200m and Aire in car park on right.

ℹ️ Parking adj to charming village with imposing château. Footpath opp. Tourist commerce 150m, below the château. Town is known as the gateway to the valley of a thousand castles. Reinspected 2016.

DOMME
35 | F9 | 24250 | T | N44°48.050' E001°13.300'

🚐 30; €3/10am-7pm; €7/7pm-10am; €9/24hrs; Pay at machine; 5m bays + 4m overhang 🚰 Euro Relais Junior; €2

▶ Le Pradal, off D46e. From D703, D46 or D50 follow blue coach/motorhome signs (not GPS). Follow signs to D50, then D46e for 8km. This route is well signed; motorhomes are banned from the town.

ℹ️ Large, popular Aire in a peaceful location with rural views. Centre of hilltop Beau Village 500m. Some parts of original fortified walls and gateways remain; also has grottes. Reinspected 2016.

SARLAT LA CANEDA
36 | F9 | 24200 | N44°53.747' E001°12.747'

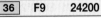

🚐 20; 1hr free; €7/24hrs; €15/48hrs; Pay at machine 🚰 Euro Relais Junior; €2

▶ Place Flandres Dunkerque 1940, on D704. From north on D704 go right at roundabout as enter town, sp 'Cahors' and signed. Aire immediately on right in car park, signed. Entrance is easy to miss.

ℹ️ Popular, sloping car park suffering constant road noise. Local commerce adj. Town 800m, large market Sat. Very popular with French motorhomers. Reinspected 2016.

VILLEFRANCHE DU PERIGORD
37 F9 24550 N44°37.844' E001°04.651'

🚐 20 Aire Services 7005; CC

➡ Rue du Nord. From west on D660, 400m after boundary sign, follow road to left, then turn left, signed. Service Point down slope on right; parking on left overlooking pond.

ℹ Pleasant parking overlooking pond and leisure space. Town centre with pleasant square and small town commerce 200m uphill. Inspected 2016.

MONPAZIER
38 F9 24540 T N44°41.107' E000°53.619'

🚐 10 Custom

➡ Lieu-dit Douelle Nord. Turn off D660 onto D53 in town centre, sp 'Belvès' and signed. Turn 1st left onto 3.5t weight restricted road, then take 1st right after passing Sapeurs Pompiers (fire station), signed. Aire immediately on right at rear of fire station, signed.

ℹ Popular, pleasant, landscaped Aire adj to fire station and cemetery. Bastide de Monpazier, Beau Village, 500m. Suggest 40 if full. Reinspected 2016.

BEAUMONT DU PERIGORD
39 F9 24440 N44°46.479' E000°45.937'

🚐 10 Flot Bleu Fontaine

➡ D660. Approach on D660 from north. Turn left as enter Beaumont du Périgord, sp 'Salle des Fêtes' and signed. Aire behind Salle des Fêtes building.

ℹ This is a large parking area located just off a main trunking route but is always likely to have space. Reinspected 2014.

BIRON
40 F9 24540 N44°37.843' E000°52.247'

🚐 10 Flot Bleu Pacific; Token (3/3); €2

➡ C203. In village turn off D53 onto C203, sp 'Vergt de Biron'. Turn immediately left into car park. Service Point on right.

ℹ Pleasant Aire with rural views and views of château. Plenty of open parking suitable for any unit configuration. Château de Biron, entry €8.20pp, and tourist commerce 100m. Market Wed am. Reinspected 2016.

ST SAUVEUR DE BERGERAC
41 E9 24520 N44°52.112' E000°35.289'

🚐 3; 7m bays Custom

➡ Route de la Rafraigne. Turn off D21, main route through, into car park past Mairie, signed.

ℹ Sloping car park with 3 designated bays in village centre; poss to overflow. Limited local commerce 150m. Dordogne river nearby. Reinspected 2016.

MONBAZILLAC
42 E9 24240 R N44°47.321' E000°29.751'

🚐 8; Grass parking Custom

➡ D13. Follow D13 through Monbazillac following sp 'Domaine de la Lande'. Aire at vineyard adj to D13, sp 'Domaine de la Lande' and signed.

ℹ Parking at small vineyard and France Passion site with views across vines. Motorhomers welcome to wine tasting at 6pm which lasts up to 1hr. Monbazillac has a château, TO, museum and numerous wine producers; worth a visit. Reinspected 2016.

BERGERAC – La Pelouse
43 E9 24100 ⛺ N44°50.948' E000°28.576'

🚐 4; €7.80/24hrs inc 10amp CEE elec; Pay at reception; Apr-Sept; Max 24hrs 👕 Custom; €3; Apr-Sept

➡ Camping de la Pelouse. From south on D936 follow sp 'Camping Municipal La Pelouse'. Turn left and left again, sp 'Camping La Pelouse'. Service Point outside Camping de La Pelouse.

ⓘ Small, Aire outside pleasant riverside campsite. Only 1.5km from Bergerac. Inspected 2016.

BERGERAC
44 E9 24100 🏛 N44°52.270' E000°30.224'

🚐 6; Outside barrier; Free; Max 24hrs; 16; Inside barrier; €5/24hr; +€0.33 tax; CC; Max 72hrs 👕 Aire Services 7010; Outside barrier; CC; €2; Aire Services Elec; Inside barrier; CC; €2/24hrs

➡ Rue du Coulobre. Exit Bergerac on D936e1 following sp 'Périgueux' and signed. As exiting town turn left, signed. Aire on right, signed.

ⓘ Popular, landscaped, commercial Aire on outskirts of Bergerac offering external and internal parking. Some road noise. Town centre 3km. Inspected 2016.

FUMEL
45 F10 47500 🏛🏢 N44°29.928' E000°58.316'

🚐 10; Very unlevel! 👕 Custom; Very custom!

➡ Place du Saulou, off D911f. Enter Fumel on D911f from east, sp 'Château de Fumel'. Aire on right after bend as enter town, signed.

ⓘ Aire in small, sloping car park. Difficult to access Service Point if car park busy. Local road noise. Voie Verte cycle path runs along river. Town commerce 300m. Reinspected 2016.

TOURNON D'AGENAIS
46 F10 47370 N44°24.113' E000°59.958'

🚐 5 👕 Custom

➡ D265. Turn off roundabout onto D265, sp 'Cahors'. Entrance to Aire 150m on right, signed.

ⓘ Small Aire just off main route. Be careful not to drive off edge when manoeuvring. WCs 150m at roundabout by steps to hilltop town commerce. Market Sun 8am-noon. Reinspected 2016.

ST GEORGES
47 F10 47370 N44°26.492' E000°56.251'

🚐 5; By Proxi convenience store 👕 Custom; Lift grid before emptying WC; 3 unmetered Cont elec points

➡ Ave St Georges de France. Turn off D102 onto C1-515, sp 'St Georges'. At end of road turn left, then turn 1st right, sp 'St Georges'. Service Point on right opp Proxi convenience store; parking behind store.

ⓘ Aire in small, peaceful, rural village adj to convenience store and restaurant. Large picnic area 200m. Reinspected 2016.

MONFLANQUIN
48 F10 47150 🏢 (A) N44°31.681' E000°45.348'

🚐 (A) 4; (B) 5 👕 Custom

➡ Approach Monflanquin on D124 from Cancon. Turn right at roundabout, sp 'Centre d'Activities de Mondesir'. Turn 1st right and Service Point in 100m, signed: N44°31.484' E000°45.382'. (A) Go straight on at roundabout, then turn 1st left, sp 'Piscine'. Designated parking on left, signed. (B) N44°32.048' E000°46.214': Continue on D124, sp 'P Bastide'. Turn left onto D150 and follow sp 'P Bastide'. Parking adj to cemetery.

ⓘ 2 pleasant parking areas with green space and signed footpaths to Bastide. (B) is closer to village and likely to be busier; will be full of cars during high season/holidays. Beau Village. Reinspected 2016.

ST SYLVESTRE SUR LOT
49 F10 47140 N44°23.765' E000°48.281'

🚐 20 🛁 Custom

➡ Rue Jean Moulin. Access from D103 or D911. Turn off D103 between D911 and river bridge. Aire behind Intermarché, designated parking by green space. Service Point by fuel station at: N44°23.733' E000°48.333'.

ℹ Popular, pleasant, peaceful Aire that can take any sized motorhome. Intermarché adj. Small town commerce 150m; market Wed am. River Lot 100m; no view but has riverside walking path. Reinspected 2016.

VILLEREAL
50 E10 47210 N44°38.271' E000°44.451'

🚐 30 🛁 Custom

➡ D104. From west on D104 go straight over roundabout, sp 'Bergerac'. Turn right, sp 'Aire de Jeux' and signed. Drive to the rear of car park for Service Point.

ℹ Aire in a peaceful location off main road. The adj water treatment plant hums quietly and local buses park here overnight, but depart swiftly at 7.30am. Town centre 250m with small town commerce and historic covered market. Market Sat am. Inspected 2016.

CASSENEUIL
51 F10 47440 N44°26.791' E000°37.136'

🚐 15 🛁 Custom

➡ Place St Pierre. Exit town on D133, sp 'Cancon' and signed. At roundabout take D225, sp 'P Tourisme'. Aire immediately on left in P Tourisme car park, opp cemetery before village exit, signed.

ℹ Pleasant parking under deciduous trees on edge of town overlooking river. Local traffic creates limited noise during day. Picnic and fishing area adj. Town centre with local commerce 250m across river. Reinspected 2016.

STE LIVRADE SUR LOT
52 F10 47110 N44°23.760' E000°35.490'

🚐 5 🛁 Custom

➡ Place du Lieutenant Colonel Jean-François Calas. From south on D113 turn right at roundabout with Casino supermarket down 3.5t weight restricted road lined with plane trees, sp 'Trésor Public', 'Sapeurs Pompiers' and signed. Aire at end of road, past Terres du Sud.

ℹ Designated parking opp Service Point outside fire station. Old railway station building adj, tracks now a Voie Verte cycle path. Small town commerce 400m. Reinspected 2016.

MONBAHUS
53 E9 47290 N44°32.825' E000°32.101'

🚐 2 🛁 Custom; 2 unmetered CEE elec points (Work when floodlights on)

➡ Rue du Château d'Eau. Turn off D124 in village centre to view point, signed. Drive up very steep, single lane hill. Aire in car park just past footpath to view point. There is very little space to turn around at top, so will be difficult for large motorhomes.

ℹ Shaded parking within a small car park below superb 360° view with interpretation, 150m uphill via footpath. Village with local commerce 300m downhill. Reinspected 2016.

LAUZUN
54 E9 47410 N44°37.658' E000°27.589'

🚐 2; Max 48hrs; Max 8m 🛁 Water tap and WCs only

➡ Rue St Colomb. From Miramont-de-Guyenne approach on D1. Turn off D1 at village boundary, sp 'Camping'. Follow road around past sports facilities and campsite and take 1st turning on left. Parking on left just before village, signed.

ℹ Small, pleasant, designated parking backing onto road with local traffic. Adj to and overlooking lake and recreational area. Village centre 150m, dominated by château, with local commerce and restaurants. Reinspected 2016.

MIRAMONT DE GUYENNE
55 | E9 | 47800 | 🏨 | N44°36.216' E000°21.727' | SP

🚐 20 🛖 Custom; 4 CEE elec points

▶ Blvd Gambetta. Approach from north on D933 following sp 'Mont de Marsan' and 'Miramont de Guyenne-Centre'. Turn left off D933 onto D1, sp 'Lauzun' and signed. Turn left, signed, and entre through barrier. Coded access, check barrier as may be open; otherwise code from Hôtel de Ville.

ⓘ Aire in gravel parking just off main route and only 300m from town centre. Some road noise. Inspected 2016.

DURAS
56 | E9 | 47120 | 🏨 | N44°40.678' E000°10.639' | SP

🚐 9; €6.30/night Jul-Aug; Free for rest of year 🛖 Custom; 12 unmetered elec points; Jul-Aug

▶ Off D708. From south on D708 follow road around village, passing château. Turn next left into C6, sp 'Château' and 'Aire de Camping-Car'. Follow road downhill and after 150m fork left, sp 'Aire de Camping-Car' and 'Camping Municipal'. Aire in bays before height barriered campsite entrance.

ⓘ Aire in bays adj to basic municipal camping field with no reception. Campsite open Jul-Aug; parking free, but no services or WC rest of year. Château adj. Reinspected 2016.

CANCON
57 | F9 | 47290 | 🏛 | N44°32.192' E000°37.530' | SP

🚐 10 🛖 Custom; 1 5amp Cont elec point; Honesty box

▶ Rue des Écoles. Turn off N21 in centre onto D124, sp 'Villereal' and signed. Go straight across at next junction, past Mairie, into town square. Service Point against barn wall, signed.

ⓘ Aire in part of large square/cattle market; can take a virtually unlimited number of motorhomes subject to local events. Small town commerce 250m. In nut and prune growing region. Village has medieval quarter, 200m; walk through it to panoramic viewpoint. Reinspected 2016.

LE TEMPLE SUR LOT
58 | E/F10 | 47110 | 🏨 | N44°22.809' E000°31.607' | SP

🚐 5; Between trees 🛖 Custom

▶ Avenue de Verdun. Just off D911 on left as enter village from Ste Livrade sur Lot. It is possible to turn 1st left at traffic lights, then left again to reach it. Not signed on D911.

ⓘ Convenient Aire just off D911. Pleasant park adj but constant noise from D911 as HGVs stop/start at traffic lights. Local commerce 200m. Reinspected 2016.

MONSEGUR
59 | E9 | 33580 | 🏛 | N44°39.056' E000°05.038' | SP

🚐 10; Max 48hrs 🛖 Custom; Difficult access

▶ Ave Porte des Tours. From east turn off D668 as enter town and go straight on as main road bears left, sp 'Centre Ville' and 'Halte Camping-Car'. Turn 1st left opp park. Service Point to right and parking at end, signed. Do not attempt to drive through town as narrow and difficult due to parked cars.

ⓘ Aire in large, open car park. Town centre, 300m, has small town commerce in the arcade around an interesting covered market which hosts small market Tue am. Park opp Aire with view over town. Path from town to river. Reinspected 2016.

LA REOLE
60 | E9 | 33190 | 🏢 | N44°34.847' W000°01.815' | SP

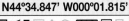

🚐 10; €4/night Apr-Sept; Collected; Grass parking 🛖 Custom; By road; 6 16amp elec points

▶ D1113. From town centre head east on D1113, sp 'Langon'. Aire on right by small, round tower, signed.

ⓘ Popular Aire adj to main route through; some local traffic noise. Grass parking and some shade. Viewpoint overlooking railway with river glimpses. Town 500m with local commerce. Reinspected 2016.

FONTET

| 61 | E9 | 33190 | | N44°33.721' W000°01.406' | SP |

🚐 10; €10/night inc 16amp CEE elec; €250/month; Pay at marina ☂ Custom; Showers €1

➤ Halte Nautique. Turn off D9 onto D9e6, sp 'Fontet' and 'Base de Loisirs Halte Nautique'. Follow road and turn left, sp 'Base de Loisirs Halte Nautique'. Follow lane to end and turn left, then immediately right. Park outside gate and enquire for entry.

ⓘ Directly adj to canal basin at marina. Swimming lake and restaurant adj. Ideal long stay base. Reinspected 2016.

MARMANDE 1

| 62 | E9 | 47200 | | N44°29.904' E000°09.626' | SP |

🚐 3; Nov-Mar only; See 63 ☂ Custom

➤ Place du Moulin. From south exit D933 at roundabout onto D933e1, sp 'Marmande-Centre Ville'. Cross river and turn right at traffic lights, sp 'Plaine de Loisirs' and signed. Follow road to left, sp 'Plaine de Loisirs', and after 225m turn left into Quai des Capucins. Service Point immediately on right, signed.

ⓘ Small Aire which motorhomes are only allowed to park in Nov-Mar; also see 63 . Reinspected 2016.

MARMANDE 2

| 63 | E9 | 47200 | | N44°29.696' E000°09.769' | SP |

🚐 36; €8/night; +€0.60pp; Inc 16amp elec; Collected; Apr-Oct; Grass parking; 3 reinforced bays ☂ Custom; Only 24 16amp CEE elec points

➤ Rue de la Filhole. From south exit D933 at roundabout onto D933e1, sp 'Marmande-Centre Ville'. Cross river and turn right at traffic lights, signed. Follow road to left, then turn right, signed. Follow road to left past height barriered car parks. At roundabout turn right, signed. Aire at end of road on left just before barrier, signed.

ⓘ Popular Aire shaded by deciduous trees on old campsite in pleasant woodland setting adj to large leisure park. Town 800m. Reinspected 2016.

CAUBEYRES

| 64 | E10 | 47160 | | N44°15.312' E000°12.047' | SP |

🚐 5; Grass and gravel parking ☂ Custom

➤ D285. Turn off D11 onto D285, sp 'Caubeyres'. Follow road for 2.5km, passing through Caubeyres, then turn left, signed. Service Point immediately on left.

ⓘ Aire adj to recreation huts on edge of woods. Space likely; when huts not in use, you will be alone. Inspected 2016.

CAUMONT SUR GARONNE ✳

| 65 | E10 | 47430 | | N44°26.506' E000°10.781' | SP |

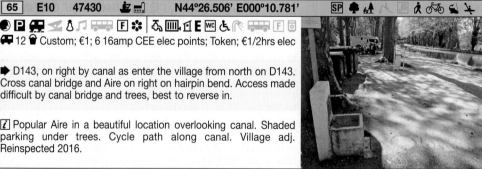

🚐 12 ☂ Custom; €1; 6 16amp CEE elec points; Token; €1/2hrs elec

➤ D143, on right by canal as enter the village from north on D143. Cross canal bridge and Aire on right on hairpin bend. Access made difficult by canal bridge and trees, best to reverse in.

ⓘ Popular Aire in a beautiful location overlooking canal. Shaded parking under trees. Cycle path along canal. Village adj. Reinspected 2016.

VILLETON

| 66 | E10 | 47400 | | N44°21.844' E000°16.376' | SP |

🚐 8; €3/night Nov-Mar; €4/night Apr-Oct; Collected ☂ Flot Bleu Fontaine; 4 8amp CEE elec points; €1/hr; Pay shower

➤ D120, by river bridge. Aire located behind Mairie at small marina, sp 'Musée de la Mémoire Paysanne' and 'Aire Camping Car'. Park only in designated space on left adj to river, signed.

ⓘ Pleasant, shaded parking adj to canal, no views. Pizza restaurant and museum adj, entry €4pp. Reinspected 2016.

VIANNE
67 E10 47230 T N44°11.889' E000°19.379'

🚐 15 🚰 None; See **69** and **245**

➡ Ave de la Gare. Approach Vianne on D642 from Buzet sur Baïse. Turn left when you see the city wall and designated parking is on the left, signed.

ℹ Designated parking next to the intact walls of fortified town; worth a visit. Inspected 2016.

CASTELJALOUX
68 E10 47700 🏛 N44°18.657' E000°04.760'

🚐 4; Max 48hrs 🚰 Custom

➡ Rue de St Michel. From D933 turn off south of town onto D291, sp 'St Michel de Castelnau' and signed. Aire 120m on left.

ℹ Thermal town 700m. E.Leclerc supermarket 350m. Aire advertised at Lac les Clarens is a holiday village charging €10/night: N44°17.567' E000°04.416'. Reinspected 2013.

BUZET SUR BAISE ⭐
69 E10 47160 ⚓ N44°15.473' E000°18.329'

🚐 20; €7/night inc token; Pay at machine at Capitainerie 🚰 Euro Relais Box; Token (ER); €2; From machine

➡ D12, at Port de Buzet. Follow D642, main route, sp 'Port Fluval'. Stay on D642 and turn right, sp 'Port Fluval'. Cross bridge and turn right onto D12, sp 'Port Fluval'. Turn right, sp 'Bienvenue en Lot-et-Garonne'. Follow road through picnic area to Aire, signed.

ℹ Very pleasant, popular Aire at pleasure marina. There are 6 official bays closest to Service Point plus plenty of grass overflow parking. Convergence of 2 navigable waterways with cycling and walking trails. Boat and bike hire at Capitainerie. Reinspected 2016.

MONTETON
70 E9 47120 🏢 N44°37.377' E000°15.407'

🚐 7; Grass parking 🚰 Euro Relais Junior; 1 unmetered CEE elec point (Not working)

➡ D423. Turn off D668 onto D423, sp 'Monteton'. Aire on right just off D423 as enter village, signed. Service Point past recycling bins.

ℹ Pleasant, popular, summer Aire adj to pleasant hilltop village. No designated parking but motorhomes parked on grass overlooking nut trees. Reinspected 2016.

CASTELCULIER
71 F10 47240 🏢 N44°10.488' E000°41.680'

🚐 2 adj; Other parking avail 🚰 Custom; Token; €2/300L water; Connect hose

➡ Rue du Champ de Baze. Approach from Valence on D813 following sp 'Agen'. As enter town turn off D813 at roundabout onto C1, sp 'Mairie de Castelculier' and 'Villascopia'. Turn left at roundabout, signed, and then 1st right, signed. Service Point at bottom of hill, signed.

ℹ Pleasant Aire in small town with local commerce. Most motorhomers choose to park by tennis courts. Agen town has every possible commerce avail in easy to access retail parks. Reinspected 2016.

LAYRAC
72 F10 47390 🏢 N44°07.938' E000°39.573'

🚐 5; Max 3 days 🚰 Custom

➡ Rue du 19 Mars 1962, off N21. At traffic-lighted junction opp D17 turn off N21 down road beside rusty metal cross, signed. Then turn 1st right, signed. Aire on left, signed.

ℹ Small, peaceful Aire with little overhang and no overflow opportunities. The bays graduate from 6m-9m (closest to Service Point). Small town commerce 250m. Market Fri am. Reinspected 2016.

ATLANTIC

NERAC
73 E10 47600 N44°08.040' E000°20.134'

🚐 Unlimited; See info 🛍 Custom

➡ Boulevard Jean Darlan. Turn off D930 in town centre at traffic lights onto D656, sp 'Mézin'. At next traffic lights turn left, sp 'P du Foirail (Gratuit)'. Aire on far side of barns, on left, signed.

ℹ Large car park/exhibition area with loads of unrestricted parking suitable for any unit configuration; subject to events. Supermarket adj. Town commerce 500m with impressive medieval buildings, inc castle for Henry IV, and picturesque river with boat hire. Reinspected 2016.

ASTAFFORT
74 F10 47220 N44°03.939' E000°38.938'

🚐 10; No notices about payment 🛍 Custom; CC; €3; Pay at Urba Flux; WC emptying point lock released on payment

➡ N21. Approach on N21 from Layrac. After entering Astaffort turn right in 400m, immediately after crossing bridge, sp 'Boulodrome' and signed. Service Point adj to campsite entrance.

ℹ Service Point outside municipal campsite with plenty of unrestricted parking, some partly shaded. Lovely riverside picnic spot opp overlooking weir. Inspected 2016.

LAVARDAC
75 E10 47230 N44°10.734' E000°17.954'

Parking

🚐 3; 6m bays and obstructed by trees 🛍 Custom

➡ Rue de la Victoire. Turn off D930, main road through, onto D258, sp 'Stade-Tennis', 'Salle Polyvalente' and signed. The Aire is 200m on the left, signed. Parked cars may make it difficult to manoeuvre large motorhomes into Service Point.

ℹ Local commerce 150m. Parking poss along Rue de la Victoire, 300m from Aire: N44°10.635' E000°18.167'. Reinspected 2016.

ST HILAIRE DE LUSIGNAN
76 E10 47450 N44°13.495' E000°30.814'

🚐 2 designated, room for 4; Max 24hrs 🛍 Custom; CC; €3; WC emptying point has electronic lock openable after payment

➡ D813, between Porte Ste Marie and Agen on D813. Service Point adj to D183 and river at the southern edge of St Hilaire-de-Lusignan, signed.

ℹ Parking shaded by deciduous trees overlooking green space with glimpses of Garonne river. Limited parking provision and all parking is close to noisy road. Reinspected 2016.

LE MAS D'AGENAIS
77 E10 47430 N44°24.384' E000°13.204'

🚐 8; €2/night; + €0.60pp tax; Collected; Jun-Sep 🛍 Custom; 8 16amp CEE elec points

➡ D143. Turn off D6 onto D143, sp 'Lagruère'. Turn left in 300m, sp 'College'. Aire immediately on left.

ℹ Popular, small Aire adj to football ground. Suffers local road noise due to proximity to main route. Large motorhomes poss, but only when space allows. Village with local commerce 500m. Inspected 2016.

AILLAS
78 E10 33124 N44°28.515' W000°04.369'

🚐 7 🛍 Custom

➡ D9. Approaching from La Réole on D9, turn right immediately after village boundary, sp 'Stade' and signed. Turn right into Aire by tennis courts.

ℹ Pleasant village Aire adj to open access sports fields. Village 250m; undergoing development which is due to be completed Mar 2017. Inspected 2016.

ROQUEFORT | 79 | E10 | 40120 | ⛺ | N44°02.850' W000°19.321'

🚐 6; €7/night when campsite open; €4/night when campsite closed; +€0.22pp; Collected; Grass/sand parking; Max 48hrs ⛺ Custom; Lift circular cover left of water point

➡ Allée de Nauton. Exit village on D932n, sp 'Bordeaux'. Turn left, sp 'Camping' and signed. Aire 50m on right past campsite, signed.

ℹ Aire adj to municipal campsite and sports facilities in small residential area. Local commerce 2km down D932n. Reinspected 2016.

LABASTIDE D'ARMAGNAC ✱ | 80 | E10 | 40240 | | N43°58.321' W000°11.159'

🚐 50; Grass/sand parking; Max 72hrs ⛺ Custom

➡ D11. Turn off D626 in the village onto D11, sp 'Betbezer d'Arc' and signed. In 400m turn left into Aire, signed.

ℹ Popular, pleasant, large, open grass/sand parking. Suitable for any unit configuration. Village centre with local commerce 250m. Voie Verte cycle route through village. Reinspected 2016.

MONT DE MARSAN | 81 | D10 | 40000 | 🏃 | N43°54.394' W000°28.542'

🚐 41; €0.50/1hr; €7/24hrs Jun/Sept; €5/24hrs Oct-May; CC ⛺ Urba Flux Tall; CC; €1/5 mins; 16amp elec; CC; €0.50/hr

➡ D1. Turn off D932/D932e roundabout east of town onto D932, sp 'Mont de Marsan-Centre' and signed. Follow road towards town for 2km, then turn right at edge of park, signed. Entrance through Urba Flux barrier.

ℹ Pleasant, landscaped, commercial Aire adj to animal petting park. Town 3km. Updated 2016.

VILLENEUVE DE MARSAN | 82 | E10 | 40190 | | N43°53.239' W000°18.355'

🚐 7; In marked bays; Max 48hrs ⛺ Custom; 2 CEE elec points

➡ Rue Roger Lamothe. Approach on D1 from Mont de Marsan. Turn right as enter town, signed. Follow road and Aire on left, signed. Well signed from all directions.

ℹ Popular, open, landscaped Aire adj to sports facilities on edge of town. Small town commerce 600m. Reinspected 2016.

AIRE SUR L'ADOUR | 83 | E11 | 40800 | 🏃 | N43°42.162' W000°15.323'

🚐 24; €3/night Sept-Jun; €4/night Jul-Aug; Collected; Max 72hrs ⛺ Urba Flux; €1

➡ Place 19 Mars 1962. From north follow sp 'Centre Ville' and 'Pau' onto D824, main route through. After crossing river bridge turn left, sp 'Camping' and signed. Follow road left of TO, then turn left past bull ring, sp 'Camping' and signed. Aire 500m beyond campsite entrance on left, signed. Drive past Service Point down to river for very large open parking.

ℹ Large, open Aire suitable for any unit configuration. River with slipway adj, some bays have river views. Town centre 700m. May be closed for fête 3rd weekend in June. Reinspected 2016.

EUGENIE LES BAINS | 84 | E11 | 40320 | ⛺ | N43°41.432' W000°22.370'

🚐 6; €3/night; Pay at campsite ⛺ Custom; Inside campsite; €3; 10amp elec €3/night

➡ Route du Mouliot. Follow sp 'Camping' in village. Designated parking 50m past campsite entrance, signed.

ℹ Designated motorhome parking adj to campsite which was partly used as a materials store. The small town, 800m, is a pretty and popular tourist village with thermal baths. Poss to park nearer town: N43°41.694' W000°22.630'. Reinspected 2016.

AIRE POUR CAMPING-CARS DE PASSAGE
- Parking seul : 3 € la nuitée
- Branchement 10 ampères : 3 € la nuitée
- Plein + vidanges : 3 €

L'installation sur cette aire ne donne pas accès aux équipements à l'intérieur du camping (bloc sanitaire, piscine, espace détente, etc.).

- Avant 18h30 : se présenter à la réception
- Après 18h30 : appeler le 06.89.75.13.87

GRENADE SUR L'ADOUR · 85 · D10 · 40270 · N43°46.483' W000°26.100'

🚐 30; Max 24hrs ♟ Custom

➡ Place 19 Mars 1962. Approach on D824 from Mont-de-Marsan. Turn right before town centre after Carrefour Contact, sp 'P Rugby' and signed. At end of road go straight on and Service Point is on right adj to cemetery, signed.

i Dead quiet parking in large open car park next to rugby pitch on edge of town. Small supermarket adj, small town commerce 500m. Reinspected 2016.

ST SEVER · 86 · D10 · 40500 · N43°45.694' W000°34.529'

🚐 5 ♟ Custom

➡ Rue du Dr Louis Fournier. Exit D933s onto D944, sp 'St Sever-Ville'. In 1.1km turn left onto D132, sp 'Montaut'. In 1.1km turn left by Crédit Agricole, sp 'Sortie de Ville' and signed. For Service Point turn left beside war memorial. Service Point in gravel car park outside school building, signed: N43°45.544' W000°34.547'. For parking pass car park and turn right. Follow road 150m to parking on left.

i Small town commerce and historic centre adj. Town 150m through alley. Reinspected 2016.

MUGRON · 87 · D10 · 40250 · N43°44.892' W000°45.047'

🚐 4 ♟ Aire Services Plastic; 4 16amp CEE elec points (Turned off)

➡ D32e. In town turn onto D3, sp 'Donzacq', 'Voie Verte de Chalosse' and signed. Follow road to left, where it becomes D32e. In 220m turn right into Aire, sp 'Voie Verte de Chalosse'. Service Point on left.

i Aire shaded by deciduous trees adj to picnic area and designated cycle path to St Sever (17.9km) and Dax (31.6km). Local road noise. Local commerce 400m. Reinspected 2016.

ARZACQ ARRAZIGUET · 88 · D11 · 64410 · N43°32.094' W000°24.624'

🚐 20 ♟ Custom

➡ Place du Marcadieu. Aire in car park on corner near D32/D944 junction. Drive to rear of car park and Service Point behind building, signed.

i Local commerce adj. Bastide town. Adj to covered market building. Always likely to have space. Updated 2016.

SAUVAGNON · 89 · D11 · 64230 · N43°24.233' W000°23.176'

🚐 8; Large bays ♟ Custom

➡ D216, near junction with D616. From south on D216 drive through town and Aire is past the church in car park on right before you reach D616, signed. Service Point behind Centre Festif. Some narrow corners but passable, walk first if unsure.

i Small town commerce adj. Centre Festif has many events, but Aire is peaceful afterwards. Alternative designated parking behind Mairie: N43°24.172' W000°23.220'. Updated 2015.

BENEJACQ · 90 · E11 · 64800 · N43°11.405' W000°12.564'

🚐 10 ♟ Euro Relais Junior; Token (ER); €2; No drive over drain

➡ Impasse de la Fontaine. Turn off D936, main route through, into Impasse de la Fontaine, signed. Turn next left into Aire, signed. Well signed through town.

i Pleasant Aire tucked away from main route adj to streamside park. At time of inspection a local fleet of HGVs were using the Aire to park/store vehicles, could be noisy when they depart/arrive. Local commerce adj. Inspected 2016.

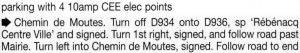

REBENACQ
91 D/E11 64260 N43°09.407' W000°23.822'

🚐 4; Max 48hrs; See info 🔧 Custom; Water in corner at end of parking with 4 10amp CEE elec points

➡ Chemin de Moutes. Turn off D934 onto D936, sp 'Rébénacq Centre Ville' and signed. Turn 1st right, signed, and follow road past Mairie. Turn left into Chemin de Moutes, signed. Follow road to end and Aire on left, signed.

ℹ Pleasant Aire on edge of Bastide town in the foothills of the Pyrénées. Whilst there are 4 designated open bays there is space for more. Open access sports fields adj, and steps up to the Bastide with local commerce. www.rebenacq.com Inspected 2016.

BRUGES
92 E11 64800 N43°07.432' W000°18.348'

🚐 10 🛒 None; See 91

➡ Chemin du Stade. Turn off D35 in central square, sp 'Stade' and signed. Follow road straight on, then after crossing river bridge turn right, signed. Aire on right opp entrance to sports grounds, signed.

ℹ Designated parking adj to open access sports fields. Occasional road noise from D35. Local commerce in village centre. Space likely. Inspected 2016.

BIELLE
93 D11 64260 N43°03.411' W000°25.389'

🚐 30 🛒 None; Service at 91 before arriving

➡ Lac de Castet. North of town on D934 turn off at roundabout, sp 'Lac de Castet' and follow road to right. Drive parallel to D934, then turn left before bridge, sp 'Entrée'. Follow road, then dirt track to large parking area.

ℹ Pleasant hardstanding and grass parking shaded by deciduous trees adj to leisure lake, no view. Ideal summer parking, make sure tanks are empty/full before arriving. Large motorhomes subject to track overgrowth, check before approaching. Inspected 2016.

ARUDY
94 D11 64260 N43°06.322' W000°25.357'

🚐 5 🛒 Euro Relais Junior; €2

➡ Rue Baulong. Exit D934 onto D287, sp 'Arudy'. Cross river bridge and follow road for 800m. Turn right up small road, sp 'Piscine' and 'Camping'. In 200m at end of football pitch turn right. Follow road straight on and Aire in car park next to fire station, signed.

ℹ Aire adj to sports facilities and river just 400m from local commerce. Reinspected 2016.

ARUDY / SEVIGNACQ MEYRACQ
95 D11 64260 N43°06.430' W000°24.962'

🚐 20; €10/night; Collected; Feb-Nov 🔧 Custom; €3; Elec €2

➡ Aire du Gave D'Ossau. From Pau on D934 continue through Sevignacq. Just past picnic spot on right, turn sharp right into minor road (long motorhomes should approach from Laruns). Do not take road over bridge for Arudy, but follow sp 'Camping Car' past marble works to site.

ℹ Commercial Aire/rural campsite. Onsite laundry, €6. Regional products for sale. Close to small town of Arudy. Reinspected 2013.

LARUNS
96 D12 64440 N42°59.300' W000°25.500'

🚐 42; €6/24hrs; CC 🔧 Euro Relais Junior; Inside barrier; Token; €3.50

➡ Ave de la Gare, off D934. Aire in town centre at rear of car park. Enter through Urba Flux barrier.

ℹ Open commercial Aire with pleasant views. Small town commerce adj, market Sat am. Updated 2015.

LES EAUX CHAUDES | 97 | D12 | 64440 | N42°57.117' W000°26.417'

🚐 Poss; Out of season 🚰 Euro Relais Junior; Token (2/1); €3.50

➡ D934. In small lay-by beside D934, signed.

ℹ Aire and area subject to change. Tokens from Larun or Fabrèges TO. For parking see Laruns 96. Updated 2016.

GOURETTE | 99 | E12 | 64440 | SKI | N42°57.784' W000°20.352'

🚐 50; €10/night; €15/night inc elec; Collected 🚰 Custom

➡ Parking de Recommande, adj to D918. Turn off D918 before Gourette, sp 'Parking de Recommande' and signed. Follow road downhill towards gondola, then turn right. Parking in summer campsite/winter Aire.

ℹ This Aire is situated at the bottom of the gondola station. Updated 2016.

ARETTE PIERRE ST MARTIN | 100 | D12 | 64570 | SKI | N42°58.733' W000°44.883'

🚐 40; €10/night inc unmetered elec; Collected 🚰 Custom; Inc; 44 elec points

➡ Braca de Guilhers, off D132 at ski station. Turn off D132 and follow to ski station, sp 'Station de Ski Pierre St Martin'. Pass through large car park and turn right at 1st roundabout into Aire.

ℹ Ski station adj. Adj to ski lift. Free WiFi at TO. Reinspected 2013.

Photo: Keith & Sue Lawrence

ARETTE | 101 | D11 | 64570 | N43°05.700' W000°42.951'

🚐 5 🚰 Custom; Adj to main road, difficult access

➡ D918. Exit D132 onto D918, sp 'Asasp' and signed. Follow road past TO on right and Mairie on left. Service Point on right by zebra crossing. Parking past Service Point in square to right.

ℹ Aire in small town at the foot of the Pyrénées. Local commerce. Small market Wed am adj to Aire. Inspected 2013.

OGEU LES BAINS | 102 | D11 | 64680 | N43°09.210' W000°30.130'

🚐 6 🚰 Custom; Token

➡ D416. Turn off D920 in Ogeu les Bains onto D416, sp 'Aire Camping Cars'. Cross railway on bridge and Aire on right just past stadium.

ℹ Village centre 800m with local commerce. Small supermarket 650m from Aire on D920 towards Oloron. Updated 2015.

OLORON STE MARIE | 103 | D11 | 64400 | N43°11.032' W000°36.511'

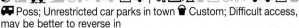

7; Max 48hrs 🛎 Aire Services 3000; Token; €4; 8 CEE elec points

➡ Rue Adoue. From Asasp Arros in south enter town on N134. Follow road straight on over 2 roundabouts. Aire after Total fuel station on right, signed. Entrance is restricted on both sides by wall, but is possible for most motorhomes.

ℹ Pleasant parking. Token from TO, 800m. Town commerce. River adj, but no views. Updated 2015.

NAVARRENX | 104 | D11 | 64190 | T | N43°19.205' W000°45.426'

🚐 Poss; Unrestricted car parks in town 🛎 Custom; Difficult access, may be better to reverse in

➡ Turn off D936 onto D947, sp 'Navarrenx'. Follow road around walled town and at roundabout turn right, sp 'Monein'. Follow road, signed, then turn left onto D2, sp 'Monein' and signed. Immediately turn right in front of Carrefour Express, signed. Service Point 50m on right opp fuel station gas bottles, signed.

ℹ Service Point at supermarket in a pretty, walled town. There is suitable parking in the town, suggest: N43°19.270' W000°45.657'. Inspected 2013.

SALIES DE BEARN | 105 | D11 | 64270 | N43°28.393' W000°56.033'

24; €6/night inc elec; CC 🛎 Custom; Inside barrier; CC; €2

➡ Lieu-Dit Herre. In town centre turn off D17 at roundabout, sp 'Office Notarial'. Pass Casino Hotel and turn right at next roundabout, sp 'Office Notarial' and signed. Turn left after Office Notarial, sp 'Aire Camping-Cars'. In 100m turn left into Aire, signed.

ℹ Commercial Aire on outskirts of small spa town. Very low amp elec. Inspected 2013.

SAUVETERRE DE BEARN | 106 | D11 | 64390 | N43°24.073' W000°56.343'

20 🛎 Custom

➡ Sauterisse. Turn off D933 at roundabout north of the town, sp 'Mairie'. Follow road and Service Point is on the left as enter town, signed. Parking adj to tennis court. Turn right opp Service Point, sp 'Stade', and parking 100m: N43°24.053' W000°56.497'.

ℹ Peaceful village with riverside walks and medieval centre. Boulangerie 100m. Reinspected 2013.

ST PALAIS | 107 | D11 | 64120 | N43°19.733' W001°01.933'

5; No parking Thurs pm-Fri am (Market) 🛎 Custom

➡ Place Sante-Elisabeth. Turn off D933 at roundabout, sp 'St Palais'. Follow road across river and straight on into town. Turn right into 2nd car park with covered market building. Drive past 1st building and the Service Point is on the rear of the 2nd building, signed. Adj parking is not designated and is popular with locals.

ℹ Covered animal market adj. Busy town car park. Town commerce adj. Reinspected 2013.

ST JEAN PIED DE PORT | 108 | D11 | 64220 | N43°09.923' W001°13.948'

40; €5.50; Pay at machine 🛎 Custom; 12 unmetered CEE elec points

➡ D933/Ave du Jai Alai. Turn off D933 at roundabout, sp 'P Jai Alai'. Aire is on right at end of road near Carrefour supermarket and sports facilities, signed. Service Point behind building, signed.

ℹ This is the only car park in town that allows motorhomes. WCs in sports hall. Updated 2015.

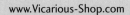

AMOU

| 109 | D11 | 40330 | ⛺ | N43°35.350' W000°44.583' |

🚐 €6/night; Collected 🚰 Custom; Apr-Oct

➤ Ave de la Digue. Turn off D13 at roundabout, sp 'Hagetmau' and signed. Go straight over next roundabout, sp 'Camping'. Turn right as exit town onto D346, sp 'Camping'. Turn right again, sp 'Camping'. Follow road through sports facilities and drive through campsite behind stadium stands and Service Point on left, signed.

ⓘ Riverside campsite in pleasant woodland setting. Hardstanding parking at stadium out of season. Reinspected 2013

HAGETMAU

| 110 | D11 | 40700 | 🏢 | N43°39.247' W000°35.898' |

🚐 15 🚰 Custom

➤ Rue de Piquette. Turn off D933s bypass, sp 'ZI de Piquette' and signed. Follow road and turn 1st right into Rue de Piquette. Aire in car park on right, signed. Note: Very complicated one-way system through town and limited parking.

ⓘ Aire in industrial area, most of which is not in use. Adj to river, limited views but good for fishing. Town commerce 350m. Inspected 2012.

POMAREZ

| 111 | D11 | 40360 | 🏢 | N43°37.697' W000°49.700' |

🚐 6; Max 72hrs 🚰 Custom; 12 unmetered Cont elec points

➤ D15. From centre follow sp 'Amou'. Aire opp D15 junction to Amou on central gravel parking area in front of bull ring. Service Point beside roadside building, signed.

ⓘ Aire will not be accessible during bull fights/events due to parked cars (approx 20 days per year). Small town commerce adj. Reinspected 2013.

POUILLON

| 112 | D11 | 40350 | 🏰 | N43°36.595' W000°59.514' |

🚐 Tolerated; See info 🚰 Custom

➤ D322. Follow sp 'Camping' in town and exit town on D322, sp 'Mimbaste' and 'Camping'. Service Point outside municipal campsite, opp large 'Maïsadour' building as exit village, signed.

ⓘ Service Point outside municipal campsite. Tolerated parking at lake, off D22, follow sp 'Lac du Luc': N43°35.639' W001°00.942'. Leisure lake has pleasant walk, restaurants, and gîtes. Reinspected 2016.

PEYREHORADE

| 113 | D11 | 40300 | ⚓ | N43°32.584' W001°05.996' |

🚐 10 🚰 Custom; Tap difficult, hose needed

➤ D817/Quai du Sablot. From river bridge exit town on D817, sp 'Pau'. Aire on left in town parking opp river near Carrefour market, signed.

ⓘ Suitable night halt but transitory road traffic makes it very noisy. Carrefour supermarket adj. Only 4km from motorway. Reinspected 2016.

ANGLET 1

| 114 | C11 | 64600 | ⚓ | N43°30.427' W001°32.059' |

🚐 60; €10/night Jul-Aug; €6/night Apr-June/Sept-Nov; Pay at machine; Max 48hrs 🚰 Custom

➤ Parking des Corsaires, off D405/Blvd des Plages. From Anglet follow sp 'Anglet-Océan' or 'Plages' and signed. At the sea turn right onto D405, sp 'La Barre'. Turn left into Aire, signed. Entrance up steep slope. Service Point and ticket machine to right, parking to left.

ⓘ Oversubscribed, large, unlevel, landscaped, commercial Aire. Surfing beach 400m downhill. Police inspect tickets. 114 and 115 are best avoided May-Sept. Reinspected 2016.

ANGLET 2	115	C11	64600		N43°31.584' W001°30.900'

🌐 P 🚐 ⛵ 👜 🎵 🚌 F ❄ | 🗝 🏭 🔋 E WC 👦 🏠 🚌 F ▣

🚐 50; €10/night Jul-Aug; €6/night Apr-Jun/Sept-Nov; CC; Pay at meter beside Service Point 👕 Custom

➡ Parking des Barre. Follow D405 past 114, straight over roundabouts and past La Barre parking area. The Aire will be visible to the left. At the next roundabout turn left (almost right around), signed. The Service Point is straight on and parking is past the Service Point almost adj to La Barre parking.

ℹ Large, open, oversubscribed Aire offering level space; some bays have water views. Can take any sized unit. Road noise. All other car parks restricted. 114 and 115 are best avoided May-Sept. Reinspected 2016.

HAVE YOU VISITED AN AIRE?

GPS co-ordinates in this guide are protected by copyright law

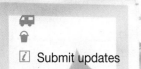

ℹ Submit updates
- Amendments
- New Aires
- Not changed

Visit www.all-the-aires.co.uk/submissions.shtml
to upload your updates and photos.

Take at least 5 digital photos showing
- Signs
- Service Point
- Parking
- Overview
- Amenities

LABENNE OCEAN	117	C11	40530		N43°35.685' W001°27.278'

🌐 P 🚐 ⛵ 👜 🎵 🚌 F ❄ | 🗝 🏭 🔋 E WC 👦 🏠 🚌 F ▣

🚐 70; €10/night; Collected; Apr-Oct; Max 2 nights 👕 Custom

➡ D126. From D810 at Labenne turn onto D126 at traffic lights, sp 'Labenne-Océan'. Turn right as enter Labenne-Océan, signed; GPS taken here. Follow bumpy road 150m to Aire, signed. Actual GPS: N43°35.760' W001°27.302'.

ℹ Large parking area in cork trees offering parking on either grass, sand or gravel. Watch for soft sand. Always likely to have space. Adventure park adj with waterslide and ropes course. Reinspected 2016.

ONDRES PLAGE	118	C11	40440		N43°34.589' W001°29.215'

🌐 P 🚐 ⛵ 👜 🎵 🚌 F ❄ | 🗝 🏭 🔋 E WC 👦 🏠 🚌 F ▣

🚐 41; €8/night Sept-Jun; €10/night Jul-Aug; Collected; Max 48hrs 👕 Customised Flot Bleu Pacific; 12 16amp Cont elec points on left

➡ D26/Ave de la Plage. From Ondres follow D26, sp 'Ondres Plage'. In car parks at end of road drive to far end, then turn left into Parking 3, signed. Barriers have been built, but were removed at the time of inspection; could be reinstated.

ℹ Popular Aire adj to pleasant beach commerce. Sandy surfing beach down slope with beach restaurant. Nice place to watch or catch the surf. Cycle/walking path to local commerce. Reinspected 2016.

CAPBRETON	119	C11	40130		N43°38.143' W001°26.809'

🌐 P 🚐 ⛵ 👜 🎵 🚌 F ❄ | 🗝 🏭 🔋 E WC 👦 🏠 🚌 F ▣

🚐 133; €8.50/night Mar-Apr/Oct-Nov; €11.50/night May-Jun/Sept; €13.50/night Jul-Aug; Inc 10amp CEE elec; Pay at hut/Collected 👕 Custom x2; Inside/past hut

➡ Allée des Ortolans, at beach. On D28 follow sp 'Centre Ville'. Pass the Mairie on the left, then go straight over roundabout, sp 'P Le Piste'. At next roundabout go straight on, sp 'Les Plages'. Turn left, signed, and cross carriageway, signed. Turn right, signed. Turn right again, signed. Aire at beach on left.

ℹ Large, popular, open, commercial Aire on beachside car park. Sand dune and view of surfing beach with strong currents adj. Town commerce 1.5km. Reinspected 2016.

BIARRITZ	120	C11	64200		N43°27.990' W001°34.302'

🌐 P 🚐 ⛵ 👜 🎵 🚌 F ❄ | 🗝 🏭 🔋 E WC 👦 🏠 🚌 F ▣

🚐 50; €12/night; CC; Max 48hrs 👕 Custom x2; 24 16amp CEE elec points on 6 bollards; Inside barrier

➡ Ave de la Milady. To avoid central Biarritz enter from south by following sp 'Bidart'. In Bidart turn left at roundabout onto D655, sp 'Biarritz'. At end of road turn right, then follow D655 to Biarritz, where it becomes D911. Turn right at roundabout, opp Hôtel de Milady, signed. Enter through barrier.

ℹ Oversubscribed Aire, busy all year. Motorhomes banned from all town parking. Road noise. Beach 500m. Supermarket 1.5m; Biarritz centre 3.5km. Reinspected 2016.

ST JEAN DE LUZ

| 121 | C11 | 64500 | | N43°23.112' W001°39.780' |

🚐 20; €6 Apr-Oct; €4 Nov-Mar; Pay at machine; Max 48hrs 🚰 Euro Relais Junior; €2

➡ Pont Charles de Gaulle, D810. From south on D810 cross river bridge and Aire immediately on right before roundabout, signed.

ℹ Oversubscribed Aire in noisy location between road and railway, best avoided. Reinspected 2016.

HENDAYE PLAGE

| 122 | C11 | 64700 | | N43°22.213' W001°45.887' |

🚐 20; €10/24hrs; CC 🚰 Aire Services 7005; Outside barrier; €4; Pin code required

➡ Rue d'Ansoenia. Enter town from south on D912. Turn right onto Rue des Rosiers and follow to end. Turn right again and left at roundabout. Aire is on left by train station. Enter through barrier.

ℹ Popular, landscaped, commercial Aire adj to train station, noise from trains. Town 1.4km. D912 coast road a pleasant drive. Reinspected 2016.

ST PEE SUR NIVELLE

| 123 | C11 | 64310 | | N43°20.983' W001°31.283' |

🚐 62; €5/12hrs; €9/24hrs; CC; 8m bays 🚰 Flot Bleu Fontaine; Outside barrier; Token/CC; €2; Flot Bleu Elec; Inside barrier; Token/CC; 3 tokens/12hrs elec

➡ Promenade du Parlement de Navarre. On east side of town turn off D918 at roundabout, sp 'Le Lac'. At next 2 mini roundabouts go right and follow road along lake edge, signed. Aire adj to lake, access via Flot Bleu Park barrier.

ℹ Overlandscaped, commercial Aire adj to large, attractive leisure lake. Pleasant walks, swimming and pedalos. Reinspected 2016.

SARE

| 124 | C11 | 64310 | | N43°18.737' W001°35.038' |

🚐 20; €8/night; Pay at machine; Max 48hrs 🚰 Custom

➡ D406. Follow sp 'Ascain' past Sare on D4. Go straight on at roundabout, signed. Aire is on left in car park, signed.

ℹ Level Aire offering longest bays on roadside edge, limited local traffic at night. Sare is a picturesque Basque Beau Village. Col de St Ignace on D4 has cog tourist train and large car parks. Reinspected 2016.

COL D'IBARDIN

| 125 | C11 | 64122 | | N43°18.583' W001°41.133' |

🚐 20; Tolerated 🚰 None; Poss at nearby AVIA fuel station

➡ D404, at Ibardin on the border of France and Spain. From Urrugne take D4 to Col d'Ibardin and follow signs to the border along D404. Border at the summit of the hill. Turn right and parking on the right adj to road and shops.

ℹ Popular parking on Spanish border. Numerous commerce and cheap fuel. Worth a look. Reinspected 2016.

ESPELETTE

| 126 | C11 | 64250 | | N43°20.319' W001°26.854' |

🚐 5 🚰 None

➡ D918. Adj to D918/D249 roundabout on main route through, signed.

ℹ Motorhome and bus parking adj to chocolate shop and other local producers. Reinspected 2016.

VIEUX BOUCAU LES BAINS 1

127   C10   40480   N43°46.815' W001°24.071'

120; €7/night Oct-Apr; €13/night May-Sept; Inc elec and WiFi; Max 48hrs; No trailers; Custom; Inside barrier; Inc

➡ Ave des Pêcheurs. From south on D652 turn left at large roundabout, sp 'Lac de Port d'Albret' and signed. Entrance to Aire 350m on right, no option to turn around at barrier. Enter through barrier; pay on exit.

ℹ Large, commercial Aire with parking between trees. Long lead needed for elec. Local commerce and golf course adj. Wind and kite surfing on lake; beach 350m. Reinspected 2016.

VIEUX BOUCAU LES BAINS 2

128   C10   40480   N43°47.675' W001°24.322'

35; €6/night Oct-Apr; €12/night May-Sept; Max 48hrs; Custom; Inside barrier; Inc

➡ Blvd du Marensin, north of town near Plage des Sablères. Follow sp 'Municipal Camping des Sablères'. Go past the entrance to small parking area. Take ticket, pay on exit.

ℹ Uninspiring and undesirable. Reinspected 2016.

SEIGNOSSE

129   C11   40510   N43°41.447' W001°25.536'

30; €8.40/night Sept-Mar; €10.80/night Apr-Aug; Inc CEE elec and WiFi; CC; Grass/sand parking; Euro Relais Junior; Inside barrier

➡ D79. Adj to D79 coast road, signed. Enter through PARKNIGHT barrier.

ℹ Commercial Aire located between noisy D79 coast road and a large campsite. Grass parking under evergreen trees. Reinspected 2016.

SOUSTONS PLAGE

130   C11   40140   N43°46.518' W001°24.628'

82; €7/night Oct-Apr; €13/night May-Sept; Inc 16amp elec; Pay at machine; Max 72hrs; Max 10m; Euro Relais Junior; Inside barrier

➡ Ave de la Petre. From D652 turn off at roundabout, sp 'Soustons Plage' and signed. Follow road to end, signed. Enter through Urba Flux barrier.

ℹ Very pleasant, peaceful, commercial Aire with open and shaded parking. Some bays with beach views. Direct access to Lac Martin beach and the sea. Nicest Aire in area. Tourist commerce adj, resort 800m. Reinspected 2016.

MOLIETS PLAGE

131   C/D10   40660   N43°51.040' W001°22.952'

40; €7/24hrs mid Mar-Apr/Oct-mid Nov; €13/24hrs May-Sept; Max 10m; Max 7 days; Custom; CEE elec points; Inside barrier

➡ Rue du Tuc. Turn off D652 at roundabout onto D117, sp 'MAA', 'Plage' and signed. Follow road and turn left, sp 'Le Tuc'. Cross road and Aire immediately on left. Entry through barrier, signed. Be careful of low trees.

ℹ Pleasant, commercial Aire with parking under trees. Some road noise. Sea, restaurants and bars all 300m at sand dune. Golf adj. Reinspected 2016.

LEON

132   D10   40550   N43°53.037' W001°19.086'

50; €11/10pm-9am; Pay at machine; Custom

➡ D409/Route de Puntaou. In Léon turn off D652 at roundabout onto D409, sp 'Le Lac'. At lake turn left and follow road for 450m, signed. Parking area signed 250m from lake.

ℹ Pleasant, large, open grass parking area with partial lake views. Lake has tourist commerce, swimming beach and pedalo hire. One of the nicest Aires in the area. Reinspected 2016.

MESSANGES | 133 | D10 | 40660 | N43°48.975' W001°24.041'

🚐 35; Max 2 days 🚽 None; WC adj

➡ D82. In Messanges turn off D652 at roundabout onto D82, sp 'Moisan' and 'Plages'. Follow road for 2km, then turn right into 1st car park, not signed.

ℹ Car park 300m from beach with commerce accessible up sand dune, no view. Sections of car park closest to beach are 1.9m and 2.3m height restricted and ban motorhomes overnight. Enjoy Aire while it lasts and expect change. Inspected 2016.

VIELLE ST GIRONS | 134 | D10 | 40560 | N43°57.185' W001°21.478'

🚐 48; €9.90/night Sept/Apr-Jun; €15.95/night Jul-Aug; Apr-Sept; Pay at campsite reception 🚽 Aire Services 7005; Inside barrier; Token (3/3)/€; €4

➡ Aire Camping-Car Les Tourterelles, off D42. Turn off D652 at traffic lights onto D42, sp 'St Girons-Plage'. Follow road towards sea, then turn right at roundabout, signed. Turn right again into Aire, signed. Enter through barrier. Report to reception of Camping Les Tourterelles for access.

ℹ Open, landscaped, commercial Aire run by adj campsite. Sandy beach 450m; tourist commerce open high season. Reinspected 2016.

CONTIS PLAGE | 135 | D10 | 40170 | N44°05.600' W001°19.117'

🚐 80; €9/night Mar-May/Oct-Nov; €13/night Jun-Sept; Inc service; CC; Free Dec-Feb; Max 48hrs 🚽 Euro Relais Junior; Inside barrier; 26 CEE elec points (Max 1hr battery charging!); Showers and washing up sink

➡ Ave du Phare. On D652 turn onto D41 at roundabout, sp 'Contis Plage'. After entering Contis Plage turn right, sp 'Parking Plage' and signed. Aire on left, signed. Enter through CC-operated barrier.

ℹ Pleasant, large, open commercial Aire surrounded by pine trees. Beach 500m over dune (uphill). Town commerce 600m. Reinspected 2016.

AZUR | 136 | D11 | 40140 | N43°47.307' W001°18.718'

🚐 30; €9.60/night; CC 🚽 Euro Relais Junior; Inside barrier; Inc; 35 10amp CEE elec points

➡ Route du Lac. On D50 turn onto Route du Lac at roundabout by church, signed. Turn left into Aire before lake. Enter through PARKNIGHT barrier.

ℹ Landscaped, open, commercial Aire 100m from the northern edge of Lake Soustons, no view. Picnic area and tourist commerce adj. Local commerce 1.4km at Azur. Inspected 2016.

ST PAUL LES DAX 1 | 137 | D10 | 40990 | N43°44.052' W001°04.604'

🚐 9; Max 48hrs 🚽 Custom

➡ Ave du President Salvador Allende. In St Paul les Dax follow sp 'Lac de Christus'. Turn off at roundabout by Lac de Christus, signed. Follow road for 2km past 2nd lake. When road bends left, fork to right, signed. Follow road into woods to Aire.

ℹ Popular Aire providing shaded, individual bays in a woodland setting at the end of lake road. Lovely lake walks. No lakeside parking 10pm-6am. Reinspected 2016.

ST PAUL LES DAX 2 | 138 | D11 | 40990 | N43°43.653' W001°03.650'

🚐 10; No parking Mon-Fri am 🚽 Custom

➡ Rue René Loustalot. Turn off D824 onto D947 and follow sp 'St Paul les Dax'. At roundabout take the 1st exit, sp 'Lac de Christus' and 'Casino'. Follow sp 'Lac de Christus' and 'Casino' and at the end of road turn right, then immediately left, signed. Service Point on left.

ℹ Service Point only except Fri and Sat nights. Mon-Thurs parking is reserved for municipal staff who arrive early in the mornings. Cemetery adj. Reinspected 2016.

DAX

| 139 | D11 | 40100 | | N43°42.833' W001°02.950' | SP |

🚐 7; Max 72hrs ⚓ Custom

▶ Blvd Albert Camus. From south on D947 follow sp 'Dax' and 'St Vincent'. At roundabout next to bull ring turn right (do not cross river), sp 'Bordeaux', 'St Paul les Dax' and signed. At mini roundabout turn left, sp 'St Vincent' and signed. Aire immediately on right, signed.

ℹ Small, very popular Aire adj to riverside park; no overflow opportunity. Suffers constant main route road noise. Adj thermal spa claimed to be the first in France. KFC adj. Town centre across river, 450m. Reinspected 2016.

HOSSEGOR

| 140 | C11 | 40150 | | N43°40.329' W001°25.169' | SP |

🚐 85; €6/night Oct-May; Max 15 days; €12/night Jun-Sept; Max 4 days ⚓ Urba Flux Tall; €2; WC; All pin code and inside barrier

▶ Route des Lacs. Turn off D152 at roundabout northwest of Hossegor, sp 'Lac et Océan' and signed. Aire on left, signed. Enter through Urba Flux barrier.

ℹ Pleasantly landscaped commercial Aire near Lac d'Hossegor. Sign states max 7.5m length, but much longer motorhomes inside; assess before entering. Hossegor centre 2km. Tourist commerce along lake edge; free shuttle bus to lake from Aire Jul-Aug. Inspected 2016.

MIMIZAN PLAGE 1

| 141 | D10 | 40200 | ! | N44°12.839' W001°16.938' | SP |

🚐 60 ⚓ None; See 142

▶ D626. Turn right at roundabout as enter Mimizan Plage from Mimizan, sp 'Camping Municipal' and signed. Entrance to Aire 230m on right.

ℹ Large, open parking which has recently been renovated. New Service Point expected summer 2017. Constantly opening and closing; expect change. Municipal campsite, next right, signs an exterior Flot Bleu Service Point, but does not have one. Reinspected 2016.

MIMIZAN PLAGE 2

| 142 | D10 | 40200 | | N44°12.291' W001°17.829' | SP |

🚐 80; €3/1hr; €9.50/24hrs; Inc service and CEE elec; CC; No trailers ⚓ Flot Bleu Pacific x2; Inside barrier; WC behind Service Point

▶ Rue des Gourbets. From Mimizan follow sp 'Plage' along D626 to Mimizan Plage. Turn left, sp 'Station Camping Car', and follow sp 'Station Camping Car' over bridge. Follow road to end and Aire in large car park adj to beach. Entrance through Flot Bleu Park barrier.

ℹ Large, popular, open Aire adj to sand dune. Sandy beach 150m over dune; seaside resort with cafés/restaurant; surfing beach. No trailers. Reinspected 2016.

STE EULALIE EN BORN

| 143 | D10 | 40200 | | N44°18.362' W001°10.915' | SP |

🚐 40; €4.50/night Apr/Oct; €5.50/night May; €7/night Jun-Sept; Free Nov-Mar; See info ⚓ Custom; Apr-Oct

▶ Route du Port, off D652. Turn off D652 onto Route du Lac, sp 'Le Lac', and follow for 1.9km, then turn left opp campsite. Aire on left and Service Point at end of road on left. Pay at campsite reception opp.

ℹ Informal Aire overlooking marina. Parking on grass on left, do not park on right. No services when free. Seasonal café. Reinspected 2016.

GASTES ★

| 144 | D10 | 40160 | | N44°19.714' W001°09.057' | |

🚐 75; €2/24hrs Jan-mid Mar/mid Nov-Dec; €4.50/24hrs mid Mar-May/Oct-mid Nov; €8/24hrs Jun-Sept; Inc service; CC ⚓ Custom; Inside barrier; Washing sinks at Service Point

▶ Ave du Lac. In Gastes turn off D652, sp 'Le Lac'. At end of road turn left and follow road along lake edge to Aire on left. Enter through pop-up bollard.

ℹ Large, popular Aire with many bays having views across boats to lake. Area has a pleasant, lively feel and seasonal commerce. Swimming beach and lakeside recreation area adj. Reinspected 2016.

CAZAUX

145 D9 33260 N44°31.906' W001°09.616'

🚐 30; €12/24hrs inc elec; CC; Max 4.5t Euro Relais Mini; 32 6amp CEE elec points; All inside barrier

➡ Rue Guynemer. From La Teste-de-Buch follow D112, sp 'Cazaux'. In Cazaux go straight over roundabout, sp 'Camping du Lac' and signed. Turn right, sp 'P Le Lac'. Aire on right, signed. Enter through barrier.

ℹ Commercial Aire adj to, and operated by, slightly officious campsite. Only 1m between bays; would feel cramped if full. WiFi €8/day; showers €2pp. Lac de Cazaux et de Sanguinet 350m, no views. Inspected 2016.

PARENTIS EN BORN

146 D10 40160 N44°20.653' W001°05.907'

🚐 20; €8.50/night inc service and elec; CC Euro Relais Junior; Inside barrier; 6 Cont elec points; 6 10amp CEE elec points

➡ Route des Campings. From centre follow sp 'Le Lac'. Just before lake turn right, signed. Aire 100m on right. Enter via pop-up bollard.

ℹ Parking opp lake, no view. Marina, lake and restaurants 150m. Reinspected 2016.

MORCENX

147 D10 40110 N44°02.321' W000°54.576'

🚐 50; Grass/sand parking Custom

➡ Chemin de L'Abattoir. From town follow D77 towards Sabres. In 200m turn right, signed. Follow road to end and the Service Point is on left.

ℹ In large, open grass area adj to sports facilities and noisy mainline train track. Trains 6am-11pm; regular departures to Bordeaux (1hr). Town centre with small town commerce, 700m. Reinspected 2016.

NAVARROSSE

148 D10 40600 N44°25.920' W001°09.958'

🚐 80; €8/night Oct-May; €12.50/night Jun/Sept; €16/night Jul-Aug; CC; Max 3 days Custom; €4; Pin code; 10amp elec mix of CEE and Cont

➡ Port de Navarrosse. Turn off D652 onto D305 at roundabout, sp 'Navarrosse'. Follow road, then turn right, sp 'Port Navarrosse' and signed. Follow road, then follow signs to Aire on right, signed. Enter through barrier; take ticket, pay on exit.

ℹ Parking overlooking small marina or amongst trees. Shop open in summer. Reinspected 2016.

BISCARROSSE PLAGE

149 D10 40600 N44°27.422' W001°14.449'

🚐 80; €8/night Oct-May; €12.50/night Jun/Sept; €16/night Jul-Aug; CC Custom; €4

➡ Aire du Vivier, Rue du Tit. From Arcachon follow D218. At 1st roundabout at Biscarrosse Plage turn right, signed. At next roundabout turn left, then turn right, signed. Entry through barrier. Take ticket, pay on exit.

ℹ Parking among pine trees on sand. Beach adj, through trees. Local commerce 200m. Reinspected 2016.

SANGUINET 1

150 D9 40460 N44°29.037' W001°05.495'

🚐 10; €8/night Custom

➡ Aire des Bardets, Ave de Losa. From town follow sp 'Le Lac'. Turn left at lake, past **151**. Follow road around past campsite and turn left, sp 'Camping Car', into designated motorhome parking.

ℹ Sailing school, campsite and lake adj. Further from beach and day-trippers. Reinspected 2013.

SANGUINET 2

| 151 | D9 | 40460 | ⚓ | N44°29.160' W001°05.049' | SP |

⊕ 🅿 🚐 ... 🚌 F ❄ | 🔧 ⊞ 🏠 E WC ... 🚌 F
🚐 10; €9/night 🏠 None; See 150

➡ Ave de Losa, at lake. From town follow sp 'Le Lac'. Turn left at lake, then take 1st turning to left by Le Pavillion restaurant opp beach, sp 'Parking'.

ℹ Small pleasant parking shared with cars under overhanging trees. Lake and beach adj. Restaurant. Some soft ground. Updated 2015.

GPS Co-ordinates for SatNav

The GPS Co-ordinates published in this guide were taken onsite by our inspectors. We consider them a valuable and unique asset and at the time of publishing have decided not to publish them as electronic files for use on navigation devices. You have permission to type in the co-ordinates of an Aire you intend to visit but not to store or share them. For the security of our copyright:

- **Do not compile them into lists**

- **Do not publish, share or reproduce them anywhere in any format**

LA TESTE DE BUCH 1

| 153 | D9 | 33260 | 🏢 | N44°36.999' W001°06.831' | SP |

⊕ 🅿 🚐 ... 🚌 F ❄ | 🔧 ⊞ 🏠 E WC ... 🚌 F
🚐 12 🏠 Urba Flux Tall; €2/10mins water or 15 mins elec

➡ Ave de l'Europe. Turn off N250 at roundabout onto D652, sp 'Sanguinet'. At roundabout turn right, sp 'E.Leclerc'. Go straight over next roundabout. Aire on left by E.Leclerc supermarket fuel station, signed.

ℹ Designated parking in out of town retail park. Road noise. Ideal as a night halt. Inspected 2016.

LA TESTE DE BUCH 2

| 154 | D9 | 33260 | 🏢 | N44°38.126' W001°09.167' | SP |

⊕ 🅿 🚐 ... 🚌 F ❄ | 🔧 ⊞ 🏠 E WC ... 🚌 F
🚐 1; Other parking avail 🏠 None; See 153

➡ Centre Commercial Cap Océan. Exit La Teste centre on D217. Turn right off D217 at roundabout, sp 'Centre Commercial Cap Océan'. Turn left at next roundabout into Intermarché supermarket. Drive behind supermarket to designated parking, signed.

ℹ Single designated bay in supermarket car park; further parking avail. Town centre 1km. Inspected 2016.

LE TEICH 1

| 155 | D9 | 33470 | ☎ | N44°37.984' W001°01.585' | SP |

⊕ 🅿 🚐 ... 🚌 F ❄ | 🔧 ⊞ 🏠 E WC ... 🚌 F
🚐 5; Also see 156 🏠 Euro Relais Tall; €5; CC

➡ Rue de l'Industrie. In Le Teich turn off D650, main route, by church, sp 'P la Gare' and signed. At roundabout turn right, sp 'Gare'. Follow road past train station and Aire on left, signed.

ℹ Designated parking adj to railway and station; electric trains cause some noise. Frequent trains to Arcachon (17 mins). Also see 156. Reinspected 2016.

LE TEICH 2

| 156 | D9 | 33470 | ⛵ | N44°38.426' W001°01.180' | SP |

⊕ 🅿 🚐 ... 🚌 F ❄ | 🔧 ⊞ 🏠 E WC ... 🚌 F
🚐 30 🏠 Tap; WC and free WiFi at café; See 155

➡ Rue du Port. Turn off D650 at roundabout in Le Teich, sp 'Réserve Ornithologique'. Follow road, then at roundabout turn left. Designated parking in 1st car park on right, signed.

ℹ Pleasant, designated parking in peaceful location adj to Réserve Ornithologique, bird sanctuary/reserve; entry €8.90pp. Marina and café adj. Inspected 2016.

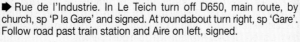

ARCACHON | 157 | D9 | 33120 | | N44°39.096' W001°08.893' | SP

🚐 15; Max 24hrs 🚽 Euro Relais Junior; 2 CEE elec points (Not working)

➡ D650. Enter Arcachon from La Teste de Buch on D650. Go straight over roundabout with LIDL on left and turn around at next roundabout, turn right into Aire opp Citroën/Total garage in front of sp 'Parking Ralentissez'.

ℹ Popular Aire despite being far from ideal; adj to busy, noisy main road. Stadium adj. Lots of local cycle paths. Reinspected 2016.

LEGE CAP FERRET - L'Herbe | 158 | D9 | 33950 | | N44°41.176' W001°14.723' |

🚐 20; 8pm-9am only 🚽 Tap by steps in cemetery, 60m; See 160

➡ D106/Ave de Bordeaux. Follow D106 towards Cap Ferret. After entering L'Herbe turn right at roundabout, sp 'Cap Ferret' and signed. In 600m turn left into cemetery car park, signed. Turn immediately right into parking.

ℹ Dead quiet parking, except for local road noise from D106. Ideal night halt after exploring Cap Ferret. Inspected 2016.

LEGE CAP FERRET - Claouey 1 | 159 | D9 | 33950 | | N44°45.121' W001°11.298' | SP

🚐 20; 8pm-9am only 🚽 None; See 160

➡ Ave Édouard Branly. Exit Arès on D3 towards Lège Cap Ferret. Turn left at roundabout onto D106, sp 'Cap Ferret'. Follow road for 5km, then turn right at roundabout by Super U, sp 'Camping les Embruns'. Follow road to left, then turn right before Camping les Embruns. Parking on left under trees, signed.

ℹ Pleasant parking under trees adj to campsite. Only likely to be busy Jul-Aug when parking will also be used by holiday hut renters. More peaceful than 160. Walking path adj. Inspected 2016.

LEGE CAP FERRET - Claouey 2 | 160 | D9 | 33950 | | N44°45.106' W001°10.821' | SP

🚐 30; 8pm-9am 🚽 Flot Bleu Fontaine

➡ D106. Exit Arès on D3 towards Lège Cap Ferret, then follow D106 for 5km towards Claouey. Turn left at roundabout by Super U, sp 'Camping Municipal' and signed. Turn immediately left, signed.

ℹ Aire in semi industrial area adj to main road with supermarket opp. Intended as night halt. Also see 159. Super U fuel station with LPG opp: N44°45.041' W001°10.821'. Reinspected 2016.

TAUSSAT | 161 | D9 | 33138 | | N44°43.035' W001°04.180' |

🚐 14 🚽 Custom, at WCs; No drive over drain

➡ Avenue Albert Pitres. From Audenge turn off D3 into lane, sp 'Centre de Vacances'. Follow road for 550m then turn left, sp 'Port Ostréicole de Taussat'. Aire 100m on left in small parking area before port, signed. Service Point on left 10m past parking.

ℹ Popular, small Aire next to recycling. Small tidal fishing harbour and beach 50m. Bird watching over mud flats when tide out. Village with local commerce 300m. Reinspected 2016.

ANDERNOS LES BAINS | 162 | D9 | 33510 | | N44°44.652' W001°06.516' | SP

🚐 80; €10/night; CC; Pay at Service Point and display ticket; Max 48hrs 🚽 Urba Flux Tall; CC; €3/20 mins

➡ Ave du Commandant Allègre. Enter Andernos-les-Bains on D3 from Arès. Turn right off D3 at roundabout, sp 'Église St Eloi'. Turn right into harbour, sp 'Aire de Camping Car'. Turn right and Service Point 100m on left. Parking 100m past Service Point under pine trees.

ℹ Pleasant parking adj to small working harbour, no view, with numerous restaurants. Town with tourist commerce 700m. Motorhomes banned in all other town parking. Reinspected 2016.

LE HUGA
| 163 | D9 | 33680 | | N45°00.365' W001°09.925' |

150; €13.50/24hrs inc 16amp CEE elec; CC 🔔 DEPAGNE and custom; Inside barrier; Inc

➡ Allée de Sauviels, off D6. In Le Huga turn off D6, signed. Aire is on both sides of road with Service Points at each. Entrance through barrier.

ℹ Large landscaped commercial Aire. Updated 2016.

CARCANS
| 164 | D9 | 33121 | | N45°05.106' W001°08.904' |

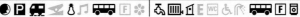

30; €5.80/night; Collected; Jun-Sept 🔔 Flot Bleu Fontaine

➡ Route de Bombannes. Exit Carcans on D207 at D207/D3 roundabout, sp 'Bombannes'. Follow sp 'Bombannes'. After exiting Maubuisson Aire is 1.5km on left, signed.

ℹ Lovely wooded area near lake. Motorhomes banned from all other parking at night. Reinspected 2013.

HOURTIN PORT
| 165 | D9 | 33990 | | N45°10.841' W001°04.885' |

54; €8.30/night; CC 🔔 SISTAL; Inside barrier; Elec €2/24hrs

➡ Avenue du Lac. From south on D3 turn left in Hourtin onto D4, sp 'Hourtin Port'. Continue over roundabout and follow road for 2km. 500m after Camping les Ormes, turn left to Aire, signed. Entry through barrier.

ℹ Beach and marina adj. Individual pitches. Pay for elec at cycle hire adj to mini golf. Self service laundry in Hourtin centre. Reinspected 2013.

MONTALIVET LES BAINS
| 166 | D8 | 33930 | | N45°22.535' W001°09.431' |

60; €6.50/night; Collected 🔔 None; Poss Service Point between boules court and ALDI: N45°22.505' W001°08.643'

➡ Aire Plage Sud, adj to seafront. From north enter town on D102e1. Follow road straight on along sea past miles of unrestricted parking. At Montalivet go straight on along seafront. Aire in car park on right as road bends away from sea, signed.

ℹ Close to beach, but no shade. Town 400m. Sun market in town. Updated 2015.

GRAYAN ET L'HOPITAL
| 167 | D8 | 33590 | | N45°25.995' W001°08.625' |

12; Max 48hrs 🔔 Euro Relais Junior; Token (ER); €3.50

➡ Route de l'Océan. Turn off D101 onto C202, sp 'Le Gurp' and 'Camping Municipal du Gurp'. Follow C202 all the way towards sea, going straight over roundabout, and the Service Point is on the right adj to Camping Municipal du Gurp, signed.

ℹ Parking on a large, level grassy verge alongside road adj to municipal campsite and facilities. 700m from a vast sandy beach with WWII bunkers, small store, beach commerce and restaurants. Updated 2016.

SOULAC SUR MER
| 168 | D8 | 33780 | | N45°30.001' W001°08.325' |

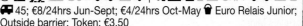

45; €8/24hrs Jun-Sept; €4/24hrs Oct-May 🔔 Euro Relais Junior; Outside barrier; Token; €3.50

➡ Blvd de l'Amélie. Follow sp 'L'Amélie', then sp 'Camping Les Sables'. Aire on right adj to and sp 'Camping les Sables d'Argent'. Enter through Aire Service Barrier, Service Point outside barrier.

ℹ Direct access to beach and tourist town accessible via cycle path. 167 only 11.5km drive. Reinspected 2013.

LE VERDON SUR MER | 169 | D8 | 33123 | N45°32.722' W001°03.263'

🚐 56; €5/night Oct-May, €8/night Jun-Sept; CC; Max 72hrs 🚰 Urba Flux Tall; CC; €2; Outside barrier

➡ Allée des Baines/D1e4. From south on D1215 turn right onto D1e4, sp 'Le Verdon sur Mer'. Follow road to end (later part on cobbles). Aire in parking areas A and B on left, enter through barrier. Service Point outside barriers. Aire well signed through town.

ℹ Sandy beach opp. Motorhomes banned all other local parking. Local commerce 300m. Ferry to Royan. Reinspected 2013.

ST ESTEPHE ✳ | 170 | D8 | 33180 | N45°15.850' W000°45.483'

🚐 100; Grass parking 🚰 Euro Relais Junior; Token (ER); €5

➡ D2e2. From Ste Estèphe follow D2e2 through village to estuary, all roads are quiet and passable. Turn right and Aire on left of road on grassy area overlooking Gironde estuary, signed.

ℹ Lovely parking area with 180° views along Gironde estuary. Some noise from adj road and restaurant. Local commerce 1.3km. Updated 2016.

MACAU | 171 | D9 | 33460 | N45°00.433' W000°36.767'

🚐 4; 6m bays 🚰 Flot Bleu Océane; Token (required for elec only)

➡ Chemin du Mahoura. From D2 turn into Macau at the roundabout, sp 'Macau-Centre', and follow the road straight on. At the crossroads in the centre turn right onto D210, sp 'Ludun'. Take the next left, sp 'P Mahoura' and signed. The Aire is in the car park on the left, signed.

ℹ Small car park with small bays and very sloping. Very old Service Point. Reinspected 2013.

ST JEAN D'ILLAC | 172 | D9 | 33127 | N44°48.641' W000°46.489'

🚐 3 🚰 Flot Bleu Euro (Not working); CC; €2; Lift grid for WC emptying

➡ Allée JJ Rousseau, off D106 roundabout at Casino supermarket. Near LIDL, signed. 3 designated bays to left of Casino supermarket, signed. Service Point in fuel station: N44°48.615' W000°46.495'.

ℹ LIDL and supermarket adj. No parking at sports centre. Reinspected 2016.

BERNOS BEAULAC | 173 | E10 | 33430 | N44°22.181' W000°14.556'

🚐 5; €4/9pm-9am; CC; Pay at Service Point 🚰 Urba Flux Tall; CC; €2

➡ N524, at Halte Nautique. From Bazas take N524 south and Aire is just south of village on left, sp 'Halte Nautique'.

ℹ Pleasant lay-by sheltered from adj main road. Leisure facilities inc open access BBQ and picnic area overlooking weir and pond. Kayak hire adj. Gorges du Ciron adj. Reinspected 2016.

BAZAS | 174 | E11 | 33430 | N44°26.022' W000°12.912'

🚐 10; 7.30pm-7am only Mon-Fri; No restriction at weekends 🚰 Euro Relais Mini

➡ D655e1/Cours Gambetta. From west follow D3 into town. In town follow D3 into one-way system, sp 'Tarbes'. Follow one-way system for 500m, then turn left by cark park on left before 19t weight restricted road. Parking on left; Service Point on left adj to disused weighbridge. Turn left just after Service Point and back to parking.

ℹ Only night parking allowed. In town centre car park that suffers local road noise. Cathedral in centre. Reinspected 2016.

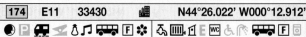

SAUTERNES
175 | E9 | 33210 | N44°32.087' W000°20.573'

🚐 7 Custom; Lift front cover for WC; Be very careful when exit

▶ D125e1. From Langon take D8 south. Turn right onto D125, sp 'Sauternes'. At village square/one-way system continue into village on D125e1, sp 'Bommes'. Turn right to Service Point, signed: N44°32.050' W000°20.617'. For parking follow road immediately past church. Designated parking in 2nd car park on right, signed.

ℹ Aire on edge of pretty tourist village with local commerce and wine tasting. Reinspected 2016.

CAPIAN
176 | E9 | 33550 | N44°42.769' W000°19.775'

🚐 4 Aire Services 3000; €2; 4 CEE elec points; €2/55 mins elec

▶ D13. From Créon take D13, sp 'Cadillac' and 'Capian'. Turn left as enter village into 1st car park, signed. Aire at far end of car park, signed.

ℹ Pleasant, landscaped village Aire overlooking vines. Local sports and community facilities adj. A 5km circular walk departs from village centre, which has no commerce. Reinspected 2016.

CADILLAC
177 | E9 | 33410 | N44°38.319' W000°19.011'

🚐 12; Max 3 nights Custom; 4 5amp CEE elec points; €2/3hrs elec

▶ Ave du Parc. Turn off D10 at roundabout onto D11, sp 'Targon' and signed. Turn left, signed, and follow one-way street. Aire located in the 2nd car park. Designated parking signed at far end. Access difficult due to parked cars Sat am (market).

ℹ Popular Aire occupying section of small car park. Large motorhomes subject to popularity. Cadillac, a beautiful walled town surrounded by vines, 300m. Popular market Sat am. Reinspected 2016.

SAUVETERRE DE GUYENNE
178 | E9 | 33540 | N44°41.635' W000°04.792'

🚐 5; 6m bays plus unlimited overhang; Poss grass parking in summer Urba Flux Tall; WCs 150m, to rear of boules building

▶ Rue de la Vignague. Follow one-way ring road around town. After passing Gendarmerie on left, turn 1st right, signed. Turn 1st left and follow road to end. Turn right and Aire on right outside sports facilities, signed.

ℹ Aire on edge of town in a peaceful location adj to vines. Sports facilities adj. Town with old gateways 500m. Voie Verte cycle path to Créon. Reinspected 2016.

PELLEGRUE
179 | E9 | 33790 | N44°44.694' E000°04.483'

🚐 4; Additional parking in adj lay-by Raclet; 2 unmetered CEE elec points

▶ D16e/Rue du Lavoir. Clearly signed at the D15/D16 crossroads north of town. Signed from all directions.

ℹ Aire in small lay-by adj to old wash house and peaceful village road. Town, 150m uphill, has interesting Victorian covered market and pleasant narrow pedestrianised streets with small town commerce; worth a wander. Bins collected Tue 6.30am. Reinspected 2016.

PORT STE FOY ET PONCHAPT
180 | E9 | 33220 | N44°50.532' E000°12.547'

🚐 4; Marked bays Custom

▶ Rue Notre-Dame. From west on D936 go straight over roundabout onto D936e2, sp 'Port Ste Foy et Ponchapt'. Cross railway, then go straight over 2nd roundabout onto D708, signed. Turn right before traffic lights, signed. Service Point is straight on: N44°50.513' E000°12.463'. For parking turn left, then right by church, signed.

ℹ Adj to river, partial views; riverside walk along Dordogne adj. Church opp; bells silenced 9pm-8am. Wine museum 50m. Ste-Foy-la-Grande 500m over river bridge with town commerce. Reinspected 2016.

CREON	181	E9	33670	🏛	N44°46.578' W000°20.920'

🌐 P 🚐 ⛽ 🛁 ♫ 🚌 F ❄ | ♿ 🚰 🔌 E WC ♿ ⛽ 🚌 F

🚐 5; Max 5 nights; Please report registration number to wooden cabin ☎ Flot Bleu Océane; Token/€; €3/150L water + 3hrs elec; 2 unmetered Cont elec points

▶ Blvd Victor Hugo. In Créon follow D121e5 ring road. Aire in car park adj to ring road, signed. Drive to far end of car park. Move barrier to enter; replace barrier after entry.

ℹ Popular, small Aire adj to noisy ring road. Voie Verte cycle route adj, 25km to Bordeaux. Pizza cabin adj. Town 250m. Next village, La Sauve, has a ruined abbey. Reinspected 2016.

JUGAZAN	182	E9	33420	🏨	N44°46.914' W000°08.576'

🌐 P 🚐 ⛽ 🛁 ♫ 🚌 F ❄ | ♿ 🚰 🔌 E WC ♿ ⛽ 🚌 F 🔲

🚐 4; Max 3.5t ☎ None; See 189

▶ D128. Follow D128 east from town for 3km and Aire just after junction with D119 in lay-by on D128 at Labric, small hamlet adj to Jugazan.

ℹ Unlevel parking in lay-by overlooking vines on D128 in Labric, hamlet next to Jugazan. Better parking at 183. For services see 189 Reinspected 2016.

GREZILLAC	183	E9	33420	🏨	N44°49.034' W000°12.989'

🌐 P 🚐 ⛽ 🛁 ♫ 🚌 F ❄ | ♿ 🚰 🔌 E WC ♿ ⛽ 🚌 F 🔲

🚐 10 ☎ None; See 189

▶ Le Bourg, off D11. Turn off D936 onto D11, sp 'Grézillac'. In village turn left after church opp Foyer Rural and Mairie, signed. Park in gravel parking area on left.

ℹ Pleasant parking overlooking vines and open countryside on edge of village. Can also park in nearby Daignac at Bergerie de Daignac, a sheep dairy with caves, €3/night inc water and elec: N44°48.123' W000°14.937'. Reinspected 2016.

NAUJAN ET POSTIAC	184	E9	33420	🏨	N44°47.223' W000°10.755'

🌐 P 🚐 ⛽ 🛁 ♫ 🚌 F ❄ | ♿ 🚰 🔌 E WC ♿ ⛽ 🚌 F 🔲

🚐 3; Plus grass parking ☎ None; See 189

▶ Off D128. From Branne follow D19 south for 4.5km. Turn left onto D128, sp 'Naujan et Postiac'. Drive through village and turn right, sp 'Stade' and signed. Aire in small gravel parking area on left adj to stadium and grass area, opp vines.

ℹ Pleasant picnic parking overlooking vines in rural hamlet. Grass parking opp for 15 motorhomes. Wine château opp. Local commerce at far end of village. Voie Verte cycle route from Bordeaux to Sauvetere de Guyenne signed in village. Reinspected 2016.

CABARA	185	E9	33420	🚢	N44°49.627' W000°09.492'

🌐 P 🚐 ⛽ 🛁 ♫ 🚌 F ❄ | ♿ 🚰 🔌 E WC ♿ ⛽ 🚌 F 🔲

🚐 5 ☎ WC 100m; See 189

▶ Ave du Port. From Branne follow sp 'Cabara'. Take D18 all the way into Cabara to riverside parking on left, not signed; 5t weight restricted.

ℹ Riverside parking in village adj to and overlooking Dordogne river. Parking is also used by locals. Lovely area, enjoy it while it lasts. Inspected 2016.

FRONTENAC	186	E9	33760	🏨	N44°44.225' W000°09.772'

🌐 P 🚐 ⛽ 🛁 ♫ 🚌 F ❄ | ♿ 🚰 🔌 E WC ♿ ⛽ 🚌 F 🔲

🚐 30; Grass and hardstanding ☎ Custom; Apr-Sept

▶ D231. In centre of village turn opp church and next to Mairie. Aire behind Mairie, signed. Service Point next to hexagonal building. More parking at end of road on grass.

ℹ Beautiful 10 hectares of communal land adj to village and local commerce. Toilet block with outdoor sinks in high season. Updated 2014.

DAIGNAC

| 187 | E9 | 33420 | | N44°47.892' W000°14.953' |

🚐 10 ☗ None; See **189**

➡ D239. Village centre at the war memorial opp Bar-Tabac.

ℹ Parking in large, peaceful car park in village centre. Large green adj with CEE elec points, working at time of inspection. Local commerce adj. Village is surrounded by vines, no views. Parking poss at nearby Bergerie de Daignac, a sheep dairy with caves, €3/night inc water and elec: N44°48.123' W000°14.937'. Inspected 2016.

ST PEY D'ARMENS

| 188 | E9 | 33330 | | N44°51.176' W000°06.406' |

🚐 20; €5/night; Max 48hrs; Grass or gravel parking ☗ Custom; 8 5-20amp Cont elec points; Elec €3

➡ Château Gerbaud, off D936e7. At St Pey D'Armens turn right onto D936e7, sp 'Château Gerbaud' and signed. Turn left, signed, then right past building and Aire in vines in 150m, very well signed.

ℹ Pleasant, peaceful parking in grape vines at small wine producer. St Emillion wine area; daily tours and tastings onsite 10am and 5pm. Very pretty town with local commerce. Reinspected 2016.

BRANNE

| 189 | E9 | 33420 | | N44°49.905' W000°11.326' |

🚐 10; Riverside ☗ Euro Relais Junior; Token (ER); €2

➡ Rue Mateau. Turn off D936 by fuel station of Carrefour supermarket. Follow road and parking at end. For Service Point turn off D936, main road through, beside river bridge onto D18, sp 'Cabara'. Service Point on left adj to river Dordogne after TO, signed: N44°49.920' W000°11.070'; there is no parking allowed here.

ℹ Parking adj to Dordogne river on edge of town down dead end. River views from end bays. Supermarket 500m. Reinspected 2016.

POMEROL

| 190 | E9 | 33500 | | N44°55.941' W000°11.955' |

🚐 5 ☗ Euro Relais Box; Token (ER); €2

➡ C1/Rue de Tropchaud. In centre of Pomerol at the community hall, signed. Drive towards the church and the Service Point is adj to the modern community hall.

ℹ Aire in the heart of St Émilion wine area; wine producers everywhere. Marked walks exploring locality. Inspected 2016.

LUSSAC

| 191 | E9 | 33570 | | N44°56.777' W000°05.703' |

🚐 7 ☗ Flot Bleu Fontaine; 2 unmetered Cont elec points in WC, other side of wooden shed

➡ Lieu-Dit la Grange. Enter on D17 from south. Take the 2nd turning on the left, sp 'Aire Touristique'. Follow road and Aire on left, signed.

ℹ Pleasant Aire adj to green space on outskirts of village adj to vines. Local commerce and wineries 350m. Market Thurs am. Reinspected 2016.

ST EMILION

| 192 | E9 | 33330 | T | N44°53.816' W000°09.421' |

🚐 7 ☗ None; WC €0.50, at parking entrance

➡ Grand Pontet. Approach from Libourne on D243. In St Émilion, turn left at roundabout, signed. Turn left, sp 'Creche' and signed. Turn left and follow sp 'P' to rear car park.

ℹ Tolerated parking in car park 500m from St Émilion, a historic and picturesque town and centre of St Émilion wine region. Local road noise. Inspected 2016.

LUGAIGNAC | 193 | E9 | 33420 | | N44°48.705' W000°11.523' | SP

10; Accessed via lanes None; See 189

➤ Canoye. In village follow sp 'Mairie'. Large parking area behind Mairie, not signed.

ℹ️ Parking in large, peaceful car park adj to Mairie. Village surrounded by vines, no views. Ideal parking if you like to get away from the crowds. Inspected 2016.

BLASIMON | 194 | E9 | 33540 | | N44°44.903' W000°04.529' | SP

4; Large motorhomes poss, but not practical Urba Flux Tall; WC 50m, towards Mairie, then left down alley

➤ Rue Abbé Greciet. From south on D17, enter village and follow D17 left, sp 'Rauzan'. Turn next left onto D129, sp 'Mairie-Stade'. Drive past Mairie and turn right, sp 'Parking' and signed. Aire immediately on left.

ℹ️ Peaceful village Aire just 500m from local commerce. Parking area is small and subject to parked local cars; turning around may be difficult for large motorhomes. Adj green space excludes dogs. Poss to park at vineyard, Chateâu la Peyraude, with free tastings; closed late Aug-early Sept: N44°44.011' W000°05.889'. Inspected 2016.

ST ROMAIN LA VIRVEE | 195 | E10 | 33240 | | N44°57.827' W000°24.106' | SP

5 Custom

➤ Route de Asques. From village centre on D737 follow sp 'Asques' and signed. Turn right as exit village, sp 'Salle des Fêtes' and signed. Follow road to bottom and the Service Point is on the left and the parking is on the right, signed.

ℹ️ On edge of village at sports facilities. Local commerce 250m uphill. Only 5km from A10, but peaceful and space likely. Updated 2014.

MARCENAIS | 196 | E9 | 33620 | | N45°03.484' W000°20.317' | SP

2; Max 48hrs Cont WC 50m

➤ Le Bourg. Turn off D18 towards Marcenais, signed. Follow road for 400m turning 2nd right, sp 'Ecole'. Continue through village past Mairie. Turn left opp school sign, signed. Aire in large, red gravel car park, signed.

ℹ️ Large, open car park that can take any sized unit. Small rural village has 12th century Templar church, 100m. Local commerce adj to D18. Reinspected 2016.

MARSAS | 197 | E9 | 33620 | | N45°04.057' W000°23.055' | SP

2; Max 48hrs None; See 207

➤ D142/Rue Étienne Chaignaud. Turn off D18 at roundabout onto D142, sp 'Marsas'. At next roundabout go straight over, sp 'Cubnezais'. Turn left in 50m opp church and cemetery, signed. Aire in car park opp church, signed.

ℹ️ Parking allowed in large village car park with 2.5t weight restriction. Small village with local commerce. Convenient night halt just 850m from N10 creating distant road noise as a result. Reinspected 2016.

LARUSCADE | 198 | E9 | 33620 | | N45°06.409' W000°20.692' | SP

5; Max 48hrs None; See 207

➤ Lac des Vergnes. Exit N10 onto D22 and follow sp 'Laruscade'. Enter village and in 150m turn right through car park, sp 'Lac des Vergnes' and signed. Turn down 3.5t weight restricted road and parking is on left just before lake. Reverse in between bollards.

ℹ️ Shady parking adj to private lake with partial views. Attended swimming in lake Jul-Aug. Village centre 400m with local commerce and small market Thurs and Sat am. Reinspected 2016.

ST MARIENS
199 | E9 | 33620 | 🏛 | N45°06.915' W000°23.947'

🚐 2; Max 48hrs 🚰 Tap at WC

➡ D22, just off D18/D22 roundabout. Exit St Mariens on D22 towards Laruscade. After crossing D22/D18 roundabout turn 1st right and 1st right again, both sp 'Aire des Lagunes'. Designated parking in Aire de Repos.

ℹ Pleasant parking adj to picnic area. Toilet block with outdoor sink adj. Some road noise. Convenient night halt. Reinspected 2016.

CUBNEZAIS
200 | E9 | 33620 | 🏠 | (A) N45°04.507' W000°24.529'

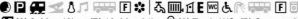

🚐 (A) 2; Max 48hrs; (B) 10; Max 24hrs 🚰 (A) Tap in WC; (B) Custom; 2 20amp CEE elec points

➡ (A) D248. Exit N10 and follow sp 'Cubnezais'. Enter village on D248 and follow D248, sp 'St Savin'. Turn left, sp 'Cezac' and signed. Aire on right in 100m, signed. Poss to turn around in large car park on left if Aire is missed! (B) N45°04.559' W000°24.801': Go 400m past Aire and turn left into château. Park to right, signed.

ℹ (A) Small, designated area in large car park adj to recycling; views of vines. Small park and bus stop adj. Winery, 300m, offers motorhome parking. (B) Further parking and Service Point at Château Bertinerie vineyard. www.chateaubertinerie.com Reinspected 2016.

(B) *(A)*

CEZAC
201 | E9 | 33620 | 🏠 | N45°05.475' W000°25.201'

🚐 2; Max 48hrs 🚰 WC at church

➡ Le Bourg. In village at traffic-lighted crossroads turn off D249 onto D248 towards church, sp 'St Mareins'. Turn left immediately in front of church, sp 'Mairie'. Turn right in front of no entry sign into car park. Aire in car park, signed.

ℹ Parking adj to picnic area, dojo and open access sports field on edge of village. Village centre with church and local commerce 100m. Reinspected 2016.

CAVIGNAC
202 | E9 | 33620 | 🏠 | N45°06.009' W000°23.507'

🚐 2; Max 48hrs 🚰 None; See **207**

➡ Rue de la Paix. Turn left off D18 into Rue de la Paix next to La Poste, sp 'Eglise' and signed. Turn left in 150m, sp 'Rue de la Paix 80 places'. Aire behind Maison de la Petite Enfance, signed.

ℹ Dead quiet parking overlooking vines. Small town commerce 100m. LIDL at north end of town; Super U south of town. Reinspected 2016.

CIVRAC DE BLAYE
203 | E9 | 33920 | 🏠 | N45°06.736' W000°26.691'

🚐 2; Max 48hrs; Grass parking 🚰 Tap with non-drinkable water; See **207**

➡ D135/Parc de Mairie. From St Mariens take D135, sp 'Civrac de Blaye'. After entering Civrac de Blaye turn right in 300m beside cross into 'Parc de Mairie', signed. Parking on grass, signed.

ℹ Pleasant grass parking adj to small park and pond. Reinspected 2016.

BOURG SUR GIRONDE
204 | D9 | 33710 | ⛴ | N45°02.407' W000°33.855'

🚐 30; Grass parking 🚰 Being installed, make unknown; See **254**

➡ Lieu-dit Le Roc. From east follow D669 past Bourg centre. Turn left at west side of town, sp 'P Eglise' and signed. Turn immediately right onto 15t weight restricted road, sp 'Cambes' and signed. DO NOT drive into town. Drive downhill, then turn 1st left at bottom into Aire, signed.

ℹ Pleasant, open parking on edge of town. Distant glimpses of Dordogne river. Town 600m via adj leisure park; interesting city walls and steps plus small town/tourist commerce. Motorhomes are banned from parking at port at night. Inspected 2016.

ST VIVIEN DE BLAYE | 205 | D9 | 33920 | 🏕🛏 | N45°05.900' W000°31.050' | SP 🌳🏕🏃📷🧍🚴🛶✈

🌑 P 🚐 🛶 🎵♫ 🚌 F ❄ | 🧑‍🦽 ▥ 🏠 E WC ♿🏪 🚌 F ▣
🚐 2; Max 48hrs 👕 None; See 207

▶ D132. From St Christoly follow D132 south, sp 'St Vivien de Blaye'. At end of road turn right onto D135, sp 'Bourg'. At church turn left onto D132, signed. Aire next to church, signed.

ℹ Dead quiet gravel/grass parking area by church. Pond adj. May feel isolated if alone. Start point for 60 min fitness course. Reinspected 2016.

ST CHRISTOLY DE BLAYE | 206 | D9 | 33920 | 🛏 | N45°09.202' W000°28.526' | SP 🌳🏕🏃📷🧍🚴🛶✈

🌑 P 🚐 🛶 🎵♫ 🚌 F ❄ | 🧑‍🦽 ▥ 🏠 E WC ♿🏪 🚌 F ▣
🚐 2; Max 48hrs 👕 Custom; Tap and WC at parking

▶ Lacs de Moulin Blanc. From St Christoly de Blaye/St Savin follow signs to 'Lacs du Moulin Blanc'. Both routes have 3.5t weight restriction. Once at lake follow signs to swimming beach. Aire has 2 marked bays, signed. For Service Point follow D22 into St Christoly de Blaye and turn off in village centre by church. Drive past church and Service Point is on left by sports field, signed: N45°07.804' W000°30.473'.

ℹ Lovely woodland space in recreation area by swimming lake, partial views. Fishing in smaller lake. May feel isolated if alone. Service Point in village with local commerce adj; parking restricted here to 30 mins. Reinspected 2016.

ST SAVIN | 207 | E9 | 33920 | 🛏 | N45°08.277' W000°26.804' | SP 🌳🏕🏃📷🧍🚴🛶✈

🌑 P 🚐 🛶 🎵♫ 🚌 F ❄ | 🧑‍🦽 ▥ 🏠 E WC ♿🏪 🚌 F ▣
🚐 2; Max 48hrs 👕 Custom, at TO

▶ Rue de la Cure, off D18. Approach St Savin from east on D250. At 1st roundabout in St Savin take D18, sp 'St Savin-Centre' and signed. After Stop junction turn left, signed. Turning may be diff due to parked cars. Designated parking on left, signed. For Service Point return to roundabout and turn left, signed. Turn 1st left, then left again, both signed. Service Point behind TO, signed: N45°08.396' W000°26.516'.

ℹ Small town commerce 50m. Intermarché 350m with self-service laundry. Service Point adj TO which has free internet connection; must take own computer. Reinspected 2016.

ST GIRONS D'AIGUEVIVES | 208 | D9 | 33920 | 🛏 | N45°08.383' W000°32.567' | SP 🌳🏕🏃📷🧍🚴🛶✈

🌑 P 🚐 🛶 🎵♫ 🚌 F ❄ | 🧑‍🦽 ▥ 🏠 E WC ♿🏪 🚌 F ▣
🚐 2; Max 48hrs 👕 Cont WC; Very old

▶ Place du 19 Mars 1962. Aire in car park behind war memorial, opp church.

ℹ Lovely, open, dead quiet Aire overlooking grassy area to cemetery. Suitable for any unit configuration. Depart point for walking circuit. Bus stop 100m around corner. Reinspected 2016.

GENERAC | 209 | D9 | 33920 | 🏕🛏 | N45°10.822' W000°32.898' | SP 🌳🏕🏃📷🧍🚴🛶✈

🌑 P 🚐 🛶 🎵♫ 🚌 F ❄ | 🧑‍🦽 ▥ 🏠 E WC ♿🏪 🚌 F ▣
🚐 2; Max 48hrs 👕 None; See 207

▶ D137e4. Follow sp 'Générac' through country lanes. Aire adj to church, not signed through village.

ℹ Pleasant, rural Aire on edge of village overlooking vines and countryside. Morning shade from conifer hedge. Depart point for forest walking circuit. Reinspected 2016.

SAUGON | 210 | D9 | 33920 | 🛏 | N45°10.678' W000°30.281' | SP 🌳🏕🏃📷🧍🚴🛶✈

🌑 P 🚐 🛶 🎵♫ 🚌 F ❄ | 🧑‍🦽 ▥ 🏠 E WC ♿🏪 🚌 F ▣
🚐 2; Max 48hrs 👕 Tap at Mairie; See 207

▶ D252. Follow sp 'Saugon' on country roads. Aire adj to D252, main route, behind church and Mairie, adj to tennis courts. There are 2 large bays marked on ground.

ℹ Rural village. Aire adj to playing fields. Local commerce 50m. Reinspected 2016.

ST PAUL | 211 | D9 | 33390 | | N45°08.875' W000°36.289' |

3; Parallel opp Service Point Aire Services Plastic; Token (3/3)

➡ Place du Souvenir Français. Turn off D137 onto D737, sp 'St Paul' and signed, and follow into village. Turn left towards the church, then immediately left into car park behind the 1914-1918 memorial, both signed.

ℹ Small Aire in small village. Local commerce and bus stop adj. Reinspected 2016.

ST CAPRAIS DE BLAYE | 212 | D8 | 33820 | | N45°17.470' W000°34.146' |

7; €7/18hrs; CC Custom; Inside barrier; Inc

➡ D137. Turn off D137 onto D23, sp 'St Ciers' and signed. Turn 1st right, signed, into roadside lay-by. Aire in far end of car park. Access through Aire Services barrier.

ℹ Aire at end of roadside lay-by, suffers road noise. Picnic area adj. Shop, TO and restaurant on site. There are 2 free designated 8m spaces on right in entrance before barrier, signed. Reinspected 2016.

DONNEZAC | 213 | E9 | 33860 | | N45°14.934' W000°26.583' |

2; Max 48hrs Cont WC, other side of church

➡ Le Bourg. In Donnezac turn behind the church and the Aire is on the right at front of Salle des Fêtes, signed.

ℹ Lots of green space. Small village with bread vend by church. Depart point for forest walking circuit. Reinspected 2016.

ST YZAN DE SOUDIAC | 214 | E9 | 33920 | | N45°08.432' W000°24.613' |

2; Max 48hrs None; See 207

➡ D250. From St Savin take D250 east, sp 'St Yzan de Soudiac'. Aire on left in 3.5t restricted car park in village centre, opp school and next to Mairie.

ℹ Small village with market on Wed am. Numerous commerce at St Savin. Reinspected 2016.

BLAYE ⭐ | 215 | D9 | 33390 | T | N45°07.536' W000°39.961' |

50; €3/noon-noon None

➡ Cours du Port. Follow D669 through Blaye, sp 'Citadelle'. Once alongside citadel walls turn off, sp 'Halte Nautique'. Designated motorhome parking in car park closest to river, signed.

ℹ Popular Aire which is always likely to be full; park considerately. River views from some bays. Open access citadel up adj hill with tourist commerce. Town commerce 250m. Reinspected 2016.

BLAYE - Chateau Marquis de Vauban | 216 | D9 | 33390 | | N45°08.230' W000°39.909' |

20; Grass and hardstanding parking; Max 48hrs Custom; 16amp CEE elec points

➡ Route des Cônes. Turn off D669 at roundabout onto D937, sp 'Paris'. Continue straight onto D255, sp 'Braud et St Louis'. Turn off, signed. Aire at Château Marquis de Vauban, signed. Drive past gates and turn right. Park in visitor car park and report through gates.

ℹ Pleasant, popular Aire at vineyard. Parking in visitor car park all year for any unit, or on grass between vines in summer; English spoken. Shop adj. Tourist train and horse and cart trips to Blaye for wine tasting from €6. Ideal for rallies. www.voyages-grand-cru.fr Inspected 2016.

ST MEDARD DE GUIZIERES | 217 | E9 | 33230 | N45°00.925' W000°03.472'

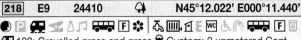

🚐2; Max 8m 🚽 Custom; Empty WC under tap

➡ D1089/Rue de la République. From Libourne follow D1089 east. At St Medard de Guizieres pass church and turn right opp junction with D21 to Coutras, sp 'P Mairie' and signed. Aire on left in small car park with difficult entrance, signed.

ℹ Small Aire just off main shopping area with local commerce. Church adj. Noise from adj road. Reinspected 2016.

ST VINCENT JALMOUTIERS | 218 | E9 | 24410 | N45°12.022' E000°11.440'

🚐100; Gravelled grass and grass 🚽 Custom; 2 unmetered Cont elec points (Turned off)

➡ Moulin de Rafalie. Turn off D44 in village, sp 'Village Vacances' and signed. Cross river bridge and immediately turn right into Aire.

ℹ Pleasant, peaceful Aire on large grass field adj to shallow river. Picnic area adj. Village centre 100m with local commerce. Reinspected 2016.

ST ANTOINE CUMOND | 219 | E9 | 24410 | N45°15.350' E000°12.031'

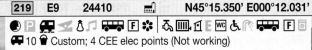

🚐10 🚽 Custom; 4 CEE elec points (Not working)

➡ D43. From Aubeterre-sur-Donne follow D2, sp 'Riberac'. Turn right onto D43, sp 'St Astier'. Follow D43 through town centre, then turn left after Mairie into car park. Aire at rear of car park, not signed.

ℹ In village centre with local commerce 100m. Ideal if Poitou **164** is full. Reinspected 2016.

VANXAINS | 220 | E9 | 24600 | N45°12.710' E000°17.036'

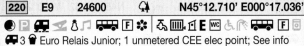

🚐3 🚽 Euro Relais Junior; 1 unmetered CEE elec point; See info

➡ D708. Exit Vanxains on D708 to south. 450m after exiting the village turn right into parking area, sp 'Stade' and signed. Aire on right above boules court, signed.

ℹ Aire in small parking lay-by adj to out of town residential area, boules court and recycling point. Elec on, but WC locked and water off during inspection; suspect water will work if WC unlocked. Bus stop adj. Local commerce 500m up main road. Reinspected 2016.

ST AQUILIN | 221 | E9 | 24110 | N45°11.154' E000°29.315'

🚐5 🚽 Custom, on right side of building; WC and sink unusable

➡ D43. Turn left as exit village on D43 to west, sp 'P'. Aire 20m on right at municipal service building.

ℹ A forgotten Aire at a municipal works building in a remote village. Service Point dilapidated; may fall out of use. Local commerce 300m. Reinspected 2016.

ST LEON SUR L'ISLE | 222 | E9 | 24110 | N45°06.904' E000°30.029'

🚐5; Also 15 adj to river 🚽 Custom; Very slow tap

➡ Route de la Lande. Turn off D3 onto D41e2, sp 'St Leon s l'Isle'. Turn right after crossing river bridge into parking adj to river: N45°07.202' E000°29.781'. For Service Point follow road through village and Service Point is adj to Maison des Associations, signed.

ℹ Service Point parking in village centre adj to local commerce. Further parking on edge of village overlooking fishable river, riverside path and skateboard park. Reinspected 2016.

NEUVIC SUR L'ISLE
223 | E9 | 24190 | N45°06.469' E000°28.181'

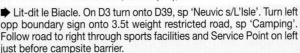

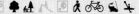

🚐 10 🚰 Euro Relais Junior; Token (2/1); €3

➤ Lit-dit le Biacle. On D3 turn onto D39, sp 'Neuvic s/L'Isle'. Turn left opp boundary sign onto 3.5t weight restricted road, sp 'Camping'. Follow road to right through sports facilities and Service Point on left just before campsite barrier.

ⓘ Service Point outside municipal campsite. Motorhomes are allowed to park overnight in the surrounding unrestricted car parks. Riverside cycle route adj. Camping Le Plein Air Neuvicois offers pitches from €9.50 + €4.50pp Apr-Jun/Sept and €15.50 + €5.50pp Jul-Aug. Inspected 2016.

SOURZAC
224 | E9 | 24400 | N45°03.097' E000°23.715'

🚐 10 🚰 Euro Relais Junior; Token (ER); 1 Cont elec point in WC (Not working)

➤ Ave du 11 Juin 1944. In Sourzac turn off D6089 onto D3e5, sp 'Douzillac'. Aire immediately on left before river bridge, signed.

ⓘ Riverside parking at picnic spot with views across river and over surrounding countryside. Constant road noise, but a convenient halt just off D6089 and A89. Local commerce and Voie Verte route adj. Reinspected 2016.

RIBERAC
225 | E9 | 24600 | N45°15.416' E000°20.545'

🚐 20 🚰 Custom

➤ Aux Deux Ponts Ouest, off D708. From east on D710 turn right at roundabout onto D708, sp 'Nontron'. Turn 1st left after crossing river Dronne, signed. Then turn left into Aire, signed.

ⓘ Aire in parking outside small, tired, seasonal municipal campsite. River Dronne adj, obscured view. Road noise. Seasonal kayak hire. Large town commerce 500m. Reinspected 2016.

DOUCHAPT
226 | E9 | 24350 | N45°15.083' E000°26.600'

🚐 5; €5; Pay at Accueil (bar) 🚰 Euro Relais Junior; Token (ER)/€; €2

➤ C1/Beauclair, off D710. From Ribérac take D710 east for 8km, sp 'Périgueux'. After passing through village of St Méard de Drône turn left, sp 'Village de Beauclair' and signed. Follow lane for 500m and Aire on right through gates, signed. Aire 1st turning on right after gates.

ⓘ Aire in grounds of municipal holiday village with swimming lake, no view. Aire surrounded by pleasantly landscaped grounds. Washing machine available. Reinspected 2016.

MENSIGNAC
227 | F9 | 24350 | N45°13.378' E000°33.931'

🚐 3 🚰 Flot Bleu Fontaine; €2

➤ Rue du Stade, off D710. From Périgueux take D710 towards Ribérac. Just before Mensignac boundary turn left, sp 'Stade' and 'Aire de Service'. Follow road for 200m past sports ground to Aire on right, signed.

ⓘ Aire with 3 10m concrete bays shaded by trees and surrounded by grass. Some local road noise. Small town commerce 400m. Reinspected 2016.

CHATEAU L'EVEQUE
228 | F9 | 24460 | N45°14.667' E000°41.233'

🚐 8 🚰 Raclet; Token (ER); €2; May-Oct

➤ Place du Jardin Public. Approach on D939 from south. Turn left at roundabout, sp 'Centre Ville'. Cross railway line and turn 1st right into car park. Service Point on left and parking on right past the railway station, signed.

ⓘ Landscaped area with gardens and footpath. Train station adj. Some train and road noise. Trains run from 7am-12am; sporadic departures throughout day towards Bordeaux. Village with local commerce 200m. Reinspected 2016.

ATLANTIC

TOCANE ST APRE — 229 — E/F9 — 24350 — N45°15.436' E000°29.676'

🚐10 Euro Relais Junior; Token (ER); €2; Taps to left of Service Point by building

▶ D103/Rte de Montagrier. In town turn off D710 onto D103, sp 'Montagrier' and signed. After 250m, Aire on right through gate before village boundary, signed.

ℹ Aire adj to municipal sports facilities and rear of municipal campsite (open mid Jun-Aug). Walkway through sports facilities to river 150m, or small town commerce 300m. Reinspected 2016.

BOURDEILLES — 230 — F8 — 24310 — N45°19.383' E000°35.000'

🚐50; €4/24hrs; +€0.55pp tax; Collected; Grass parking Euro Relais Mini; Token (ER)

▶ D106. From Brantôme take D78 to Bourdeilles. In village turn left onto D106e2, sp 'St Just' and signed. Cross river bridge and turn right, signed. Turn right, signed, and drive past Mairie. Turn right after Service Point and follow signs around football pitch to grass parking by river on edge of village.

ℹ Aire on large, grass, riverside field; some hardstanding near Service Point when wet, also riverside. Fishing permits from Tabac. Pretty and historic centre with fortified château and small town commerce, 300m across pedestrianised river bridge. Market Sun am. Seasonal canoe hire. Reinspected 2016.

PAUSSAC ST VIVIEN — 231 — E8 — 24310 — N45°20.865' E000°32.309'

🚐3; €3.70/24hrs; +€1.60pp, +€0.33pp tax; Collected Euro Relais Junior; Token (2/1); €2; Taps on bollard past Service Point; 4 20amp Cont elec points; 16amp CEE elec points (Not working)

▶ Le Bourg. From Bourdeilles follow sp 'Paussac St Vivien'. At the church turn left on D92, sp 'Leguillac de C'. In 60m turn right, signed. Aire 20m on right.

ℹ Small Aire at tiny town campsite. Village centre 150m has local commerce. Reinspected 2016.

BRANTOME — 232 — F8 — 24310 — N45°21.641' E000°38.883'

🚐130; €1/5hrs; €6.05/24hrs; Collected; Grass/gravel parking Custom; Outside barrier; €2/12 mins

▶ Chemin du Vert Galant. From south on D939 turn right at roundabout onto D939e2, sp 'Brantôme-Centre Ville'. Follow road and turn left before river bridge into car parks, sp 'P Motorcycles' and signed (low down). Follow left road for 400m and Aire on right after children's play area. Enter through barrier.

ℹ Popular, commercial Aire in a peaceful location on edge of town by riverside park. Abbey and small town commerce 400m. Market Fri. Reinspected 2016.

SORGES — 233 — F8 — 24420 — N45°18.332' E000°52.371'

🚐15 Euro Relais Junior; Lift flap near road for WC emptying point; Hose needed; No drive over drain; 1 CEE elec point (Not working)

▶ N21, as exit town to south. Aire opp Écomusée de la Truffe, truffle museum, signed. Service Point in exit/entry road of lay-by adj to picnic area, signed: N45°18.246' E000°52.355'.

ℹ Large parking area in multiple sections; the signed parking is furthest from the road. TO with truffle museum opp, €5pp. Local commerce 200m. Lay-by with Service Point suitable for any unit configuration. Walking and cycling path departs from Service Point lay-by. Reinspected 2016.

SARLIAC SUR L'ISLE — 234 — F9 — 24420 — N45°14.155' E000°52.448'

🚐10 Custom; Lift up drain for WC emptying

▶ N21 and D705, at roundabout junction to south of town. Turn off roundabout, sp 'Sarliac-Centre', and make immediate right, sp 'Stade'. Service Point adj to former WC, not signed.

ℹ Aire in town car park, suffers road noise as traffic navigates adj roundabout. Large, open access football pitches adj. Small town commerce adj. Market Fri 3.30-6.30pm. Reinspected 2016.

PERIGUEUX | 235 | F9 | 24000 | N45°11.260' E000°43.864'

🚐 41; €6/24hrs; CC; Max 4 nights; 7m bays plus overhang on some
⛲ Aire Services 3000; Inside barrier

➡ Rue des Prés. From east on N21 follow road straight on onto D6021, sp 'Périgueux Centre Ville'. Keep following road straight on, sp 'Centre Ville'. Then fork left, sp 'Toutes Directions' and signed. Turn left at traffic lights and cross bridge, signed. At roundabout turn far left, signed. At end of road turn left, then right, both signed. Drive along river and Aire on right, signed. Enter through barrier.

ℹ Popular Aire adj to river, but no views and overlooked by flats. Historic town 1km along river path. Sat/Wed am market in town. Reinspected 2016.

All of the listings in this section are Service Points without designated parking. The majority are located either at supermarkets or outside campsites.

Height barriers are rare at supermarkets and overnight parking should be possible. Always park considerately. Supermarket Service Points often lack a waste water drain.

Most campsites are municipally owned. Parking outside may be possible when campsites are closed. Acquiring tokens in rural locations may be difficult or impossible, especially in low season.

Remember to be a responsible tourist whenever offsite parking.

NONTRON | 236 | F8 | 24300 | N45°32.167' E000°40.000'

⛲ Euro Relais Junior; €2

➡ Ave Jules Ferry, off D675. From D675 turn onto Ave Jules Ferry, sp 'Super U' and signed. At roundabout turn left into Super U. Service Point in middle of car park facing the shop. Access may be difficult in peak shopping hours. Reinspected 2013.

THENON | 237 | F9 | 24210 | N45°08.459' E001°04.063'

⛲ Euro Relais Box; Token (ER)/€; €2

➡ D6089. Service Point at Carrefour supermarket adj to D6089. Reinspected 2016.

VERGT | 238 | F9 | 24380 | N45°01.350' E000°42.634'

⛲ Urba Flux Tall; €2

➡ D8. From centre exit on D8, sp 'Bergerac'. Turn off D8 just before Intermarché supermarket entrance. Service Point on left adj to supermarket car park, signed. Inspected 2012.

ST CYPRIEN | 239 | F9 | 24200 | N44°51.789' E001°02.430'

⛲ Flot Bleu Marine; €2; No drive over drain or WC emptying

➡ D703/Voie de Vallée. Service Point adj to D703 at Carrefour supermarket just southwest of town. Reinspected 2016.

STE NATHALENE | 240 | F9 | 24200 | N44°54.788' E001°15.902'

⛲ Euro Relais Mini; €5

➡ Maillac-le-Petit. From Ste Nathalène follow sp 'Camping de Maillac' through the lanes. Service Point outside campsite. Reinspected 2016.

VILLENEUVE SUR LOT | 241 | F10 | 47300 | N44°24.511' E000°44.062'

⛲ Aire Services Plastic

➡ D911. Enter town on D911 from Fumel. Service Point in E.Leclerc fuel station in retail park on right. Drive through 24/24 fuel pumps to access. Reinspected 2016.

ST PARDOUX ISAAC | 242 | E9 | 47800 | N44°36.816' E000°21.585'

⛲ Custom

➡ C201, at Intermarché. Exit Miramont-de-Guyenne to north on D933 and turn right onto C201, sp 'St Pardoux Isaac' and 'Intermarché'. Aire on right adj to car wash at Intermarché supermarket with fuel station and self-service laundry. Reinspected 2016.

PONT DES SABLES | 243 | E10 | 47200 | N44°27.657' E000°08.334'

⛲ Custom

➡ D933, at Emeraude Navigation. From Marmande drive 3.5km south on D933 and Aire on left immediately over canal bridge. Service Point only as parking is very unlevel and full of boat hire customer's cars. Bike and canoe hire adj. Reinspected 2016.

STE BAZEILLE | 244 | E9 | 47180 | N44°31.670' E000°06.178'

⛲ Euro Relais Mini; €2

➡ D813. Turn off D813 at roundabout into Super U car park, signed. Service Point behind fuel station and car wash, signed. Poss to park in 3 bays opp Service Point. Reinspected 2016.

LAVARDAC · 245 · E10 · 47230 · N44°10.235' E000°17.595'

Euro Relais Junior; €2

➡ D408. From town follow D930, sp 'Nérac'. At roundabout turn left to stay on D930, sp 'Nérac', then turn 1st right onto D408, sp 'Mézin'. Turn right into Super U supermarket car park and Service Point between fuel station and car wash, signed. Car wash poss for high vehicles. Reinspected 2016.

LESCAR · 246 · D11 · 64230 · N43°19.537' W000°26.550'

Custom

➡ Ave du Vert Galant. From Artix on D817 take 1st exit at roundabout onto D501, sp 'Saragosse'. Pass ALDI and turn right into Impasse du Vert Galant; GPS taken here. Service Point on right of turning circle, signed. Tolerated parking at P Verdun central Pau: N43°17.951' W000°22.581'. Reinspected 2013.

MORLAAS · 247 · E11 · 64160 · N43°20.971' W000°15.760'

Urba Flux Tall; €2

➡ Avenue Gaston IV Le Croise. From Pau enter Morlaàs on D943, then D923. Follow through centre and at traffic lights turn left, sp 'Piscine'. Follow road and Service Point on left outside municipal campsite. Inspected 2013.

ST VINCENT DE TYROSSE · 248 · D11 · 40230 · N43°40.113' W001°16.888'

Custom; Token (2/2)

➡ D810, at Netto supermarket. Enter in front of McDonald's at the E.Leclerc supermarket roundabout and follow road around to Netto. Reinspected 2013.

MIMIZAN · 249 · D10 · 40200 · N44°13.178' W001°13.786'

Flot Bleu Pacific; €2

➡ D87. Service Point at municipal campsite adj to D87 as exit town to north. Reinspected 2013.

PARENTIS EN BORN · 250 · D10 · 40160 · N44°20.920' W001°03.950'

Raclet; €2; No drive over drain

➡ D43, at Super U. Service Point in Super U car park adj to pizza kiosk near car wash. Reinspected 2016.

AUDENGE · 251 · D9 · 33980 · N44°41.066' W001°00.293'

Euro Relais Junior; Token (ER); €4

➡ D5e5, in municipal campsite car park. From D3 turn onto D5e5 at roundabout, sp 'Lubec'. At next roundabout turn into campsite adj to roundabout. Service Point outside municipal campsite. Camping €14-€24/night. Tokens available from TO or campsite. Reinspected 2016.

LE PORGE · 252 · D9 · 33680 · N44°52.549' W001°04.714'

Flot Bleu Océane

➡ D3, at Intermarché supermarket. Service Point adj to fuel station, signed. Reinspected 2016.

LIBOURNE · 253 · E9 · 3500 · N44°54.393' W000°14.032'

Flot Bleu Pacific; €2

➡ Off D670, at Intermarché supermarket. Turn off D670 at large Intermarché sign. Follow road 150m, beside stadium, to Intermarché supermarket entrance. WC emptying poss at all times. Suggest St Émilion to east for overnight parking: N44°53.820' W000°09.421'. Reinspected 2016.

BOURG · 254 · D9 · 33710 · N45°02.323' W000°33.606'

Raclet; Token (ER); €2

➡ Rue du Roc. Turn off D669, sp 'Le Port' and 'Halte Nautique', and follow road downhill. Turn right at the crossroads, sp 'Camping', and follow road to end. Service Point on left, outside small, pleasant riverside campsite; €8-€15/night. Reinspected 2016.

LA ROCHE CHALAIS · 255 · E9 · 24490 · N45°08.788' E000°00.340'

Euro Relais Junior; €2; Drive over drain in car wash

➡ D674. Turn off D674 in town into Intermarché supermarket. Service Point adj to car wash; diff access. Inspected 2012.

LISLE · 256 · F8 · 24350 · N45°16.878' E000°32.408'

Euro Relais Junior; Token (ER); €2; May-Sept

➡ Les Sonneries, off D1. Turn off D78 onto D1, sp 'Grand Brassac'. In 300m turn right, sp 'Camping Municipal'. Service Point on left outside municipal campsite. Reinspected 2016.

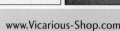

PERIGUEUX 257 F9 24000 N45°10.875' E000°43.360'

☗ Custom; Obstructed by parked cars

➦ Rue de l'Ancienne Préfecture. From south on D2 turn onto D6089 at roundabout, sp 'Centre Ville'. Follow road straight on and after crossing river bridge turn 2nd right into car park. Service Point in 50m on left, signed. Service Point still fully functioning, but is always parked on by local vehicles. Parking on quayside prohibited for vehicles >4.8m, except Sat/Wed 5am-1pm. Reinspected 2016.

PUGNAC 258 D9 33710 N45°04.537' W000°29.912'

☗ Aire Services 7005; Token; €3

➦ D249. Turn off D137 onto D249 at roundabout, sp 'Tauriac'. Turn 1st right into Intermarché supermarket and Service Point immediately on left, signed. Reinspected 2016.

HOSTENS 259 D9/10 33125 N44°29.591' W000°37.742'

☗ Flot Bleu Euro (In disrepair); CC

➦ Rue de Chantegrue. From D651/D3 traffic-lighted junction take D3, sp 'Bazas'. Turn left in 400m, sp 'Camping'. Follow road and Service Point on right before campsite. Inspected 2016.

COUTRAS 260 E9 33230 N45°02.985' W000°07.401'

☗ Custom; Token; €3 or free if spend €20 in store

➦ Rue des Muguets, just off D674. Follow sp 'Intermarché' through town from D10. Drive to right of supermarket, signed. Service Point adj to side of supermarket, signed. Inspected 2016.

LE PIAN 261 D9 33290 N44°57.300' W000°37.766'

☗ Flot Bleu Pacific

➦ D2. Turn off D2 at McDonald's roundabout into E.Leclerc car park. Service Point to left adj to car wash. Inspected 2016.

GPS Co-ordinates for SatNav

The GPS Co-ordinates published in this guide were taken onsite by our inspectors. We consider them a valuable and unique asset and at the time of publishing have decided not to publish them as electronic files for use on navigation devices. You have permission to type in the co-ordinates of an Aire you intend to visit but not to store or share them. For the security of our copyright:

• **Do not compile them into lists**

• **Do not publish, share or reproduce them anywhere in any format**

Caumont-sur-Garonne

Vicarious Shop

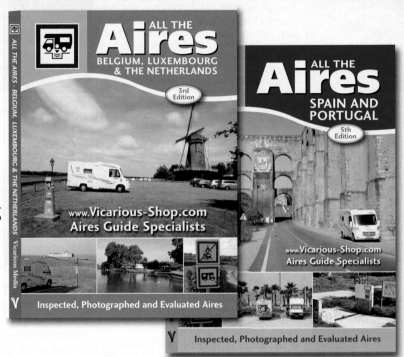

- 500 Aires for Spain and Portugal
- 190 Aires for the Netherlands
- 127 Aires for Belgium, plus 12 for Luxembourg
- Extensive LPG listings for every country

Sample Spain and Portugal entry. Entries for Belgium, Luxembourg and the Netherlands follow the same format.

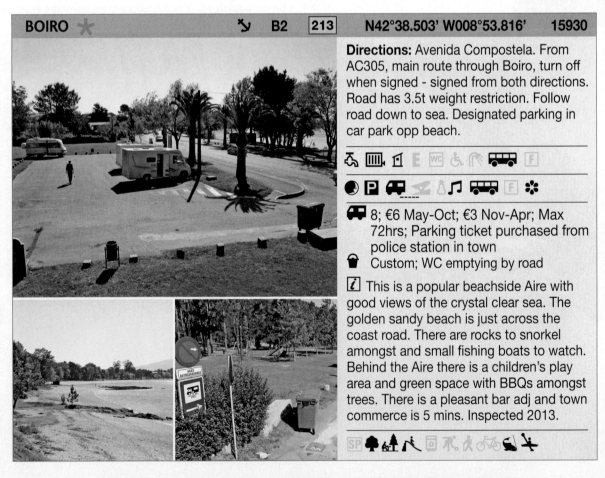

BOIRO ✶ ⚓ B2 213 N42°38.503' W008°53.816' 15930

Directions: Avenida Compostela. From AC305, main route through Boiro, turn off when signed - signed from both directions. Road has 3.5t weight restriction. Follow road down to sea. Designated parking in car park opp beach.

🚐 8; €6 May-Oct; €3 Nov-Apr; Max 72hrs; Parking ticket purchased from police station in town

Custom; WC emptying by road

ℹ️ This is a popular beachside Aire with good views of the crystal clear sea. The golden sandy beach is just across the coast road. There are rocks to snorkel amongst and small fishing boats to watch. Behind the Aire there is a children's play area and green space with BBQs amongst trees. There is a pleasant bar adj and town commerce is 5 mins. Inspected 2013.

To order, give us a call or visit our website to buy online.

Tel: 0131 208 3333 www.Vicarious-Shop.com

Marsac

LIMOUSIN & AUVERGNE

Treteau

LIMOUSIN & AUVERGNE

CHATEAU SUR ALLIER | 1 | H7 | 03320 | ⚲ | N46°45.826' E003°01.831'

🌓 P 🚐 🛥 🜊 🎵 🚌 F ❄ | ♿ 🏧 🚪 E WC ♿ 🚹 🚐 F ⌀

🚐 4 ☂ Aire services 7010; Token (3/3)

➡ D13. Turn off D978a onto D13, sp 'Château s/ A' and 'Sancoins'. Aire immediately on left, signed.

ℹ Landscaped Aire in rural location on edge of village, adj to water treatment. 4 hardstanding bays, additional grass parking in summer. Local commerce 1km. Inspected 2016.

ST BONNET TRONCAIS | 2 | H7 | 03360 | 🏭 | N46°39.530' E002°41.538'

🌓 P 🚐 🛥 🜊 🎵 🚌 F ❄ | ♿ 🏧 🚪 E WC ♿ 🚹 🚐 F ⌀

🚐 10; Max 48hrs; Grass parking ☂ Custom; Token; €1.50/50L water; 1 unmetered Cont elec point (Not working)

➡ D39. Turn off D978a onto D39, sp 'St Bonnet-Tais'. Service Point in 2.5km on left at sports ground, signed: N46°39.609' E002°41.824'. For parking drive past Service Point and follow sp 'Braize'. Turn off at roundabout by TO into gravel area. Drive past building to grass parking behind the car park in the village, opp TO.

ℹ Large grass parking area suitable for any unit configuration. Creche adj, TO 50m, local commerce 100m. Surrounded by Tronçais forest, a large forest with marked trails and day parking. Reinspected 2016.

LURCY LEVIS ✳ | 3 | H7 | 03320 | 🛥 | N46°44.293' E002°56.336'

🌓 P 🚐 🛥 🜊 🎵 🚌 F ❄ | ♿ 🏧 🚪 E WC ♿ 🚹 🚐 F ⌀

🚐 6 hardstanding; Overflow grass parking in summer ☂ Aire Services Plastic; Token (3/3)

➡ Plan d'Eau des Sezeaux, Rue du Fontgroix. In town follow sp 'Sancoins' and signed onto D1. Turn right, sp 'Plan d'Eau des Sézeaux' and signed. Aire at lake.

ℹ Pleasant popular Aire with every bay having a view over leisure lake and surrounding park. Fishing €8/day. Seasonal café and pedalo hire adj. Small town commerce 400m. Reinspected 2016.

ST LEOPARDIN D'AUGY | 4 | H7 | 03160 | 🏭 | N46°41.053' E003°06.452'

🌓 P 🚐 🛥 🜊 🎵 🚌 F ❄ | ♿ 🏧 🚪 E WC ♿ 🚹 🚐 F ⌀

🚐 3; Max 9m ☂ Aire Services 7005; Token (3/3)

➡ D256. From Limoise take D13, sp 'Couzon', then turn left onto D256, sp 'St Léopardin sur A'. In St Léopardin sur Augy turn left to stay on D256, sp 'Aubigny'. Aire on right just before exit village adj to pond, signed.

ℹ Small, landscaped Aire overlooking village pond. Each bay is divided by grass with a picnic bench. Local commerce 300m. Inspected 2016.

BOURBON L'ARCHAMBAULT | 5 | H7 | 03160 | 🏢 | N46°35.010' E003°03.985'

🌓 P 🚐 🛥 🜊 🎵 🚌 F ❄ | ♿ 🏧 🚪 E WC ♿ 🚹 🚐 F ⌀

🚐 5 ☂ Flot Bleu Océane

➡ D953. Follow D953 bypass around Bourbon d'Archambault. Aire at the former railway station, clearly signed from both directions.

ℹ Aire on outskirts of spa town dominated by ruined château; worth a visit, 900m downhill. Local produce market Sat. Supermarket 450m. Inspected 2016.

LIMOISE | 6 | H7 | 03320 | 🛥 ⚲ | N46°40.540' E003°03.071'

🌓 P 🚐 🛥 🜊 🎵 🚌 F ❄ | ♿ 🏧 🚪 E WC ♿ 🚹 🚐 F ⌀

🚐 6 ☂ Aire Services 7010; Token; €3; WC 50m, in car park

➡ D1. Aire at far end of main village car park adj to D1, signed.

ℹ Pleasant Aire with open and shaded parking overlooking fishing pond. Suitable for any unit configuration. Picnic and park adj. Local commerce 50m. Inspected 2016.

Photos: Stephen & Janet Davies

PARAY LE FRESIL
7 | **H7** | **03220** |  | N46°39.282' E003°36.775'

🚐 3 📍 Aire Services 7005

➡️ D238, adj to roundabout by church. From Chevanges take D238 to Paray-le-Fresil. At Paray-le-Fresil follow sp 'St Martin des Lais' around church. Aire located off roundabout opp church, signed.

ℹ️ Located adj to church, with daytime bells, in a small rural village. Reinspected 2016.

MOULINS
8 | **H7** | **03000** | | N46°33.506' E003°19.506'

🚐 30; €2.40/24hrs; CC; Pay at Flot Bleu Park; Grass parking 📍 Flot Bleu Pacific; CC/Token (FB); €2/20 mins service or 4hrs elec

➡️ Chemin de Halage. Approach Moulins on D13 from Montilly. At roundabout go straight over, sp 'Montlucon' and signed. In 100m turn left, signed. Turn left again, signed, and follow road to Aire. Service Point on right. Parking accessed through Flot Bleu Park barrier.

ℹ️ Former municipal campsite turned commercial Aire. Town centre 1km across river bridge. Reinspected 2016.

CHEVAGNES
9 | **H7** | **03230** |  | N46°36.598' E003°33.125'

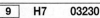
🚐 4 📍 Aire Services 7005; Aire Services Elec; 4 unmetered CEE elec points

➡️ Rue de l'Ancienne Poste. Exit village on D779 towards Bourbon-Lancy and turn off just after Mairie and La Poste, signed. Aire in far right corner, signed.

ℹ️ Located behind Mairie which obscures main road. Village with local commerce 100m. Reinspected 2016.

BEAULON
10 | **I7** | **03230** | | N46°36.219' E003°39.490'

🚐 5 📍 Aire Services 3000; Aire Services Elec; 4 unmetered CEE elec points

➡️ Base Nautique. Turn off D15 at roundabout onto D298, sp 'Chevagnes', 'Base Nautique' and signed. Follow D298 across canal bridge and Aire is on left, signed.

ℹ️ This Aire is in a rural location adj to canal but with no view. Canal walks/cycle path with picnic area opp. Reinspected 2016.

DIOU
11 | **I7** | **03920** | ⛺ | N46°32.118' E003°44.631'

🚐 6; Grass parking 📍 Aire Services 3000; Aire Services Elec; 4 unmetered elec points

➡️ Place du Marché, adj to campsite. Exit N79/E62 at Junction 26, sp 'Diou'. At roundabout take 3rd exit onto D779, sp 'Diou' and signed. Enter village and drive past church, then take next left, signed. Aire in 150m, signed.

ℹ️ Peaceful Aire adj to Camping Gué de Loire and leisure area near river Loire. Small town commerce 150m. www.campingguedeloire.com Inspected 2015.

DOMPIERRE SUR BESBRE
12 | **I7** | **03920** |  | N46°31.108' E003°41.089'

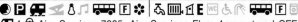
🚐 7 📍 Euro Relais Mini; Donation; Self-cleaning WC adj

➡️ D779. Exit N79 at Junction 26 and turn onto D779, sp 'Dompierre s/ B'. After crossing the river, take 1st left, sp 'Espace Boudeville'; 3.5t weight restricted. Aire on left in 50m.

ℹ️ Large parking area now subdivided with an area designated for motorhomes. River adj. Supermarket and local commerce 350m. Inspected 2016.

MOLINET

| 13 | I7 | 03510 | | N46°28.238' E003°56.490' |

🚐 12 🚰 Flot Bleu Euro; CC; €2; Inspection cover

▶ D779/Route de Moulins. From Digoin take D779 west. Cross the canal and keep right at the roundabout. Aire 100m on right, signed

ℹ️ Aire at Halte Nautique on the Loire canal, some bays have canal views. It is a more peaceful and picturesque town to visit than Digoin, but without the facilities. Inspected 2016.

THIEL SUR ACOLIN

| 14 | H7 | 03230 | | N46°31.330' E003°35.242' |

🚐 11 🚰 Aire Services 7005; Aire Services Elec; 4 CEE unmetered elec points

▶ Route de Dompierre. Exit village on D12 towards Dompierre-sur-Besbre. Turn left immediately before cemetery. Aire on left in 10m.

ℹ️ Landscaped Aire with bays divided by neat hedges. Local commerce 400m. Reinspected 2016.

BESSAY SUR ALLIER

| 15 | H7 | 03340 | | N46°26.461' E003°21.862' |

🚐 10 🚰 Flot Bleu Fontaine

▶ D102/Rue Réné Fallet. Follow N7 north from Moulins and turn onto D102 in Bessay sur Allier, sp 'Gouise' and 'Treteau'. Aire on left in 200m, signed.

ℹ️ Gravel parking area in centre of town adj to 12th century church, hell's bells on the hour. Parking shared with local cars; some shade. Useful stopover 100m from N7. Local commerce 100m. Inspected 2016.

CRESSANGES

| 16 | H7 | 03240 | | N46°26.816' E003°09.641' |

🚐 4 🚰 Euro Relais Box; €2

▶ Grand Rue. Exit N79 to Cressanges. In Cressanges follow D18, sp 'Service Station'. Turn right onto D137, sp 'Moulins'. Aire on left in 20m, signed.

ℹ️ Landscaped Aire adj to town square with rural views from the 4 marked bays. Village with local commerce 250m. Updated 2015.

VILLEFRANCHE D'ALLIER

| 17 | H7 | 03430 | | N46°23.736' E002°51.431' |

🚐 4 🚰 Urba Flux; Token; €2/10 mins water or 2hrs elec; See info

▶ D16. From D16/D33 traffic lighted junction in town centre exit to south on D16, sp 'Bezenet'. Aire is on left in 50m, signed.

ℹ️ Aire in large car park adj to sports facilities. Water free at time of inspections. Centre with local commerce 150m. Reinspected 2016.

MONTMARAULT

| 18 | H7 | 03390 | | N46°19.087' E002°57.309' |

🚐 5 🚰 Euro Relais Junior; Token (ER); €2; No drive over drain; 5 CEE elec points; Token

▶ Rue de Turenne. Enter town on N79 from Le Montet. At roundabout turn left onto D204, sp 'Blomard'. Turn right onto D68, sp 'Centre Ville', and in 20m turn left into large car park. In 30m turn right into Aire, signed.

ℹ️ Small, landscaped Aire 200m from town centre with small town commerce. Adj parking holds market Weds 6am-3pm. Updated 2016.

ST MARCEL EN MURAT
19 | H7 | 03390 | N46°19.304' E003°00.462'

🚐 10 🚰 Euro Relais Junior; Token (ER); €2

➡ D429. Approach on D429 from the west. The Aire is on the left on entering the village, opposite the Mairie, signed.

ℹ Very pleasant rural location with farmland views. Only a restaurant in the village. Tokens available from Mairie and restaurant. Visited 2012.

Photo/Infos: Charlie Tulk

ST POURCAIN SUR SIOULE ★
20 | H7 | 03500 | N46°18.715' E003°17.708'

🚐 70; Gravel and grass parking 🚰 Flot Bleu Pacific (Green); €4 (2 x €2); Flot Bleu Elec; €4/4hrs elec; 8 CEE elec points

➡ Rue des Béthères. Turn into Rue de la Moutte at La Poste. Turn right at the end of the road into Rue des Béthères. Well signed.

ℹ Popular Aire adj to river; some pitches have river views. Town 450m. Reinspected 2016.

Photo: Patricia & Geoff Houghton

VARENNES SUR ALLIER
21 | H7 | 03150 | N46°18.777' E003°24.272'

🚐 20; No parking Tue 6am-1pm (Market) 🚰 Raclet; Token (ER); €2

➡ Place Charles de Gaulle, Rue de Beaupuy. From south on N7 follow sp 'Centre Ville'. Aire in town centre car park to right of Hôtel de Ville. 3.5t weight restriction in car park.

ℹ In tree-lined square adj to town centre. Reinspected 2016.

MONTOLDRE
22 | H7 | 03150 | N46°19.962' E003°26.831'

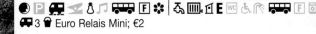

🚐 3 🚰 Euro Relais Mini; €2

➡ D268. Turn off D21 onto D268 and follow into village. Aire 600m in village centre opp Mairie, signed.

ℹ Village with local commerce 350m. Reinspected 2016.

TRETEAU ★
23 | H7 | 03220 | N46°22.086' E003°31.048'

🚐 5; €3.50/night Mar-Oct; 6th night free; Collected; Grass parking 🚰 Euro Relais Junior; €2

➡ Chemin du Vieux Moulin. From D21 turn onto D463 in town, signed. Take 1st right turn, signed. At end of road turn right again and follow road to Service Point.

ℹ Pleasant Aire overlooking village pond. Village centre 700m. Reinspected 2016.

JALIGNY SUR BESBRE
24 | H7 | 03220 | N46°22.898' E003°35.492'

🚐 5 🚰 Aire Services 3000; 5 unmetered CEE elec points

➡ Off D989. From south on D480 turn right onto D989 at traffic lights, sp 'Jaligny-Centre'. Cross river and turn 1st left by war memorial. Follow road to riverside and Aire on left, signed.

ℹ Aire overlooking park and river; canoe hire and snack bar in season. Lovely small town with château and local commerce 150m. Reinspected 2016.

Photos: Ken & Jean Fowler

ST GÉRAND DE VAUX
25 | H7 | 03340 | N46°23.041' E003°23.909'

🚐20 🛒 Euro Relais Box; Token; €2/100L water or 1hr elec

➡ Moulin du Saint-Gérand. From Moulins on N7 turn onto D32, sp 'St Gérand de Vaux'. In village take 1st left. In 550m enter the former campsite on the right, signed.

ℹ A peaceful location with views of a fishing lake. Village and local commerce 750m. Inspected 2016.

LAPALISSE 1
26 | I7 | 03120 | N46°14.956' E003°38.407'

🚐10; Max 12hrs 🛒 None; See **27**

➡ Off D990a. Turn off the roundabout by the river bridge onto D990a, sp 'Bert' and 'Château Lapalisse'. Follow the road up hill and turn beside church. Parking is behind church.

ℹ Ideal if **27** closed. Château and church adj. Town 200m downhill. Updated 2013.

Photo: Rita Renninghoff

LAPALISSE 2
27 | I7 | 03120 | N46°15.000' E003°38.133'

🚐10 🛒 Euro Relais Juior; Token (ER); €2

➡ Place Jean Moulin. From west on D707 turn left in town centre near river bridge, sp 'P 200 Places' and signed. In 300m turn right, signed. Aire at end of road.

ℹ Popular Aire by shallow river. Town 250m. Impressive château 400m uphill. Updated 2013.

PERIGNY
28 | H7 | 03120 | N46°15.122' E003°33.237'

🚐8 🛒 Custom

➡ Rue de l'Eglise. Turn off N7 in Perigny, sp 'D472' and 'Servilly'. Turn 1st left and the Aire is 100m on the left.

ℹ By shallow river; Town 400m; impressive château further 150m uphill. Market Fri from 3pm. Inspected 2012.

BILLY
29 | H7 | 03260 | N46°14.201' E003°25.878'

🚐3; Max 48hrs; Weekends/school holidays only Apr-Oct 🛒 Custom; Lift covers; Male hoselock connector required

➡ Montée d'Almandière, off N209. Service Point is behind bus stop in Place de l'Ancien Marché, adj to N209 in village centre, signed: N46°14.159' E003°25.833'. For parking continue north on N209 and take 1st right on one-way system, signed.

ℹ Service Point with inadequate parking in separate location adj to school. Village has castle to explore and local commerce, 200m from parking. Reinspected 2016.

CREUZIER LE VIEUX
30 | H7 | 03300 | N46°09.270' E003°25.879'

🚐5 🛒 Euro Relais Junior; €2; Token (ER)

➡ D258. Exit village on D558, sp 'Vichy', then turn left onto D258, sp 'Vichy'. The Service Point is 400m on left, signed. There is a small car park directly behind the Service Point and one 100m further back from the road: N46°09.259' E003°25.925'. Turn left after Service Point and the parking is on the left, signed.

ℹ Local commerce adj, closed Mon. Vichy centre 3km south. Inspected 2012.

LE MAYET DE MONTAGNE | 31 | H7 | 03250 | N46°04.321' E003°39.983'

🚐 10 👕 Raclet; €2

▶ Avenue de la Libération. Enter town on D7 from north. Turn off D7 at 2nd right after the church into Avenue de la Libération, sp 'Le Pré Colombier' and 'Centre Social'. The Aire is in the large car park on the right.

ℹ Village 1 min with local commerce; D7 very scenic drive. Updated 2012.

BELLERIVE SUR ALLIER | 32 | H7 | 03700 | N46°06.940' E003°25.807'

🚐 35; €10/night; Pay at campsite 👕 Custom; Inside barrier

▶ Rue Claude Decloitre. Turn off D131 at roundabout by LIDL, sp 'Stades' and 'Berge de l'Allier'. Follow road to right, then left, sp 'Riv'Air Camp'. Follow road to right along river and past numerous campsites. Aire on right opp Camping Beau Rivage, signed. Enter through barrier.

ℹ Landscaped, commercial Aire run by adj campsite. Some facilities at adjoining campsite available for use, confirm on arrival. Close to River Allier with canoeing and swimming, no views. Bellerive and Vichy within easy walking distance. Visited 2015.

Info/photos: Elizabeth Cook

RANDAN | 33 | H8 | 63310 | N46°00.973' E003°21.070'

🚐 5 👕 Euro Relais Junior (Not working); Token (ER); €2

▶ D59/Rue du Puy de Dôme. From centre turn onto D59, sp 'Riom'. Aire on left in 200m, signed.

ℹ Intermarché supermarket 150m. Town 450m. Reinspected 2016.

LE CHEIX SUR MORGE | 34 | H8 | 63200 | N45°57.088' E003°10.695'

🚐 6; Max 48hrs 👕 Custom

▶ D425/Rue du Faubourg. From D2009 in village turn onto Rue du Stade. At end of road turn right onto D425/Rue du Faubourg towards Varennes sur Morge. Aire immediately on right. Well signed.

ℹ Aire in countryside setting within walking distance of village. Beautiful spot. Reinspected 2016.

Photo: Carol Weaver

AIGUEPERSE | 35 | H8 | 63260 | N46°01.561' E003°12.192'

🚐 10 👕 Raclet; €2

▶ From Grande Rue/D2009 turn onto D984 at roundabout. Turn right at next roundabout and take 2nd left into Rue de la Porte aux Boeufs. Aire situated at junction with Boulevard Charles de Gaulle.

ℹ Aire adj to children's play area and green space with benches. Town 150m. Reinspected 2016.

EBREUIL | 36 | H7 | 03450 | N46°06.590' E003°04.537'

🚐 20; At sports stadium 👕 Aire Services 3000; Token (3/3); €2

▶ D915. On D998 follow sp 'Campings' and 'Camping Municipal' through town and onto D915. Parking on right in 850m adj to playing fields, signed. For Service Point take road opp parking to municipal campsite, signed: N46°06.656' E003°04.855'.

ℹ Playing fields adj. Village with tourist commerce 1.3km. Reinspected 2016.

LIMOUSIN & AUVERGNE

POUZOL
37 | H7 | 63440 | N46°06.189' E002°55.854'

🚐 8; May-Oct 🚰 Flot Bleu Pacific; €2/20 mins

➡ Le Pont de Menat. Turn off D2144 near Pouzol, sp 'La Passerelle' and signed. The entrance is quite steep. Drive through the gates into Le Pont de Menat. Take the 1st turning on the left, signed, and follow the road to the right, signed.

ⓘ Aire in a pleasant rural location adj to the Gorges de la Sioule and Gorges de la Chouvigny. Distant road noise. Updated 2015.

ST ELOY LES MINES
38 | H7 | 63700 | N46°09.337' E002°50.152'

🚐 30; Max 48hrs 🚰 Custom

➡ D2144. Adj to D2144 as enter from south, signed. Parking near large lake.

ⓘ Views over lake limited by trees. Town centre 800m. Swimming, boating and fishing adj. Reinspected 2016.

Photo: Carol Weaver

MONTAIGUT
39 | H7 | 63700 | N46°10.624' E002°48.376'

🚐 5 🚰 Flot Bleu Pacific; Token; €2

➡ Off D988. In town turn south onto D988 at traffic light junction, sp 'Pionsat' and to truck parking. Turn left as exit town, sp 'Tennis'. Aire adj to tennis courts.

ⓘ Aire on edge of village adj to sport facilities. Town centre 450m. Reinspected 2016.

MARCILLAT EN COMBRAILLE
40 | H7 | 03420 | N46°09.785' E002°38.240'

🚐 18 🚰 Custom

➡ Rue de l'Economique, off D1089. In village centre at roundabout take D1089, sp 'Poinsat'. Aire next to Gendarmerie (police station), signed.

ⓘ A lovely, typical French village with local commerce and convenience store 750m. Inspected 2016.

Photo: Roy Geddes

ST JULIEN LA GENESTE
41 | H7 | 85540 | N46°01.937' E002°45.459'

🚐 15; €8/24hrs inc service 🚰 Custom; 15 elec points

➡ D532/Les Marceaux. Best approached from St Gervais d'Auvergne on D532. Aire on left 5.7km from St Gervais d'Auvergne, sp 'Les Marceaux' and signed.

ⓘ Seasonal private Aire set in deep countryside a long way from civilisation. Perfect for getting away from it all. Inspected 2016.

ST PARDOUX
42 | H7 | 63440 | N46°03.624' E002°59.710'

🚐 4 🚰 Euro Relais Junior; Token (ER)

➡ Turn off D2144 at village boundary, sp 'Accueil Camping-Car'. Drive 1.5km and turn left onto track, sp 'Etang des Cayers' and 'Accueil Camping-Car'; GPS taken here. Follow track down hill and around lake, 800m. Actual GPS: N46°03.553' E002°59.438'.

ⓘ A beautiful, remote and rural location. Not suitable for RVs. May feel isolated if alone. Reinspected 2016.

ST GERVAIS D'AUVERGNE | 43 | H8 | 63390 | N46°01.845' E002°49.249'

🚐 15; In village centre 🏠 Euro Relais Junior; €2

➡ D417. Turn off D534 in town, sp 'P Covoiturage'. Parking immediately on left opp Carrefour supermarket and Sapeurs Pompiers (fire station). For Service Point travel north on D534, then D987, sp 'St Eloy les Mines' and 'Base de Loisirs - Étang Philippe'. Service Point at Base de Loisirs: N46°02.203' E002°49.107'.

ℹ Unrestricted parking in very ordinary town centre car park opp supermarket. Service Point at very pleasant leisure lake. Campsite adj, open Apr-Sept. Reinspected 2016.

SAURET BESSERVE | 44 | H8 | 63390 | N45°59.544' E002°48.441'

🚐 5 🏠 Euro Relais Junior; €2

➡ D523. Near the church, adj to D523 in tiny village.

ℹ Tiny village near Gorges de la Sioule. Reinspected 2016.

MANZAT | 45 | H8 | 63410 | N45°57.724' E002°56.296'

🚐 20 🏠 Custom

➡ D148. Turn off D227 onto D418, sp 'Pulverières' and signed. Aire 50m on right, signed.

ℹ Aire in large gravel car park. Town centre and local commerce 300m. Reinspected 2016.

CHARBONNIERES LES VARENNES | 46 | H8 | 63410 | N45°53.076' E002°58.814'

🚐 4; Between trees 🏠 Aire Services 3000; Token (3/3); €2

➡ D90. Turn off D943 west of Volvic onto D16, sp 'Paugnat' and signed. Follow road for 4km to roundabout and turn left onto D90, sp 'Les Ancizes'. In 500m turn left into Aire, signed.

ℹ Alt 800m. Pleasant hedged bays tucked off main route. Although close to habitation, Aire is shielded by trees and feels remote. In national park famous for springs, inc Volvic mineral water. Reinspected 2016.

ORCINES | 47 | H8 | 63870 | N45°47.271' E003°00.578'

🚐 51; €6/24hrs Oct-Apr; €8/24hrs May-Sept; +€0.50 tax; CC; Pay at machine 🏠 Euro Relais Junior; Outside barrier; €2; Flot Bleu Euro; Token; €2; Inspection cover; Flot Bleu Elec; Token; €2; 1 Token/4hrs elec; Both inside barrier

➡ D941. The Service Point is located adj to D941 as exit the town towards Pontgibaud. Turn off near electricity pylon, signed. Service Point immediately to left. Parking and additional Service Point through Flot Bleu Park barrier.

ℹ Formerly Service Point only outside campsite, now landscaped commercial Aire. Original Euro Relais still in situ outside barrier, but may be removed. Sports facilities adj. Reinspected 2016.

ORCINES - Le Puy de Dome | 48 | H8 | 63870 | N45°46.176' E002°59.081'

🚐 20; Day parking only 🏠 Custom; Seasonal WC

➡ Panoramique des Domes. Follow sp 'Le Puy de Dome' onto D68. Turn off, sp 'P Panoramique des Domes', and follow road around parking area to designated coach and motorhome parking, signed.

ℹ Alt 903m. Large parking area intended for visitors of Grand Site Le Puy, adj to visitor centre and tourist train to summit. Numerous walking and cycling trails. Popular tourist attraction. Reinspected 2016.

ST OURS - Vulcania
49 | H8 | 63230 | N45°48.742' E002°56.931'

65; €10/night 5pm-noon; €18/2 nights 5pm-noon; €2/hr noon-5pm; CC; Apr-Oct; Max 2 nights Euro Relais Box; Token/CC; €2/100L water or 6hrs elec; Apr-Oct

▶ D559/Route de Mazayes. From D941 turn off at roundabout onto D559, sp 'Vulcania'. Drive past the entrance and follow road for 250m. Entrance to Aire on right, signed. Enter through barrier.

ℹ Landscaped Aire with multiple Service Points. Reserved for visitors to Vulcania, a volcano-themed amusement park, and only open when park open; park entry €24.50pp. Day parking €2/hr on Aire, but free day parking inside the park for visitors. www.vulcania.com Inspected 2016.

CLERMONT FERRAND
50 | H8 | 63100 | N45°47.884' E003°06.794'

7; €4.70; Max 1 night; See Accueil, 20m, for access 6.30am-8.30pm Mon-Sat Euro Relais Mini; Inside barrier

▶ P+R Les Pistes. Approach Clermont Ferrand from north on D2009. At traffic-lighted roundabout go straight on, sp 'Le Mont Dore' and 'P+R Les Pistes'. Turn 1st right and cross tramway, sp 'P+R Les Pistes' and signed. Aire 2nd entrance on right through barrier, signed.

ℹ Barrier lifts automatically on exit. Adj tram stop direct to town (€2.60 return). Reinspected 2016.

AYDAT
51 | H8 | 63970 | N45°39.630' E002°58.628'

30; €9.50/night inc unmetered elec; CC; Pay on entry; Grass parking Custom; Inside barrier

▶ Rue du Stade, off D90. Turn behind the church and entrance 150m, signed. Aire signed from Ponteix on D213. Enter through Urba Flux barrier.

ℹ Aire within former municipal campsite 300m from large leisure lake. All parking around lake bans motorhomes 8pm-8am. WiFi avail. Reinspected 2016.

PERIGNAT LES SARLIEVE
52 | H8 | 63170 | N45°44.214' E003°08.310'

6; 8m bays Euro Relais Junior; Token (ER); €2

▶ Rue Marcel Margard. Turn off D978 north edge of village, sp 'Ateliers Municipaux' and signed. Follow road to left and turn left, then turn immediately right, all signed.

ℹ Aire in centre of village. Walk through adj park to reach local commerce. Convenient stop near A75 motorway. Clermont Ferrand has reasonably priced fuel. Reinspected 2016.

COURNON D'AUVERGNE
53 | H8 | 63800 | N45°44.397' E003°13.366'

15; €4.70/24hrs; Collected; Max 24hrs Flot Bleu Pacific; Token (FB); Lift cover for waste water disposal

▶ Rue des Laveuses, at the campsite. Follow D52 around town following sp 'Camping' and 'Zone de Loisirs'. The Aire is outside the campsite.

ℹ Aire in gravel car park adj to campsite. Leisure lake and river adj, no views. All other parking restricted 8pm-8am. Reinspected 2016.

PONT DU CHATEAU
54 | H8 | 63430 | N45°48.070' E003°15.693'

5 Aire Services 3000; Token (3/3)

▶ D1093b/Route de Vichy. In town turn off D2089 at roundabout onto D1093b, sp 'Cimitière'. Aire on left outside cemetery.

ℹ Service Point in large, unrestricted car park adj to main road and cemetery. Space likely. Inspected 2016.

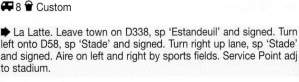

ST DIER D'AUVERGNE | 55 | H8 | 63520 | N45°40.368' E003°28.452'

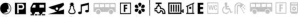

🚐 8 ♛ Custom

➡ La Latte. Leave town on D338, sp 'Estandeuil' and signed. Turn left onto D58, sp 'Stade' and signed. Turn right up lane, sp 'Stade' and signed. Aire on left and right by sports fields. Service Point adj to stadium.

ℹ Large, flat gravelled area on outskirts of town by the open access sports fields. Small river beside parking. Small town commerce 700m. Visited 2016.

Photos/Info: Alan Potter

VOLVIC | 56 | H8 | 63530 | N45°52.355' E003°02.813'

🚐 5; Max 6m ♛ Aire Services 3000; €2

➡ Rue de Chancelas. Turn off D986, sp 'Camping'. Aire is outside the campsite.

ℹ Designated parking located directly outside campsite; €11/2 people. Volvic has walking trails. Reinspected 2016.

CHATEAUGAY | 57 | H8 | 63119 | N45°50.964' E003°05.077'

🚐 Poss; Busy during school run ♛ Aire Services 3000; €2; Self-cleaning WC adj

➡ Place Charles de Gaulle. Turn off D402, main route through, opp La Poste into car park just before exit village towards Volvic, sp 'Ecole Maternelle'. Service Point in far right corner, signed.

ℹ Adj to school, no designated parking but should be poss out of school hrs and at weekends. Privately owned château, 210m, has a restaurant. www.aubergeduchateau-chateaugay.fr Reinspected 2016.

CHATEL GUYON | 58 | H8 | 63140 | N45°55.024' E003°03.466'

🚐 14; €5/night Apr-Oct; Pay at machine; Free Nov-Mar ♛ Aire Services 3000; Token (3/3); €2; Aire Services Elec; Token (3/3); €2/2hrs

➡ D15/Avenue de Russie. Approach Châtel-Guyon from south on D455 and at roundabout junction with D15 follow sp 'Châtel-Guyon Centre' into Avenue de Russie. Aire on left in 500m. Signed from both directions.

ℹ Former Aire relocated and Service Point blocked. Well laid out Aire in a popular spa town. Town centre with a wide range of commerce 650m. Inspected 2016.

ST BONNET PRES RIOM | 59 | H8 | 63200 | N45°55.635' E003°06.832'

🚐 3; Max 24hrs ♛ Custom

➡ Place de la Liberté, off D2144. Turn off D2144 at church into Place de la Liberté and stay to right at fork (higher road). Aire between church and Salle Municipal.

ℹ Aire adj to town with local commerce. Views of countryside. Reinspected 2016.

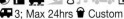

RIOM | 60 | H8 | 63200 | N45°53.680' E003°07.497'

🚐 4; Max 48hrs ♛ Urba Flux; €2/15 mins elec and water

➡ Route d'Ennazat. From Volvic approach on D986 and follow sp 'Riom', then turn left at traffic lights, sp 'Riom-Centre'. Follow sp 'Ennazat', 'A71' and signed onto D224. Cross railway bridge and the Aire is directly across the roundabout, signed.

ℹ Landscaped Aire adj to road which can be noisy during day. Riom town commerce 700m across railway bridge, within fortified town. Reinspected 2016.

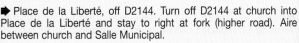

LIMOUSIN & AUVERGNE

LEZOUX
61 | H8 | 63190 | N45°49.630' E003°23.141'

🚐 15 Custom

▶ Musée de Céramique/Rue de la République. Turn off D2089, sp 'Musée de Céramique' and signed. Turn right and right again into Aire, sp 'Parking Visiteurs Gratuit'.

ℹ Lezoux is famous for Samian ware pottery; major ceramics producer since Roman times. Ceramic museum adj. Inspected 2014.

ST REMY SUR DUROLLE
62 | H8 | 63550 | N45°53.718' E003°35.838'

🚐 5 Custom

▶ At Lac des Moines, off D201. Exit town to north on D201. Turn off to Lac des Moines by the Elan garage, sp 'Plan d'Eau'. Drive down to the lake and follow sp 'Village Vacances' and signed.

ℹ Service Point and unrestricted parking on terrace overlooking leisure lake, unrestricted parking around lake. Tourist commerce in season, may feel isolated if alone. Village with local commerce 1km. Reinspected 2014.

THIERS
63 | H8 | 63300 | N45°52.255' E003°29.057'

🚐 10 Custom (in yellow box)

▶ D44, at the Base de Loisirs ILOA. Turn off D906 onto D44 at roundabout junction near A89/E70, sp 'Dorat'. Follow D44 for 1.8km and turn left, sp 'Base de Loisirs ILOA'. The Service Point is in 200m on left, signed.

ℹ Aire with parking under trees or on gravel at activity centre/leisure lake. Popular carp fishing. Municipal campsite adj. Updated 2016.

CHABRELOCHE
64 | H8 | 63250 | N45°52.767' E003°41.911'

🚐 5 Custom

▶ D324/Rue St Thomas. Turn off D2089 onto D324, sp 'Col St Thomas' and signed. Turn right just past village boundary sign, sp 'Terrain de Petangue'. Service Point immediately on right opp cemetery, signed.

ℹ Pleasant Aire at the tennis and boules courts, outside cemetery and behind church. Small town commerce 200m. Inspected 2014.

ARCONSAT
65 | I8 | 63250 | N45°53.279' E003°42.773'

🚐 2 None; See **64** or **72**

▶ Place du 19 Mars 1962, off D64. From Chabreloche follow sp 'Arconsat'. Designated parking on right in Arconsat centre, signed.

ℹ 2 designated bays in rural village. 42 cycling circuits. 5km cross country skiing trails in winter. Inspected 2014.

PALLADUC
66 | I8 | 63550 | N45°54.284' E003°37.802'

🚐 2 None; See **64** or **72**

▶ D201. Adj to D201 as exit village to northeast, sp 'P Camping Cars'. Near D201/D64 junction.

ℹ Sports facilities adj. Remote mountain village. Reinspected 2014.

LA MONNERIE LE MONTEL
| 67 | I8 | 63650 | | N45°52.174' E003°36.393' |

🚐 10; No parking Sat 5am-1pm (Market) 🏕 Campsite bollard; Dilapidated

➡ D2089. Adj to and signed off D2089. Parking located between main road and railway line.

ℹ Aire located between train track and main road. Service Point in disrepair, but working. Town centre with commerce adj, shop here and then stay at 65 or 66. Reinspected 2014.

VISCOMTAT
| 68 | I8 | 63250 | | N45°49.636' E003°40.533' |

🚐 10 🏕 None; See 64 or 72

➡ Place du 19 Mars 1962. In car park in centre of village behind shop, signed.

ℹ Peaceful Aire in a rural French village off the beaten track. Local commerce adj. Inspected 2014.

VOLLORE MONTAGNE
| 69 | I8 | 42440 | | N45°47.393' E003°40.978' |

🚐 4 🏕 WC and sink; See 64 or 72

➡ Plan d'Eau. Turn off D42 in Vollore-Montagne onto D312, sp 'Noiretable' and signed. Turn left and follow road to left, sp 'Plan d'Eau' and signed. Follow road past houses and down to the pond. Designated parking to right, signed.

ℹ 4 landscaped designated parking bays adj to the village recreational facility which includes a pond, no views. May feel isolated if alone. Inspected 2014.

STE AGATHE
| 70 | H8 | 63120 | | N45°49.243' E003°36.721' |

🚐 2 🏕 WC 15m; See 64 or 72

➡ D131a. Aire on left adj to D131a as exit village towards Escoutoux (south), signed.

ℹ Designated parking in tiny village. Inspected 2014.

CELLES SUR DUROLLE
| 71 | H8 | 63250 | | N45°51.357' E003°38.202' |

🚐 3 🏕 None; See 64 or 72

➡ Ave du Bois de la Donne. Turn off D2089 onto D7, sp 'Celles s Durolle'. Turn off D7 at south end of Celles sur Durolle, signed. In 400m turn right, sp 'Mairie' and signed. Parking outside Mairie and La Poste.

ℹ Parking outside Mairie in village centre car park. Small picnic area adj. Inspected 2014.

LAC D'AUBUSSON
| 72 | H8 | 63120 | | N45°45.241' E003°36.859' |

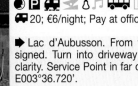

🚐 20; €6/night; Pay at office 🏕 Custom

➡ Lac d'Aubusson. From town follow sp 'Lac d'Aubusson' and signed. Turn into driveway and follow road, GPS taken here for clarity. Service Point in far corner of car park, signed: N45°45.186' E003°36.720'.

ℹ Aire at large leisure lake with big swimming beach, no views. Masses of green space with BBQ areas and picnic tables. Restaurant adj. Popular with locals on hot days and holidays. Updated 2016.

Photos: Alan Potter

JOB | 73 | I8 | 63990 | N45°37.225' E003°44.707'

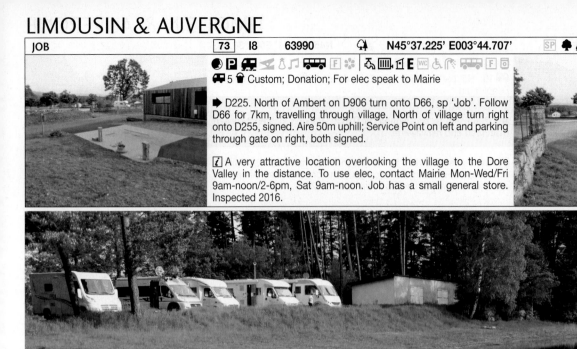

🚐5 🏠 Custom; Donation; For elec speak to Mairie

➤ D225. North of Ambert on D906 turn onto D66, sp 'Job'. Follow D66 for 7km, travelling through village. North of village turn right onto D255, signed. Aire 50m uphill; Service Point on left and parking through gate on right, both signed.

ℹ️ A very attractive location overlooking the village to the Dore Valley in the distance. To use elec, contact Mairie Mon-Wed/Fri 9am-noon/2-6pm, Sat 9am-noon. Job has a small general store. Inspected 2016.

Serviers le Chateau

VERNET LA VARENNE | 75 | H8 | 63580 | N45°28.406' E003°26.933'

🚐15 🏠 Raclet; €2

➤ D999. Aire in large car park adj to D999 in village, signed.

ℹ️ Alt 800m. Leisure/swimming lake adj. In small village with château. Reinspected 2016.

ST GERMAIN L'HERM | 76 | H8 | 63630 | N45°27.602' E003°32.631'

🚐20 🏠 Euro Relais Junior; May-Sept

➤ D37. Adj to D37 at junction with D999 to east of town, signed.

ℹ️ Village with local commerce 350m. Reinspected 2016.

ARLANC | 77 | I8 | 63220 | N45°24.718' E003°43.102'

🚐5 🏠 Euro Relais Junior; Token; €2

➤ D300. Exit town to west on D300, sp 'St Bonnet'. Aire is adj to the sports pitch, signed.

ℹ️ Nice parking under trees in picnic area. Outdoor swimming pool, swimmable river and sports facilities adj. Reinspected 2016.

CHOMELIX | 78 | I8 | 43500 | N45°15.707' E003°49.544'

🚐10 🏠 Euro Relais Junior; Token (2/1)

➤ D135. Turn off D1 in village centre onto D135, sp 'Estables'. In 10m turn left, sp 'Multi Activities'. Service Point immediately on left. Parking 10m on right.

ℹ️ Located adj to sports facilities, 1 min from village centre and commerce. Inspected 2012.

CRAPONNE SUR ARZON
79 | I8 | 43500 | N45°20.034' E003°51.043'

15 Euro Relais Junior; €2; Closed in winter

▶ Place de la Gare, D498. Follow D498 out of town to the northeast. The Service Point is adj to D498 at old train station, signed.

ℹ Aire adj to old railway station in semi industrial area. Town 500m downhill. Updated 2012.

VALPRIVAS
80 | I8 | 43210 | N45°18.627' E004°02.697'

5 Euro Relais Junior; €2

▶ Rue du Lavoir. Turn off D42 onto D44, sp 'Valprivas'. Turn right in 100m, sp 'Valprivas'. Follow road and the Aire is on the right as enter village.

ℹ Located on edge of village 100m from centre with bar. Inspected 2012.

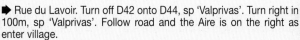

TIRANGES
81 | I8 | 43530 | N45°18.421' E003°59.457'

6 Euro Relais Junior; €2

▶ Heading north on the D24. Turn right in the village centre, sp 'Eco Point' and signed. Aire on right in 400m.

ℹ Located on edge of small hamlet 300m from centre. Park opp. Inspected 2012.

BAS EN BASSET
82 | I8 | 43210 | N45°18.454' E004°07.097'

5 Euro Relais Junior; €2

▶ Camping La Garenne. Turn off D42 onto D12 to Bas-en-Basset. At the roundabout turn right, sp 'La Garenne'. Service Point on right outside Camping La Garenne.

ℹ Adj to campsite entrance and overlooking carp fishing lake. Campsite €16/night. Reception confirmed that it was OK to stay overnight at the Aire. Town 550m. Inspected 2012.

ST ANDRE DE CHALENCON
83 | I8 | 43130 | N45°16.357' E003°58.215'

4; Residents use car park Euro Relais Junior; €2

▶ In village centre turn opp church, the Aire is visible at this point. Aire is 10m on right, signed.

ℹ Sweeping views from parking, but access may be obstructed by local vehicles. Bar 1 min. Inspected 2012.

VOREY
84 | I9 | 43800 | N45°11.200' E003°54.283'

3 Custom; Token; €3

▶ Chemin des Félines, next to Camping les Moulettes. Turn off D103 north of the river, signed. Pass the campsite and Aire is alongside the river.

ℹ Adj to river overlooking sports field. Town centre 350m. Inspected 2013.

RETOURNAC
| 85 | I9 | 43130 | | N45°12.259' E004°02.712' |

🚐 6 🚰 Custom; Push down red tops for water

➤ Rue de l'Industrie. Turn off D9 at river bridge, sp 'Aire de Pique Nique' and signed. Follow sp 'Aire de Pique Nique' and the Aire is adj to the picnic area, signed. Service Point 100m by WC.

ℹ️ A popular Aire adj to river suitable for fishing, but no view. Riverside park with picnic tables adj. Town centre and commerce 1.3km. Inspected 2012.

BEAUZAC
| 86 | I9 | 43590 | | N45°15.717' E004°06.115' |

🚐 15 🚰 Euro Relais Mini

➤ D42. Turn off D42 at north side of village, sp 'Espace la Doriliere'. Follow road straight on and the Aire is on the lower terrace, signed.

ℹ️ Adj to function hall. Slightly protected from road noise due to high banks. Local commerce 450m, adj to main route and in citadel. Market Sun 8am-noon. Inspected 2012.

ST ROMAIN LACHALM
| 87 | I8 | 43620 | | N45°15.849' E004°20.149' |

🚐 4 🚰 Flot Bleu Pacific; Token; Flot Bleu Electric; 1 Token/4hrs

➤ From the large D45/D23 roundabout take the D25, sp 'St Romain Lachalm' and signed. Follow road to right and turn right in 200m, before La Poste, signed. Exit town and Aire 100m on left, signed.

ℹ️ Landscaped Aire on edge of town with rural views. Local commerce 200m. Inspected 2012.

RAUCOULES
| 88 | I9 | 43290 | | N45°11.178' E004°17.862' |

🚐 4 🚰 Flot Bleu Pacific; Token; Flot Bleu Electric; 1 Token/4hrs

➤ Turn off D61 onto D66, sp 'Raucoules' and signed. Follow road and turn left immediately after cemetery, signed. Aire on right in 20m, signed.

ℹ️ Landscaped Aire on edge of town with rural views. Butcher opp, local commerce 250m. Inspected 2012.

ST BONNET LE FROID
| 89 | I9 | 43290 | | N45°08.481' E004°26.064' |

🚐 6; €4/night inc elec 🚰 Custom; Water in wooden bin box; 16amp elec in lockable box

➤ Lotissement Herbier des Boenes. Approach on D105 from Montfaucon-en-Velay. In village turn right, signed, and drive up hill into residential area. At top of hill turn left. In 200m turn left again at end of garages, signed.

ℹ️ Landscaped Aire overlooking town square. Key for elec and Service Point from local commerce (Bar les Genets d'Or/Boucherie Chatelard) on receipt of payment. Inspected 2012.

TENCE
| 90 | I9 | 43190 | | N45°06.943' E004°17.549' |

🚐 10 🚰 Raclet; 2 unmetered CEE elec points

➤ Off D18. Follow D18 one-way system through town. Turn off D18 down a narrow road which quickly widens, sp 'Parking le Fieu' and 'Maison de Retraite'. Aire in car park on left.

ℹ️ Large car park at rear of town; Service Point turned off in winter, but elec points working when inspected in Nov. Updated 2013.

LA CHAISE DIEU

| 91 | I8 | 43160 | | N45°18.986' E003°41.799' |

🚐 8; €3/night; €2pp; Collected 🛒 Euro Relais Box; €2; Elec €2.50; Tap at railway building

➡ Rue Pablo Picasso. Enter town from South on D906, parking immediately on first right at old railway station.

ℹ Aire in open car park adj to former railway station. Local commerce adj. Visited 2016.

Photos/Info: Chris & Angela Irving

LES ESTABLES

| 92 | I9 | 43150 | | N44°54.155' E004°09.427' |

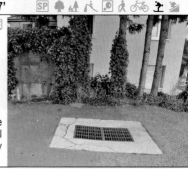

🚐 20; Opp Service Point 🛒 Custom; Free if buy fuel

➡ D36. Situated in the village centre at fuel station, signed.

ℹ Alt 1343m. Service Point at small 24/24 fuel station. Large unrestricted parking opp suitable for any unit configuration. Small town commerce and TO 100m. Walking, biking and cross country skiing area. Reinspected 2016.

LE MONASTIER SUR GAZEILLE

| 93 | I9 | 43150 | | N44°56.228' E003°59.584' |

🚐 25 🛒 Flot Bleu Océane; €2 (2 x €1)

➡ Rue Augustin Ollier. North of town turn off D535 onto D27 and follow sp 'Centre Ville'. Turn off in town centre by chapel, sp 'Camping' and signed. Follow road for 300m, then turn left into Rue Augustin Ollier. Aire on left next to tennis courts, signed.

ℹ Alt 900m. Pleasant, popular Aire adj to sports facilities and with rural views. Town 300m uphill with small town commerce. Cross country skiing in winter. Reinspected 2016.

SOLIGNAC SUR LOIRE

| 94 | I9 | 43370 | ⛺ | N44°57.880' E003°52.826' |

🚐 21; €7/night inc water and elec; Access via magnetic card from Mairie (€50 deposit); Grass parking 🛒 Euro Relais Mini; Inside gate

➡ Rue d l'Iris. Turn off D27, main route through town, onto D276, sp 'Cayres' and signed. Turn left into Rue d l'Iris, signed. Follow road for 300m and Aire on right adj to sports facilities. Enter through electronic gates, code from town.

ℹ Former campsite revamped as a commercial Aire. Adj to sports and play area, may feel isolated if alone. Small town commerce 800m. Voie Verte cycle route to Brives-Charensac. Inspected 2014.

PRADELLES

| 95 | I9 | 43420 | | N44°46.537' E003°53.244' |

🚐 20; Max 48hrs; Grass parking 🛒 Custom; 6amp CEE elec €2; Pay at shop

➡ N88. On N88 to north of town at local produce shop 'Saveurs des Montagnes', next to the football pitch. Opp side of road to boucherie and charcuterie 'Saveurs des Montaunes'.

ℹ Alt 1200m. Aire/France Passion at local produce shop; English spoken. Adj to road, some road noise. Reinspected 2016.

COUBON

| 96 | I9 | 43700 | ⚓ | N44°59.836' E003°55.006' |

🚐 10; Max 6m; Must park in marked bays 🛒 Custom; €2.50; Mar-Nov

➡ D37/Route du Plan d'Eau. In Coubon centre by the river bridge at the village car park, beside the church and cemetery.

ℹ Aire in popular local car park adj to river and lovely park. Small town commerce adj. Reinspected 2014.

AIGUILHE
97 | **I9** | **43000** | **T** | **N45°03.038' E003°53.017'**

🚐 6; Max 24hrs; Max 9m 🚽 None; See **289**

➡ D13. From N88 turn onto D13, sp 'Aiguilhe Camping'. At roundabout go straight on, sp 'Vichy'. Go all the way around the next elongated roundabout, then turn right into car park. Designated parking on left, signed.

ℹ Adj to busy main road in parking at bottom of religious pilgrimage site, Rocher St Michel, €3.50pp. www.rochersaintmichel.fr Footpath to top with many steps. Puy centre 700m. Updated 2016.

BEAULIEU
98 | **I9** | **43800** | | **N45°07.602' E003°56.815'**

🚐 6 🚽 Custom

➡ Lois Saux. Turn off D103 at traffic lights in Lavoûte-sur-Loire onto D7, sp 'Beaulieu'. In Beaulieu turn off D7 just after Elan fuel station, sp 'La Galoche' and signed. Aire immediately on right.

ℹ This Aire has moved and is adj to the main road. Village centre with local commerce 500m. Updated 2014.

AIRE de SERVICE RESERVEE UNIQUEMENT aux CAMPING-CARS

Cette aire de stationnement vous est proposée gratuitement
MERCI de la laisser propre pour les futurs occupants

BEAULIEU VOUS ACCUEILLE A TITRE GRACIEUX

Vous trouverez au bourg:
- une boulangerie epicerie
- un bar-tabac-journaux
- une coiffeuse
- un medecin..........Merci de penser à eux ...

Pour tous renseignements complémentaires
s'adresser à la MAIRIE: 04.71.08.53.60

ST CHRISTOPHE SUR DOLAISON
99 | **I9** | **43370** | | **N44°59.881' E003°49.293'**

🚐 5 🚽 Euro Relais Mini; Token (ER); €2; Tap at WC

➡ D31. Turn off D906 onto D31 in St Christophe sur Dolaison. Drive through village and Service Point is situated against a building behind Mairie, signed.

ℹ Pleasant village with local commerce. On St Jacques de Compostelle pilgrimage route. Reinspected 2014.

LOUDES - Aerodrome
100 | **I9** | **43320** | | **N45°04.488' E003°45.671'**

🚐 5 🚽 Euro Relais Mini; Token (ER)

➡ D906, at Aérodrome. Turn off D906, sp 'Loudes Airport' or follow sp 'Aérodrome de Loudes'. Aire at picnic area on left.

ℹ Overlooking airfield; Parachuting poss. Reinspected 2014.

LE VERNET
101 | **I9** | **43320** | | **N45°02.117' E003°40.193'**

🚐 40; €3 inc service; Collected 🚽 Custom; €3; Collected; 10 CEE elec points; Elec €3

➡ D48. Aire located on right as exit village on D40 towards St Berain, signed.

ℹ Large parking area adj to wood with adventure activities, maps from TO 150m. Village and bar adj. Inspected 2014.

SIAUGUES ST MARIE
102 | **H9** | **43300** | | **N45°05.572' E003°37.660'**

🚐 5; Underneath pylon 🚽 Euro Relais Junior; €2

➡ D590. Adj to D590 by 24hr unmanned fuel pump, signed.

ℹ Centre of mountain bike area. Village adj with small selection of shops. Very small campsite 100m. Reinspected 2014.

CHANTEUGES
103 H9 43300 N45°04.310' E003°31.817'

🚐 10 🚰 Custom

➡ The old train station, off D585. Turn off D585, main route through, signed. Follow road then turn right before railway track. The Service Point is 200m on left in children's play area. Parking is outside the old train station.

ℹ Pleasant Aire tucked away at the former railway station. Views to town and monastery. Marked info panels. Inspected 2014.

SAUGUES
104 H9 43170 N44°57.587' E003°32.641'

🚐 20 🚰 Euro Relais Mini

➡ Place du Breuil. Exit town centre, sp 'Langeac'. Turn left and left again both, sp 'Centre Culturel - Aire Camping-Car'. Aire on left in large car park, signed.

ℹ Aire in large car park. Small town commerce, tourist/walking shops and restaurants 1 min. Inspected 2012.

CHANALEILLES
105 H9 43170 N44°51.567' E003°29.431'

🚐 5 🚰 Custom

➡ D587. Enter village from Sauges and the Aire on left adj to D587, signed.

ℹ Landscaped Aire on edge of village adj to stream and has rural views. Gîte adj. Inspected 2012.

CHAUDES AIGUES
106 H9 15110 N44°50.986' E003°00.182'

🚐 20 🚰 Raclet; €2

➡ Off D981. Turn off D921 onto D989 in town, sp 'Fournels' and signed. In 50m do not follow road to left across river bridge, but drive straight on through gap into large car park behind, signed.

ℹ Aire in large, open, sloping and unglamorous, but well located car park. Some road noise. Town commerce 200m, Town has natural spring water of 82°F and associated thermal commerce, 150m. 2hrs in the thermal waters €15.50pp. www.caleden.com Reinspected 2016.

RUYNES EN MARGERIDE
107 H9 15320 N45°00.075' E003°13.437'

🚐 20; Plenty of parking space 🚰 Aire Services 3000; €2

➡ D4. Turn off D4 as exit village towards Paulhav, signed. Service Point in corner on left beside trees, opp houses.

ℹ Small park adj. Village with local commerce 1 min. Inspected 2012.

FAVEROLLES
108 H9 15320 N44°56.339' E003°08.858'

🚐 5 🚰 Aire Services 3000; €2

➡ D248. Turn off D13 onto D248, sp 'St Marc'. Aire on left in 200m, signed.

ℹ In town square adj to Mairie. Local commerce adj. Château, 650m, open 2-6pm. Viaduc de Garabit, 5km north, goes over D909 and was designed by Gustave Eiffel, of the Eiffel Tower. Inspected 2012.

ST FLOUR 1

| 109 | H9 | 03100 | | N45°02.157' E003°05.905' |

🚐 10 ♻ Euro Relais Maxi; €2

➡ Rue Marie-Aimée Méraville. Exit A75 at Junction 28, sp 'St Flour'. At roundabout follow sp 'St Flour'. Follow road until enter town (at bottom of hill). Turn right, signed. Follow road, turning left across bridge, and Aire is then on right.

ℹ Alt 800m. Aire in residential area with views of hilltop town. Only likely to be busy when events on at 110. Lower town commerce 300m. Reinspected 2016.

ST FLOUR 2

| 110 | H9 | 15100 | | N45°02.059' E003°05.251' |

🚐 50 ♻ Euro Relais Maxi; €2; No drive over drain

➡ Cours Chazerat. Take D926 up hill, sp 'Haute Ville'. At top of hill go straight on at roundabout and through car park. Turn left at roundabout and then next left into Cours Chazerat. Service Point in Cours Chazerat, outside hospital.

ℹ Alt 879m. Service Point located in centre of hilltop town with town commerce adj. Large car park, but parking subject to local events. Reinspected 2016.

PIERREFORT

| 111 | H9 | 15230 | | N44°55.306' E002°50.512' |

🚐 15 ♻ Euro Relais Tall; CC/Token; €2

➡ Côte de Chabridet, off D990. Turn off D990 in the town onto Côte de Chabridet, signed. Service Point on right in 300m next to Centre Medico-Social: N44°55.331' E002°50.494'. Parking 100m past Service Point on right, signed.

ℹ Alt 959m. Large open parking area adj to sports facilities; suitable for any unit configuration. Small town commerce 300m downhill; market Wed am. Motorhome parking poss in: Cezens, Gourdieges, Brezons, Iradour, Ste Mairie, Lietades and Narnhac. Reinspected 2016.

PAULHAC

| 112 | H9 | 15430 | SKI | N45°00.387' E002°54.246' |

🚐 3; Best parking adj to water trough ♻ Custom; No drive over drain; 1 unmetered Cont elec point

➡ Place des Chasseurs, off D34. At church turn off D34 onto D44, sp 'Plomb du Cantal'. Turn 1st left at water trough and Service Point immediately on left, signed.

ℹ Alt 1115m. Small Aire in small village with local commerce near the Volcans d'Auvergne national park. Walking in summer, cross country skiing in winter. Reinspected 2016.

GPS Co-ordinates for SatNav

The GPS Co-ordinates published in this guide were taken onsite by our inspectors. We consider them a valuable and unique asset and at the time of publishing have decided not to publish them as electronic files for use on navigation devices. You have permission to type in the co-ordinates of an Aire you intend to visit but not to store or share them. For the security of our copyright:

- **Do not compile them into lists**

- **Do not publish, share or reproduce them anywhere in any format**

VALUEJOLS

| 114 | H9 | 15300 | | N45°03.216' E002°55.782' |

🚐 15; €3/night inc service; Collected ♻ Euro Relais Mini; €3 service only; Honesty box

➡ Place du 19 Mars 1962, off D134. Follow D34, sp 'Paulhac' and signed. Then turn onto D134 in the village, signed. Aire is at the Centre d'Accueil, next to the cemetery, signed.

ℹ Alt 1066m. Aire in large car park with hardstanding and grass parking, behind hedge adj to cemetery. Rural village centre 300m. Cross country skiing in winter, walking in summer. Reinspected 2016.

TALIZAT
| 115 | H9 | 15170 | | N45°06.846' E003°02.754' |

🚐2 🚰 Raclet; Token (ER); No drive over drain

➥ Turn off D679 in village. Drive past Mairie, signed. Aire immediately on right, Service Point up against and obscured by building.

ℹ️ Alt 986m. Impractical Aire with very limited parking. Local commerce adj. Cycle route marked on sign. Suggest 116. Reinspected 2014.

COLTINES
| 116 | H9 | 15170 | | N45°05.754' E002°59.142' |

🚐5 🚰 Euro Relais Junior; Token (ER); May-Sept

➥ D40. Exit the village on D40, sp 'Celles' and signed. The Aire is on the right after the water tower opp the sports facilities, signed.

ℹ️ Alt: 970m. Pleasant gravel Aire offering far reaching views adj to a rural French farming community with local commerce. Reinspected 2014.

MURAT
| 117 | H9 | 15300 | | N45°06.563' E002°52.147' |

🚐3 parking areas in town 🚰 Raclet; €2

➥ N122. From south on D926 turn left onto N122 immediately after crossing train tracks, sp 'Aurillac'. Service Point at far side of train station car park in 200m. Parking: Stade, opp train track: N45°06.531' E002°52.240'. Swimming pool: N45°06.503' E002°51.713' or Car park at D3 roundabout: N45°06.859' E002°51.747'.

ℹ️ Aire at train station. Large town ideal for servicing motorhome and stocking up before visiting Le Lioren ski resort. Reinspected 2016.

NEUSSARGUES MOISSAC
| 118 | H9 | 15170 | | N45°08.065' E002°58.881' |

🚐5 🚰 Euro Relais Tall; CC/Token (ER); Apr-Sept

➥ N122/D679 junction. Turn off N122 to Neussargues-Moissac and Aire is on the right, signed.

ℹ️ On edge of village near main road. Local commerce 100m. Reinspected 2016.

VEDRINES ST LOUP
| 119 | H9 | 15100 | | N45°04.048' E003°16.528' |

🚐10 🚰 Aire Services Plastic; €2

➥ At the sports facility. From south on D990 turn onto D901 and follow into town. After 350m turn left in town and follow road to sports facilities. Aire on left after football pitch and tennis court, opp pond.

ℹ️ Alt 1038m. Pleasant Aire overlooking pond and countryside on the edge of a rural village. D590/D990 a very pleasant drive. Fishing Jul-Aug only €5/day. Inspected 2014.

ALLY
| 120 | H9 | 43380 | | N45°09.661' E003°18.796' |

🚐5 🚰 Euro Relais Junior; €2

➥ Off D22. In the village follow sp 'Moulin Panoramique'. The Aire is to north of village just before the road to Moulin Panoramique (windmill), behind the buildings.

ℹ️ Alt 1000m. Small windmill adj. Service Point virtually impossible to use due to raised platform. Updated 2013.

LA CHAPELLE LAURENT | 121 | H9 | 15500 | | N45°10.830' E003°14.635'

🛏10; Grass parking 🚰 Custom; €1; Turned off in winter

➡ D10. On D10 as exit town towards St-Laurent-Chabreuges (north). 11.5km from A75 Junction 25.

ℹ Alt 970m. Grass parking adj to sports facilities on edge of town. Local commerce, 300m, inc a very large cheese shop. Car park, 300m, provides good winter parking. Reinspected 2014.

ALLANCHE | 122 | H9 | 15160 | | N45°13.788' E002°55.892'

🛏25 🚰 Euro Relais Box

➡ Chemin de la Roche Marchal. Exit town to north on D9, sp 'Vernols'. Aire 300m from centre of town, adj to D9 at old train station (La Gare), signed.

ℹ TO and former railway track, now a Vélo-Rail, adj. www.velorail-cantal.com Small town commerce 400m. Reinspected 2016.

ST SATURNIN | 123 | H9 | 15190 | | N45°15.520' E002°48.143'

🛏20; May-Sept; Pay in high season 🚰 Euro Relais Mini

➡ D21A. Follow sp 'Camping' from town. Service Point is in the entrance to the municipal campsite.

ℹ Service Point in entrance of very basic municipal campsite. Bar and lake opp. Village centre 800m. Inspected 2012.

SEGUR LES VILLAS | 124 | H9 | 15300 | | N45°13.390' E002°49.111'

🛏8; Grass parking 🚰 Euro Relais Junior; Token (ER)

➡ Turn off D3 into Segur-les-Villas. Turn off main route through at Vival convenience store and drive along side of store, signed. In 250m turn right, signed.

ℹ Alt 1200m. Aire located adj to sports pitch in an isolated mountain village with local commerce. Inspected 2012.

VALETTE | 125 | H9 | 15400 | | N45°16.198' E002°36.135'

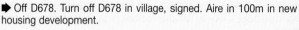

🛏5; 8m bays 🚰 None; Service Point removed

➡ Off D678. Turn off D678 in village, signed. Aire in 100m in new housing development.

ℹ Aire landscaped by hedges which have overgrown making bays narrow. Service Point has been removed. Expect change. Updated 2016.

BLESLE | 126 | H8 | 43450 | T | N45°19.013' E003°10.461'

🛏6; Max 48hrs; Large motorhomes dependent on parking 🚰 None; See 127

➡ D8. Exit A75 at Junction 23 and at roundabout turn right, sp 'Blesle'. Turn off D909 onto D8 and follow sp 'Blesle'. As enter Blesle turn left into parking, signed.

ℹ Designated parking at entrance to medieval Beau Village. Only 7.3km from A75, so ideal stop en route. Inspected 2014.

MASSIAC
| 127 | H9 | 15500 | | N45°15.209' E003°11.599' | SP |

🚐 10 grass; 5 hardstanding 🚰 Custom; Water €2

➤ Rue Jacques Chaban Delmas. In town follow sp 'Murat' onto N122. Cross railway track and river then turn 1st right onto D21, sp 'Allanche' and signed. Turn 1st right, sp 'Gymnase' and signed. Follow road along river where there are 10 marked bays, signed. Service Point and hardstanding parking 100m on left.

ℹ Pleasant Aire with 10 bays adj to shallow river in a peaceful location just 350m across pedestrian bridge to town commerce inc numerous cafés. Updated 2016.

CHALET (MASSIAC)
| 128 | H8 | 43450 | | N45°16.332' E003°11.933' | SP |

🚐 30 🚰 None; See 127

➤ Chapelle Ste Madeliene. Exit Massiac to north following sp 'Claremont Ferrand'. At roundabout by A75 and Intermarché supermarket, turn right onto C55, sp 'Chalet' and signed. Follow lane up hill to end. Parking in large grass area at top.

ℹ Alt 700m. Parking at scenic view point. Chapelle Ste Madeliene, 200m, is perched on the clifftop overlooking Massiac. Ideal lunch stop but may feel isolated if alone overnight. Inspected 2014.

ST GERMAIN LEMBRON
| 129 | H8 | 63340 | | N45°27.331' E003°14.208' | SP |

🚐 10 🚰 Custom; Lift cover

➤ Rue de la Ronzière, off D214. Turn off D909, main route through, onto D214, sp 'Ardes s/ Cruze'. Turn left in 200m, sp 'Salle Polyvalente' and signed. Service Point on left adj to the Salle Polyvalente, signed.

ℹ Aire in community building car park. Small town commerce 300m. Preferable stop to 132. Inspected 2014.

VIEILLE BRIOUDE
| 130 | H9 | 43100 | | N45°15.925' E003°24.349' | SP |

🚐 9; 8m bays; Parallel parking required 🚰 Euro Relais Maxi (Burgundy); CC

➤ Exit N102 onto D912, sp 'Vieille Brioude'. Follow road across river bridge and into town. Turn right opp hotel into car park, sp 'Mairie' and signed. Service Point is on right, for parking continue through car park then turn left, sp 'P'.

ℹ Designated parking just 100m from rural village centre adj to boules club and sports facilities. Local commerce in centre. Town surrounded by lovely countryside. Reinspected 2016.

BRIOUDE
| 131 | H8 | 43100 | | N45°17.679' E003°23.256' | SP |

🚐 20 🚰 Flot Bleu Pacific (Burgundy); Token; €2

➤ D588. From N102 enter Brioude on D588 from roundabout. Go under 4m bridge following sp 'Centre Ville', then turn right, sp 'P Centre Historique' and signed. Service Point 50m on right, parking adj. Sp 'P Centre Historique' throughout town.

ℹ Adj to city wall. Town 300m uphill or via lift. Nearby Lavaudieu is a Beau Village with parking: N45°15.840' E003°27.501'. Free WiFi at TO. Reinspected 2016.

LE BREUIL SUR COUZE
| 132 | H8 | 63340 | | N45°28.142' E003°15.663' | SP |

🚐 5 🚰 Custom

➤ Allée des Treize Vents, just past railway station. West of town centre turn right off D726a after crossing train tracks, sp 'Gare SNCF', 'Mairie' and signed. Follow road past Mairie and Aire on right.

ℹ Aire adj to railway line in residential area. Always likely to have space, but 129 may be more peaceful. Town with local commerce 500m. Reinspected 2014.

SOLIGNAT | 133 | H8 | 63500 | N45°31.026' E003°10.245'

🚐 15; Grass parking 🚰 Raclet; €2

➡ Route de Florat, off D32. Follow signs in village from D32, main road through, onto Rue de Lotissement La Cherelle. Follow this road to left, signed, and at end of road turn left, signed. Aire 20m on left opp cemetery. Do not follow GPS.

ℹ New building, poss primary school, being built at Aire. Service Point barriered off during building work. Future unknown. There is also parking at the Table d'Orientation: N45°31.240' E003°09.831'. Reinspected 2014.

MONTPEYROUX | 134 | H8 | 63114 | T | N45°37.489' E003°12.041'

🚐 10; Large motorhomes poss if not busy 🚰 Aire Services 3000; Token (3/3); €2.50; Seasonal day WC at TO

➡ Parking Obligatoire. Exit A75 at Junction 7 and follow sp 'Montpeyroux'. Turn left before village, sp 'Parking Obligatoire', and park in the furthest section, adj to petting farm.

ℹ Aire in visitor parking, 4 landscaped car parks with open grassland adj. Convenient stop off A75; distant hum. TO adj. Beau Village with tourist commerce 300m; two walled inner villages and dominating tower; opening hrs vary, €2.50pp. Reinspected 2016.

TOURZEL RONZIERES ✳ | 135 | H8 | 63320 | N45°31.701' E003°08.038'

🚐 15 🚰 Custom; 1 unmetered Cont elec point

➡ D23/Rue du Dauphiné D'Auvergne. As enter village on D23 from southwest Aire on left, signed. Steep initial acess. GPS given at entrance for clarity.

ℹ Grass or asphalt parking on 5 terraces which ensures every bay enjoys 180° views. Bronze and Iron Age remains found in the surrounding area, information boards adj. Updated 2016.

MUROL | 136 | H8 | 63790 | N45°34.372' E002°56.480'

🚐 10; No parking mid Jun-Aug 🚰 None

➡ D5. Car park opp junction with D168, by TO.

ℹ Village centre with small park adj. Ski hire shop opp. Reinspected 2016.

CHAMPEIX | 137 | H8 | 63320 | N45°35.293' E003°06.886'

🚐 10 🚰 Raclet; Token (2/1); Lift cover for drive over drain; May-Sept

➡ D996. Exit town to west on D996 towards Mont Dore. Turn left after Gendarmerie and cross bridge, signed. Follow road to right. Service Point on left in compound, parking past compound, signed.

ℹ Aire in roadside lay-by sheltered from road by trees, may feel isolated if alone. Service Point in fenced compound, closed Oct-Apr. Town 1.3km. Market Fri am. Reinspected 2014.

CHAMBON SUR LAC | 138 | H8 | 63790 | N45°34.209' E002°54.285'

🚐 50; €6/night; Collected 🚰 Flot Bleu Fontaine; Token; €3

➡ Off D996. In Chambon sur Lac turn off D996, main route, sp 'Camping les Bombes' and signed. Service Point directly adj to campsite entrance. Designated parking is 100m on left, signed.

ℹ Aire 1.2km from lake via footpath, no views. All lakeside parking bans motorhomes. Reinspected 2016.

MUROL LAC CHAMBON — 139 — H8 — 63790 — ⛺ — N45°34.295' E002°55.775'

🚐30; €14.50 low season; €21 high season; Grass parking; Apr-Sept 🔧 Custom; Inside barrier; Elec €5; Pay at campsite; Apr-Sept

➡ Allée de la Plage, off D996. From Murol take D996 west towards Lac Chambon. At roundabout take 2nd exit, sp 'Lac Chambon Plage Est'. Aire on right in 400m just before the campsite entrance. Enter through barrier.

ℹ Seasonal Aire run as part of a campsite. Very basic Service Point. Lakeside beach 500m. Motorhomes discouraged from parking in bays with lake views. Inspected 2016.

LA BOURBOULE — 140 — H8 — 63150 — N45°35.143' E002°44.115'

🚐 10 🔧 Aire Services 7010; CC; €5

➡ Chemin de la Suchére. Enter La Bourboule from east on D996. At 2nd roundabout take 4th exit and cross river. Turn left immediately into one-way street, then turn 1st right. Keep right into Chemin de la Suchére and Aire on left in 100m.

ℹ Aire adj to stables amongst houses, but may feel isolated if alone. Busy spa town with casino 550m. Inspected 2016.

LE MONT DORE — 141 — H8 — 63240 — SKI — N45°34.637' E002°48.263'

🚐80; €9.50/night; CC 🔧 Flot Bleu Pacific; €2; Outside barrier; Custom; Inside barrier; No drive over drain

➡ Ave des Crouzets, off D130. Approach on D130 from La Bourboule. Aire outside Camping Les Crouzets, signed. Drive towards campsite barrier and Service Point on right, signed. Parking to left. Enter through barrier.

ℹ Large Aire with limited shade adj to campsite. River nearby. Town commerce, with large market Friday and railway station, 350m. Ski resorts close by. Updated 2016.

Info/photos: Mick & Babs Bartle

SUPER BESSE — 142 — H8 — 63610 — SKI — N45°30.219' E002°51.294'

🚐200; €6.30/24hrs (Summer); €10.40/24hrs (Winter); Long stay discounts 🔧 Flot Bleu Euro; Outside barrier; Flot Bleu Elec; Inside barrier; 1 Token/4hrs 16amp CEE elec; €2.50

➡ D149. Adj to D149 as exit resort to west. Aire in car park P6 and P7 south of Lac des Hermines, signed. Pay with credit card at entrance barrier.

ℹ Alt 1276m. Ski resort with resort commerce 1km; ski bus stop adj. Cheaper for longer stays. Motorhomes are not allowed to park anywhere else in resort. www.sancy.com Updated 2016.

Photo: Mike and Jenny Woodthorpe

CHASTREIX — 143 — H8 — 63680 — SKI — N45°30.744' E002°44.083'

🚐5 🔧 Custom

➡ Off D615, behind the church in the centre of small village. Local ski resort also offers motorhome parking: N45°32.125' E002°46.610'.

ℹ Alt 1064m. Very small parking area behind church in small village. La Tour d'Auvergne 144 has better parking. Ski resort 7km, parking poss. Reinspected 2016.

LA TOUR D'AUVERGNE — 144 — H8 — 63680 — N45°31.957' E002°40.911'

🚐20 🔧 Euro Relais Box; €2

➡ Off D47. Enter La Tour from southwest on D47. Aire on left near Sapeurs Pompiers (fire station). Signed from both directions.

ℹ Well laid out Aire on the edge of a lake; limited views. Village 750m. Free WiFi at TO. Inspected 2016.

Photos: Mick & Babs Bartle

St Mathieu

MURAT LE QUAIRE | 146 | H8 | 63150 | N45°36.174' E002°44.251'

🚐 37; €5/5hrs; €9.60/24hrs; +€1.10 tax; Inc service and 10amp elec; CC 🚽 Urba Flux Tall; Shower €1/10 mins (Seasonal)

➤ Route de la Banne d'Ordanche. Turn off D219 opposite church in centre of Murat le Quaire. Follow road and Aire is on right before the lake. Enter through PARKNIGHT barrier.

ⓘ Aire near lake up in the hills. Seasonal shower and toilet block. Local commerce 850m. Inspected 2016.

LES GANNES (MESSEIX) | 147 | G8 | 63750 | N45°36.935' E002°33.389'

🚐 7 🚽 Aire Services 3000; Token (3/3)

➤ Place des Pins. Turn off D987 at Les Gannes onto D73c, sp 'Messeix' and signed. Aire in car park 200m on left, signed.

ⓘ Located in a small hamlet adj to small park (no dogs) and local commerce. Inspected 2012.

ST GERMAIN PRES HERMENT | 148 | G8 | 63470 | N45°43.716' E002°32.711'

🚐 5 🚽 Flot Bleu Pacific; €2

➤ D98. Visible and signed off D98 between Lastic and Verneugheol on one of two roads to the lake etang. Service Point 30m on left.

ⓘ Lake 100m and restaurant perhaps open in season. Very nice place off beaten track. May feel isolated out of season. Visited 2012.

Photo/Info: Carol Weaver

LA COURTINE | 149 | G8 | 23100 | N45°42.351' E002°15.545'

🚐 10; Max 24hrs 🚽 Euro Relais Junior; Token

➤ Impasse Jacques Bayle. From La Courtine take D982 towards Aubusson. Turn right at tabac into Impasse Jacques Bayle, before D25. Aire on right in 250m, signed.

ⓘ In small town centre. Tokens free from local commerce, 150m. Large lake 175m with foot/cycle paths. Town within Millevaches national park; guided walks Jun-Oct. www.pnr-millevaches.fr Inspected 2015.

USSEL | 150 | G8 | 19200 | N45°32.865' E002°17.013'

🚐 10 🚽 Raclet; €2

➤ D157/Route de Ponty. Exit Ussel on D1089 towards Tulle. After crossing river turn right onto D157, sp 'Chaveroche' and 'Centre Touristique de Ponty'. Aire in 2km at Centre Touristique de Ponty at the lake, opp Camping Municipal de Ponty.

ⓘ Adj to TO and picnic area by lake. Bar/restaurant with children's play area and sandy beach adj to lake. Fishing poss, buy licence from TO. www.ot-ussel.fr Reinspected 2015.

ST MERD LES OUSSINES
151 G8 19170 N45°38.097' E002°02.184'

🚐 20 Euro Relais Mini; Token (ER)

➡ D109. Turn off D164 in centre onto D109, sp 'Tarnac' and signed. Follow road out of village, then turn left into Aire, signed.

ℹ Alt 837m. Peaceful, open Aire suitable for any unit configuration. Shade from conifers poss in summer. Village with local commerce 450m. Inspected 2016.

MEYMAC
152 G8 19250 N45°31.500' E002°07.657'

🚐 20 Custom

➡ Base Nautique de Sèchemaille. From Meymac follow D36 south. At roundabout turn off, sp 'Lac de Sèchemailles' and signed. Aire in parking area 750m on right, signed.

ℹ At leisure lake with sandy swimming beach, bar/restaurant and good walks; steep access. Fishing and boat hire poss. Likely to be busy Jul/Aug. Updated 2013.

EGLETONS
153 G8 19300 N45°24.233' E002°02.850'

🚐 16 Euro Relais Box; €2

➡ Parking de l'Espace Ventadour, Rue Docteur Henri Dignac. In town centre turn off D1089 onto Rue Docteur Henri Dignac, signed. Follow road downhill. Parking in fenced area on right and Service Point in separate drive through area to left of parking, both signed.

ℹ Very attractive town with numerous commerce. Free WiFi at TO. www.tourisme-egletons.com Reinspected 2015.

PEROLS SUR VEZERE
154 G8 19170 N45°35.142' E001°59.010'

🚐 2 hardstanding; 18 grass parking Aire Services 7010; Token (3/3)

➡ Lieu-dit au Ciolle. Turn off D979 onto D979e1, sp 'Pérols s/ V' and signed. Turn 1st left, signed, and follow track to Aire.

ℹ Pleasant Aire on edge of village. Large, open, mostly grass parking at picnic area behind Mairie. Suitable for any unit configuration. Conveniently close to D979. No commerce in village. Roman Ruins at Site des Cars, 5.4km: N45°36.336' E002°01.601'. Inspected 2016.

LAC DE NEUVIC (LIGINIAC)
155 G8 19160 N45°23.460' E002°18.214'

🚐 10 Urba Flux

➡ Turn off D982 north of Neuvic onto D183, sp 'Yeux'. Follow D183 around lake edge towards Liginiac. Turn off D183, sp 'Le Maury' and follow road downhill. Service Point on left, signed. Unrestricted parking with lake view further down hill.

ℹ Adj to reservoir with swimming beach and sports facilities. Parking adj to water does not exclude motorhomes even though there is a campsite nearby. Inspected 2012.

CHAMPAGNAC
156 G8 15350 N45°21.455' E002°23.956'

🚐 Poss, in village square by church Euro Relais Mini

➡ D12. Turn onto D12 between the church and the war memorial, sp 'St Pierre'. Take next right, signed, and Service Point is on right.

ℹ In remote village near Dordogne river. There is no designated parking or parking by the Service Point. Updated 2013.

BORT LES ORGUES | 157 | G8 | 19110 | N45°23.950' E002°29.833'

🚐 5; 7pm-7am only 🚽 Custom; Lift grate for WC emptying

▶ Rue Font Grande. Best access via D979. Turn off D979 into town. Turn right before river bridge by Gendarmerie, sp 'Complex Sportif' and signed. Follow road along river to Aire. Aire is signed on all routes through town. Some routes are narrow with difficult turns.

ℹ️ Dordogne river adj, nice views. Town commerce 100m; hypermarket within walking distance. Motorhomes can only park on Aire 7pm-7am. Reinspected 2016.

CHAMPS SUR TARENTAINE MARCHAL | 158 | G8 | 15270 | N45°23.672' E002°33.486'

🚐 1 hardstanding; Additional grass parking 🚽 Euro Relais Mini

▶ D679. Adj to D679 through gate to house 16, signed. Nearly opp Elan garage, specializing as HGV mechanic.

ℹ️ Start of Gorges de la Rhue drive. Village with local commerce 250m. Reinspected 2016.

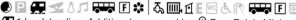

CONDAT | 159 | H8 | 15190 | N45°20.335' E002°45.766'

🚐 5 🚽 Flot Bleu Pacific; Token

▶ D678. Adj to D678 just beside roundabout junction with D679, by river bridge. The Service Point is visible from roundabout.

ℹ️ Sign suggests for your security you should stay in campsite, but does not ban motorhomes. Reinspected 2016.

MAURIAC | 160 | G9 | 15200 | N45°13.110' E002°19.311'

🚐 30 🚽 Euro Relais Tall; Token (ER) or CC

▶ Lac du Barrage d'Enchanet. Turn off D922 at roundabout onto D678, sp 'Pleaux'. At next roundabout turn onto D782, sp 'Plan d'Eau'. Turn right, sp 'Plan d'Eau'. Follow road and Aire in car park on left, signed.

ℹ️ Aire in parking for leisure lake, no views. Swimming lake, play area, walks, golf and campsite all adj. Motorhomes restricted in all other car parks. May feel isolated if alone. Reinspected 2014.

DRUGEAC | 161 | G9 | 15140 | N45°10.026' E002°23.203'

🚐 8 🚽 Euro Relais Maxi; €2; No drive over drain; Apr-Nov

▶ D29e. Turn off D933 onto D29, sp 'Drugeac' and signed. Cross the railway track (Velo Rail) and turn 1st right, sp 'Ally' and signed. Aire 250m on left opp old railway station, signed.

ℹ️ Aire in peaceful residential area adj to Velo Rail, hire available Jul-Aug only. Village 350m downhill. Waterfall walk near Salins, parking adj to D922. Reinspected 2014.

SALERS | 162 | G9 | 15140 | N45°08.909' E002°29.927'

🚐 30; €5.50; Pay at campsite; 9 (day parking); €3; Pay at machine 🚽 Aire Services 3000; Token; €2

▶ Off D680. Follow sp 'Camping' through village. Service Point is outside Camping Le Mourial, sp 'Camping Municipal'. Parking is adj to campsite and sports facilities, signed. Day parking on D680 ring road to north of town, signed: N45°08.417' E002°29.676'.

ℹ️ Alt 992m. Day parking avail for visiting pretty cobbled Beau Village. Aire a pleasant 1.5km walk from village. Cold Sept-May due to altitude. May feel isolated if alone. Reinspected 2014.

ST MARTIN VALMEROUX

163 | **G9** | **15140** | N45°06.958' E002°25.231'

🚐 10 ☕ Euro Relais Maxi

➡ D37/Rue de Montjoly. Turn off D922 in the village onto D37, sp 'Loupiac' and 'Camping'. The Service Point is in 450m past the campsite, signed, 3.5t weight restriction on car park.

ℹ Aire adj to pleasant riverside campsite on the edge of town. Small town commerce 450m. Reinspected 2014.

ST CERNIN

164 | **G9** | **15310** | N45°03.191' E002°25.584'

🚐 1 ☕ Euro Relais Junior

➡ D160. Follow main route south out of town. At 1st fork, stay left, sp 'Aurillac'. At next fork stay left onto D160, sp 'Route des Crêtes'. Aire on right in 600m.

ℹ Really just a Service Point with picnic area and small boules court adj. Reinspected 2014.

LE LIORAN

165 | **H9** | **15300** | SKI | N45°05.218' E002°44.866'

🚐 70 ☕ None; See **168**

➡ Off D67. Turn off N122 onto D67 at the roundabout before the tunnel. Follow D67 750m, then turn left into parking area adj to Sapeurs Pompiers (fire station). Also poss unrestricted parking in Combe Negre (1500m): N45°05.112' E002°44.010'.

ℹ Alt 1206m. Aire in popular ski area. Parking has been relocated slightly further, 400m, from slopes with chairlifts. Local commerce in ski season or high summer, 300m. Reinspected 2016.

MANDAILLES ST JULIEN

166 | **H9** | **15590** | N45°04.157' E002°39.368'

🚐 5; Max 24hrs ☕ Euro Relais Mini; Token (ER); €3.50

➡ D17. Follow D17 from Aurillac. In Mandailles follow D17 across river bridge, then turn left, signed. Aire 200m at far end of car park, signed.

ℹ Landscaped bays adj to river. Remote village en route to Puy Mary. Poss to drive across Puy Mary in a motorhome between midnight-noon. Motorhomes completely banned (moving or stationary) noon-midnight. Inspected 2014.

VELZIC

167 | **H9** | **15590** | N45°00.110' E002°32.777'

🚐 6; Max 24hrs ☕ Euro Relais Mini; Token (ER)

➡ From Aurillac turn left off D17 in Velzic, signed. Drive past Mairie and follow road. The Aire is adj to the river, signed.

ℹ Pleasant riverside Aire in rural village. Puy St Mary restricts motorhomes from visiting/driving between noon and midnight. Reinspected 2014.

THIEZAC

168 | **H9** | **15800** | N45°00.961' E002°39.762'

🚐 5; Max 24hrs ☕ Raclet; Token; €3.50

➡ D59. Turn off N122 onto D59 or D759 into Thiézac. Follow road through village and the Aire is by the river bridge, signed.

ℹ Alt 800m. Aire in wooded dell adj to stream, no view. Mountainside village with local and tourist commerce 200m. Reinspected 2014.

VIC SUR CERE | 169 | H9 | 15800 | N44°58.942' E002°37.891'

🚐 10 🚰 Euro Relais Junior; Token (ER)

➡ Place de l'Egalité, Avenue des Tilleuls. Turn off N122, sp 'Camping' and 'Aire de Camping-Car'. Turn left in front of cemetery, signed. Follow road past campsite and the Aire is on the right.

ℹ Pleasant Aire with landscaped bays. Peaceful location with river and park adj, no views. Small town commerce 650m. Reinspected 2014.

AURILLAC | 170 | G9 | 15000 | N44°55.790' E002°26.971'

🚐 10; Max 24hrs 🚰 Euro Relais Junior; Token (ER)

➡ Champ de Foire, off D17. Follow sp 'Puy Mary' through town, then 'Aire de Camping Car'. In town near river, well signed.

ℹ Designated parking under nesting rooks in a popular town centre car park near river, obstructed views. Town commerce 200m. Route to Puy Mary adj. Reinspected 2014.

LACAPELLE VIESCAMP | 171 | G9 | 15150 | N44°55.275' E002°15.820'

🚐 4; Only when campsite closed 🚰 Euro Relais Junior; Token (ER); €2

➡ D18, on the outskirts of the village at the entrance to municipal campsite opp local shop. Turn into campsite between hedges and Service Point is to the right.

ℹ Large reservoir with limited parking considering its size. No parking has lakeside views. Lake predominantly used by fishermen. Reinspected 2014.

VEZAC | 172 | G9 | 15130 | N44°53.425' E002°31.073'

🚐 2; Max 24hrs 🚰 Euro Relais Mini; Token (ER)

➡ D206. Turn off D990 onto D206, sp 'Labrousse', 'Golf' and signed. The Aire is on the left in 600m, signed.

ℹ Golf course opp. Restaurant 1 min. Reinspected 2014.

MARCOLES | 173 | G9 | 15220 | N44°46.818' E002°21.248'

🚐 4; €8.40/night; mid Jun-Sept 🚰 Custom; 4 CEE elec points at Service Point (long lead needed)

➡ D66. Follow D66 through village. Turn off into sports facilities, signed. Service Point on the right and parking 20m further on the right, signed.

ℹ Aire at sports facilities adj to municipal camping field. 4 designated bays are unlevel, but there is plenty of other parking. Views over open access sports facility. Inspected 2014.

MONTSALVY | 174 | G9 | 15120 | N44°42.477' E002°29.792'

🚐 10; plus 10 overflow 🚰 Euro Relais Junior; €2; Showers €1

➡ Off D19. From north turn off D920 onto D19 into town. Aire 250m on left before Centre de Secours.

ℹ Very landscaped Aire adj to amenity space. Bays have grass and hedges giving optimum privacy; hedge dictates which way to park. Old bays now turn around/overflow area. Local commerce 500m. Inspected 2014.

VIEILLEVIE | 175 | G9 | 15120 | 🛥 | N44°38.662' E002°25.064' | SP

🚐5 🚰 Euro Relais Junior; €2; Closed in winter

➡ D141. Adj to D141 in the centre of the village opp TO, signed. D141 is a narrow, but passable, gorge road.

ℹ Very pleasant Aire with partial river views in small village with tourist commerce. D141 to Entraygues-sur-Truyere a pleasant drive with riverside lay-bys and canoe hire. Reinspected 2014

CASSANIOUZE | 176 | G9 | 15340 | 🏛 | N44°41.629' E002°22.949' | SP

🚐6 🚰 Euro Relais Junior; €2; Closed in winter

➡ Lieu-Dit le Bourg Nord. Turn off D601 in the village, signed. Turn right and right again, signed.

ℹ Landscaped Aire in very rural village. Reinspected 2014.

CALVINET | 177 | G9 | 15340 | 🚶 | N44°42.607' E002°21.526' | SP

🚐6; €6/night; Collected 🚰 Euro Relais Junior; €2; Elec €2/night

➡ Adj to Camping Municipal de Calvinet and sports fields, off D66. Turn off D66 in town, sp 'Tennis' and signed. Turn left past tennis courts, signed, and the Aire is on the left.

ℹ A confused Aire adj to camping field overlooking open access sports fields. Prices quoted are for the campsite. Inspected 2014.

MONTMURAT | 178 | G9 | 15600 | 🏭 | N44°37.685' E002°11.860' | SP

🚐20 🚰 Flot Bleu Fontaine; €2

➡ D345. From Maurs on D663 turn right onto D45 at St Constant. Turn right onto D345, sp 'Montmurat'. Follow D345 and Aire on left just before village. DO NOT take motorhome into village, very narrow and steep.

ℹ Picnic area and viewpoint above Aire with 360° views. May feel isolated if alone. Reinspected 2014.

MAURS LA JOLIE | 179 | G9 | 15600 | 🏛 | N44°42.872' E002°11.762' | SP

🚐6 🚰 Euro Relais Junior; Token (ER)

➡ D19/Route de Quézac. Enter Maurs from north on N122 and turn off in town, signed. Follow road beside Hotel Bar Le Plaisance and continue for 500m. Aire on left outside cemetery, signed.

ℹ Adj to cemetery with additional parking opp. Town commerce 300m. Reinspected 2014.

CAYROLS | 180 | G9 | 15290 | 🏭 | N44°49.803' E002°13.973' | SP

🚐30 🚰 Euro Relais Junior; Token (2/1)

➡ D51, at sports facilities. On main route through village, signed. Parking has 5.5t weight restriction.

ℹ Pleasant location by community sports facilities with plenty of parking. Local commerce in village. Reinspected 2014.

LIMOUSIN & AUVERGNE

ST MAMET LA SALVETAT `181` G9 15220 N44°51.422' E002°18.596'

🚐 3 🍞 Euro Relais Junior; Token (ER)

➡️ Allée des Coudercs. Turn off N122 onto D32, sp 'St Mamet'. Follow D32 into village. Go straight over roundabout onto D20, signed. Aire on left in 400m.

ℹ️ Peaceful location on edge of village. Picnic area 100m; local commerce 300m. Inspected 2012.

YTRAC `182` G9 15000 N44°54.902' E002°21.816'

🚐 4; Max 24hrs 🍞 Raclet; Token (ER)

➡️ Impasse Jean de la Fontaine, off D18 at Parking Centre Culturel et Sportif. Aire adj to D18, signed as enter village from north. Follow road in front of cultural building and Aire behind building.

ℹ️ At community building/sports facility. Local commerce 200m. Reinspected 2014.

SANSAC DE MARMIESSE `183` G9 15130 N44°53.036' E002°20.805'

🚐 5; Max 24hrs; Grounding of overhang likely due to bank 🍞 Euro Relais Junior; Token (ER)

➡️ Rue de la Vidalie, off N122. Adj to N122 at the local shops/retail area, signed.

ℹ️ Local commerce adj. Convenient night halt just off N122. Big motorhomes poss, but must reverse into bays and overhang space is banked too high. Reinspected 2014.

ST PAUL DES LANDES `184` G9 15250 N44°56.562' E002°19.008'

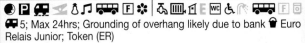

🚐 7; Max 24hrs 🍞 Euro Relais Mini; Token (ER)

➡️ D53. Turn off D120 onto D53. Aire signed on right.

ℹ️ Aire located just off D120 in a residential area; Some road noise. Local commerce 150m. Always likely to have space. Reinspected 2014.

CRANDELLES `185` G9 15250 N44°57.529' E002°20.512'

🚐 5; Max 24hrs 🍞 Raclet; Token (ER)

➡️ Off D59, at Lac des Genevrières. At Crandelles follow sp 'Lac des Genevrières' and signed. Aire overlooking lake.

ℹ️ Pleasant Aire overlooking leisure lake with swimming beach and bar. Village adj. Reinspected 2014.

JUSSAC `186` G9 15250 N44°59.327' E002°25.158'

🚐 5; Max 24hrs; No parking Jul-Aug 🍞 None; See `188`

➡️ Promenade des Sports, off D922. Turn off D922 in Jussac, sp 'Salle Polyvalente'. Aire at sports facilities, signed.

ℹ️ Designated parking adj to sports facilities. No parking Jul-Aug when campsite open. Small town commerce 100m. Reinspected 2014.

AYRENS

187 **G9** **15250** | N44°59.138' E002°19.627'

🚐 5; Try **185** 1st ♙ Euro Relais Mini; Token (ER); No drive over drain

➡ Off D53c. At D52/D53 junction in village turn onto D53, sp 'Jassac'. Follow road behind church and turn left, sp 'Terrain de Sports'. Aire in 100m.

ℹ Limited parking in tiny village adj to small wood yard. Local commerce 190m. Reinspected 2014.

NAUCELLES

188 **G9** **15000** | N44°57.393' E002°25.044'

🚐 20 ♙ Euro Relais Mini; Token (ER)

➡ Rue du Terrou. Turn off D922 onto D253 at roundabout south of Naucelles, sp 'Crandelles'. In 200m turn right, sp 'Mairie'. At the Stop junction turn right, signed. Turn right at next junction and Service Point is on left side of car park.

ℹ Located 300m from D922 in centre of village but is surrounded by sports facilities and amenity grass. Local commerce 300m. Reinspected 2014.

LAROQUEBROU

189 **G9** **15150** | N44°57.892' E002°11.803'

🚐 1 designated; 10 opp ♙ Flot Bleu Fontaine; €2

➡ D653. Enter town from east on D653. Service Point is against the road on the right opp D18 turning to 'Lacapelle V.' and campsite.

ℹ Service Point near pleasant riverside municipal campsite on edge of riverside town. Parking possible in lay-by opp. Reinspected 2014.

PLEAUX

190 **G9** **15700** | N45°08.141' E002°13.708'

🚐 50 opp Service Point ♙ Custom

➡ Place d'Empeyssine, off D666. Approach from north on D680 and take the 1st left turn, sp 'D666', 'Centre Ville' and signed. The Aire is adj to the square on the left.

ℹ Aire located adj to stock pens in a large car park adj to central square. Likely to be busy if livestock market is in progress. Small town commerce adj. Reinspected 2014.

ST PRIVAT

191 **G9** **19220** | N45°08.406' E002°05.860'

🚐 8 grass parking (summer); 4 hardstanding (winter) ♙ Euro Relais Junior; €2

➡ Rue des Chanaux, off D13. Follow sp 'Aire Service' through town. Aire on outskirts of village, well signed.

ℹ Pleasant grass parking near centre with small town commerce. Town serves as centre for rural/agricultural area, popular market Sat am. Reinspected 2014.

SERVIERES LE CHATEAU ★

192 **G9** **19220** | N45°08.670' E002°02.201'

🚐 15 ♙ Euro Relais Junior; €2

➡ Lac de Feyt. From Servières le Château follow sp 'Centre Touristique du Lac de Feyt' for several kms. Follow road to left at campsite, signed. Aire 400m after holiday chalets at end of road.

ℹ Pleasant Aire set in woodland overlooking leisure lake. Boating and swimming in season. May feel isolated if alone out of season. Reinspected 2014.

FORGES
193 G9 19380 N45°09.205' E001°52.265'

🚐31; €12/night; CC 🚰 Euro Relais Junior; Inside barrier

➡ Rue Pierre et Marie Curie. Exit D1120, sp 'Camping Municipal'. Aire on left. Enter through PARKNIGHT barrier.

ⓘ Commercial barriered Aire replacing former municipal campsite and being installed at time of inspection. Reinspected 2014.

BEAULIEU SUR DORDOGNE
194 G9 19120 N44°58.590' E001°50.464'

🚐20; €5/night Sept-Jun, €10/night Jul-Aug; Collected 🚰 Custom; Tap under green cover, hose connection needed; Turned off in Oct

➡ Rue Gontrand Roye. Turn off D940 near TO onto D41, sp 'Astaillac'. Turn left off D41 as exit town, sp 'Du Pont (Municipal)'. Aire 50m.

ⓘ Aire adj to canoe slalom course. Town centre, 400m, bans motorhomes but has town commerce. Updated 2016.

BEYNAT
195 G9 19190 N45°07.338' E001°43.534'

🚐30 🚰 Euro Relais Mini; Token (ER); Tokens free from commerce

➡ Rue de la Châtaigne. Turn off D921 at roundabout onto D169, sp 'Beynat Centre Bourg' and signed. In 700m turn right at Stop junction onto D130, sp 'Meyssac'. Turn right into car parks, signed. Aire on left.

ⓘ Aire in large car park by school adj to woods. Local commerce 300m uphill. Inspected 2014.

LANTEUIL
196 G9 19190 N45°07.731' E001°39.698'

🚐10 🚰 Aire Services 3000; WC and bins locked

➡ Le Doux. Turn off D921 at roundabout by telephone box, sp 'Le Doux'. Cross bridge and Aire is on right, signed.

ⓘ Aire adj to main route in small village. Small stream adj. Local commerce 200m. Inspected 2014.

TURENNE
197 F9 19500 N45°03.233' E001°34.837'

🚐14; Max 48hrs 🚰 Euro Relais Junior; 2 unmetered CEE elec points

➡ Turn off D8 at Turenne and drive behind TO, signed. Follow lane down hill then turn right into parking, signed. Be careful not to tail swipe wall at bottom of hill.

ⓘ Views from Aire of hilltop Beau Village with château at top open to public, €4.80, www.chateau-turenne.com. A pleasant place to wander for a few hours. Updated 2016.

COLLONGES LA ROUGE
198 F9 19500 N45°03.523' E001°39.551'

🚐40; €5/24hrs; Collected 🚰 Custom

➡ P Le Marchadial. From Meyssac follow D38 west towards Brive. Turn off D38, sp 'P Le Marchadial'. Turn 1st right, signed. Follow lane and Aire on left, signed.

ⓘ Pretty Beau Village 700m with tourist commerce; very popular with French tourists. Maison de la Sirène museum and guided village tour, €3; must book, www.tourismecorreze.com. Small town commerce at Meyssac. Updated 2016.

DAMPNIAT

| 199 | G9 | 19360 | | N45°09.763' E001°38.258' |

🚐 5 ⛽ Euro Relais Junior; €4; 2 unmetered CEE elec points

➡ From church in Dampniat centre follow signs to Aire. Located down narrow lane at sports facilities, 1km from centre.

ℹ Aire located in pleasant rural location adj to a few houses with panoramic rural views. Most parking reserved for adj sports facilities. Local commerce 1km. Reinspected 2014.

BRIVE LA GAILLARDE

| 200 | F9 | 19100 | | N45°09.903' E001°32.500' |

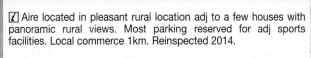

🚐 10; €8/24hrs; CC ⛽ Flot Bleu Pacific; Token/CC; €2; Flot Bleu Elec; Token; €2/6hrs; All inside barrier

➡ Blvd Michelet. On D1089 on north side of river turn off roundabout by cinema, sp 'Park des Sports'. In 100m turn left, just past Mr Bricologe, signed. Aire 10m on right. Enter through Flot Bleu Park barrier.

ℹ Commercial Aire adj to riverside walk/park. Town centre 1.2km across bridge. Adj commerce inc supermarket and cinema. May feel vulnerable if alone. Inspected 2014.

LISSAC SUR COUZE

| 201 | F9 | 19600 | | N45°05.933' E001°27.810' |

🚐 40; €4/night; Token (ER); CC ⛽ Euro Relais Mini; Token (ER); €4; 1 Token/6hrs elec or 100L water; WC on beach

➡ Le Bourg. In LIssac sur Couze turn off roundabout, sp 'Le Soulier' and 'Table du Lac'. Follow road downhill and fork right towards lake. Fork right again, sp 'Parking des Peupliers'. Aire in parking on right. Enter via token-operated barrier. Purchase tokens from Euro Relais token machine adj to barrier.

ℹ Commercial Aire offering shaded parking under deciduous trees. Lake adj, trees obscure view. Large leisure lake with swimming beach, likely to be busy high days and holidays. May feel isolated if alone. Inspected 2016.

Photo: David Statham

DONZENAC

| 202 | F9 | 19270 | | N45°13.126' E001°31.140' |

🚐 10 ⛽ Euro Relais Mini; Elec €3.40/night (Not working)

➡ Off D170. Exit A20 at Junction 48 and follow sp 'Donzenac'. In town turn right onto D920, sp 'Ussac'. Follow road out of town and at roundabout turn right onto D170, sp 'Ussac' and 'La Rivière'. Turn right in 300m and Aire just before campsite barrier on left, signed.

ℹ River adj, no view. Campsite adj. Intermarché supermarket 300m. Historic town 1.5km uphill. Updated 2015.

SADROC

| 203 | F8 | 19270 | | N45°16.983' E001°32.918' |

🚐 6; Max 24hrs; 6m bays ⛽ Custom; 4 unmetered 16amp CEE elec points

➡ D9, in the village centre by the church. Follow sp 'Sadroc' from A20. In Sadroc centre turn right by tabac, signed, and right again to Aire, signed.

ℹ In small, well maintained village centre. 16th century church and local commerce adj. www.sadroc.fr Reinspected 2015.

ALLASSAC

| 204 | F8 | 19240 | | N45°15.531' E001°28.410' |

🚐 4; Max 3 days; 6m bays, no overhang ⛽ Euro Relais Junior; 2 unmetered CEE elec points

➡ Ave du Saillant, off D9 opp train station. Follow sp 'Gare SNCF' in town. Aire opp train station, 200m from centre.

ℹ Train station adj. Pretty town centre with small town commerce 300m. Reinspected 2014.

OBJAT

205 F8 19130 N45°16.267' E001°24.717'

€6.60/24hrs Apr-Oct; €8.60/24hrs Nov-Mar; Inc 16amp elec; Pay TO; Max 72hrs Euro Relais Junior; Token (3/3); €2; Showers €2 via Token

➤ D148e3/Ave Jules Ferry. From D901 turn onto D148e3 in Objat. Follow road north out of town towards Les Grandes Terres following sp 'Aire de Camping-Car'. Aire on right, signed. Enter through barrier, access code from TO in village by war memorial: N45°15.869' E001°24.591'.

Small lake nearby. If Aire full, additional max 24hrs parking near lake. Follow sp 'Centre aquarécréatif'. TO, 1km, has internet access and supplies tokens. www.tourismeobjat.com Reinspected 2015.

AYEN

206 F8 19310 N45°14.988' E001°19.410'

5; Additional grass parking; See info Custom

➤ Exit village to north on D39 towards St Robert. Turn left by Centre D'incendie et de Secours building on outskirts of village, sp 'Ayen-Bas' and signed. The Aire is behind the Secours building outside the Atelier Municipal, works yard.

Small Aire with rural views on edge of small village. Additional grass parking in hedged bays at former campsite, 150m: N45°14.964' E001°19.317'. Follow sp 'Aire Naturelle'. Peaceful, but remote. www.ayen.fr Inspected 2015.

CONCEZE

207 F8 19350 N45°21.285' E001°20.744'

5 Custom

➤ D56e, in small village. Turn off D901 onto D56e heading east into town. Turn by church and Aire is 10m on left, signed.

Adj to orchard in centre of small village. Restaurant/bar 150m. On Limousin apple orchard route. Local parking by church. Grass parking has been blocked off. Reinspected 2015.

VIGEOIS - Lac de Pontcharal

208 F8 19410 N45°22.049' E001°32.037'

10 Euro Relais Junior; Token (ER); €2

➤ D7. Exit A20 at Junction 45 and follow sp 'Vigeois' onto D3. In Vigeois turn left onto D7, sp 'Lac de Pontcharal'. Aire on left adj to D7, signed.

Leisure lake adj, no views from parking adj to Service Point. Other parking unrestricted with views over beach and diving platform. Lovely area but may feel isolated if alone. Inspected 2014.

UZERCHE ★

209 G8 19140 N45°25.471' E001°33.968'

20; Max 48hrs; No parking Sat (Market) Custom; WC emptying in WC; 40 unmetered CEE/Cont elec points

➤ D3, at Place de la Petite Gare. Turn off A20 at Junction 44 and follow sp 'Uzerche' onto D920. In town turn left off D920, sp 'Treignac'. Follow road and at the roundabout turn left onto D3, signed. Aire 150m on right, signed.

Very popular Aire at old train station; cycle/walk along old track. Sat market on Aire; no parking Sat am, on the 20th of each month or during fair. River adj, no views. Small town commerce 250m. Reinspected 2014.

CONDAT SUR GANAVEIX

210 G8 19140 N45°28.090' E001°35.618'

10 Custom; No water, flushing drive over drain only; Cont WC by church (underground)

➤ D26. At the church in the centre of the village turn onto D26, sp 'Salon la Tour'. Turn right into parking after old fuel station and Service Point is immediately on right. Drive to top and turn left for parking.

Pleasant parking behind school adj to open access sports facilities. Rural views. Local commerce adj to Service Point. Inspected 2016.

ST YBARD
211 F8 19140 N45°26.948' E001°31.341'

🚐 4; Tolerated 🚿 Custom; WC emptying down round inspection cover meter to left of tap

➡ Rue des Fontaines. Exit A20 at Junction 44 and follow sp 'St Ybard' onto D20e7. Turn left onto D902, sp 'St Ybard'. Turn right onto D54e2, sp 'St Ybard'. After entering village turn right into Aire, sp 'Foyer Rural'.

ℹ Tolerated motorhome parking and Service Point in peaceful village with local commerce. Pleasant park adj, leads downhill to pond; fishing poss, day ticket required. Cascades de Bialet nearby. Conveniently close to A20 motorway. Inspected 2016.

TREIGNAC
212 G8 19260 N45°32.684' E001°48.069'

🚐 50; €1/24hrs; Pay at Service Point; CC 🚿 M-INNOV; CC; €2.50

➡ Parking des Rivières. Turn off D940 at roundabout by industrial estate, signed. Follow road downhill. Service Point is in far-right corner adj to WC: N45°32.616' E001°47.953'.

ℹ Large, open gravel and grass parking suitable for any unit configuration. Shallow river with canoe club boat launch adj. Local commerce 1.5km. Large leisure beach at lake, 2km; motorhomes banned overnight. Reinspected 2016.

CHAMBERET 1
213 G8 19370 N45°34.767' E001°43.236'

🚐 4; 12m bays 🚿 Custom; WC emptying at stade WC when open; See **214**

➡ Route de la Font Blanche. Exit village to west on D3, sp 'Masseret' and 'M.A.S. Stade'. Turn left onto Rte de la Font Blanche, signed. Aire at sports ground, opp cemetery.

ℹ Aire overlooking sports field. Small town commerce 150m. New Aire outside campsite, expect change. Additional designated parking in town off D16, signed: N45°35.071' E001°43.155', 700m north of Aire. Reinspected 2016.

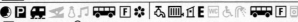
Photo: Alan Potter Designated parking

CHAMBERET 2
214 G8 19370 N45°34.749' E001°42.520'

🚐 7 🚿 Euro Relais Box; 1 unmetered CEE elec point

➡ D132e4. Turn off D3 in town centre onto D3e4, sp 'Limoges' and signed. In 175m turn left, signed. Follow sp 'Camping' out of town on D132e4. Turn right and follow road up hill, sp 'Camping'. At high ropes course turn right, sp 'Camping'. Aire on left before campsite.

ℹ Small pleasant Aire adj to campsite and high ropes course. Town centre with small town commerce 1.3km. Inspected 2016.

ST VITTE SUR BRIANCE
215 F8 87380 N45°37.526' E001°32.762'

🚐 2; Max 5 days; €5/day over 5 days 🚿 Custom; 4 unmetered CEE elec points (long cable needed)

➡ Place de la Mairie, adj to D31. Just off D31 next to the Mairie in the centre of the village. Service Point behind Mairie.

ℹ Small village centre parking area. Service Point may be obstructed by parked cars. Nearby St German les Belles signs motorhomes, but Centre de Tourism Montréal is a campsite. Reinspected 2014.

MEUZAC
216 F8 87380 N45°32.936' E001°26.312'

🚐 15 🚿 Custom

➡ Rue 11 Novembre 1918. Exit A20 at Junction 42 and follow D7bis, sp 'Meuzac'. In Meuzac turn left onto D243, sp 'Benayes'. Service Point 250m on right, signed. Parking 100m further on left in car park overlooking lake: N45°32.882' E001°26.406'.

ℹ Pleasant Aire on edge of residential area adj to leisure lake with swimming beach, signed walks and picnic facilities. Local commerce 500m. Ideal for both overnight stays and leisurely days. Updated 2015.

Photo: Rod Poxon

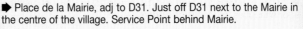

Bellac

ST YRIEIX LA PERCHE	220	F8	87500	🏢	N45°30.753' E001°12.380'	SP

🚐 Poss 🛢 Euro Relais Mini; Token (2/1); €3.50

➡ D704/Ave Gutenberg. At roundabout junction of D704/D901 turn onto D704, sp 'Limoges'. Service Point in 3rd entrance to car park on left, signed.

ℹ Service Point in a very unlevel town car park with 5m bays and limited overhang; better parking with overhang adj to park, 150m to left after Service Point. Medieval town 400m. www.tourisme-saint-yrieix.com Reinspected 2015.

GLANDON	221	F8	87500	🔒	N45°28.621' E001°13.718'	SP

🚐 2 🛢 Euro Relais Mini; Token (2/1); €3.50

➡ CD18. Exit town to south on D18. Aire is adj to D18 just past the sports facilities by the weigh bridge.

ℹ Village 100m; local parking available. Service Point signed as out of order at time of inspection, but WC rinse still functioning and drive over drain still available. Reinspected 2015.

PIERRE BUFFIERE	222	F8	87260	⛺	N45°41.370' E001°22.260'	SP

🚐 10; Park at stade when campsite open 🛢 Custom; No drive over drain; 1 CEE elec point (Not working)

➡ Turn off A20 at Junction 40, sp 'Pierre Buffiere', then follow sp 'Stade'. Drive through the building complex and the Aire is on the left.

ℹ Service Point with 2 parking bays opp municipal camping field (May-Sept €10.50/night) and gîtes. More parking before campsite at stade. Convenient night/lunch halt as only minutes from A20. Elec out of order since 2014. May feel isolated if alone. www.pierre-buffiere.com Reinspected 2015.

NEXON

223 F8 87800 △ N45°40.255' E001°10.866'

🖳 3 🛒 Custom

▶ Near Étang de la Lande, between D11 and D15a1. In town turn off D11 onto D15, sp 'Châlus' and signed. In 850m turn left onto D15a1, sp 'Étang de la Lande' and signed. In 650m turn left, sp 'Étang de la Lande' and signed. In 550m, past lake, turn right, signed. Aire on right.

ℹ Service Point outside campsite near small lake/swimming pond. Less commercial than **224**. www.nexon.fr Reinspected 2015.

ST HILAIRE LES PLACES

224 F8 87800 ⚓ N45°38.053' E001°09.700'

🖳 20 🛒 Raclet; 2 16amp CEE elec points (Not working)

▶ At Lac Plaisance. In town turn off D11 by church, sp 'Lac Plaisance'. Follow sp 'Lac Plaisance' for 1.6km. At campsite entrance keep left through gates. Service Point at bottom of hill on right, signed. Parking in top (barriered) and bottom car parks, signed.

ℹ Adj to campsite at leisure/swimming lake; views from both parking areas. Children's play area, crazy golf and waterslide by lake. www.sainthilairelesplaces.fr Reinspected 2015.

CHALUS

225 F8 87230 🏢 N45°39.656' E000°59.286'

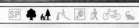

🖳 15 🛒 Custom; €2; Showers €2; See info

▶ N21. Exit town on N21 towards Limoges. Aire on right, sp 'Aire des Energies' and signed. Designated parking behind building, signed.

ℹ Adj to N21, but sheltered by banks. This is a motorway style fuel station which also appeals to HGVs. There is a small shop and café on site. Service Point accepts cash or tokens, which can be bought by cash/CC from machine. www.chalus87.fr Reinspected 2015.

PAGEAS

226 F8 87230 ⛟ N45°40.690' E001°00.135'

🖳 10; Grass parking 🛒 Euro Relais Junior; Token (ER); €2

▶ N21. From north on N21 turn right at bottom of hill before village onto D141a, sp 'Pageas'. Aire immediately on right in large, flat grass parking area. Limited hardstanding for winter use.

ℹ Well kept Aire within easy walking distance to village. Small lake and restaurant adj. Play area in adjoining park. www.pageas.fr Reinspected 2015.

ORADOUR SUR VAYRES

227 F8 87150 ⛟ N45°43.963' E000°51.942'

🖳 5 🛒 Custom

▶ Rue Jean Giraudeau, off D901. Turn off D901 by the Hotel de Ville/Mairie, opp D75 junction, sp 'Relais de la Vaynes' and signed. Service Point 50m on left, undesignated parking opp.

ℹ Local commerce 1 min. Hell's Bells all night. Voie Verte cycle/walking route to Chalus from town. Inspected 2014.

CUSSAC

228 F8 87150 ⛟ N45°42.318' E000°50.957'

🖳 3 🛒 Euro Relais Junior; Token (ER); €2

▶ Rue du 8 Mai 1945, off D73. From west on D669 turn right alongside cemetery onto D73, sp 'Marval'. Turn 1st left opp cemetery parking. The Aire is 75m on right, signed.

ℹ Very small Aire adj to boules court. Pleasant village with local commerce adj. Inspected 2014.

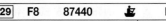

ST MATHIEU
`229` F8 87440 N45°42.912' E000°47.242'

🚐20 🛒 Depagne; €2

➡ C65. Turn off D675 in St Mathieu onto D699, sp 'Limoges'. Turn off D699 onto D127, sp 'Centre Tourisme du Lac'. Turn off D127 onto C65, sp 'Centre Tourisme du Lac'. Turn left into Centre Tourisme du Lac. Aire is on right, signed.

ℹ Aire adj to leisure lake with walks and boat hire. Views of lake from the very uneven parking. Adj campsite open May-Sept. Inspected 2014.

ST LAURENT SUR GORRE
`230` F8 87310 N45°45.922' E000°57.390'

🚐30; Grass parking between trees 🛒 Euro Relais Mini and Euro Relais Box; €2; 5 elec points; €2/4hrs

➡ Allée des Lilas. Exit town on D34, sp 'Vayres' and signed. Turn left in front of Gendarmerie, sp 'La Cote' and signed. After passing the stade municipal turn left and follow road to lake. Aire in former municipal campsite, sp 'Accueil Camping-Cars Les Chenes'.

ℹ Former campsite turned commercial Aire beside small leisure lake and park. Local commerce 650m, partially uphill. www.saint-laurent-gorre.fr Reinspected 2015.

LES SALLES LAVAUGUYON
`231` F8 87440 N45°44.412' E000°42.037'

🚐6; €4/24hrs; Honesty box 🛒 Flot Bleu Fontaine; 1 CEE elec point on timer (Not working)

➡ D33. Exit village on D33, sp 'St Mathieu'. Turn right after cemetery, signed. Aire in 20m on lower road.

ℹ Pleasant country Aire located on the Richard the Lionheart route. Covered picnic area adj. Village with local commerce 650m. Inspected 2014.

ROCHECHOUART
`232` F8 87600 T N45°49.320' E000°49.208'

🚐5 in adj car park marked with 5m bays; Other parking avail 🛒 Flot Bleu Océane; Token; €2; WC 150m

➡ Place du Château. Turn off D675, sp 'P Hotel de Ville' and 'Château'. Follow road up hill and Service Point is in car park opp château and adj to Hotel de Ville.

ℹ Central car park which will be busy in summer on château open days. Château open Wed-Mon, €4.60pp, www.museum-rochecouart.com. Alternative adj roadside parking may be more practical or car park on D675: N45°49.454' E000°49.316'. Updated 2016.

SEREILHAC
`233` F8 23400 N45°46.054' E001°04.732'

🚐10 🛒 Aire Services Plastic; Token (3/3); €2

➡ From Limoges on N21 turn right just after entering town, sp 'Aire de Service Camping-Car'. Drive through parking area to Aire at end.

ℹ A calm and quiet location just off busy main route. Ideal for overnight stopover or for lunch. Views of country park with lake . Local commerce 300m. www.sereilhac.com Inspected 2015.

ST PRIEST TAURION
`234` F8 87480 N45°53.158' E001°23.759'

🚐17 🛒 Custom

➡ Stade Municipal. Follow D29 through town towards Royeres. After crossing river bridge turn right in 100m into stade municipal, signed. Drive to the right and the Service Point is close to the river.

ℹ Adj to river with limited views, but does have interesting disused lock. Fishing is private. Sports ground adj. Local commerce 200m on D29. http://mairie.spt87.pagesperso-orange.fr Reinspected 2015.

NIEUL

235 F8 87510 N45°55.553' E001°10.318'

22; Max 72hrs; Grass parking ♀ Custom; WC emptying down toilet

➤ Rue de la Gare. Turn off D28 into car park opp château, signed. Service Point in car park, parking on grass behind car park.

ℹ Pleasant parking area with views of château, which has open access gardens in one direction and grassland in the other. Local commerce 250m. Updated 2014.

ORADOUR SUR GLANE

236 F8 87520 N45°56.129' E001°01.531'

27; Double bays ♀ Euro Relais Junior; €2

➤ From north on D3 turn right on entering town, signed. Follow road, then turn right, signed. Aire in 50m on one-way loop. Always popular, each bay is designed for two motorhomes.

ℹ Memorial at opp end of town (1.3km) commemorating 642 people killed during a Nazi attack on the town on June 10, 1944: N45°55.727' E001°02.114'. Open Feb-mid Dec 9am-5pm, later in spring/summer; €7.80pp. Reinspected 2014.

JAVERDAT

237 F8 87520 R N45°57.145' E000°59.158'

4; Max 72hrs ♀ Aire Services Plastic; Token; Aire Services Elec; 1 Token/55 mins

➤ C8. Turn off D711 in village centre by church onto C8, signed. Aire on right as exit village, signed.

ℹ Landscaped Aire in a small village. Onsite toilet block. Local commerce 100m, tokens free from Auberge bar. Reinspected 2016.

BUSSIERE POITEVINE

238 F7 87320 N46°14.187' E000°54.103'

20 ♀ Euro Relais Box; Token (ER)

➤ D942. Turn off N147 onto D942, sp 'Gueret'. Turn right in 700m, just past village boundary sign. Service Point in 10m, behind WC. Parking adj to road and on other side of lake.

ℹ Pleasant parking adj to park with pond and walk. Distant road noise, but ideal stop if transiting along N147. Local commerce 300m. Inspected 2014.

RAZES - Lac de St Pardoux

239 F8 87640 N46°02.050' E001°17.892'

10 ♀ Aire Services 3000; Token (3/3); €3.50; WC adj

➤ Lac de St Pardoux. From Razes follow D44, sp 'Lac de St Pardoux'. Turn off D44, sp 'Lac de St Pardoux', and Service Point is in 1st parking area on left.

ℹ Aire in small section of large car park for adj leisure lake. Development includes new swimming pool. Swimming beach, boating and 24km (6hrs) cycle/walk around lake. Reinspected 2016.

BESSINES SUR GARTEMPE

240 F7 87250 N46°06.568' E001°22.183'

5 ♀ Euro Relais Junior; No drive over drain; 2 unmetered CEE elec points

➤ Parking Champ de Foire, Rue d'Ingolsheim. In village turn beside Mairie, signed. Aire in car park in 100m.

ℹ Aire located in the central square parking. Constant comings and goings of vehicles when commerce open. Local commerce 150m. Reinspected 2014.

CIEUX

| 241 | F8 | 87520 | N45°59.500' E001°02.966' |

🚐 20; Grass parking 🚰 Euro Relais Box; Token (ER); Campsite has 8 CEE elec points, WC and shower

➡ Allée Bel Air, off D711. Follow D711 east through the village towards Nantiat. As exit village turn right off D711 onto Allée Bel Air, sp 'Aire Naturelle'. Aire is adj to Aire Naturelle municipal campsite.

ℹ Pleasant, open access, seasonal, basic campsite. Village with local commerce 200m. Down a lane directly opp is a very large lake with fishing available; permits from Mairie. Reinspected 2016.

BELLAC 1

| 242 | F7 | 87300 | N46°06.956' E001°03.086' |

🚐 5 🚰 Custom

➡ Rue des Tanneries. Approach from south on N147. Exit roundabout onto D947, sp 'Bellac'. Turn left onto D3, sp 'Blond' and signed. Turn right, signed. Follow road to Service Point on right, signed. Parking is on left before Service Point: N46°06.891' E001°03.128'.

ℹ Beautiful riverside park in tranquil setting. Roman bridge and marked walks adj. Town with commerce 500m uphill; market Sat. Updated 2016.

BELLAC 2

| 243 | F7 | 87300 | N46°07.283' E001°02.764' |

🚐 5+5 🚰 None; See 242

➡ Rue Louis Jouvet. From north turn off N147 at roundabout onto D947, sp 'St Junien' and 'Bellac'. After 4.3kms turn 1st right past village boundary sign, signed. Designated parking in car park 700m on right opp Hotel de Ville, signed. Other designated 3.5t parking adj to D947 by Maison de Association and TO: N46°07.253' E001°03.034'.

ℹ Two designated parking areas in town centre. School opp 1st, TO opp 2nd. Town commerce adj. Inspected 2014.

RANCON

| 244 | F7 | 87290 | N46°07.653' E001°10.885' |

🚐 10; Grass and gravel; Summer only 🚰 Custom

➡ D1. Exit village on D1 towards Bellac (south). Aire on right in lay-by as exit village, signed. Parking is in the stade (sports stadium) through adj gate and up steep slope: N46°07.698' E001°10.830'.

ℹ Slightly isolated parking on edge of small village, avail summer only. Limited local commerce 350m. Sports facilities adj. 12th century Lanterne des Morts 600m at former cemetery: N46°07.933' E001°10.950'. Reinspected 2014.

MARSAC

| 245 | G7 | 23210 | N46°05.995' E001°34.780' |

🚐 4 hardstanding; 15 grass parking 🚰 Custom

➡ Lavaud, off D42. From village centre follow D42, sp 'Fursac' and signed. Follow road out of village, then turn right, signed, and follow road uphill alongside campsite. Service Point to left, signed. Parking 100m adj to sports field.

ℹ Pleasant Aire with parking on grass under trees in summer, or hardstanding when necessary. Open access sports field adj. Campsite adj. Local commerce 300m. Reinspected 2016.

BOSMOREAU LES MINES

| 246 | G8 | 23400 | N45°59.957' E001°45.144' |

🚐 25 🚰 Euro Relais Mini

➡ Ave de la Gare. From Bourganeuf on D912 turn right onto D61 and follow sp 'Vélo-rail de la Mine' for 5km. Turn left before railway line and the Aire is on the left beyond former railway station.

ℹ Large, open, peaceful Aire adj to old railway station which is now a Velorail. Velorail bike hire, €25/5 people. www.veloraildelamine.fr Mine museum in village, 500m. www.museedelamine.fr Reinspected 2016.

ST DIZIER LEYRENNE

247 | G8 | 23400 | | N46°01.390' E001°43.032'

🚐 5; Max 48hrs; No parking Tue pm-Wed am (Market) 🛒 Custom

➡️ D912. From south follow D912 towards St Dizier Leyrenne. Aire on right adj to D912 when enter village, next to municipal campsite and Étang de la Valodie.
.

ℹ️ Pleasant parking adj to open access sports field. Lake walk adj. Local commerce 700m. Reinspected 2016.

CHATELUS LE MARCHEIX

248 | G8 | 23430 | | N45°59.931' E001°36.198'

🚐 5 🛒 Raclet; €2

➡️ Off D8. Exit the village to the west on D8, sp 'Ambazac' and signed. Turn left at the edge of the village, signed. The Service Point is in 50m on the left, outside municipal campsite.

ℹ️ Lovely rural views. Parking available when campsite closed (Sept-Jun); campsite €11.50/night inc elec, open Jul-Aug. http://chateluslemarcheix.fr Reinspected 2015.

BOURGANEUF

249 | G8 | 23400 | | N45°57.265' E001°45.460'

🚐 5; Max 48hrs; No parking Tue 9pm-Wed 2pm (Market) 🛒 Euro Relais Mini

➡️ D912. Enter town from north on D912. Turn left in front of turreted building, signed. Turn right in car park, signed.

ℹ️ Pleasant town with multiple commerce 200m uphill. Reinspected 2016.

MONTBOUCHER

250 | G8 | 23400 | | N45°57.089' E001°40.866'

🚐 10 🛒 Euro Relais Mini

➡️ Off D36, in village centre. Turn off D941 onto D36, sp 'Montboucher'. Follow signs to Aire. In village centre follow road behind church and to right.

ℹ️ Located in a rural village centre. Outdoor sinks and WC in adj building. Tennis court adj. Reinspected 2015.

SAUVIAT SUR VIGE

251 | G8 | 87400 | | N45°54.559' E001°36.911'

🚐 20 🛒 Urba Flux; €2

➡️ D941. Adj to D941 as enter village from northeast. Aire on left in large parking area, signed.

ℹ️ Aire in large parking adj to main route. Suitable for any unit configuration. Popular HGV parking and suffers road noise. Reinspected 2016.

ST JUNIEN LA BREGERE

252 | G8 | 23400 | | N45°52.944' E001°45.174'

🚐 5 🛒 Custom

➡️ D13, off D940. In village turn off D940 onto D13. In 100m turn right, signed.

ℹ️ Rural views. Some road noise from D940. Village 400m. Reinspected 2015.

PEYRAT LE CHATEAU
253 G8 87470 N45°48.881' E001°46.251'

🚐 10 Custom; Token; €2

➤ Place du Pré de l'Age. Turn off D940 main road in town centre opp TO. Aire 100m on left.

ℹ Rural views. Village 100m with local commerce, museum and lake. Reinspected 2016.

BUJALEUF
254 G8 87460 N45°48.297' E001°38.207'

🚐 5 Custom

➤ D16. Exit village on D16, sp 'Cheissoux' and 'Lac de Ste Hélène'. Parking in 1.5km adj to lake, signed. For Service Point exit village on D14 towards Eymoutiers. In 250m turn left into Rue du Champ de Foire. Service Point 250m on left, signed: N45°47.850' E001°37.878'.

ℹ Parking adj to large open space and leisure lake/reservoir. Local commerce in village, 1.5km. www.bujaleuf.fr Reinspected 2015.

AURIAT
255 G8 23400 N45°52.716' E001°38.574'

🚐 3; See info Euro Relais Mini; Seasonal WC

➤ In Sauviat-sur-Vige turn off D941 onto D5, sp 'Auriat'. Follow road for 4km, then turn right, sp 'Auriat' and 'Etang d'Auriat'. In 1.5km turn left just past cemetery into Aire, sp 'Etang d'Auriat'. If approach from village there is a difficult turn not suitable for motorhomes longer than 8m.

ℹ Pleasant rural landscaped Aire at fishing lake, no views; no swimming and fishing permits required. Unrestricted grass parking adj to lake, be careful of rocks. Signed walks to megaliths. Inspected 2016.

LAC DE VASSIVIERE - AUPHELLE
256 G8 87470 N45°48.323' E001°50.584'

🚐 50; €4.20/24hrs Apr-Nov; €6/24hrs Jul-Aug; Grass parking Urba Flux Tall; €2.50; 1 CEE elec point; €6/4hrs; Both outside barrier

➤ Route de Barrage. Turn off D222 onto D233, sp 'Royère de Vassivière'. In Auphelle turn into Aire opp campsite, signed. Service Point on left. Enter through barrier; wait in parking to left if barrier down.

ℹ Campsite controlled commercial Aire in former campsite land. Shaded and open parking. Large leisure lake and campsite across road. Inspected 2016.

ROYERE DE VASSIVIERE
257 G8 23460 N45°50.403' E001°54.668'

🚐 7; Max 48hrs; No parking adj to Service Point Tue 6am-2pm (Market) Euro Relais Mini; Closed Mon 9pm-Tue 2pm (Market)

➤ D3. Exit the village to south on D3, sp 'Gentious'. The Aire is adj to D3 in the car park by the Proxi mini market, signed.

ℹ Pleasant village with local commerce adj. Parking poss on either side of road. Hell's bells all night adj to car park with Service Point; car park opp has area suitable for any unit configuration and is furthest from bells. Reinspected 2016.

FELLETIN
258 G8 23500 N45°52.923' E002°10.546'

🚐 5 Euro Relais Mini

➤ Rue des Fosses. Located off D10 and D982, sp 'Crocq'. Well signed from all directions. Service Point accessible from slope at rear of car park.

ℹ Town with commerce 200m. Market Fridays. Free WiFi at TO. www.felletin.fr Reinspected 2015.

CROCQ
259 | G8 | 23260 | N45°51.812' E002°22.125'

6; Grass parking but other hardstanding parking poss 🏺 Euro Relais Junior; Token (ER)

➡ Route de la Bourboule. Follow D996, main route, through Crocq towards Giat. The Aire is at the sports facilities adj to D996, signed. Entrance is narrow but passable with care.

ℹ Located adj to sports facilities and fire station. Local commerce 550m. Inspected 2012.

AUBUSSON
260 | G8 | 23200 | N45°57.407' E002°10.514'

20 🏺 Euro Relais Junior

➡ Place du Champ de Foire, off D988, signed. Enter town from north on D990. Turn onto D988, sp 'Aubusson D94a'. Follow road past Intermarché and Aire is in car park 100m on left, signed.

ℹ Large town 300m; Do not attempt to drive through town in anything but van-style motorhome. Intermarché supermarket 900m. www.tourisme-aubusson.com Reinspected 2015.

SOUBREBOST
261 | G8 | 23250 | T | N45°59.071' E001°51.189'

10 🏺 Euro Relais Mini

➡ D13. Turn off D941 in Pontarion onto D13, sp 'Soubrebost' and signed. Follow road for 1.5km, then turn right into Aire, signed.

ℹ Pleasant Aire with rural views at former house of Martin Nadaud, now museum; open Apr-Oct, €6pp. www.martinadaud-martineche.com Walk or cycle 1km to Pierre aux Neuf Gradins, the mysterious stone bowls that Martin Nadaud used to visit; parking: N45°58.572' E001°51.403'. Inspected 2016.

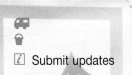

CHENERAILLES
263 | G7 | 23130 | N46°06.641' E002°10.683'

5 🏺 Euro Relais Junior; Token (ER)

➡ D990. Exit town towards Aubusson and the Aire is on the left, signed.

ℹ Between main road and housing estate. Village centre 200m with local commerce. www.chenerailles.fr Reinspected 2015.

CRESSAT
264 | G7 | 23140 | N46°08.363' E002°06.610'

5; 8m bays 🏺 Raclet; Token (2/1)

➡ Off D990. As enter Cressat from Chénérailles, Aire just past lake on left, signed.

ℹ Lake adj, but no view. Village 150m uphill. Reinspected 2015.

GOUZON
265 | G7 | 23230 | N46°11.486' E002°14.412' | SP

10 Raclet

➡ Place du Champ de Foire, Rue d'Alcantera. Drive out of Gouzon on D997, sp 'Aubusson'. Turn off, sp 'Camping'. Before road splits turn left, sp 'Parking Ombragé: Pique-Nique' and signed.

ℹ Shaded parking under trees. Town and restaurants 250m. Updated 2013.

JARNAGES
266 | G7 | 23140 | N46°11.064' E002°04.870' | SP

5 Euro Relais Junior; €2

➡ D65. In Jarnages turn right at La Poste onto D65, sp 'Accueil Camping Car'. Service Point adj to play area and lake.

ℹ Lake, crazy golf and tennis court adj. Village commerce 300m. Market Sunday am. Reinspected 2015.

ST LAURENT
267 | G7 | 23000 | N46°09.983' E001°57.700' | SP

4; 8m bays Euro Relais Junior; 2 unmetered elec points

➡ D3. Turn onto D3 in village centre at rear of church, sp 'Bourne Camping-Car'. Aire 50m on right in car park, adj to church.

ℹ Good stopover. Local commerce under construction at time of inspection. Reinspected 2015.

GUERET - Aire des Monts de Gueret
268 | G7 | 23000 | N46°10.945' E001°50.918' | SP

16; Not recommended Euro Relais Junior; €2

➡ D942/DN145. Exit N145 at Junction 49, sp 'Guéret Ouest', and follow sp 'Aire des Monts de Guéret'. Aire located at motorway services behind main building, signed.

ℹ Designated parking that is technically off the motorway, but as with all motorway Aires we advise you not to stay overnight. Shop/café and WC inside building. Reinspected 2015.

BOUSSAC
269 | G7 | 23600 | N46°20.867' E002°13.242' | SP

10 Euro Relais Box

➡ D997. Follow D997 through town towards Gueret. Aire on left adj to large car park/livestock market, signed.

ℹ Adj to livestock market and D997, both of which can be busy and noisy. Small town commerce 1 min. Updated 2016.

PREMILHAT
270 | H7 | 03410 | N46°20.081' E002°33.518' | SP

8; Max 72hrs Euro Relais Maxi; CC; €5/150L water; Euro Relais Elec; €2.50/10hrs

➡ Route de l'Etang de Sault. Exit Montluçon following sp 'Limoges' and 'Guéret'. After passing retail park with large Auchan supermarket, turn left at roundabout onto D605, sp 'Prémilhat'. Follow road and Aire is on left opp lake, signed.

ℹ Landscaped Aire with partial lake views over road and through willows. Pleasant lakeside park and swimming beach opp. Reinspected 2016.

MONTLUCON
271 | G7 | 03100 | N46°21.301' E002°35.188'

50; No parking Thurs 6am-3pm (Market) ♂ Euro Relais Maxi; 2 elec points on Service Point

➤ Place de la Fraternité. Enter town on D943. Aire just off D943 in large square, signed. Just before D916/D301 junction if coming from north.

ℹ Aire in large car park; elec bollards throughout car park intended for market, Thurs 6am-3pm. Small park adj. Drive over drain access may be diff for wide motorhomes due to bollards. Town centre 2km. Reinspected 2016.

ESTIVAREILLES
272 | H7 | 03190 | N46°25.499' E002°36.933'

20 ♂ Custom; Near entrance

➤ Off D3. From D2144 turn onto D3 at Estivareilles, sp 'Herisson'. The Aire is 100m on left, sp 'Salle Polyvalente' and signed.

ℹ Aire in large, uninspiring car park. Village with local commerce 250m. Reinspected 2016.

CHAMBLET
273 | H7 | 03170 | N46°20.018' E002°42.150'

5 ♂ Custom; No drive over drain; 4 CEE elec points (Not working)

➤ Rue St Maurice. Turn off D2371 at traffic-lighted crossroads, sp 'P Mairie' and signed. Turn right in 50m, sp 'P Mairie' and signed. Turn right again in 20m opp church, signed. Service Point immediately on right, signed.

ℹ Aire located in village centre adj to D2371 which may be noisy. Local commerces 1 min. Inspected 2012.

COMMENTRY
274 | H7 | 03600 | N46°17.392' E002°45.614'

10 ♂ Euro Relais Junior

➤ Rue des Platanes, off D69. Turn off D998 at the roundabout onto D69, sp 'Moilins'. In 300m take road on right and Aire on left in 50m.

ℹ Adj to D69; suffers road noise. Really only a suitable night halt or Service Point only. Green space opp. Reinspected 2016.

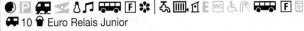

NERIS LES BAINS
275 | H7 | 03310 | N46°17.207' E002°39.137'

6; €8 inc 10amp elec and showers; Pay at campsite; Max 3 nights; Apr-mid Nov ♂ Raclet; Token (2/1); €2.50

➤ D155, at Camping du Lac. Follow sp 'Camping du Lac' through town. Located directly on D155 on west side of town.

ℹ In thermal spa town. Beautiful town centre 600m, worth a visit. Parking available when campsite open, Apr-mid Nov. Reinspected 2016.

All of the listings in this section are Service Points without designated parking. The majority are located either at supermarkets or outside campsites.

Height barriers are rare at supermarkets and overnight parking should be possible. Always park considerately. Supermarket Service Points often lack a waste water drain.

Most campsites are municipally owned. Parking outside may be possible when campsites are closed. Acquiring tokens in rural locations may be difficult or impossible, especially in low season.

Remember to be a responsible tourist whenever offsite parking.

LES ANCIZES COMPS
276 | H8 | 63770 | N45°56.392' E002°47.993'

♂ Flot Bleu; CC; €3

➤ Le Moulin, off D62. Take D62 north from Les Ancizes. 900m after the town boundary sign turn left, sp 'Comps'. Service Point outside campsite 200m on right. Inspected 2016.

ST GEORGES `277` H9 15100 N45°01.905' E003°08.107'

🛁 ▥ 🚽 **E** WC ♿ ⛽ 🚌 F ▯
🚰 Euro Relais Junior; €2

➤ D909. Turn off A75 motorway at Junction 29 and follow sp 'St Flour'. Service Point on right at Esso fuel station. Inspected 2016.

NANTIAT `278` F8 87140 N46°00.286' E001°09.179'

🛁 ▥ 🚽 **E** WC ♿ ⛽ 🚌 F ▯
🚰 Euro Relais Box; Token (ER); €2

➤ D711. Turn off D711 into Camping Les Haches. Service Point on left before open access campsite.

ORCIVAL `279` H8 63210 N45°40.919' E002°50.570'

🛁 ▥ 🚽 **E** WC ♿ ⛽ 🚌 **F** ▯
🚰 Urba Flux Tall; CC; €2

➤ D27. Adj to D27 above village. Visited 2016.

Info/photos: Alistair & Helen MacFadyen

AINAY LE CHATEAU `280` H7 03360 N46°42.322' E002°41.654'

🛁 ▥ 🚽 **E** WC ♿ ⛽ 🚌 F ▯
🚰 Flot Bleu Océane; €2 (2 x €1)

➤ D953. South of the town adj to D953 at Intermarché supermarket, signed. Reinspected 2016.

AVERMES `281` H7 03000 N46°35.218' E003°18.907'

🛁 ▥ 🚽 **E** WC ♿ ⛽ 🚌 F ▯
🚰 Flot Bleu Euro; CC; €2

➤ Rue Alphonse Daudet off D707, at the E'Leclerc fuel station. Well signed from town centre. Follow sp 'Nevers' from south. Updated 2016.

CHAMBON SUR VOUEIZE `282` G7 23170 N46°11.170' E002°26.035'

🛁 ▥ 🚽 **E** WC ♿ ⛽ 🚌 F ▯
🚰 Euro Relais Junior; €2

➤ Rue du Stade, off D915. Exit village on D915, sp 'Evaux les B' and 'Camping Municipal'. Turn off at Intermarché supermarket, signed. Service Point in 200m on left at entrance to the campsite. Reinspected 2016.

BELLENAVES `283` H7 03330 N46°12.325' E003°04.666'

🛁 ▥ 🚽 **E** WC ♿ ⛽ 🚌 F ▯
🚰 Aire Services 3000; €2

➤ D68. Exit Bellenaves on D68, sp 'Louroux de Bouble' and 'Vernusse'. Service Point adj to D68 on left outside campsite. Inspected 2012.

ST GEORGES DE MONS `284` H8 63780 N45°56.393' E002°50.573'

🛁 ▥ 🚽 **E** WC ♿ ⛽ 🚌 F ▯
🚰 Euro Relais Junior; €2

➤ Place des Anciens Combattants. Turn off D19 onto D19 ring road. Turn off before town centre, sp 'Camping'. Service Point directly outside camping municipal. Reinspected 2016.

BROMONT LAMOTHE `285` H8 63230 N45°50.394' E002°48.821'

🛁 ▥ 🚽 **E** WC ♿ ⛽ 🚌 F ▯
🚰 Raclet; Token (2/1); €3; May-Sept

➤ Off D941. Turn off D941 to west of village, sp 'Camping' and signed. Service Point outside campsite, accessible May-Sept when campsite open. Reinspected 2016.

AMBERT `286` I8 63600 N45°32.369' E003°43.724'

🛁 ▥ 🚽 **E** WC ♿ ⛽ 🚌 F ▯
🚰 Euro Relais Junior; €2; May-Sept

➤ D906. Service Point adj to D906 outside Camping Les 3 Chênes, south of Ambert. Reinspected 2016.

MARSAC EN LIVRADOIS `287` I8 63940 N45°28.800' E003°43.855'

🛁 ▥ 🚽 **E** WC ♿ ⛽ 🚌 F ▯
🚰 Aire Services 3000; €2

➤ D252, outside campsite. Follow D252 east out of town towards river. Aire adj to D252, sp 'Gandrif' and 'Camping de la Graviere'. Reinspected 2016.

ST JULIEN CHAPTEUIL `288` I9 43260 N45°02.347' E004°03.713'

🛁 ▥ 🚽 **E** WC ♿ ⛽ 🚌 **F** ▯
🚰 Custom

➤ D28. Exit town to north on D28, sp 'Yssingeaux' and 'Camping'. Turn right at edge of town, sp 'Camping'. Service Point adj to municipal campsite, signed. Reinspected 2014.

LE PUY EN VELAY | 289 | I9 | 43000 | N45°02.979' E003°53.394'

🔧 Euro Relais Mini; Token (ER); No drive over drain

➤ D13/Boulevard de Cluny. From N88 turn onto D13, sp 'Vichy'. Service Point 200m on right before Super U fuel station, signed. Reinspected 2014.

ST PAULIEN | 290 | I9 | 43350 | N45°07.223' E003°47.607'

🔧 Urba Flux Tall; €3

➤ D25. Turn off D906 in St Paulien by the church onto D13, sp 'Allegre'. Turn left onto D25, sp 'Loudes' and 'Camping'. Service Point on left outside campsite entrance. Inspected 2012.

BRASSAC LES MINES | 291 | H8 | 63570 | N45°24.811' E003°20.118'

🔧 Flot Bleu Pacific (Green); €2

➤ Place du Muse, by D34/D34a junction. Follow sp 'Jumeaux' and signed as exit town to east on D34. Service Point on right. Reinspected 2016.

BAGNOLS | 292 | H8 | 63810 | N45°29.844' E002°38.093'

🔧 Custom; Apr-Oct

➤ Outside Camping La Thialle, off D25. Turn off D47 at church onto D25, sp 'Camping' and signed. Follow road for 400m, then turn right, sp 'Camping' and signed. Service Point to right of campsite entrance, signed. Reinspected 2016.

MEYMAC | 293 | G8 | 19250 | N45°31.803' E002°08.521'

🔧 Flot Bleu Euro; CC; €2

➤ D36, outside Casino supermarket. From D979 in Meymac turn onto D36, sp 'Égletons'. Aire on left in 750m. Reinspected 2015.

MARCILLAC LA CROISILLE | 294 | G9 | 19320 | N45°15.725' E002°00.343'

🔧 Euro Relais Junior; No drive over drain

➤ At corner of Rte du Puy Nachet and Promenade du Lac. 2km from village at Barrage de la Valette. Follow sp 'Lac du Valette' from village. Inspected 2015.

MAURIAC | 295 | G9 | 15200 | N45°12.864' E002°20.801'

🔧 Flot Bleu Marine; €2/20 mins; No drive over drain

➤ D922. Exit town on D922 towards Aurillac. Turn off roundabout into Carrefour supermarket and the Aire is located in the car park near the fuel station. Reinspected 2014.

TULLE | 296 | G9 | 19000 | N45°16.494' E001°46.440'

🔧 Euro Relais Box (Not working); Token (ER)/€; €2

➤ Quai Victor Continsouza, at Intermarché fuel station. From centre follow D23 north along river towards Corrèze. Drive past Intermarché supermarket, then turn immediately right across river bridge. Service Point in Intermarché fuel station 200m on left, signed. Reinspected 2015.

LUBERSAC | 297 | F8 | 19210 | N45°26.201' E001°23.803'

🔧 Euro Relais Junior

➤ D901, at the Super U. ON D901 turn off at roundabout with big apple adj to Super U supermarket and fuel station. Service Point in fuel station. Reinspected 2015.

EYMOUTIERS | 298 | G8 | 87120 | N45°44.293' E001°44.108'

🔧 Flot Bleu Fontaine; 2 unmetered elec points; No drive over drain

➤ D979. Exit town to west on D979 towards Limoges. The Service Point is located at the Casino supermarket fuel station on the left as exit town. Reinspected 2015.

LA CELLE DUNOISE | 299 | G7 | 23800 | N46°18.534' E001°46.459'

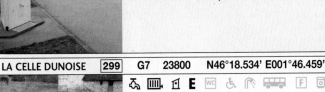

🔧 Euro Relais Junior; €2

➤ D48a/Rte du Canard. Exit village to south on D22, sp 'Gueret' and signed. Turn left onto D48a, signed. Service Point is on left outside municipal campsite. Inspected 2010.

MAZET ST VOY | 300 | I9 | 43520 | N45°03.246' E004°15.261'

🔧 Raclet; €7.50; Closed in winter

➤ Off D7. From town centre follow sp 'Camping' east on D7 out of town. Take 2nd left turn. At end of road turn left and follow to campsite. Aire outside Camping Surnette. Inspected 2012.

LIMOUSIN & AUVERGNE

MAGNAC BOURG	301	F8	87380	N45°37.051' E001°26.063'

♿ 🔢 🔼 E 🚾 ♿ 🔽 🚌 F ▣

🛖 Custom

➡ Route du Moulin, off D82. Exit A20 at Junction 41 and follow D82 into town, sp 'Centre Bourg'. At the roundabout turn right, sp 'Centre Bourg'. Turn immediately into 3.5t restricted parking on right and the Service Point is at the bottom by pond. Reinspected 2014.

AHUN	302	G7	23150	N46°04.797' E002°02.648'

♿ 🔢 🔼 E 🚾 ♿ 🔽 🚌 F ▣

🛖 Euro Relais Mini

➡ Route de Limoges. In village centre on D942 turn onto D13, sp 'Camping Municipal' and signed. Service Point 850m on left outside municipal campsite, signed. Small, municipal campsite has been closed since July 2014. Signs forbid motorhome parking. Village with local commerce 850m. Reinspected 2015.

Tourzel Ronzieres

Turenne

Canyon du Verdon

MEDITERRANEAN

Les Salles sur Verdon

MEDITERRANEAN

CASTELNAUDARY

1   G11   11490   🏢   N43°18.843' E001°56.947'   SP

🚐 9; €8.40/24hrs Sept-Jun; €9.60/24hrs Jul-Aug; CC 🚽 Euro Relais Junior; Inside barrier; 19 CEE elec points; All inc

➡ D624. Approach on D624 from south to avoid driving through town. Aire adj to D624 on left before Gendarmerie, signed. Enter through PARKNIGHT barrier.

ℹ Commercial Aire adj to Canal du Midi, no views; access on foot. Aire suffers road noise. Small town commerce 250m. Day parking adj to Canal du Midi: N43°21.130' E001°49.442'. Reinspected 2016.

SALLES SUR L'HERS

2   G11   11410   N43°17.534' E001°47.259'   SP

🚐 10 🚽 Depagne; Tap requires male hose connector; 2 unmetered CEE elec points

➡ Rue des Écoles. From south on D625 turn right past La Poste, sp 'Borne Camping Car'. Follow road to bottom of hill on one-way system. Aire in 70m outside sports grounds, signed.

ℹ Sloping parking adj to sports stadium on edge of village. Stream adj and footpaths into open countryside. Very pleasant shady spot. Reinspected 2016.

BELPECH

3   G11   11420   N43°11.915' E001°44.709'   SP

🚐 5; Grass parking 🚽 Bollard; No drive over drain; 2 unmetered Cont elec points

➡ Rue du Stade. Approach on D502 from Marty (west). At Stop junction turn left onto D102, sp 'Belpech'. Turn right opp CA bank into Rue du Stade. Follow road and turn left into sports stadium after houses. Aire to right, not signed. Counter lever barrier should be open.

ℹ If the barrier is closed there is hardstanding space avail outside. Open access sports ground adj. Small town commerce 400m. Inspected 2013.

FANJEAUX

4   G11   11270   N43°11.176' E002°01.952'   SP

🚐 12; Max 48hrs 🚽 Bollard; No drive over drain; WC opp TO

➡ Chemin des Fontanelles. From Carcassonne on D119 enter village via unrestricted weight route. Pass through arch, then take 1st right. Follow road uphill, then turn left at T-junction, signed. Drive past TO and follow road uphill. In 300m turn left by crucifix, signed. Aire immediately on left.

ℹ Popular Aire at medieval hilltop village. Small town commerce and TO all 300m downhill. Reinspected 2016.

VILLASAVARY

5   G11   11150   N43°13.117' E002°01.952'   SP

🚐 11; €8.40/24hrs Sept-Jun; €9.60/24hrs Jul-Aug; Inc service and elec; CC 🚽 Euro Relais Junior; 10 CEE elec points; Inside barrier

➡ Ave du Dr Combes. Turn off D623 in village centre into Ave du Dr Combes, sp 'Stade - Tennis'. Follow road down hill and past sports ground on right. Aire 180m on right, signed. Enter through PARKNIGHT barrier.

ℹ Landscaped, open commercial Aire on edge of village. Local commerce 650m. Unrestricted day parking at sports grounds 180m. Inspected 2016.

CARCASSONNE 1

6   G11   11000   🏢   N43°12.402' E002°21.530'   SP

🚐 20; €20/24hrs; CC 🚽 None; See **7**

➡ P2, Allée des Jardins du Beal. Approach from east on D6113. Turn off D6113 at roundabout following sp 'La Cité' and 'Limoux'. In 3km turn right at roundabout, sp 'P2 Port d'Aude' and signed. Follow signs to right into one-way street. At end turn left, signed, then turn right, sp 'P2' and signed. Enter through barrier.

ℹ Motorhome parking allowed in barriered car park 450m from historic Carcassone; uphill walk. This is the closest motorhomes are allowed to park to La Cité, expect change. Inspected 2016.

CARCASSONNE 2

7 G11 11000 N43°11.982' E002°21.162'

🚐 38; €12/24hrs; +€0.20pp tax; Max 8m ♿ Urba Flux Tall; Inside barrier; €2; 4 CEE elec points

➡️ D104. Approach from east on D6113. Turn off D6113 at roundabout following sp 'La Cité' and 'Limoux'. In 3km turn right at roundabout, sp 'P2 Port d'Aude', 'Camping de la Cité' and signed. Turn left, sp 'Camping de la Cité' and signed. Drive past the campsite, then turn right, signed. Aire on right. Enter through Urba Flux barrier.

ℹ️ Landscaped commercial Aire adj to and run by campsite on outskirts of Carcassonne. Exit Aire to right and turn right for riverside path to Carcassonne, 1.5km; the last 300m are uphill to La Cité. Some road and airplane noise. Inspected 2016.

VILLENEUVE MINERVOIS

8 G11 11160 N43°18.900' E002°27.850'

🚐 5; Max 48hrs; Designated bays ♿ Bollard

➡️ D111. From D111 turn into the car park in the town centre, opp Mairie and next to the Spar shop. Once in car park, turn right and Service Point in far right corner. Designated parking before Service Point, signed.

ℹ️ Small, peaceful village. Local commerce adj. Shaded parking in summer. Inspected 2013.

HOMPS

9 H11 11200 N43°16.191' E002°43.063'

🚐 20; Max 24hrs ♿ None

➡️ Rue du Lac. From east turn off D610, sp 'Homps'. Turn right and follow sp 'Olonzac'. After crossing canal turn left, sp 'Lac de Jouarres', then turn left again, sp 'Le Lac'. At roundabout turn left and bear to right down mud track to canal. Park to right of roadway as signed.

ℹ️ Parking overlooking a small boat marina on Canal du Midi. Local commerce across bridge. Market in Olonzac Tues am. Area granted planning permission Nov 2015 allowing residential and commercial construction; expect change. Suitable lay-bys on D11 between Homps and Cabezac. Inspected 2016.

MONZE

10 G11 11800 N43°09.294' E002°27.518'

🚐 4; Max 48hrs ♿ None

➡️ Rue de Cabernet. From Lagrasse turn off D3, sp 'Étape Camping-Car'. Follow road straight on, then in village turn left, then right, both sp 'Étape Camping-Car'. Cross bridge and turn left to designated parking, signed.

ℹ️ Pleasant, peaceful designated parking backing onto acres of grape vines. Medieval village with beautiful Roman bridge adj. Series of excellent long and short walks signed from village. Flowering orchids in spring. Inspected 2016.

LAGRASSE

11 H11 11220 N43°05.563' E002°37.245'

🚐 40; €4/24hrs Oct-May; €6/24hrs Jun-Sept; Collected ♿ Custom

➡️ Parking 2, Avenue des Condomines. Follow D3 through village towards Trèbes, ignoring sp 'P Obligatoire'. Turn right just before exit village, sp 'P2'. Turn next left into car park. Service Point and parking down slope, signed.

ℹ️ Popular and pleasant grass and hardstanding parking. Beau Village with abbey and tourist commerce 100m. Reinspected 2016.

VILLEROUGE TERMENES

12 H11 11330 (A) N43°00.287' E002°37.601'

🚐 (A) 3; (B) 5 ♿ (A) Tap in WC; (B) Bollard; No drive over drain

➡️ D613. (A) Villerouge-Termenès: Adj to D613, beside shop at rear corner of château parking, signed. (B) N42°59.225' E002°36.776': Felines-Termenès: From (A) travel 2.7km south on D613. Aire on left in village car park as exit village towards Mouthoumet, just before D39 junction, not signed.

ℹ️ 2 parking options on D613: (A) Shop selling local products adj. Entrance to 13th century château on opp side of road, signed. Info panels direct you around château and the onsite restaurant recreates medieval dishes. (B) Pleasant car park under trees. Village centre 200m. Very old Service Point, water turned off in winter. Reinspected 2016.

(A)

(B)

MEDITERRANEAN

GPS co-ordinates in this guide are protected by copyright law

[i] Submit updates
- Amendments
- New Aires
- Not changed

Visit www.all-the-aires.co.uk/submissions.shtml
to upload your updates and photos.

Take at least 5 digital
photos showing
- Signs
- Service Point
- Parking
- Overview
- Amenities

LIMOUX | 14 | G11 | 11300 | N43°03.475' E002°12.888'

🚐20 🛒 Custom

➡ Rue Louis Braille. Best approached from north on D118. On entering town fork left following sp 'Centre Ville', then turn left into Rue Louis Braille, sp 'Gamme Vert'. The Aire is on the left, signed. Not signed from other directions.

[i] Riverside parking, no view, suitable for any unit configuration. Town centre 550m with large market Fri am. Town makes a famous sparkling wine. LPG avail at E.Leclerc on D118 at Centre Commercial. Reinspected 2016.

ESPERAZA | 15 | G12 | 11260 | N42°56.028' E002°12.949'

🚐20; On grass under trees 🛒 Custom

➡ Avenue François Mitterrand. Turn off D118 onto D46, sp 'Espéraza' and 'Camping'. Follow D46 into town and turn left before river bridge, signed. Follow road along river for 400m and parking is on the right under pine trees. Service Point on left, signed.

[i] Pleasant parking under trees adj to suburb and small river, partial views but access adj. Town 600m. Inspected 2013.

QUILLAN | 16 | G12 | 11500 | N42°52.450' E002°10.950'

🚐5 🛒 Custom; Token (2/0); €3.20

➡ La Gare, D117. Turn off D117, main route through, into car park, sp 'Le Gare' and signed. Parking also for railway station and buses.

[i] Parking under trees. Market in parking Sat am. Small town commerce opp. Train to Carcassone. Inspected 2013.

LAPRADELLE PUILAURENS | 17 | G12 | 11140 | N42°48.583' E002°18.517'

🚐Poss 🛒 Custom

➡ Rue de la Devèze, off D117. Turn off D117 at viaduct. Aire between viaduct and fire station, signed. Be careful to avoid bollard in entrance.

[i] Poss parking adj to fire station. Views of mountains and château. Inspected 2013.

DUILHAC SOUS PEYREPERTUSE | 18 | G12 | 11350 | N42°51.683' E002°33.917'

🚐20 🛒 Custom

➡ D814. From Maury take D19, sp 'Château de Queribus'. After passing the château turn left onto D14, sp 'Duilhac-s/s-P'. At entrance to village turn left onto D814, sp 'Duilhac-s/s-Peyrepertuse 0.7' and 'Château de Peyrepertuse'. Follow road past cafés and Aire is in car park on left, signed.

[i] Beautiful views of surrounding mountains. Village centre with cafés 250m. Castle 3.5km by road; adults from €6. Medieval fête in town 2nd week of Aug. Inspected 2013.

BELESTA

19 H12 66720 ▦ N42°42.925' E002°36.562' SP

🛞 8; €5/night; Collected; Hedged bays 🚰 Flot Bleu Pacific; Token (FB); Flot Bleu Elec; 1 Token/4hrs elec

➡ D21. Exit Ille-sur-Têt to north following sp 'Belesta'. As enter village turn right down narrow road on 20% hill, signed. At bottom of hill turn left, signed. Service Point on right, parking past tennis court and children's play area, signed. Actual GPS: N42°42.982' E002°36.477'.

ℹ Aire adj to picnic area on outskirts of village. Drive up on D21 has some unusual rocky landscape. Inspected 2013.

VERNET LES BAINS

20 G12 66820 ▦ N42°32.567' E002°23.433' SP

🛞 20 🚰 Flot Bleu Océane; Token (FB); €2

➡ Chemin de la Laiterie. Turn off D116 at roundabout at far end of village, signed. Cross river bridge and turn left past pink hotel, sp 'Aire Camping Car'. Follow road to right of car park. Aire at end of road, signed.

ℹ Parking on two levels overlooking thermal spa town. Inspected 2013.

PUYVALADOR

21 G12 66210 SKI N42°39.076' E002°04.622' SP

🛞 20 🚰 Custom

➡ Rue des Sources. Turn off D118 onto D32g and follow signs to Puyvalador ski station. Aire on left in 'Parking 3'. Access road in poor condition.

ℹ Service Point in very poor condition. Tap missing at time of 2010 inspection. www.puyvalador.fr Updated 2017.

LES ANGLES PLA DEL MIR

22 G12 66210 ▦ N42°33.787' E002°04.008' SP

🛞 40 🚰 Customised Aire Services; Token; €3

➡ Pla del Mir ski lift station. Turn off D118 onto D32, sp 'Les Angles'. D32 is a very wide road and a scenic drive. In Les Angles turn off D32 opp large car park banning motorhomes, sp 'Parc Animaler' and 'Parking Camping Car'. Follow road up hill and Service Point is to the left of the ski lift, signed. Designated parking is to the right, signed.

ℹ Alt 1791m. Ski lift station adj; 3 ski runs finish adj to Aire. Tokens from adj animal park. May feel isolated if alone out of season. Inspected 2013.

MONT LOUIS ★

23 G12 66210 T N42°30.409' E002°07.345' SP

🛞 50; €7/4pm-10am; Collected 🚰 Custom; Under arch; Inc

➡ Parking des Remparts. Turn off N116 into car park on right-hand side of arched entrance into town (do not drive through arch into town), sp 'Parking Entrée'. Pass through barriers, not in use at time of inspection, and Aire is at rear of car park. Also possible to walk to town from N116 lay-by.

ℹ Parking adj to impressive citadel walls, numerous commerce inside citadel. Town in the foothills of the Pyrénées. Updated 2016.

SAILLAGOUSE

24 G12 66800 ▦ N42°27.467' E002°02.250' SP

🛞 5 🚰 Flot Bleu Pacific; Token; €4; Flot Bleu Elec (Not working)

➡ Lieu-Dit Village. Turn off N116, opp Hôtel de Ville, by fun statues in village centre, signed. Aire 10m on left in car park.

ℹ Town centre adj, small cheese market Wed am. There are 3 Flot Bleu elec points dotted about town, but this is the only signed parking. Inspected 2013.

THUES ENTRE VALLS

25 G12 66360 N42°31.333' E002°13.283'

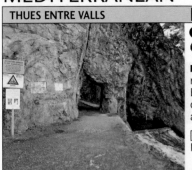

🚐 10; €8/day inc service; Pay at machine 🚰 Custom; Inside barrier

➡ Turn off N116, sp 'Gorges de la Carança'. Cross 3.5t weight restricted bridge, turn left and follow sp 'Gorges de la Carança'. Enter car park through barrier, then follow signs to large grass area on left. Go with flow by entering in morning/departing in afternoon as approach roads are narrow with few passing places.

ℹ Adj to cool gorge walk to grotto. Café in car park in season. Inspected 2013.

CASTEIL

26 G12 66820 N42°32.017' E002°23.517'

🚐 10 🚰 None; See **20** and **261**

➡ D116. Small parking area on left before village adj to D116, signed.

ℹ Pleasant woodland setting. Tap and WC up steps in car park but not accessible by motorhome due to height barrier. Inspected 2013.

Sete

ST MARSAL

28 H12 66110 N42°32.250' E002°37.400'

🚐 5; €3/night; Pay at La Poste, open 9.30-11.30am 🚰 Tap only

➡ D618. From Amélie-les-Bains-Palalda take D618 to St Marsal; this road is a shorter, easier drive than from Bouleternère. Turn right into village car park and take road to right, signed. Turn 1st left and Aire on left, signed.

ℹ Isolated village with just a village shop. Showers €1, but sign does not indicate location. Updated 2016.

AMELIE LES BAINS

29 H12 66110 N42°28.717' E002°40.433'

🚐 5; €6/night; Max 48hrs 🚰 Raclet Maxi; Token (ER); €4; No drive over drain

➡ Rue des Lledoners. Turn off D115, sp 'Camping Municipal'. Aire on right adj to campsite, signed

ℹ Next to popular campsite. Short walk to pretty spa town nestled in wooded hills. Inspected 2013.

STE MARIE LA MER

30 G12 66470 N42°43.955' E003°01.529'

🚐 120; €6/24hrs Sept-Jun; €9.50/24hrs Jul-Aug; CC/€; Inc water and WiFi 🚰 Custom; Service only €2-€4/12 mins water low-high season; 16amp CEE elec €3-€4 low-high season; Pay at bollard

➡ D81. Take D81 south from Le Barcarès. At 1st roundabout take 1st exit before the D12 St Marie la Mer turning. Aire immediately to right, signed. Enter through barrier.

ℹ Commercial Aire in large, open gravel car park adj to main route. P1 suffers road noise; P2 is more protected. Self-service laundry and supermarket adj. Town and beach 900m via cycle path. www.night4campingcar.com Inspected 2016.

LE BOULOU

31 H12 66160 N42°31.636' E002°50.229'

🚐 21; Max 24hrs 🚾 Aire Services Plastic (Not working); €2; No drive over drain; Tap in cemetery; See info

▶ Chemin du Moli Nou. Exit Boulou towards Perpignan on D900 and turn right, sp 'P. Cimetière' and signed. Take next left turn, signed. Aire in 50m by the cemetery.

ℹ️ Very popular Aire adj to stadium with football pitch. Service Point no longer working and WC locked, but still poss to empty WC. Town with numerous commerce 400m. Market Thurs/Sun am. Reinspected 2015.

ST ANDRE

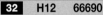

32 H12 66690 N42°33.135' E002°58.396'

🚐 6; €2.30/night; Collected; Free during day; Max 3 nights 🚾 Flot Bleu Océane; Token; €2; Flexi hose for wastewater

▶ Rue de Taxo. Exit D914 at Junction 11, sp 'St André'. Follow sp 'St André'. Turn right into Intermarché supermarket car park, signed. Drive behind supermarket and turn left, signed. Aire 100m past cemetery, signed. If approaching from other directions, do not follow GPS off main route through town.

ℹ️ Supermarket 200m. Town 150m. Reinspected 2013.

COLLIOURE

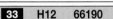

33 H12 66190 N42°31.517' E003°04.100'

🚐 40; €10/24hrs Oct-Apr; €15/24hrs May-Sept; Pay at kiosk 🚾 Custom; Inside barrier; 12 CEE elec points on lower terrace

▶ D86/Route de Madeloc. Turn off D914 at Junction 14, sp 'Collioure'. Follow road straight across roundabout, sp 'Camping'. Aire on left adj to tennis club, entry through barrier.

ℹ️ Shuttle bus to village every 30 mins May-Sept. Elec points suggest use should be 2hrs. Inspected 2013.

PORT VENDRES

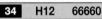

34 H12 66660 N42°31.063' E003°06.815'

🚐 40; €10/night inc service; Collected 🚾 Sani Station; Token (Provided on payment)

▶ Route de la Jetée. Turn off D914 onto D86b, sp 'Port de Commerce' and signed. Follow road to port entrance and turn right at roundabout. Aire 100m on right, signed. May need to reverse in/out.

ℹ️ Popular Aire adj to sea and harbour, no views. Beach adj, but swimming banned. Town 1.3km. Updated 2014.

ST CYPRIEN

35 H12 66750 N42°37.076' E003°02.103'

🚐 50; €4.10/12hrs or €6.10/24hrs Dec-Mar; €6.20/12hrs or €8.20/24hrs Apr-Jun/Sept-Nov; €9/12hrs or €12/24hrs Jul-Aug; CC 🚾 Flot Bleu Océane; Inside barrier; Flot Bleu Elec

▶ Rue Jean de la Fontaine. Turn off D81 at roundabout, sp 'St Cyprien-Le Port'. At roundabout turn right, sp 'Le Port'. Follow road past LIDL, then turn right. At roundabout turn left, sp 'P Le Port'. Follow road to left along marina edge and Aire on left, signed. Entry through Flot Bleu Park barrier.

ℹ️ Barriered Aire adj to and partially overlooking large pleasure boat marina. Restaurants adj, tourist commerce 900m. Unrestricted beachside parking on D81a towards Canet-en-Roussillon. Reinspected 2016.

LATOUR BAS ELNE

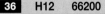

36 H12 66200 N42°35.998' E003°00.438'

🚐 40; €10/night inc service and elec; Collected; No access Sun 10am-6pm; Grass parking 🚾 Custom

▶ Parking Camping Cars Rousillon. Turn off D81 at roundabout, sp 'Latour Bas Elne' and signed. Follow road for 1.5km and Aire on left, signed.

ℹ️ Aire at motorhome dealer with workshop, some English spoken. Security gates locked at night. Updated 2016.

MEDITERRANEAN

FITOU
37 H12 11510 🏢 N42°53.559' E002°59.803'

🅿️ 10; €5/12hrs; €7/24hrs; Collected 🛎️ Flot Bleu Océane; Inside gateway; Token (FB); €2; Elec €2; 4 elec points; WC 9am-11pm

➡️ D900/D6009, at hotel. Aire adj to D900/D6009, on right as exit Fitou towards Perpignan and south of the D50/D6009 junction, signed.

ℹ️ Commercial Aire in Fitou wine region run by Hotel l'Aragon. Sandwiched between main route and railway line so can be noisy. Pleasantly old fashioned bar/restaurant adj. Local commerce 500m. Inspected 2016.

LE BARCARES - Port
38 H12 66420 ⚓ N42°48.089' E003°02.019'

🅿️ 49; €9.60/night Sept-Jun; €12/night Jul-Aug; Inc service and 16amp CEE elec; CC 🛎️ Euro Relais Junior; Inside barrier

➡️ Quai Alain Colas. From south on D83 exit at Junction 11, sp 'Port'. Follow sp 'Le Port', then turn left at roundabout. At roundabout by marina go straight on, sp 'LIDO'. Cross bridge and turn left at roundabout, signed. Drive alongside marina and Aire at end of road through PARKNIGHT barrier.

ℹ️ Aire adj to harbour with one end enjoying views of water leading to marina (Bassin de la Tourette). Free WiFi. WC, 250m, locked and only for boaters. Seaside resort with tourist commerce 700m. Motorhomes banned from all other local parking. Reinspected 2016.

LE BARCARES
39 H12 66420 ☀️ (A) N42°48.667' E003°02.067'

🅿️ **(A)** 2; 5.5m bays; 1 bay has overhang; **(B)** 3; 6m bays; **(C)** 3; 5m bays + overhang 🛎️ None; See **38**

➡️ **(A)** Exit D83 at Junction 12. At roundabout take 3rd exit, sp 'Le Lydia'. Aire at far end of parking on left adj to woods. **(B)** N42°50.067' E003°02.267': Exit D83 at Junction 14. At roundabout turn left, sp 'Cap de Front'. Follow road parallel to D83 for 400m. Designated bays on left just past bus stop. **(C)** N42°49.454' E003°01.823': Exit D83 at Junction 13. At roundabout take 1st exit, sp 'Nautica'. Aire on right overlooking lake, signed.

ℹ️ **(A)** Designated parking adj to pine woodland with cycle/walking path. **(B)** D83 adj, some road noise. Cycle track adj; beach 400m. **(C)** Designated parking overlooking lake with kite/windsurfers. 4hr parking restriction signs at **(A)** and **(B)** removed. Despite signed bays it appears town will ban motorhomes; expect change. Reinspected 2016.

(A)

(B)

LEUCATE
40 H12 11370 🏭 N42°54.817' E003°01.200'

🅿️ 100; €10.20/24hrs Nov-Mar; €10.80/24hrs Apr-May/Oct; €13.80/24hrs Jun-Sept; CC 🛎️ Flot Bleu Fontaine; Inside barrier

➡️ D327. From south exit D627, sp 'Leucate village'. Turn left onto D327, sp 'Caves'. Pass under road bridge and Aire on left, signed. Enter through Urba Flux barrier.

ℹ️ Terraced Aire overlooking lake with distant views of mountains beyond. Windsurf school and café. Pay WiFi. Popular with windsurfers. Updated 2016.

LEUCATE PLAGE
41 H12 11370 ⚓ N42°54.010' E003°03.156'

🅿️ 200; €10.20/24hrs Nov-Mar; €10.80/24hrs Apr-May/Oct; €13.80/24hrs Jun-Sept; CC 🛎️ Flot Bleu Fontaine; Inside barrier

➡️ From south on D627 turn onto D327, sp 'Leucate Plage', and then turn right, sp 'Leucate Plage' and signed. Turn right in 500m, sp 'Leucate Plage', then follow road to right, signed. Aire past campsite, on both sides of road. Enter through Urba Flux barrier.

ℹ️ 15 sea/beach view bays. Direct access to beach on left side. No shade. Updated 2015.

LA PALME
42 H12 11480 ⚓ N42°58.843' E003°01.170'

🅿️ 48; €9.60/24hrs inc WiFi; CC 🛎️ Euro Relais Junior; Inc; Inside barrier; 48 6amp CEE elec points

➡️ D709. From Port-la-Nouvelle take D709 towards Fitou. Turn left at flagpole, then immediately right, both signed. Enter through PARKNIGHT barrier.

ℹ️ Remote commercial Aire adj to Étang de La Palme; no views. Lagoon is popular with kite surfers and surrounding area has a range of walking/cycling routes. Some road noise. Seasonal tourist commerce inc bar and tourist train. Traditional French bread vending machine available, €1. Inspected 2016.

PORT LA NOUVELLE
43 H11 11210 ⚓ N43°00.817' E003°02.450'

🚐100; €4/day Apr-Jun/Sept-Nov; €9/day Jul-Aug; Pay at kiosk 8-10am/4-8pm; Apr-Nov 🕿 Flot Bleu Euro; CC; €2; Flot Bleu Fontaine

➡ Chemin des Vignes. From Sigean take D6139 to Port la Nouvelle. At the roundabout turn right onto D709, sp 'Centre Ville'. At roundabout by ALDI turn left, sp 'Centre Ville 3.5t'. After crossing railway on bridge, turn left, signed. Turn left again, sp 'Gare SNCF', and Aire on left, signed. Entrance through counter lever barrier, open when Aire open.

ℹ Large, popular, open gravel Aire adj to railway and main road, noisy at times. Can accommodate any unit configuration. Flot Bleu Fontaine is for WC emptying. Town centre 600m. Reinspected 2016.

PEYRIAC DE MER
44 H11 11440 ⚓ N43°05.551' E002°57.749'

🚐6; €5/night; CC 🕿 Custom; Adj to 1st building; Inside barrier

➡ D105. Turn off D6009 onto D105, sp 'Peyriac de Mer'. Follow road through village, signed. Exit village on D105, sp 'Bages'. Aire on left, signed. Enter through Urba Flux barrier.

ℹ Aire adj to sports facilities and basic campsite. Inland sea and beach opp, but no view. Village has local commerce and 30 mins motorhome parking is allowed. Reinspected 2016.

GRUISSAN PLAGE
45 H11 11430 ⚓ N43°05.754' E003°06.591'

🚐100; €9/noon-noon inc service; Pay at kiosk; Mar-Sept 🕿 Urba Flux; Inside barrier

➡ Avenue de la Jetée. Enter Gruissan from north on D32. Go straight over roundabout, sp 'Gruissan-Centre'. Follow road to right, sp 'Gruissan-Village' and 'Le Port'. Go straight over roundabout, past **46**, following sp 'Plage de Chalets'. Parking is 1.9km at end of road, signed. Barrier manned by guardian in adj hut.

ℹ Ideal beach holiday location adj to sandy beach. Popular area for water sports, inc kitesurfing/windsurfing. Can be noisy until 3am. Cycle path to town adj. Updated 2016.

GRUISSAN PORT
46 H11 11430 🏭 N43°06.256' E003°05.983'

🚐100; €9/noon-noon inc service; Pay at kiosk; Mar-Nov 🕿 Urba Flux; Inside barrier

➡ Quai de la Tramontane. Enter Gruissan from north on D32. Go straight over roundabout, sp 'Gruissan-Centre'. Follow road to right, sp 'Gruissan-Village' and 'Le Port'. At roundabout turn left then left again, both sp 'Aire des 4 Vents'. Follow road to end and Aire on left at marina. Entry has manned hut and manual barrier.

ℹ Adj to marina with views across water/boats. Town 800m. Updated 2016.

NARBONNE PLAGE
47 H11 11100 ⚓ N43°08.828' E003°09.249'

🚐100: €10/night; Pay at kiosk; Accessible 8am-8pm; Apr-Oct 🕿 Custom; Inside barrier; 8am-7pm

➡ Off D332. At D168/D332 roundabout south of town turn onto D332, sp 'Gruissan'. Turn left, sp 'Aire Camping Car' and 'Aqua jet'. Aire on right in 20m. Barrier at entry, opened by warden 8am-8pm.

ℹ Commercial Aire adj to vast beach which is popular with wind/kite surfers. Aqua park adj. No facilities 8pm-8am. Reinspected 2013.

ST PIERRE LA MER
48 H11 11560 🏭 N43°11.388' E003°11.805'

🚐100; €3/2hrs; €8/24hrs; Inc service; CC 🕿 Flot Bleu Océane; Inside barrier; 1 Token/4hrs elec

➡ Enter town from Narbonne on D1118. Turn left on Blvd des Embruns and follow it along the seafront. At the roundabout turn right, signed. Follow road past municipal campsite and Aire is adj to the height barriered car park, signed. Enter via Flot Bleu Park barrier.

ℹ Commercial Aire with informal feel. Sailing school adj. In sea marsh with footpaths through to beach/naturist beach. Updated 2015.

LES CABANES DE FLEURY | 49 | H11 | 11560 | | N43°12.910' E003°14.088'

🚐 50; €6.50/night; Collected; Free 9am-3pm 🚰 Flot Bleu Océane; Token; €2

➤ Ave Eric Tabarly, off D718. From Fleury follow D718, sp 'Les Cabanes de Fleury'. Follow road to right, then straight on past campsite towards marina. Aire on right past marina, signed.

ℹ️ Small river/creek marina adj, partial views. Beach adj, no views. Local commerce adj. Reinspected 2013

VINASSAN | 50 | H11 | 11110 | | N43°12.278' E003°04.451'

🚐 10; €8/24hrs inc 16amp elec; CC 🚰 Aire Services 3000; Inside barrier

➤ D31/Ave du Docteur Etienne Montestruc. Follow D31 through town towards Coursan and Aire on left, signed. Enter through Aire Services barrier.

ℹ️ Aire located in former municipal campsite under trees providing deep shade. Village with local commerce 150m. Reinspected 2016.

NARBONNE | 51 | H11 | 11100 | | N43°10.834' E003°01.419'

🚐 34; €9/24hrs inc elec; CC; Max 72hrs 🚰 Flot Bleu Euro; Inside barrier; CC; €2

➤ Parking 'La Narbonette', Ave de la Mer. To avoid town, enter Narbonne from east on D168 from Narbonne Plage and follow sp 'Centre Historique'. Aire opp Parc des Expositions, signed. Enter via Flot Bleu Park barrier.

ℹ️ Popular commercial Aire. Road noise from adj main route. Free shuttle bus to Narbonne from theatre Mon-Sat 7.40am-7.20pm. Cycle path to centre adj. 1.5km to busy lively town. Reinspected 2016.

OUVEILLAN | 52 | H11 | 11590 | | N43°17.533' E002°58.208'

🚐 5 🚰 Custom

➤ Rue de la Coopérative, off D13. As enter town from north turn left at roundabout, sp 'Cave Coopérative' and signed. Take road to left, then in 10m turn left next to orange house, signed. Access road is narrow and may be obstructed by bushes. Walk in first and check there is space.

ℹ️ Small popular Aire; parking restricted by trees. Local wine production adj. Village with local commerce 400m. Reinspected 2016.

LA SALVETAT SUR AGOUT | 53 | H11 | 34330 | | N43°36.021' E002°40.749'

🚐 20; Max 48hrs; Grass parking close to lake, hardstanding in previous lay-by 🚰 Custom; Apr-Oct

➤ Sailing school car park. Turn off D907 south of La Salvetat-sur-Agout onto D14e1, sp 'Lac de la Raviège' and 'Base Touristique des Bouldouïres'. In 2.8km turn left, sp 'Base Touristique des Bouldouïres'. Follow road past the campsite to the sailing school car park adj to lake.

ℹ️ Aire on sloping parking adj to large leisure lake/reservoir, no views. Sailing and sandy beach, swimming poss. May feel isolated out of season. Inspected 2014.

FRAISSE SUR AGOUT | 54 | H11 | 34330 | | N43°36.267' E002°47.750'

🚐 10; €7/24hrs; Collected; Grass parking 🚰 Flot Bleu Compact; 6 unmetered CEE elec points

➤ Chemin de la Salvetat á Fraisse. From west on D14 turn right just before village, sp 'Île sur l'Agout' and signed. Aire on right in 180m.

ℹ️ Pleasant riverside Aire. Riverside park includes BBQ point. TO and local commerce 300m. Aire can flood in winter. Inspected 2014.

BEDARIEUX

55 H11 34600 N43°36.644' E003°09.206'

🚐 15; Max 4 nights ⛽ Urba Flux Tall

➤ Quai de la Passerelle. From east on D908 follow sp 'Centre Ville' through a series of roundabouts. As approach town turn left, sp 'P Av. J. Moulin' and signed. Follow road to right, then turn left. Follow road straight on along river edge and the Aire is on the right, opp a college, signed.

ℹ Open gravel Aire adj to river Orb. Small town commerce 650m along shallow river. Updated 2016.

Photos: Jean & Ken Fowler

LUNAS

56 H11 34650 N43°42.351' E003°11.179'

🚐 30 ⛽ Custom; WC inside leisure lake facility

➤ D35. On right as approach Lunas from Le Bousquet d'Orb, sp 'Base de Loisirs' and signed. Approach from east is very narrow and winding with a sheer drop.

ℹ Popular Aire adj to small leisure lake, entry €4/pp. Café adj. Footpath to village with local commerce. Updated 2015.

MOUREZE

57 H11 34800 N43°37.040' E003°21.661'

🚐 15; €6/24hrs; €2 day parking; Pay at kiosk ⛽ WC only

➤ D8. From Clermont l'Hérault turn off D908 onto D8e1a, sp 'Mourèze'. Follow road for 2.1km and Aire in car park by TO, signed.

ℹ This is simply pay parking where motorhomes are allowed to stay overnight. Walks from 1-4hrs around Cirque de Mourèze, follow appropriate colour marker. Inspected 2013.

VAILHAN

58 H11 34320 N43°33.324' E003°17.930'

🚐 5; €5/night; Collected ⛽ Custom

➤ Lieu Dit l'Eglise. Approach Vailhan from Roujan. Follow D125 through the village, sp 'Fournols' and signed. Aire on left, adj to the church before the village boundary, signed.

ℹ Remote village near reservoir. Walking paths adj. Restaurant nearby. Inspected 2013.

SALASC

59 H11 34800 N43°37.068' E003°19.027'

🚐 2; Max 1 night; Grass parking, but hardstanding available ⛽ None

➤ D148. Turn off D908 onto D148, sp 'Salasc'. Follow the road to the village and turn right into parking area as enter village, sp 'P'. Two bays in the middle of the car park are assigned to motorhomers. D8 between Salasc and Mourèze has a 2.2m width restriction.

ℹ Salasc is a pretty picture postcard French village with local commerce. Walking trails. Inspected 2013.

LAC DU SALAGOU - Rives de Clermont

60 H11 34800 N43°38.811' E003°23.350'

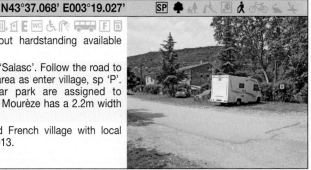

🚐 6; €7.50/night Oct-May; €8.50/night Jun/Sept; €10/night Jul-Aug; Inc elec; Pay at campsite ⛽ Custom; Token; €2; 4 16amp CEE elec points

➤ Lac du Salagou/Rives de Clermont. From Clermont l'Hérault turn off D908 onto D156e4, sp 'Lac du Salagou'. Follow sp 'Rives de Clermont'. Turn right before height barriered car park, sp 'Base de Plein Air' and signed. Service Point on right and parking beyond, signed.

ℹ Adj to café and busiest part of the lake, 150m with swimming beach. All other lake parking banned 10pm-8am. Day parking 400m east at Rives de Liausson: N43°38.609' E003°23.278'. www.grandsitesalagoumoureze.fr Updated 2016.

LAC DU SALAGOU - Village des Arts — 61 · H11 · 34800 · N43°39.253' E003°19.069'

Photos: Rod Poxon

🚐 5; €6/night inc service; Additional day parking opp 🛒 Custom; Token; €6

➡ Off D148, adj to picnic area. Turn off D148, sp 'Village des Arts'. Designated parking just past picnic area on left, signed.

ℹ Small landscaped parking area adj to picnic area; no lake views. All other lake parking banned 10pm-8am. Day parking only adj to lake at Rives d'Octon, 1.2km: N43°39.065' E003°19.484'. Inspected 2015.

LAC DU SALAGOU - Rives des Vailhes — 62 · H11 · 34700 · N43°40.268' E003°21.280'

🚐 16; €7/night low season; €9/night high season; Max 1 night 🛒 Custom; Tap, drain, WC emptying destroyed; Elec not working

➡ D148e5. On north of Lac du Salagou turn off D148/D148e4 onto D148e5, sp 'Les Vailhés'. Turn left in 600m before lakeside parking, sp 'Les Vailhés', then take 1st right. Aire on left before campsite, signed.

ℹ Partial lake views. Lake has slipway and swimming beach. Basketball hoop and table tennis table. All other lake parking banned 10pm-8am. Updated 2016.

ANIANE — 63 · I11 · 34150 · N43°41.183' E003°34.950'

🚐 12 🛒 None; See 269

➡ D32. In Aniane follow D32 towards St Jean de Foz. Turn left, sp 'Sapeurs Pompiers'. Turn left, then immediately right, and follow road to end. Aire in parking at end of road, signed. Also signed from 'P Centre Ville' parking by La Poste in town.

ℹ Large parking area suitable for all motorhomes, always likely to have space. Local commerce 200m. Reinspected 2013.

MONTAGNAC — 64 · H11 · 34530 · N43°28.517' E003°29.467'

🚐 4 🛒 Custom

➡ At D613/D5e11 junction. Approach town from Mèze on D613. Turn right onto D5e11 as the dual carriageway ends at Montagnac boundary sign, signed. Turn immediately right to Aire, signed.

ℹ Small, uncongested parking area adj to a dual carriageway. During the day you will be on your own. Some road noise, but tolerable. Reinspected 2016.

PORTIRAGNES PLAGE — 65 · H11 · 34420 · N43°16.527' E003°21.105'

🚐 30; €5/night; Pay at TO; Max 48hrs 🛒 Custom; Tap at parking behind clearway sign

➡ Ave de la Grande Maïre. Turn off D37 at roundabout, sp 'Plage OUEST' and signed. Turn right, sp 'Plage OUEST' and signed. Follow road to left; Service Point is here on right, signed: N43°16.781' E003°21.096'. For parking continue straight over roundabout. Designated parking on left, signed. If barrier locked get padlock code from TO.

ℹ Large open gravel parking area with a sandy beach 200m through car park. WC 150m. Large wetland area with paths adj, no view. Roadside parking banned. Inspected 2016.

LE CAP D'AGDE — 66 · H11 · 34300 · N43°17.148' E003°31.037'

🚐 22; €5/24hrs Nov-Mar; €10/24hrs Apr-Oct; Collected; 7m bays 🛒 Flot Bleu Euro; CC; €2

➡ Parking de la Bavière. Exit D612, sp 'Le Cap d'Agde'. At 1st roundabout turn left, then turn right at 2nd roundabout. Aire 20m on right, signed.

ℹ Aire adj to road in residential area. Sea and sandy beach 500m. Marina 650m. Updated 2016.

SERIGNAN - Les Plages
67 H11 34410 ⚓ N43°16.135' E003°19.912'

🚐 49; €9.60/night Mar-Jun/Sept-Oct; €12/night Jul-Aug; CC; Inc service and WiFi; Mid March-mid Oct 🛒 Euro Relais Junior; Inside barrier

▶ D37e11. Approach Sérignan Plage on D37e11. As enter Sérignan Plage turn right, sp 'P 450 Places'. Turn immediately right and enter through PARKNIGHT barrier. Service Point opp, across adj D37e11: N43°16.169' E003°19.881'. Enter through PARKNIGHT barrier, signed.

ℹ️ Landscaped commercial Aire at entrance of resort. Parking is open and suffers road noise from passing local traffic. Local commerce adj. Service Point across adj main route. Mediterranean Sea 500m. Inspected 2016.

MARSEILLAN PLAGE
68 I11 34340 🏢 N43°19.149' E003°32.928'

🚐 122; €4/24hrs Jan-Mar/Nov-Dec; €6/24hrs Apr-Jun/Oct; €12/24hrs Jul-Sept; CC 🛒 Urba Flux Tall; Outside barrier; CC; €2/10 mins; Male connection required

▶ Rue des Goélands. From Sète on D612 turn left at roundabout, sp 'Marseillan Plage' and signed. Go straight over next roundabout, then turn left in 50m at next roundabout, both signed. Aire on left, signed. Service Point past Urba Flux barrier entrance.

ℹ️ Popular Aire at former municipal campsite. Can take any size unit. Seaside resort and beach 1.6km. www.marseillan.com Reinspected 2016.

MEZE
69 I11 34140 ⚓ N43°26.453' E003°35.700'

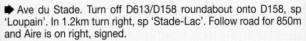

🚐 20; See info 🛒 Custom; Be careful not to drop off left side

▶ Ave du Stade. Turn off D613/D158 roundabout onto D158, sp 'Loupain'. In 1.2km turn right, sp 'Stade-Lac'. Follow road for 850m and Aire is on right, signed.

ℹ️ Aire providing roadside parking, but adj road has poor surface increasing traffic noise. At time of inspection parking in unsigned area behind poss for small units, allowing larger motorhomes to occupy roadside. Sports facilities adj. Small town commerce 2.4km. Reinspected 2016.

BALARUC LES BAINS
70 I11 34540 ⚓ (A) N43°26.739' E003°40.665'

🚐 (A) 6; (B) 6; (C) 6; All €7/night; Collected 🛒 (A) Aire Services Plastic; Token (3/3); 2 CEE elec points; Free at time of inspection

▶ Ave des Hespérides. Turn off D2 onto D2e11, sp 'Balaruc les Bains' and signed. Go straight ahead at roundabout, then follow sp 'Camping-Cars' and signed at next 2 roundabouts. In 800m turn right, signed. Aire on right, signed. Additional 6 designated bays at both (B) N43°26.734' E003°40.602' and (C) N43°26.711' E003°40.510'; see map at (A).

ℹ️ Popular designated parking adj to thermal spa. Reinspected 2016.

SETE
71 I11 34200 ⚓ N43°22.019' E003°36.962'

🚐 70; €6.66/24hrs Nov-Mar; €9.66/24hrs Apr-Jun/Sept-Oct; €11.66/24hrs Jul-Aug; Max 72hrs; 6mx3.5m bays 🛒 Aire Services 3000; Outside barrier; CC; €1

▶ N112. From Agde follow N112 beach road for 6km towards Sète. Aire on right off roundabout, signed. Enter through barrier, signed.

ℹ️ Commercial Aire in an isolated location off main road adj to railway. Large sandy beach adj, access via footpath. Reinspected 2016.

VILLENEUVE LES MAGUELONE
72 I11 34750 ⚓ N43°31.769' E003°52.092'

🚐 42; €9/night Oct-Apr; €14/night May-Sept; Inc 16amp elec; CC; Pay at barrier 🛒 Custom; 26 16amp CEE elec points; Inside barrier

▶ Rue René Bert. From Palavas les Flots approach on D185. Turn left at roundabout, sp 'Villeneuve M Centre'. Turn left again, sp 'Plage' and signed. Follow road for 400m, then turn left alongside cycle path on gravel track, sp 'Arenes' and signed. Aire straight on after Stop junction, enter through gate.

ℹ️ Commercial Aire with clearly defined bays on asphalt. Partial view of water from 2 bays. Favoured by large motorhome users as no obstacles to impede access. Updated 2015.

PALAVAS LES FLOTS 1 `73` I11 34250 N43°31.808' E003°55.471'

🛒 126; €11/4pm-4pm Oct-May; €14/4pm-4pm Jun-Sept; Inc service and elec; +€0.22pp tax; >8m +€3; Pay at reception 🛒 Custom; Inside barrier; Elec €2

➡️ Rue Frédéric Mistral. On D986 from north go straight over roundabout, sp 'Halte Camping Cars'. Take next left, sp 'Halte Camping Cars'; road turns back on itself under 3.7m bridge. GPS taken from top of road. Actual GPS: N43°31.855' E003°55.438'. Enter through barrier.

ℹ️ Large commercial Aire at pleasure boat marina, many bays have marina views. Road noise in some areas. Bike hire at reception. Updated 2016.

PALAVAS LES FLOTS 2 `74` I11 34250 N43°31.948' E003°55.630'

🛒 130+; €11.70/night; Pay guardian 🛒 Custom; 12amp elec €2

➡️ Ave de l'Abbé Brocardi. From D986 turn off at roundabout, sp 'Office de Tourisme' and signed. Cross bridge and turn off at roundabout with multi-storey car park, signed. Turn left, signed, and follow signs to Aire. Guardian will direct you to a pitch, on a Segway.

ℹ️ Large municipally run commercial Aire that resembles an airport car park. The adj multi-storey car park provides shaded parking. 24hr guardian. www.palavaslesflots.com. Updated 2015.

CARNON PLAGE `75` I11 34280 N43°33.033' E003°59.633'

🛒 18; €11.50/night Sept-Jun; €13/night Jul-Aug; Inc elec; CC 🛒 Custom; Inside barrier

➡️ From Palavas les Flots take D62e2, sp 'Carnon'. In Carnon turn onto D59, sp 'Carnon Est'. Follow road to end, then turn left, sp 'Le Grand Motte'. Turn left in 150m, sp 'Les Saladelles'. Turn right into Camping Les Saladelles. Aire to left of campsite, enter through barrier.

ℹ️ Aire outside campsite with furthest bays suffering road noise. Only 80m from sandy Mediterranean beach with snack bars and boardwalks; popular with kite surfers. Price includes use of showers and campsite facilities. Reinspected 2016.

LA GRANDE MOTTE `76` I11 34280 N43°34.033' E004°04.467'

🛒 30; €11/night Oct-Apr; €13/night May/Sept; €16/night Jun-Aug; CC; Max 72hrs 🛒 Custom; Inside barrier; Inc; Plenty of 16amp elec points

➡️ Ave de la Petite Motte. From Le Grau du Roi follow sp 'La Grande Motte' at numerous roundabouts onto D62e1. Turn left, sp 'Centre Ville' and signed. Go straight on at traffic lights, then turn 1st right at traffic lights, signed. Turn right at 2nd set of traffic lights, sp 'Petite Motte' and signed. Aire on right at end of road past campsites. Enter through barrier.

ℹ️ Popular shaded Aire in part of a campsite dedicated to motorhomes. There are showers and plenty of elec. Riding stables opp. The town is a seaside resort with the beach 1.8km. Reinspected 2016.

LE GRAU DU ROI 1 `77` I11 30240 N43°32.314' E004°08.480'

🛒 15; €4/4hrs or max €6 9am-midnight; CC/€; Pay at machine; Free midnight-9am 🛒 Aire Services 3000; €2

➡️ D979/Rue du Stade. From Aigues-Mortes take D979 to Le Grau-du-Roi. Go straight over roundabout, sp 'Centre Ville', staying on D979; 3.5t weight restricted. Turn 1st left at the bull statue, sp 'Halte Nautique'. Aire in car park on right, signed.

ℹ️ Designated parking on edge of car park. Standard car size bays, so it will be necessary to occupy several bays. Bays closest to Service Point have views of marina. Car park could be busy during events at adj bullring. Inspected 2016.

LE GRAU DU ROI 2 `78` I11 30240 N43°32.437' E004°08.011'

🛒 40; 2hrs free (must get ticket), €1.50/1st pay hr, €0.80/hr additional hrs; Pay at machine 🛒 Aire Services 3000; €2

➡️ Parking de la Plage, D62a. Enter town on D62a from La Grande Motte. Go straight over roundabout, sp 'Le Grau du Roi'. At next roundabout turn off into car park, sp 'Parking de la Plage' and signed. Aire straight on in only non-height barriered part of Parking de la Plage.

ℹ️ Popular Aire in beachside car park. Gets very busy on hot days and holidays; cars will park in camper section. Standard width bays with overhang over adj green space. Pleasant town centre 500m. Reinspected 2016.

AIGUES MORTES 1
79 | I11 | 30220 | T | N43°33.919' E004°11.811'

🚐 40; €0.50/15 mins; €15.30/24hrs; CC/€; Pay at machine
👕 Custom; Inside barrier

➡ P4, Blvd Diderot. Enter Aigues-Mortes on D979. In town follow sp 'P4' and signed around the walled town. Designated parking in P4. Enter through barrier.

ℹ Popular Aire adj to walled town on edge of Camargue. Charming town centre and pristine walls make Aigues-Mortes an established spot on the tourist trail. Walking and cycling routes follow Sète canal to Le Grau-du-Roi. Motorhomes banned from all other local parking. Inspected 2016.

AIGUES MORTES 2
80 | I11 | 30220 | 🏢 | N43°34.646' E004°11.921'

🚐 10 👕 None; See **78**; WC key avail after purchase

➡ D979, parking at Intermarché. On northern outskirts of town at roundabout junction of D62/D979/D46. On entering car park turn right and parking signed at rear of Intermarché against grass bank.

ℹ Parking to rear of supermarket adj to D62 main route, constant road noise. Aigues Mortes, walled city, 1.5km. Ideal parking/night halt if **79** full. Supermarket with LPG adj. Reinspected 2016.

LES STES MARIES DE LA MER 1
81 | I11 | 13460 | ⚓ | N43°27.326' E004°25.649'

🚐 30; €10/night <7.5m; €20/night >7.5m; Collected; Max 48hrs
👕 Custom; Water avail 8.30-11.30am/4.30-7.30pm

➡ Rue Crin Blanc, adj to D570/Ave d'Arles. At end of pony rides/ranches go across roundabout. Turn left in 20m, opp pond.

ℹ Aire in town centre with tourist commerce. Beach 850m. Pony rides in area. Gypsy Fair closes Aire for 2 weeks mid May. Updated 2016.

Photo: Keith & Sue Lawrence

LES STES MARIES DE LA MER 2
82 | I11 | 13460 | ⚓ | N43°27.222' E004°26.231'

🚐 84; €12/night; Pay at manned barrier 8.30am-5.30pm; Max 48hrs 👕 Custom; Water avail 8.30am-5.30pm

➡ Vallée des Lys, Ave Jacques-Yves Cousteau. At end of pony rides/ranches turn left at roundabout. Follow road straight over next roundabout, then turn left onto Ave Jacques-Yves Cousteau. Aire just off roundabout after campsite turning, sp 'Plage Est'.

ℹ Exposed spot adj to beach and sea, no view due to sea wall. Promenade along sea wall into town (closer than **83**). Pony rides in area. Gypsy Fair closes Aire for 2 weeks mid May. Updated 2016.

Photo: Maureen & David Abbott

Photo: Chris & Angela Irving

LES STES MARIES DE LA MER 3
83 | I11 | 13460 | ⚓ | N43°26.997' E004°24.344'

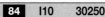

🚐 30; €10/night <7.5m; €20/night >7.5m; Collected; Max 48hrs
👕 Custom; Inside barrier

➡ D38. From town exit to west on D38. Turn left off D38, sp 'Camping Front de Mer'. Aire in large car park on left, signed. Pay guardian upon entering.

ℹ Exposed spot adj to beach and sea, no view due to sea wall. Promenade along sea wall into town. Pony rides in area. Updated 2016.

SOMMIERES
84 | I10 | 30250 | 🏛 | N43°47.183' E004°05.233'

🚐 5 👕 Euro Relais Mini; Token (ER); €3.30

➡ Outside Camping Municipal Le Garanel. Turn off D6110 onto D40, sp 'Nîmes'. At roundabout turn right, sp 'Nîmes', and follow road onto 3.5t one-way system through town. Turn right at river, sp 'Camping Municipal'. Follow road to right, then turn left, sp 'Camping Municipal'. Road opens into large parking area. Service Point in far corner to the right of the campsite entrance.

ℹ Medieval riverside town. Campsite open Apr-Sept. River 100m with stepping stone causeway. Inspected 2014.

MEDITERRANEAN

ST MATHIEU DE TREVIERS

85 | I10 | 34270 | 🏛 | N43°45.733' E003°51.634'

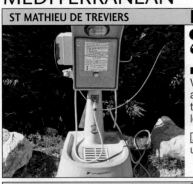

🚐 10; €5/24hrs; Collected 🛒 SOS; 9 16amp elec points

➡ Chemin de la Ville. Turn off D17 at roundabout, sp 'St Mathieu-Village de Haut' and signed. Follow road straight on for 200m, then at stop junction go straight over and turn diagonally left and drive through white gate. Aire on right through additional gate. Gate locked 10pm-8am.

ℹ Very peaceful Aire adj to sports centre in gravel car park with unmarked bays. Market Sun am. Inspected 2013.

AVEZE

86 | I10 | 30120 | 🏭 | N43°58.545' E003°35.931'

🚐 5; Oct-May; When campsite closed 🛒 Euro Relais Mini

➡ Le Pouchounet. Turn off D999 onto D48, sp 'Avèze'. Turn right before river bridge, sp 'Salle Polyvalente' and signed. Service Point on approach road, unrestricted parking adj.

ℹ Pleasant area with access to shallow river. Café and municipal facilities adj inc sports facilities and campsite. Updated 2015.

ARRE

87 | H10 | 30120 | 🏭 | N43°58.055' E003°31.262'

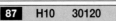

🚐 5 🛒 Euro Relais Mini; €2

➡ D999. Aire adj to D999 at eastern end of the village, 200m from Mairie, signed.

ℹ Local commerce within 500m. Walking and cycling on old railway track 100m. Inspected 2013.

SAUVE

88 | I10 | 30610 | T | N43°56.390' E003°57.160'

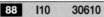

🚐 10; Max 6m 🛒 Custom

➡ D999. Turn off D999 in village into roadside car park, signed. Turn left and Aire on left adj to road wall, signed. Car park floods.

ℹ Pleasant parking under plane trees. Must park in designated space. Local commerce adj. Medieval village access via archway opp Service Point. Inspected 2013.

ST MAMERT DU GARD

89 | I10 | 30730 | 🏛 | N43°53.381' E004°11.422'

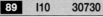

🚐 5 🛒 Custom; Reverse in

➡ Rue du Gres, off D1. Turn off D999 onto D22, sp 'St Mamert du G'. In 4km turn left onto D1, sp 'St Mamert du Gard'. Service Point 300m on left behind recycling, signed: N43°53.084' E004°11.418'. For parking, exit Service Point to left onto D1. Turn right in centre, sp 'Mairie' and 'P Gratuit'. Turn 1st left, then 1st left again, both signed. Parking on right, signed.

ℹ Peaceful parking with no shade. Village with local commerce 400m. Inspected 2013.

ANDUZE

90 | I10 | 30140 | T | N44°02.890' E003°59.110'

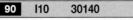

🚐 30 🛒 Aire Services 3000; €2

➡ Place de la Gare. Follow D907 through town and turn into train station car park, sp 'Gare'. For Service Point follow road to left through car park. Service Point on left: N44°03.001' E003°59.090'. For parking follow signs behind building, signed.

ℹ At train station for tourist steam train to St Jean du Gard (40 mins), runs Apr-Oct. Tourist commerce 750m. St Jean du Gard **92** a more charming town. Updated 2015.

ALES

Photo: Rod Poxon

91 | I10 | 30100 | N44°07.208' E004°04.927'

🚐 12 Depagne

➡ Ave Jules Guesde. To avoid town approach from south on N106. At roundabout turn left, sp 'Alès-Centre' and 'La Prairie'. After crossing river bridge turn right, sp 'Centre Ville' and 'La Prairie'. Follow road along river. Go straight over roundabout, sp 'La Brésis' and signed. Aire 100m on right, signed.

ℹ 3 end bays suit larger motorhomes. Adj river is more of a storm drain. Large town commerce 550m. Updated 2015.

ST JEAN DU GARD ✳

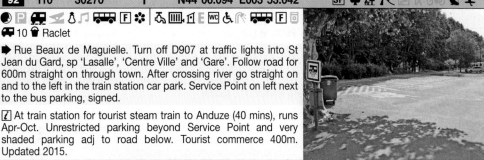

92 | I10 | 30270 | T | N44°06.094' E003°53.042'

🚐 10 Raclet

➡ Rue Beaux de Maguielle. Turn off D907 at traffic lights into St Jean du Gard, sp 'Lasalle', 'Centre Ville' and 'Gare'. Follow road for 600m straight on through town. After crossing river go straight on and to the left in the train station car park. Service Point on left next to the bus parking, signed.

ℹ At train station for tourist steam train to Anduze (40 mins), runs Apr-Oct. Unrestricted parking beyond Service Point and very shaded parking adj to road below. Tourist commerce 400m. Updated 2015.

FLORAC

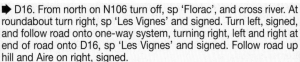

93 | I10 | 48400 | N44°19.528' E003°35.414'

🚐 20; Max 24hrs Raclet; €2

➡ D16. From north on N106 turn off, sp 'Florac', and cross river. At roundabout turn right, sp 'Les Vignes' and signed. Turn left, signed, and follow road onto one-way system, turning right, left and right at end of road onto D16, sp 'Les Vignes' and signed. Follow road up hill and Aire on right, signed.

ℹ Popular Aire located in a peaceful location on a terraced car park above the town. Parking on Service Point terrace can take all sized motorhomes. Inspected 2014.

ISPAGNAC

94 | H10 | 48320 | N44°22.256' E003°32.202'

🚐 None; See info Custom; Token (2/1); Difficult access

➡ Chemin des Plots. As enter village from north turn right off D907bis (Gorges du Tarn) at the 'Information' sign into car park, signed. Aire is through car park and on the left just beyond the WC, signed. 3.5t weight restriction on parking.

ℹ Service Point in town centre car park. Parking moved near to campsite: N44°22.313' E003°31.773'. On start/end Gorges du Tarn, a must see (subject to height restrictions). Inspected 2014.

LA CANOURGUE

95 | H10 | 48500 | N44°25.993' E003°12.705'

🚐 25; Max 24hrs Custom

➡ D998. Exit A75 at Junction 40 and follow sp 'Banassac' and 'La Canourgue' onto D998. Follow road into La Canourgue and Aire 500m on right through gateway, signed.

ℹ Very convenient Aire to A75 with plenty of parking. Supermarket 300m. Local commerce adj. Inspected 2014.

ST GERMAIN DU TEIL

96 | H10 | 48340 | N44°28.746' E003°10.311'

🚐 10 Custom

➡ D52. Exit A75 at Junction 40 and follow sp 'St Germain du Teil' onto D809 then D52. Follow D52 to village then turn right in front of 8 à Huit, sp 'Gendarmerie'. Aire in car park behind 8 à Huit.

ℹ Alt 800m. Aire in car park between commerce and community hall, always likely to have space. Pleasant rural community with local commerce adj. Cross country skiing nearby in winter. Inspected 2014.

LE MONASTIER
97 H10 48100 N44°30.534' E003°15.104'

📦 4 🛒 Raclet

➤ N809, at the train station. From A75 turn off at Junction 39, sp 'Le Monastier', and follow road down hill. At roundabout turn left onto D809. Aire is 150m on right at train station, signed.

ℹ️ Landscaped Aire located between main road and train station. Builder's yard adj. Likely to have space. Reinspected 2014.

MARVEJOLS
98 H9 48100 T N44°33.244' E003°17.216'

📦 30 🛒 Custom

➤ Lotissement Pre de Suzon. Enter Marvejols from south on D809. At city wall gatehouse turn left. Follow road and when it bends to the right, go straight on. Service Point adj to WC, signed, car park to left has 115 spaces.

ℹ️ Peaceful residential area; marked with car bays, 5 bays with poss overhang. Medieval walled city 500m, laundry in gatehouse. Wolf park 8.6km north in Ste Lucie, entry €7.80pp. www.loupsdugevaudan.com Inspected 2014.

MENDE
99 H10 48000 N44°31.248' E003°29.724'

📦 25; 9 riverside; Max 96hrs 🛒 Aire Services 3000; €2

➤ Rue du Faubourg Montbel. Follow N88 into town from west. At D42/N88 roundabout turn left, sp 'Base de Canoë-Kayak' and signed. Follow road along river and Aire in car park just after river bridge, signed. Service Point near exit, signed, and parking in far corner, signed.

ℹ️ Aire located adj to river weir and old bridge. Large town adj. On transitory route to Gorges du Tarn and Mediterranean coast. Locals park in spare bays during day when adj car park full. Inspected 2014.

ST CHELY D'APCHER
100 H9 48200 N44°48.050' E003°16.473'

📦 2 🛒 Euro Relais Junior; Token (ER)

➤ Avenue de la Gare, adj to D809. Turn off D809/Blvd Guerin d'Apcher into car park adj to roundabout, signed. Service Point on right.

ℹ️ Small, busy town centre car park. Tokens from TO, 200m. Supermarket 400m. Updated 2011.

Photos: Keith & Sue Lawrence

LE MALZIEU VILLE
101 H9 48140 N44°51.302' E003°20.003'

📦 5 🛒 Custom

➤ Place du Foirail. From D989 follow signs into Rue du Barry. At end of road turn left and the Aire is on right.

ℹ️ Pleasant spot on edge of pretty, medieval walled town adj to river. Medieval festival in May/June. Updated 2014.

Photos: Keith & Sue Lawrence

POMEYROLS
102 I9 48300 N44°46.113' E003°49.861'

📦 3 🛒 None

➤ Lou Pouon. From Langogne head north on D26. After crossing dam turn right, sp 'Pomeyrols'. Follow road uphill 2.9km to Pomeyrols. At Pomeyrols turn 1st right, sp 'P 50m'. Parking in 50m, not signed.

ℹ️ Alt 1100m. Pleasant parking in small rural hamlet parking area. An ideal place to get away from it all. Inspected 2016.

LANGOGNE PLAGE
103 | I9 | 48300 | N44°43.518' E003°50.307'

🚐 5; Max 8m 🔑 None; See **105**

➡ Route de la Tuilerie. On N88 following sp 'Mende', turn onto D26, sp 'Auroux'. Follow road and turn left, sp 'Camping Hotel'. Turn left, sp 'l'Oasis', then immediately right into parking, signed.

ℹ Alt 953m. Popular, landscaped lakeside parking before height barriered car park, always full in season. Be careful of ditch on bankside parking. Tourist commerce 100m down towards lakeside. Inspected 2016.

LANGOGNE 1
104 | I9 | 48300 | N44°44.177' E003°50.092'

🚐 40; €9.10/night Nov-Feb; €10.30/night Mar-Oct; Inc service and elec; CC 🔑 Euro Relais Junior; Inside barrier; 17 6-16amp CEE elec points; WC and shower at Base Nautique, 20m

➡ Plan d'Eau de Naussac, off D26. Turn off N88 onto D26, sp 'Lac de Naussac'. Follow sp 'Lac de Naussac' along D26, then turn left, sp 'Base Nautique' and signed. In 20m turn right and enter through PARKNIGHT barrier.

ℹ Pleasant, popular terraced Aire adj to and overlooking lake, some views obscured by trees. Shaded and open mostly grass parking. Tourist commerce and sailing school adj. Reinspected 2016.

LANGOGNE 2
105 | I9 | 48300 | N44°43.368' E003°51.250'

🚐 7; Also see **106** 🔑 Euro Relais Junior; Token (ER); €3; Water tap outside adj blue building

➡ Chemin de la Côte. From south on D906 drive past turning to **106** (A) on right, then turn left, sp 'P Gratuit'. Follow road to large parking area by sports ground.

ℹ Alt 908m. Open Aire on edge of town adj to sports ground. Tokens from TO. Town commerce 500m. Inspected 2016.

LANGOGNE 3
106 | I9 | 48300 | (A) N44°43.337' E003°51.453'

🚐 (A) 3; (B) 3 🔑 None; See **105**

➡ (A) Foirail: From south on D906 turn right, sp 'Marché aux Bestiaux'. In 10m turn left and follow road to very large parking area. (B) N44°43.966' E003°51.407' Gare: Follow N88 through town sp 'Le Puy'. Turn left, sp 'Gare'. Parking adj to train station with level bays at end of road.

ℹ Alt 939m. (A) Large open residential space that can accommodate any unit configuration. (B) Adj to train station, parking is limited and used by patrons of local bars. Inspected 2016.

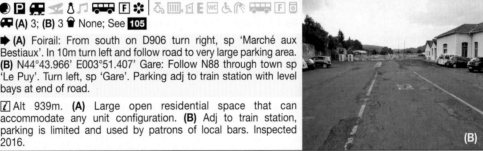
(A) (B)

CHEYLARD L'EVEQUE - Sagnerouse
107 | I9 | 48300 | (A) N44°40.655' E003°48.298'

🚐 (A) 2; (B) 2 🔑 (A) Tap around corner; (B) None

➡ (A) Sagnerouse. Turn off N88, sp 'Sagnerouse Cheylard l'Evèque'. Follow road for 1.3km. Designated parking in unkempt area adj to farm. (B) N44°38.825' E003°48.202': From (A) follow lane straight on for 1.3km, sp 'Cheylard l'Evèque', then join D71. Follow D71 for 1.5km into village. Parking in village centre adj to boules court. Neither signed.

ℹ Alt 1148m. 2 parking places allotted in 2 unsuitable places. One feels like a farmer's yard whilst the other has very limited parking. Inspected 2016.

(A) (B)

LES MAGES
108 | I10 | 30960 | N44°14.082' E004°10.184'

🚐 10 🔑 Custom

➡ Off D904. Turn off D904 north of Les Mages, sp 'Les Mages'. Aire 220m on left.

ℹ Aire in roadside lay-by with bus stop. Small town commerce 750m. Inspected 2014.

FONS SUR LUSSAN
109 | I10 | 30580 | N44°11.135' E004°19.912'

🚐5 Urba Flux Small; Token

➡ D187. From Lussan take D187, sp 'Fons s Lussan'. As approach village turn right opp bus stop into community/sports facility. Follow gravel road and Aire on far side of basketball court.

ℹ Peaceful rural Aire on edge of small village with local commerce. Bus to Lussan, a walled town, adj. Concluses of Lussan offers lovely walking and scenery. Inspected 2014.

MEJANNES LE CLAP
110 | I10 | 30430 | N44°13.553' E004°21.042'

🚐20; Max 72hrs Custom

➡ D167. Aire on left as exit village on D167, sp 'St Andre'. Turn left into large car park by TO and Aire in far corner, signed.

ℹ Aire in large car park adj to TO. Numerous signed walks through the adj 3000 hectares of scrub forest. Ideal stop for outdoor enthusiasts. Inspected 2014.

BARJAC
111 | I10 | 30430 | N44°18.347' E004°20.634'

🚐10 Aire Services Plastic; Token (3/3); €3; 1 CEE elec point on WC wall

➡ D901. Enter town from south on D979. At roundabout turn right onto D901, sp 'Bagnols s/c'. Turn left in 50m. Service Point on left against building, parking down slope past Service Point.

ℹ Adj to busy main road. Restaurant adj. WC and water fountain adj. Town centre 300m uphill. Reinspected 2014.

ST LAURENT DE CARNOLS
112 | I10 | 30200 | N44°12.612' E004°31.853'

🚐4; Max 48hrs; Need to reverse out Urba Flux Tall; Token; €2

➡ D166. Turn off D980 onto D166, sp 'St Laurent de Carnols' and signed. Aire 700m on right, signed.

ℹ Landscaped Aire in Côtes du Rhône wine area. Adj to wine seller. Rhône and Ardèche rivers nearby. Reinspected 2014.

ST ALEXANDRE
113 | I10 | 30130 | N44°13.648' E004°37.369'

🚐3 Custom

➡ Route des Remparts. Turn off N86 and follow sp 'St Alexandre' onto D311. Follow D311 to St Alexandre, drive past cemetery and turn left into car park adj to cemetery. Aire at far end of car park, signed.

ℹ Views over vines and hills from Aire. Local commerce in village. France Passion site signed on other side of cemetery. Inspected 2013.

LA ROQUE SUR CEZE
114 | I10 | 30200 | T | N44°11.754' E004°31.359'

🚐25; €9.60/24hrs Sept-May; €12/24hrs Jun-Aug; +€0.40 tax; CC
24 6amp elec points

➡ D166. North of Bagnols-sur-Cèze on N86 turn onto D980 at roundabout, sp 'Barjac'. Follow road for 8.4km, then turn left onto D166, sp 'La Roque s/ Cèze'; 3.5t weight and 2.1m width restricted. Follow road for 1.2km to car park. New PARKNIGHT Aire; barrier being constructed at time of inspection. Motorhomes banned from village, do not approach any other way.

ℹ Peaceful mud/grass parking under deciduous trees in car park close to riverside. Restaurant 150m. Beau Village with ruined castle and cobbled streets 700m across river. Cascades du Sautadet 850m south along river. Inspected 2016.

CHUSCLAN

115 J10 30200 N44°08.733' E004°40.644'

🚐6; Poss overflow parking for 20+ 🚽 Custom

▶ D138. From N580 turn onto D138 at roundabout, sp 'Chusclan'. Turn right to stay on D138, sp 'Chusclan'. Follow road for 1.7km and Aire on left opp Côtes du Rhône producer, signed.

ℹ️ Popular private Aire in large, level car park with 6 landscaped bays at Côtes du Rhône seller; open daily 9am-noon/2-6.30pm Sept-Apr, 9am-12.30pm/2.30-6.45pm May-Aug, 9am-1pm Sun all year. Tasting at 7pm. Poss to overflow on other side of car park. Views and signed walks across vines. Reinspected 2016.

BAGNOLS SUR CEZE

116 J10 30200 N44°10.102' E004°37.178'

🚐6; Max 24hrs 🚽 Flot Bleu Fontaine

▶ Rue du Moulinet. Enter town from north on N86. Cross river, then at the roundabout turn left, sp 'Avignon' and signed. Turn right in 100m, signed, then immediately right again, signed. Follow road for 100m to Aire on right, signed.

ℹ️ Level Aire that can take any unit configuration. Adj to noisy main road, but it is an acceptable stop close to town. Commerce 400m. Pleasant open park along riverside hosts 2 blues and reggae summer festivals. Reinspected 2016.

LAUDUN L'ARDOISE 1

117 J10 30290 N44°06.476' E004°39.327'

🚐3 🚽 Customised Flot Bleu; No drive over drain

▶ Place du 19 Mars 1962. From D6086 turn onto D9 at roundabout, sp 'L'Ardoise'. After 3.5km turn left onto D9ex, sp 'Laudun'. Follow road straight over roundabout. Turn left, follow road uphill and turn left again, both sp 'Camp de César'. Aire in car park on right, signed.

ℹ️ 350m downhill to pretty town. Côtes du Rhône producing area. Space likely. Reinspected 2013.

LAUDUN L'ARDOISE 2

118 J10 30290 N44°06.228' E004°39.829'

🚐10; Max 24hrs 🚽 Custom

▶ Vignerons de Laudun, D121. Exit village on D121, sp 'Roquemaure' and 'Cave de Laudun' on wall. Aire 200m on left on the far side of Vignerons de Laudun, signed. Parking past Service Point under trees.

ℹ️ Pleasant grass/gravel parking under trees at wine producer. Will fill your bottles with wine (price/litre or kg). Worth the experience, open 9am-noon/2-6.30pm. Inspected 2013.

L'ARDOISE

119 J10 30290 N44°05.717' E004°42.083'

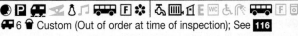

🚐6 🚽 Custom (Out of order at time of inspection); See **116**

▶ Place de la Resistance, off N580. Turn off N580 by La Poste, signed. Follow road through square past Mairie and La Poste. Service Point adj to tennis court, signed.

ℹ️ Conveniently located in a large municipal car park that can accommodate any unit configuration. Sandwiched between N580 and train track, buildings reduce road noise. La Poste and police station adj. Reinspected 2016.

REMOULINS

120 I10 30210 N43°56.258' E004°33.321'

🚐Tolerated; See info 🚽 Flot Bleu Euro; CC; €5

▶ D981. Turn off at roundabout with D986l and D6086, signed. Service Point on D981. Free unrestricted parking across bridge on right: N43°56.287' E004°33.521' or pay day parking at Pont du Gard aqueduct: N43°56.961' E004°32.586'.

ℹ️ Service Point only, but motorhomes tolerated in unrestricted parking adj to river and canoe hire. Poss to canoe 3.4km up river to aqueduct. All day parking and entry to Pont du Gard site for up to 5 people, €18. www.pontdugard.fr Updated 2016.

MEDITERRANEAN

COMPS
121 J10 30300 N43°51.257' E004°36.488'

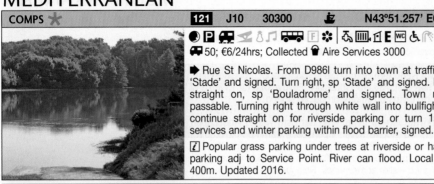

🚐 50; €6/24hrs; Collected 🚽 Aire Services 3000

▶ Rue St Nicolas. From D986l turn into town at traffic lights, sp 'Stade' and signed. Turn right, sp 'Stade' and signed. Follow road straight on, sp 'Bouladrome' and signed. Town narrow but passable. Turning right through white wall into bullfighting arena, continue straight on for riverside parking or turn 1st right for services and winter parking within flood barrier, signed.

ℹ️ Popular grass parking under trees at riverside or hardstanding parking adj to Service Point. River can flood. Local commerce 400m. Updated 2016.

VALLABREGUES
122 J10 30300 N43°51.464' E004°37.586'

🚐 6 🚽 Euro Relais Junior, Token (ER); €2

▶ D183a/Route d'Aramon. Exit Vallabrègues to north on D183a, sp 'Avignon'. Aire is 300m on left, signed. Service Point in entrance, parking beyond.

ℹ️ Landscaped Aire with plenty of space adj to road. River Gard nearby, but no views. Very basic crazy golf and picnic area adj. Inspected 2013.

BARBENTANE
123 J10 13570 N43°54.202' E004°44.481'

🚐 20; €5/night; CC; Pay at Service Point 🚽 Urba Flux Tall; CC

▶ Turn off D35 near bull ring, sp 'Arenes Stade' and signed. Aire is 300m on right, signed.

ℹ️ Aire located in gravel car park at rear of sports facility adj to municipal storage area. Large car park adj to Abbaye St Michel de Frigolet on D81: N43°51.602' E004°43.707'. Inspected 2014.

Abbaye St Michel de Frigolet

BEAUCAIRE
124 J10 30300 N43°48.371' E004°38.250'

🚐 9; Subject to Rhône flooding 🚽 Euro Relais Junior Tall; Token (ER)

▶ Quai de la Paix Nord. From Redessan follow D999 into town. In town turn right at roundabout onto D986l, sp 'Arles' and 'Centre Historic'. Follow D986l aross river bridge and turn 1st right, signed. Aire 150m on right, signed.

ℹ️ Small Aire adj to river marina. Large motorhomes subject to space. Unrestricted car park at Château de Tarascon: N43°48.338' E004°39.297'. Inspected 2014.

Château de Tarascon

AVIGNON
125 J10 84000 N43°57.340' E004°47.939'

🚐 25; €11/24hrs Sept-Apr; €14/24hrs May-Jun; €18/24hrs Jul-Aug; CC; Max 48hrs 🚽 Flot Bleu Océane; Inside barrier; Token; €2.50

▶ Chemin de la Barthelasse. Approach from north on D6580 following sp 'Avignon'. After passing under railway bridge, turn right, then left, sp 'Aramon'. Turn left, sp 'Nimes'. Follow river 800m, then turn left onto D900, sp 'Avignon'. Cross river bridge, then turn 1st right, sp 'P&R'. Turn 1st right, signed, then 2nd right, sp 'Camping Bagatelle 400m'. Aire immediately on left through Flot Bleu Park barrier.

ℹ️ Commercial Aire run by Camping du Pont Avignon. Grass parking separated from river Rhône by road. Adj P&R is height barriered, but has buses to historic town - a UNESCO World Heritage site. Inspected 2016.

BELLEGARDE
126 I10 30127 N43°44.657' E004°31.135'

🚐 20; Max 48hrs 🚽 Euro Relais Maxi; Token (ER); €2

▶ Port de Bellegarde. Approach from south on D6113. At roundabout turn left, then immediately right into Ave Eric Tabarly, both sp 'Port de Plaisance' and signed. Follow road straight on over bridge then turn left in 150m at bottom of hill onto gravel track, signed. Follow road to end.

ℹ️ Parking overlooking pleasure boats just off main road. All other riverside parking is restricted. Small town with local commerce 1.5km. Updated 2016.

ARLES

127 J11 13200 N43°41.026' E004°37.821'

🚐 6; Do not park in bus bays 👤 None; See **126**

➡ Rue Jean Gorodiche. Exit N113 at Junction 7, sp 'Arles-Z.I. Port'. Turn left at roundabout, sp 'Arles-Centre'. After 1.7km turn right at traffic lights by city wall, sp 'Gare Ferroviaire'. After 700m go straight over roundabout into car park, signed. Follow road to river and turn right. Parking 100m along river at lion statues, signed.

ℹ Oversubscribed Aire. Service Point removed, expect change. Beautiful historic town with Roman amphitheatre, historic monuments and commerce 400m. Reinspected 2016.

FONTVIEILLE

128 J11 13900 N43°43.174' E004°42.703'

🚐 30; €6.50/24hrs inc service; CC 👤 Urba Flux Tall; Inside barrier

➡ P Moulin de Daudet. In Fontvieille centre turn off D17 onto D33, sp 'Moules', 'Moulin de Daudet' and signed. Follow road for 750m then turn left, sp 'Moulin de Daudet' and signed. Aire on right through Urba Flux barrier.

ℹ Very pleasant Aire in former quarry with a very Mediterranean feel. Steps to Moulin de Daudet. Château 1km. Town centre with tourist commerce 750m. Updated 2016.

ST MARTIN DE CRAU

129 J11 13310 N43°38.309' E004°48.823'

🚐 3; Max 24hrs 👤 Urba Flux Tall

➡ N1453. Enter from east on D113. At roundabout follow sp 'St Martin de Crau'. Go straight over next roundabout. At traffic lights turn right, sp 'Mouries', then immediately left opp Gendarmerie. Aire in large car park adj to toilets, signed.

ℹ Despite being a large car park, only 3 bays have been allocated to motorhomes. Town centre, 250m, has 3.5t weight restriction. Library opp. Reinspected 2016.

SALIN DE GIRAUD

130 J11 13129 N43°24.739' E004°43.851'

🚐 20 👤 Custom WC disposal; Flot Bleu Elec/Water; Token (FB)

➡ Rue de la Bouvine. From Arles follow D36. 400m after traffic lights turn right, sp 'Centre Ville' and signed. Turn left at Medi@site and then right just before fire station, signed.

ℹ Aire on designated gravel car park tucked away from town. Local commerce 500m. Local rice growing area. Chain ferry (takes all vehicles) across Rhône, €5. Reinspected 2014.

PORT ST LOUIS DU RHONE

131 J11 13230 N43°23.062' E004°49.155'

🚐 70; €6.25/24hrs; CC; Pay at barrier 👤 Urba Flux; Inside barrier

➡ Avenue de la 1ère D.F.L. From north follow D35 through town on main road, signed. At marina follow road to right then take 2nd left. Cross lift bridge and go straight over roundabout, signed. Aire 800m on left, signed. Enter through Urba Flux bollard.

ℹ Aire located in an exposed riverside location in the desolate old dock area. 4 riverside bays. 1km to marina, 1.5km to town. May feel isolated if alone. Inspected 2014.

ISTRES

132 J11 13800 N43°30.930' E004°59.564'

🚐 12; €3.10/2hrs; €8.20/24hrs; Inc service; CC; Pay at machine; Max 48hrs 👤 Custom; Seasonal WC

➡ Chemin du Castellan. Follow D16, 3.5t weight and 3.8m height restricted lakeside road, from St Chamas. Follow road for 800m, then turn right at roundabout, sp 'Centre Ville'. Turn right, sp 'Centre de Secours', then right again at end of road, sp 'P Castellan'. Follow road to Aire on left. Enter through pop-up bollard.

ℹ Landscaped commercial Aire adj to Ètang de l'Olivier; partial views. Town centre 700m. Inspected 2016.

MEDITERRANEAN

ST CHAMAS

133 | J11 | 13250 | N43°32.782' E005°01.955'

🚐8; See info 🛒 Euro Relais Box; Token (ER); Seasonal WC

➤ Ave Marx Dormoy. Turn off D10 at roundabout, sp 'Saint Chamas - Centre'. Turn left before LIDL, sp 'Ecole de Voile'. Follow road, then turn right at roundabout, sp 'Centre Ville'. Follow road for 450m and Aire on left, sp 'Parking' and signed.

ℹ Popular lakeside Aire with 8 landscaped bays, but room for 8 more motorhomes. Official bays have views across car park to lake and small beach with adj port. Small town commerce 400m. Inspected 2016.

CARRO

134 | J11 | 13500 | N43°19.758' E005°02.416'

🚐60; €8/24hrs Oct-May; €10/24hrs Jun-Sept; €12/24hrs Jul-Aug; CC; Pay at barrier 🛒 Depagne; Inside barrier

➤ Quai Jean Vérandy. Turn off D49b into Carro and follow main route through town to marina. Follow road around marina and Aire on right. Enter through Urba Flux barrier.

ℹ Aire at end of harbour; 40 bays have views to the sea on one side or the marina on the other. Exposed spot popular with windsurfers. Local commerce 100m. Updated 2015.

SAUSSET LES PINS

135 | J11 | 13960 | N43°20.294' E005°06.513'

🚐16; Max 72hrs 🛒 Urba Flux Tall; €2; No drive over drain

➤ Stade Michel Hidalgo. Enter Sausset les Pins from north on D5. At roundabout turn left, sp 'Stade M Hidalgo'. The Aire is 450m on the left, sp 'Stade M Hidalgo' and signed.

ℹ Very sloping Aire in a small space shared with HGV parking. Harbour 1km downhill. Reinspected 2014.

CARRY LE ROUET

136 | J10 | 13620 | N43°20.300' E005°09.534'

🚐4; Max 48hrs; 10m bays 🛒 None; Tap by sign (Not working)

➤ D5c. Turn off A55 at Junction 8 onto D9, sp 'Châteauneuf les Martigues'. Exit D9 onto D5c, sp 'Carry le R'. After 350m pass Carry le Rouet boundary sign and turn right, sp 'P Gendarmerie'. Designated parking immediately on right, signed.

ℹ Aire with 4 designated bays in car park/roadside lay-by adj to gendarmerie. The 4 spaces are close to the road and back onto a railway track; other parking avail inc coach/HGV bays. Town centre 2.5km. Inspected 2016.

PELISSANNE

137 | J11 | 13330 | N43°37.699' E005°09.225'

🚐22 🛒 Custom

➤ Chemin de la Prouvenque. Turn off D572 at roundabout onto D17, sp 'Prouvenque' and signed. Turn left, signed, and Aire on right, signed.

ℹ Popular Aire providing designated parking in large unrestricted car park adj to football pitch and skate park. Small town commerce 300m; market Sun am. Reinspected 2016.

PUYVERT

138 | J10 | 84160 | N43°44.828' E005°20.247'

🚐4; Max 72hrs 🛒 Aire Services 3000; €2

➤ D973. From Lauris follow D973, sp 'Puyvert'. Turn off D973 at roundabout, sp 'Centre Commercial' and signed. Turn left into Super U car park and go straight over roundabout, signed. Aire on right behind car wash adj to laundry.

ℹ Supermarket adj. Parking adj to self-service laundry, car wash and garage backing onto recycling, all of which can be noisy. Reinspected 2016.

SENAS

`139` J10 13560 🏭 N43°44.644' E005°04.853'

🚐 10 🚰 Euro Relais Junior; Token (ER)

▶ Ave des Jardins. Turn off D7n at roundabout, sp 'La Capellette', 'Centre de Secours' and signed. Follow road and the Aire is on left alongside school, signed.

ℹ Outside school, best avoided during school hours. Village 400m. Reinspected 2014.

GORDES 1

`140` J10 84220 T N43°54.961' E005°11.857'

🚐 30; €8/24hrs; Collected 🚰 Aire Services Plastic; Inside; €3; Speak to attendant for access

▶ Off D15, approx 2km from D15/D2 junction. Aire is at far end of car park, sp 'Bus Parking'. Approaching from other directions requires navigating narrow village roads.

ℹ Aire in large car park 600m from Gordes, a stunning Beau Village clinging to the side of a cliff. Best viewed from viewpoint on D15. Inspected 2014.

GORDES 2

`141` J10 84220 🛎 N43°54.067' E005°11.583'

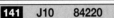

🚐 50 🚰 None; See `140`

▶ D2. From D900 turn onto D2 at Coustellet, sp 'Gordes' from west and 'Musée de la Lavande' from east. Aire on left after 5.6km, just before Village des Bories, signed.

ℹ Large gravel car park near Village des Bories, a pleasant undulating 1.5km walk on lanes, entrance €6. Gordes 2km uphill on main road. Inspected 2014.

ROUSSILLON

`142` J10 84220 T N43°53.782' E005°17.760'

🚐 10; €2/8am-10pm; €5/10pm-8am; CC; Pay at machine; Max 48hrs 🚰 WC and water tap in bus car park opp

▶ D149. Turn off D4 onto D104, sp 'Roussillon'. Follow road to village and at roundabout turn left onto D149, signed. Designated car park immediately on left, enter through barrier.

ℹ Designated parking outside Beau Village. Motorhomes banned from village centre. Tourist commerce in centre 800m. Ochre dye museum on D104. Inspected 2014.

FONTAINE DE VAUCLUSE ⭐

`143` J10 84800 ⚓ N43°55.218' E005°07.453'

🚐 27; €9.60/24hrs Nov-Mar; €12/24hrs Apr-Oct; Inc service; CC 🚰 Euro Relais Junior; Inside barrier; 2 unmetered CEE elec points

▶ D24. Follow D25 through town. Pass car parks and cross river. Aire 500m on right. Enter through PARKNIGHT barrier. Alternatively turn off D25 before town onto D57, sp 'Camping'. Turn left onto D24, sp 'Camping'; this route is sometimes temporarily no entry.

ℹ Commercial Aire 900m from village with pretty weir; popular at weekends. Canoe hire in season. Mysterious source of river Sorgue (water highest in spring). The site of Petrarch's house is now a museum, open Apr-Oct; entry from €1.50pp. Inspected 2014.

L'ISLE SUR LA SORGUE

`144` J10 84800 🏢 N43°55.059' E005°02.841'

🚐 30 🚰 WC outside train station

▶ Gare SNCF. Approach on D901 from Avignon as other roads have 3.1m height restrictions. Turn off D901 at roundabout, sp 'Gare SNCF'. At next roundabout turn right. Parking in large car park adj to train track. Access diff Sunday due to market in town.

ℹ Large car park adj to train station. Town has numerous antique shops and halls and a market/brocante every Sun which is very popular. Arrive Sat and do not expect to depart until Mon. Poss to park at: N43°55.463' E005°03.168', 450m from town. Updated 2016.

MEDITERRANEAN

BEDARRIDES

| 145 | J10 | 84370 | 🏛 | N44°02.347' E004°54.191' |

🚐 4; Max 72hrs; Max 9m 🛒 Aire Services Inox; Token (3/3); No drive over drain or WC point

➡ Chemin des Sences. From town centre turn left at roundabout before old river bridge, signed. Aire 200m on right, signed.

ℹ Designated parking in a peaceful location adj to scent garden which leads to river. Small town commerce 350m. Châteauneuf du Pape wine village nearby: N44°03.357' E004°49.910'. Inspected 2014.

CARPENTRAS

| 146 | J10 | 84200 | 🏢 | N44°02.653' E005°03.284' |

🚐 10 🛒 Aire Services 3000

➡ Ave Pierre de Coubertin, adj to Camping Lou Comtadou. Heading towards St Didier on D4 turn right at Y-junction before roundabout, sp 'Complexe Sportif' and 'Parking'. After 850m turn left through outer gate of municipal campsite, sp 'P de Coubertin'. Aire on right, signed.

ℹ Aire adj to municipal facilities and campsite. Bus stop adj. Town with numerous commerce 1.5km. Reinspected 2013.

SARRIANS

| 147 | J10 | 84260 | 🏕 | N44°04.776' E004°58.671' |

🚐 10; €3/night; Collected 🛒 Euro Relais Junior; Token (3/1); €2

➡ Off D221, at Camping de la Ste Croix. Turn off D950 at Intermarché roundabout at southern edge of town, sp 'Camping Municipal' and signed. Turn right into campsite and drive past entrance into parking area, signed.

ℹ Aire adj to campsite, BMX bike track and tennis courts. LIDL 350m. Town commerce 800m. Reinspected 2013.

GIGONDAS

| 148 | J10 | 84190 | 🏭 | N44°09.808' E005°00.179' |

🚐 3; Max 48hrs 🛒 Flot Bleu Océane; Token; Tap at parking (Turned off); Do not use elec in parking area

➡ Chemin de la Limade. Turn off D977 onto D7, sp 'Sablet'. At roundabout go straight on, then turn left onto D80, both sp 'Gigondas'. Turn right, sp 'La Poste' and 'Tennis'. Service Point by tennis court 150m on right, signed: N44°09.927' E005°00.111'. For parking continue around bend uphill. Turn 2nd right and follow road behind La Poste, both signed. Designated parking on right, signed.

ℹ Designated parking with limited shade. 100m from charming village with many local wine producers open to public. Do not use elec in parking area. Poss to park adj to Service Point. Inspected 2016.

Service Point

VAISON LA ROMAINE

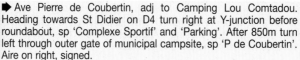

| 149 | J10 | 84110 | T | N44°14.786' E005°04.445' |

🚐 30; €7/24hrs; +€0.55pp; Collected 🛒 Custom

➡ Avenue André Coudray. Turn off D975, main route through, at roundabout opp amphitheatre into Avenue André Coudray, signed. At T-junction at end of road turn left and Aire is 150m on left, signed. Motorhomes banned from all other local parking.

ℹ Popular open Aire near medieval village. Voie Verte cycle route nearby. Town commerce 1km. Motorised tourist train in summer from centre of village. Reinspected 2016.

MALAUCENE

| 150 | J10 | 84340 | 🏛 | N44°10.652' E005°07.792' |

🚐 20; €3/day; Collected 🛒 Custom

➡ Ave Charles De Gaulle, off D938. Turn left off D938 between plane trees as enter town, signed. Follow road for 200m to Aire at rear of Gendarmerie near sports facilities, signed.

ℹ Large open Aire. Motorhomes banned from all other local parking. Town commerce 300m; market Wed. Inspected 2013.

MALEMORT DU COMTAT

151 J10 84570 N44°01.311' E005°09.425'

Info/photo: Chris & Shelagh Partington

🚐 10 🕳 Custom

➡ D5. Aire on right as enter town on D5 from St Didier en Vaucluse, sp 'Salle des Fêtes' and signed.

ℹ Aire outside the village hall. Peaceful, apart from people visiting the recycling bins. Some shade. Nice village with local commerce 160m. Visited 2015.

BEDOIN

152 J10 84410 N44°07.483' E005°10.333'

🚐 40; €3/night; Collected; Max 72hrs 🕳 Aire Services 3000; €2

➡ Chemin de Bédoin á Malaucène. From south on D974 turn left at roundabout onto D138, sp 'P Municipal Gratuit'. Follow road left, then turn right, sp 'Camping Municipal' and signed. Follow road to left and Service Point on right. Parking 150m by entrance to municipal campsite, signed.

ℹ Aire adj to municipal swimming pool. Tourist village with local commerce 950m. D19 popular with cyclists. Inspected 2013.

SAULT

153 J10 84390 N44°05.664' E005°24.758'

🚐 20 🕳 Euro Relais Mini; €2

➡ D950. Enter town from north on D950 and go straight over roundabout. Turn left opp Saupers Pompiers, sp 'P P3' and 'Cimitière'. Aire in Parking P3, signed.

ℹ Popular, open Aire with very limited shade. Small town commerce, inc self-service laundry, in old town 500m downhill. Town produces lavender related goods from local lavender fields which flower May-Jul. Inspected 2016.

REILLANNE

154 K10 83560 N43°52.805' E005°39.855'

🚐 3; Max 48hrs 🕳 Euro Relais Box; 1 unmetered CEE elec point; Apr-Oct

➡ D14. Southeast of village turn off D4100 onto D14, sp 'Reillanne'. Follow road for 2.3km. Aire on right before village and after car share car park, signed.

ℹ Very small Aire with limited parking on edge of village. Small picnic area adj. Local commerce with TO in centre, 200m; market Thurs am. Water from Service Point maybe unavailable due to local water shortage. Inspected 2016.

BANON

155 K10 04150 N44°02.393' E005°37.811'

🚐 10; €4/night; Collected; Max 7 days 🕳 Custom; Must not use elec points

➡ Rue de la Grande Fontaine. Turn off D950, sp 'P Centre Village 50 places'. Service Point on 1st terrace. There is parking here or poss to drive to 2nd lower terrace and park, signed.

ℹ Aire on 2 terraces: Lower has tap and elec, green space adj, suited to large motorhomes. Upper used by cars. WC and small town commerce 100m uphill/steps; market Tue am. Drive through lavender fields on D950 towards Sault, flowering Jun-Jul. Inspected 2016.

ST ETIENNE LES ORGUES

156 K10 04230 N44°02.461' E005°46.933'

🚐 5 🕳 Urba Flux Tall; 5 unmetered Cont elec points

➡ D12. From town follow D12, sp 'Fontienne'. Aire on left in 450m adj to D12 and outside municipal swimming pool, signed.

ℹ Pleasant, popular Aire adj to municipal swimming pool. Parking shaded by small deciduous trees. Do not block road when parking as coaches deliver children to pool. Small town commerce and WC 150m. Pool open Jul-Aug Tue-Sun 11am-6.45pm, €3pp. Inspected 2016.

CHATEAU ARNOUX ST AUBAN

157 K10 04160 N44°05.762' E006°00.603'

🚐 15; Max 48hrs; Market Thurs noon-8pm 🔧 Custom; Push down hard on red tops

➡ D4096. Turn off D4096 north of town into car park, sp 'P Resistance' and 'Salle des Fêtes'. Park near the war memorial, Service Point 50m further on, signed.

ℹ Aire in large car park with open and shaded parking. Parc du Château behind war memorial. Adj to a busy and very noisy road. Small town commerce through adj park 250m. Reinspected 2016.

SISTERON 1

158 K10 04200 N44°11.478' E005°56.732'

🚐 10; €4/24hrs; CC/€ 🔧 Flot Bleu Euro; Token/CC/€; €3; Inspection cover; Flot Bleu Elec; 1 Token/4hrs; 4 CEE elec points

➡ D4085. Approach Sisteron from south on D4085 following sp 'Sisteron'. Turn right on outskirts of town, sp 'Gare SNCF' and signed. Enter parking area and go to left to Aire, signed.

ℹ Small Aire in front of 1.9m height barriered car park sandwiched between noisy main road and railway. View of tracks from most bays, some bays adj to tracks. Local commerce adj. Historic citadel 1.2km. Inspected 2016.

SISTERON 2

159 K10 04200 N44°12.019' E005°56.631'

🚐 5; Max 6m 🔧 Flot Bleu Standard Plus; €2; Cont WC opp

➡ D4085/Cours Melchior Donnet. From south follow D4085 through town. After tunnel turn right into car park, Aire at far end, signed.

ℹ Aire at far end of busy car park. Noise from adj main road and constant car parking. Path to citadel opp, 1km uphill. Town commerce at other end of tunnel. Reinspected 2016.

MALIJAI

160 K10 04350 N44°02.654' E006°01.780'

🚐 7 🔧 Custom

➡ Impasse des Bugadières. Turn off D4 at roundabout, sp 'Malijai' and signed. Cross river bridge and turn 1st left, signed. This is a difficult turn made harder by parked cars, assess before attempting. Drive straight on, Service Point on left and parking on right. Best summer parking at end past boules court: N44°02.716' E006°01.712'.

ℹ Pleasant Aire in car park with several parking options; nearest used by local vehicles, furthest shaded. Some road noise from D4. River adj; very shallow in summer, no swimming. Local commerce and Château de Malijai, now town hall, 200m. Inspected 2016.

MISON

161 K10 04200 N44°15.925' E005°51.445'

🚐 7; 5m bays with overhang 🔧 Custom

➡ Les Armands Sud. Turn off D4075 opp La Poste, sp 'P Parking'. Follow road to left and Aire 150m on left past play area and basketball court.

ℹ Peaceful Aire just off main route in landscaped car park with parking under trees. School adj, parking busy at pick up/drop off times but deserted in school holidays. Green space adj with play area and open access basketball court. Local commerce 250m. Inspected 2016.

LARAGNE MONTEGLIN

162 K10 05300 N44°18.745' E005°49.568'

🚐 20; Max 48hrs 🔧 Custom; WC 80m

➡ C12/Chemin des Vergers. From south on D1075 turn left onto C12 at roundabout, sp 'Gorges de la Méouge' and 'Parking Gratuit'. Aire 200m on right. Service Point in far left corner.

ℹ Popular Aire in large open car park part shaded in afternoon by deciduous trees. Aire suitable for any unit configuration and shared with HGVs. Park adj. Town commerce 200m. Shallow river through trees behind Aire. Reinspected 2016.

ROSANS

163 J10 05150 ⛺ N44°23.585' E005°28.447'

🚐 Poss 🔧 Depagne; Tap and compost WC at parking

➡ D994. Turn off D994 in Rosans, sp 'Camping' and signed. Service Point immediately on left: N44°23.368' E005°28.253'. For parking turn right from Service Point, then turn left onto D25, sp 'Village Medieval' and 'TO'. Follow road, then turn left over bridge and parking is on left, not signed.

ℹ️ Pleasant, peaceful, open car park on edge of medieval village. Suitable for any unit configuration. Picnic and play area adj. TO and medieval village 250m. Discover surrounding countryside on any of 11 circular footpaths departing from car park. Inspected 2016.

TRESCLEOUX

164 K10 05700 N44°21.327' E005°42.597'

🚐 3; Max 2 nights; Large motorhomes will have to reverse out if busy 🔧 Custom

➡ Impasse du Dégoulavour. Turn off D949 in Trescléoux, signed. Aire 10m on right.

ℹ️ Small Aire with gravel parking in rural village. Local commerce 100m. Inspected 2016.

LA BEAUME DES ARNAUDS

165 K9 05140 N44°33.127' E005°38.164'

🚐 10 🔧 Flot Bleu Standard Plus; €2; Inspection cover to rear; Cont WC

➡ D993. Approach on D993 from Aspres-sur-Buëch in east. As enter village cross bridge, then turn 1st left into car park. Service Point immediately on left. For most practical parking drive straight on past boules court, then to left: N44°33.140' E005°38.100'.

ℹ️ Alt 882m. Aire in car park adj to D993 and railway line; trains 6am-10pm. Unlevel 5m bays by Service Point; popular with locals. Recommended parking in large, open gravel space suitable for any size motorhome, 100m; closest to railway line. Working laverie, traditional washing pond, and local commerce in village, 150m. Terrible Cont WC; EU grant for village so WC may improve. Inspected 2016.

ASPRES SUR BUECH

166 K9 05140 N44°31.214' E005°45.241'

🚐 15 🔧 Custom; WC at TO

➡ Avenue de la Gare. Turn off D1075, sp 'Office du Tourisme' and signed. Follow road past the TO and alongside the railway line and the Aire is on left, signed.

ℹ️ Aire adj to railway station in large municipal car park. Open and shaded parking. Small town commerce and TO (open am all year) 100m. TO has English language leaflet of village walk. Trains depart to Gap, Grenoble and Veynes-Dévoluy. Inspected 2016.

VEYNES

167 K9 05400 🏛 N44°31.074' E005°47.921'

🚐 30; €6/night Jun-Sept; Collected; Max 48hrs 🔧 Custom; Difficult access; WC adj

➡ Plan d'Eau des Iscles, off D994. Enter town from Gap on D994. Cross roundabout junction with D48 and Service Point in Place du 19 Mars 1962 on left, signed: N44°31.997' E005°49.367'. For parking continue on D994. Turn right to turn left, sp 'Plan d'Eau'. Follow sp 'Plan d'Eau' to right and follow road to end, then turn left. Designated parking on left, signed.

ℹ️ Popular designated parking in large open car park adj to swimming lake, no views. Recreation facilities inc gravel beach, boules court and café with public WCs; no pets allowed. Reinspected 2016.

TALLARD

168 K9 05130 ⛴ N44°27.709' E006°03.582'

🚐 3; Roadside parking by picnic area opp 🔧 Flot Bleu Euro; CC; €2.50; Inspection cover; Access diff if canoe hire busy

➡ D46. In town turn off D942 onto D46, sp 'Curbans' and 'La Durance Base de Tallard'. Follow road to river bridge. Service Point outside La Durance Base de Tallard canoe hire, signed.

ℹ️ Service Point adj to canoe hire, be careful of people if accessing when area busy. Roadside parking poss at picnic area opp. Small town commerce 400m. Château de Tallard 550m; opening times vary, €4.50pp. www.chateau-tallard.fr Inspected 2016.

LA ROCHE DES ARNAUDS

169   K9   05400   N44°33.683' E005°57.387'

🚐 5; Max 24hrs 🅿 None; See **166**

➡ D994. From Gap turn right off D994 into 3.5t weight restricted car park just after river bridge, signed.

ℹ Designated parking in roadside car park adj to main route, suffers road noise. Local commerce adj. Further parking and Service Point at **166**. Petit Buëch river is home to a variety of wildlife inc birds, bats and butterflies. Inspected 2016.

SUPERDEVOLUY

170   K9   05250   SKI   N44°40.662' E005°55.871'

🚐 10 🅿 Flot Bleu Pacific; Token (FB)/€; €2 (2 x €1); Inspection cover

➡ D17b. From Corps turn left off D537 (becomes D937) onto D117, sp 'Superdévoluy'. Follow D117 through St-Étienne-en-Dévoluy onto D17b, sp 'Superdévoluy'. Follow road uphill, then turn right at roundabout, sp 'Ski de Fond P' and 'P Couvert'. Aire on right, signed.

ℹ Alt 1488m. Aire on edge of large ski resort which offers facilities inc indoor pool, ski school, dogsledding and skijoring. Resort commerce complex 600m. Four ski lifts depart from resort up towards 53 slopes. TO open mid Dec-mid Apr/Jul-Aug. Inspected 2016.

LA JOUE DU LOUP

171   K9   05250   SKI   N44°41.489' E005°53.659'

🚐 10 🅿 None; WC 400m

➡ D17c. Turn off D17 onto D17c, sp 'La Joue de Loup'. Follow road for 850m and designated parking is on right in roadside lay-by P1 before all car parks, signed on info board.

ℹ Alt 1450m. Parking on edge of ski resort which offers facilities inc ski school, toboggan run, and cinema. Resort commerce 500m. Ski lift 600m gives access to Superdévoluy, one of the largest ski resorts in the southern French Alps. Inspected 2016.

GAP 1

172   K9   05000   N44°32.537' E006°03.694'

🚐 5; Max 48hrs 🅿 Custom

➡ Ave de Traunstein. From Gap on N85 turn off at traffic lights 400m after roundabout with McDonald's, sp 'C.F.A Régional' and signed. If you get to the Total fuel station you have gone too far. Turn left in front of Stade Nautique and left into P+R car park, signed. Aire to rear of car park.

ℹ Oversubscribed Aire in large, open car park on outskirts of Gap. Sports facilities adj. Free Park and Ride bus to town centre. Cycle path to Gap on main road. Inspected 2016.

GAP 2

173   K9   05000   N44°34.171' E006°06.155'

🚐 6; Max 48hrs 🅿 Custom

➡ Ave d'Embrun. On N94 follow sp 'Briançon'. Turn left at roundabout with Géant Casino supermarket and Renault Minute, signed. Aire on right, signed.

ℹ Aire sandwiched between main road and railway line in industrial area, therefore noisy. Space likely. Out of town retail commerce adj. Inspected 2016.

GAP 3

174   K9   05000   N44°33.900' E006°05.033'

🚐 3 🅿 Flot Bleu Euro; CC; €2

➡ Parking Dumont, N85. On N85 follow sp 'Grenoble'. Aire on right just past Intermarché supermarket, signed. Turn right before sign into car park and Aire on left.

ℹ Aire adj to noisy main route, but closest Aire to town centre, 1km. Neogothic 19th century Notre-Dame-et-Saint-Arnoux in centre has 70m-high bell tower and impressive organ inside. Reinspected 2016.

LAYE | 175 | K9 | 05000 | N44°38.422' E006°05.142'

🛒 10; Max 36hrs ⚑ None; See **174**

➡ Off N85. From Gap follow N85 north for 11km. Ignore the turning for Laye ski station (D88) to the left. Continue on N85 for 800m then turn right, sp 'Monument de la Resistance'. Aire on right in 50m.

ℹ Alt 1174m. Gravel car park adj to small hamlet with local commerce and lovely views of surrounding mountains. Parking not allowed beyond yellow line. Resistance memorial, 200m, acknowledges fallen marquis of nearby Champsaur and Valgaudemar during WWII. Reinspected 2016.

ST ETIENNE LE LAUS | 176 | K9 | 05130 | N44°30.169' E006°09.476'

🛒 5; On lower terrace ⚑ Euro Relais Maxi; Token (ER)/CC; €4; Max 3.5t

➡ D942. Turn off D942 into roadside lay-by, sp with the picnic symbol and signed. Service Point up 3.5t weight restricted hill adj to WCs, signed.

ℹ Aire in roadside lay-by with local convenience store/bar. Road noise from main route adj. Convenient night halt. Inspected 2016.

PONT DU FOSSE | 177 | K9 | 05260 | N44°40.200' E006°14.317'

🛒 49; €10/night inc 6amp elec and WiFi; CC ⚑ Euro Relais Junior; Inside barrier; 60 6amp Cont and CEE elec points

➡ Off D944. From river bridge in Pont-du-Fossé follow D944 northeast for 900m. Turn right opp D481 junction and before Toyota garage, signed (GPS given is at this turning for clarity). Follow road to right and Aire in 500m. Actual GPS: N44°40.077' E006°14.094'. Enter through PARKNIGHT barrier.

ℹ Alt 1134m. Very pleasant Aire in woodland setting adj to river with beautiful mountain views. River can cause flood risk. Small town commerce accessible by footpath; market Fri am. Reinspected 2016.

ORCIERES | 178 | K9 | 05170 | SKI | N44°41.704' E006°19.565'

🛒 24; €18/24hrs (Winter); €10/24hrs (Summer); Pay attendant/TO; 16amp elec €6/4hrs; Max 8m ⚑ Raclet; Inside barrier

➡ Les Balcons d'Orcières. From west take D944 to Orcières. In Orcières follow sp 'Merlette Station' onto D76. Follow road uphill to Merlette; some hairpin bends. Drive into Merlette, then 450m past cinema turn right off D76, sp 'Casse Blanche P2' and signed. Turn 1st right into Aire in car park on upper floor. Enter through barrier.

ℹ Alt 1811m. Dramatic top floor car park at ski resort. Stunning mountain views from front bays. Main ski resort/lifts 400m. Resort virtually deserted in summer, but some ski lifts still run. www.orcieres.com Reinspected 2016.

PUY SAINT VINCENT STATION 1600 | 179 | K9 | 05290 | SKI | N44°49.187' E006°29.198'

🛒 15; €6/day; €35/week; Collected; Max 2 weeks ⚑ Custom; Inc; 10 10amp CEE elec points

➡ D804, Station 1600. From N94 follow D994e, sp 'Puy St Vincent'. From D994e either turn left onto 3.5t restricted road or continue to Vallouise and follow sp 'Puy St Vincent' for wider unrestricted D4 road with hairpins. At Puy St Vincent turn onto D804 following sp 'Station 1600'. Aire in 1st parking on left as enter one-way system, signed.

ℹ Alt 1653m. Popular, small landscaped Aire with views over mountains. Nice ski/summer walking resort in Écrins National Park. www.ecrins-parcnational.fr Resort commerce 450m uphill. Reinspected 2016.

PELVOUX | 180 | K9 | 05340 | SKI | N44°51.910' E006°29.226'

🛒 50 ⚑ Euro Relais Junior; €2; Drive over drain 10m

➡ Station La Blanche. Follow D994e past Vallouise, sp 'Pelvoux'. Continue on road to St Antoine, then turn left, sp 'Station la Blanche'. Follow road to left and Aire on left, signed. Service Point inside wooden bin cover, signed.

ℹ Alt 1239m. Pleasant summer location with green fields and mountain views. Avalanche of parking options adj to La Blanche ski lift, inc at its very base. Ski commerce adj inc lift pass shop and ski season TO. Local commerce 100m. Inspected 2016.

MEDITERRANEAN

BRIANCON 1

| 181 | L9 | 05100 | | N44°53.418' E006°37.767' |

🚐 4; €6/12hrs; €12/24hrs; Pay at Service Point; Max 24hrs 🚽 Euro Relais Maxi; Token (ER)/CC; €2; Working tap adj to parking

➡ Rue Georges Bermond-Gonnet. From south on N94 turn right at roundabout onto D36b, sp 'Villard'. Cross bridge and turn left at roundabout, sp 'Briançon Sud'. Follow road straight on over roundabout, sp 'Park de Sports'. Continue on road for 1km, then turn right, sp 'Park des Sports' and signed. Aire in car park on right, signed in 100m. Alternative parking at 182.

ℹ Alt 1201m. Large car park on outskirts of town with 2 Service Points. Once had 4 designated bays, but now allows motorhomes to park everywhere. Reinspected 2016.

BRIANCON 2

| 182 | K9 | 05100 | T | N44°54.095' E006°38.780' |

🚐 11; €1/1hr; €6/8hrs +€0.70/additional hr; CC/€; Max 24hrs; Pay at machine 🚽 WC adj; See 181

➡ Route du Fontenil. Follow N94 through Briançon, sp 'Turin'. Go straight over roundabout adj to fort, follow road to end of car park and turn right, sp 'Le Fontenil', to designated parking, signed. Alternative parking and Service Point at 181.

ℹ Alt 1347m. Popular designated parking offering open and shaded parking. Green space adj and small town commerce adj. Some road noise. Briançon centre 550m. Ski lifts 2km. Local area has collection of Vauban fortifications, one adj; many are UNESCO World Heritage sites. Inspected 2016.

LE MONETIER LES BAINS

| 183 | K9 | 05220 | SKI | N44°58.285' E006°30.748' |

🚐 50; €4.80/day; Long stay discounts; Collected 🚽 Euro Relais Maxi; 2 CEE elec points (Not working)

➡ Off D1091. From Briançon enter town on D1091. Just after town boundary sign turn left, sp 'Espace Loisirs' and signed. Follow lane, turning left across bridge into parking, sp 'Depart des Pistes'. Aire on left, signed.

ℹ Alt 1467m. Large open Aire in sloping car park with mountain views. Further parking poss in adj car park. Ski lift 100m. Poss to ski back to motorhome from piste. Very scenic drive over Col du Lautaret (2058m). Reinspected 2016.

SERRE CHEVALIER - Le Bez

| 184 | K9 | 05240 | SKI | N44°56.648' E006°33.366' |

🚐 18; €10-€18/night low-high season; Access 8am-10pm 🚽 Euro Relais Junior, behind wooden fence; 18 6amp CEE elec points; No drive over drain

➡ Chemin du Marquis. Turn off D1091 at roundabout, sp 'Le Bez'. Follow road straight on uphill for 400m and turn right, then immediately left into road marked no entry. Aire immediately on right, signed.

ℹ Alt 1409m. Small, privately run commercial Aire at rear of small village. Adj ski lift runs in summer and nearby Chantemerle has cable car. Tourist commerce 200m downhill; charming old village 300m uphill. Inspected 2016.

LA SALLE LES ALPES

| 185 | K9 | 05240 | SKI | N44°56.867' E006°33.333' |

🚐 20; €8/24hrs inc elec; Register at TO for electronic gate key, pay when key returned 🚽 Raclet; Ouside barrier; No drive over drain; WC at ski lift

➡ Chemin des Preras. From south on D1091 turn left as exit village towards La Grave, sp 'P Pontillas' and 'Plan d'Eau'. Cross river, then turn right at roundabout, sp 'Plan d'Eau'. Aire immediately on left, signed.

ℹ Alt 1388m. Pleasant Aire adj to small swimming lake with pedalos and rafting. Ski lift adj and ski run finishes nearby. Adj modern resort has nice feel and is active in summer. Charming old village 400m uphill. Reinspected 2016.

MONTGENEVRE

| 186 | L9 | 05100 | SKI | N44°56.094' E006°44.154' |

🚐 280; €10/day inc 10amp elec; Rate decreases 2-7 days, increases 8+; Pay on exit 🚽 Custom; Inside barrier; €5; Pay at machine

➡ Voie du Collet. From Briançon follow N94, sp 'Turin'. Follow N94 up a series of hairpin bends to Montgenèvre. In Montgenèvre go straight over roundabout, sp 'Montgenèvre'. Go through tunnel, then straight across roundabout, sp 'Turin'. Turn 1st left, signed. Follow road uphill for 400m, then turn right into Aire, signed. Enter through barrier.

ℹ Alt 1859m. Large, open, popular Aire on 2 terraces. Pleasant summer views over ponds and green fields to lively resort with summer events. Good walking and mountain biking. Excellent skiing. Aire 100m from slopes. Free shuttle bus to/from Aire. Italy 1.4km. Reinspected 2016.

ST CREPIN

187 K9 05600 N44°42.337' E006°36.076'

🚐 24; €8/night; +€0.40pp; Additional charges for extra people/animals; Collected 🍺 Custom; 3-10amp Cont elec €3.80; Showers inc

➡ D138. From south on N94 turn right to turn left onto D138, sp 'Aerodrome'. Follow road over railway. Parking on right before river bridge. For Service Point and WC cross river bridge and turn left immediately towards aerodrome buildings. Service Point on left: N44°42.250' E006°36.055'. Signed on N94 from south, but not from north.

ℹ Alt 901m. Convenient location just off N94. Designated motorhome parking on part shaded marked pitches in tired part of campsite. Facilities inc WC and showers. Poss better to stay in campsite. Canoe hire and light aircraft adj. Distant road noise. Inspected 2016.

RISOUL 1850

188 L9 05600 SKI N44°37.398' E006°38.338'

🚐 22; €15/night; €60/week +€0.20pp 🍺 Custom; 22 CEE/Cont elec points

➡ Rue des Pourrières. From Guillestre follow sp 'Risoul', then follow D186 11.2km up to Risoul ski station, sp 'Risoul 1850'. On arrival follow road to left, sp 'Centre Station'. Continue for 350m, then turn left, sp 'P2', 'P3' and signed. Aire 100m on right, signed.

ℹ Alt 1866m. Aire on edge of lively ski resort in terraced parking area, no views. Inconvenient location for ski lifts. Road cyclists and mountain bikers in summer. Resort commerce 450m. Resort activities inc toboggan run and year-round ice rink. Inspected 2016.

CROTS

189 K9 05200 N44°32.298' E006°27.292'

🚐 40; €9.60/night Sept-June; €10.80/night Jul-Aug; +€0.40/night tax; Inc service, elec and WiFi 🍺 Aire Services 3000; Inside barrier; Aire Services Elec; 16 6amp CEE elec points

➡ Plage de Chanterenne. Turn off N94 opp Crots turning, sp 'Plage de Chanterenne' and signed. Follow road, eventually driving past Chanterenne beach, signed. Follow road to left and Aire straight on, signed. Enter through PARKNIGHT barrier.

ℹ Aire to the rear of parking for leisure beach, partial views. Rear overflow parking is rough, unkempt gravel with no access to elec. Leisure beach is part of large lake adj. Inspected 2016.

VARS LES CLAUX ✶

190 L9 05560 SKI N44°34.534' E006°40.675'

🚐 50 🍺 Custom; In building

➡ Off D902, in car park P5 at the top of the resort.

ℹ Alt 1600m. Popular large open Aire at ski resort. Free summer chairlift. Good local walking. Free WiFi at TO. Updated 2016.

Photos: Alistair & Helen MacFadyen

CHORGES

191 K9 05230 N44°32.750' E006°16.800'

🚐 15; €5/noon-noon; Collected 🍺 Custom

➡ Chemin la Butte. To avoid route through town, which is passable but one-way and narrow, approach from Rousset in south on D3. Turn right when the town is on your left, signed. In 100m turn left into Place du Champ de Foire, signed. Continue between gendarmerie and Salles des Fêtes and Aire on right in 150m, signed.

ℹ Alt 878m. Popular large open Aire surrounded by community facilities inc fire station and boules court. Small town commerce 400m. WC adj to boules court. Reinspected 2016.

SAVINES LE LAC

192 K9 05160 N44°31.483' E006°24.033'

🚐 17; €9.50/24hrs inc elec; CC/€; Pay at machine; Max 10m 🍺 Custom; €2; 14 elec points

➡ D954/Avenue du Faubourg. From west on N94, after crossing lake on long bridge, take 1st right onto D954/Avenue du Faubourg, sp 'P Camping Cars'. Aire on left in 180m, signed.

ℹ Aire adj to road, but just 50m from Lac de Serre-Ponçon, a large water sports and activity lake, no views. Village centre 100m with beach (water freezing in summer!) and local and tourist commerce; boat trips avail. Day parking at multiple lakeside lay-bys on N94 towards Chorges. Reinspected 2016.

LA BRÉOLE
193 K9 04340 N44°27.466' E006°17.518'

🚐9 Flot Bleu Fontaine

➤ D707. From west on D900b turn left onto D707, sp 'La Bréole' and signed. Aire 40m on left, signed.

ℹ Alt 933m. Pleasant village Aire with rural views. Tourist commerce adj and local commerce 200m. Large reservoir nearby. Inspected 2016.

SELONNET
194 K10 04140 N44°22.101' E006°18.912'

🚐7 Aire Services 3000; Token (3/3); Free water tap on adj bike wash; WC in wooden shed, 10m

➤ Saint-Domitien. Turn off D900, sp 'Selonnet'. Turn left onto D1, sp 'Station de Chabanon'. Turn immediately left in village and drive past WC on right, signed. Aire 400m on left, signed.

ℹ Alt 1071m. Aire on edge of village, adj to municipal works. Village centre 400m with local commerce. Public BBQ by adj river. Space likely and ideal stop if Lac de Serre Poncon Aires (**189**, **191**, **192**) full. Reinspected 2016.

LES ORRES
195 K9 05200 SKI N44°29.980' E006°33.435'

🚐50; Max 15 days Flot Bleu Pacific; Token (FB); No drive over drain

➤ Parking Bas de Champs Lacas, off D40. From Embrun turn off N94 onto D40 at roundabout, sp 'Les Orres'. Follow D40 for approx 16km, then turn left as approach resort, signed. Follow road and Service Point on left by bins before parking: N44°29.976' E006°33.338'. Parking at end of road in large parking area, sp 'Parking B', below chairlift ticket office, well signed.

ℹ Alt 1564m. Motorhomes allowed to park in large car park at base of ski lift. Seasonal restaurants adj. Good summer stop near lake to escape the heat. Reinspected 2016.

LE LAUZET UBAYE
196 K9 04340 N44°25.686' E006°26.044'

🚐7; Max 10m None

➤ Le Village. Turn off D900 at monument in Le Lauzet-Ubaye. Follow road immediately down slope to left, then back to right at bottom of slope. Drive through boules court and Aire on right, signed. Access poss blocked during boules events. If so, follow sp to 'Le Lac' on other side of village.

ℹ Alt 903m. Convenient Aire just off main route. Tourist commerce 350m on D900. Beautiful deep leisure/swimming lake adj. Some road noise. Inspected 2016.

JAUSIERS
197 L9 04850 N44°24.712' E006°43.750'

🚐4 Flot Bleu Euro; CC; €3

➤ D900. From Barcelonnette on D900 turn right down gravel track after passing village boundary sign, signed. Aire in small roadside lay-by, entrance and exit both sides.

ℹ Alt 1214m. Small rough roadside lay-by. Village with local commerce and market Sun am 1.1km. Restricted motorhome parking over river bridge; permanent flood risk. Border with Italy via Col de Larche on D900. Follow sp 'Nice' to cross highest route in France. Reinspected 2016.

BARCELONNETTE
198 L10 04400 N44°22.917' E006°39.483'

🚐15; €8/night; CC; Pay at machine Euro Relais Junior; Token (ER); 2 tokens inc with parking ticket

➤ Chemin des Alpages. From west on D900 turn right to cross river on D902, sp 'Pra Loup'. Immediately after crossing river turn left by recycling bins, signed. Follow road along river for 600m, then turn right, signed. Aire on left behind stadium. Well signed from D900.

ℹ Alt 1149m. Popular Aire adj to sports stadium on edge of town. Parking on grass/sand among trees with mountain views. Drag lift 100m. 2 Service Point tokens inc with parking and given at parking payment machine. www.barcelonnette.com Reinspected 2016.

BARCELONNETTE (ST PONS)

199 L10 04400 N44°23.190' E006°38.049'

🚐 4; Max 48hrs 🔧 Custom

▶ Allée des Pins. On west side of town turn off D900, sp 'Zone Artisanale du Chazelas'. Follow road left to designated parking, signed. For Service Point continue west on D900 for 2km, then turn onto D609 by plane, sp 'Aerodrome' and signed. Turn 1st left, signed. Service Point on right before Services Techniques: N44°23.141' E006°36.550'. Access difficult, large vehicles can park roadside.

ℹ️ Alt 1135m. Convenient parking adj to local commerce. Service Point 2km along D900 by Dassault 312 passenger plane. Inspected 2016.

PRA LOUP 1600

200 L10 04400 SKI N44°22.054' E006°36.367'

🚐 20 🔧 Flot Bleu Standard Plus; €3; Inspection cover; No drive over drain

▶ D109. As enter resort on D109 turn 2nd right into car park, signed. Parking to left, Service Point to right.

ℹ️ Alt 1574m. Large car park, but motorhomes restricted to one side, signed. Some parking along edge has steep drop, but amazing views. Free bus/ski lift adj running in winter. Not a pretty resort, but good skiing. www.praloup.com Reinspected 2016.

LA FOUX D'ALLOS

201 K10 04260 SKI N44°17.738' E006°34.135'

🚐 Poss 🔧 Flot Bleu Euro; CC

▶ D908. From south on D908, follow the upper road at resort. Service Point is on left immediately after exiting tunnel. Approach from north via Col d'Allos not advised due to 7m length and 3.5t weight restriction for 24km of virtually single track road.

ℹ️ Alt 1842m. Flot Bleu behind wooden toilet block, under ski lift. Only really a roadside Service Point, but parking unrestricted within resort. Nearest parking other side of tunnel. Reinspected 2016.

ALLOS

202 L10 04260 SKI N44°14.583' E006°37.367'

🚐 20; Max 72hrs 🔧 Flot Bleu Standard Plus; Token (FB)/CC; €2; Flot Bleu Elec; 1 Token/4hrs; 12 CEE elec points; WC at ski lift, 100m

▶ Parc de Loisirs, off D908. From south on D908 go through town and turn left, sp 'Parc de Loisirs' and signed. Follow road and Aire on left as enter car park, signed. Approach from north via Col d'Allos not advised due to 7m length and 3.5t weight restriction.

ℹ️ Alt 1416m. Open Aire at base of ski gondola lift and cross country ski depart. In summer cable car runs walkers to top. Recreation area adj, entry €8pp, with popular leisure lake and high wire course. www.valdallos.com Reinspected 2016.

COLMARS LES ALPES

203 L10 04370 N44°10.761' E006°37.577'

🚐 20; Max 24hrs 🔧 Flot Bleu Euro; CC; €3; Blue inspection cover adj; No drive over drain

▶ Place de la Tour. Turn off D908 opp the Garage des Alps, signed. Turn left before river bridge, signed. Service Point on left just past WC. Approach from north via Col d'Allos not advised due to 7m length and 3.5t weight restriction.

ℹ️ Alt 1241m. Pleasant but unlevel parking under deciduous trees in visitor car park. River/flood ditch adj. Interesting, well preserved walled town 200m with local and tourist commerce. Footpath to Cascade de la Lance. Reinspected 2016.

DIGNE LES BAINS

204 K10 04000 N44°04.796' E006°15.637'

🚐 20 🔧 Euro Relais Junior; Token (ER); €2.50

▶ D20/Ave des Thermes. In town follow sp 'Les Thermes' and 'Piscine les Eaux Chaudes' onto D20. Follow this road past Intermarché supermarket and for a further 1.5km. Follow one-way system, sp 'Therme'. Aire is on right before thermal spa, signed. Riverside day parking (8am-10pm): N44°05.419' E006°13.718'. Between the two road bridges on other side of river.

ℹ️ Large, open Aire adj to thermal baths 3km from town. Can accommodate any unit configuration. No water in winter. Poss to park in town at one one-way system out of town opp self-service laundry. Reinspected 2016.

MEDITERRANEAN

ST ANDRE LES ALPES

205 K10 04170 N43°57.921' E006°30.439'

🚐 23; Max 7m; No parking Wed/Sat 6am-2pm (Market) ⛽ Flot Bleu Euro; Token (FB)/CC; €3; Inspection cover; No drive over drain

➤ D2/Grand Rue. From south turn off N202 at roundabout, signed. Aire 100m on left, signed.

ℹ️ Alt 900m. Large, unshaded, sloping asphalt parking area. Large leisure lake nearby, no views. Acceptable day parking in lay-bys on N202 with full and partial lake views. Reinspected 2016.

ANNOT

206 L10 04240 N43°57.793' E006°39.860' SP

🚐 25 ⛽ Urba Flux Tall; Laundry sink

➤ Chemin de la Colle Basse. From south on D908 turn left in village centre and drive through car park, sp 'Aire de Camping Car'. Cross river and turn right, then immediately left, signed. Follow road and signs for 300m, past gendarmerie and uphill. On edge of village turn left into wood and Aire, signed.

ℹ️ Popular, peaceful and pleasant Aire under deciduous trees. Part-shaded hardstanding and grass parking options. Small town commerce 400m; market Tues. Stunning mountain railway journey to Nice departs from station, 1km, €26.60pp return. www.trainprovence.com Inspected 2016.

GUILLAUMES

207 L10 06470 N44°05.308' E006°51.178' SP

🚐 20 ⛽ Euro Relais Junior; Token (ER); WC up steps behind Service Point

➤ Place de Provence. Turn off D2202 by pharmacy near river bridge, sp 'P 60 places' and signed. Follow road downhill, then turn left into Aire. Service Point on left.

ℹ️ Pleasant, peaceful Aire in large, open gravel car park suitable for any unit. Aire has unfenced steep drops to rivers on 2 sides; river rafting poss. Small town commerce 150m. Gorges de Daluis, on D2202, a pleasant drive. Inspected 2016.

VALBERG

208 L10 06470 SKI N44°05.766' E006°56.204' SP

🚐 21; €10 inc service and elec; +€0.70pp/night; Max 9m ⛽ Custom; 24 16amp CEE elec points

➤ D528a. Turn off D28 at roundabout, sp 'Ecole des Neiges'. Follow road uphill, forking 1st left, then turning immediately right, both signed with small signs; do not go around hairpin bend. Follow road and Aire is on right in 250m, clearly signed.

ℹ️ Alt 1713m. Popular Aire in peaceful location 300m from busy ski resort. Most of resort open in summer. www.valberg.com Stunning scenery through Gorges de Daluis on approach via D2202. Reinspected 2016.

PUGET THENIERS

209 L10 06260 N43°57.210' E006°53.966' SP

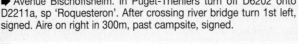

🚐 20; €4/24hrs; Max 48hrs; Pay at campsite ⛽ Urba Flux Tall

➤ Avenue Bischoffsheim. In Puget-Théniers turn off D6202 onto D2211a, sp 'Roquesteron'. After crossing river bridge turn 1st left, signed. Aire on right in 300m, past campsite, signed.

ℹ️ Aire in open car park opp river with slipway. Small village set in French Alps. Local commerce, visitor centre and train station with classic trains 400m. Steam train journeys to Annot Sun May-Oct/Fri Jul-Aug. Historic fortified Entrevaux adj and next stop on train line, €3.40pp return. Inspected 2016.

ROUBION - Les Buisses

210 L10 06420 SKI N44°05.061' E007°02.547' SP

🚐 14; 9m bays plus overhang; Max 5 days ⛽ Urba Flux Tall

➤ Clogaglia. From Beuil turn off D30/M30 before hairpin bend, sp 'Station de Ski' and 'Les Buisses'. At roundabout turn left into car park. Aire at far end, signed. Approach from St-Sauveur-sur-Tinée is winding, narrow gorge road.

ℹ️ Alt 1210m. Aire at small ski station; pleasant summer location. Drag and ski lift 200m; ski lift runs in summer. Snow shoe trekking and bike trails; mountain bike hire poss. 1.4km footpath to teetering medieval, mountain-top village; no suitable motorhome parking. Inspected 2016.

ENTREVAUX

211 L10 04320 N43°57.888' E006°47.142'

6 None

➡ Zone Artisanale, behind Intermarché. Exit Entrevaux towards Annot on D4202. Turn right at bridge, sp 'Zone Artisanale' and signed. Follow narrow road to Intermarché supermarket, well signed. Designated parking to right in large bays.

ℹ Designated parking at remote supermarket, no shade. May feel isolated and will be alone. Self-service laundry adj, €4/8kg. Poss to park in Parking de la Gare car park on opp side of railway line in Entrevaux: N43°56.933' E006°48.833'. Inspected 2016.

ST MARTIN VESUBIE

212 L10 06450 N44°03.628' E007°15.585'

15 Urba Flux Tall; CC; €3

➡ M2565. Adj to M2565 at southern town boundary, signed.

ℹ Open Aire adj to main route. Small town commerce 1.5km. In the Alps, near the Italian border. Visited 2016.

Info/photos: Alistair & Helen MacFadyen

SOSPEL

213 L10 06450 N43°52.734' E007°26.562'

7; €5/night; Pay at campsite; Jul-Aug Custom

➡ D2204. Turn off D2204, sp 'Stade Municipal Camping'. Follow road past campsite. Parking and Service Point are on the left, signed.

ℹ Aire adj to and run by small campsite only open Jul-Aug. Nice old town 350m. Trains run to Nice. Visited 2016.

Info/photo: Alistair & Helen MacFadyen

ST PAUL DE VENCE

214 L10 06570 N43°42.136' E007°07.022'

6; Max 48hrs; Max 7m, absolutely no overhang None

➡ Chemin des Gardettes. Approach on D536/D7 from Cagnes-sur-Mer, following sp 'Vence St Paul'. Stay left to join D7d at St Paul de Vence boundary sign. At roundabout turn left, sp 'Fondation Maeght'. Follow road uphill for 350m to designated parking on right just after town boundary, signed.

ℹ Roadside bays on hill at edge of town. Road noise and 7am bells. Contemporary art exhibits at Foundation Maeght, 200m; open daily Oct-Jun 10am-6pm, €15pp. www.fondation-maeght.com Local commerce 600m downhill; hilltop town centre 3.5km. Inspected 2016.

ST LAURENT DU VAR

215 L10 06700 N43°41.119' E007°11.116'

5; Max 7 days; Not suitable for motorhomes with trailers Custom; Slow tap

➡ Route des Pugets. Exit A8 at Junction 49 and follow sp 'St Laurent-Centre'. Go straight on at roundabout, sp 'Cimetière St Marc' and signed. Go straight on, sp 'Parc d'Activities'. Turn left at next roundabout, sp 'Cimetière St Marc' and signed. Turn left at roundabout, sp 'Cimetière', then left again, sp 'Cimetière St Marc'. Aire 400m on right, signed.

ℹ Popular, level Aire in a hillside location opp cemetery (faster tap at cemetery) and overlooking industrial park. Town commerce 1km uphill. Reinspected 2016.

ANTIBES

216 L10 06600 N43°36.900' E007°07.249'

35; €25/day; CC Flot Bleu Pacific; Token (FB)/CC; €3; Inspection cover; Flot Bleu Elec; Token (FB); €3; 3 elec points; Inside barrier

➡ Chemin des Groules. Approach on D6007 from Nice following sp 'Antibes'. As approach Antibes turn right at roundabout onto D4, sp 'Biot'. Turn right at next roundabout, sp 'P1 Parc Marineland'. Enter through left-hand barrier, signed.

ℹ Designated motorhome parking in car park for Marineland, water park and fun fair. Adj to main road. Inspected 2016.

MEDITERRANEAN

FAYENCE

217 L11 83440 🏛 (A) N43°37.380' E006°41.412' SP

🚐 **(A)** 2; **(B)** 2; **(C)** 3; Max 48hrs; Max 7m 🚽 **(A)** Urba Flux; €4/15 mins

➡ Enter town from south on D19 or D563. At roundabout follow D563, sp 'Mons' and 'Centre Ville'. After roundabout: **(A)** Turn immediately left, signed. Service Point on left, 2 designated bays on right, signed. **(B)** N43°37,314' E006°41.589': Turn right, sp 'Centre Ville'. Turn right off 1st hairpin bend into parking, signed. **(C)** N43°37.481' E006°41.802': Turn right, sp 'Centre Ville', and follow D563 through town, then turn left, sp 'P3 P4'. Drive through car park onto upper terrace. Parking on left, signed.

ℹ 3 parking places at hilltop town. **(A)** By TO, furthest from town. 1 bay obstructed by tree. **(B)** Parking la Ferrage: 2nd furthest from town (uphill) adj recycling bins. **(C)** P3: 100m from town and most popular. 1 bay obstructed by tree. Reinspected 2016.

CAILLE

218 L10 06750 N43°46.733' E006°43.997' SP

🚐 3 🚽 Flot Bleu Pacific; €4 (2 x €2); No drive over drain

➡ Junction of Rue St Pons and Rue des Ecuries, off D79/D80. Turn off D6085 onto D79, sp 'Caille' and signed. Turn right to enter village, sp 'Centre Ville' and signed with sp 'Bas du Ville'. Continue through village and Aire on left, signed.

ℹ Alt 1138m. Very small Aire with rural views. Located in ancient village with local commerce and 2 restaurants. Not suitable for large motorhomes. Ski resort l'Audibergue la Moulière 5km. http://stations-greolieres-audibergue.com Reinspected 2016.

LAC DE THORENC

219 L10 06750 🏛 N43°47.967' E006°48.500' SP

🚐 20 🚽 Flot Bleu Euro; CC; €5

➡ Lac de Thorenc. Turn off D2 into parking, sp 'Lac de Thorenc' and signed. Parking on right and Service Point 100m on left, by WC.

ℹ Alt 1122m. Large peaceful parking area that can accommodate any unit. Pony rides on small Shetlands opp. Pleasant woodland walks around lake. Reinspected 2016.

CASTELLANE 1

220 L10 04120 N43°50.763' E006°30.950' SP

🚐 40; €6.50/24hrs; Pay at barrier; Max 48hrs 🚽 Custom; Inside barrier; Inc

➡ D4085/D952. Aire on right as enter town on D4085 from Grasse, next to river under 184m-high rock with chapel on top, sp 'Parking Obligatoire Camping Cars'. Enter through barrier; correct change needed.

ℹ Very popular Aire beneath Chapelle Notre Dame du Roc. River and old bridge adj. Historic town with small town commerce 150m. Motorhomes are banned from all town car parks. Reinspected 2016.

CASTELLANE 2

221 K10 04120 N43°51.287' E006°30.023' SP

🚐 49; €5.50/24hrs inc WiFi; Collected 🚽 Custom; €2; Elec €3/24hrs

➡ Plan de la Palud. Exit Castellane on D4085, sp 'Grenoble' and 'Barrême'. Turn left in 300m after exiting town, sp 'Musée de la Résistance' and signed. Follow road to right to Aire, signed.

ℹ Open, private commercial Aire adj to Musée de la Résistance; open May-Sept 9.30am-7pm, €4pp. Outdoor activity company inc rafting adj. Can accommodate any unit configuration. Castellane 1.5km. Inspected 2016.

CASTELLANE 3

222 K10 04120 N43°52.320' E006°30.667' SP

🚐 20; €7/night; Collected; Mar-Nov 🚽 Custom; Water is untreated and from natural source; 16amp CEE elec poss via generator as elec is not connected to mains supply

➡ Aire de Castellane Camping-Car, D402. Approach from north on D955. Drive past lake, then turn right onto D402, sp 'Blaron' and signed. Aire immediately on right, signed.

ℹ Alt 907m. Popular, shaded, private, commercial Aire with a relaxed atmosphere. Leisure lake with boat hire 800m. Castellane 3.5km downhill. Inspected 2016.

COMPS SUR ARTUBY
223 K10 83840 N43°42.375' E006°30.392'

🚐 19; Max 24hrs; Max 9m Custom; Token; €3/15 mins; Lift square cover for WC emptying

➡ D955. From south on D955 turn left immediately after Comps-Sur-Artuby boundary sign on bend, signed. Aire in lay-by, signed.

ℹ Alt 894m. Conveniently situated Aire in lay-by adj to D955. Landscaped shaded or open parking with views over valley. Picnic area adj. Token available from adj Le Rouable pizzeria. Village 500m. Reinspected 2016.

TRIGANCE
224 K10 83840 N43°45.611' E006°26.495'

🚐 5; €5/night; Max 72hrs; Apr-Oct Aire Services 7010; Token (3/3); Apr-Oct

➡ D90. Turn off D955 onto D90, sp 'Trigance'. Cross bridge and turn left, sp 'Trigance'. Follow road and Aire is located just off a hairpin bend on this road, sp 'Trigance' and 'P'. Service Point at end of car park.

ℹ Most of car park is small and unlevel. Drive past Service Point for level parking suitable for large motorhomes; other parking only suitable for 6m motorhomes. Pretty, historic village adj. Lay-by en route with views of village. D952 and D23 follow alongside stunning Gorges du Verdon, 7.5km. Reinspected 2016.

MOUSTIERS STE MARIE
225 K10 04360 T N43°50.617' E006°13.100'

🚐 30; €8.50/8pm-8am; Max 48hrs Urba Flux; Inside barrier; 1 unmetered elec point

➡ D952. Follow D952 from Riez. Go straight over roundabout, then in 350m turn right, signed. Aire in car park on left through barrier. Barrier out of use at time of inspection.

ℹ Aire located in a charming Beau Village, 500m uphill. Has suspended star across gorge. Inspected 2014.

RIEZ
226 K10 04500 N43°49.445' E006°05.634'

🚐 50; €5/night; Collected Custom; Hose needed for water

➡ D953. Exit town on D953, sp 'Digne', 'P de l'Auvestre' and signed. After passing supermarket on left, turn right, sp 'P de l'Auvestre' and signed (GPS taken here for clarity). Follow road to right, then turn off into car park, signed. Designated parking to right, signed. Exact GPS: N43°49.316' E006°05.560'.

ℹ A pleasant Aire on the outskirts of town with parking on 3 terraces. Small town commerce 650m; market Sat am. Inspected 2014.

LES SALLES SUR VERDON 1
227 K10 83630 N43°46.463' E006°13.062'

🚐 17; €9/night inc service; +€0.20pp; Pay at shop Custom; €3.50 service only; 5amp elec €4

➡ D957. Turn off D957 at the l'Ermitage hotel, near junction with D71, signed. Aire behind shop/fuel station, signed.

ℹ Commercial Aire in small space behind shop on a terrace above D957 main route. Very busy high season. Facilities inc showers, WC and use of small onsite swimming pool. Shop and restaurant on site. Inspected 2016.

LES SALLES SUR VERDON 2
228 K10 83630 N43°46.648' E006°12.856'

🚐 25 None; See **227**

➡ D957. After D71 junction turn 1st right into parking, signed. Aire 10m on left, signed.

ℹ Popular designated parking on outskirts of Les Salles-sur-Verdon. Limited shaded parking; some road noise. Large lake 500m, lake leisure facilities 1km. Stunning Verdon Gorge 4.8km; continues adj to D952 towards La Palud-sur-Verdon. Inspected 2016.

MEDITERRANEAN

STE CROIX DE VERDON
229 K10 04500 ⚓ N43°45.651' E006°09.058'

🚐 22; €6.50/10pm-8am; Collected; Free in winter; Max 48hrs
🛒 Custom; Turned off in winter; 2 unmetered elec points by boules court

➡ D111a. From Quinson on D11 drive past lavender fields and turn onto D111. Follow sp 'Ste Croix du Verdon' onto D111a and downhill towards lake. Do not turn right to village, continue downhill, sp 'Camping Municipal'. Aire on right, signed.

ℹ A peaceful Aire offering views of the large Lac de Ste Croix for 8 motorhomes. Local commerce 350m. Canyon du Verdon nearby. Lavender flowering June, harvested mid July. Inspected 2014.

QUINSON
230 K10 04500 N43°41.881' E006°02.347'

🚐 7 🛒 Custom; Water marked non potable

➡ P du Musée. From south on D13 turn right after passing lake, sp 'Parking du Musée'. Turn left, sp 'P du Musée'. Aire on left before height barrier. Parking must not obstruct car park entrance or coach parking; large motorhomes subject to space. May need to reverse out.

ℹ Parking near Prehistoric museum. River Verdon with tourist commerce 200m. Hire a canoe (€8/hr), pedalo (€12) or electric boat (€23) and meander through the Gorges du Verdon to Lac d'Esparron. Inspected 2014.

GREOUX LES BAINS
231 K10 04800 ⚓ N43°45.336' E005°53.314'

🚐 71; €9/24hrs inc service and 6amp elec; Pay at machine; Max 3.5t/8m; No trailers/cars 🛒 Custom; Inside barrier

➡ Chemin de la Barque. On D952 from Riez turn left at roundabout onto D8, sp 'St Julien'. Follow road for 500m then turn right immediately before river bridge, signed. Follow road uphill for 200m and turn right, signed. Turn right again, signed, and enter through barrier.

ℹ Former municipal campsite turned commercial Aire offering shaded parking on multiple treed terraces. Town is a spa resort with tourist commerce and casino. Updated 2016.

VILLENEUVE
232 K10 04180 N43°53.773' E005°51.705'

🚐 12; Max 48hrs 🛒 Custom; No water Dec-Feb

➡ At cemetery. Turn off D4096 at roundabout, sp 'Villeneuve'. Follow sp 'P Cimetière' and signs up the hill, then out of village. Turn right towards cemetery, then follow road and signs downhill around the cemetery, signed.

ℹ Popular Aire under trees next to cemetery; dead quiet. Hilly walk to village centre 300m, which has local commerce and convenience store. Reinspected 2014.

STE TULLE
233 K10 04220 🏃 N43°47.073' E005°45.824'

🚐 10; €5/night; Collected; 3 CEE elec points on campsite bollard by road 🛒 Custom; WC locked 7.30pm-8am

➡ Parc Municipal des Sports. Enter St Tulle from Mirabeau on D996/D4096. On entering town turn 1st left, then turn right at Stop junction, sp 'Parc des Sports'. Turn into 1st car park on left. Service Point on far side against WC.

ℹ Parking under plain trees in municipal sports area. Some open grass parking at far end overlooking adj park. Boules court and other sports facilities adj. Small town commerce 400m. Reinspected 2016.

ST PAUL LES DURANCE
234 K11 13115 🏛 N43°41.255' E005°42.243'

🚐 6; Marked bays 🛒 Flot Bleu Fontaine

➡ Chemin du Retour. Turn off D96 at roundabout onto D952, sp 'St Paul-lès-Durance'. After passing St Paul-lès-Durance boundary sign, turn left and cross irrigation canal, signed. Turn 1st left, signed, and follow road to end. Turn into residential campsite and follow road to right. Aire at end of road. Actual GPS: N43°41.241' E005°42.336'. DO NOT drive through town, it is one-way and impassable.

ℹ Aire surrounded by residential caravans in all states, which makes the area resemble a shanty town although we believe it is a municipal campsite offering very long term pitches. Small town commerce 400m. Distant road noise. Reinspected 2016.

SILLANS LA CASCADE
235 K11 83690 N43°34.047' E006°10.932'

🚐 10; Max 24hrs 🅿 Urba Flux; Token; €3

➡ D560/Route de Salernes, on main road south of village. 3.5t weight restriction on Aire.

ℹ Aire in roadside lay-by. 1km signed walk to famous waterfall from TO, or 450m from Aire. Walled town 450m. On historic villages cycle route. Inspected 2014.

SALERNES
236 K11 83690 N43°33.529' E006°14.011'

🚐 5 🅿 Custom

➡ Route des Quatre Chemins. Exit town on D31, sp 'Entrecasteaux' and 'Terra Rosa'. Turn 1st right and cross bridge, then follow road to left. Aire 150m on left just past entrance to Terra Rossa ceramic museum.

ℹ Peaceful Aire 100m from ceramic museum. Town centre 650m with small town commerce. Visited 2014.

Info/photos: Lynne Watson

GREASQUE
237 K11 13850 N43°25.996' E005°32.044'

🚐 20 🅿 Custom; Tap at parking

➡ Route de la Chapelle. Turn off D96 at roundabout onto D46, sp 'Gréasque'. Go straight over next roundabout, then turn right at roundabout, sp 'Gardanne'. At next roundabout turn left, sp 'Hély d'Oissel' and signed. Follow road uphill to mine, well signed. Official parking to left next to skateboard ramps, Service Point to the right.

ℹ Very popular Aire which can take any unit configuration. Overflow into other car parks currently tolerated in low season, accommodating another 40 motorhomes. Mining museum adj. Supermarket 700m. Motorhomes banned from all other parking within a 12km radius. Reinspected 2016.

VAUVENARGUES
238 K11 13126 N43°33.262' E005°35.860'

🚐 4; Max 24hrs; 5m bays, no overhang 🅿 None; Tap inside cemetery gate

➡ D10. Approach on D10 from Aix-en-Provence. After Vauvenargues boundary turn right. Follow road to parking at bottom of hill, signed.

ℹ Dead quiet Aire located in small car park. Only suitable for 5m motorhomes during day and at peak times; bigger motorhomes will need to occupy multiple bays and should arrive late and depart early. Small town commerce 250m. Inspected 2016.

GEMENOS
239 K11 13420 N43°17.877' E005°37.760'

🚐 3; Max 24hrs 🅿 Custom

➡ Cours Sudre. From D396, main route through town, turn off, sp 'La Ste Baume' and signed. At end of road go straight on into left car park and follow road around car park. Turn right in front of La Poste, signed. Aire is behind La Poste; Service Point to left, parking to right.

ℹ Aire in tucked away location that can be difficult to access due to badly parked cars. Local commerce adj. Market Wed am. Reinspected 2014.

CUGES LES PINS
240 K11 13780 N43°16.868' E005°42.350'

🚐 20; €4.50/24hrs; Collected 🅿 Custom; €2; Elec avail from generator

➡ Le Cros Reynier. Turn off D8n in Cuges les Pins at the traffic lights by the TO, sp 'Espace Socioculturel' and signed. Follow road straight on up rough but very passable roads with passing places, signed. Follow road to left around park and Aire on left, signed.

ℹ Commercial Aire in the wooded hills with parking on terraces. Pleasant park adj with walking trails. Local commerce 650m through park. Updated 2016.

MEDITERRANEAN

LA ROQUEBRUSSANNE
241 K11 83136 N43°20.164' E005°58.775' SP

P 200 Places

🚐 4 ⛽ Euro Relais Maxi; Token; €2 (Free at time of inspection); No drive over drain; 2 CEE elec points

➡ Ave St Sébastien, off D5. Approach from Brignoles on D5; there are some hairpin bends, but the road is wide. Follow bypass past La Roquebrussanne, then at roundabout turn left, sp 'Néoules'. Turn immediately right, signed, and Aire on right, signed. Do not drive through town centre as street furniture makes it narrow.

ℹ Small Aire that is really just a Service Point. Road noise from adj bypass. Small picnic area adj. Village centre, 300m, has 3.5t weight restriction. Better parking on bypass opp fuel station, 200m, sp 'P 200 places': N43°20.233' E005°58.637'. Reinspected 2016.

SIX FOURS LES PLAGES
242 K11 83140 N43°06.752' E005°48.714'

🚐 Poss ⛽ Custom; Unhygienic and tricky; No access Sun am May-Sept

➡ Sq Hippolyte Cesmat. In town follow sp 'Six Fours' onto one-way dual carriageway along seafront of Six-Fours-les-Plages. After TO turn left, sp 'Bureau de Poste', and immediately left again. Accessible only from behind TO. After servicing have to reverse out into road.

ℹ All non-height barriered parking is unrestricted and overnight parking is allowed. Tourist resort with large shingle beach. Reinspected 2016.

OLLIOULES
243 K11 83190 N43°08.489' E005°50.913'

🚐 8; €3/24hrs; CC; Max 48hrs ⛽ Custom; WC emptying by pay machine; Tap opp by gate; No drive over drain

➡ DN8. Adj to DN8 at Ollioules. Enter through barrier, signed.

ℹ Open, gravel parking adj to main route; road noise. Room for 16. Charming town with delightful narrow streets to explore 350m; Thurs/Sat am market, 500m around storm drain. Inspected 2016.

TOULON
244 K11 83000 N43°07.601' E005°56.191'

🚐 6; €2.50/day; Pay at machine; 7m bays ⛽ None

➡ Ave des Lices. Exit A57 at Junction 1b, sp 'Toulon Centre'. Follow sp 'Centre Ville', then in 500m bear right, sp 'Toulon Nord' and 'Gare SNCF'. Stay in right-hand lane and at traffic lights follow road to left then turn immediately right into car park, sp 'P des Lices'. Designated parking on right, signed.

ℹ Designated parking on outskirts of town in busy car park. Pleasant, historic harbour with tourist commerce and National Maritime Museum, 1.5km; open all year 10am-6pm except Tues Sept-May, €6pp. Rugby union team RC Toulonnais play their home games at Stade Mayol, 1.6km. Inspected 2016.

ST MANDRIER SUR MER
245 K11 83430 N43°04.661' E005°54.262' SP

🚐 6; Max 48hrs; Max 8m ⛽ SOS

➡ Ave Charles de Gaulle, off D18. From west on D18 turn right at roundabout, sp 'Complex Sportif'. Follow road to right and Service Point on right just after roundabout: N43°04.636' E005°54.326'. Exit Service Point to right and take 1st right to parking, signed.

ℹ Popular but difficult parking, may have to reverse out onto road. Additional parking on seafront which can accommodate 12 motorhomes: N43°04.742' E005°54.013', sp 'P Obligatoire pour Remorques'. Reinspected 2016.

LA LONDE LES MAURES
246 K11 83250 N43°07.905' E006°13.836'

🚐 4; Max 24hrs ⛽ Flot Bleu Euro; CC

➡ Rond Point Ducourneau. Turn off N98, sp 'La Londe Les Maures'. At next roundabout go straight over, sp 'Port-Plages' and signed. Service Point and parking adj to roundabout 'Ducourneau'.

ℹ Adj to road and roundabout. Local commerce 500m. Reinspected 2014.

COLLOBRIERES

247 K11 83610 T N43°14.237' E006°18.170'

🚐 30 🏠 Euro Relais Box; €2

➡ D14. From west on D14 turn right at village boundary, sp 'Sapeurs Pompiers' and signed. Aire 20m, signed. Parking on other side of village: N43°14.198' E006°18.886', well signed through village. Alternative approaches are along narrow, twisting roads with no barriers!

ℹ Pleasant tourist village with restaurants and craft shops 200m. Park at Aire and walk in. Reinspected 2014.

LE THORONET

248 K11 83340 N43°27.052' E006°18.253'

🚐 5; 5m bays on far side of car park: N43°27.059' E006°18.162'
🏠 Custom; Token

➡ D79. Service Point adj to D79 at TO, signed.

ℹ Token from TO. Parking in car sized bays with no overhang. Suitable as a transitory night halt. Abbaye du Thoronet nearby. Inspected 2014.

LA MOTTE 1

249 L11 83920 N43°29.318' E006°32.521'

🚐 10; Max 24hrs 🏠 Euro Relais Box; Token (ER); €2; Also see **250**

➡ Off D47/Route de Trans. From Le Muy exit onto D25 towards Callas. Turn left at D25/D47 roundabout, sp 'La Motte'. Follow road to tennis courts, turning left before the town, signed. Drive around the tennis courts and Aire through gateway and on left, signed.

ℹ Aire located at sports facility in a residential area. Local commerce 750m. Popular walking and cycling area. Reinspected 2016.

LA MOTTE 2

250 L11 83920 N43°29.776' E006°31.879'

🚐 6; Max 24hrs 🏠 Urba Flux Tall

➡ D47/Route de Trans. From Le Muy exit onto D25 towards Callas. Turn left at D25/D47 roundabout, sp 'La Motte'. Follow road through town, max 10m long, then turn left, sp 'Trans'. Aire on right, not signed.

ℹ Aire on edge of village en route to Gorges du Verdon. Local commerce 500m. New Aire nearby, this Aire may close. Reinspected 2016.

LA GAILLARDE

251 L11 83370 N43°21.934' E006°42.720'

🚐 50; €11/24hrs inc service; €1.50/hr day parking; Pay at kiosk
🏠 Custom; 4amp elec €3/night

➡ N98/D1098, Chez Marcel. Signed off N98; 100m from main road at La Gaillarde. Pay guardian at entrance.

ℹ Well located commercial Aire in a good location for a beach holiday with a sandy beach and sea view snack bar just across the road. Shower €0.50. Washing machine €5. Reinspected 2014

STE MAXIME

252 L11 83120 N43°19.025' E006°37.799'

🚐 30; €5 Oct-Mar; €10 Apr-Sept; Max 48hrs; Pay at machine
🏠 Urba Flux; Outside barrier

➡ D25, just off large roundabout with McDonald's. If approach from St Tropez (south) on N98 follow sp 'Le Muy' to large roundabout and turn off roundabout before McDonald's, signed. Aire on left, enter through Vinci barrier.

ℹ Large gravel Aire adj to ring road and McDonald's. LIDL 300m. Town and beach 1.2km. Water taxi from harbour to St Tropez, €13.50 return in high season. www.bateauxverts.com Reinspected 2014.

MEDITERRANEAN

ST TROPEZ
253 L11 83990 🏛 N43°15.819' E006°40.303'

🌐 P 🚐 ⚓ 🔥 🎵 🚌 F ❄ | ♿ 🔲 🚾 E WC ♿ 🚐 F 🔲

🚐 40 in 2 locations; €16/night inc 16amp elec; Trailers €2; Cars €2
🚿 Custom; Water €2; Shower (Token)

➡ Take D61, then D98a to St Tropez. Follow sp 'La Moutte Les Salins' along narrow, but passable, 3.5t weight restricted roads. Turn off road only when signed into 'Les Mas du Valinco'. Aire 200m, signed, one parking area to right, one straight on. Actual GPS: N43°15.889' E006°40.333'.

ℹ Commercial Aire close to St Tropez. 150m from Cannebiers beach. Walk into St Tropez along coast. Bus nearby. Updated 2016.

PORT GRIMAUD
254 K11 83310 🏭 N43°16.792' E006°34.716'

🌐 P 🚐 ⚓ 🔥 🎵 🚌 F ❄ | ♿ 🔲 🚾 E WC ♿ 🚐 F 🔲

🚐 10; €13/24hrs; Pay at machine 🚿 Euro Relais Maxi; 2 unmetered CEE elec points

➡ N98. From St Tropez on D98 Aire is signed after junction with D14.

ℹ Aire located in lay-by adj to busy, noisy main road. Boulangerie and restaurant adj. Suggest beachside campsite 500m towards Ste Maxime instead. Reinspected 2014.

RAMATUELLE 1
255 L11 83350 ⚓ N43°12.676' E006°39.731'

🌐 P 🚐 ⚓ 🔥 🎵 🚌 F ❄ | ♿ 🔲 🚾 E WC ♿ 🚐 F 🔲

🚐 50; €5/night Nov-Mar; €8/night Apr-Oct; Inc service; Collected/Pay at kiosk; Max 48hrs 🚿 Custom; Inside barrier; 7.30am-5pm; Cold water showers

➡ Route de Bonne-Terrasse. From D93, St Tropez to La Croix Valmer, turn off, sp 'Déchetterie' and signed. Follow road, crossing bridge, signed. Aire entrance is on left before beach. 5.5t weight restriction on road.

ℹ Large open commercial Aire ideal for a beach holiday. Cove with sandy beach and tourist commerce 100m. Reinspected 2014.

RAMATUELLE 2
256 L11 83350 ⚓ N43°14.341' E006°39.693'

🌐 P 🚐 ⚓ 🔥 🎵 🚌 F ❄ | ♿ 🔲 🚾 E WC ♿ 🚐 F 🔲

🚐 56; €10 Sept-Jun; €18 Jul-Aug; 9am-9am (day parking half price) 🚿 Custom; Inside; 1 Token/100L water; €2; 6amp elec €5 Sept-June; €7 Jul-Aug; Cold water shower on beach

➡ Route des Tamaris. Turn off D93 between St Tropez and Pampelonne, sp 'Les Tamaris'. Parking on left near end of road.

ℹ Large open landscaped commercial Aire adj to beach with numerous tourist commerce and activities. Ideal for a beach holiday. Inspected 2014.

CAVALAIRE SUR MER
257 L11 83240 🏭 N43°11.700' E006°32.844'

🌐 P 🚐 ⚓ 🔥 🎵 🚌 F ❄ | ♿ 🔲 🚾 E WC ♿ 🚐 F 🔲

🚐 Tolerated in cemetery car park; Arrive late, depart early 🚿 Euro Relais Mini; €2

➡ From La Croix Valmer take D559, sp 'Cavalaire'. Turn right just past Total Access fuel station, sp 'Cimetière'. Follow road through cemetery car park and up hill. At Stop junction turn left, then left again. Follow road for 350m and Service Point is on left.

ℹ Service Point only near recycling/municipal yard. Parking at cemetery is not restricted but will be if abused. May feel isolated if alone. Inspected 2014.

CAVALIERE
258 K11 83980 ⚓ N43°09.124' E006°25.842'

🌐 P 🚐 ⚓ 🔥 🎵 🚌 F ❄ | ♿ 🔲 🚾 E WC ♿ 🚌 F 🔲

🚐 100; €16/24hrs inc service and 16amp elec; Collected 🚿 Custom; Inside; Inc

➡ D559, adj to main road. From west on D559 parking on left at rear of large gravel car park when sea is visible on right, entrance sp 'Camping-Car'.

ℹ Large partially terraced commercial Aire. Sea across road. Local and tourist commerce 100m. Reinspected 2014.

PERNES LES FONTAINES `259` J10 84210 N43°59.980' E005°03.429'

🚐 8 🚰 Flot Bleu Fontaine; Mid Mar–mid Oct

➡ P Frédéric Mistral, Cours Frizet. Enter town on D938. In centre turn off at roundabout, sp 'P'. Designated parking 200m on right, signed. For Service continue past parking and turn 2nd right, sp 'Complexe Sportif Paul de Vivie'. In 500m turn onto D28 at roundabout, sp 'St Didier'. Follow road left, then turn left, sp 'Camping Municipal Coucourelle'. Turn right, sp 'Camping' and signed, and follow road behind sports facilities. Service Point just prior to campsite: N43°59.989' E005°04.097'.

ℹ Open Aire backing onto small streamside green space and bridge to a warren of medieval streets. Small town commerce 200m. Updated 2016.

All of the listings in this section are Service Points without designated parking. The majority are located either at supermarkets or outside campsites.

Height barriers are rare at supermarkets and overnight parking should be possible. Always park considerately. Supermarket Service Points often lack a waste water drain.

Most campsites are municipally owned. Parking outside may be possible when campsites are closed. Acquiring tokens in rural locations may be difficult or impossible, especially in low season.

Remember to be a responsible tourist whenever offsite parking.

EGAT `260` G12 66120 N42°29.850' E002°00.800'

🚰 Euro Relais Junior; €2; No drive over drain

➡ D618, at Super U in Égat. Located at the roundabout junction of D618 and D33f, southwest of Égat. Service Point at the supermarket fuel station, signed. Inspected 2013.

BOLQUERE PYRENEES 2000 `261` G12 66210 N42°30.867' E002°03.733'

🚰 Flot Bleu Euro; CC; €2

➡ D618, at Casino supermarket. Located on D618, Mont Louis to Égat road, north of Bolquère. Inspected 2013.

VERNET LES BAINS `262` G12 66120 N42°33.395' E002°23.043'

🚰 Euro Relais Mini; Token (ER); €2.50; Drive over drain in car wash poss

➡ D116, at Intermarché supermarket. On right as enter town on D116, opp campsite. Service Point adj to fuel station. Inspected 2013.

ST PAUL DE FENOUILLET `263` H12 66220 N42°48.633' E002°30.267'

🚰 Flot Bleu Euro; CC; €3; No drive over drain

➡ Place St Pierre. Turn off D117 into car park in town centre, sp 'Gare SNCF' and signed. Service Point against road edge. Inspected 2013.

LA FRANQUI PLAGE `264` H12 11370 N42°56.625' E003°01.830'

🚰 Custom; Token; €5

➡ Chemin de las Pitchinos. From D627 turn off, sp 'La Franqui'. Then follow sp 'Les Cousseles'. Follow road across bridge onto island and round to right. Service Point adj to campsite entrance. Reinspected 2013.

PORT LA NOUVELLE 1 `265` H11 11210 N43°00.977' E003°02.958'

🚰 Aire Services Plastic; €2

➡ Rue Vincent Auriol. From south take D709 to Port la Nouvelle. At the roundabout turn right, sp 'Centre Ville 3.5t'. Go straight on, past `43` and `266`, go over roundabout and at the next roundabout turn left. Service Point at far end of Super U car park near self-service laundry. Reinspected 2016.

PORT LA NOUVELLE 2 `266` H11 11210 N43°00.890' E003°02.779'

🚰 Flot Bleu Euro; CC; €2

➡ Blvd Francis Vals, outside municipal campsite. From south take D709 to Port la Nouvelle. At roundabout turn right, sp 'Centre Ville 3.5t'. After crossing railway on bridge, turn left at next roundabout, sp 'Le Golfe'. Service Point on left outside Camping Municipal du Golfe, in 3.5t weight restricted area. Reinspected 2016.

NARBONNE `267` H11 11100 N43°10.550' E002°59.656'

🚰 Flot Bleu Euro; CC; €2

➡ Ave du Général Leclerc. From south on D6009 dual carriageway follow sp 'Centre Ville'. Service Point at fuel station of Casino supermarket just after turning sp 'Narbonne Plage'. Reinspected 2016.

SERIGNAN `268` H11 34410 N43°16.140' E003°17.020'

🚰 Aire Services Plastic; €2

➡ D64. Approach from north on D64. At roundabout turn right off D64 towards Carrefour supermarket. At next roundabout turn left. Drive past fuel station, follow road to left, then turn left into fuel station. Service Point on right, signed. Reinspected 2016.

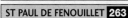

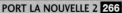

MEDITERRANEAN

VILLENEUVE LES BEZIERS 269
H11 34420 N43°18.994' E003°17.076'

♿ IIII, 🔒 **E** WC 🚻 🏕 🚌 F ⊡

🚰 Custom; €2

➡ Promenade des Vernets, adj to canal outside Camping des Berges du Canal. From town centre cross canal on D37e13 and turn immediately right, sp 'Les Berges du Canal'. Follow road along canal and Service Point 100m on left. Reinspected 2016.

GIGNAC 270
H11 34150 N43°39.716' E003°33.522'

♿ IIII, 🔒 **E** WC 🚻 🏕 🚌 F ⊡

🚰 Euro Relais Mini; Token (ER)

➡ Chemin de la Meuse, outside Camping La Meuse. Take D32 north out of village, sp 'Aniane'. Turn left, sp 'La Meuse' with the campsite symbol. Service Point to the left of campsite entrance. Reinspected 2013.

VILLEFORT 271
I10 48800 N44°26.033' E003°55.833'

♿ IIII, 🔒 **E** WC 🚻 🏕 🚌 F ⊡

🚰 Euro Relais Junior; €2

➡ Rue du 19 Mars 1962. From south on D901 turn left just before town, sp 'Les Sédariès', 'Camping' and signed. Follow road uphill and Service Point on left before campsite, just past Gendarmerie. Reinspected 2016.

REDESSAN 272
I10 30129 N43°49.526' E004°29.754'

♿ IIII, 🔒 **E** WC 🚻 🏕 🚌 F ⊡

🚰 Flot Bleu Euro; CC; €2

➡ D999. Service Point in fuel station of Casino supermarket adj to D999/D3 roundabout, signed. Reinspected 2014.

ST LAURENT DES ARBRES 273
J10 30120 N44°03.554' E004°42.672'

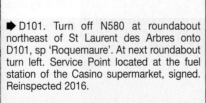

♿ IIII, 🔒 **E** 🚻 🏕 🚌 F ⊡

🚰 Flot Bleu Euro; CC

➡ D101. Turn off N580 at roundabout northeast of St Laurent des Arbres onto D101, sp 'Roquemaure'. At next roundabout turn left. Service Point located at the fuel station of the Casino supermarket, signed. Reinspected 2016.

ST PAULET DE CAISSON 274
I10 30130 N44°15.947' E004°35.861'

♿ IIII, 🔒 **E** 🚻 🏕 🚌 F ⊡

🚰 Urba Flux; Token; €2

➡ Chemin du Plane. Turn off D256, sp 'Cave Cooperative' and signed. Follow road behind cave and Service Point at rear, signed. Inspected 2014.

BOLLENE 275
J10 84500 N44°19.317' E004°44.650'

♿ IIII, 🔒 **E** WC 🚻 🏕 🚌 F ⊡

🚰 Flot Bleu Pacific

➡ D26, at E'Leclerc supermarket. Turn off D26 at roundabout north of town, sp 'Centre Commercial'. Drive around past fuel station to rear of supermarket and Service Point is in a roadway within the parking. Reinspected 2016.

BEDOIN 276
J10 84410 N44°07.927' E005°10.239'

♿ IIII, 🔒 **E** WC 🚻 🏕 🚌 F ⊡

🚰 Euro Relais Mini; Token; €2

➡ D19. From Bédoin follow D19 north for 1.3km. Service Point is on left of road outside Camping le Pastory. Inspected 2013.

LA BRILLANNE 277
K10 04700 N43°55.922' E005°53.409'

♿ IIII, 🔒 **E** WC 🚻 🏕 🚌 F ⊡

🚰 Flot Bleu Pacific; 1 Token/20 mins

➡ D4096. Adj to main route through town at the fuel station of the Carrefour supermarket. Exit difficult due to bollards. Reinspected 2016.

AURIOL 278
K11 13390 N43°22.081' E005°38.483'

♿ IIII, 🔒 **E** WC 🚻 🏕 🚌 F ⊡

🚰 Flot Bleu Pacific (Green); Token

➡ D560, at Casino supermarket entrance. Exit Auriol towards Péage on D560. Service Point adj to supermarket fuel station. Reinspected 2016.

LE BEAUSSET 279
K11 83330 N43°11.900' E005°48.371'

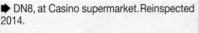

♿ IIII, 🔒 **E** WC 🏕 🚌 F ⊡

🚰 Flot Bleu Euro; CC; €2

➡ DN8, at Casino supermarket. Reinspected 2014.

BRIGNOLES 280
K11 83170 N43°24.579' E006°03.722'

♿ IIII, 🔒 **E** WC 🏕 🚌 F ⊡

🚰 Flot Bleu Pacific (Green); Token (FB)

➡ D2007. From DN7 at roundabout take D1007 towards town centre. At traffic lights turn right onto D2007 and 1st right into Casino supermarket. Service Point at fuel station. Reinspected 2016.

SOLLIES PONT 281 K11 83210 N43°12.137' E006°02.813'

🚿 ▥ 🛁 E ᵂᶜ ♿ ☂ 🚌 F ⊡
🚰 Flot Bleu Euro; CC; €2

➤ Ave Jean Brunet. Heading south on A57 exit at Junction 8. At roundabout turn left, sp 'Centre Commercial'. Turn right, then drive through car park and turn left, then right. Service Point adj to Casino fuel station. Supermarket adj. Motorway adj. Reinspected 2016.

HYERES 1 282 K11 83400 N43°06.478' E006°07.710'

🚿 ▥ 🛁 E ᵂᶜ ♿ ☂ 🚌 F ⊡
🚰 Flot Bleu Euro (Green); CC; €3

➤ D559/Ave Geoffroy St Hilaire, at the Casino supermarket. From Toulon go across roundabout on A570 then at traffic lights turn right onto D559. The Aire is down this road on right. Narrow access. Not signed from road. Inspected 2014.

HYERES 2 283 K11 83400 N43°06.782' E006°06.952'

🚿 ▥ 🛁 E ᵂᶜ ♿ ☂ 🚌 F ⊡
🚰 Flot Bleu Euro; CC; €1.50; Can lift grid to empty WC

➤ Hyper E'Leclerc. From Toulon turn right off A570 at roundabout, then fork right. At roundabout take 2nd exit and follow advert to the Hyper E'Leclerc. Service Point adj to fuel station. Inspected 2014.

LA LONDE LES MAURES 284 K11 83250 N43°08.303' E006°14.259'

🚿 ▥ 🛁 E ᵂᶜ ♿ ☂ 🚌 F ⊡
🚰 Flot Bleu Euro (Green; not working); CC

➤ D559, at Casino supermarket fuel station. Aire on right on D559 as exit town towards Bormes les Mimosas. Reinspected 2014.

LA FAVIERE 285 K11 83230 N43°07.494' E006°21.708'

🚿 ▥ 🛁 E ᵂᶜ ♿ ☂ 🚌 F ⊡
🚰 Raclet; Token (ER); €2

➤ Blvd du Port, off D198. From west on D198 follow sp 'Port' through town. At port turn left, sp 'Toutes Directions', and follow road to 'Le Lavandou'. Service Point 100m from port, adj to road and park. Reinspected 2014.

LES ARCS SUR ARGENS 286 K11 83460 N43°27.161' E006°29.463'

🚿 ▥ 🛁 E ᵂᶜ ♿ ☂ 🚌 F ⊡
🚰 Flot Bleu Euro; CC; €2

➤ D555. Turn off DN7 onto D555, sp 'Draguignan'. At the next roundabout turn left, sp 'ZA le Pont Rout'. At either of the next two roundabouts turn left into the Hyper U supermarket complex. The Service Point is at the rear of the fuel station. Reinspected 2016.

FREJUS 287 L11 83600 N43°26.367' E006°44.671'

🚿 ▥ 🛁 E ᵂᶜ ♿ ☂ 🚌 F ⊡
🚰 Flot Bleu Euro; CC; €5

➤ D100/Avenue André Léotard, at Casino supermarket. As enter Fréjus from north on D37 take 3rd exit at roundabout onto DN7, sp 'Fréjus-Centre'. Supermarket on left at next junction. Service Point adj to fuel station. Reinspected 2014.

CALLIAN 288 L11 83440 N43°36.251' E006°45.290'

🚿 ▥ 🛁 E ᵂᶜ ♿ ☂ 🚌 F ⊡
🚰 Urba Flux; Token; €2

➤ Off D562. Turn off D562 east of town at roundabout towards McDonald's, sp 'Chemin de Combes'. Drive past McDonald's entrance and turn left, signed. Continue straight, then turn left at roundabout. Service Point on left adj to car wash, signed. Reinspected 2016.

CANNES 289 L11 06150 N43°33.002' E006°58.236'

🚿 ▥ 🛁 E ᵂᶜ ♿ ☂ 🚌 F ⊡
🚰 Flot Bleu Euro; CC; €2; Inspection cover

➤ D6007. Exit A8 at Junction 41 and follow sp 'Cannes-La Bocca' onto D6007. Continue following sp 'Cannes-La Bocca' and drive past the Hyper Casino. Go around roundabout and retrace steps to Hyper Casino. Service Point by fuel station of Hyper Casino supermarket, 30m from car park entrance. Reinspected 2016.

CASTELLANE 290 K10 04120 N43°51.150' E006°30.500'

🚿 ▥ 🛁 E ᵂᶜ ♿ ☂ 🚌 F ⊡
🚰 Flot Bleu Pacific; Token (FB); Inspection cover

➤ D955, at Casino supermarket. On northern edge of town at roundabout junction of D955 and D4085. Service Point adj to fuel station with own access road. Reinspected 2016.

EMBRUN 1 291 K9 05200 N44°32.773' E006°28.815'

🚿 ▥ 🛁 E ᵂᶜ ♿ ☂ 🚌 F ⊡
🚰 Flot Bleu Pacific; €2

➤ N94, at Intermarché supermarket. From Embrun take N94 south. After crossing river turn right at roundabout, sp 'Centre Commercial'. Follow road straight on over roundabout and continue until road bends left. Service Point on left outside Intermarché fuel station. Reinspected 2016.

EMBRUN 2 292 K9 05200 N44°33.047' E006°29.374'

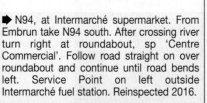

🚿 ▥ 🛁 E ᵂᶜ ♿ ☂ 🚌 F ⊡
🚰 Flot Bleu Euro; CC; No drive over drain

➤ Lieu-dit Entraigues. From Embrun take N94 south. After crossing river turn right at roundabout, sp 'Embrun'. Turn 1st right again, sp 'Embrum'. Follow road going straight over roundabout and past commerce. Service Point on left at far end of Super U. Service Point sealed up and building notice at site; will move location. See 291. Inspected 2016.

MEDITERRANEAN

GAP | 293 | K9 | 05000 | N44°32.664' E006°03.994'

🛗 🎛 1️⃣ E WC ♿ 🚰 🚌 F ⭕

🚾 Euro Relais Junior; €2; Self-cleaning WC adj, 8am-8pm

➡ Chemin de Châteauvieux. Follow sp 'Sisteron' through town. Turn left at roundabout between building with mirrored glass and McDonald's. Follow road to right through shopping complex, then turn left at roundabout, sp 'Crématorium'. Drive past Auchan, then turn right into Auchan car park. Service Point behind fuel station, signed. Self-service laundry and WC adj. Inspected 2016.

VILLARS COLMARS | 294 | K10 | 04370 | N44°09.642' E006°36.357'

🛗 🎛 1️⃣ E WC ♿ 🚰 🚌 F ⭕

🚾 Custom; €3; Pay at campsite

➡ D908. From south turn right into car park of La Haut Verdon campsite before Total fuel station. Service Point at far end of car park adj to D908, signed. Inspected 2016.

AUPS | 295 | K11 | 83630 | N43°37.019' E006°13.193'

🛗 🎛 1️⃣ E WC ♿ 🚰 🚌 F ⭕

🚾 Flot Bleu Pacific; €2 (1 x €2); Inspection cover

➡ D31. Exit Aups on D22, sp 'Carcès'. Turn right just after D22/D31 roundabout into Intermarché car park, then turn immediately right to Service Point. Inspected 2016.

SISTERON (NORTH) | 296 | K10 | 04200 | N44°14.208' E005°54.701'

🛗 🎛 1️⃣ E WC ♿ 🚰 🚌 F ⭕

🚾 Flot Bleu Pacific; Token/20 mins

➡ Follow D4085 north out of Sisteron. At roundabout junction with E712/D4075 turn right to stay on D4085, sp 'Gap'. At next roundabout turn left, sp 'Zone Commercial'. At next roundabout turn left into Super U. Service Point is near fuel station adj to car wash, signed. Reinspected 2016.

AVIGNON | 297 | J10 | 84000 | N43°56.520' E004°49.596'

🛗 🎛 1️⃣ E WC ♿ 🚰 🚌 F ⭕

🚾 Euro Relais Box; €2; No drive over drain

➡ Ave de Colchester. Approach from south on N7. Turn right onto D907, sp 'Orange'. Turn first right off D907, then turn right at traffic lights, sp 'Centre Ville'. Go through next 2 sets of traffic lights and turn right into Intermarché. Drive to rear and Service Point is adj to Le Drive. There is limited space for manoeuvring; entrance and exit are narrow. Inspected 2016.

GUILLESTRE | 298 | K9 | 05600 | N44°39.407' E006°37.953'

🛗 🎛 1️⃣ E WC ♿ 🚰 🚌 F ⭕

🚾 Custom; €4.60; Pay at campsite

➡ Route de la Gare. Turn off N94, sp 'Guillestre'. Go straight over roundabout, then turn right, sp 'Piscine - Tennis'. Follow road and Service Point on right opp municipal campsite, signed. Inspected 2016.

PONT DE CLANS | 299 | L10 | 06420 | N43°58.625' E007°08.412'

🛗 🎛 1️⃣ E WC ♿ 🚰 🚌 F ⭕

🚾 Flot Bleu Océane; Token (FB)

➡ Route de la Tinée. Turn off M2205 in Pont de Clans at roundabout towards small retail/industrial area, sp 'Vival' and signed. Service Point on right, to left of Vival entrance. Inspected 2016.

VINON SUR VERDON | 300 | K10 | 83560 | N43°43.764' E005°48.202'

🛗 🎛 1️⃣ E WC ♿ 🚰 🚌 F ⭕

🚾 Flot Bleu Pacific; Token (FB)

➡ Chemin du Pas de Menc. Exit Vinon-sur-Verdon on D852 following sp 'Manosque'. At roundabout turn left, sp 'Zone d'Activités Pas de Menc'. Go straight ahead at next 2 roundabouts. Turn 1st left into Carrefour supermarket fuel station. Service Point behind car wash. Inspected 2016.

SALLELES D'AUDE | 301 | H11 | 11590 | N43°15.967' E002°56.927'

🛗 🎛 1️⃣ E WC ♿ 🚰 🚌 F ⭕

🚾 Flot Bleu Euro; CC

➡ D418. Service Point at Casino Supermarket on left as approach town on D418 from Ouveillan. Service Point immediately on right, signed. Inspected 2016.

LA MALENE | 302 | H10 | 48210 | N44°18.000' E003°18.761'

🛗 🎛 1️⃣ E WC ♿ 🚰 🚌 F ⭕

🚾 Aire Services 3000; CC; €4

➡ D907bis. Exit La Malène on D907bis, sp 'Millau'. Service Point on left in 650m, signed. Visited 2016.

Info/photo: Frank Butler

VALRAS PLAGE | 303 | H11 | 34350 | N43°14.600' E003°16.903'

🛗 🎛 1️⃣ E WC ♿ 🚰 🚌 F ⭕

🚾 Aires Services 3000; €2/50L water

➡ Boulevard Pierre Giraud. Enter town on D19. At the roundabout turn right, sp 'Casino'. At the traffic lights turn right, sp 'Casino'. Turn right in 600m before road bends left, Service Point on right in 10m, signed. Follow road as bends to sea for unofficial parking in 100m: N43°14.529' E003°16.906'. Reinspected 2016.

AGDE | 304 | H11 | 34300 | N43°17.954' E003°28.259'

🛗 🎛 1️⃣ E WC ♿ 🚰 🚌 F ⭕

🚾 Euro Relais Mini; Token (ER); €2.50

➡ Route de Guiraudette, at Hyper U. Exit D612, sp 'Grau d'Agde'. At roundabout turn left, crossing over D612, sp 'Grau d'Agde'. At next roundabout turn right, then right again into Hyper U. Updated 2015.

Lac de L'uby

MIDI-PYRENEES

Lacroix Barrez

GIGNAC
| 1 | F9 | 46600 | | N45°00.350' E001°27.400' |

🚐 15 ☕ Custom

➡ Place des Troubadours. Turn off D820 onto D34, signed. In village join D87. After 300m turn right into Rue Pierre Cerou, signed. Aire at rear of Salle des Fêtes, signed.

ℹ Aire in car park on edge of small rural village. Local commerce 150m. Always likely to have space. Reinspected 2016.

CARENNAC
| 2 | G9 | 46110 | T | N44°55.034' E001°43.839' |

🚐 20; €6/24hrs; Pay at machine at P Omberge, 200m: N44°55.041' E001°43.982' ☕ Custom; 4 CEE unmetered elec points (Turned off)

➡ D20. In Bétaille turn off D803 onto D20, sp 'Gramet'. Follow road, crossing river and turning right, sp 'Gramet'. At Carennac stay on D20, sp 'Gramet'. Drive past P Omberge, where ticket machine is, then turn left, sp 'P3' and signed. Aire at end of road, signed.

ℹ Aire on edge of Beau Village, footpath to village at end of road. Dordogne river nearby. Inspected 2016.

SOUILLAC
| 3 | F9 | 46200 | | N44°53.497' E001°28.574' |

🚐 45 ☕ Flot Bleu Euro; CC; €3; Also see 235

➡ Parking du Baillot. From D820 turn into D804 in town centre at traffic lights, sp 'Sarlat'. In 250m turn left, sp 'Baillot' and signed. Turn 1st right into Parking du Baillot, signed. Aire 200m on right, signed.

ℹ Popular Aire in a residential area. The Byzantine cathedral is a must see, 400m. Town commerce 450m. Reinspected 2014.

GOURDON
| 4 | F9 | 46300 | | N44°44.067' E001°23.116' |

🚐 8 ☕ Custom; €1; 8 12amp elec points; €1/1.5hrs

➡ Place du Foirail. Follow one-way system in town, sp 'Figeac' or 'Rodez' and signed. After passing the church on the right, turn right, sp 'Quartier du Foirail'. Follow signs through car park and down slope to Aire on right.

ℹ Pleasant landscaped Aire on edge of attractive hilltop town. Restaurant adj. Town centre 650m. Reinspected 2014.

MARTEL
| 5 | G9 | 46600 | | N44°56.379' E001°36.504' |

🚐 25; On rear gravel section ☕ Custom; Taps permanently removed

➡ D23. Follow sp 'Les Quatre Routes' through town onto D23. As exit town turn right, sp 'P Parking'. Designated overnight parking on lower terrace, signed. For Service Point follow D23 into town. Go straight over 2 roundabouts. In 140m turn right and Service Point on right: N44°56.098' E001°36.404'.

ℹ Aire on edge of medieval town famed for its 7 towers. Town and tourist commerce 300m. Steam train to St Denis along the Dordogne, €10.50pp. Expect change. Reinspected 2016.

Photo: Rod Poxon

GLUGES (Montvalent)
| 6 | G9 | 46400 | | N44°54.502' E001°37.470' |

🚐 13 ☕ Custom; WC down drain behind building

➡ D840. From south follow D840 through Montvalent towards Martel. Just before river bridge turn left, sp 'Zone de Loisirs' and signed. Turn 1st right and Service Point is 20m on left, signed, parking 100m, signed.

ℹ Dordogne river adj, no views; may flood in winter. Walk chairs to riverside park. Swimmers, boaters and fishermen will be happy all day. May feel isolated if alone. Seasonal commerce. Reinspected 2016.

LABASTIDE MURAT

7 G9 46240 N44°39.004' E001°34.237'

🚐 5; Closest to Service Point 🛢 Custom

➡ D677. Exit town on D677, sp 'Gramat'. Turn left as exit town into Carrefour supermarket car park. Service Point located behind supermarket in what is believed to be municipal space.

ℹ This Aire feels different to most supermarket stops because of the views and the rural location; but parking is near delivery point, can be noisy during deliveries. Pleasant town centre with local commerce 350m. Reinspected 2016.

ROCAMADOUR

8 G9 46500 T N44°48.013' E001°36.933' SP

🚐 25; Tolerated 🛢 None; See **9**

➡ Parking Le Château. From west on D673 turn right onto D200 in L'Hospitalet, sp 'Parking Le Château' and 'Remparts'. Parking at coach park in 700m just beyond funicular railway station. DO NOT attempt to drive through lower Rocamadour village.

ℹ Must see amazing town clinging onto cliff. Walk or funicular railway to village adj, €4.20 return. Grotto in town adj to TO. All local parking unrestricted. Reinspected 2014.

ALVIGNAC

9 G9 46500 N44°49.502' E0001°41.827' SP

🚐 15 🛢 Raclet

➡ D673/Route de Padirac. From south on D840 turn right onto D673, sp 'Alvignac'. Follow road through centre and Aire on right on inside of bend 150m after junction with D20, signed.

ℹ Former campsite turned Aire on edge of town adj to a pleasant park, no dogs. WC closed in winter. Local commerce 200m. Rocamadour **8** should be visited. Reinspected 2016.

GRAMAT

10 G9 46500 N44°46.789' E001°43.705' SP

🚐 20; Max 48hrs 🛢 Euro Relais Junior; 2 unmetered elec points

➡ Avenue Paul Mazet. From D840 turn onto D807 at roundabout, sp 'Gramat Centre'. At roundabout turn left, signed. Follow road and Aire on left.

ℹ Aire located on a peaceful residential street. Town commerce 300m. Reinspected 2016.

ST CERE

11 G9 46400 N44°51.250' E001°54.006' SP

🚐 6 🛢 Flot Bleu Fontaine; No drive over drain

➡ D19. From south on D48 turn right onto D19 150m after town boundary sign. Aire on left in 100m.

ℹ Large open parking area near river Brave, no view. Town centre commerce 950m. Visited 2016.

Info/photos: David Hayward

SOUSCEYRAC

12 G9 46190 N44°52.361' E002°02.201' SP

🚐 10 🛢 Euro Relais Junior; 1 unmetered elec point; No drive over drain

➡ D653. Adj to D653 in village centre car park facing La Poste and Mairie. Service Point behind toilet block, not visible from road.

ℹ Aire located in centre of town adj to small town commerce. Plenty of parking, but parking closest to Service Point may be obstructed at times. Tiny medieval centre adj. Reinspected 2016.

LATRONQUIERE

| 13 | G9 | 46210 | | N44°47.951' E002°04.741' |

🚐15 Euro Relais Junior; 1 unmetered CEE elec; No drive over drain

➡ Place du 19 Mars 1962. Follow D31 through town centre towards Figeac. Turn left before Salle des Fêtes, sp 'Le Rouget (RN 122)'. Turn 1st right, sp 'La Poste'. Service Point behind La Poste.

ℹ Aire in town parking adj to boules and mini golf. Small town commerce 150m. Inspected 2014.

MONTET ET BOUXAL

| 14 | G9 | 46210 | | N44°44.471' E002°01.169' |

🚐15 Euro Relais Junior; Potable water near fuel pumps; 1 unmetered CEE elec point; No drive over drain

➡ D653. From north on D653 the Service Point is on the right between car wash and 24hr fuel station.

ℹ Aire in small rural village. Parking behind Service Point is large but mostly sloping. It is possible to level near the top. Reinspected 2014.

LEYME

| 15 | G9 | 46120 | | N44°47.046' E001°53.989' |

🚐7 Aire Services 3100; 1 unmetered CEE elec point; WC at parking

➡ Off D48. From south on D48 Service Point at 24hr fuel station on right at entry to village, opp church: N44°47.001' E001°54.044'. For parking continue north on D48, then turn 1st left at church, sp 'Complex Sportif' and signed. Designated parking in car park on left, signed.

ℹ Parking adj to sports grounds in large open carpark just 150m from local commerce. Bus stop adj, WC well kept. Open access sports grounds and park 50m downhill, parking adj. Pleasant beech wood with pleasant lay-by to south on D39. Reinspected 2016.

LACAPELLE MARIVAL

| 16 | G9 | 46120 | | N44°43.685' E001°55.799' |

🚐30 Euro Relais Junior; €2; No drive over drain

➡ D653/Place Larroque. From D840 turn onto D940, sp 'Lacapelle Marival'. In town turn right onto D653, sp 'Latronquière'. Follow road to large parking area. Aire on right at rear of car park.

ℹ Aire in large car park in town. Thriving Mon am market does not affect Aire. Many historic buildings in town, inc 13th century château. Leisure lake with unrestricted parking to north adj to D39. Reinspected 2016.

THEMINES

| 17 | G9 | 46120 | | N44°44.466' E001°49.784' |

🚐2; Limited and very sloping Euro Relais Junior; 1 unmetered elec point; No drive over drain

➡ D40, outside the church. Turn onto D40 at Thémines, sp 'Halle de Thémines'. Turn left at covered market, opp Mairie. Service Point at top of hill just past church.

ℹ Small, very sloping parking outside church; hell's bells all night. Ancient covered market adj. Nearby Aynac has old fuel pumps at fuel station on D40. Reinspected 2016.

CARDAILLAC

| 18 | G9 | 46100 | T | N44°40.755' E001°59.874' |

🚐10 Euro Relais Junior; €2; No drive over drain

➡ Off D15, by the church in village centre. Signed from D15 main route through village. 100m of narrow turns to access. May be difficult to manoeuvre on busy days when car park full.

ℹ Well maintained, pretty, medieval fortified Beau Village 400m down main street. Adj village has shabby chic charm, ensure you wander down the alleys and back streets. Inspected 2014.

AUTOIRE

19 | G9 | 46400 | **T** | N44°51.358' E001°49.316'

🚐30 Euro Relais Box; €2

▶ Lieu-Dit La Roque Maynard, adj to D38. Turn off D30 onto D38, sp 'Autoire'. Follow road for 2.3km and the Aire is on the right as enter village, signed. Drive down slope and Service Point is on right adj to WCs. Additional parking on D30 at KM30 in Aire de Repos d'Autoire.

ℹ Aire adj to Beau Village, 300m up path. Walk to Autoire waterfall and Cirque d'Autoire, visible from village. Updated 2015.

Photos: Rod Poxon

FIGEAC

20 | G9 | 46100 | | N44°36.661' E002°02.213' | **SP**

🚐40 Euro Relais Junior; €2

▶ From N122 or D13 at roundabout exit onto D19, signed. Service Point is 300m on right in small car park with trees against town wall, signed. For better parking continue across next roundabout into Parking du Foirail: N44°36.721' E002°02.095'.

ℹ Service Point difficult to access if car park busy. Large town. Motorhomes can park anywhere. Reinspected 2014.

BOUILLAC

21 | G9 | 12300 | | N44°34.372' E002°09.459' | **SP**

🚐10; Max 24hrs Custom; Token; €3

▶ Adj to D840. From Figeac on D840 the Aire is on the right in roadside lay-by 280m after 'Bienvenue à Aveyron' sign, signed.

ℹ Aire in attractive roadside picnic area alongside noisy main road. River views and access. Reinspected 2014.

BOISSE PENCHOT

22 | G9 | 12300 | | N44°35.517' E002°12.333' | **SP**

🚐8 Euro Relais Junior; Token (ER); €3

▶ Off D42. Turn off D840 onto D42, sp 'Boisse Penchot' and signed. After 1.3km turn left, signed, and Aire on right in 125m.

ℹ Pleasant Aire with 8 landscaped bays. River Lot and riverside park 10m, partial view from some bays. Local commerce adj. Reinspected 2014.

CRANSAC LES THERMES

23 | G10 | 12110 | | N44°31.367' E002°16.433' | **SP**

🚐6; Max 48hrs Custom; Token; €3/100L water or 1hr elec; 2 Cont elec points

▶ D11e/Avenue de la Gare. In Aubin turn onto D11, sp 'Cransac'. Turn right off D11, sp 'Cransac' and 'Casino'. Drive past supermarkets, then turn right at traffic lights into Ave de la Gare, sp 'Gare SNCF'. Aire on right opp campsite before you cross the railway track, signed.

ℹ 6 landscaped bays separated by shrubs. Train noise from adj track. Thermal town with associated commerce inc casino. Thermes 1.5km uphill behind casino, where treatments feature the use of natural gas created with the thermal water. www.chainethermale.fr Reinspected 2016.

CAPDENAC GARE

24 | G9 | 12700 | | N44°34.395' E002°04.385' | **SP**

🚐40; €9.60/24hrs inc service and elec; CC Euro Relais Junior; Inside barrier; Mix of CEE and Cont elec

▶ D86. From west on D840 cross river bridge on D994, sp 'Capdenac Gare'. Turn right immediately after crossing bridge onto D86, sp 'Cajarc'. Aire on right in 300m by TO. Enter through PARKNIGHT barrier.

ℹ Riverside commercial Aire in former campsite. Some hardstanding and some grass parking. Supermarket 150m, small town commerce 650m. Visited 2016.

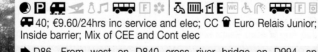

Info/photos: David Hayward

PEYRUSSE LE ROC
25 | G10 | 12220 | N44°29.683' E002°08.333'

7 Custom; Inaccessible drive over drain

➤ D87. Follow D87 out of village, sp 'Naussac' and signed. Aire on right down slope, signed.

i Pleasant Aire adj to quaint medieval village with local commerce. Lovely spot with views. Reinspected 2016.

VILLENEUVE
26 | G10 | 12260 | N44°26.467' E002°02.224'

8; €5/night Custom; €3; 4 CEE elec points; Elec €2/2hrs

➤ D40. From Figeac turn left off D922, sp 'Villeneuve - Centre' and signed. Turn left onto D48, signed. Then turn left again onto D40, sp 'Salles Courbaties', 'Camping' and signed. Aire on right in entrance to campsite just past sports facilities, signed.

i Service Point and overnight parking at campsite. 500m from pretty walled town, poss to park for day in car park adj to La Poste: N44°26.292' E002°01.969'. Reinspected 2016.

PREVINQUIERES
27 | G10 | 12350 | N44°22.447' E002°13.598'

15 Custom

➤ D118. Turn off D1 onto D61, sp 'Prévinquières' and signed. Follow D61 to Prévinquières. In centre turn right onto D118, sp 'Compolibat' and signed. Aire on right just before exit village, signed.

i Peaceful Aire suitable for any unit configuration on edge of small old village with local commerce. Inspected 2016.

LANUEJOULS
28 | G10 | 12350 | N44°25.600' E002°09.670'

14; €5/night Custom; Drive over drain and WC outside barrier; 12 unmetered CEE elec points and water inside barrier

➤ Impasse des Bleuets. Turn off D1 by church onto D635, sp 'Pachins' and signed. Follow road uphill for 130m, then turn left, signed. Aire immediately on right. Enter through barrier; barrier opened via card available to purchase from commerce in town.

i Aire just off centre with small town commerce. Overcomplicated access; cards difficult to obtain at night. WC and showers also accessed via cards. Reinspected 2016.

VILLECOMTAL ★
29 | G10 | 12580 | N44°32.135' E002°33.853'

24; Extra grass parking in season Custom; 18 unmetered Cont elec points

➤ D904. Aire adj to D904 at former municipal campsite, signed.

i Very pleasant former municipal campsite turned Aire. 24 large hedged bays adj to shallow river; Mixture of grass and gravel parking. Get here whilst it's still good. Inspected 2014.

RIGNAC
30 | G10 | 12390 | N44°24.272' E002°17.379'

10; No parking 10am-7.30pm mid Jun-Aug; €5/7.30pm-10am Jun-Aug Euro Relais Mini; Turned off in winter

➤ Parc de la Peyrade. From Rodez on D994 take 1st exit at roundabout onto D997, sp 'Rignac'. Follow D997 through town, then turn left onto D75, sp 'Odalys' and signed. Turn right off D75, sp 'Camping'. Drive downhill past camping and Aire on left after crossing bridge, signed.

i Pleasant Aire by park with numerous walks. Restrictions in place during summer camping season mean that the pleasant park cannot be enjoyed. Reinspected 2016.

BELCASTEL

31 G10 12390 T N44°23.134' E002°19.820'

5; Grass parking 🛒 Custom; 6 unmetered CEE elec points

➡ D285. Turn off D997 onto D285, sp 'Belcastel'. Aire on right in 2km. Entrance is a difficult turn down steep slope, not signed. Assess before attempting.

ℹ Former municipal campsite with grass parking alongside river, can be muddy if wet. Shower in toilet block. Follow path across bridge to Beau Village, car parks don't allow motorhomes at night. Reinspected 2016.

ST CYPRIEN SUR DOURDOU

32 G10 12320 N44°33.159' E002°24.596'

14 🛒 Flot Bleu Pacific; €2; Inspection cover; Flot Bleu Elec; €1/2hrs; 8 CEE elec points

➡ D901. Exit village on D901, sp 'Conques'. 400m after town boundary turn right into fuel station, signed. Drive through fuel station and at exit go straight on down lane opp, signed. Turn 1st left into Aire, signed.

ℹ Landscaped Aire 400m from village with small town commerce. Historic UNESCO village of Conques with Ste Foy Abbey, an important stop on the pilgrimage to St Jacques, 7km. Inspected 2016.

ENTRAYGUES SUR TRUYERE

33 H9 12140 N44°38.406' E002°34.162'

50; Gravel and grass parking 🛒 Euro Relais Junior; Token (ER)

➡ D904. Turn off D920 south of town onto D904, sp 'Campuac'. Cross river bridge then turn right, signed. For parking turn right and follow road downhill. Service Point: N44°38.557' E002°33.976'. Turn left and follow road for 220m and Service Point on right, signed.

ℹ Very pleasant Aire adj to river. Steep bank and trees obscure views and access. Canoe hire in season. Town commerce 650m, other side of river. Amenity space and pedestrian river bridge by Service Point. Inspected 2014.

MONTEZIC

34 H9 12460 N44°42.617' E002°38.633'

8; +€0.30pp tax; Honesty box behind sink; Max 48hrs 🛒 Custom

➡ Les Prades, off D504. From south on D97 turn right onto D504 at church, sp 'St Gervais' and signed. After 300m turn right, signed. Aire 175m on left, signed.

ℹ Small, peaceful Aire adj to sports facilities. Village with local commerce 400m. D97 from village takes scenic drive through Gorges de la Truyere with lay-bys and vistas. Reinspected 2016.

LACROIX BARREZ

35 H9 12600 N44°46.675' E002°37.890'

20; €2.50/night; +€0.20pp; Apr-Oct; Max 72hrs; Grass parking 🛒 Flot Bleu Compact; Apr-Oct; 6 Cont and CEE elec points

➡ D505. Turn off D904 onto D505, sp 'Murols' and signed. Turn right in 200m, signed, and Aire on left in 100m. Parking signed behind service Point.

ℹ Lovely Aire in former municipal campsite. 6 hedged bays with elec plus additional open parking. Sports facilities adj. Local commerce 500m. 5 mins of fun: Interesting old lava flows, 1km: N44°46.215' E002°37.945'. Adj to D97 with parking, continue on this road for scenic drive past Château Valon to Gorges de la Truyere. Reinspected 2016.

MUR DE BARREZ

36 H9 12600 N44°50.483' E002°39.567'

8 🛒 Euro Relais Junior; Token (ER)

➡ Place du Foirail, adj to Parc de la Corette. Turn off D904, sp 'Centre Ville' and signed. Turn 1st left and follow road to right, signed. Turn left to Service Point, signed.

ℹ Alt 800m. Aire adj to pleasant hilltop park with picnic tables, play area and viewpoints on edge of village. Map of walks and cycle routes at park. Local commerce 200m. www.carladez.fr Reinspected 2016.

THERONDELS `37` H9 12600 N44°53.897' E002°45.420'

🚐5; Grass parking; 5 additional in centre 🚰 Flot Bleu Pacific; Water tap (near ground), WC and 4 CEE elec points past picnic tables

➡ Rue du Mars 1962. From Mur de Barrez take D900, sp 'Barrage de Sarrans'. In Brommat turn left onto D18, sp 'Thérondels'. In Thérondels, 10.6km, take 1st right, signed, and Service Point is 200m on right: N44°53.900' E002°45.567'. Parking past picnic tables opp Service Point or at Vival mini market in centre: N44°53.709' E002°45.477'.

ℹ Alt 936m. Pleasant Aire with grass parking adj to pond with rural views. Hardstanding parking in centre. Small town commerce 200m. Reinspected 2016.

STE GENEVIEVE SUR ARGENCE `38` H9 12420 N44°48.117' E002°45.733'

🚐10 🚰 Flot Bleu Pacific; €2; 4 6amp CEE elec points (Night use only, don't split)

➡ Rue de l'Argence. From D900 heading south, or D78 heading east, turn into Rue de l'Argence (which connects the two roads). The parking is adj to the river, signed.

ℹ Aire in a pleasant spot adj to small river. Notice requests that no electricity cables should be connected during the day. Local commerce 400m. Leisure lake and park adj to D900. Reinspected 2016.

CAMPUAC `39` H9 12580 N44°34.091' E002°35.368'

🚐4 🚰 Custom; Adj to WCs beside cemetery

➡ Off D46. From south on D904 turn right onto D46, sp 'Campuac'. After 3.7km turn right between church and cross. Parking on left at end of road. For Service Point drive 225m further on D46 straight over mini roundabout. Service Point straight ahead: N44°34.200' E002°35.483'.

ℹ Parking located in a small gravel area only suitable for 7m motorhomes. Village centre with local commerce adj. Reinspected 2014.

LAGUIOLE SKI STATION `40` H9 12210 SKI N44°40.343' E002°55.471'

🚐25; €10/7pm-7am in winter season; €40/week; Free rest of year 🚰 Seasonal WC; 25 Cont 10amp elec points €5/night

➡ Lieu-Dit le Bouyssou, off D15. From Laguiole take D15, sp 'Aubrac' and 'Station de Ski de Laguiole le Bouyssou'. Follow road for 9.8km and Aire on right at 'Station de Ski de Laguiole'. Day parking during season on left, 8.45am-5.30pm: N44°40.383' E002°55.649'. Compulsory night parking straight on at bottom of slopes, signed.

ℹ Alt 1300m. Large parking area in small ski resort. Ski hire and local seasonal commerce. Lots of summer walks with well-marked footpaths. Ski lifts to beginner and intermediate runs adj. Laguiole has a knife museum and several commercial knife forges open to public, 10km. Reinspected 2016.

AUBRAC `41` H9 12470 N44°37.233' E002°59.200'

🚐20 🚰 Flot Bleu Fontaine; Taps removed; No drive over drain; WC 150m

➡ D533. Turn off D987 onto D533, sp 'St Chély d'Aubrac'. Aire on right in 150m on edge of village.

ℹ Alt 1299m. Pleasant open parking area on edge of village suitable for any unit configuration. Botanical gardens with regional product shop and TO opp. www.aubrac-jardin.org St Jacques de Compostella path runs through village. Festival of Transhumance, moving Aubrac cows up to pasture, held annually on weekend closest 25 May. Expect change. Reinspected 2016.

ESPALION `42` H10 12500 N44°31.296' E002°46.156'

🚐20; €9.60/24hrs Sept-Jun; €10.80/24hrs Jul-Aug; Inc service and elec 🚰 Euro Relais Junior; 9 6amp CEE elec points; Inside barrier; WC 90m, by play area

➡ Ave Pierre Monteil. From north on D920 follow across bridge and turn left, sp 'Camping' and signed. Turn 1st left, sp 'P Forail'. Follow road, narrow in places, and Aire is on right opp tennis courts before roundabout, signed. Enter through PARKNIGHT barrier.

ℹ Commercial Aire. Motorhomes banned from all other local parking at night. 500m from town commerce. Exit Aire to right and walk/cycle along river on St Jacques de Compostela route to St Come d'Olt, Beau Village with pleasant riverside campsite €14/night. www.camping-bellerive-aveyron.com Inspected 2016.

STE EULALIE D'OLT
43 H10 12130 T N44°27.883' E002°56.950'

🚐 16; €7/night inc elec; CC 🛒 Custom; 16 16amp CEE elec point; All inside barrier

➡ Rue de la Grave. Turn off D988 onto D597, sp 'Camping la Grave' and signed. Follow road for 700m, then turn right as road bends left, sp 'Camping' and signed. Turn right before river bridge and Aire is 200m to right of Camping Municipal La Grave. Enter through Aire Services barrier.

ℹ Commercial Aire adj to campsite. River on other side of campsite, no views. Pretty historic Beau Village 300m. Day parking, 8am-10pm: N44°27.800' E002°56.634'. Motorhomes banned from all car parks at night. Reinspected 2016.

BOZOULS
44 G/H10 12340 T N44°28.326' E002°43.264'

🚐 10 🛒 Custom

➡ Rue Marc André Fabre, adj to D20. Turn off D20, sp 'Bibliothèque' and 'Mediathèque'. Aire immediately on left in large car park, signed.

ℹ Well located Aire. Continue down lane on foot into pedestrianised street and follow to left for commerce, gorge and views across to a cliff top commune. Poss to walk past waterfall and up through gorge. Reinspected 2014.

CAMPAGNAC
45 H10 12560 N44°25.185' E003°05.313'

🚐 5; €3/night; Collected 🛒 Custom

➡ Off D37. In village centre turn off D202 onto D37, sp 'St Laurent d'Olt' and 'Gendarmerie'. Turn 1st right past Gendarmerie and the Aire is on the right directly behind the Gendarmerie.

ℹ Peaceful village with local commerce. Unmetered elec in grassed area, long cable needed. Reinspected 2014.

LAISSAC
46 H10 12310 N44°23.140' E002°49.282'

🚐 6 🛒 Custom; €2; Honesty box

➡ From N88 turn onto D28, sp 'Laissac'. Take 1st right, signed. Drive around Intermarché and turn right, signed.

ℹ Aire sandwiched between large livestock market area, market Tue am, and noisy N88. Constant road noise, but more sheltered parking adj to market. Supermarket 150m, small town commerce 300m past market. Reinspected 2016.

RODEZ
47 H10 12000 N44°21.467' E002°35.647'

🚐 6; Max 72hrs 🛒 Custom

➡ D162, opp ZI Cantaranne. Turn off N88 at roundabout onto D217/Ave de la Roquette. After 2km do not turn left over railway line, but carry straight on, sp 'Rodez'. After a further 1.6km turn left at large junction, sp 'Ste Radegonde'. Aire 750m on right, signed.

ℹ Pleasant landscaped Aire surrounded by green fields with walk/cycle to Rodez adj. Rodez historic centre 1.8km uphill. Reinspected 2016.

SEGUR
48 H10 12290 N44°17.441' E002°50.104'

🚐 5 🛒 Custom; €2; Honesty box; Shower; Token

➡ Rue de la Mairie, off D95. From Rodez take D29 21.7km to Ségur. In village turn right onto D95, sp 'Segur', then turn 1st left. Service Point signed at sports facilities; parking to left beyond Service Point. Well signed through village.

ℹ Parking poss in village car park. Local commerce adj. Reinspected 2016.

PONT DE SALARS
`49` H10 12290 N44°16.688' E002°43.706'

5; Max 72hrs Custom; Token; €5/80L; May-Oct; Seasonal WC

➡ Place de la Rivière, in village centre. Turn off D911, sp 'Pont de Salars'. Turn off main route into large car park, sp 'Aires'. Aire at far side of car park, signed; WC to left, Service Point to right.

ℹ Landscaped Aire in hedged bays to rear of large car park. Boules court and river adj. Small market Thurs am. Local commerce 100m. Reinspected 2016.

SALLES CURAN ★
`50` H10 12410 N44°12.016' E002°46.558'

40; €11/night inc 10amp CEE elec; CC; Free in winter Flot Bleu Compact; €4; Inside barrier; Water on numerous pitches; No services in winter

➡ D243. From north on D993 turn right onto D243, sp 'Les Vernhes'. After 1.6km turn left into Aire, signed. Enter through Flot Bleu park barriers.

ℹ Alt 814m. Former municipal campsite turned Aire adj to and overlooking beach and lake; direct access. Terraces allow most pitches to have excellent lake views. This is the best located Aire around the lake and a lovely place for a holiday. Inspected 2016.

Photos: Elizabeth O'Leary

ARVIEU
`51` H10 12120 N44°11.526' E002°39.569'

12; Max 72hrs; Apr-mid Nov Custom; Token; €3; Apr-mid Nov; WC at far end

➡ Route de la Rivière. From Canet de Salars enter Arvieu on D56. Turn right opp lake before bridge, signed. Follow road down and around boules court, signed. Access bumpy, may be difficult for motorhomes with long overhang.

ℹ Large parking area adj to open access boules court on edge of village. Only likely to be busy during boules competitions. Small town commerce 200m. Reinspected 2016.

CANET DE SALARS
`52` H10 12290 N44°13.946' E002°44.851'

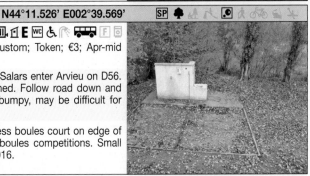

5 hardstanding; 10 grass; €6/24hrs inc elec; Collected; May-Oct Custom; Token; €2; 18 Cont elec points; May-Oct

➡ D176. Exit Canet de Salers on D176, sp 'Arvieu'. Aire adj to D176 on left at village boundary, signed.

ℹ Alt 872m. Aire in peaceful location at former municipal campsite next to sports field. Village with local commerce. Near Lac de Pareloup. Inspected 2016.

Photo: Frank Butler

BARAQUEVILLE
`53` G10 12160 N44°16.711' E002°26.018'

12 Euro Relais Junior; Token (ER); €3

➡ Rue de la Mairie. On N88 turn right at roundabout, sp 'Tous Commerces' and signed. Turn 1st left into car park and turn left again at rear of car park in front of Mairie. Turn 1st right, signed, and follow road 240m to Aire, signed.

ℹ Pleasant landscaped Aire overlooking fields with a lake in the distance. On terrace above livestock market. Small town commerce 250m. Inspected 2016.

CASTANET
`54` G10 12240 N44°16.734' E002°17.365'

4; €8; Pay Mairie/Honesty box Custom; Each bay has 16amp CEE elec point and tap

➡ D613. Turn off D911 onto D542, sp 'Castanet'. Follow road for 3.8km to Castanet, then turn right onto D613, sp 'Centre Ville'. Aire on right just past Mairie, signed.

ℹ Pleasant small Aire in small rural village. No commerce in village. Reinspected 2016.

SAUVETERRE DE ROUERGUE

| 56 | G10 | 12800 | T | N44°12.960' E002°19.014' | SP |

🚐15; May-Oct 🛢 Custom; Elec €2/24hrs; Shower €1.50; Pay at TO

➡ D997. On right of D997 as enter town from Naucelle, signed.

ℹ️ Former municipal campsite turned Aire. Beau Village 400m. Roadside parking surrounds Beau Village, which has a large, central arcaded square. www.sauveterre-de-rouergue.fr Reinspected 2016.

NAJAC

| 57 | G10 | 12270 | T | N44°13.289' E001°58.041' | SP |

🚐12; €2/2hrs; €6/24hrs Oct-Apr; €8/24hrs May-Sept; CC 🛢 Euro Relais Junior; 8 CEE elec points; All inside barrier

➡ Le Pontet. From Villefranche follow D47, sp 'Najac'. Turn left onto D39, sp 'Najac' and signed. In 4km turn right, signed, and Aire 150m on right. Enter through barrier.

ℹ️ Peaceful commercial Aire by picnic area and sports facilities. 1.5km steep climb to ridgetop Beau Village with château and church, visible from Aire. Inspected 2016.

LAGUEPIE

| 58 | G10 | 82250 | 🚢 | N44°08.709' E001°58.212' | SP |

🚐30; Max 24hrs; Grass and hardstanding bays 🛢 Custom; Seasonal WC; CEE/Cont elec turned off

➡ Chemin de St Cambraire. From west follow D958 into town. In Laguépie turn right immediately before river bridge, signed, and follow road downhill (GPS taken here). Follow road to left and along river edge. Aire on left in the old municipal campsite. Actual GPS N44°08.764' E001°58.357'.

ℹ️ Well located Aire at former municipal campsite. River adj with steps and slipway, partial views. An ideal summer spot with shade from deciduous trees. Riverside walks. Small town commerce on other side of river. Reinspected 2016.

LE SEGUR

| 59 | G10 | 81640 | | N44°06.533' E002°03.517' | SP |

🚐4; Opp Service Point 🛢 Custom; No drive over drain; Shower with WC at Mairie

➡ Maison du Temps Libre, off D27. From Mirandol Bourgnounac turn off D905 onto D80 and follow sp 'Le Ségur'. At roundabout in Le Ségur turn right onto D27, sp 'Mairie'. Turn right again, sp 'Mairie' and signed. Aire is 150m on right outside Mairie, signed.

ℹ️ Aire located in small village; space likely. Local commerce 100m. Reinspected 2016.

MIRANDOL BOURGNOUNAC

| 60 | G10 | 81190 | | N44°08.513' E002°10.000' | SP |

🚐15 🛢 Custom; Flexi hose for waste water; Cont WC adj

➡ Place du Foirail. Turn off D905 in centre, signed. Service Point to rear of car park against covered market building, signed.

ℹ️ Aire in central car park also used for livestock markets; access will be difficult if livestock market is trading. Suitable for any unit configuration. Small town commerce adj. 2 cycling routes depart from town, 17km and 25km; see sign. Reinspected 2016.

MONTEILS

61 G10 12200 N44°16.021' E001°59.802'

5 Custom

➡ D47. Follow D47 from Villefranche, sp 'Monteils'. Aire 600m on right after entering Monteils, signed.

ℹ Small, overly landscaped Aire adj to stream in small park with trees. Watch for rocks when parking. Pretty, well kept village with local commerce 100m. Inspected 2016.

CAYLUS

62 G10 82160 N44°14.022' E001°46.282'

20 Custom; Cont WC 50m opp

➡ D19. On D19 as exit Caylus towards St Antonin. On left opp Maison du Patrimoine, signed.

ℹ Aire on edge of town opp park with fishing pond and free entry ecomusée. Town centre 500m uphill through interesting historic streets. Covered market is listed monument. Local commerce in central square and on main route through. Reinspected 2016.

ST ANTONIN NOBLE VAL

63 G10 82140 N44°09.144' E001°45.085'

20 Custom; WC emptying dysfunctional, use drive over drain or inspection cover

➡ Chemin de Roumégous. From north on D19 turn right onto D958, sp 'Autres Directions'. Turn 1st left back onto D19, sp 'Varen'. Turn 1st right, then left opp cemetery, sp 'P'. Service Point immediately on left as enter car park, signed; 3t weight restriction.

ℹ Pleasant, popular Aire with parking shaded by deciduous trees. Town commerce 150m. Seasonal canoe hire and riverside picnic area 250m. Gorges de l'Aveyon start from town. Reinspected 2016.

Photos: Keith & Sue Lawrence

CORDES SUR CIEL

64 G10 81170 T N44°03.855' E001°57.474'

20+; €6/night inc 1 Token; Pay at machine Custom; 1 Token/3hrs elec or 100L water

➡ Parking les Tuileries. From D600, main route through, turn off onto D8, sp 'Bournazel' and signed. Follow road down hill and to the right. Just after village boundary sign turn right, sp 'P' and signed. Aire is 700m on right in Parking les Tuileries, signed.

ℹ Pleasant Aire offering parking on 3 terraces. Town, 1.6km uphill, is a Grands Sites de Midi Pyrénées. Modern commerce closer than town. Updated 2016.

MONESTIES

65 G10 81640 T N44°04.269' E002°05.628'

4; Mid Sept-mid Jun; See info Custom; Flexi hose for waste water

➡ From Carmaux take D91, sp 'Monestiès'. Turn off D91, sp 'Camping'. Turn right, sp 'Camping Municipal', and cross bridge. Aire on left outside Camping Municipal les Prunettes, signed.

ℹ A very pretty Beau Village. Motorhomes must use pleasant municipal campsite 15 June-15 Sept: €3.50pp, €2 camper; €2.60 elec. Reinspected 2014.

CAHUZAC SUR VERE

66 G10 81140 N43°58.923' E001°54.667'

5 Custom

➡ Place du Mercadial. From south on D922 turn right as enter town, signed. At end of road turn left, signed. Continue straight on into Place du Mercadial. Service Point on left, signed, parking on right.

ℹ Aire in a peaceful location on dead end road opp boules court. Communal washing lines adj. Small town with municipal campsite and local commerce. Reinspected 2014.

CARMAUX

67   G10   81400   N44°03.021' E002°09.879'

🚐 20 🛒 Custom

➡ Turn off N88 onto D91 and follow sp 'Carmaux'. Follow road to right, then turn right into Rue Gambetta. Drive round main square and turn off, sp 'Aire Camping-Car'. Follow road to right, sp 'Rosières'. As road bends left, go straight on and Aire is on left, signed.

ⓘ Aire adj to sports facilities, 650m from town centre with town commerce. Market Friday am. Some noise from local industry during day. Updated 2015.

VALDERIES

68   G10   81350   N44°00.725' E002°14.014'

🚐 10 🛒 Custom; Flexi hose for waste water

➡ D91. Follow D91 through town and Aire is the large car park opp Mairie, by La Poste and taxi parking.

ⓘ Aire adj to central car park. Peaceful at night, but school adj and area busy at drop off and pick up times. Local commerce adj. Reinspected 2014.

ALBI 1

69   G10   81000   N43°55.886' E002°08.152'

🚐 10 🛒 Aire Services 3000; CC; €2

➡ Rue René Cassin. From large traffic-lighted roundabout by river bridge turn off, sp 'Base de Loisirs de Pratgraussals' and signed. Turn right at end of road, then left and after following road around sewerage works turn right, all signed. Service Point immediately on right, parking around corner on left.

ⓘ Roadside parking adj to cemetery and leisure park. View of Albi cathedral steeple, Albi 1.6km along river Tarn. Leisure park attracts youthful behaviour. May feel isolated if alone. Inspected 2014.

ALBI 2

70   G10   81000   N43°55.630' E002°08.458'

🚐 9; Max 48hrs 🛒 None; See **69** , **240** , **241** or **242**

➡ P Cathédrale, Blvd du Général Sibille. From **69** cross bridge and turn right in 600m when road opens to square. At next junction turn right and follow road for 300m. Turn left at roundabout, signed, then immediately right into P Cathédrale. Follow road to left downhill, sp 'École Européenne…'. Aire on the left, sp 'Sauf Camping-Cars'.

ⓘ Excellently located pleasant Aire at the base of Albi cathedral, the largest brick structure in world. Historic centre adj. Updated 2016.

ALBAN

71   G10   81250   N43°53.230' E002°27.545'

🚐 15 🛒 Euro Relais Junior; €2

➡ Rue Italo Zaccaron. From D999 turn off in Alban, sp 'Complexe Sportif' and signed. Follow road down hill and Aire on left before sports stadium. 3.5t weight restriction on some parking.

ⓘ Pleasant Aire away from the road noise overlooking open access sports ground. Small town commerce 280m uphill on D999. Reinspected 2014.

REQUISTA

72   G10   12170   N44°02.073' E002°32.163'

🚐 6 hedged bays plus additional parking 🛒 Custom

➡ Place François Fabié. From north on D902 turn left into Place François Fabié opp Renault garage. Aire adj to Salle des Fêtes.

ⓘ Aire in large unlevel car park. Alternative level parking in next car park. Small town commerce 250m. Very scenic drive on D902 along river Tarn to **76** via Brousse le Château, a Beau Village. Reinspected 2014.

PAMPELONNE 73 | G10 | 81190 | N44°07.334' E002°14.651'

🚐 5 ⛺ Custom; Flexi hose for waste water missing; No drive over drain; Cont WC

▶ Place du Foirail. Follow D78 through village and turn onto D53, sp 'Tanus'. The Aire is on right at edge of village green, with weighbridge and public WCs.

ℹ Parking under topiary plane trees overlooking village green. Local commerce adj. Reinspected 2016.

TANUS 74 | G10 | 81190 | N44°06.150' E002°19.006'

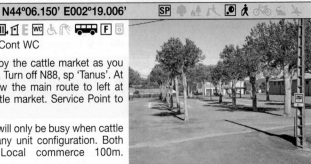

🚐 40 ⛺ Custom; No drive over drain; Cont WC

▶ Rue de Tanus le Vieux. The Aire is by the cattle market as you exit the village on D688 towards Rodez. Turn off N88, sp 'Tanus'. At roundabout turn left, sp 'Tanus'. Follow the main route to left at church, then turn left into car park/cattle market. Service Point to left.

ℹ Aire in a large gravel car park which will only be busy when cattle market on; space likely. Suitable for any unit configuration. Both shaded and unshaded parking. Local commerce 100m. Reinspected 2016.

ST JUST SUR VIAUR 75 | G10 | 12800 | N44°07.433' E002°22.533'

🚐 4; Max 48hrs ⛺ Euro Relais Junior; 2 unmetered CEE elec points

▶ Place des Fêtes. From N88 turn onto D10, sp 'Castelpers'. In 11km turn right onto D532, sp 'St Just'. Aire on left in 2km, signed.

ℹ Pleasant rural location with BBQ and riverside park. Suitable for any unit configuration. On the Gorges du Viaur road and close to the Viaduc du Viaur. Reinspected 2016.

BROQUIES 76 | H10 | 12480 | N44°00.294' E002°41.617'

🚐 15 ⛺ Custom; 1 unmetered elec point

▶ From Vabres L'Abbaye follow D25 to Broquiès. In village centre turn left onto D54. Turn next left into Place de la Mairie, then 1st right into Rte de Mazies/D200e. Aire on left in 140m as road bends left.

ℹ Aire in a pleasant location situated on a terrace overlooking the wooded hills of the Tarn Valley. 3 further elec points in recycling area. Local commerce 200m uphill. Reinspected 2014.

MILLAU 77 | H10 | 12100 | N44°05.750' E003°05.133'

🚐 32; €12/night; CC ⛺ Euro Relais Junior; Inside barrier; Inc; 24 CEE elec points

▶ Rue de la Saunerie. From south follow D809 across river, sp 'Millau-Centre'. Take 1st slip road on right, sp 'P Centre Historic' and signed. Follow under D809 and go straight on, sp 'P La Grave'. Pass Parking La Grave then turn right at mini roundabout, signed. Turn right. Enter through PARK NIGHT barrier.

ℹ Popular landscaped commercial Aire adj to main road. Millau 450m. Viewpoint underneath Millau bridge: N44°04.807' E003°01.299'. Reinspected 2014.

LA COUVERTOIRADE 78 | H10 | 12230 | N43°54.776' E003°18.970'

🚐 30; €3; Pay on exit; Mar-Nov ⛺ Nearest Service Point at Caylar; €2.50; See info

▶ Off D55. Enter 1st car park and follow signs to motorhome area. Enter through barrier.

ℹ Within 200m walk of large 12th century fortified Templar Beau Village. www.lacouvertoirade.com Private restaurant Aire with pay Service Point adj to D609 near Caylar, signed: N43°52.191' E003°18.886'. Updated 2017.

Photos: Rod Poxon

LA CAVALERIE

79 H10 12230 N44°00.520' E003°09.145'

🛇 32; €12/night; CC ♻ Euro Relais Junior; Inside barrier; Inc

➡ D277. Exit A75 at Junction 47 and follow sp 'La Cavalerie' onto D999. As approach Le Cavalerie turn right onto D277, signed. Aire immediately on right, enter through PARKNIGHT barrier.

ℹ A landscaped commercial Aire within earshot of the A75. Ideal night halt when heading south. Village 450m has Templar ruins. Inspected 2014.

ROQUEFORT SUR SOULZON

80 H10 12250 T N43°58.867' E002°58.867'

🛇 10 ♻ Custom; WCs down steps

➡ D23, at entrance to village next to TO. From Millau take D992/D999 then D23, sp 'Roquefort'. Aire is on left as you enter village.

ℹ Popular Aire located on a sloping car park with panoramic views. TO adj. The village is a short walk uphill with numerous Roquefort cheese cave tours. The 'Société' Roquefort cave tour is recommended. Inspected 2014.

ST JEAN D'ALCAS

81 H10 12250 T N43°55.600' E003°00.517'

🛇 10 ♻ Custom

➡ D516. Aire next to cemetery on east/southeast edge of village, signed.

ℹ A basic Aire which is always likely to have space. Village centre, 300m downhill, has an amazing fortified town with info panels in English, audio tour available. Inspected 2014.

VABRES L'ABBAYE

82 H10 12400 N43°56.728' E002°50.367'

🛇 20 ♻ Euro Relais Mini; Token (ER); €2

➡ Rue de la Vigne. From St Affrique on D999 turn left at 1st roundabout, sp 'Vabres l'Abbaye'. Follow road, then turn left into Rue du Coustel at village hall and pharmacy, signed. Follow road to right, then turn right, signed. Service Point immediately on right.

ℹ Pleasant town Aire in large car park at rear of village hall with open and shaded parking. Bells noisy when they chime. Local commerce 250m. Reinspected 2014.

COUPIAC

83 G10 12550 N43°57.100' E002°35.033'

🛇 5; Grass parking ♻ Custom

➡ Off D90, at rear of 'Station Service'. From D999 turn onto D33, sp 'Réquista'. After 12km turn right onto D60, sp 'Coupiac'. In village turn right onto D60, sp 'Montclar' and signed. Turn right over bridge onto D90, sp 'Martrin' and signed. Turn right again in 400m and Service Point on left adj to 24hr fuel station.

ℹ Pleasant Aire on grass between trees. 200m from medieval village and château. Background factory noise/smells. Reinspected 2014.

ST SERNIN SUR RANCE

84 H10 12380 N43°53.205' E002°36.103'

🛇 5; Max 72hrs ♻ Custom

➡ From east on D999 pass through village and turn right immediately before high river bridge, signed. Follow road downhill and Aire on right under bridge, signed. Access road steep with a sharp bend at end which could be difficult in icy conditions.

ℹ This is a very pleasant Aire adj to stream and away from road noise, but may feel isolated if alone. 800m up the road to village which has local commerce. Reinspected 2014.

CAMARES

85 | H10 | 12360 | N43°49.017' E002°52.883'

🚐 25; Max 72hrs 🏠 Custom

➤ Base de Loisirs, Chemin des Zizines. Turn off D902 just south of village, sp 'Plan d'Eau', 'Base de Loisirs', and signed. Cross bridge and turn right into Chemin des Zizines. After 430m turn left and Aire in car park for swimming lake.

ℹ Basic Aire which is always likely to have space. The village centre, 350m downhill, has an amazing fortified town with info panels in English, audio tour available. Inspected 2014.

MURAT SUR VEBRE

86 | H11 | 81320 | N43°41.250' E002°51.201'

🚐 5 🏠 Custom

➤ D622. Aire adj to D622 as exit village towards Lacaune. In lay-by on left, signed.

ℹ A traditional French village Aire in local parking area adj to boules court. Local commerce within 200m, butcher adj has interesting range of sausages and hams. Inspected 2014.

LAC DU LAOUZAS ✱

87 | H11 | 81320 | N43°38.815' E002°46.938'

🚐 20; €7.50/night Mar-Oct; €8.50/night July-Aug; Collected 🏠 Custom; 16 CEE elec points dotted through parking for battery charging, do not stay permanently connected

➤ D162. From northeast on D162 the Aire is on north shore of lake 3km after junction with D162c, signed.

ℹ Popular pleasant Aire along shore of lake, all bays with lake views. Water access for swimming, boating and fishing. Busy at weekends. Updated 2016.

BELMONT SUR RANCE

88 | H10 | 12370 | N43°48.979' E002°45.164'

🚐 3; Max 24hrs 🏠 Flot Bleu Fontaine

➤ Adj to D32 in car park, opp Mairie.

ℹ Popular Aire with lovely garden. No animals allowed in garden. Interesting village with old church. Local commerce adj. Reinspected 2014.

RAYSSAC

89 | G10 | 81330 | N43°49.067' E002°24.950'

🚐 10; Max 24hrs 🏠 Flot Bleu Compact; €3.05 inc elec; Pay Mairie; 2 unmetered elec points

➤ From D81 turn onto D59, sp 'Rayssac'. Aire on right on entry to village in small car park adj to Mairie, signed. Approach from north not advised, very narrow roads.

ℹ Aire in open car park adj to Mairie; suitable for all unit configurations. WC and tap at large BBQ. Reinspected 2016.

MONT ROC

90 | G11 | 81120 | N43°48.189' E002°22.299'

🚐 10 🏠 Flot Bleu Standard Pacific; €2; No drive over drain

➤ Rue du Village. Turn off D81 onto D81a, sp 'Montroc' and signed. In 500m turn right into car park adj to Mairie, signed. Service Point is behind the Mairie, best parking to right by picnic tables.

ℹ Aire behind Mairie adj to community hall and picnic area. Shaded and open parking. Suitable for any unit configuration. 5 mins of fun: Walk through village to the table d'Orientation, for impressive 360° views. Inspected 2016.

VABRE
91 G11 81330 N43°41.658' E002°25.528'

🚐 5 🛏 Custom

▶ Rue du Garric. Follow D55 through centre, sp 'Castres'. After crossing river bridge turn 1st left, sp 'Piscine' and signed. Drive past swimming pool and Service Point on right before tennis court, signed; parking behind and adj to tennis courts.

ℹ️ Parking adj to river at bottom of impressive stone bridge. Small town commerce across bridge, accessed via steps from Aire. Inspected 2016.

FERRIERES - La Ramade
92 G11 81260 N43°39.711' E002°26.892'

🚐 3 🛏 Custom; On side of toilet block; 1 Cont elec point at WC

▶ D53. From Vabre follow D53, sp 'Ferrieres'. Aire on right after entering La Ramade, signed.

ℹ️ Motorhome Service Point and limited parking in roadside lay-by and picnic area in small hamlet. Museum to Protestantism 300m, €4pp. http://mprl.fr Inspected 2016.

ANGLES
93 G11 81260 N43°33.932' E002°33.924'

🚐 3 🛏 Custom

▶ D68. Aire adj to D68 to the south of town by the local fuel station, signed.

ℹ️ 3 designated bays at the local 24/24 fuel station on the edge of a rural town. Small town commerce inc TO 500m. Inspected 2014.

MAZAMET
94 G11 81200 N43°29.450' E002°22.800'

🚐 20+ 🛏 Custom

▶ Parking Champ de la Ville, Rue du Bassin. From Labruguière follow N112 towards town. At traffic lights turn right and follow sp 'Centre Ville'. At end of road in town centre turn right at traffic lights. Then turn left, sp 'P Champ de la Ville'. At roundabout turn right into car park. Service Point on lower terrace, level parking on top terrace.

ℹ️ Centrally located Aire in town centre car park shaded by plane trees. Car park is virtually empty at night, but busy Sat am (market). Town commerce 450m. Reinspected 2014.

MAZAMET LAC DES MONTAGNES
95 G11 81200 N43°27.916' E002°20.502'

🚐 10 🛏 Custom; Seasonal WC and outdoor cold showers

▶ Lac des Montagnes. From Mazamet take D118, sp 'Carcassone' and 'Lac des Montagnes'. After 5.8km turn right, sp 'Lac des Montagnes' and signed. Turn 1st left for Service Point, signed, on right before height barrier: N43°27.733' E002°20.800'. For parking carry straight on. Turn left further around lake, sp 'Parking 2'. Designated parking on bottom terrace.

ℹ️ Pleasant Aire adj to picnic area at swimming lake with sandy beach and pontoon, limited views. Shade from conifer trees. Pleasant park with seasonal WC and BBQ adj. Reinspected 2016.

LABRUGUIERE
96 G11 81290 N43°31.996' E002°15.366'

🚐 35; €2/1hr; €6/24hrs; Inc elec and service; CC; Pay at machine
🛏 Custom; CC; 15 CEE elec points; All inside barrier

▶ Parc du Montimont. Approach from Puylaurens on D621. Turn right before railway track, sp 'Domaine d'En Laure'. Follow road to right, then turn left, both sp 'Domaine d'En Laure'. Aire on left at Domaine d'En Laure, to right of gateway, signed. Enter through barrier.

ℹ️ Landscaped commercial Aire on edge of town adj to leisure park with fishing lakes. Town commerce 1km. Reinspected 2016.

LACROUZETTE

97 G11 81210 N43°39.779' E002°20.919'

🚐 10 ⛽ Flot Bleu Océane; Token; €2; 3 Cont elec points to left of Service Point

➡ Place du Theron. Approach Lacrouzette from Roquecourbe on D30. Follow road through town, turning right onto one-way system, sp 'Toutes Directions'. Turn left, sp 'Brassac'. Turn next left, sp 'P Place du Theron'. Aire on right behind sculpture.

ℹ Aire in large open car park with plenty of space in granite cutting town. Local commerce 100m. Near national park and gorges. Interesting granite glacial boulder deposits and TO 5km south on D30. www.lacrouzette.fr Reinspected 2016.

LAUTREC

98 G11 81440 N43°42.239' E002°07.830'

🚐 50 ⛽ Euro Relais Junior; Token (ER); €2

➡ Espace Aquatique Base de Loisirs. Approach on D83 toward Castres. Turn off D83 onto D92, sp 'Vielmur', 'Base de Loisirs' and signed. Follow road then turn left, signed. Turn left again and Aire is on right, signed. Town centre has 3.5t weight restriction.

ℹ Aire on outskirts of hilltop town adj to leisure park, lakes (no views) with swimming beach, picnic area and recreational facilities. Beau Village with local commerce 1.5km up hill. Reinspected 2016.

SAIX

99 G11 81710 N43°34.897' E002°08.698'

🚐 12; €2/1hr; €7/24hrs; CC ⛽ Custom; Inside barrier

➡ VC11. Turn off N126 onto VC11, sp 'Base de Loisirs' and 'Les Etangs'. Follow road and Aire is on left at far end of parking. Enter through barrier.

ℹ Small, uninspiring Aire surrounded by gravel car parks adj to several leisure lakes, no view. Plenty of parkland and walking begins 100m from Aire, no view. Bike trails/BMX course adj, noise poss. Seasonal tourist commerce adj, Saix centre 3.7km. Suggest **98** as a better leisure lake to stop at. Inspected 2016.

CASTRES

100 G11 81100 N43°37.225' E002°15.203'

🚐 20; 5pm-10am Sept-Jun; 7pm-9am Jul-Aug; Max 1 night ⛽ Custom; Cont WC at parking

➡ D89. Enter town from north on D89, then turn left into Parc de Loisirs de Gourjade. Follow road to car park. For Service Point exit Castres on N126, sp 'Toulose'. Turn left at roundabout by Nissan dealer and Service Point on right, signed: N43°35.431' E002°12.398'.

ℹ Service Point with no parking in industrial estate, or night only parking at leisure facilities. Suggest **98** as a better stop. Reinspected 2016.

PUYLAURENS

101 G11 81700 N43°34.122' E002°00.725'

🚐 15 ⛽ Custom; Tap in middle; WC in hedge

➡ Rue Albert Thorel. In town turn off D926 onto D84, sp 'Revel' and signed. Follow road downhill, then at roundabout turn left, signed. Aire 300m on right through gateway, signed.

ℹ Pleasant, peaceful landscaped Aire on part of an old campsite with some hedged pitches and some shade. Outdoor swimming pool adj. Market Wed. Horse fair in town 1st Sun of each month. Reinspected 2016.

SOREZE

102 G11 81540 N43°27.017' E002°03.928'

🚐 7 ⛽ Custom

➡ P Gratuit 250. Approach Sorèze on D85 from Revel. At roundabout adj to U Express turn right onto C18, sp 'P Gratuit 250' and 'TO'. Follow road to left and Service Point on left, parking on right before height barriered parking.

ℹ Pleasant Aire backing onto green space. Small town commerce, TO, glass museum and monastery museum all 250m. Walking trail around town in English. Inspected 2014.

DURFORT

| 103 | G11 | 81540 | | N43°26.358' E002°03.909' |

🚐 10 🛒 Custom

➡ D44. Exit D85 onto D44, sp 'Durfort'. Follow road and as enter village turn right signed, into large car park. Service Point to left.

ℹ Pleasant tranquil Aire in ample car park close to village centre. Local/tourist commerce 100m. Rural views of surrounding national park. Nicknamed Cité du Cuivre (the copper city); copper museum in town. Reinspected 2014.

REVEL

| 104 | D4 | 31250 | | N43°27.222' E002°00.841' |

🚐 28; €9/night Jun-Aug; €7/night Sept-May; +tax and inc elec (16 points); CC 🛒 Custom; Inside barrier; Inc; €3

➡ Chemin des Peupliers. From town centre ring road follow sp 'Halte Camping-Cars'. Turn left into gravel track, signed. Aire at end of track. Enter through Urba Flux barrier.

ℹ Isolated position away from town in the middle of sports fields and trout farm. Unsuitable gravel parking on some bays, remaining on grass. Free access to swimming pool, show receipt. Reinspected 2014.

LAVAUR

| 105 | F11 | 81500 | | N43°41.177' E001°49.083' |

🚐 5 🛒 Custom

➡ Chemin d'en Trabouillou. Exit town on D112 towards Castres. Turn off D112 onto D87, sp 'Caraman'. Go straight over roundabout, sp 'Caraman'. In 200m turn left, sp 'Cuisine Centrale' and signed. In 100m turn left, signed.

ℹ Parking behind school. Small town commerce 1.5km. Market Saturday am. Inspected 2012.

LISLE SUR TARN

| 106 | G10 | 81310 | | N43°51.729' E001°49.106' |

🚐 15 🛒 Euro Relais Box; Token; €2

➡ Rue des Aulnes. As enter town from Gaillac on D988 turn left at roundabout onto D14b, sp 'Lisle sur Tarn'. Turn 1st left, signed, then follow road to right, signed. Aire straight on, signed.

ℹ Popular, pleasant Aire adj to leisure lake, no views. Plenty of green space surrounding Aire and leisure lake. Carp fishing. Small town commerce 1.5km. Reinspected 2016.

BRENS

| 107 | G10 | 81600 | | N43°53.448' E001°54.639' |

🚐 4; Max 72hrs 🛒 Custom; Water marked non-potable; 4 CEE elec points at parking

➡ Rue des Rives. From north on D964 cross Tarn river and turn 1st left onto D4, sp 'Cadalen'. Follow D4 through town, then turn left, signed. Service Point 100m on left: N43°53.390' E001°54.567', signed. Parking further round to right, signed.

ℹ Pleasant Aire next to peaceful road and adj to river, no access and partial view. Local commerce 300m. Inspected 2016.

GAILLAC

| 108 | G10 | 81600 | | N43°53.977' E001°53.696' |

🚐 20 🛒 Custom

➡ Parking Rives Thomas in Rue des Silos. From south on D964 follow road into town. At centre follow sp 'P Rives Thomas'. Service Point at bottom of large unrestricted car park on several levels.

ℹ Gaillac is a pleasant, traditional French town with a historic centre and town commerce, 250m up short slope. Reinspected 2014.

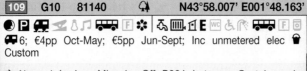

CASTELNAU DE MONTMIRAL 1

`109` G10 81140 N43°58.007' E001°48.163'

🚐 6; €4pp Oct-May; €5pp Jun-Sept; Inc unmetered elec ♿ Custom

➡ Aire privée Les Miquels. Off D964 between Castelnau de Montmiral and Puycelci. Very clearly sp 'Les Miquels' from both directions.

ℹ Family run pleasant commercial Aire in rural location at gîte/restaurant. Use of swimming pool inc. Breakfast avail. Castelnau-de-Montmiral is visible and walking distance, 2km uphill. Inspected 2014.

CASTELNAU DE MONTMIRAL 2

`110` G10 81140 T N43°57.954' E001°49.119'

🚐 10; No overnight parking Jul-Aug ♿ WCs only; See `109`

➡ Turn off D964 at roundabout and follow sp 'P Bus Motorhome' (symbols) along road around outside of town. Parking on gravel partly under trees on left, not signed. These are the largest bays and parking allowed anywhere around the city walls.

ℹ Unrestricted parking at a Beau Village. Historic hilltop town adj with tourist commerce, pedestrianised central square. Inspected 2014.

SALVAGNAC

`111` G10 81630 N43°54.910' E001°41.156'

🚐 8; €5-€10/night; Apr-Oct ♿ Aire Services Plastic; Outside barrier; Apr-Oct

➡ Base de Loisirs de Sourigous, off D999. North of town turn off D999, sp 'Base de Loisirs les Sourigous' and signed. Follow road straight on and Service Point is to left; parking straight on through Aire Services barrier.

ℹ Service Point outside seasonal Aire Naturelle just off D999, signed as an Aire; some road noise. Adj to leisure lake and recreation area with fishing; 10 trouts max. When closed there is a 3.5t restricted car park adj to D999. Inspected 2016.

VILLEMUR SUR TARN

`112` F10 31340 N43°51.176' E001°29.879'

🚐 3; 1 bay obstructed by tree ♿ Aire Services 3000; Token (3/3)

➡ Ave du Général Leclerc. Turn off D630 onto D14, sp 'Villemur sur Tarn'. Follow road and Aire adj to D14 before town on right, signed.

ℹ Aire in small section of car park adj to main road and sports facilities. Noisy and busy at times. Town centre 300m. Reinspected 2016.

LA MAGDELAINE SUR TARN

`113` F10 31340 N43°48.611' E001°32.407'

🚐 4; Additional grass parking ♿ Aire Services 3000; Token (3/3)

➡ Chemin du Lac. Turn off D630 onto D15, sp 'La Magdelaine'. Follow road to roundabout and turn right onto D61, sp 'Montjoire'. Follow road straight on, then turn right into Chemin du Lac. Follow road and Aire is on left, signed.

ℹ Pleasant, peaceful Aire adj to and overlooking leisure lake. Grass parking when dry. Local commerce 300m. Short Voie Verte cycle track from D630. Reinspected 2016.

VENERQUE

`114` F11 31810 N43°26.010' E001°26.406'

🚐 10 ♿ Custom; WCs

➡ Base de Loisirs/Allées du Duc de Ventadour. Exit Le Vernet on D19. Cross river and enter Venerque. Turn left before river bridge, sp 'Base de Loisirs' and signed. Parking on right between trees, Service Point to left.

ℹ Pleasant parking on a plane tree lined avenue. Suitable for all motorhomes. Boules adj. Canoe hire in season. Local commerce 250m. Updated 2015.

AUTERIVE
115 F11 32550 🏛 N43°21.100' E001°28.583'

🚐 12; 6m bays plus overhang 🚰 Custom

▶ Rue des Docteurs Basset. Turn off D820 at traffic lights onto D622, sp 'Nailloux'. Go straight over roundabout and cross river. Turn 1st right, signed, for Service Point. 100m down dead end road: N43°21.011' E001°28.637'. For parking turn 1st left after crossing river bridge into car park before D35 junction.

ℹ Pleasant canalside parking with river Ariège across adj gardens. Well maintained town with small town with commerce 300m. Reinspected 2014.

VILLEFRANCHE DE LAURAGAIS
116 G11 31290 🏛 N43°23.798' E001°42.580'

🚐 10; €13/night inc elec and WiFi; Pay at house 🚰 Custom; 10amp Cont elec

▶ 10 Chemin de Magnauques. Turn off D622 by the village boundary sign into Chemin de Magnauques, not signed. In 100m turn left into No. 10, the pink house, signed. Stop at barrier and report to house.

ℹ Privately owned Aire located behind house. Limited English, but very friendly. Pleasant parking around small lawn with BBQ point. Washing machine €3. Canal du Midi nearby. Commerce 500m. Inspected 2016.

MONTGEARD NAILLOUX
117 G11 31560 ⛺ N43°21.346' E001°38.896'

🚐 20; €6/night; Pay at barrier; Sept-Jun 🚰 Euro Relais Junior; Inside barrier; €2

▶ Camping de la Thésauque. On D622 turn onto D25 at roundabout, sp 'Lac de la Thésauque' and signed. Turn right before bridge, sp 'Lac de la Thésauque'. Follow road past lake to campsite entrance. Enter through barrier.

ℹ Campsite offering motorhome Aire in low season; asphalt parking. Campsite open all year and offers discounts. Pleasant lake with walks adj. Inspected 2016.

SAVERDUN
118 F11 09700 🚶 N43°13.556' E001°36.226'

🚐 20 🚰 Euro Relais Junior; Token (ER); €2.50

▶ D14. Service Point located in the Aire de Repos roadside lay-by adj to D14 south of town, signed. Service Point directly behind shop.

ℹ Aire located in very pleasant roadside lay-by with large picnic area, TO and café. Tokens from TO. Noise from road and trucks parking. Recommend **115**. Inspected 2014.

MIREPOIX
119 G11 09500 🚶 N43°05.126' E001°52.333'

🚐 25 🚰 Custom

▶ Allée des Soupirs. From Franjeaux follow D119, sp 'Foix'. Go straight over roundabout by cemetery and fuel station, then follow road straight on through gateway, signed. Service Point to left before old train station: N43°05.097' E001°52.453'. Best parking past old train station at end of road.

ℹ Aire located in large car park at old railway station; suitable for any unit configuration. Some road noise. Railway track now a Voie Verte cycle route and station building is a music school. Small park adj. 500m to beautiful medieval centre with original arcaded market square and town commerce. Laundry at fuel station. Inspected 2016.

FOIX
120 G12 09000 T N42°57.671' E001°36.665'

🚐 10 🚰 Custom

▶ Quarter Beau-Rivage. Exit N20 at Junction 11, sp 'Tarbes', and follow sp 'Foix'. At elongated roundabout over railway turn left, sp 'Tarbes' and signed. Turn left onto D8h, sp 'Ferrières' and signed. Take 2nd right, signed. Follow road to left, then turn right, sp 'Centre Culturel'. Follow road downhill and turn left into Aire, signed.

ℹ Open Aire on outskirts of Foix, 700m to square with covered marked and start of the pedestrianised old town. Château open to public, €5.60pp. www.sites-touristiques-ariege.fr Inspected 2016.

MONTFERRIER

`121` G12 09300 N42°53.554' E001°47.522' SP

🚐 10 🔧 Custom

➡️ Lieu-dit Labarous. From Lavelanet follow sp 'Foix' and 'Station d'Olmes' onto D117. Turn left onto D9, sp 'Montferrier' and 'Station d'Olmes'. Follow D9 past Montferrier, sp 'Camping' and signed. After bridge on right turn right off D9, sp 'Camping La Fount de Sicre' and signed. Drive to right of campsite alongside river to Aire on right, signed.

ℹ️ Open Aire adj to hunting lodge in small mountain village en route to mountain passes and Station d'Olmes ski resort. Hunting dogs can be noisy at weekends during season. Inspected 2016.

AX LE THERME

`122` G12 09110 N42°43.567' E001°49.884' SP

🚐 25; €6/24hrs; €10/48hrs; €14/72hrs; CC 🔧 Aire Services 7005; Inside barrier; 1hr elec and 100L water inc

➡️ La Capelette, adj to N20 on the left-hand side as approach the town. Aire is located next to railway station car park. Enter through Aire Services barrier.

ℹ️ Popular ski resort. Busy traffic on adj N20 to Andorra and local railway line adj. Town commerce and hot springs 1km. Day parking allowed in town 6am-6pm. Inspected 2013.

Photo: Dot Palastangal

L'HOSPITALET PRES L'ANDORRE

`123` G12 09390 N42°35.335' E001°47.985' SP

🚐 27 🔧 Euro Relais Maxi; CC; Water €2; Elec €6/6hrs

➡️ Les Fountanals. From north on N20, turn left onto N22 opp electricity plant, sp 'Pas de la Case' and 'Mairie'. Cross railway track and turn immediately left into car park, signed. The Aire is adj to railway station car park, signed.

ℹ️ L'Hospitalet is a village in a narrow valley amid snowy mountains near Andorra and the Spanish border. Local commerce adj. Inspected 2013.

LES CABANNES

`124` G12 09310 N42°47.067' E001°40.967' SP

🚐 30; €4/night; Pay at machine 🔧 Custom; €2

➡️ Quartier la Bexane. From E9/N20 take D522, sp 'Les Cabannes'. Follow signs to Aire adj to Gendarmerie. Both well signed.

ℹ️ Very scenic location. Updated 2016.

Photos: Carol Weaver

VICDESSOS

`125` F12 09220 N42°46.133' E001°30.150' SP

🚐 20; €6; Pay at Mairie 🔧 Custom; Inc; 12 Cont unmetered elec points

➡️ Rue de l'Eglise. Turn off D8 into D708/Rue de l'Eglise, sp 'Parking Camping Cars'. Immediately turn right, passing 8 à Huit supermarket. Aire just beyond the shop.

ℹ️ Adj to river on outskirts of village amid beautiful scenery. Updated 2016.

Photo: Sue & Trevor Smith

AULUS LES BAINS

`126` F12 09140 N42°47.340' E001°20.158' SP

🚐 15; €2/day; Pay at TO adj to roundabout; Max 72hrs 🔧 Euro Relais Junior; No parking

➡️ D8f. From Oust follow D32, an easy, wide valley drive that slowly rises 300m to 757m. Service Point as enter Aulus les Bains on D32, before the campsite, but must approach from opp direction: N42°47.729' E001°19.847'. For parking continue on D32 and turn onto D8f at roundabout, sp 'Ustou'. Parking is on right in 100m, signed.

ℹ️ Pleasant parking within a mountain valley on edge of thermal village. TO and local commerce at roundabout, 150m. Thermal baths 230m, €9pp. www.thermes-aulus.fr No parking is allowed at Service Point. Inspected 2016.

SEIX

127 F12 09140 🏛 N42°51.747' E001°12.154'

🚐 10 ⚑ Euro Relais Box

▶ Place de l'Allée. From Oust follow D3, sp 'Station de Guzet'. Pass campsite and go straight across roundabout, sp 'Station de Guzet'. Service Point on left, sp 'Nouveau Cimetière' and signed: N42°51.972' E001°12.439'. Continue into Seix on D3. Turn left in large car park, signed. Follow road to right around car park, then turn left, signed, and immediately left again. Designated parking on upper terrace, signed.

ℹ Open Aire tucked away in mountain town with town commerce across bridge in narrow streets. En route to Guzet ski station. Inspected 2016.

CASTELNAU DURBAN

128 F12 09420 🏢 N42°59.996' E001°20.398'

🚐 30; Max 48hrs ⚑ Urba Flux; €2

▶ D117. Turn off D117 in centre, opp church, signed. Service Point to left outside WC, parking to right.

ℹ Aire next to main road, road noise, and church, hell's bells all night. Popular car park; visitors may park close to WC and obstruct access to Service Point. Parking shaded by plane trees, adj to small river, no view, and Voie Verte cycling/walking path. Local commerce adj. Inspected 2016.

RIEUX VOLVESTRE

129 F11 31310 ⚓ N43°16.149' E001°10.701'

🚐 7; Report to campsite, 100m ⚑ Custom; WC emptying in cupboard; 2 Cont elec points

▶ Route du Plan d'Eau. Turn off D627, sp 'Camping' and 'Piscine'. Follow road to end and drive through car park on one-way system to top terrace. Aire on right, signed.

ℹ Aire on upper terrace adj to Plan d'Eau swimming pool, park and river. Cars may obstruct Service Point and parking during events/hot days and holidays. The town is very pretty with an interesting octagonal tower, but is 2.5km away. Inspected 2016.

MONTESQUIEU VOLVESTRE

130 F11 31310 🏢 N43°12.326' E001°13.510'

🚐 10 ⚑ Flot Bleu Océane

▶ Rue de la Chutere. Exit town on D40, sp 'St Christaud'. Turn left, sp 'Salle Polyvalente', then immediately left again into parking. For Service Point drive past parking and follow road to right. Service Point on left: N43°12.240' E001°13.360'.

ℹ Open car park adj to municipal hall. Riverside park opp. Historic centre with arcades, covered market and unusual 17th century octagonal cathedral tower 700m. Inspected 2016.

ST CROIX VOLVESTRE

131 F11 09230 ⛺ N43°07.600' E001°10.250'

🚐 30; Grass parking; Limited hardstanding ⚑ Custom

▶ D35. Approach on D35 from Cazères, sp 'Ste Croix Volvestre'. Turn right at entrance to village, signed, and follow road through gateway at end. Service Point to left against building.

ℹ Aire adj to rugby pitch on edge of village. Lovely open grass parking in summer. Limited hardstanding parking in winter, which is inaccessible weekends of games. Small village with some local commerce 500m. Reinspected 2016.

CAZERES SUR GARONNE

132 F11 31220 ⚓ N43°12.230' E001°05.189'

🚐 30 ⚑ Urba Flux Tall; 2 unmetered CEE elec points; Cont WC

▶ Ave Gabriel Peri. Turn off D10 onto D6, sp 'Ste Croix V', 'Base Nautique' and 'Camping'. Turn right before river bridge, sp 'P'. Service Point to rear of 1st car park on left, but best parking is in adj car park.

ℹ Aire adj to Garonne, partial views. Noise from road in parking adj to Service Point, but additional peaceful parking poss. Town commerce 200m, market Sat 7am-1pm. Inspected 2016.

BOUSSENS

`133` F11 31360 N43°10.666' E000°58.482'

🚐2 hardstanding; 4 grass parking between trees 🚰 Custom; Water at rock; Lift cover

➡ Turn off D817 at roundabout onto D62n, sp 'Boussens' and 'Du Lac'. At roundabout turn left, sp 'Du Lac' and 'Camping'. Turn right at end of road, sp 'Camping', then left, signed. Service Point on left before campsite, signed.

ℹ Riverside Aire with picnic benches. Bird watching on river. Constant hum from motorway and cement works. Reinspected 2016.

MARTRES TOLOSANE

`134` F11 31220 N43°12.134' E001°00.665'

🚐4; Roadside at cemetery 🚰 Bollard

➡ D10. From central one-way system turn onto D10, sp 'Alan'. Service Point on right opp cemetery, signed.

ℹ It is possible to stay overnight outside cemetery, but really this is just a Service Point. Suggest `135` and `136` as alternatives. Reinspected 2016.

AUZAS

`135` F11 31360 N43°10.200' E000°53.217'

🚐9; €4/night inc unmetered CEE elec; Collected 🚰 Custom; Lift cover by sign; Water, elec and WC at parking

➡ D33r. From St Martory on D52 turn left onto D33r, sp 'Auzas'. After 900m turn left to lake, sp 'Lac'. Follow road downhill to lower terrace, signed. Service Point in 100m opp church, signed: N43°10.158' E000°53.102'.

ℹ Aire adj to small leisure lake, 3 parallel bays have lake views. Leisure facilities inc outdoor gym, mini golf and boats in summer. Best to walk WC to Service Point, 150m, as parking very impractical. Updated 2016.

MAZERES SUR SALAT ★

`136` F11 31260 N43°08.080' E000°58.579'

🚐8 🚰 Custom; 1 Cont elec point (Not working)

➡ Le Pre Commune. At traffic lights in town centre turn off D13 onto D52, sp 'Cassagne'. Just before river bridge turn left. Follow road along river to Aire.

ℹ Aire in a beautiful location overlooking fish ladder and weir with views of the Pyrénées beyond. Open winter parking and shaded summer parking. Park with BBQ adj. Small town commerce 300m. Reinspected 2016.

ST MARTORY

`137` F11 31360 N43°08.507' E000°55.726'

🚐7; €3/24hrs; Collected/Pay at Mairie opp (in letterbox) 🚰 Custom; Lift grid; CEE elec points in parking

➡ D817, in car park adj to D817 near D52/D117 junction.

ℹ Pleasant Aire overlooking river and old river bridge. Local commerce adj and market on Aire Fri, but does not impede Aire if parked on river edge. Reinspected 2016.

ST GIRONS

`138` F12 09200 N42°59.303' E001°08.366'

🚐6 🚰 Urba Flux; €2

➡ D117, at rear of old station building. From St Gaudens on D117 Aire on right adj to large Renault/Peugeot garage, signed. If approaching from other directions follow D117, sp 'Tarbes'. DO NOT drive through town.

ℹ Aire in urban area 650m from historic town. St Lizier, 1.8km, is a Grand Site of Midi Pyrénées and is dominated by the 17th century bishop's palace. Voie Verte cycle path from St Girons to Foix, 45km. www.tourisme-stgirons-stlizier.fr Inspected 2016.

BONAC

| 139 | F12 | 09800 | | N42°52.527' E000°58.489' |

🚐 11; €7night Sept-Jun; €8/night Jul-Aug; +€0.30pp tax; Collected 🛒 Custom; 10 unmetered elec points

➡ D4. From St Girons take D618 to Castillon-en-Couserans, then continue on D4 to Bonac. Drive through village and turn left beyond lake. Aire on opp side of lake, signed.

ℹ Landscaped commercial Aire by lake; Lovely mountain scenery. Very small village with limited local commerce. Updated 2015.

Info/photos: Jean & Ken Fowler

BAGNERES DE LUCHON

| 140 | E12 | 31110 | | N42°47.706' E000°35.920' |

🚐 30; €4; Collected; 7m bays 🛒 Custom; Token; €4

➡ Rue Jean Mermoz. Approaching from north on D125 turn left, sp 'D125', 'Espagne', and 'Accueil Camping Car' on very small sign at road level. Take the next left and follow this road. The Aire is on the left, opp the sports ground.

ℹ Path to Lac de Badech from Aire. LIDL nearby. Thermal baths. Town 950m. Tokens from TO. Updated 2014.

Photos: Keith & Sue Lawrence

ST LARY SOULAN

| 141 | E12 | 65170 | SKI | N42°49.348' E000°19.397' |

🚐 34; €6/7pm-8am; Collected 🛒 Euro Relais Junior; €2

➡ D19, at Parking du Stade. From north on D929 take 1st exit at roundabout as enter town onto D116. At next roundabout turn left onto D19. Aire 100m on right in car park, opp stadium.

ℹ Ski resort with all necessary facilities. Cable car 500m from Aire. Convenient stop en route to Spain via Bielsa Tunnel. Updated 2015.

Photos: Keith & Sue Lawrence

PIAU ENGALY

| 142 | E12 | 65170 | SKI | N42°47.181' E000°09.464' |

🚐 100; €15/day inc elec 🛒 Custom; €6 for 4amp elec in ski season

➡ D118. From north on D929 turn right onto D118 after Aragnouet, sp 'Piau Engaly'. Follow road up to ski station and Aire is adj to Parking 1, signed through resort.

ℹ Alt 1855m. Aire at ski resort with stunning mountain views. Parking may be free in spring/autumn. www.piau-engaly.com Updated 2016.

Photos: Keith & Sue Lawrence

LOUDENVIELLE

| 143 | E12 | 65510 | | N42°48.083' E000°24.650' |

🚐 20 🛒 Euro Relais Junior; Token (ER); €2

➡ D25/Chemin du Hourgade. From north take D618. Turn off onto D25 and continue south approx 3.5km. Aire adj to lake on right.

ℹ Adj to Lac de Genos-Loudenvielle; Thermal baths. Updated 2015.

Info/photos: Carol Weaver

ARREAU

| 144 | E12 | 65240 | | N42°54.437' E000°21.549' |

🚐 15; €2/night; Collected 🛒 Custom; No drive over drain

➡ Avenue de la Gare. Turn off D929 into Ave de la Gare, sp 'Volerie: Les Aigles d'Aure', and cross river bridge. Aire in car park on left within 150m.

ℹ Pretty, small village en route to Bielsa Tunnel to Spain. Updated 2015.

Photo: Keith & Sue Lawrence

Photo: Carol Weaver

STE MARIE DE CAMPAN

145 E12 65710 N42°58.955' E000°13.694'

🚐 5; Max 48hrs 🚽 Custom

➡ D918. Follow D935 from Campan, sp 'Col d'Aspin'. In Ste Marie de Campan turn left onto D918, sp 'Arreau'. Aire 100m on left, signed.

ℹ Alt 853m. Aire adj to D918 at base of Col d'Aspin, a popular tourist drive and cycle to 1489m. Ideal stop if **157** full. Reinspected 2014.

PAYOLLE

146 E12 65710 N42°56.309' E000°17.498'

🚐 19 🚽 Custom

➡ D113. From east on D918 turn left in Payolle, sp 'Lac de Payolle'. In 700m turn right to Aire near end of road before small Complexe Touristique.

ℹ Peaceful rural location in clearing surrounded by trees with glimpses of lake. Cattle wandering about. Additional parking on upper terrace. Visited 2016.

Info/photos: Ian Lones

LA MONGIE 1900 STATION

147 E12 65200 SKI N42°54.750' E000°10.733'

🚐 20; Tolerated 🚽 None

➡ Place Pène Nègre. From Ste Marie de Campan follow D918 to La Mongie ski station. Turn sharp right just before 'Le Choucas' restaurant. Follow road uphill for 500m to Place Pène Nègre. May be signed 'Parking 4' in ski season.

ℹ Alt 1750m. All parking in ski resort is unrestricted. Lovely views and lots of walking. Cable car to Pic du Midi de Bigorre in summer: €30. Updated 2016.

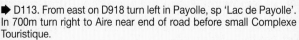
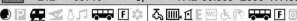

Photo: Keith & Sue Lawrence

LA MONGIE

148 E12 65200 SKI N42°55.168' E000°11.403'

🚐 100; Tolerated 🚽 None

➡ Just off D918 between Artigues-Campan and La Mongie in large gravel parking area, sp 'P'. May be signed as 'Parking 5' in ski season.

ℹ Alt 1575m. Rural mountain Aire just below ski resort of La Mongie, with cable car to summit of Pic du Midi de Bigorre with stunning scenery. Updated 2016.

Photos: Keith & Sue Lawrence

GAVARNIE

149 E12 65120 SKI N42°44.317' W000°01.167'

🚐 50; €10 in season; Collected 🚽 Custom

➡ D923. From Gavarnie turn onto D923 from D921. Parking on left opp monument in 3km.

ℹ Large popular open Aire with dramatic mountain views. Popular walk to Cirque de Gavarnie and waterfalls. Updated 2015.

Photos: Carol Weaver

MONTREJEAU

150 E11 31210 N43°05.059' E000°34.306'

🚐 5 🚽 WC only

➡ D817. Just off main road near centre of town at Place de Verdun, around octagonal, covered car park.

ℹ Well located designated parking just moments from small town commerce. Good patisserie and popular and reasonably priced restaurant adj. Viewpoint across to the Pyrénées adj. Sheltered from road noise, surprisingly peaceful stop. Reinspected 2014.

PIERREFITTE NESTALAS 151 E12 65260 N42°57.572' W000°04.608'

🚐 15; Max 8 nights ♿ Walther; €1; Cont WC

➡ Rue Victor Hugo. From D921 turn off by the Mairie, sp 'Aire de Pique-Nique' and signed. At end of road turn right to Aire, signed.

ℹ Popular Aire adj to picnic area. Voie Verte foot/cycle path to Cauterets, 6km, or Lourdes, 15km. Local commerce 600m. Inspected 2016.

CAUTERETS 1 152 E12 65110 SKI N42°53.576' W000°06.804'

🚐 42; €10.70/24hrs inc service and elec; Pay at Machine ♿ Custom; 42 3amp CEE elec points; WC 100m, at bus station

➡ D920/Route de Pierrefitte. From Soulom turn right off D920a as enter town, sp 'Pantinoire' and signed. Turn left in 150m into Aire, signed.

ℹ Alt 897m. Located on level ground adj to central ski resort action and near bus station. A better winter Aire; closest to gondola up to downhill and boarding resort, and bus to mostly Nordic Station Pont d'Espagne. Ski pass valid at 8 resorts, €35/day. www.n-py.com Inspected 2016.

CAUTERETS 2 153 E12 65110 SKI N42°53.183' W000°06.917'

🚐 32; €10.70/night inc service and elec; Pay at machine ♿ Custom; 32 3amp CEE elec points

➡ Avenue du Docteur Charles Thierry, off D920. From south on D920 follow sp 'Toutes directions', then 'Pont d'Espagne'. Aire on left at rear of casino just before leaving town, signed; designated parking on lower level.

ℹ Alt 941m. Adj to old town in a peaceful car park with some shade and views of mountains. Town has thermal spa, Les Thermes de Cauterets, and a wellness centre, Les Bains du Rocher, €18.50/2hrs. www.bains-rocher.fr Pont d'Espagne, Cascades and Lac de Gaube, 6km, all have lovely walks. Inspected 2016.

ARRENS MARSOUS 154 E12 65400 N42°57.520' W000°12.436'

🚐 15 ♿ Euro Relais Junior; Elec €2

➡ D918. Exit village on D918 towards Argelès-Gazost. Parking area on right, turn right beside EDF building, signed with a small sign on road edge. Follow road to parking area, Service Point on left.

ℹ Alt 864m. Aire sheltered from limited road noise by buildings. Adj to mountain road leading to Col d'Aubisque. Local commerce: convenience store, 150m; village centre, 600m; and local producers selling cheese and meat nearby. Parking at Lac de Tech, 7.3km on D105: N42°54.674' W000°15.536'. Inspected 2016.

Photo: Ian Lones — Lac de Tech

ARGELES GAZOST 155 E11 65400 N43°00.281' W000°05.183'

🚐 20 ♿ Flot Bleu Pacific; Token

➡ D100. On Turn off D821 at large roundabout junction with D100, sp 'Thermes' and 'Casino'. At next roundabout turn into the Carrefour supermarket. Service Point by fuel station, parking beyond, signed.

ℹ Designated parking in own section of supermarket car park. Inspected 2016.

LANNEMEZAN 156 E11 65300 N43°07.651' E000°22.859'

🚐 30 ♿ Aire Services 3000; 1 unmetered CEE elec point

➡ Espace du Nebouzan. Turn off D817 at roundabout onto D939, sp 'Galan'. Follow sp 'Galan' and 'P 200 places' (not HGV route sp 'Galan'). As exiting town turn left into car park. After driving through car park turn right, then turn left, signed. Follow road through entrance and behind building.

ℹ Aire located on a terrace behind the sports facility. May feel isolated if alone. Town commerce 500m. Market Wed am. Reinspected 2016.

CAMPAN
157 E11 65710 N43°01.099' E000°10.687'

🚐 5; Max 48hrs 🔧 Custom; Push tap down hard

➤ D8. From Bagnères de Bigorre follow sp 'Campan' onto D935. In Campan turn left off D935 just before church, signed. Follow road to left and Aire on right. Service Point on left by crucifix and parking on right, signed.

ℹ️ Alt 653m. Aire in the foothills of the Pyrénées. Small farm and its collection of machinery, fodder and cats surround the Aire and give it a quaint feel. Reinspected 2014.

BAGNERES DE BIGORRE
158 E11 65200 N43°04.396' E000°09.139'

🚐 30 🔧 Euro Relais Mini

➤ Allée René Descartes. Approach from Pouzac on D935. Turn left at roundabout, sp 'Ordizan' and 'Zones d'Activités'. Turn 3rd right into industrial estate, signed. Turn 1st left, signed, and Aire on right.

ℹ️ This well used Aire is located in a large car park in a semi industrial area. Views of the Pyrénées from all parking areas. Interesting large town with a Basque feel, 1.2km. Reinspected 2016.

LOURDES 1
159 E11 65100 N43°05.296' W000°03.161'

🚐 50; €10/24hrs; Pay guardian; Apr-Oct 🔧 Custom; €5

➤ Esplanade du Paradis. From south on D821 follow blue signs sp 'P Arrouza'. Cross river and take 3rd exit at roundabout. Turn 1st left into Blvd Georges Dupierris, then 2nd left into Blvd du Gave, then 2nd left again, all sp 'P Arrouza' on blue sign. Cross river and Aire immediately on left at rear of coach parking.

ℹ️ 24hr-manned Aire by river. Sanctuary Notre Dame 1.2km. This is only official overnight parking. Reinspected 2016.

LOURDES 2
160 E11 65100 N43°06.264' W000°02.014'

🚐 26; €15/24hrs inc 6amp elec and WiFi; CC 🔧 Aire Services 7005; Outside barrier; CC; €3

➤ Route de Julos. Follow D821 around city. North of town turn off, sp 'Julios' and 'Le Vieux Berger'. Follow road straight on into Camping Le Vieux Berger. Service Point to left and parking to right. Enter through Aire Services barrier. Tolerated day parking adj to WC in P Lapacca on Blvd du Lapacca: N43°05.900' W000°02.517'.

ℹ️ Landscaped commercial Aire outside campsite. Use of some campsite facilities is permitted. Noise from adj main road. Sanctuary Notre Dame 1.8km. www.campingvieuxberger.fr Undesignated, but tolerated parking in P Lapacca; expect change. All Lourdes parking restricted to day parking. Submitted 2016.

P Lapacca

Library photo

AGOS VIDALOS
161 E11 65400 N43°02.131' W000°04.244'

🚐 29; €10.60/24hrs Sept-Jun; €11.80/24hrs Jul-Aug; CC 🔧 Euro Relais Junior; Inside barrier; 12 6amp CEE elec points

➤ D921b. Exit D821 and follow sp 'Agos Vidalos'. Aire on right beside Camping Soleil du Pibeste. Enter through PARKNIGHT barrier.

ℹ️ Commercial Aire with grass and gravel parking located in a mountain valley 8km north of Lourdes, bus stop adj. If you are just looking for a lunch stop there is a convenient lay-by just off the dual carriageway. Inspected 2016.

TARBES 1
162 E11 65000 N43°13.116' E000°04.354'

🚐 10; Tolerated 🔧 Flot Bleu Euro; CC; €3

➤ N21. Follow sp 'Toutes Directions'. Service Point just past N21/D935 roundabout opp stadium, signed. Parking: N43°13.282' E000°04.493'. From Service Point turn right, then left at the next two roundabouts. Unrestricted parking under trees on right.

ℹ️ Parking area under trees between park and stadium. Reinspected 2014.

TARBES 2 | 163 | E11 | 65000 | 🏛 | N43°14.577' E000°04.080' | SP

🚐20; €10/night inc 5amp elec; €8/night inc water; Collected Custom; €5/water+2hrs elec if not staying

➡ Ave de la Libération. Approach Tarbes from north on D935. Turn right at the traffic lights by the Intermarché supermarket, sp 'Cimetière Nord' and signed. In 600m turn left at traffic lights, sp 'Laubadère' and signed. Follow road across traffic lights. Aire on left, signed.

ℹ Aire adj to garage in a residential area. Local commerce adj. Tarbes centre 2km, large park near centre. Reinspected 2014.

MIELAN | 164 | E11 | 32170 | 🏛 | N43°25.994' E000°18.519'

🚐6; Additional parking 🚰 Custom

➡ Rue du Cubet. Approach town on N21 from Mirande. Turn left as enter town, signed. Follow road for 300m and Aire is in car park on left, signed.

ℹ Just off N21 but sheltered from road noise. Town with small town commerce and historic covered market 350m. Reinspected 2014.

VIC EN BIGORRE | 165 | E11 | 65500 | 🏛 | N43°23.085' E000°02.956' | SP

🚐6; Under trees 🚰 Custom

➡ Rue du Stade. From town centre follow sp 'Pau'. After crossing river bridge turn left onto D61, sp 'Montaner' and signed. Turn immediately right, signed, and Aire immediately on right under plane trees, signed.

ℹ Parking is possible with care under low plane trees that provide excellent shade on hot summer days. Noisy main road adj. Town centre commerce 250m. Reinspected 2016.

MAUBOURGUET | 166 | E11 | 65700 | 🏢 | N43°26.584' E000°02.493'

🚐6 🚰 Flot Bleu Pacific; €2; Inspection cover; Flot Bleu Elec; €1/3hrs; 4 CEE elec points

➡ D935. Turn off D935 south of town to Super U supermarket. Aire adj to fuel station, signed.

ℹ Designated parking adj to supermarket just off main route; road noise. Reinspected 2016.

VILLECOMTAL SUR ARROS | 167 | E11 | 32730 | | N43°24.154' E000°11.918'

🚐20 🚰 Euro Relais Box; Token (ER); €2

➡ Chemin de la Fontaine. Turn off N21 near river bridge, sp 'Ecole' and signed. Aire 100m, but have to drive around parking to get to it.

ℹ Aire in large open car park sheltered from main route. School adj, parking likely to be busy at pick up/drop off times. Inspected 2016.

MARCIAC | 168 | E11 | 32230 | T | N43°31.602' E000°09.455' | SP

🚐45 🚰 Flot Bleu Euro; CC; €3; Inspection cover (Bolted down); Flot Bleu Elec; Token; €3; 1 Token/4hrs; 8 CEE elec points

➡ Chemin de Ronde. Approach on D3 from Nogaro. At Marciac follow D3 to right, sp 'Autres Directions' and signed. Turn right onto D255, sp 'Juillac' and signed. Turn right into Aire, signed; GPS taken here. Actual GPS: N43°31.650' E000°09.527'.

ℹ Pleasant open Aire adj to picnic area that leads through to leisure lake. Marciac is a Grand Site of the Pyrénées and has a pleasant central square, 550m. www.marciactourisme.co.uk Inspected 2016.

EAUZE
`169` E10 32800 🏛 N43°51.546' E000°06.222'

🚐 4; See info ⛽ Urba Flux Tall; CC; €2

➡ Rue de Rochefort. From Nogaro follow sp 'Agen' onto D931. Follow D931 through town, then turn right by Crédit Agricole bank, sp 'P Belle Mairie' and signed. Aire on left side of car park on left, signed.

ℹ 4 designated bays in large open car park suitable for any unit configuration. Historic centre with museum of Roman archaeology and town commerce 200m. www.tourisme-eauze.fr Inspected 2016.

BEAUMARCHES
`170` E11 32160 🏛 N43°35.243' E000°05.536'

🚐 7; Limited hardstanding ⛽ Custom

➡ Chemin de Ronde. Turn off D3 onto D946, sp 'Beaumarchés'. Follow road uphill, then turn left into Chemin de Ronde, signed. Follow road and then turn left, signed. Parking immediately on left, Service Point at far end of building.

ℹ Small mostly grass parking adj to municipal works building on edge of village. Reinspected 2016.

BARBOTAN LES THERMES
`171` E10 32150 🏢 N43°56.967' W000°02.600'

🚐 16; €8.50/10pm-6am; Collected ⛽ None; See `172`

➡ Off N524, at the casino. Turn off N524, sp 'Parking Nocturne Payant' and 'Casino'. Bear left and park in front of casino, signed.

ℹ Popular large parking area adj to town centre, ideal night stop. For longer stays see `172`. WC and free WiFi at TO adj. Inspected 2016.

LAC DE L'UBY - Barbotan les Thermes
`172` E10 32150 ⚓ N43°56.150' W000°01.950'

🚐 49; €8.50/night inc CEE elec; Pay at TO in advance ⛽ Custom; Inside barrier

➡ Lac de l'Uby. Must pay at TO by `171` first. From TO turn right at roundabout onto N524 and continue over roundabout. In 500m turn left, sp 'Lac de l'Uby' and signed. After 1.8km turn right onto track (GPS taken here). Aire in car park beyond height barriers. Actual GPS: N43°56.053' W000°01.873'.

ℹ Very popular Aire adj to large leisure lake with swimming beach and fishing swims; some bays have lake views. Insufficient elec points, long leads required for some bays. Aire may be closed during rowing competitions in Mar-Apr. Reinspected 2016.

MONTREAL
`173` E10 32250 T N43°57.222' E000°11.835'

🚐 20; 10 additional ⛽ Custom; Water tap and WC at town parking

➡ D29. In centre turn onto D29, sp 'Fources'. Follow D29 and just before exit turn left, sp 'Stade' and signed. Service Point to left, parking on right. Additional terraced parking in town: N43°57.061' E000°12.055'; convenient for visiting town, but not as peaceful as parking by Service Point.

ℹ Town parking just 100m from centre of Beau Village with pleasant town centre arcades accommodating small town commerce. At Service Point there is large, open parking suitable for any unit configuration. Open access sports field adj. Reinspected 2016.

FOURCES
`174` E10 32250 T N43°59.649' E000°13.765'

🚐 6; €7/night inc service and elec; Grass parking ⛽ Custom; 6 CEE elec points

➡ D114. Turn off D29 onto D114, sp 'Fources-Village'. Follow road past village green, sp 'Aire de Camping-Car'. In 50m turn right, sp 'P Autos'. Follow road and parking on grass before Service Point.

ℹ Grass parking between small trees to rear of grass park. 150m level walk to charming village centre with a central village green surrounded by arcades with tourist commerce. Hardstanding poss in low season. Reinspected 2016.

CONDOM | 175 | E10 | 32100 | N43°56.917' E000°21.821'

🚐 12; Max 3 nights 🛒 Custom; Water tap badly designed

➡ Rue Boileau. Exit town on D931, sp 'Pau'. Turn left, sp 'Camping l'Argente'. Turn left in 50m and drive up slope to Aire.

ℹ Pleasant landscaped Aire above campsite adj to camping huts. Outdoor swimming pool complex adj, noisy on hot days and holidays. Condom centre 2km through park: walk downhill past campsite, cross 2 river bridges, then turn left and follow river to town. Reinspected 2016.

VALENCE SUR BAISE | 176 | E10 | 32310 | N43°52.383' E000°23.267'

🚐 4 🛒 Custom; Cont WC

➡ D930. On D930 in lay-by picnic area as enter town from Auch, signed. Further parking on grass behind Service Point.

ℹ Convenient night halt in picnic area adj to main road, occasional road noise. Local commerce 850m, village centre 1.2km. Reinspected 2016.

ST PUY | 177 | E10 | 32310 | N43°52.557' E000°27.742'

🚐 4; Max 6m 🛒 Custom; 2 Cont elec points on lamp post

➡ Grande Rue. From Valence sur Baïse follow sp 'St Puy' onto D142. In 6.4km turn left onto D42, sp 'St Puy'. Go straight over junction, signed. In 50m turn right between trees just after Boulangerie, signed. Difficult access between concrete posts.

ℹ Small Aire with difficult access, difficult to turn around inside and difficult exit. Free WiFi. Village centre with local commerce adj, charming covered market with chandeliers 100m. Reinspected 2016.

FLEURANCE | 178 | F10 | 32500 | N43°50.842' E000°40.318'

🚐 15 hardstanding; 30 grass parking 🛒 Flot Bleu Océane; Token; €2; Inspection cover

➡ D953. From N21 at roundabout take D953, sp 'St Clar'. Turn right immediately after crossing river bridge. Aire on right, signed.

ℹ Pleasant Aire with grass and hardstanding parking adj to river, some views; fishing requires day pass. Park, lake, and swimming pools accessed over river footbridge. Town centre 850m with town commerce and a big, busy market on Tue am, which is worth visiting. Reinspected 2016.

PREIGNAN | 179 | F11 | 32810 | N43°42.748' E000°38.053'

🚐 5 🛒 Custom

➡ Rue Emile Zola. From Auch on N21 turn right at 1st roundabout, sp 'Parc Municipal des Sports'. Follow road for 1.5km and Aire on right, signed. Parking limited to the 5 marked bays to left of the car park; Service Point opp.

ℹ Aire in peaceful location adj to sports facilities. Local commerce 1km downhill. Reinspected 2016.

AUCH | 180 | E11 | 32000 | N43°38.192' E000°35.325'

🚐 48; €8/24hrs inc service; CC; Long stay discount €1/day 🛒 Aire Services 7010; Service only €2; Aire Services Elec; €4/24hrs; 16amp CEE elec

➡ Rue du Général de Gaulle. From south on N21 turn right at traffic lights, sp 'Salle du Mouzon' and 'Camping'. Turn right between two river bridges into Aire (former campsite), signed. Enter through Aire Services barrier.

ℹ Large commercial Aire in former campsite; hedged bays with elec on end of rows. Local commerce 100m on N21. Riverside park opp. Walk through park following river and crossing it twice to impressive Monumental Steps, 374 steps leading to Auch historic centre, cathedral and town commerce, 1.2km. Reinspected 2016.

LOMBEZ
181 F11 32220 N43°28.485' E000°54.959'

🚐 40 Custom

➡ D632. Enter Lombez on D634/D632 from Samatan. Aire is in car park on right just after the D626 junction and before the Gendarmerie, signed.

ℹ Aire located in very large car park adj to sports stadium. Park opp with a walk. Busy during sporting events and used as night parking by HGVs. Reinspected 2014.

SAMATAN
182 F11 32130 N43°29.296' E000°55.628'

🚐 10; €3/night; +€0.20pp/night; Collected Custom; Pay; Water tap in box

➡ D39. From Samatan turn onto D39, sp 'Lombez'. At the roundabout turn left into Les Rivages, signed. Turn left and the Aire is at the end, signed.

ℹ Aire between D39 and holiday rentals. Complex has lake with walks, no views. Small town shops in centre, 350m. Reinspected 2014.

ST LYS
183 F11 31470 N43°30.920' E001°10.553'

🚐 5 Custom; Poss obstructed by cars

➡ Route de Saiguede. From town centre turn off by church, sp 'Fontenilles'. Turn left onto D12, sp 'L'Isle Jourdain' HGV route and 'Le Moulin'. Service Point is 10m on right, poorly signed and may be obstructed by parked cars. For suitable overnight parking follow road round bend and turn right into car park.

ℹ Parking adj to boules courts. Town with numerous commerce 250m uphill. Service Point is very old and underused. Inspected 2012.

L'ISLE JOURDAIN
184 F11 32600 N43°37.174' E001°04.335'

🚐 5 Custom

➡ Allée du Lac. Exit town to west on D161. Turn right, 500m from town, onto D654, signed. Turn left in front of railway track into Allée du Lac. Service Point immediately on left, signed. Unrestricted parking before Service Point.

ℹ At leisure lake with waterskiing, indoor swimming pool and other water related sports. No designated parking, but unrestricted parking available. Updated 2013.

GIMONT
185 F11 32200 N43°37.810' E000°52.187'

🚐 10 Bollard

➡ N124. From town on A24 follow sp 'Auch'. After crossing river bridge turn immediately right into Aire, signed.

ℹ Trucking hell! The Aire has a lovely outlook overlooking a fishing pond, but that is completely overshadowed by the noise from the traffic within 15m. For a more peaceful stop, try **187**. Updated 2015.

CADOURS
186 F11 31480 N43°43.368' E001°02.916'

🚐 1 hardstanding; 5 on grass Custom

➡ Chemin d'En Cornac. Exit town to south on D24, sp 'Garac'. At roundabout turn left down small lane, signed. Follow road to right, signed, and Aire on right, signed.

ℹ A small, poorly positioned Aire overlooking sports stadium. Suitable for a night halt, but might feel isolated if alone. Town commerce 650m. Reinspected 2014.

SARRANT

187 F11 32120 T N43°46.537' E000°55.679'

🚐15 Custom; Lift plastic cover on drive over drain for WC emptying; Slow water

➡ D165. From north on D165 the Aire is on the left as you enter village, signed.

ℹ Very pleasant Aire overlooking a large grass area. Small fortified Beau Village with local commerce worth a wander. Reinspected 2016.

COLOGNE

188 F11 32430 N43°43.470' E000°58.627' SP

🚐7 Custom

➡ D227. Turn off D654 onto D165, sp 'St Anne'. Turn 1st right onto D227, sp 'St Anne'. Follow road straight on for 200m and Aire on left at village boundary, behind green fenced water treatment plant. Service Point on left by bins.

ℹ Aire adj to recycling bins and community bins behind water treatment plant that gurgles constantly. Bastide village 400m. Inspected 2016.

MAUVEZIN

189 F11 32120 N43°43.933' E000°52.486' SP

🚐4 Custom

➡ Rue des Petites Garennes. Turn off D928 onto D40, sp 'Montfort' and 'St Clar'. Turn right before river bridge, signed. Follow road and Service Point is on right, signed. Parking further on up 5t weight restricted hill: N43°43.929' E000°52.586'; reverse in.

ℹ Pleasant Aire adj to small park with children's play area and covered picnic area. There is some parking by the Service Point and further parking up hill. Small town commerce 100m up hill. Inspected 2016.

ST CLAR

190 F10 32380 N43°53.474' E000°46.375' SP

🚐15; Max 4 days Custom; WC with shower on terrace above

➡ D13. Exit St Clar on D13, sp 'Lavit'. Turn immediately left into Aire, signed.

ℹ Pleasant landscaped Aire with rural views. Hardstanding bays between the grass amongst fruit trees. Local commerce and pleasant historic centre 450m. Reinspected 2016.

LECTOURE 1

191 F10 32700 N43°56.109' E000°38.516' SP

🚐10 Euro Relais Box; 1 unmetered CEE elec point

➡ N21. Exit town on N21 to north. Turn off N21 into Intermarché supermarket. For Service Point turn left, signed, and drive behind fuel station. Service Point opp car wash, signed: N43°56.142' E000°38.607'. Follow road uphill and parking is adj to and opp self-service laundry, signed.

ℹ Service Point and designated parking adj to large supermarket. Parking near delivery point and pick up point, some road noise. Large green space with picnic adj. Reinspected 2016.

LECTOURE 2

192 F10 32700 N43°56.179' E000°37.558' SP

🚐10; Grass parking Water tap, WC and shower

➡ Rue Victor Hugo. Turn off roundabout near town centre into Rue Victor Hugo, signed; one-way and 3.5t weight restricted. Follow road downhill, then turn right at roundabout, signed. Aire on right in 100m, signed. Follow road downhill to parking.

ℹ Aire on outskirts of town adj to walking club and open access sports field. Small town commerce 500m, market Fri am. Thermal spa 800m; half day access to pool and two treatments €38. www.valvital.fr Reinspected 2016.

ST ANTOINE

193 F10 32340 N44°02.149' E000°50.542'

🚐 10 🛠 Custom

➡ D953. Enter St Antoine from Valance on D953. As enter village turn 1st left, signed. Follow arrows behind stone barns on gravel track. Parking on right, arrowed.

ℹ Aire in a peaceful location behind the village with views of countryside. Local commerce 200m in medieval streets. Pilgrims continue the centuries old tradition and pass through the village en route to Santiago. Updated 2015.

BEAUMONT DE LOMAGNE

194 F10 82500 N43°52.824' E000°59.452'

🚐 10 🛠 Custom; Lift plastic cover on drive over drain for WC waste; Slow water

➡ D3. Enter town on D928 from Larrazet. At the roundabout turn right onto D3, sp 'Centre Ville'. Cross railway track and turn 1st right. Aire on right, signed. 3.5t weight restricted parking.

ℹ On the edge of town adj to D928 and railway track. Local cars use car park, but there should always be space. Town centre 450m uphill. Reinspected 2016.

GRISOLLES

195 F10 82170 N43°49.759' E001°17.884'

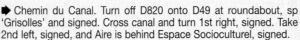

🚐 10 🛠 Custom; €2

➡ Chemin du Canal. Turn off D820 onto D49 at roundabout, sp 'Grisolles' and signed. Cross canal and turn 1st right, signed. Take 2nd left, signed, and Aire is behind Espace Socioculturel, signed.

ℹ Popular Aire in a large car park behind social centre. Village centre 100m with commerce. Canal 100m for walks and cycling. Updated 2016.

GRENADE

196 F11 31330 N43°46.300' E001°17.817'

🚐 10 🛠 Custom

➡ Quai de la Garonne. From D17/D29 roundabout follow D17 towards Ondes, signed. Turn left at recycling point, signed. Service Point in front of recycling. Parking: N43°46.103' E001°17.710'. At D17/D29 roundabout turn left onto D2, sp 'Toulouse'. Turn 2nd right, sp 'Salle des Fêtes'. Parking immediately on right.

ℹ Market Sat am and adj school can make Service Point access difficult. Parking suitable to visit town centre, 500m. Updated 2015.

ST NICOLAS DE LA GRAVE 1

197 F10 82210 N44°03.828' E001°01.494'

🚐 10 🛠 Euro Relais Mini

➡ Rue Bouchotte, off D26. Enter town on D26, D15, or D67 and follow sp 'Centre Ville'. Drive behind church and follow signs to Aire.

ℹ Convenient, centrally located town Aire. Always likely to have space. Small town commerce 150m. Town has interesting architecture including the former Château Richard Coeur de Lion (Richard the Lionheart). Birthplace of Lamothe Cadillac, founder of Detroit, USA; free museum open Jul-Aug. Reinspected 2016.

ST NICOLAS DE LA GRAVE 2

198 F10 82210 N44°05.062' E001°01.661'

🚐 15 🛠 Aire Services 7005; €2; Aire Services Elec; €3.50/24hrs; 12 CEE elec points

➡ D15. Exit town on D15, sp 'Moissac'. Turn right, sp 'Base de Loisers Tarn et le Garranne' and signed. Turn immediately right again and Aire is in 200m, signed.

ℹ Popular Aire adj to leisure lake and recreation area, no views. Marked walks and swimming lake. Use **197** to shop locally or if full. Inspected 2016.

CASTELSARRASIN
199 F10 82100 N44°02.314' E001°06.136'

30; €3/24hrs; CC Aire Services 3000; Inside barrier; €2.50; Aire Services Elec; €2.50/24hrs; 16 CEE elec points

➤ Allee de la Source. Exit E72/A62 Junction 9. Take D813 and follow sp 'Toulouse' onto one way system. Turn right into Rue du Gaz, signed. Take 1st right into Allee de la Source, signed. Aire on left, access via Aire Services barrier.

ℹ Popular commercial Aire located in peaceful residential streets. Can accommodate any unit configuration. Town centre 500m. Reinspected 2016.

MALAUSE
200 F10 82200 N44°05.483' E000°58.402' SP

5 Flot Bleu Océane; Token (FB)

➤ D4. Turn off D813 at the roundabout by the church onto D4, sp 'Boudou'. Turn immediately left into the car park by the church and the Service Point is on the right.

ℹ Convenient night halt in town centre car park just off D830 trunking route, some noise. Local commerce adj. Reinspected 2016.

BARDIGUES
201 F10 82340 N44°02.316' E000°53.551' SP

4 Custom; €2

➤ Between D89 and D11, outside cemetery. Signed off D11, but more easily accessible from D89 as road doesn't go through village. Exit D89 from either direction, sp 'Bardigues'. Aire at top of hill by cemetery. Open unlocked gates to enter.

ℹ Landscaped Aire with rural views in a tranquil village. Local commerce 200m uphill. Updated 2015.

MOISSAC
202 F10 82200 N44°05.920' E001°05.606' SP

42; €8/night; CC Custom; Inside barrier; €3

➤ Promenade Sancert. Turn off D813 at river bridge, sp 'berges du Tarn', 'Port-Canal' and signed. Follow road straight on for 900m and Aire is on left, signed. Enter through Urba Flux barrier.

ℹ Commercial Aire between river Tarn and canal, no views of either. Bike and canoe hire adj. Towpath along canal. Visited 2016.

Info/photos: Phil and Julie Hutchins

DONZAC
203 F10 82340 N44°06.855' E000°49.239' SP

20 Custom; WC down well!

➤ D30, at Lac des Sources. From north on D813 turn right onto D30 at Lamagistère, sp 'Donzac' and signed. Cross river and Aire on right at lake, signed.

ℹ Aire at pleasant picnic area with pond and arboretum. Local commerce in village centre, 450m. River Garonne 800m. Power station 1.4km. Updated 2015.

VALENCE D'AGEN
204 F10 82400 N44°06.342' E000°53.168' SP

20 Aire Services 3000; €4/15 mins water and 2hrs elec; Showers Apr-Oct

➤ Rue des Tanneries. Turn off D813 onto D11e, sp 'Centre Ville' and signed. Drive into town and turn right, sp 'Mairie' and 'Port Canal'. Turn right at roundabout, signed. Turn left and cross canal. Aire on right, signed.

ℹ Popular Aire in peaceful spot adj to canal, but no view. Showers and WC in former abattoir, now an info centre. Small town commerce 400m. Reinspected 2016.

VAZERAC `205` F10 82220 N44°11.370' E001°17.160' SP

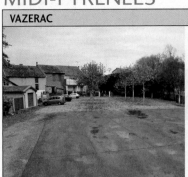

🚐 7 🚰 Tap only

➡ Rue Antonin Perbosc. Turn off D20 onto D109, sp 'Vazerac'. In 4.3km turn left at end of road onto D34 and drive into Vazerac. Aire at rear of parking 200m on right, signed.

ℹ Designated open or shaded parking just off main route adj to recycling bins. Sewerage treatment 100m. Local commerce 450m. Inspected 2016.

MONTJOI `206` F10 82400 R N44°11.868' E000°55.347' SP

🚐 10 🚰 Custom

➡ D46. Turn off D953 onto D46, sp 'Montjoi'. Follow sp 'Montjoi' on pleasant, wide country roads. Aire just off D46 in village by church, signed.

ℹ Recommended off-the-beaten-track stop 10km from D813. Pleasant and peaceful village Aire with rural views that can take any size unit and is always likely to have space. Circular village walk and other good walking. Reinspected 2016.

CASTELSAGRAT `207` F10 82400 N44°11.008' E000°56.675' SP

🚐 25 🚰 Aire Services 3000; Token (3/3)

➡ Cooperative Agricole. Turn off D953 at the roundabout onto D7, sp 'Castelsagrat'. In 2.5km turn left onto D28, 'Castelsagrat'. At village turn right, sp 'Valance'. Turn left, sp 'Cooperative Agricole'. Turn right and Aire at end of road.

ℹ Pleasant Aire on large gravel area with rural views. Idyllic village centre, 350m, with charming covered walkways which houses local commerce. Updated 2015.

MONTAUBAN `208` F10 82000 N44°00.435' E001°20.519' SP

🚐 10; €8/24hrs inc service; +€0.46 tax; Pay at Capitainerie 🚰 Aire Services 7010; Inside barrier; See info

➡ Rue Clos de Lauzun. Approach Montauban on D958 from west. Go straight over roundabout, sp 'Port-Canal'. In 900m turn right, sp 'Port-Canal'. Go under railway, 3.8m height restriction, and turn left, sp 'Port-Canal'. Take the next left, then follow road through marina. Aire on left, enter through Aire Services barrier.

ℹ Over landscaped commercial Aire adj to small river marina, no views. Very pleasant marina with tourist commerce and bike hire. Noisy commercial train track runs adj. Barrier appears to have been disabled, therefore Aire is open access. Reinspected 2016.

NEGREPELISSE `209` F10 82800 N44°04.442' E001°31.582' SP

🚐 6 🚰 Custom

➡ D958. Approach from east. At the D115/D65/D958 roundabout take D958 following sp 'Centre Ville' and signed. Turn left at next roundabout continuing on D958, signed. Entrance to Aire 200m on right between hedges, adj to D958, signed.

ℹ Aire just 100m from centre. Small town commerce includes a laundry. Market Wed am. Walking and cycle paths and picnic areas along river Aveyron. Inspected 2014.

LAUZERTE 1 `210` F10 82110 N44°16.026' E001°08.447' SP

🚐 10 🚰 Custom

➡ From Montcuq travel south on D653, which becomes D953. At D953/D2 junction go straight on into small lane. Turn immediately right into picnic area adj to junction. Service Point signed on WCs.

ℹ Aire in shaded picnic area with BBQ area adj to river with views. Road noise from main route but no HGV parking. 1.7km to Lauzerte, a Beau Village. Reinspected 2014.

LAUZERTE 2	211	F10	82110	T	N44°15.251' E001°08.192'	SP

3; No parking Wed am (market) ♟ Custom

➡ From Montcuq travel south on D653 which becomes D953. At D953/D2 junction turn onto D2, sp 'Lauzerte-Centre'. Follow road into village, then follow to left, signed. Aire on right in small car park, signed.

ℹ Aire in small Beau Village. No real overnight parking as car park too small and sloping, see 210. Market Wed am. Reinspected 2014.

MONTCUQ	212	F10	46800		N44°20.452' E001°12.151'	SP

20 ♟ Euro Relais Junior; Token (ER); €2

➡ D653. Aire in roadside lay-by adj to D653, signed.

ℹ Ideal lunch stop to visit Montcuq. At night the parking is shared with HGVs. Road gets noisy from HGVs around 6am. 210 (10km) is a more peaceful stop. Reinspected 2014.

ROQUECOR	213	F10	82150	R	N44°19.393' E000°56.651'	SP

6; 10m bays ♟ Custom

➡ On D656 from Tournon d'Agenais take 1st turning on left by two plane trees, sp 'Roquecor'. Drive into village and Aire on left, signed.

ℹ Pleasant, peaceful Aire offering rural views over the open access leisure facilities. Always likely to have space. The village centre is charming and has local commerce. Reinspected 2016.

MAUROUX	214	F10	46700		N44°27.099' E001°02.870'	SP

10; Apr-Oct ♟ Custom

➡ Aire de Repos 'La Garenne', D5. Approx 180m south of village in woodland, but hardcore roads and parking spots.

ℹ Parking under deciduous trees at picnic spot on edge of village. Kitchen/BBQ available to use Apr-Oct. Poss to park opp adj to sport facilities and main road. Local commerce 150m. Reinspected 2016.

PUY L'EVEQUE	215	F10	46700		N44°30.406' E001°08.141'	SP

30 ♟ Custom; Tap and drain next to bench

➡ D28/Rue Henri Dunant. From Cahors on D811, turn right off D811 opp Mairie, sp 'La Poste' and signed. Follow road past La Poste on the left, and Aire is on right, signed.

ℹ Aire occupies a large open car park. Medieval centre and small town commerce 350m. Small market Tue am by Mairie. Updated 2015.

PRAYSSAC	216	F10	46220		N44°30.199' E001°11.502'	SP

6 landscaped; 15 overflow ♟ Custom; Water under green cover; Hose/tap adaptor needed

➡ D811. Turn off D811 into Ave des Acacias, sp 'Residence les Plantades'. Turn 1st right, Aire immediately on left. If turn off where signed, turn left and follow road. Aire on right.

ℹ A pleasant, landscaped Aire set back from the main road. Large open overflow car park adj. Small town commerce 250m. Reinspected 2014.

ALBAS
217 F10 46140 N44°28.488' E001°13.965'

🚐 20 🛠 Custom

➡ D8. Exit Albas to north on D8. After 800m turn right, sp 'Camping Pech Del Gal'. Aire outside campsite, adj to river. Signed on entry to village from north.

ⓘ Aire in unrestricted parking overlooking dammed section of river Lot. Noise from dam control, but very interesting. D8 a pleasant drive. Adj municipal campsite only open in high season. Inspected 2014.

LUZECH (CAIX)
218 F10 46140 N44°29.431' E001°17.702'

🚐 20; €8.50/night inc elec; Collected 🛠 Bollard; €2

➡ D9. From Luzech take D9/Quai Lefranc de Pompignan along the river Lot, sp 'Caix' and signed. Turn right after 2km into campsite, visible from road, sp 'Restaurant le Capitaine' as enter Caix. Drive into campsite entrance, then turn right into Aire.

ⓘ Commercial Aire adj to scruffy campsite which swings into action in Jul/Aug. River 50m no views. Canoe hire in season (€6/hr). Reinspected 2014.

CASTELNAU MONTRATIER
219 F10 46170 N44°16.473' E001°21.123'

🚐 10 🛠 Euro Relais Junior; Token (2/1); €2

➡ Causse du Moulin à Vent. Exit town on D659 towards Lalbenque. At the windmill on the right, turn left and follow the road uphill. Aire on left, signed.

ⓘ Adj to a line of windmills and municipal campsite. Village centre with local commerce and convenience store 650m downhill. Reinspected 2016.

LABASTIDE MARNHAC
220 F10 46090 N44°23.163' E001°23.856'

🚐 10 🛠 Custom

➡ Between D7 and D67. Turn off D7 onto D67, sp 'l'Hospitalet' and signed. Turn immediately left, signed, then 1st right. Aire on left.

ⓘ Adj to picnic area and tennis courts. Bar/restaurant adj. On popular GR65 walking route. Reinspected 2014.

CAHORS
221 F10 46000 N44°26.420' E001°26.468'

🚐 3 riverside; 40 in overflow; Max 86hrs 🛠 Custom

➡ Parking St Georges. Approach Cahors from south on D820. Follow sp 'Cahors-Centre' onto D620. Turn off to P St Georges at roundabout before river bridge, signed. Service Point and 3 bays on right, signed. Additional parking: N44°26.324' E001°26.464'.

ⓘ Limited riverside parking, additional riverside parking tolerated between Service Point and additional parking. Historic town adj with amazing pedestrianised medieval river bridge, 1.5km. Reinspected 2014.

ARCAMBAL
222 F10 46090 N44°27.412' E001°30.966'

🚐 10 🛠 Euro Relais Junior; Token (ER); €2

➡ D8. At Arcambal centre turn onto D8 at traffic lights, sp 'St Cirq Lapopie'. Aire immediately on right behind Mairie.

ⓘ Aire located in village centre just off D911. Boules court and park adj. Water tap by hairdressers. Reinspected 2014.

VERS

223 | F10 | 46090 | N44°29.131' E001°33.302'

🛏 10; €5/night; Collected 🛒 Custom

➡ Off D662. From St Géry on D662 turn left on entering village, sp 'Camping'. For parking turn right at tennis courts, signed. Service Point: N44°29.175' E001°33.391'. Go past tennis courts down gravel track.

ℹ Pleasant location at old station with access to WCs and a warm shower. Picnic park adj. Local and tourist commerce inc restaurant with river views. Market Thur am. Reinspected 2014.

ST GERY

224 | G10 | 46330 | N44°28.702' E001°34.895'

🛏 30 🛒 Custom

➡ D662. Adj to D662 in village centre, signed.

ℹ Pleasant location just off village centre with local commerce. Miniature train and museum 250m. No river access. Reinspected 2014.

BOUZIES

225 | G10 | 46330 | N44°28.993' E001°38.716'

🛏 15 🛒 Euro Relais Box; Token (ER)

➡ D40. Turn off D662 onto 10t weight and 2.3m (wheelbase) width restricted bridge to D40, sp 'Bouziers'. Turn left and left again. Service Point in car park on left. Overnight car park to right adj to river. To avoid bridge approach from St-Cirq-Lapopie.

ℹ Adj to river park. Partial views through trees to river. Canoe hire adj. D662, a pleasant river drive under rocky overhangs and tunnels. Reinspected 2014.

ST CIRQ LAPOPIE 1

226 | G10 | 46330 | T | N44°27.864' E001°39.810'

🛏 40; €3; Pay at machine; 9am-9pm only 🛒 None; See **227**

➡ D8. Parking off D8 north of village (uphill walk on way back) or bottom of village: N44°27.964' E001°40.700' (downhill walk on way back).

ℹ Aire near medieval town and Beau Village with tourist commerce. Lots of interesting buildings, roadways and a viewpoint over the river Lot. Inspected 2014.

ST CIRQ LAPOPIE 2

227 | G10 | 46330 | N44°28.233' E001°40.830'

🛏 50; €7/night; Collected 🛒 Raclet; €2; Showers €2

➡ La Plage. Turn off D662 at roundabout in Tour de Faure onto D181, sp 'St Cirq Lapopie' and signed, and cross river Lot and go straight onto D8. After 150m turn right, sp 'Parking de la Plage'. At river, Service Point and shaded bays to right, open parking to left.

ℹ Aire adj to river Lot in riverside park with views through trees to river. Canoe hire in season (€5/hr). St Cirq Lapopie is a must see, see **226**. Reinspected 2014.

CAJARC

228 | G10 | 46160 | N44°29.075' E001°50.744'

🛏 10 🛒 Custom; €1

➡ Avenue de la Gare. Follow ring road around town turning at D117/D17 roundabout onto D17, sp 'Figeac'. Turn right immediately, sp 'P la Gare' and signed. Aire 50m, signed.

ℹ Aire adj to old train station, now a youth centre. Town commerce 250m. Reinspected 2014.

CATUS ★ | 229 | F9 | 46150 | N44°33.346' E001°20.344' | SP

🚐 10 🏠 Custom

▶ Off D6. In Catus at the D6/D5 junction by the old market turn onto D6, sp 'Cahors'. Turn left before river bridge, signed, and follow road along river through car park. Service Point on right.

ℹ Aire full of French charm 200m from small town commerce. Small market Tue am on adj street, locals park at Aire but still accessible. Reinspected 2014.

Photos: Rod Poxon

DEGAGNAC | 230 | F9 | 46340 | N44°40.073' E001°18.565' | SP

🚐 20 🏠 Euro Relais Box; Token (ER)

▶ D6. From north on D6 turn left by the tennis courts towards the leisure lake. Parking is in this car park, signed. Service Point: N44°39.971' E001°18.910'. Exit parking to left and turn left in 250m onto D2, sp 'St Germain'. Take 1st left to Service Point.

ℹ Parking is in a large gravel car park overlooking the leisure lake. Service Point is in the village, park here to shop in the village before retiring back to the lake. Inspected 2014.

Lake Parking

All of the listings in this section are Service Points without designated parking. The majority are located either at supermarkets or outside campsites.

Height barriers are rare at supermarkets and overnight parking should be possible. Always park considerately. Supermarket Service Points often lack a waste water drain.

Most campsites are municipally owned. Parking outside may be possible when campsites are closed. Acquiring tokens in rural locations may be difficult or impossible, especially in low season.

Remember to be a responsible tourist whenever offsite parking.

LES QUATRE ROUTES DU LOT | 231 | G9 | 46110 | N44°59.425' E001°39.139'

🏠 Custom

▶ D32. Turn off D96 by railway track onto D32, sp 'St Denis' and signed. In 800m turn left into campsite entrance, signed. Service Point on right. Inspected 2014.

SOUILLAC | 232 | F9 | 46200 | N44°53.958' E001°28.480'

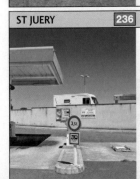

🏠 Aire Services Plastic; Token (3/3)

▶ Off D103/Ave Jean Jaurès. Turn off D820 at the LIDL roundabout onto D103, sp 'Sarlat'. In 100m turn right. Service Point in Casino fuel station on right. Inspected 2014.

LAGUIOLE | 233 | H9 | 12210 | N44°40.917' E002°51.250'

🏠 Custom

▶ Lieu-dit Le Griffoulet, outside Camping Les Monts D'Aubrac off D921. From south turn right off D921, signed. Follow road to campsite, signed. Alt 1035m, but notice states open all year. Reinspected 2016.

ST GENIEZ D'OLT | 234 | H10 | 12130 | N44°28.183' E002°59.000'

🏠 Aire Services Plastic; €1

▶ D503/Route de la Cascade. Turn off D988, sp 'Pomayrols' and 'Camping Boissière'. Turn 1st right, sp 'Camping'. Turn left into campsite entrance and the Service Point is immediately on right. Do not drive through town; passable, but narrow in places. Reinspected 2016.

LE GARRIC (Carmaux) | 235 | G10 | 81400 | N44°00.858' E002°08.080'

🏠 Custom

▶ Off D25. Exit Carmaux to south on D988, sp 'Cap' Découverte'. In 3.8km at roundabout turn right onto D25, sp 'Cap' Découverte'. At next roundabout turn left into Cap' Découverte. Follow road past car parks and across roundabout, signed. Service Point on left before campsite. Inspected 2014.

ST JUERY | 236 | G10 | 81160 | N43°57.043' E002°12.597'

🏠 Euro Relais Junior; Token (3/3)

▶ D100. From centre exit St Juéry on D100, sp 'Albi'. Service Point at fuel station of Carrefour supermarket before river bridge. Reinspected 2014.

ALBI 1 | 237 | G10 | 81000 | N43°55.856' E002°10.669'

🏠 Flot Bleu Océane; Token; €2

▶ Rue Jean Rostand, at Kercher branded car wash. Service Point directly behind 2.8m car wash bays. Safest entrance is through exit; must reverse out. Inspected 2014.

ALBI 2 · 238 · G10 81000 · N43°55.159' E002°06.458'

Aire Services 3000; CC; €2

➡ Z.A. Fonlabour. Turn off N88 at Junction 13 and follow sp 'Z.A. Fonlabour'. In 2km turn left at roundabout. Service Point signed at E.Leclerc Express Drive. Reinspected 2014.

ALBI 3 · 239 · G10 81000 · N43°56.761' E002°09.071'

Custom; WC emptying at waist height

➡ D988. From north on N88 turn onto D988 at roundabout, sp 'Albi Centre'. Service Point is on the right in 700m, signed. Reinspected 2014.

LACAUNE · 240 · H11 81230 · N43°42.576' E002°42.446'

Custom; Token (3/3)

➡ Rue de la Belmette. Turn off D607 in town, sp 'Les Vidals' and 'Camping'. Turn left, sp 'Camping'. Service Point on left outside campsite entrance, signed. Inspected 2014.

REVEL · 241 · G11 31250 · N43°27.779' E002°00.318'

Aire Services 3000; Token (3/3); Free from supermarket

➡ Chemin d'En Besset. Follow ring road around town, sp 'Castres'. On north side of ring road turn off at roundabout onto D622, sp 'Castres'. At next roundabout turn left, sp 'Hyper Casino'. Turn right into supermarket. Service Point in fuel station by gas bottles. Reinspected 2014.

LABARTHE SUR LEZE · 242 · F11 31860 · N43°27.261' E001°23.696'

Euro Relais Box; Token or €2

➡ D4. Adj to D4 at the western edge of town near its junction with D19. Visited 2013.

ST SULPICE SUR LEZE · 243 · F11 31410 · N43°19.812' E001°18.999'

Euro Relais Junior; €2

➡ D622. Aire is adj to D622 as you enter town from A64. The Service Point is in the fuel station of the Intermarché supermarket, next to the car wash. Reinspected 2014.

ST GAUDENS · 244 · F11 31800 · N43°06.610' E000°42.493'

Custom; Jun-Sept; 1 unmetered Cont elec point

➡ Rue des Chanteurs du Comminges. Exit St Gaudens towards Montréjeaux on D817. Turn right at roundabout junction with D39a, sp 'Le Belvédère' with the campsite symbol. Service Point in 100m. Reinspected 2014.

NAUCELLE · 245 · G10 12800 · N44°11.830' E002°20.510'

Custom; WC by La Poste

➡ Place du Ségala, at back of village square. From D997 turn onto D52 by water fountain, public WCs and La Poste, sp 'Crespin'. Service Point 100m on left, signed. The parking is very impractical, so really just a Service Point. Reinspected 2016.

GOURDAN POLIGNAN · 246 · E11 31510 · N43°03.611' E000°35.529'

Euro Relais Junior; €2

➡ D825. Service Point at Super U just off D8/A645/D825/N125 roundabout. The Service Point is in the fuel station. Inspected 2014.

ARGELES GAZOST · 247 · E11 65400 · N43°00.562' W000°05.129'

Flot Bleu Pacific (Pink); €2

➡ Turn off D821 at roundabout junction with D100, sp 'Déchetterie' and signed. Turn 1st left, signed, and Service Point 350m on right at car wash, signed. Reinspected 2016.

POUZAC · 248 · E11 65200 · N43°04.750' E000°08.482'

Euro Relais Mini; €2

➡ D935, at Intermarché supermarket. From north on D935 Service Point on left behind fuel station, adj to self-service laundry. Reinspected 2016.

MASSEUBE · 249 · E11 32140 · N43°26.566' E000°34.687'

Custom

➡ D929. Exit town to north on D929. At roundabout turn into Super U supermarket car park. Service Point adj to self-service laundry. Reinspected 2014.

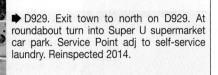

PLAISANCE 250 — E11 32160 N43°36.491' E000°02.918'

♿ ▥ 🔁 E WC ♿ 🚿 🚌 F

🚰 Euro Relais Mini

➡ Place des Arenes. Turn off D946 by river bridge into car park, signed. Opp outdoor swimming pool. Drive behind bull ring and Service Point is on left, signed. Reinspected 2016.

MIRANDE 251 — E11 32300 N43°30.801' E000°24.501'

♿ ▥ 🔁 E WC ♿ 🚿 🚌 F ⬛

🚰 Custom; Token

➡ Chemin du Batardeau. Turn off N21, sp 'Chalets L'ile du Pont', and follow sp 'L'ile du Pont'. Service Point to right of campsite entrance. Inspected 2012.

BEAUMONT DE LOMAGNE 252 — F10 32500 N43°53.543' E001°00.695'

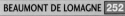
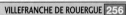

♿ ▥ 🔁 E WC ♿ 🚿 🚌 F

🚰 Flot Bleu Euro; CC/Token; €2/20 mins

➡ D928, at the car wash in the Casino supermarket car park. Aire adj to D928 as enter town from Larrazet in the east. Reinspected 2016.

ST BENOIT (MOISSAC) 253 — F10 82200 N44°05.776' E001°05.317'

♿ ▥ 🔁 E WC ♿ 🚿 🚌 F ⬛

🚰 Custom

➡ D72/Route de Gandalou. Turn off D813 before Moissac at roundabout onto D72, signed. Follow road and Service Point on left, outside campsite, signed. Reinspected 2014

CAHORS 254 — F10 46000 N44°27.689' E001°27.033'

♿ ▥ 🔁 E WC ♿ 🚿 🚌 F ⬛

🚰 Custom; Token; €2

➡ Avenue Édouard Herriot. From Cahors centre follow D911, sp 'Rodez'. 70m after Total fuel station turn left into Rue Jean Racine. Aire at Intermarché at end of road, currently in car wash on left side of car park, signed. Reinspected 2014.

PRADINES 255 — F10 46090 N44°27.762' E001°25.242'

♿ ▥ 🔁 E WC ♿ 🚿 🚌 F ⬛

🚰 Flot Bleu Pacific; €2

➡ D8. Follow D820 south towards Cahors. Cross river and turn 1st right, sp 'D8' and 'Luzech'. At roundabout turn right onto D8, sp 'Cahors'. At next roundabout turn right into L'Auto fuel station. Service Point is directly on left next to car wash, to access drive behind car wash. Inspected 2014.

VILLEFRANCHE DE ROUERGUE 256 — G10 12200 N44°21.369' E002°01.487'

♿ ▥ 🔁 E WC ♿ 🚿 🚌 F ⬛

🚰 Custom

➡ D911. Enter from west on D911. Turn right at traffic lights into Intermarché supermarket. Follow road uphill and Service Point on corner of supermarket building. Inspected 2016.

IBOS 257 — E11 65420 N43°14.295' E000°01.088'

♿ ▥ 🔁 E WC ♿ 🚿 🚌 F ⬛

🚰 Flot Bleu Pacific; Token; Inspection cover

➡ Zone Commercial Méridien. Turn off D817 onto D64, sp 'Ibos' and 'Zone Commercial'. At roundabout turn left and Service Point adj to car wash outside L'Auto. Inspected 2016.

BESSIERES 258 — G10 31660 N43°48.100' E001°35.526'

♿ ▥ 🔁 E WC ♿ 🚿 🚌 F ⬛

🚰 Aire Services 7010; €2

➡ D630. On D630 turn off at roundabout into Super U. Service Point at the fuel station, signed. Inspected 2016.

BOULOC 259 — F11 31620 N43°47.039' E001°24.144'

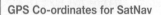

♿ ▥ 🔁 E WC ♿ 🚿 🚌 F ⬛

🚰 Euro Relais Junior; €2

➡ D4. On D4 turn off at roundabout into Intermarché supermarket. Service Point at the fuel station to rear of the supermarket. Inspected 2016.

CABRERETS 260 — G10 46330 N44°30.463' E001°39.736'

♿ ▥ 🔁 E WC ♿ 🚿 🚌 F ⬛

🚰 Custom; Apr-Oct

➡ D41. Follow D41 north of the village. Service Point outside Camping Familial Cantal. Adj to basic riverside campsite set into gorge. €3.50 pitch + €2.80pp, elec €2.50. Inspected 2012.

GPS Co-ordinates for SatNav

The GPS Co-ordinates published in this guide were taken onsite by our inspectors. We consider them a valuable and unique asset and at the time of publishing have decided not to publish them as electronic files for use on navigation devices. You have permission to type in the co-ordinates of an Aire you intend to visit but not to store or share them. For the security of our copyright:

- **Do not compile them into lists**

- **Do not publish, share or reproduce them anywhere in any format**

Bougon

POITOU

Mortagne sur Gironde

MAULEON

1 | D6 | 79700 | N46°55.070' W000°45.133'

🚐 3 🛒 Custom

➡ Rue de la Bachelette. Follow sp 'Niort' south out of town on D744. Turn right up lane after exiting town, sp 'Complexe Sportif' and signed. Follow lane into housing estate until reach sports fields. Aire signed on left.

ℹ Small Aire by entrance to sports complex with 2m height barriered parking. Sports field and swimming pool with waterslide adj. Town with château and impressive church 700m. Reinspected 2016.

ST AMAND SUR SEVRE 1

2 | D6 | 79700 | N46°52.154' W000°47.998'

🚐 5; Reinforced grass parking; Max 48hrs 🛒 Custom; Roadside

➡ C56. From D154 follow sp 'Centre Ville'. Turn off in village centre, signed. Drive past Mairie and church, then turn left onto C56, sp 'Les Chateliers-Chateaumur'. Aire on right adj to C56, signed.

ℹ Small, pleasant Aire adj to streamside picnic area. Service Point to right on main road as exit parking. Local commerce in village centre 600m. Reinspected 2016.

ST AMAND SUR SEVRE 2

3 | D6 | 79700 | N46°53.033' W000°49.546'

🚐 20; €10/night inc elec; Collected; Grass parking 🛒 Custom; 16 6amp Cont elec points

➡ C2, between St-Amand-sur-Sèvre and Treize-Vents. Turn off D34 by large cross in St Amand sur Sevre, sp 'Treize-Vents'. In 2.5km turn left, sp 'Bar Moulin de Chaligny' and signed. Follow road to Aire at end.

ℹ Pleasant, peaceful, private Aire at bar surrounded by fields located at beautiful riverside spot. Suitable for any unit configuration. Basic facilities. Reinspected 2016.

COURLAY

4 | D6 | 79440 | N46°46.814' W000°34.233'

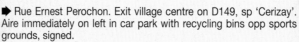

🚐 15 🛒 Custom

➡ Rue Ernest Perochon. Exit village centre on D149, sp 'Cerizay'. Aire immediately on left in car park with recycling bins opp sports grounds, signed.

ℹ Aire on edge of village opp sports ground and only likely to be busy during weekend events. Suitable for any unit configuration. Local commerce in centre 300m. Inspected 2016.

ST MAURICE LA FOUGEREUSE

5 | E6 | 79150 | N47°01.974' W000°30.509'

🚐 4 🛒 Custom; 2 unmetered CEE elec points in WC

➡ Espace de la rivière Juliot. Turn off D748 in La Fougereuse onto D161, sp 'St Maurice'. In St Maurice turn right into car park, opp D33 junction, sp 'Espace de la rivière Juliot'.

ℹ Aire adj to pleasant village pond and park. Local commerce 100m. Updated 2016.

BOISME

6 | E6 | 79300 | N46°46.655' W000°26.007'

🚐 15 🛒 Custom; WC adj to Service Point

➡ Rue des Essarts. From north on D139 turn left in Boismé onto D135, sp 'Chiché' and signed. Follow road around lake and Aire in car park at far end of lake, signed.

ℹ Aire with both hardstanding and summer grass parking adj to pleasant lake and park, no view. Depart point for 28km/46km cycling circuits and 9km circular walking route. Walk around lake to local commerce in village centre, 800m. Reinspected 2016.

LA CHAPELLE ST LAURENT | 7 | E6 | 79430 | N46°44.871' W000°28.544' | SP

🚐 20 🏺 Custom; WC 20m, at picnic area

➡ D748. Turn off D748 opp fuel station and drive past La Poste, signed. Aire 100m, signed.

ℹ Large, popular Aire with grass and hardstanding parking suitable for any unit configuration. Just far enough away from D748 to be pleasant. Landscaped park adj with picnic area and pond, no view. Local commerce 50m. Voie Verte cycle/walking route 200m; Bressuire 11km and Parthenay 23km. Reinspected 2016.

CLESSE | 8 | E7 | 79350 | N46°42.955' W000°24.326' | SP

🚐 10 🏺 Custom; WC 50m, at church

➡ D19. At roundabout by church turn onto D19, sp 'Parthenay'. Parking on right, signed. For Service Point drive past parking and turn left onto D177, sp 'Chiché' and signed. Service Point 100m on left, signed: N46°43.082' W000°24.257'.

ℹ Designated parking in village centre with local commerce. Aire offers grass and hardstanding parking and is popular on hot summer days as it has shade. Service Point is at municipal storage buildings but has no parking. Reinspected 2016.

L'ABSIE | 9 | D7 | 79240 | N46°37.987' W000°34.642' | SP

🚐 10 🏺 Custom; 4 unmetered CEE elec points; WC 20m, up steps to left

➡ Rue des Halles, adj to D949bis. From D949bis turn onto D179 at mini roundabout, sp 'La Chapelle St Etienne' and signed. Aire on right in central square below HGV parking, signed.

ℹ Sloping Aire conveniently located in central village square, 100m off main route. Suitable for any unit configuration. Most level parking by Service Point. Local commerce adj. Reinspected 2016.

VERNOUX EN GATINE | 10 | E7 | 79240 | N46°38.196' W000°30.882'

🚐 6; Grass parking; Max 7m 🏺 Custom; 6 unmetered elec points (Turned off)

➡ D143. From D949bis in village turn onto D143, sp 'Neuvy-Bouin'. Turn left before church, signed. Entrance to Aire beside mausoleum, signed.

ℹ Small grass parking Aire beside church, hell's bells. Elec has been permanently turned off. Local commerce 400m. Reinspected 2016.

LA FORET SUR SEVRE | 11 | D7 | 79380 | N46°46.510' W000°38.842' | SP

🚐 30 🏺 Custom; 4 unmetered Cont elec points in covered seating

➡ Rue de Beauchêne. Turn off D744 at roundabout into town, sp 'La Forét s/ S.' and signed. Turn right in 100m, signed. Aire 200m on left, signed. Entrance has passable bollards.

ℹ Very pleasant space at former campsite offering grass and hardstanding parking. Also used by boules club. Covered seating area, BBQ area and fishable river. Reinspected 2016.

PARTHENAY | 12 | E7 | 79200 | N46°38.437' W000°15.982'

🚐 8; €9/24hrs inc service and elec; Pay at campsite for exit code; Apr-Oct 🏺 Custom; 4 unmetered CEE elec points just behind Service Point in campsite

➡ Rue de Boisseau. As enter Parthenay on D949bis turn left, sp 'Base de Loisirs de Parthenay'. Enter the village of Boisseau. Aire on right, signed. Coded barrier at exit. Must pay at campsite for exit code.

ℹ Popular, small, commercial Aire run by the adj campsite. Overlooks fishing lake and park; pleasant lakeside footpath with picnic benches. Walled old town 2km. Reinspected 2016.

POITOU

AZAY SUR THOUET
13 | E7 | 79130 | N46°37.319' W000°21.076'

🚐 5; €7/night inc elec; +€0.50pp; May-mid Oct; Free mid Oct-Apr
🛒 Custom; 4 unmetered CEE elec points just behind Service Point in campsite

➡ Rue des Rocs. In Azay-sur-Thouet turn off D949bis onto D139, sp 'St Pardoux' and signed. Turn left before bridge, signed. Service Point is beside campsite entrance.

ℹ Aire at picnic area outside basic municipal campsite with toilet block and shower. Pitches €4/night +€2.70pp; €3.50/night for elec. Local commerce 50m. Inspected 2016.

VASLES
14 | E7 | 79340 | N46°34.402' W000°01.394'

🚐 10 🛒 Custom; WC emptying by WC

➡ Rue de la Cité. From D59 follow sp 'Parking' and 'Espace Mouton Village', both with sheep heads. Aire at large parking area near stadium, between D59 and D121.

ℹ Aire in car park of Parc Mouton (sheep) Village with lots of items celebrating sheep; entry to park €10pp in high season. www.moutonvillage.fr Open access municipal sports facility adj. Excellent small town commerce 100m, walk through large car park towards church. Reinspected 2016.

MENIGOUTE
15 | E7 | 79340 | N46°29.887' W000°03.450'

🚐 7 🛒 Custom

➡ Rue des Vignes. From the village centre take D21, sp 'La Pagerie'. Turn immediately right into Rue des Vignes. Drive past SPA supermarket and Aire is on left.

ℹ Peaceful Aire in centre with SPA supermarket adj and other local commerce. Large open access park and sports field adj. Gallo-Roman ruins 3km, €5.50pp. www.sanxay.fr Reinspected 2016.

AYRON
16 | E7 | 86190 | N46°39.370' E000°05.398'

🚐 30; €3.50/night; Collected 🛒 Flot Bleu Pacific; €2; Apr-Oct; Water tap adj, drive over drain diff

➡ Off N149/E62, outside campsite at Étang de Fleix. Take N149/E62 east out of town, sp 'Poitiers'. After town boundary turn right off N149, sp 'Base de Loisirs', 'Camping' and signed. Parking on right, signed. Service Point adj outside campsite: N46°39.382' E000°05.286'.

ℹ Large, open parking on grass or hardstanding just moments from main road; distant road noise. Suitable for any unit configuration. Fishing lake, no swimming, and café 200m downhill, no view. Reinspected 2016.

ST LOUP LAMAIRE
17 | E6 | 79600 | N46°47.128' W000°09.850'

🚐 30; Grass parking 🛒 Flot Bleu Océane; €3 (3 x €1); See info

➡ Places des Tanneries. From west follow D46. Cross the river and after passing under the railway bridge turn off D46 onto D121, sp 'Clémille' and signed. Aire on left in 100m.

ℹ Large, popular, grass parking suitable for any unit configuration. Located near river, no views, on outskirts of pretty village with local commerce. Leisure lake nearby. Service Point instructs you to insert 3 x €1, then press refund button and receive €2 back. Reinspected 2016.

AIRVAULT
18 | E6 | 79600 | N46°49.506' W000°08.578'

🚐 5 🛒 Custom; WC to right of Service Point

➡ Rue de la Gare. Approach from south on D46 and at roundabout take D725e, sp 'St Varent'. Turn right across railway track onto D27, sp 'Airvault' and signed. At next roundabout go almost completely around and enter car park on left, signed. Aire at far end. Route through centre is narrow and 3.5t weight restricted.

ℹ Aire located on the edge of town in a peaceful car park. Bus stop adj. Town is a charming Petite City of Character with a Sat market. Reinspected 2016.

ST VARENT

19 | E6 | 79330 | N46°53.326' W000°14.534'

🚐 7 🔧 None

➡️ Route de Pierrefitte. Turn off D28 onto D135, sp 'Pierrefitte' and signed. Follow road and Aire on right in lay-by picnic area on edge of town, signed.

ℹ️ Grass and gravel parking at picnic area on edge of town. Shaded and open parking suitable for any unit configuration. River runs adj to parking. Small town commerce 650m. Reinspected 2016.

LA BOURELIERE (LUCHE THOUARSAIS)

20 | E6 | 79330 | N46°54.384' W000°17.939'

🚐 4; Max 1 night 🔧 Aire Services 3000; CC; €2

➡️ Rue du Village. Turn off D938ter in St Gemme onto V4, sp 'Luché-Thouarsais' and 'Base de Loisirs'. Follow road past entrance to Base de Loisirs, then turn immediately left into Aire.

ℹ️ Small Aire adj to, but fenced off from, leisure lake with swimming beach; obscured views. Seasonal café, WCs and outdoor showers 100m. Fishing on far side of lake. Inspected 2016.

THOUARS

21 | E6 | 79100 | N46°58.579' W000°12.702'

🚐 8; 7m narrow bays 🔧 Campsite bollard

➡️ Place Ferdinand Buisson, outside old city wall. Turn off D938 at roundabout, sp 'Centre Ville'. Follow sp 'Centre Ville'. After passing the cemetery follow sp 'Autre Directions', then 'P Cemetery'. Aire 200m on left, signed.

ℹ️ Pleasant location against town ramparts; motorhomes restricted to small part of car park. Town with various historical sites, 500m uphill. Reinspected 2016.

ST MARTIN DE SANZAY

22 | E6 | 79290 | N47°05.524' W000°12.038'

🚐 50; Grass parking; Jul-Aug 🔧 Custom; 12 unmetered CEE elec points

➡️ La Zona de Loisirs La Ballastière, at Étang la Ballastière. On D158 head north from St-Martin-de-Sanzay, following sp 'Étang la Ballastière' and signed. Aire at leisure lake.

ℹ️ Large, open Aire at former municipal campsite suitable for any unit configuration. Sports facilities and boules court adj. Fishing lake adj, no views. Reinspected 2016.

OIRON

23 | E6 | 79100 | N46°56.875' W000°04.954'

🚐 10 🔧 Custom; Token; €1

➡️ Salle Polyvalente, in village centre. Follow D64/D145 south, sp 'Salle Polyvalente' and signed. Parking is on right by recycling before Salle Polyvalente. Service Point on adj building, signed.

ℹ️ Open parking suitable for any unit configuration; additional unrestricted parking behind. Rural views and small park with picnic area adj. Pretty village with local commerce 450m. Château d'Oiron in village, €7.50pp. www.oiron.fr Reinspected 2016.

LOUDUN 1

24 | E6 | 86200 | N47°00.815' E000°04.679'

🚐 Lots of unrestricted local parking; Also see **25** 🔧 Aires Services 3000; €2; Max 30 mins; Max 3.5t

➡️ Place de la Porte Saint Nicolas. From Thouars on D759 turn left at roundabout onto D347, sp 'Angers'. Turn 5th right off D347, on northwest side of town, not signed. At end of road turn immediately left to Aire, signed.

ℹ️ Service Point with 3.5t weight and 30 min time restriction. Plenty of unrestricted local parking. Reinspected 2016.

LOUDUN 2

25 | E6 | 86200 | N47°01.108' E000°05.313'

🚐 4 🚰 Flot Bleu Standard Plus (Yellow); €2

➡ Avenue de Ouagadougou. Enter Loudun from north on D147 and follow sp 'Z.I. Nord', then 'Ave de Ouagadougou'. Follow this road for 650m and the Service Point is at the car wash on the right.

ⓘ Aire in open car park to rear of car wash in urban industrial estate; 1 car wash suitable for motorhomes. Green space and picnic area adj. Plenty of suitable motorhome parking near town centre to visit commerce. Reinspected 2016.

CHALAIS

26 | E6 | 86200 | N46°57.510' E000°06.279'

🚐 8; Overflow poss 🚰 Custom; 4 unmetered 10amp CEE elec points

➡ Turn off D347, sp 'Aire de Repos de la Briande'. Aire at rear, signed.

ⓘ Landscaped Aire with hedged bays to rear of roadside lay-by just off the noisy D347 main route. Large restaurant and TO with local products for sale; free WiFi at TO. Area is due for remodel in 2017. Reinspected 2016.

MIREBEAU

27 | E6 | 86110 | N46°46.836' E000°11.639'

🚐 8; €7/night; €12/night inc elec; Collected 🚰 Custom; €2; Elec €5; 4 16amp Cont elec points; All inside gate

➡ 14 Rue du Pas Martin. Turn off D347 at Mirebeau onto D15, sp 'Thurageau' and signed. Follow road for 700m then turn right onto Rue du Pas Martin, signed. Turn into gate before no entry sign, signed.

ⓘ Landscaped, private Aire owned by adj house; regional products for sale. Road noise. Troglodyte cave nearby. Walled town of Mirebeau 1km. Other signed Aire is France Passion site at Agressais. Inspected 2016.

LENCLOITRE

28 | E6 | 86140 | N46°49.057' E000°19.524'

🚐 20; Max 48hrs; No parking 1st Mon of the month 🚰 Custom

➡ Place du Champ de Foire. From Mirebeau on D725 enter town, then turn left onto D20, sp 'Cernay'. Turn immediately right, then left into Aire. Service Point beside WC.

ⓘ Large, popular Aire on market place with open and shaded grass and hardstanding parking; suitable for any unit configuration. Small town commerce adj. Some noise from main route. Inspected 2016.

VENDEUVRE DU POITOU

29 | E7 | 86380 | N46°43.466' E000°17.922'

🚐 2 🚰 Tap and Cont WC only

➡ D757. Adj to D757 as exit village to south towards Poitiers. Designated parking on left adj to park, signed.

ⓘ Aire with 2 small designated parking bays, but further parking poss. Adj to main road, some road noise. Overlooking l'Aire des Marais, a streamside picnic area. Les Marais de la Pallu, a 10.2km circular walking route, departs from here. Reinspected 2016.

POITIERS - FUTUROSCOPE

30 | E7 | 86360 | N46°39.813' E000°22.094'

🚐 100; 1st hr free; €7/24hrs; Pay at machine 🚰 Euro Relais Maxi; €4; See info

➡ Avenue du Futuroscope, at Futuroscope off D20d. Follow sp 'Futuroscope'. Aire adj to roundabout junction of D910 and D20d. Go through barrier, then turn right into Aire.

ⓘ Futuroscope adj. www.futuroscope.com If only visiting for 1hr, do not put ticket in payment machine, go straight to barrier. Reinspected 2016.

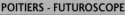

CHEZELLES — 31 — F7 — 86530 — N46°45.980' E000°30.663'

🚐 3 hardstanding; 15 grass 🛠 Custom

▶ D1c. Turn off D910 at roundabout onto D23, sp 'Vouneuil s/ V'. Cross river, then turn left onto D1c, sp 'Cenon s/ Vienne'. In 1.6km turn left at Chezelles boundary, sp 'Point Pêche'. Service Point and parking immediately on left. Follow tracks to riverside grass parking.

ℹ️ Open grass or gravel parking all year plus peaceful, shaded, riverside summer parking; ideal for anglers - fish from your motorhome! No river views, but views of ruined castle, Site du Vieux Poitiers. Castle is 5 mins of fun, open weekends 2-6pm Jun-Sept; has grass parking and numerous walks pass by: N46°45.654' E000°30.766'. Inspected 2016.

VICQ SUR GARTEMPE — 32 — F7 — 86260 — N46°43.447' E000°51.719'

🚐 10 🛠 Custom

▶ D5. Exit village on D5, sp 'La Roche Posay'. Aire is 300m on the left, signed.

ℹ️ Large parking area by boules courts. Poss road noise. Village with local commerce 250m. www.vicq-sur-gartempe.fr Inspected 2015.

MONTMORILLON — 33 — F7 — 86500 — N46°25.389' E000°52.069'

🚐 10; Max 24hrs 🛠 Urba Flux Tall; CC; €2

▶ Rue Léon Dardant. Approach on D54 from south. At traffic lights turn left onto D727, sp 'Chauvigny'. Cross river bridge and turn right at traffic lights, sp 'P'. Turn right again, then left, then right, signed. Some of these turns are narrow due to parked cars; 8m+ motorhome owners advised to inspect before attempting.

ℹ️ Pleasant, peaceful, open parking adj to river, no view. Historic town of Cité de L'Ecrit visible, 400m; has tourist commerce with 20 specialist booksellers inc an English bookshop, antique shops and a bookshop cum beer bar. From historic town cross river bridge for town commerce. www.citedelecrit.fr Reinspected 2016.

THOLLET — 34 — F7 — 86290 — N46°25.325' E001°07.259'

🚐 8 🛠 Aire Services 7010; 2 unmetered elec points (1 Cont, 1 CEE); WC through passage

▶ Route Bouchaud. Turn off D121 onto D10, sp 'Thollet'. Follow road for 1.9km and in Thollet turn 1st right before bar and church into parking, signed. Drive around behind building to Aire, signed.

ℹ️ Pleasant, open, landscaped Aire adj to large grass area to rear of large gravel car park. Pretty village with ford and local commerce 50m through passage. Walking path towards La Trimouille. Inspected 2016.

LATHUS ST REMY — 35 — F7 — 86390 — N46°19.974' E000°57.431'

🚐 8; Hedged bays 🛠 Euro Relais Junior; 1 unmetered elec point (long lead needed)

▶ D10. Exit town on D10, sp 'St Rémy' and signed. Aire 150m on right, signed.

ℹ️ Pleasant Aire with hedged bays backing onto very basic camping field. Leisure pond opp is popular fishing spot. Local commerce and WC by church, 200m. Updated 2016.

MOULISMES — 36 — F7 — 86500 — N46°19.985' E000°48.578'

🚐 80 🛠 Custom; Token (ER); €3

▶ N147. Exit town on N147 north towards Lussac les Châteaux. Aire at end of town on right, sp 'Aire de Repos'; not in the truck stop in town. Service Point by WC. Slightly more peaceful parking poss 200m away overlooking pond.

ℹ️ Very popular overnight stop. N147 is a very busy, noisy truck route. Suggest Bussière Poitevine 238 (Limo) as an alternative. Grass parking very boggy in wet weather. Snack bar in summer. Reinspected 2014.

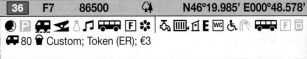

LUSSAC LES CHATEAUX

| 37 | F7 | 86320 | 🏛 | N46°24.165' E000°43.534' | SP |

🚐 30; In centre square; No parking Fri pm (Boules)/Sat am (Market)
👕 Custom; Diff drive over drain; WC at TO

➡ Place de l'Amitie, D11/Rue du Quai. Turn off N147 by TO into main town centre parking, sp 'Aire de Repos'. Service Point 20m from TO, signed.

ℹ Popular lunchtime Aire adj to main town square with numerous undesignated parking. Service Point diff to access depending on parked cars. Noise from N147. Town commerce and TO adj. Parking also tolerated adj to river: N46°24.181' E000°42.345'. Turn off N147 near river, sp 'Camping'. Unrestricted car park on right. Reinspected 2016.

LHOMMAIZE

| 38 | F7 | 86410 | 🏛 | N46°26.101' E000°35.811' | SP |

🚐 2 👕 Custom; 2 unmetered 16amp CEE elec points

➡ Off D8, near junction with N147/E62. Turn off either N147 or D8 in centre, sp 'Aire de Repos'. Aire behind Mairie and Salle des Fêtes.

ℹ Parking behind Mairie, so sheltered from road. In centre of pleasant town. River adj. www.lhommaize.fr Reinspected 2015.

CIVAUX

| 39 | F7 | 86320 | ⛺ | N46°26.949' E000°40.001' | SP |

🚐 30 👕 Custom

➡ Route de la Necropole. Turn off D749 onto D83, sp 'Civaux'. Cross river bridge and turn right at the roundabout towards the power station, sp 'Morthemer'. Turn into the parking at the power station and follow road to right. The Service Point is outside the campsite entrance.

ℹ Service Point outside campsite adj to leisure facilities at the base of the power station. Swimming pool, bowling and crocodile land all have unrestricted parking. Reinspected 2016.

ARCHIGNY

| 40 | F7 | 86210 | ⚓ | N46°40.520' E000°38.990' | SP |

🚐 10 👕 Euro Relais Box; 1 unmetered CEE elec point; Seasonal WC at lake

➡ Ave des Gazillières. Turn off D749 onto D3, sp 'La Roche Posay' and signed. Follow D3 to Archigny, then turn left at church, sp 'Chenevelles' and signed. Follow road to left and Aire on right.

ℹ Large, open Aire suitable for any unit configuration. Swimming lake, play area and picnic area 100m; no dogs allowed and no view. Inspected 2016.

FLEURE

| 41 | E7 | 86340 | 🏰 | N46°28.708' E000°31.406' | SP |

🚐 5 👕 None

➡ D2, northeast of village. Parking at the church. Aire signed from N147.

ℹ Designated parking in car park adj to church. Village 250m. Reinspected 2015.

CHAUVIGNY

| 42 | F7 | 86300 | T | N46°34.386' E000°38.812' | SP |

🚐 4 👕 WC only

➡ Rue Porte Chevreau. Turn off D951/D749 roundabout, sp 'Camping'. Turn left onto D2, sp 'Camping' and signed. Follow road up hill, then turn left, signed. Go straight on at Stop junction, then turn left, signed. Aire 50m on left beside cemetery, signed.

ℹ Aire adj to cemetery on outskirts of medieval city with narrow streets, church and château to wander around. Nearby campsite has Service Point inside and charges motorhomes €9/night without elec: N46°34.255' E000°39.206'. Reinspected 2016.

NIEUIL L'ESPOIR | 43 | E7 | 86340 | N46°29.113' E000°27.268'

🚐 10; Reinforced grass parking Euro Relais Junior; Token

➤ D1/Allée du Champ de Foire. Turn off D1 north of town centre, sp 'Aire de camping-cars'. Signed from N147.

ℹ️ Very pleasant Aire surrounded by green space in leisure area. www.nieuil-espoir.com Reinspected 2015.

USSON DU POITOU | 44 | E7 | 86350 | N46°16.540' E000°31.590'

🚐 15 Euro Relais Junior; 1 unmetered elec point

➤ D727. Turn off D741 onto D727, sp 'Usson du Poitou'. Aire on right opp cemetery, signed.

ℹ️ Aire adj to pleasant riverside picnic area, no views, in large open car park. Local commerce 300m. Inspected 2014.

ST MARTIN L'ARS | 45 | F7 | 86350 | N46°13.189' E000°31.804'

🚐 2 Euro Relais Junior; €2

➤ D741. Aire at D741/D28 crossroads opp D28, signed.

ℹ️ Service Point with enough parking for night halt only. Unrestricted parking at Plan d'Eau leisure lake on opp side of road, accessed via D28: N46°13.152' E000°32.065'. Inspected 2014.

CHIRAC | 46 | F8 | 16150 | N45°54.837' E000°39.440'

🚐 4; Max 3 nights Custom; Inspection cover; 2 16amp CEE elec points

➤ D59. Exit Chirac on D59 towards Chabanais. Turn left before river bridge into parking area. Aire at far corner of parking area adj to Mairie.

ℹ️ Small, peaceful Aire on edge of village. Park with walking trails adj. Shallow river adj, no view. Local commerce 200m. Reinspected 2016.

CONFOLENS | 47 | F8 | 16500 | N46°01.104' E000°40.519'

🚐 12; €8/night Apr-Sept; €10/night Jul-Aug; Pay at campsite Custom; €4; May-Sept

➤ D952/Avenue de Saint-Germain. From south on D948 turn right in Confolens onto D51/D952 and follow one-way system, sp 'Camping'. Turn onto D952, sp 'Saint-Germain' and 'Camping'. Aire is on left in 350m adj to Camping Municipal les Ribières, signed.

ℹ️ Aire adj to riverside campsite. Town and tourist commerce 350m, includes a fish and chip shop. Pleasant bridges over Vienne river. Updated 2016.

ESSE | 48 | F7 | 16500 | N46°01.780' E000°43.490'

🚐 5 Urba Flux Tall; €2

➤ D167. Turn off D80 opp the cemetery onto D167, sp 'St Maurice des Ls'. In 50m turn left into Aire, signed.

ℹ️ Aire adj to open access sports field and boules court. Village centre 250m, marked as a picturesque village. Updated 2016.

ST QUENTIN SUR CHARENTE (PRESSIGNAC) ★ | 49 | F8 | 16150 | N45°49.633' E000°41.287'

🚐 10; Max 72hrs 🚽 Custom; 4 unmetered elec points; Apr-Oct

▶ Lac de Lavaud. From St Quentin-sur-Charente follow D161, sp 'Pressignac' and 'Lac de Lavaud'. In 1.6km turn right onto D214, sp 'Lac de Lavaud'. Aire at end of road, signed.

ⓘ Lovely location with reservoir views from entire car park. Slipway for non motorised boats adj. Footpaths across adj dam and around lake parkland. Isolated if alone, 51 better winter stop. Reinspected 2014.

CHASSENON | 50 | F8 | 16150 | N45°51.025' E000°46.352'

🚐 3 🚽 Custom; Water point in WC

▶ D29. Off D29 as exit the village to east, sp 'Autocars' and 'Picnic Site'.

ⓘ Rural picnic area opp Parc Archéologique for Roman town of Cassinomagus; open daily mid Feb-Sept, hours vary, €6pp. www.cassinomagus.fr May feel isolated if alone. Reinspected 2014.

LESIGNAC DURAND | 51 | F8 | 16310 | N45°48.700' E000°38.283'

🚐 6; Max 72hrs 🚽 Custom; 6 unmetered elec points; Apr-Oct

▶ Off D52. Turn off D52 in village centre at the local shop, sp 'P' and signed. Drive past the vintage, but active, fuel pumps to the Aire.

ⓘ In pleasant village which overlooks Lac de Mas Chaban, partial views from Aire. Numerous walks and activities around the reservoir. Small village with local commerce adj. Inspected 2014.

MASSIGNAC | 52 | F8 | 16310 | N45°46.786' E000°39.304'

🚐 5; Large motorhomes depending on parked cars 🚽 Custom; Lift blue cover for WC emptying; 2 unmetered CEE elec points

▶ Off D163. In village centre turn onto D163 at church, sp 'Challains'. Turn immediately right beside church for Service Point, adj to Mairie, and small parking area. Additional parking next right in picnic area at rear of church: N45°46.805' E000°39.340'.

ⓘ Charming rural village with local commerce and TO. Inspected 2014.

CHATAIN BESSON (ECURAS) | 53 | E8 | 16220 | N45°40.983' E000°33.579'

🚐 10 🚽 Euro Relais Mini

▶ D699. Clearly signed off D699 in Chatain Besson, opp La Poste and Salle Municipale.

ⓘ In village centre. WC and picnic area across road at rear of Salle Municipale. www.ecuras.fr Reinspected 2015.

LA ROCHEFOUCAULD | 54 | E8 | 16110 | N45°45.053' E000°23.275'

🚐 7 🚽 Euro Relais Box; €2

▶ Route de Limoges. Exit town towards N141, sp 'Taponnat'. Aire 400m on left outside E.Leclerc Drive supermarket, opp fuel station, signed. There are two E.Leclerc supermarkets in town, the other bans motorhomes.

ⓘ Designated parking against noisy main route. All other parking has 2.5m height restriction. Supermarket adj. Reinspected 2014.

LE PONT D'AGRIS (AGRIS)
55 | E8 | 16110 | N45°47.168' E000°20.343'

🚐 5 ⚲ Urba Flux Tall; €3

➤ D6. Exit N141 onto D6, sp 'Agris'. At Agris go straight over 1st roundabout and turn right at the next roundabout, then immediately left into car park. Service Point by telephone box.

ℹ️ Pleasant Aire in centre of village opp the bar/shop. Picnic area, bus stop and walking trails adj. Ideal night stop off N141. Inspected 2014.

CELLEFROUIN
56 | E8 | 16260 | N45°53.655' E000°23.179'

🚐 30 ⚲ Custom; Service Point behind WC

➤ Off D739, to west of village. As enter village from Mansle (west) on D739 turn off, sp 'Aire de Loisirs', 'Pique-nique' and signed. Turn right before tennis court and Service Point at toilet block in far corner of car park.

ℹ️ Very pleasant large Aire adj to leisure area, inc picnic area within park, marked walks and an open access tennis court. Local commerce in village, 600m. Reinspected 2014.

CHASSENEUIL SUR BONNIEURE
57 | E8 | 16260 | N45°49.493' E000°27.100'

🚐 4 ⚲ Euro Relais Junior; €2

➤ Rue du 8 Mai 1945. Turn off D942 onto D27, sp 'Montemboeuf' and signed. Follow road past the central square, then turn left just before the Intermarché, signed. Service Point near WCs.

ℹ️ In centre of town just off main route through. Small town commerce adj. Market Wed. Inspected 2014.

ROUMAZIERES LOUBERT
58 | F8 | 16270 | N45°52.962' E000°34.351'

🚐 10 ⚲ Euro Relais Junior; 2 unmetered CEE elec points

➤ N141. Aire on N141 as exit towards La Rochefoucauld. Turn off opp D169 turning to Chantrezac, sp 'Aire de Détente' and signed.

ℹ️ Trucking hell! Aire adj to very noisy main road in a small parking area. Suitable to service but **60** much better overnight stop. Snack bar in adj picnic area. Reinspected 2014.

ST LAURENT DE CERIS
59 | F8 | 16450 | N45°56.446' E000°28.984'

🚐 7; Parking adj to Service Point impractical, park opp ⚲ Custom; Diff access; 7 unmetered CEE elec points

➤ Le Bourg, in village centre off D15. Service Point opp Champ de Foire.

ℹ️ Peaceful Aire in village centre with open and shaded parking. Champ de Foire, which is more practical parking, has 4 unmetered CEE elec points. Service Point difficult to access. Children's play area and local commerce adj. Reinspected 2016.

VERTEUIL SUR CHARENTE
60 | E8 | 16510 | N45°58.788' E000°14.122'

🚐 10; Max 48hrs ⚲ Custom; 4 CEE elec points €2/24hrs; See Mairie

➤ Rue de la Fontaine, off D26. Follow sp 'Aire de Loisirs' through town; narrow access through town. Aire on right as head down Rue de la Fontaine, signed.

ℹ️ Popular, pleasant Aire backing onto park. Pretty village with château, park, river and tourist commerce 200m. Park considerately. Reinspected 2016.

CHARROUX
61 E7 86250 T N46°08.573' E000°24.411'

🚐 15 🚰 Aire Services Plastic; Token (3/3); €2

➡ D148/Route de Limoges. From east on D148 at roundabout do not follow ring road to right but take 3rd exit towards village centre on old D148. Aire on left in 1.2km, signed. 200m before tower.

ℹ Interesting abbey ruins and Beau Village 220m. Plenty of local commerce. Tokens available from local commerce. www.charroux.com Reinspected 2015.

LIZANT
62 E7 86400 N46°05.165' E000°16.697'

🚐 8; €2/night; Collected 🚰 Euro Relais Junior; 4 unmetered elec points

➡ In centre of Lizant at D107/D104 junction around the war memorial. Follow sp 'P'. In 50m turn right into car park, signed.

ℹ In pretty rural village adj to park with picnic area and stream. Walking and cycle routes adj. Reinspected 2015.

ROMAGNE
63 E7 86700 N46°16.123' E000°18.247'

🚐 6; Max 72hrs/month 🚰 Custom; 6 5amp CEE elec points

➡ Espace Detente. In centre by church turn onto D25, sp 'Brux'. In 100m turn left onto D27, sp 'Civray' and signed. Go straight on, sp 'St Romain' and signed. Aire on right at the sports facilities, signed.

ℹ Landscaped Aire at sports facilities. Pleasant, well maintained area 300m from village centre with local commerce. Reinspected 2015.

GENCAY
64 E7 86160 N46°22.384' E000°24.703'

🚐 5; Parking banned near Service Point 🚰 Aire Services Plastic; Token; €2; WC and water at water tower

➡ Off D741. From north follow D741 through town towards Civray. Turn left just before D1 turning to Brion. Service Point on left, in car park under trees: N46°22.384 E000°24.373'. For parking drive past Service Point on D741 and turn left, sp 'Plan d'Eau de Verneuil' and signed. Follow road to right. Parking adj to lake, signed.

ℹ Aire adj to fishing lake. Paths around it used by dog walkers and includes an exercise circuit. On opp side of lake are steps up to the swimming pool with Intermarché opp and the town beyond. Updated 2016.

Photo: Glen Swatman

CHATEAU LARCHER
65 E7 86160 N46°24.869' E000°18.938'

🚐 10 hardstanding; 4 grass parking; €5/24hrs inc service and 15amp CEE elec; Collected; Mar-Oct 🚰 Custom; Cont WCs at sports ground

➡ Off D88. Turn off D88, sp 'Camping', 'Stade' and signed. Aire at sports ground. Gate has digital lock, code from TO. Gate may be open in season.

ℹ Pleasant, landscaped Aire with plenty of grass space around each bay. Open access sports ground and river adj. Nice walk through sports ground to château and village. Fishing poss at river and pond; day permit €10. Reinspected 2016.

VIVONNE
66 E7 86370 N46°25.553' E000°15.773'

🚐 2 marked bays; Additional parking adj 🚰 Aire Services Plastic; €2; WCs below TO

➡ Ave de la Plage. Turn off D4, main route through, in centre at roundabout into parking area adj to TO, signed. Aire just below TO, signed.

ℹ Aire in central square adj to small town commerce and TO. Interesting town with numerous waterways and sports. TO organises free 2hr hike from parking every Thurs at 9am; further 19 walking routes exploring village and nearby château and chapel. www.tourisme-vivonne.fr Reinspected 2016.

COUHE

67 | E7 | 86700 | 🏛 | N46°17.907' E000°10.705'

🚐 9; 5m bays 🔧 Custom; Cont WC by Service Point, standard up stairs

➡ D26/Rue de Bel-Air. Turn off D2 onto Rue du Marché at covered market. Drive through parking area and take 2nd turning on left into larger parking area. Service Point on left by WC. Designated parking at end on right, signed.

ℹ Aire on terraced car park suffering distant road noise from N10, but convenient stop. Small town commerce and lovely covered market 150m. Reinspected 2016.

SAUZE VAUSSAIS

68 | E7 | 79190 | 🏢 | N46°08.123' E000°06.399'

🚐 10 🔧 Flot Bleu Océane; Token for elec only

➡ Place des Halles, in main town square. Follow sp 'Centre Ville'. At tower turn right, sp 'Mairie', and Place des Halles is straight ahead.

ℹ In town square, adj to Mairie and Sapeurs Pompiers (fire station). Disabled WC at rear of Mairie. Reinspected 2015.

LONDIGNY

69 | E7 | 16700 | ⛪ | N46°05.010' E000°08.102'

🚐 5; Max 48hrs 🔧 Custom; 1 unmetered elec point; Mar-Oct

➡ Place de l'Église. From D26 turn onto D181, sp 'Londigny'. Follow for 1.3km towards Londigny, then turn left, sp 'Place de l'Église'. The Aire is at the church.

ℹ Very rural location; no facilities in village. Private château 500m. Bells 3 times a day. Trees obstruct some parking. Reinspected 2015.

CHEF BOUTONNE

70 | E7 | 79110 | 🚶 | N46°06.607' W000°04.626'

🚐 10; Grass parking 🔧 Custom; Water turned off Nov-Mar

➡ Rue Pierre Blanchard. Follow D737, main route, through town and turn off opp cemetery, sp 'Aire Naturelle' and signed. Aire in 120m on right.

ℹ Parking on grass, some parts slope but plenty of flat areas too. Château de Javarzay 500m; open seasonally, €4pp. Open access park and lake with 4km walking route with English info panels. Town commerce 800m. Reinspected 2015.

MELLE

71 | E7 | 79500 | T | N46°13.049' W000°08.877'

🚐 5 🔧 WCs, when mine open; See  212

➡ Chemin de Loubeau. From Niort follow D948 to Melle. At D948/D101 roundabout go straight on, sp 'Melle-Centre'. Follow road straight on, then at roundabout turn right, sp 'Paizay le Tort' and 'Mines d'Argent'. Turn right, sp 'Mines d'Argent'. Designated parking is outside Mines d'Argent, signed.

ℹ Designated parking outside tourist attraction, intended for visitors. Picnic area adj. Mines d'Argent has 30km of silver mines, one of the biggest in Europe; guided tours 3pm daily, €8.50pp. www.mines-argent.com Open access discovery walk signed from Aire. Inspected 2016.

CHAUNAY

72 | E7 | 86510 | 🏭 | N46°12.356' E000°09.823'

🚐 5; By Service Point; See info 🔧 Urba Flux x2; Lift small round grey cover by Service Point for WC emptying; 7 CEE elec points

➡ D25/Grande Rue. Turn off D25 in centre into car park, signed. Aire are rear of car park, behind WCs and school, signed.

ℹ Aire in large central car park with 2 Service Points either side of WC, both with elec points. Local commerce adj. Reinspected 2015.

LEZAY

| 73 | E7 | 79120 | | N46°15.884' W000°00.685' | SP |

🚐 20 🏠 Custom

➤ Place du Marché, Rue de Gâte-Bourse. From Chey on D950 turn left onto D45, sp 'Lezay'. Turn left at roundabout, sp 'Centre Ville', then take 2nd right in front of indoor market. Service Point against wall in gravel car park on left, signed.

ℹ Pleasant, large car park adj to indoor market. Shaded parking poss under trees. Can accommodate any unit configuration. Small town commerce and TO adj. Reinspected 2016.

ROM

| 74 | E7 | 79120 | | N46°17.463' E000°06.850' | SP |

🚐 10 🏠 Custom; Adj to WC and washing sinks

➤ D14. Turn off D14 near church, sp 'La Mere' and signed. Parking on right before basketball court; Service Point past basketball court adj to building, signed.

ℹ Pleasant, open parking surrounded by green space. Private fishing pool adj with river beyond. Cemetery with war graves adj; 34 SAS, 1 American and 7 resistance fighters were captured and executed nearby during Operation Bulbasket in 1944. Local commerce 200m. Reinspected 2016.

MESSE

| 75 | E7 | 79120 | | N46°15.822' E000°06.645' | SP |

🚐 6; Max 7 nights 🏠 Custom; Lift silver cover on right side for WC emptying; 2 unmetered Cont elec points

➤ D114. Follow D114 through Messé, sp 'Vanzay'. As exit village turn right, sp 'Étang des Marzelles'. Service Point at end of car park.

ℹ Aire in car park of private fishing lake, no views; only likely to be busy during competitions. Rural views over countryside. Community hall adj. Inspected 2016.

ROUILLE

| 76 | E7 | 86480 | | N46°25.218' E000°02.411' | SP |

🚐 7 🏠 Custom; WC adj

➤ D611. Turn off D611 in town centre opp church and covered market into 3.5t weight restricted car park, signed. Service Point past WCs on right before Sapeurs Pompiers (fire station).

ℹ Service Point in town centre car park surrounded by small town commerce. Parking is busy with locals and the road is noisy. Reinspected 2016.

LA MOTHE ST HERAY

| 77 | E7 | 79800 | | N46°21.589' W000°07.083' | SP |

🚐 5; Additional parking 300m on left as approach town 🏠 Flot Bleu Fontaine; €1; WC with wash sinks and 10amp Cont elec points

➤ D5/Rue du Pont l'Abbe. At junction between D737/D5 as enter village. Signed on building.

ℹ Aire adj to busy main road which detracts from its pleasant green space. Toilet block adj inc washing sinks. Town is a Petite City of Character; water mill, Les Moulin l'Abbé, 300m along path through arboretum with excellent specimen trees. Reinspected 2016.

PAMPROUX

| 78 | E7 | 79800 | | N46°23.770' W000°03.506' | SP |

🚐 3; 10 in town 🏠 Flot Bleu Océane; €2 (1 x €2); 2 CEE elec points; Cont WC in town; See info

➤ D329/Rue de la Cueille. Turn off D5 to west of village centre, sp 'D329' and 'Fomperron'. Follow road around to left and Aire on right, signed. Also possible to park in centre at the Champ de Foire: N46°23.785' W000°03.221'.

ℹ Aire on outskirts of town with rural views. Parking at Service Point has 3 designated bays; Service Point free at time of inspection. Town centre parking is 150m from small town commerce and is adj to park and outdoor gym: N46°23.785' W000°03.221'. Reinspected 2016.

BOUGON ✲ | 79 | E7 | 79800 | T 🏠 | N46°22.694' W000°04.125' | SP 🌳 | 🚶 🚲

🚐 10 🔧 Custom; No WC emptying; 4 unmetered CEE elec points; See 78

➡ Tumulus de Bougon. From D5 follow sp 'Tumulus de Bougon'. Service Point in car park adj to Tumulus de Bougon.

ℹ Aire in car park of 6000-year-old Neolithic burial chambers. Worth a visit. 2km walk around museum and burial chambers; open daily, €4.50pp. Parking may feel isolated if alone. Inspected 2016.

CHEY | 80 | E7 | 79120 | 🏛 | N46°18.246' W000°02.980' | 🌳 🏕 🚶 🚲

🚐 4 🔧 Custom; Lift cover on front right corner for WC emptying; Cont WC

➡ Place de la Liberté. From D950, main route, turn off near church by shop, signed. Follow road through parking, Aire at rear, signed.

ℹ Aire adj to picnic area in parking furthest from road. A convenient stop just off main route. Cemetery adj and local commerce 100m. Reinspected 2016.

MONTIGNE | 81 | E7 | 79370 | 🏛 | N46°12.752' W000°14.337' | SP 🌳 🏕 | 📷 🚲

🚐 10; Grass parking 🔧 Custom; At wooden building; Tap removed

➡ D103. Exit the village on D103 towards Perigné. Aire on right, signed. Steep access into Aire from road, may be difficult for larger motorhomes to exit; assess before entering.

ℹ Aire in a pleasant spot amongst mature trees and river in picnic/BBQ area. Boules court adj. Be aware of soft ground. Reinspected 2016.

LA CRECHE | 82 | E7 | 79260 | 🏛 🚶 | N46°21.621' W000°18.389' | 🌳 🏕 🛝 🚶 🚲

🚐 10; Max 48hrs 🔧 Flot Bleu Fontaine; WC adj

➡ Turn off D611 in centre, sp 'Cherveux' and signed. At roundabout turn immediately right into Stade Georges André Groussard. Service Point on right, parking on left.

ℹ Open parking adj to park with stream and open access sports field. Distant, but constant, road noise. Small town commerce on D611. Reinspected 2016.

CELLES SUR BELLE | 83 | E7 | 79370 | 🏛 | N46°15.754' W000°12.494' | SP 🌳 🏕 🚶

🚐 20 🔧 Custom; Water opp disposal

➡ Rue des Halles. From north follow D948. Go straight over roundabout, sp 'Celles sur Belle'. Follow road straight, then turn left, sp 'Abbaye' and signed. Drive down 300m of cobbled street, past abbey, then turn left at the bottom, signed.

ℹ Large, open Aire opp abbey with gardens, church and motorbike museum, €12pp with English audio tour. Town is a Petite City of Character. Explore town and area via 3.5km footpath. Small town commerce 150m uphill; small market Wed am. Goat's cheese made locally. Reinspected 2016.

ECHIRE | 84 | E7 | 79410 | 🏛 | N46°23.551' W000°25.114' | SP 🌳 🏕 🏘 🚶 🚲

🚐 4; Max 48hrs 🔧 Custom

➡ Chemin du Marais. From Niort on D743 turn right at roundabout, sp 'Échiré', then turn left and follow sp 'Échiré' straight on. In Échiré follow road straight on, then turn left before river bridge, sp 'Aire de Dénte' and signed. This turn may be difficult for large motorhomes. Follow road 200m to Aire at end.

ℹ Over-landscaped Aire dominated by a huge roundabout that leaves little space for parking. Constant hum from water treatment adj. Open access sports fields and riverside picnic area adj. Small town commerce 300m. Inspected 2016.

CHAMPDENIERS ST DENIS — 85 — E7 — 79220 — N46°28.978' W000°24.424'

🚐5 🚰 Custom; Lift grid or use WC for WC emptying - DO NOT use large sink!

➡ Rue du Paradis. Exit D743 onto D6 following sp 'Chamdeniers-St-Denis'. In town turn left at roundabout, sp 'Fontenay' and signed. In 300m, after passing cemetery, turn left, sp 'P Place Paradis' and signed. Aire in car park.

ℹ️ Small car park with old covered market, now used as garage for local cars. Café adj. Small town commerce 300m. Convenient night halt. Inspected 2016.

COULONGES SUR L'AUTIZE — 86 — D7 — 79160 — N46°28.812' W000°35.629'

🚐2; Max 24hrs; Limited additional parking opp 🚰 Custom; 4 unmetered CEE elec points; WC adj; Tap in WC

➡ D744. Aire adj to D744, sp 'Aire de Repos' and signed.

ℹ️ Small Aire under deciduous trees adj to busy and noisy main road. Small park adj. Town centre with small town commerce 450m. Reinspected 2016.

COULON — 87 — D7 — 79510 — N46°19.244' W000°35.464'

🚐80; €9/24hrs inc service; CC; Apr-Oct; Grass parking 🚰 Aire Services 3000; 6amp elec limited to 2hrs!; All inside barrier

➡ D123. Enter town on D1. Go across river and turn left at crossroads onto D123, signed. Aire adj to D123 as exit village to west in large, open field, signed. Enter through Urba Flux barrier.

ℹ️ Popular, commercial Aire providing grass parking. There are not enough elec points so use is limited to 2hrs/motorhome. Small town commerce 400m. Multiple boat hire options along La Sèvre Niortaise river. Reinspected 2016.

NIORT — 88 — E7 — 79000 — N46°19.763' W000°27.870'

🚐15; €7.70/24hrs inc unmetered CEE elec; Collected; Max 7 days; Must park in designated bays 🚰 Euro Relais Junior; Outside entrance

➡ Rue de Bessac, on northwest side of town centre. Enter town from west on D148/D648 following sp 'Centre Ville'. Travel south towards centre and turn left at 4th roundabout onto Blvd Main. Turn right at next roundabout and turn left onto Rue de Bessac, both signed. Follow one-way road straight on and Aire in car park on right, signed. Follow signs through car park, Aire in far left corner.

ℹ️ Popular, pleasant, landscaped Aire with most bays divided by walls. Service Point accessible at entrance. River adj; can walk directly into town over bridges from Aire. Reinspected 2016.

MAUZE SUR LE MIGNON — 89 — D7 — 79210 — N46°11.990' W000°40.857'

🚐10 🚰 Flot Bleu Pacific; Token; €4

➡ Rue du Port. Turn off N11 onto D51, sp 'Rochefort' and 'Mauzé s/ le M.'. Turn right, sp 'Mauzé s/ le M.'. Turn left onto C49, sp 'St Hilaire la Palud' and signed, and follow road straight on, sp 'St Hilaire la Palud'. Go through railway tunnels, then turn left, sp 'Camping' and signed. Follow road straight on over canal and around to Aire, signed.

ℹ️ Aire adj to 19th century canal basin. Depart point of 7km circular trail exploring surrounding monuments, churches and gardens. Pleasant municipal campsite 200m, open Jun-Aug. Small town commerce 1km. Reinspected 2016.

LA LAIGNE — 90 — D7 — 17170 — N46°12.782' W000°45.226'

🚐15 🚰 Flot Bleu Océane; €2 (2 x €1); WC and wash sink

➡ D114. From N11 follow sp 'Le Laigne' onto D114. Adj to D114, signed.

ℹ️ Service Point in popular HGV parking area. Noise from HGVs. Les Routiers restaurant adj. Reinspected 2016.

ARCAIS | 91 | D7 | 79210 | | N46°17.786' W000°41.249'

🅿 40; €8/24hrs; CC; Apr-Oct; Grass parking ☕ Custom; Outside barrier

➡ Parking du Praineau. Just off D102 in car park, signed. Located on the east edge of the village. Service Point on left; parking through Aire Services barrier.

ℹ Large grass parking area with rural views. WCs by Service Point. Overnight parking prohibited adj to Service Point. Local and tourist commerce in centre, 400m. Seasonal boat hire to explore 'Green Venice' at river. Cycle routes towards St Hilaire la Palud and St Georges de Rex. Reinspected 2016.

LA RONDE | 92 | D7 | 17170 | | N46°18.306' W000°48.294'

🅿 10; Grass parking ☕ Flot Bleu Océane; Token (FB) x 2

➡ D116/Rue du Port. Follow D116 north from village and Aire is 800m on right at Aire de Repos, signed.

ℹ Pleasant grass picnic area adj to dyke. Plenty of space subject to weather. Local commerce 400m. The area is called Marais Poitevin and is known as 'Green Venice' because of its navigable dykes. Reinspected 2016.

TAUGON | 93 | D7 | 17170 | | N46°18.363' W000°50.156'

🅿 3; See info ☕ Flot Bleu Océane; €2 (2 x €1)

➡ D109. Adj to D109 in front of cemetery as exit village towards St Jean de Liversay.

ℹ Service Point with limited parking outside cemetery or church. Suggest 92 for parking in good weather. Local commerce 250m. Reinspected 2016.

ST JEAN DE LIVERSAY | 94 | D7 | 17170 | | N46°16.237' W000°52.645'

🅿 5 ☕ Flot Bleu Océane; Token (FB); €2; 2 unmetered CEE elec points

➡ Rue des Sports. In village turn off D109 by church. Turn immediately left and drive through car park, sp 'Parking Stade', then turn left again past Mairie. Turn right, sp 'P', and park in the 2nd car park on right. For Service Point stay on D109 and take next right, sp 'St Cyr du Doret' and signed. Service Point immediately on left: N46°16.200' W000°52.349'.

ℹ Parking adj to open access sports facilities. Over engineered roadside Service Point, be careful on exit. Local commerce 400m. Reinspected 2016.

RIVEDOUX PLAGE (ILE DE RE) | 95 | D7 | 17940 | | N46°09.590' W001°15.978'

🅿 17; 45 mins free; €6/24hrs Nov-Mar; €13/24hrs Sept-Oct; €14/24hrs Apr-Jun; €17/24hrs Jul-Aug; Inc elec Apr-Sept; CC ☕ SOS; Inside barrier; Token; €3

➡ Camping Municipal Le Platin. As enter Rivedoux Plage turn off the D201/D735 roundabout, sp 'Camping Municipal' and signed. Aire in 20m adj to campsite, signed. Enter through barrier.

ℹ The only Aire on the island overlooking the sea; 7 bays with excellent views. Local commerce 200m. Reinspected 2014.

ST MARTIN DE RE | 96 | D7 | 17410 | | N46°11.955' W001°21.905'

🅿 17; €11/24hrs; CC; Max 72hrs; 8m bays ☕ Custom; Inside barrier

➡ Rue du Rampart. From south on D735 turn into St Martin de Re at roundabout, sp 'St Martin' and 'Camping Municipal'. After driving through city wall turn left, sp 'Camping Municipal'. Follow one-way road, then turn right into Aire. Enter through barrier.

ℹ Fortified town with interesting ramparts. Easy walk to town with picturesque port. Cycling all around island. Reinspected 2014.

LES PORTES EN RE

97 D7 17880 N46°13.756' W001°29.001'

🚐 7; €10/24hrs; Pay at machine; 10m bays ⚓ SOS

➡ D101/Route du Fier. Follow D101 through Les Portes-en-Ré. When road reaches coast it turns sharply to the south. Aire at the end of the road near the sea.

ℹ Parking 20m from beach, no view. Reinspected 2014.

Soubise

ST CLEMENT DES BALEINES

99 D7 17590 N46°13.662' W001°32.787'

🚐 40; €12/24hrs inc unmetered elec; CC ⚓ Euro Relais Junior; Inside barrier; Token; €2

➡ Rue de la Forêt. From south on D735 drive past St Clements des Baleines, then turn left, signed. Drive straight on, then when straight on is no longer possible turn left. Follow road and Aire on right, signed. Enter through Aire Services bollard.

ℹ This is a large open Aire which is a complete sun trap. The island is popular with cyclists and there are numerous flat cycle paths across the island. Updated 2016.

CHATELAILLON PLAGE

100 D7 17340 N46°04.358' W001°04.731'

🚐 42; €5/5hrs; €8.40/24hrs Oct-May; €10.80/24hrs Jun-Sept; Inc service, elec and WiFi; +€1.66 tax; CC; Grass parking ⚓ Euro Relais Junior; Inside barrier; 48 16amp CEE elec points

➡ Blvd Georges Clemenceau, at the race track. From centre of town follow sp 'P Hippodrome' and signed. Aire in designated section of race track parking, signed. Enter through PARKNIGHT barrier.

ℹ Aire to rear of car park, may be difficult to access during hippo racing! Town centre and beaches cyclable. Reinspected 2016.

LA ROCHELLE 1

101 D7 17000 N46°09.959' W001°09.255'

🚐 24; 7m bays; See info ⚓ Custom

➡ Esplanade des Parcs, Parc Charruyer. Turn off N237 onto D104 into town. Stay on main road going straight across all junctions and roundabouts. After 3rd roundabout turn right, sp 'Gaston Neveur' and 'Parking'. Designated parking starts from Gaston Neveur building.

ℹ Must park within designated bays or face a €35 fine. Interesting town centre 1km walk/cycle through park. Market Fri. Town parking bans motorhomes. Reinspected 2016.

LA ROCHELLE 2

102 D7 17000 N46°09.134' W001°08.390'

🚐 50; €10/24hrs Oct-Mar; €12/24hrs Apr-Sept; Inc service; CC ⚓ Aire Services 3000; Inside barrier

➡ Rue des Jars, on south side of railway station. Accessible from D937 ring road. Sp 'P+R Vieux Port' through town. Enter through barrier. GPS taken at entry to large parking complex.

ℹ Motorhome parking on either grass or gravel. Frequent P&R bus to town centre inc in price, except Sun. No access 8.15pm-7.15am Sept-Jun, 12.30am-7.15am Jul-Aug. Town parking bans motorhomes. Reinspected 2016.

LA ROCHELLE 3
103 | D7 | 17000 | N46°08.641' W001°10.301'

🚐 31; See info 🏺 None; See **218**

➤ Quai du Lazaret. Follow sp 'Les Minimes', then 'Port des Minimes'. Follow road to end and designated parking in car park along back edge, closest to boats, signed.

ℹ️ Popular, but oversubscribed designated parking between the marina and the sea; views of masts. Must park in designated bays or face a €35 fine. Local commerce 350m. Town parking bans motorhomes. Reinspected 2016.

ANGOULINS SUR MER
104 | D7 | 17690 | N46°06.248' W001°07.901'

🚐 17 🏺 Euro Relais Mini

➤ Rue du Chay. Follow D111e1, main route, west through town towards coast following sp 'Tennis Club'. Cross train tracks and Service Point 400m on left, signed: N46°06.357' W001°06.995'. From Service Point continue straight on, pass campsite and parking on right, signed. Additional parking further on for 10 motorhomes, currently not signed: N46°06.377' W001°08.151'.

ℹ️ Dedicated parking 150m from small beach and tourist commerce. Area currently being redeveloped with flood defences and improvements. Most car parks are now height barriered, expect change. Reinspected 2016.

ST GERMAIN DE MARENCENNES
105 | D7 | 17700 | N46°04.752' W000°46.997'

🚐 8; €5/day inc elec; Collected Mar-Nov; Free Dec-Feb; Max 72hrs 🏺 Custom; 8 unmetered CEE elec points; WC by tennis courts

➤ Rue de Moulin Neuf. From north on D911 turn right onto D111, sp 'St Germain de Marencennes'. Turn immediately right, sp 'Espace Loisirs Pré Bègue' and signed. Aire on left in 150m, adj to sports facilities. Service Point to left, parking to right.

ℹ️ Aire with 8 large, marked bays adj to park. Park has outdoor gym, play area and specimen trees. Footpath leads to centre with local commerce. Inspected 2016.

AIGREFEUILLE D'AUNIS
106 | D7 | 17290 | N46°07.447' W000°54.869'

🚐 20; Max 24hrs 🏺 Urba Flux Tall; Cont WC by lake

➤ Lac de Frace. Exit village on D113, sp 'Virson'. Turn off D113, sp 'Lac de Frace' and signed. Follow road straight on and across Stop junction, sp 'Lac de Frace'. Service Point on right and parking 50m on left.

ℹ️ Pleasant parking in large car park; only likely to be full on hot days and holidays. Leisure/fishing lake adj but no views from parking. Path and picnic benches around lake. May feel isolated at night. Night fishing prohibited. Reinspected 2016.

ROCHEFORT 1
107 | D8 | 17300 | N45°55.687' W000°57.289'

🚐 40; €3/24hrs; Pay at machine; Max 6 days 🏺 Custom

➤ Ave de la Charente. From south cross bridge and turn right onto D911, sp 'Rochefort'. At roundabout turn left onto D911, sp 'Rochefort'. At next 2 roundabouts turn right, sp 'Camping Municipal'. Turn left, sp 'Camping Municipal'. Drive past campsite and Aire is on left, signed.

ℹ️ Town centre with commerce and numerous historic buildings to leisurely wander 700m. May feel isolated if alone. Reinspected 2014.

ROCHEFORT 2
108 | D8 | 17300 | N45°56.648' W000°57.443'

🚐 20 at marina; 15 at overflow parking; €6/24hrs; Pay at machine 🏺 Custom

➤ Off D911. Exit D137 at Junction 32 onto D5, sp 'Rochefort-Nord'. Turn onto D911, sp 'Centre Ville'. At end of road turn right, then immediately left, sp 'Capitainerie' and signed. Turn 1st left and Service Point on left, parking straight on. Overflow parking: N45°56.818' W000°57.607'.

ℹ️ Aire in pleasant Napoleonic/regency marina overlooking boats in dry storage. LIDL 250m, town centre commerce 650m. Reinspected 2014.

ROCHEFORT SUR MER | 109 | D8 | 17300 | N45°55.106' W000°57.850'

🚐 20; Roadside 🚻 None; See 107 and 108

➡ Pont Transbordeur. Approach from south, then follow sp 'Pont Transbordeur'. At Pont Transbordeur, follow one-way route which will take you through Aire, signed.

ℹ Free overnight parking 500m from 19th century Pont Transbordeur, a tourist attraction lift bridge; €2.60pp return, free museum on Echillais side. May feel isolated if alone. Reinspected 2014.

ST SAVINIEN | 110 | D8 | 17350 | N45°52.603' W000°41.122'

🚐 15 gravel (Winter); 30 grass (Summer) 🚻 Custom

➡ D18. From St Jean d'Angély take D18 west, sp 'St Savinien'. Continue through town following sp 'Île de Oléron' and 'Camping'. Service Point 200m on left outside campsite: N45°52.682' W000°41.068'. Parking 100m past campsite; to right for winter (hiver): N45°52.702' W000°41.177', to left for summer (été): N45°52.603' W000°41.122'; both signed.

ℹ Designated parking adj to river. Winter parking is sheltered and hardstanding. Summer parking extends onto grass overlooking river; fishermen's paradise. Reinspected 2016.

ST GEORGES DES COTEAUX | 111 | D8 | 17810 | N45°46.028' W000°42.669'

🚐 10 🚻 Euro Relais Box; Token; €2

➡ D237. Turn off D137 onto D127, sp 'St Georges des Coteaux'. In 1.3km turn right at roundabout onto D237, sp 'Halte de Loisirs'. Aire is on the left in 200m, signed.

ℹ Local commerce 200m. Village 700m. A peaceful stopover going north or south on D137. www.saintgeorgesdescoteaux.fr Reinspected 2015.

ST PORCHAIRE | 112 | D8 | 17250 | N45°49.243' W000°46.946'

🚐 6; Gravel parking 🚻 Custom

➡ Place du Champ de Foire. From Saintes follow D137 north. Turn off D137 onto D237, sp 'St Porchaire'. After 1.7km turn right in village centre into Place du Champ de Foire, signed. Turn right again and Aire is at end of car park.

ℹ Pleasant Aire adj to grassy area in village centre. Reinspected 2016.

PONT L'ABBE D'ARNOULT | 113 | D8 | 17250 | N45°49.700' W000°52.348'

🚐 5 🚻 Custom; Lift grate for WC emptying

➡ Rue de la Cité. From church follow D18, sp 'Saintes'. Turn right into Rue de la Cité, signed. Service Point on corner, parking opp.

ℹ In residential location. Local commerce, decorative church and historic covered market 300m. www.tourisme-pontlabbedarnoult.fr Reinspected 2015.

ST AGNANT | 114 | D8 | 17620 | N45°51.987' W000°57.885'

🚐 10 🚻 Tap and Cont WC only

➡ Place de Verdun, off D123. Enter town on D123/Ave Charles de Gaulle. Aire in car park with memorial, sp 'Place de Verdun' and 'Médi@thèque'.

ℹ Village 200m. Old Service Point in bad state of repair and Aire no longer signed; expect change. Reinspected 2014.

ECHILLAIS
115 D8 17620 N45°53.847' W000°57.335'

🚐 10; €7.20/night inc service; Collected 👕 Custom; Service only €7.20; Pay at Mairie

➡ Place de l'Europe. From south on D733 turn right onto D238, sp 'Échillais'. At crossroads go straight on. Aire in car park on right in 350m. Well signed in village.

ℹ Aire in asphalt car park. Motorhome weather vane and town map by Service Point. Centre, with TO and ornate church, 400m. Reinspected 2016.

MURON
116 D7 17430 N46°02.176' W000°49.660'

🚐 5 👕 Custom; Cont WC at church

➡ Place du Champ de Foire. From north turn right off D911, sp 'Muron'. Follow road, then in village centre turn left before square, signed. Follow road for 150m and Aire on right, signed.

ℹ Pleasant, peaceful, small village Aire adj to park with picnic area. Small village centre with local commerce and small market Tue am, 150m. Motorhome weather vane at Aire. Reinspected 2016.

TONNAY CHARENTE
117 D8 17430 N45°56.371' W000°52.897'

🚐 16; €6/24hrs; Collected 👕 Custom

➡ Quai Auriol Roy-Bry. Approach from east on D739 to avoid town. At roundabout turn onto D137, sp 'Saintes'. Turn right onto D124, sp 'Tonnay-Charente'. Follow road for 1.5km. Pass under 4m height restricted bridge and Aire is 250m on left, signed.

ℹ Pleasant Aire outside municipal campsite, adj to river but no view. Small town 600m. Distant road noise. Reinspected 2016.

FOURAS 1
118 D8 17450 N45°58.669' W001°04.968'

🚐 12; €7/24hrs; Pay at machine; Max 48hrs 👕 Urba Flux Tall; CC

➡ Rue de l'Espérance. Well signed from town, adj to coast road and campsite.

ℹ Aire set one row back from the tidal sandy beach overlooking the campsite. Pleasant promenade to town along the seafront. Inspected 2014.

FOURAS 2
119 D8 17450 N45°59.528' W001°05.202'

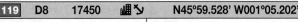

🚐 9; €7/24hrs; Pay at machine; Park on left 👕 Custom; Token; €1

➡ D937c/Avenue du Cadoret, just off roundabout outside Camping Le Cadoret. Signed from main road. 3.5t weight restriction on Aire.

ℹ Campsite and mini golf adj. Town 800m. Reinspected 2014.

FOURAS 3
120 D8 17450 N45°59.744' W001°06.355'

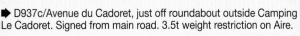

🚐 24; €6/24hrs; Pay at machine 👕 None; See **118** or **119**

➡ Rue du Bois Vert. From Fouras follow sp 'La Fumée'. Turn left at fort, sp 'P Gratuite' and 'Fort Voban'. Designated parking at rear of car park, signed.

ℹ Designated parking adj to fort ruin, no access. Beaches and picnic areas nearby. Ideal to walk/cycle to Ponte de la Fumée which has a causeway at low tide; onsite parking €36/24hrs. Inspected 2014.

SOUBISE 1 | 121 | D8 | 17780 | N45°55.703' W001°00.401'

🚐 40; €8/24hrs inc unmetered elec; Pay at machine 🛒 Custom; 24 unmetered CEE elec points in central hedge; WC and shower at Capitainerie

➡ Rue Colbert. In Soubise turn off main route, sp 'Zone Portuaire' and signed. Follow road downhill, then turn right, signed. Aire on right, signed. Open barrier to enter.

ℹ Lovely Aire with grass and gravel parking offering a very pleasant feel. Park and lake at one end. Boats wind through creeks, visible at high tides. Tourist commerce adj inc pedestrian ferry across creek; 2 voyages €2.60. Town commerce 300m uphill. Bike rental avail from TO, 450m. Reinspected 2016.

SOUBISE 2 | 122 | D8 | 17780 | N45°55.577' W001°00.911'

🚐 5 🛒 Urba Flux Tall; CC; €2.50

➡ Ave de Soubise. Exit Soubise following sp 'Port des Barques'. Aire immediately on left by village boundary in roadside picnic area, signed.

ℹ Pleasant, shaded roadside picnic area. Ideal as night halt or if 121 full. Reinspected 2016.

PORT DES BARQUES | 123 | D8 | 17730 | N45°56.800' W001°05.400'

🚐 30; €8/night; CC 🛒 Aire Services 3000; Outside barrier; CC/Token; €2

➡ Avenue des Sports, off D125/D125e3 junction. Turn left off D125 after town entrance, sp 'Plage' and signed. Follow road for 1.5km. After passing cemetery on left Aire is 100m on left. Enter through Aire Services barrier.

ℹ Commercial Aire in a peaceful location adj to boules court and sports facilities. Poss to visit Île Madame across causeway depending on tide. Reinspected 2016.

BOYARDVILLE | 124 | D8 | 17190 | N45°57.805' W001°14.680'

🚐 40; €9/night inc 6amp elec; CC; Pay at barrier 🛒 Custom; Inside barrier

➡ Allée de Fort Royer. Take D126 from Dolus d'Oleron to Boyardville. As enter town turn right, immediately right again into Camping Fort Royer and right again, signed. Enter Aire through barrier.

ℹ Commercial Aire adj to campsite on former campsite ground close to main road adj. Bays marked by elec points. One of the nicest Aires on the island. Inspected 2014.

DOLUS D'OLERON | 125 | D8 | 17550 | N45°54.717' W001°15.266'

🚐 30; €6/24hrs; Collected 🛒 Euro Relais Maxi; CC or Token (ER); €4

➡ Route du Stade. Turn off D734 at roundabout in Dolus d'Oléron onto D126, sp 'Boyardville'. In 700m turn right, sp 'Parc Aquatique'. Service Point on left by tennis courts. Parking 50m past Service Point, signed.

ℹ Pleasant grass parking with approx 14 hardstanding for winter use. Pay for both services and parking by CC on Service Point, however Service Point is broken regularly. Updated 2016.

LA BREE LES BAINS | 126 | D7 | 17840 | N46°00.508' W001°21.437'

🚐 30 🛒 Euro Relais Junior; €4.50

➡ D273e1, at ZA de la Brée les Bains. Turn off D734 into La Brée les Bains on D273e1. Turn right just before boundary sign. Aire in industrial area on right before you enter town.

ℹ Adj to recycling point and caravan sales/storage. Tokens from TO, 1km. Reinspected 2014.

ST DENIS D'OLERON — 127 — D7 — 17650 — N46°01.659' W001°22.993' — SP

160; €9 inc 5amp elec and showers; Max 4 nights; Grass parking
Custom; Inside barrier

➡ Route des Huttes. From the south approach St Denis d'Oléran on D734. 350m after passing boundary sign turn left onto Route des Huttes, signed. Follow road and Aire is on right, signed. Enter through barrier.

ℹ Commercial Aire on former campsite with grass and reinforced grass pitches between deciduous trees. Old amenities block. Town and seafront 1km. Updated 2016.

LA COTINIERE (ILE D'OLERON) — 128 — D8 — 17310 — N45°55.425' W001°20.576' — SP

5; €9/24hrs; + tax; Collected Raclet; Token; €4

➡ Ave des Pins. In St Pierre turn off D734 at traffic lights onto D274, sp 'La Cotinière'. Follow sp 'La Cotinière' to end of road. Turn right, sp 'Camping', and Aire is 50m past Camping Municipal de la Fauche-Prere, signed.

ℹ Small parking area under trees next to municipal campsite. Beach 100m through campsite. Reinspected 2014.

LE GRAND VILLAGE PLAGE (ILE D'OLERON) — 129 — D8 — 17370 — N45°51.714' W001°14.436' — SP

9; €6/24hrs; CC; Pay at Service Point Urba Flux Small; CC; €4

➡ Allée des Pins. Follow D26 to Grand Village. Turn onto D126 at roundabout, sp 'La Cotiniere'. Turn left at next roundabout, sp 'Plage'. Turn 1st right, then left in front of Camping Les Pins to Aire, signed.

ℹ Landscaped Aire under shady pine trees. Bays are unlevel and some are impractical. Reinspected 2014.

LE CHATEAU D'OLERON — 130 — D8 — 17480 — N45°53.791' W001°12.125'

100; €10.50/night inc service and 6amp elec; CC; Pay at barrier
Euro Relais Junior; Inside barrier

➡ Blvd Phillippe Daste. From bridge follow sp 'Château d'Oléron'. In Château d'Oléron follow sp 'Ors' and signed, then follow sp 'Plage' and signed. Aire on left in 1.2km. Enter through Aire Services barrier.

ℹ Large commercial Aire on former campsite. Shower water is solar heated. Tidal beach with a small stretch of sand opp. Updated 2016.

ST TROJAN LES BAINS 1 — 131 — D8 — 17370 — N45°50.624' W001°12.533'

10; Max 72hrs None; See 220

➡ Place de la Liberté, off D126. Aire in centre adj to large car park near TO.

ℹ Designated parking adj to large height barriered car park. TO and local commerce at roundabout 50m. Reinspected 2014.

ST TROJAN LES BAINS 2 — 132 — D8 — 17370 — N45°50.467' W001°12.331'

16; Max 72hrs None; See 220

➡ Rue Capitaine Patoiseau. Turn off main route through opp children's play area, then turn right into car park, signed.

ℹ Designated parking adj to main route. Town centre 250m. Park opp with recreational facilities leading to beach. Views of bridge to mainland. Inspected 2014.

BOURCEFRANC LE CHAPUS 1 | 133 | D8 | 17560 | N45°50.755' W001°08.948'

🚐 10; Max 24hrs 🛢 None; See 134

➡ Rue des Amandiers. Turn off D26 at roundabout onto C107, sp 'Bourcefranc le Chapus'. Follow road towards town and turn into large car park on left, signed. Parking adj to boules club, signed.

ℹ Large parking area in town centre. Boules club and pharmacy adj. Reinspected 2016.

BOURCEFRANC LE CHAPUS 2 | 134 | D8 | 17320 | N45°49.564' W001°08.582'

🚐 30; €7.50/10pm-9am; Pay at machine 🛢 Euro Relais Junior; Token (ER); €3

➡ Route Touristique. Exit town on C107 and go straight across D26 roundabout, sp 'Plages'. Service Point in 1.5km on left outside Camping La Giroflée: N45°49.867' W001°09.048'. Parking 600m further down road on right.

ℹ Parking adj to tidal sandy beach overlooking sea and island. Service Point on sand, some parts are deep. Tokens avail from campsite, TO and Mairie. Reinspected 2016.

HIERS BROUAGE | 135 | D8 | 17320 | (A) N45°51.759' W001°04.6620'

🚐 (A) 30; Grass parking; 8pm-9am; (B) 15; Hardstanding 🛢 Raclet; Token (ER); €4; Water not working

➡ D3. Exit Hiers north on D3. Service Point on right at bend in road by boat: N45°51.166' W001°04.636'. For (A) follow road from Service Point towards Brouage. Turn left into parking, signed. (B) N45°52.090' W001°04.056': On other side of Brouage, 1.2km.

ℹ (A) Overnight, designated motorhome parking. Dead quiet apart from local road noise. Walking paths through adj salt marshes. Fort du Bourage 700m. (B) Designated parking just 20m from entrance of fort with tourist and local commerce. Oyster production and nature reserve adj. Inspected 2016.

(A)

(B)

ST JUST LUZAC | 136 | D8 | 17320 | N45°47.950' W001°02.900'

🚐 5 🛢 Euro Relais Junior; Token (2/1); €4

➡ Avenue des Vignes, at ZI Fief de Luzac. In St Just Luzac turn off D728 at roundabout onto D241e1, sp 'Luzac'. Take 1st right into Rue des Vignes. Aire in 80m in small industrial estate.

ℹ In industrial estate, not picturesque, but suitable night halt. Only 1 bay but plenty of additional parking. Boulangerie adj. Reinspected 2016.

MARENNES | 137 | D8 | 17320 | N45°49.561' W001°05.819'

🚐 20 🛢 Euro Relais Junior; Token (ER)

➡ Rue Jean Moulin. Turn off D728, Marennes bypass, onto D3 at traffic lights, sp 'Marennes'. Turn left, sp 'Centre d'Animation et de Loisirs'. Aire 350m in car park opp Renault dealer. Do not park on the side with houses against it. Additional designated parking in supermarket opp.

ℹ Large, open gravel parking area in residential area. Adj to supermarket with designated parking. Popular tolerated parking at La Cité de l'Huitre: N45°48.781' W001°06.762'; will become controlled. Reinspected 2016.

HAVE YOU VISITED AN AIRE?

GPS co-ordinates in this guide are protected by copyright law

Visit www.all-the-aires.co.uk/submissions.shtml
to upload your updates and photos.

ℹ Submit updates
- Amendments
- New Aires
- Not changed

Take at least 5 digital photos showing
- Signs
- Service Point
- Parking
- Overview
- Amenities

LA TREMBLADE 1
139 D8 17390 🏛 N45°46.962' W001°09.141'

🚐 55; €10/night inc 10amp CEE elec; Pay at machine; Max 72hrs
Urba Flux Tall

▶ Rue Marcel Gaillardon. Turn off D728e at roundabout with D25, and the large paper boats, sp 'Le Port' and signed. Turn left, signed, then right, signed. Turn right opp recycling bins to entrance of Aire.

ℹ️ Popular, landscaped, commercial Aire in a residential area. Park in marked bays, silver dots to front, white lines to rear. Town commerce 2km; beach 2.5km. Area is famed for oysters. Reinspected 2016.

LA TREMBLADE 2
140 D8 17390 🏢 N45°45.577' W001°07.746'

🚐 20; Max 1 night Euro Relais Mini; €2

▶ Rue des Artisans. Turn off D14 south of La Tremblade at the D14/C13 roundabout into Intermarché supermarket, sp 'Intermarché' and signed. Service Point between self-service laundry and fuel station.

ℹ️ Motorhome parking limited to 1 night. Supermarket and self-service laundry adj. Inspected 2016.

LA PALMYRE 1
141 D8 17570 ⚓ N45°41.483' W001°11.352'

🚐 83; €8/24hrs; CC; Max 7 days; 10m bays Euro Relais Junior; Outside barrier; Token (ER); €2

▶ Avenue de l'Atlantique, off D25. Turn off D141e1 onto D25 at roundabout in La Palmyre, sp 'Ronce les Bains'. Turn left, sp 'Le Plage' and 'Tennis'. Aire 150m on right. Enter through Urba Flux barrier.

ℹ️ Commercial Aire located beside sand dunes in a pleasant wooded area. Sandy beach 300m through picnic area. Town centre 1km. Reinspected 2014.

LA PALMYRE 2
142 D8 17570 ⚓ N45°40.982' W001°10.818'

🚐 56; €8/24hrs; Pay at machine None; See **141**

▶ Blvd de la Plage. Turn off D141e1/D25 at roundabout, sp 'Le Port'. Follow sp 'Le Port'. Drive through port and Aire 500m further along coast road, signed.

ℹ️ Large designated parking area which is less popular than **141**. Beach and park over adj protective sand dune. Port with tourist commerce 250m. Town 700m on cycle path. Reinspected 2014.

LES MATHES
143 D8 17570 🏢 N45°42.848' W001°08.864'

🚐 40; €8; Pay at machine; Feb-Nov Custom; Token (ER); €4

▶ Rue de la Garenne. Turn off at roundabout adj to SPAR supermarket onto D141, sp 'Royan'. Turn right, sp 'Espace Multi-Loisirs' and signed. Aire on right.

ℹ️ Large uninspiring commercial Aire next to pleasant recreational facilities offering poor value for money locally. Always likely to have space. Inspected 2014.

NIEULLE SUR SEUDRE
144 D8 17600 🔓 N45°45.153' W001°00.131'

🚐 3 Euro Relais Junior; 2 unmetered CEE elec points (Not working)

▶ Place de la Mairie, off D241. From Marennes take D728 southeast. Fork right onto D131, sp 'Royan'. Then turn right onto D118, sp 'Nieulle sur Seudre'. At mini roundabout turn right onto D241 and follow road straight on. Aire on right in centre of village outside school.

ℹ️ Small parking area outside school, La Poste and Mairie. Take care using services as corner of building overhangs Service Point. Local commerce 150m. Reinspected 2016.

LE GUA

145 D8 17600 N45°43.538' W000°56.684'

2; See info ♛ Euro Relais Junior; 2 unmetered CEE elec points

➡ Place 19 Mars 1962. Turn off D733 onto D131 at roundabout, sp 'Le Gua'. Follow road and practical parking on right, sp 'P': N45°43.596' W000°56.763'. For Service Point continue straight on and at mini roundabout turn right. Service Point and 2 designated bays 50m on left.

ⓘ Service Point in small parking area just off central square. Aire has 2 designated parking bays, but there is more suitable, open parking detailed in directions. Small town commerce 100m; market Sun. Reinspected 2016.

SAUJON

146 D8 17600 N45°40.513' W000°55.905'

20; €10/24hrs inc elec; CC; Max 5.5t ♛ Euro Relais Maxi; Outside barrier

➡ Route des Écluses. Exit N150 onto D1, sp 'Saujon-La Lande', and follow sp 'Port de Ribérou'. Turn right, sp 'Port de Ribérou' and signed. Aire on left, signed. Enter through barrier. Parking has 5.5t weight restriction.

ⓘ Pleasant asphalt Aire adj to pond and river with footpath to town, 700m. Reinspected 2016.

ROYAN

147 D8 17200 N45°37.691' W001°00.718'

40; €9.60/night inc service; CC; Gravel parking ♛ Euro Relais Junior; Inside barrier; 2 unmetered CEE elec points

➡ Rue Bel-Air. Approach from east on N150. Turn right at roundabout just past D25 junction, sp 'Habitat 17'. Turn 1st right, sp 'Espace Commercial Royan 2'. Follow road to end, then turn left, immediately right across railway tracks and immediately right again, sp 'Scouts de France' and signed. Aire 150m on left. Enter through PARKNIGHT barrier.

ⓘ Popular, landscaped, commercial Aire located in a peaceful, out of town suburb. Inspected 2016.

MORNAC SUR SEUDRE

148 D8 17113 T N45°42.455' W001°01.837'

30; Grass parking ♛ None; See 145

➡ Route de Breuillet. Turn off D14 in Breuillet onto D140e1, sp 'Mornac s/ Seudre'. Follow road for 2km, then turn left immediately before train track, signed. Park on grass on left; park furthest from turning to get longest bay.

ⓘ Pleasant grass parking that can take any unit at furthest end. Train track is for a seasonal steam train; Musée Ferroviaire, a railway museum, 100m, €3.50pp. Cross railway to Beau Village with tourist commerce. Inspected 2016.

ST GEORGES DE DIDONNE 1

149 D8 17110 N45°36.178' W000°59.522'

13; €6/night Sept-Jun; €8/night Jul-Aug; Pay at machine; Max 72hrs; Max 8m ♛ None; See 150

➡ Allée des Ormes. Turn off D25 at roundabout, sp 'St Georges de Didonne-Centre'. Follow road straight on, sp 'Centre Ville'. Turn left, sp 'P Gillet'. Aire is on right in 50m. Difficult entrance due to street furniture and road layout.

ⓘ Designated parking at rear of car park backing on to cemetery. Less popular than the other designated parking within the town. Beach and tourist/town commerce 300m. Reinspected 2016.

ST GEORGES DE DIDONNE 2

150 D8 17110 N45°36.261' W000°59.974'

19; €6/night Sept-Jun; €8/night Jul-Aug; Pay at machine; Max 72hrs ♛ Euro Relais Mini

➡ Rue du Stade. From south on D25 turn off at roundabout, sp 'St Georges de Didonne-Centre'. Follow road straight on, sp 'Centre Ville'. Turn right, sp 'Marche' on road. Follow road straight on and Aire is on right in 400m.

ⓘ Popular Aire 350m from beach and town centre. Opp sports facilities. Pleasant seaside town with large sandy beach. Reinspected 2016.

ST GEORGES DE DIDONNE - Plage

151 | D8 | 17110 | N45°35.742' W000°59.502'

🚐20; €6/night Sept-Jun; €8/night Jul-Aug; CC/€; Pay at machine at far end; Max 72hrs 🚽 WC 50m; See **150**

➡ D25e. From Meschers-sur-Gironde follow D25, sp 'St Georges de D'. Just outside St Georges de Didonne turn left at roundabout onto D25e, sp 'Centre Ville' and 'Plage'. Turn right at mini roundabout and follow road for 750m to parking on right, signed.

ℹ Oversubscribed roadside parking overlooking road to large sandy beach. WC 50m past payment machine. Inspected 2016.

ST GEORGES DE DIDONNE - Port

152 | D8 | 17110 | N45°36.023' W001°00.422'

🚐18; €6/night Sept-Jun; €8/night Jul-Aug; CC/€; Pay at machine; Max 72hrs 🚽 None; See **150**

➡ Rue du Port. From Meschers-sur-Gironde follow D25 sp 'St Georges de D'. Just outside St Georges de Didonne turn left at roundabout onto D25e, sp 'Centre Ville' and 'Plage'. Turn right at mini roundabout and follow road along seafront to end (past **150**). At roundabout turn left, sp 'Le Port'. Bear left down one-way street, then in 450m turn left through gateway, sp 'P'. Designated parking immediately on right, signed.

ℹ Popular, pleasant area on clifftop with sea glimpses. Small beach and port 100m via footpath and steps. Use of tables and chairs is allowed; some bays are pleasantly large. Inspected 2016.

MESCHERS SUR GIRONDE

153 | D8 | 17132 | N45°33.377' W000°56.695'

🚐12 hardstanding; 30 grass; €8/24hrs; Pay at machine/collected 🚽 Custom; €2; 12 16amp CEE elec points, mostly for hardstanding; Cont WC

➡ Routes des Salines. From Talmont on D145 turn left on entry to Meschers sur Gironde, sp 'Le Port' and signed. Follow road to left and Aire and Service Point at end of road, signed.

ℹ Oversubscribed Aire offering year-round hardstanding parking and seasonal grass parking. Adj to working port overlooking boats in dry storage. Restaurants/bars on quay. Cycle to Talmont-sur-Gironde for a day out. Reinspected 2016.

COZES

154 | D8 | 17120 | N45°35.177' W000°49.999'

🚐8 🚽 Custom

➡ Ave de la Gare. Enter town from north on D17. Turn right after crossing railway track, sp 'Talmont'. Turn right in 50m, signed. Aire at far end of car park.

ℹ Adj to sports facilities and velo rail. Hire a velo cart in summer and pedal along the disused railway. Reinspected 2014.

ST SEURIN D'UZET ✳

155 | D8 | 17120 | N45°30.061' W000°50.097'

🚐7; €8/night inc service and elec; Collected 🚽 Custom; 14 unmetered CEE elec points

➡ Place du Créac, off D145 adj to river. Signed from D145 main road. Aire on opp side of marina to church, signed.

ℹ Small parking area overlooking river marina in village centre. Pleasant grass picnic area adj. Slipway opp. An ideal place to get away from it all. Reinspected 2016.

MORTAGNE SUR GIRONDE ✳

156 | D8 | 17120 | N45°28.550' W000°47.681'

🚐80; €8/night inc CEE elec; Collected 🚽 Custom; €1; See directions

➡ Quai des Pêcheurs, at the port. From town follow sp 'Le Port' onto D6. Follow D6 to port. At crossroads go right for Service Point: N45°28.521' W000°47.928' or straight on and then right to Aire, signed. No parking against the water's edge.

ℹ Popular Aire located in a pleasant area overlooking river marina with pleasure and working boats; charter boat trips avail. Park considerately. Part grass, part hardstanding and some parking between trees. Tourist commerce 350m. Reinspected 2016.

TALMONT SUR GIRONDE

| 157 | D8 | 17120 | T | N45°32.257' W000°54.331' |

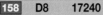

🚐 60; €2/day; €8/night; CC; Grass parking 🏠 None; See 156

➡ D145b. Turn off D145 at roundabout, sp 'Talmont' and 'Parking Obligatoire'. Turn left into car park and enter through left-hand barrier, signed. Designated parking 50m on left, signed.

ℹ Popular, designated grass parking on outskirts of Beau Village. Inspected 2016.

ST DIZANT DU GUA

| 158 | D8 | 17240 | | N45°25.840' W000°42.343' |

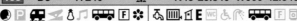

🚐 20; Grass parking 🏠 Euro Relais Junior; €2; Lift grid for waste water drain

➡ D145. Aire adj to D145 as you exit the village towards St-Thomas-de-Conac (south), signed.

ℹ Large, pleasant, open grass parking behind shop in picnic area adj to small river. Space likely and can take any unit configuration. Local commerce adj. Cycle routes around vines. Château de Beaulon, with gardens and woodland, 350m. Reinspected 2016.

ST THOMAS DE CONAC

| 159 | D8 | 17150 | | N45°23.279' W000°41.401' |

🚐 4; Max 72hrs 🏠 Custom; Donation; WC at boules court

➡ D145. Off D145, adj to village boules court. 100m from church, signed.

ℹ Small Aire with partial views over horse paddocks and countryside. Overflow parking adj to road, or on grass behind weather permitting. Local commerce 250m. Reinspected 2016.

ST GENIS DE SAINTONGE

| 160 | D8 | 17240 | | N45°29.001' W000°33.993' |

🚐 20; €6/24hrs inc service and 4hrs 6amp CEE elec; CC 🏠 Urba Flux Tall; Inside barrier

➡ Rue Fanny. Follow D137 through town towards Pons. Turn right into Rue Fanny, signed. Aire in 50m. Enter through Urba Flux barrier.

ℹ Landscaped commercial Aire 100m from town. Replaces previous Aire in town centre. Updated 2016.

JONZAC

| 161 | E8 | 17500 | | N45°26.893' W000°25.960' |

🚐 10 🏠 Euro Relais Junior; Token (ER); WC by parking

➡ Place du 8 Mai 1945. From D142/D28/D134 roundabout take D28, sp 'Cognac'. Turn right, sp 'P Mai 1945' and signed. Best parking immediately on left. Service Point 100m on left, signed: N45°26.849' W000°25.959'.

ℹ Service Point in large, unrestricted car park just off main route. Unlimited overhang. Town commerce 200m through car park. Reinspected 2016.

LEOVILLE

| 162 | E8 | 17500 | | N45°22.788' W000°20.036' |

🚐 10 🏠 Euro Relais Mini; Token (ER); €1; 1 Cont elec point

➡ Off D253e3. From D142 in village turn onto D253e3, sp 'Baignes' and 'Aire de Loisirs'. Turn right in 150m, sp 'Aire de Loisirs' and signed. Follow road to right; GPS taken here. Actual GPS: N45°22.752' W000°20.112'.

ℹ Pleasant Aire adj to park with fishing pond, picnic area and footpath to village, 150m. Village has local commerce. Viewpoint of surrounding area and landmarks up through fields at orientation table. Reinspected 2016.

MONTENDRE

| 163 | E8 | 17130 | N45°17.179' W000°24.661' |

🚐 25; Closed Tue (Market) 🚽 Aire Services 3000; Slow tap; 6 Cont elec points (Not working); Closed Tue (Market)

➡ Rue de la Motte à Vaillant. From north on D730, sp 'Centre Ville' and signed. In 350m turn right, then turn 1st right and 1st left, sp 'R.E.S.E. Bureaux'. Drive straight on, then follow road to left and uphill, sp 'R.E.S.E. Bureaux'. Stay to left and Aire in car park on right at top of hill. GPS will navigate through town, which is narrow and 3.5t restricted.

ℹ️ Aire in large car park just 50m from small town commerce. Not accessible Tue due to market. Town also has château. Inspected 2016.

CLERAC

| 164 | E9 | 17270 | N45°10.754' W000°13.693' |

🚐 6; Gravel parking 🚽 Euro Relais Junior; 1 unmetered elec point (Not working); Excellent WC

➡ D261e1/Route des Vignes. Turn off D158 in the centre of the village onto D261e, sp 'Cercoux' and signed. Drive past the boulangerie, then turn left, signed. Service Point at end of road.

ℹ️ Popular, small, peaceful Aire at picnic area on edge of village overlooking pond and countryside. Local commerce 100m. Reinspected 2016.

MONTGUYON

| 165 | E9 | 17270 | N45°13.075' W000°10.990' |

🚐 15; Max 3.5t 🚽 Custom; WC opp Service Point

➡ Rue de Vassiac. From Montlieu la Garde on D730 turn left at roundabout staying on D730, sp 'Montguyon'; 3.5t weight restriction. Go straight across next roundabout onto D910bis and follow main road around right-hand bend. Turn left onto D158, sp 'Martron' and signed. Follow road straight on for 400m, then turn right at stadium, signed. Service Point to left. Parking behind building; 3.5t weight restriction.

ℹ️ Large, open parking at sports facilities. Footpath leads through sports pitches to large park, Château de Montguyon and town, 500m. Reinspected 2016.

BROSSAC

| 166 | E8 | 16480 | N45°19.974' W000°02.738' |

🚐 4; 11m bays 🚽 Flot Bleu Euro; 1 CEE elec point (Not working); WC 100m, at stadium

➡ Rue du Château d'Eau. Turn off D731 onto D7 at roundabout, sp 'Brossac', 'Centre de Loisirs' and signed. In 600m turn sharp right into Rue du Château d'Eau, signed. In 50m turn left, signed. Aire on right.

ℹ️ Small, landscaped Aire; each bay has its own drain. Large motorhomes subject to other parked motorhomes; further parking available. Pleasant, peaceful spot by open access sports field. Small town commerce 300m; market Sat am. Reinspected 2016.

AUBETERRE SUR DRONNE

| 167 | E8 | 16390 | N45°16.162' E000°10.606' |

🚐 10; Riverside parking allowed Oct-Apr 🚽 Flot Bleu Océane

➡ D2, at Base de Loisirs. Follow D2, sp 'Ribérac'. Cross river bridge, then turn right, sp 'P'. Turn immediately left. Service Point on left and parking opp on right, signed.

ℹ️ Peaceful Aire adj to municipal sports facilities and campsite. River adj with seasonal kayak hire. Riverside parking banned May-Sept. Motorhomes banned from all other local parking. Short walk into Beau Village; local commerce 500m. Reinspected 2016.

ST SEVERIN

| 168 | E8 | 16390 | N45°18.750' E000°15.300' |

🚐 3 🚽 Custom; 4 unmetered CEE elec; Water tap on other side

➡ Rue de la Pavancelle. Turn off D709, main route through, opp SPAR supermarket, sp 'Mairie' and signed. Turn 1st left and Aire on left, signed.

ℹ️ Pleasant, small Aire under deciduous trees adj to main road. Large motorhomes subject to other parked motorhomes. Steps up to adj small town commerce which runs for about 300m. Reinspected 2016.

MONTMOREAU ST CYBARD — 169 — E8 — 16190 — N45°23.948' E000°07.963'

🚐15; Max 48hrs 🛒 Flot Bleu Pacific; €2; Inspection cover; 10 unmetered CEE elec points

➡ Rue de la Tude, off D674. From south on D674 turn right at mini roundabout into Rue de la Tude opp La Poste, signed.

ℹ Parking in open, slightly sloping square suitable for any unit configuration. Grassy area adj between parking and river Tude. Château de Montmoreau and small town commerce 100m. Very small market in square Sat am. Reinspected 2016.

VILLEBOIS LAVALETTE — 170 — E8 — 16320 — N45°28.850' E000°16.607'

🚐40 🛒 Urba Flux Tall; Token; €2 (2 x €1)

➡ Place du Champ de Foire. Approach from south on D17. Turn off D17 at large roundabout. Continue uphill and past college, then turn right, sp 'P'. Follow road downhill and into Aire. For Service Point continue for 50m past right turning to parking: N45°28.900' E000°16.583'.

ℹ Large, secluded parking area below pleasant, terraced park with plenty of open green space. WCs down steps behind Service Point. TO near Service Point. Impressive château in town; guided English tours all year, €4.50. www.chateaudevilleboislavalette.com Reinspected 2016.

MOUTHIERS SUR BOEME — 171 — E8 — 16440 — N45°33.254' E000°07.493'

🚐5 🛒 Custom

➡ Chemin de la Chauveterie. Turn off D12 at the roundabout to south of village into Place du Champ du Foire, signed. Follow road to left, then to right and the Aire is in front of the church, signed.

ℹ Pleasant Aire overlooking church. Square adj with convenience store, local commerce and small market on Thursday am. Reinspected 2015.

VOEUIL ET GIGET — 172 — E8 — 16400 — N45°35.092' E000°09.292'

🚐3 🛒 Flot Bleu Océane; €2

➡ Rue de la Mairie. Turn off D674 as exit village by covered water feature. Aire 20m on right, behind church.

ℹ In village centre opp Mairie. Restaurant adj. Pretty church and small river adj. Reinspected 2015.

SERS — 173 — E8 — 16410 — N45°35.788' E000°19.298'

🚐7; Max 48hrs; Grass parking 🛒 Euro Relais Junior; Token (ER); €3

➡ Rue du Champ de Foire. Turn off D25 onto Rue du Champ de Foire at either end of village, signed. Easiest entrance is from east. Aire just off central square, signed. Fencing and bushes look like they restrict entrance but it is over 3m wide.

ℹ Aire adj to sports facilities just off central square. Local commerce 100m. Reinspected 2016.

TOUVRE — 174 — E8 — 16600 — N45°39.657' E000°15.489'

🚐7 🛒 Aire Services 3000

➡ Route du Pontil. Follow D57 to south. After crossing railway line turn 1st right onto D408, sp 'Soyaux'. Aire 20m on right, signed.

ℹ Landscaped Aire adj to railway line. Bus stop adj; unlimited travel €3.60/day. Plan d'Eau le Grande Prairie Aire closed in 2010, night parking banned; still signed from N141. Footpath around Sources de Touvre, area of historical/ecological interest. Reinspected 2016.

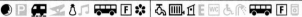

LA COURONNE

175 | E8 | 16400 | N45°36.378' E000°06.019'

🚐 5; No parking Wed/Sat am (Market) 🛒 Custom

➡ Place du Champ de Foire. Enter town on D35 from south. At roundabout turn left, sp 'Centre Socio Culturel', then turn immediately right into car park. Service Point adj to public WCs.

ℹ Aire in large town centre car park; access diff when busy and no parking during market Wed/Sat 7.30am-1pm. Traffic noise may prevent a peaceful night. Good range of local commerce adj. www.lacouronne.fr Reinspected 2015.

ROULLET ST ESTEPHE

176 | E8 | 16440 | N45°34.785' E000°02.704'

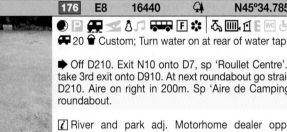

🚐 20 🛒 Custom; Turn water on at rear of water tap

➡ Off D210. Exit N10 onto D7, sp 'Roullet Centre'. At roundabout take 3rd exit onto D910. At next roundabout go straight across onto D210. Aire on right in 200m. Sp 'Aire de Camping-Car' from 1st roundabout.

ℹ River and park adj. Motorhome dealer opp. Popular and convenient stop just off N10, always likely to have space. Town 400m. www.roullet-saint-estephe.fr Reinspected 2015.

PONT A BRAC - Nonaville

177 | E8 | 16120 | N45°31.526' W000°05.399'

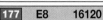

🚐 6 🛒 Urba Flux Tall; CC; €2

➡ D916. Turn off N10, sp 'D68 Nonaville'. Follow sp 'Nonaville' onto D916. Turn right into picnic area as exit Pont-à-Brac, signed. Follow road for 100m and Aire on left, signed.

ℹ Landscaped lay-by parking just minutes from N10; constant road noise. Some parking shaded by deciduous trees. There is enough overflow for another 4 motorhomes and space likely as it will only appeal as a night halt. Inspected 2016.

NERSAC

178 | E8 | 16440 | N45°37.555' E000°03.004'

🚐 7; Max 48hrs/month 🛒 Custom; 4 unmetered elec points

➡ Rue de la Foucaudie. Turn off D699, main route, by chemist, signed. Turn left adj to turreted building in village centre, signed. Follow road around walled field and Aire is on right adj to police station, signed.

ℹ Lovely, popular Aire in very nice village, 150m, that is well worth a look around. www.mairie-nersac.fr Reinspected 2015.

SIREUIL

179 | E8 | 16440 | N45°37.034' E000°00.411'

🚐 3; Grass parking 🛒 None; See **178**

➡ Chemin du Ponton. Turn off D7 north of village, sp 'Lavoir Ancien' and signed. At T-junction turn right and parking is immediately on left adj to river.

ℹ Idyllic riverside parking with BBQ and picnic area adj to corn field. Village centre 350m. May feel isolated. Reinspected 2015.

CHATEAUNEUF SUR CHARENTE

180 | E8 | 16120 | N45°35.924' W000°03.403'

🚐 7; Gravel parking 🛒 Euro Relais Junior; Token (ER); €3

➡ Rue de Genac. As enter town from southeast on D939 take 3rd exit at roundabout towards Super U supermarket, sp 'Centre Ville' and signed. Aire on left opp Super U fuel station, signed.

ℹ Supermarket opp. Large park and picnic area adj. Noise at night from adj road. Small town commerce 400m. Reinspected 2016.

ST SIMON | 181 | E8 | 16120 | N45°39.168' W000°05.119'

🚐 6 🚰 Urba Flux Tall; CC

➡ D22. Adj to D22 on right as exit village towards Jarnac, signed.

ℹ Designated landscaped parking in fenced compound on edge of village. Views over vines. In cognac region. May feel isolated if alone. Reinspected 2015.

HIERSAC | 182 | E8 | 16290 | N45°39.978' W000°00.022'

🚐 3 🚰 Urba Flux Tall; CC; €2/20 mins

➡ D14. Exit village on D14 towards Châteauneuf sur Charente. Aire on left just before village boundary.

ℹ Aire located on the edge of the village. Local commerce inc convenience store on N141, 600m. Reinspected 2014.

MAINE DE BOIXE | 183 | E8 | 16560 | N45°50.229' E000°11.250'

🚐 Poss, but not recommended; Max 24hrs 🚰 Very custom; No vehicle access

➡ N10. Turn off N10, sp 'Maine de Boixe' (travelling south) or 'Maine de Boixe Est' (travelling north). Service Point is signed at the WCs, for parking follow the caravan symbols.

ℹ Main route roadside lay-by; overnight parking not recommended. Service Points on both sides of road. Inspected 2016.

MANSLE | 184 | E8 | 16230 | N45°52.674' E000°10.894'

🚐 Poss, in unrestricted roadside bays 🚰 Raclet; €2

➡ Rue de Watlington. As enter Mansle from north on D18 turn left, sp 'Camping le Champion'. Service Point outside campsite.

ℹ Service Point is adj to pleasant municipal campsite. Seasonal noise from adj snack bar. Small town commerce 500m. Reinspected 2016.

AIGRE | 185 | E8 | 16140 | N45°53.603' E000°00.329'

🚐 15; €4 inc elec May-Oct; Collected 🚰 Bollard; 2 unmetered CEE elec points (Not working); 5 16amp Cont elec points

➡ Rue des Charrières. From west on D739 turn off, sp 'Aire de Repos' and 'Camping Car'. Aire on right. Well signed from all directions in town.

ℹ Pleasant Aire adj to park and boules courts. Open or shaded parking on hardstanding or grass. Small town commerce 300m. Reinspected 2016.

ROUILLAC | 186 | E8 | 16170 | N45°46.592' W000°03.678'

🚐 7; Gravel parking 🚰 Euro Relais Junior; Token (ER); €3

➡ Rue de Genac. As enter town from southeast on D939 take 3rd exit at roundabout towards Super U supermarket, sp 'Centre Ville' and signed. Aire on left opp Super U fuel station, signed.

ℹ Supermarket opp. Large park and picnic area adj. Noise at night from adj road. Small town commerce 400m. Reinspected 2016.

SEGONZAC
187 E8 16130 N45°36.869' W000°13.255'

🚐 4 (each with elec); Max 4 days 🚾 Custom; 4 unmetered elec points

➡ Place du Jardin Public, adj to Rue Gourry. From D763 turn onto Rue Gourry and follow to end. Aire on right. Signed from all directions.

ℹ Sign adj to Aire shows local cognac producers. Village 300m. www.segonzac.fr Reinspected 2015.

LIGNIERES SONNEVILLE
188 E8 16130 N45°33.413' W000°10.957'

🚐 20 🚾 Custom

➡ Off D90. From D699 turn onto D90 in town. Follow D90 south for 300m then turn left just before exiting village, signed. Aire on left in 100m.

ℹ Large, gravel parking area adj to football pitch and ancient restored barn. In grounds of 17th century moated château now housing Mairie. Pretty historic village 350m. Reinspected 2015.

BARBEZIEUX ST HILAIRE
189 E8 16300 N45°28.234' W000°09.637'

🚐 7; 7m bays plus 2m overhang 🚾 Euro Relais Box; Token (ER); 1 unmetered CEE elec point

➡ Rue du Commandant Foucaud. Exit N10, sp 'D917 Barbezieux-Nord'. At roundabouts follow sp 'Barbezieux' and 'Cognac' on D917. Go straight ahead at roundabout onto D731, sp 'Bordeaux'. Turn left at roundabout, sp 'Centre Ville'. Follow road 500m, then turn right through arch to Aire.

ℹ Designated, landscaped parking in entrance of supermarket car park. Constant noise from passing vehicles. Town centre 300m. Market Sat am 50m. Inspected 2016.

ARCHIAC
190 E8 17520 N45°31.205' W000°18.277'

🚐 5; Max 72hrs 🚾 Euro Relais Mini (Missing in Aug 2016)

➡ Rue du Pâtis, off D699. Aire at foot of water tower behind La Poste in village centre.

ℹ Service Point in rear right-hand corner of car park by WCs. Village adj. Small market Sat am. www.archiac-tourisme.fr Reinspected 2015.

Photo: Alistair MacFayden

GENTE
191 E8 16130 N45°37.732' W000°18.921'

🚐 5; Max 2 nights 🚾 Custom; 6 16amp unmetered elec points

➡ Off D148. From Cognac (north) on D731 turn left onto D148, sp 'Gente'. After 1.2km fork right into Lieu-Dit La Vallade. Aire on left in 400m by sports field and boules pitches.

ℹ Well maintained Aire and surroundings on edge of village; no amenities. Skate park adj. WCs at boules pavilion. Léopold Gourmel cognac producer 600m. www.leopold-gourmel.com Reinspected 2015.

BOUGNEAU (PONS)
192 D8 17800 N45°36.051' W000°32.195'

🚐 3; Max 24hrs 🚾 None; See 193

➡ Exit Bourgneau on D134, sp 'Chaniers'. Turn left, sp 'Château Renaud'. Parking in 1.5km at forested Aire de Château Renaud picnic area.

ℹ Parking adj to country lane at picnic spot by river. May feel isolated if alone. Reinspected 2014.

PONS | 193 | D8 | 17800 | 🏃 | N45°34.667' W000°33.315' | SP

🚐 4 at campsite; 50 in Salle des Fêtes parking 🚰 Raclet; Token (2/1); €6; WCs at Salle des Fêtes

▶ P de L'Europe. Turn off D137 onto D142, sp 'Camping Municipal'. Motorhome parking in large car park adj to roundabout: N45°34.868' W000°33.137'. For other parking turn right at roundabout adj to P de L'Europe, then right at next roundabout, both sp 'Camping Municipal'. Aire on left outside campsite.

ⓘ 4 designated bays at campsite. Salle des Fêtes car park can take hundreds of motorhomes, but is used for markets Mon/Thurs/Sat am. Reinspected 2014.

COGNAC | 194 | E8 | 16100 | 🏛️🏭 | N45°41.910' W000°19.962' | SP

🚐 3 🚰 Raclet; €2; 4 bays at Service Point limited to 2hrs

▶ Place de la Levade. Enter Cognac from north on D731. At roundabout turn right, sp 'Cognac-Centre'. At roundabout turn left, sp 'St Jacques'. At roundabout turn right, sp 'Centre Ville'. In 50m turn right, sp 'Parking Gratuit' and signed. Aire at end of parking on right.

ⓘ Adj to Hennessey cognac producer, walk around building for visitor centre. Pleasant riverside park adj, cross bridge for town. Inspected 2014.

DOMPIERRE SUR CHARENTE | 195 | D8 | 17610 | ⚓ | N45°42.052' W000°29.650' | SP

🚐 Poss; 5 spaces adj to D24 to right of campsite; 5 spaces behind campsite reception 🚰 Euro Relais Junior; Token (ER); €4

▶ D24. Aire adj to D24 outside the municipal campsite.

ⓘ Outside municipal campsite, Camping Fontaine du Pre St Jean, adj to lake and picnic area. Campsite open mid Jun-mid Sept. Drive past campsite and follow road to end for 3 riverside spaces adj to old chain ferry; muddy when wet. Reinspected 2015.

MONTILS | 196 | D8 | 17800 | ⛲ | N45°39.166' W000°30.380' | SP

🚐 10 🚰 Custom

▶ D233. In Montils turn off D135 onto D233, sp 'Rouffiac' and 'Salle des Fêtes'. Aire on left in 450m, signed. The Service Point is at the rear of the car park.

ⓘ Large open parking area with extensive views towards Cognac. Adj to sports fields and Salle des Fêtes. Local commerce and free WiFi in village square. Visited 2014.

SAINTES | 197 | E8 | 17100 | 🏛️ | N45°44.427' W000°37.621' | SP

🚐 10; €5/day; Pay at machine 🚰 Aire Services 3000; CC; €5

▶ Ave de Saintonge. From Cognac follow D24 to Saintes. Go straight on, sp 'Centre Ville', then turn left at roundabout always staying on D24, sp 'Office de Tourisme'. At next roundabout turn left, sp 'P Palu' and signed. Aire on right, signed.

ⓘ Large designated bays in car park opp E.Leclerc supermarket. Road noise from adj main road. Riverside park access at end of Aire with foot/cycle path into Saintes centre, 1.2km. Inspected 2014.

ST CESAIRE | 198 | E8 | 17770 | 🏚️ | N45°45.231' W000°30.444' | SP

🚐 30 🚰 Custom

▶ Rue de Lilas. From D134, main road, turn up small lane opp church, sp 'Cimitière' and signed. Aire 30m on left.

ⓘ In large car park in small village. Maison de Pays selling local produce and other local commerce 100m. www.lamaison depays17.com Reinspected 2015.

BURIE
`199` E8 17770 N45°46.317' W000°25.467' SP

🚐 5; Grass parking 🏷 Custom

➡ D131. Adj to D131 as exit village towards St Bris des Bois. Signed from D731.

ℹ Parking in deep shade under very old lime tree; open grass parking to rear. Pleasant town centre 300m with small town commerce. Map of local walks in town centre. Reinspected 2015.

CHERVES RICHEMONT
`200` E8 16370 N45°44.410' W000°21.350'

🚐 5 🏷 Aire Services Plastic

➡ Impasse du Vieux Chene. At Cherves Richemont turn off D731 onto D85, sp 'Matha'. Follow road and turn left in 500m, signed. Aire 10m on left.

ℹ 5 designated bays overlooking pony paddock. Local commerce 150m. Ideal if `194` full. Reinspected 2015.

MATHA
`201` E8 17160 N45°51.937' W000°19.321' SP

🚐 7 🏷 Custom; 5 unmetered CEE elec points; WCs locked

➡ Blvd Bossais. From west on D939 turn off at roundabout, sp 'Matha' and 'D.I. Centre d'Exploitation'. Go straight over roundabout, then at next roundabout turn right. At Stop junction go straight across. Aire is on right, signed. Service Point at end past WCs.

ℹ Shaded parking under deciduous trees with small river adj. Gatehouse of old château and pond adj. Town commerce 300m. Reinspected 2016.

ST JEAN D'ANGELY
`202` E8 17400 N45°56.722' W000°32.249'

🚐 3; Max 2 Nights 🏷 Custom; WC €0.20; Outdoor shower

➡ D18/Avenue de Marennes. From St Savinien on D18 follow road straight on, sp 'St Jean d'Angely'. Cross D739, sp 'St Jean de Angely - Centre'. Turn left into car park past skateboard ramps and before river bridge. Aire on left adj to skateboard ramps. Motorhomes are banned from all other car parks at Base Nautique.

ℹ Popular Aire at leisure lake area with park, picnic areas, outdoor activities and water sports. Very busy hot days and holidays. Baker selling bread and croissants every am 8.30am-8.45am. Reinspected 2016.

LOULAY
`203` E7 17330 N46°02.784' W000°30.587'

🚐 3 🏷 Custom

➡ D210e5. At Loulay turn off D150 into town square opp 'i'. Turn left at bottom of car park/square following sp 'P Poids Lourds' and signed. For parking turn right, follow road to end, then turn right again. Parking on left. For Service Point turn left into one-way Rue des Tilleuls (leads back to main road). Service Point on left at rear of La Poste and Mairie: N46°02.858' W000°30.688'.

ℹ Roadside Service Point in one-way street. Parking poss adj to small park just 200m from small town commerce and square. As this is not dedicated parking, park considerately and overhang the grass. Reinspected 2016.

AULNAY 1
`204` E8 17470 N46°01.344' W000°20.716' SP

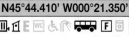

🚐 15 🏷 Custom; Lift cover for WC emptying

➡ D129/Rue de Salles. Exit town to north on D129, sp 'Chef-Boutonne'. Aire 200m on right, signed.

ℹ Large, open parking with easy access suitable for any unit configuration. Large, open shaded green space adj. Some local road noise. Small town commerce 200m with a market Sun am. Also see `205` and `206`. Reinspected 2016.

AULNAY 2 | 205 | E8 | 17470 | N46°01.407' W000°21.274'

🚐 10 ♿ WC adj, not cleaned; Water tap in WC

▶ D121/Avenue de l'Église. From D950 turn onto D121 by TO. Designated parking on left opp church, signed.

ℹ Town 800m but proximity to D950 makes this a useful night halt. TO with free WiFi 50m. Small amount of green space and sports facilities adj. Romanesque church, Église St Pierre d'Aulnay, opp; guided visits poss. Reinspected 2016.

AULNAY 3 | 206 | E7 | 17470 | N46°01.168' W000°20.824'

🚐 5 ♿ 5 unmetered CEE elec points (Not working); See 204

▶ Rue des Douves. Turn off main central square, sp 'Foyer Rural'. Motorhome parking 50m in car park, signed.

ℹ Parking just off central square full of small town commerce; car park popular with locals during trading hours, but peaceful at night. Pleasant green space and tor (tower) adj. Inspected 2016.

All of the listings in this section are Service Points without designated parking. The majority are located either at supermarkets or outside campsites.

Height barriers are rare at supermarkets and overnight parking should be possible. Always park considerately. Supermarket Service Points often lack a waste water drain.

Most campsites are municipally owned. Parking outside may be possible when campsites are closed. Acquiring tokens in rural locations may be difficult or impossible, especially in low season.

Remember to be a responsible tourist whenever offsite parking.

BRESSURE | 207 | E6 | 79300 | N46°50.670' W000°29.489'

♿ Custom; Press on top of tap

▶ Place Labate. Follow D938ter from Thouars and drive straight on into town past the supermarkets. In town turn right at roundabout, sp 'Place Labate' and signed. Go straight over 2nd mini roundabout into central road of Place Labate car park, signed. At end turn right, then left to Service Point, signed. Day parking with WC at: N46°50.250' W000°29.689'. Reinspected 2016.

LA ROCHE POSAY | 208 | F7 | 86270 | N46°47.630' E000°47.874'

♿ Aire Services Plastic

▶ D725, at Super U. Adj to D725 as you approach from Coussay les Bois. Service Point at Super U fuel station, adj to large roundabout junction of D725/D725b, signed. Reinspected 2015.

ST SAVIN | 209 | F7 | 86310 | N46°34.154' E000°52.110'

♿ Custom; €2; Pay at reception

▶ Rue du 8 Mai 1945. Turn off D951 in the town centre onto D11, sp 'Nalliers' and 'Camping-Kayak'. Follow D11, sp 'Camping-Kayak', then turn right into the campsite. Take the 1st left and the Service Point is behind the conifer bush. Inspected 2014.

MONTMORILLON | 210 | F7 | 86500 | N46°25.129' E000°51.285'

♿ Euro Relais Junior; 1 unmetered elec point

▶ D727. Approach from Lussac-les-Châteaux on D727. At roundabout turn right into E.Leclerc. Turn left and Service Point by car wash. Reinspected 2016.

CHABANAIS | 211 | F8 | 16150 | N45°52.833' E000°44.200'

♿ Euro Relais Mini; Token (ER); €2

▶ N141/E603, at Super U. From west on N141/E603 pass through Chabanais and Super U is at roundabout 1.7km east of town. Service Point and designated spaces are at rear of car wash, adj to main road. Inspected 2014.

MELLE | 212 | E7 | 79500 | N46°13.907' W000°08.643'

♿ Custom

▶ Rue de la Croix Casselin, outside municipal campsite. Turn off D737 and follow sp 'Camping'. Service Point outside campsite. Parking avail in town, follow sp 'Parking du Jardin': N46°13.361'W000°08.394'. Reinspected 2016.

MOUGON | 213 | E7 | 79370 | N46°17.574' W000°17.700'

♿ Custom

▶ Rue René Gaillard. Turn off D948, sp 'Mougon-Ouest'. Turn left onto C9, sp 'Mougon-Ouest'. Service Point in fuel station of SPAR supermarket, signed. Reinspected 2016.

MAGNE 214 E7 79460 N46°18.963' W000°33.404'

♿ IIII, ⌂ E WC ♿ ☔ 🚌 F 🔲

🚰 Aire Services Plastic; €2; No drive over drain

➤ D9, at Super U. Turn off D1 onto D9 towards Magné. Aire just off large roundabout to west of town, adj to fuel station but accessible from other side. Reinspected 2016.

MARANS 1 215 D7 17230 N46°18.759' W000°59.895'

♿ IIII, ⌂ E WC ♿ ☔ 🚌 F 🔲

🚰 Custom

➤ Quai du 11 Novembre, at the port. Turn off D105, sp 'ZI du Port'. Follow sp 'ZI du Port' and Service Point against building. Motorhomes are banned from car park nearest to town. Exit town as entered to avoid narrow streets. Reinspected 2014.

MARANS 2 216 D7 17230 N46°18.773' W000°59.529'

♿ IIII, ⌂ E WC ♿ ☔ 🚌 F 🔲

🚰 Euro Relais Mini; €2

➤ N137, at Super U supermarket. On N137 turn into Super U supermarket as exit town to north. Service Point is at the edge of the car park opp car wash, not in the fuel station. Reinspected 2014.

ESNANDES 217 D7 17137 N46°15.167' W001°07.200'

♿ IIII, ⌂ E WC ♿ ☔ 🚌 F 🔲

🚰 Custom

➤ Rue de l'Océan. Turn off D105 onto Rue de l'Océan. Service Point is 400m on right outside Camping Les Misottes. Reinspected 2014.

LA ROCHELLE 218 D7 17000 N46°09.060' W001°09.491'

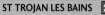

♿ IIII, ⌂ E WC ♿ ☔ 🚌 F 🔲

🚰 Custom

➤ Avenue Michel Crépeau. Follow sp 'Les Minimes', then 'Camping'. Service Point in small lay-by on main road opp Camping Le Soleil, signed. All local parking bans motorhomes. Reinspected 2016.

TAILLEBOURG 219 D8 17350 N45°49.980' W000°38.800'

♿ IIII, ⌂ E WC ♿ ☔ 🚌 F 🔲

🚰 Custom

➤ Les Douves, D127. Signed from D127/D114 junction. Cross railway line and turn immediately left. Service Point below château wall at entrance to former campsite. Difficult to turn around in space due to bins. Inspected 2016.

ST TROJAN LES BAINS 220 D8 17370 N45°49.632' W001°13.059'

♿ IIII, ⌂ E WC ♿ ☔ 🚌 F 🔲

🚰 Urba Flux Tall; CC; €5

➤ Avenue des Bris. From D126 turn off at roundabout, sp 'Plage de Gatseau'. Follow sp 'Plage de Gatseau' and fork left when road divides. Service Point on right at ZI les Bris. Inspected 2014.

LA MORELIERE 221 D7 17650 N46°02.651' W001°23.924'

♿ IIII, ⌂ E WC ♿ ☔ 🚌 F 🔲

🚰 Flot Bleu Euro (Not working) and Custom; Token/CC; €5

➤ D734. North of St Denis d'Oléron adj to D734, signed. Flot Bleu provides water adj to custom WC emptying point. Flush standing behind wall if you don't want wet feet! Inspected 2014.

MARENNES 222 D8 17320 N45°49.399' W001°06.127'

♿ IIII, ⌂ E WC ♿ ☔ 🚌 F 🔲

🚰 Euro Relais Mini; Token (ER); €3

➤ Rue Ovide Beillard. Turn off D728, Marennes bypass, onto D3 at traffic lights, sp 'Marennes'. Follow road for 900m, then turn left, sp 'Hôtel des Impôts' and 'E.Leclerc'. Follow road behind E.Leclerc fuel station and up behind gas bottles. Service Point 10m, signed. Reinspected 2016.

CRITEUIL LA MAGDELEINE 223 E8 16300 N45°32.279' W000°12.906'

♿ IIII, ⌂ E WC ♿ ☔ 🚌 F 🔲

🚰 Euro Relais Junior; 1 unmetered CEE elec point

➤ Off D151. From west on D699 turn right onto D151, sp 'Criteuil'. At right-hand bend continue straight onto C2 into village. Aire on right in village centre by school and behind Mairie, signed. Reinspected 2015.

LES PORTES EN RE 224 D7 17880 N46°14.902' W001°29.569'

♿ IIII, ⌂ E WC ♿ ☔ 🚌 F 🔲

🚰 SOS (Not working)

➤ Route de la Pointe À Chabot, outside campsite. Follow D101 east from town and turn left, sp 'Camping Municipal' and 'Salle Polyvalente'. In 300m turn right, sp 'Camping', and Service Point outside Camping La Prée. Inspected 2014.

GPS Co-ordinates for SatNav

The GPS Co-ordinates published in this guide were taken onsite by our inspectors. We consider them a valuable and unique asset and at the time of publishing have decided not to publish them as electronic files for use on navigation devices. You have permission to type in the co-ordinates of an Aire you intend to visit but not to store or share them. For the security of our copyright:

- **Do not compile them into lists**

- **Do not publish, share or reproduce them anywhere in any format**

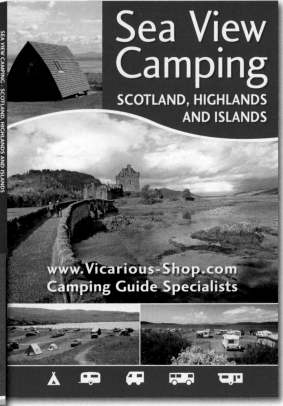

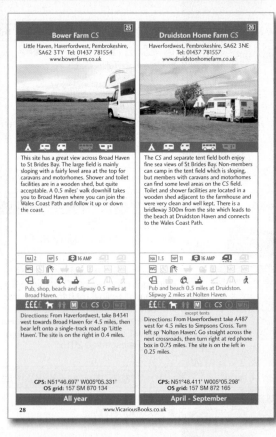

Plaine Joux

RHONE-ALPS

Thueyts

ST MARTIN D'ESTREAUX

| 1 | I7 | 42620 | | N46°12.434' E003°47.888' |

🚐 6 in adj parking area; Max 48hrs 🛒 Custom

➡️ D52. From south on N7 take 3rd exit at roundabout, sp 'St Martin D'Estréaux'. Follow road through town and turn right opp D207 onto D52, sp 'Sail les Bains' and signed. Follow road to right and Aire is on right, signed.

ℹ️ Aire in peaceful residential area and is a convenient stop when travelling north/south on N7. Small town commerce 250m. Inspected 2014.

LE CROZET

| 2 | I7 | 42310 | | N46°10.164' E003°51.448' |

🚐 2; Max 72hrs 🛒 Custom; €2; Elec €2/4hrs

➡️ D35. Exit N7 at Junction 59, sp 'La Pacaudière'. Follow road to La Pacaudière and turn right onto D35, sp 'Le Crozet'. Follow road under 3.8m arched railway bridge up towards village. Turn sharp left, signed. Aire on left, signed. Best to reverse in.

ℹ️ A difficult Aire to access due to its location and size. 150m from medieval village. Inspected 2014.

ST RIRAND

| 3 | I7 | 42370 | | N46°04.503' E003°51.015' |

🚐 3; Max 9m 🛒 Custom

➡️ Le Moulin, off D41 opp church. From Renaison take D9, then turn left onto D41, sp 'St Rirand'. At start of village turn left into Lieu-Dit Le Moulin opp church, signed. Aire 100m on left.

ℹ️ Small Aire in lovely, rural setting on edge of village. Covered picnic benches on decking 'islands'. Small wetland park with paths or longer walk around reservoir. Inspected 2014.

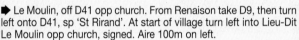

AMBIERLE

| 4 | I7 | 42820 | | N46°06.392' E003°53.623' |

🚐 5 🛒 Custom

➡️ Rue du 19 Mars 1962. Turn off D8, sp 'Ambierle'. In centre by church turn right, sp 'Le Musée', 'Salle Municipale' and signed. Follow road straight on, signed. Parking on right overlooking cemetery, Service Point to the left behind municipal hall, signed.

ℹ️ Parking with views across cemetery to vast valley beyond. Ambierle is a Petite Village of Character. Interesting Benedictine priory complex in centre with ornately tiled roof, 300m. Reinspected 2014.

ST GERMAIN LESPINASSE

| 5 | I7 | 42640 | | N46°06.317' E003°57.737' |

🚐 3; More parking adj 🛒 Custom

➡️ D18. From south on N7 exit onto D4, sp 'St Germain Lespinasse'. In town turn right onto D18. Aire in car park on left just beyond village centre, signed.

ℹ️ Small designated parking area with some shade and lovely views across open countryside. Additional parking with overhang and HGV sized bays adj. Small town commerce adj. Market Thurs. Inspected 2014.

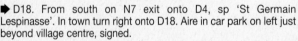

LA BENISSON DIEU

| 6 | I7 | 42720 | T | N46°09.053' E004°02.766' |

🚐 2 🛒 None; See 4; WC near TO

➡️ D4. Turn off D4 in La Benisson Dieu, sp 'Abbaye Cistercienne' and signed. Drive towards church and designated parking on left overlooking church, signed.

ℹ️ Designated parking overlooking abbey with ornate roof and spire; free entry, €3 to climb some of the bell tower. TO at abbey. On Santiago (St Jacques) pilgrimage route. School adj, busy at drop off and collection times. Inspected 2014.

POUILLY SOUS CHARLIEU 1

| 7 | I7 | 42720 | | N46°08.589' E004°06.515' |

🚐 10; No parking Sun 6am-1pm (Market) 🛢 Aire Services Plastic

➡ D482/Rue de la République. From D4 turn onto D482, sp 'Roanne'. Aire 200m on left opp mini Casino market and just before D35 junction, sp 'Espace Loisirs' and signed.

ℹ Aire adj to park. Town 100m with commerce. Also check 8 , may be preferable. Reinspected 2014.

POUILLY SOUS CHARLIEU 2

| 8 | I7 | 42720 | | N46°08.829' E004°05.998' |

🚐 4 🛢 None; See 7

➡ D4. Exit town on D487/D4 towards Briennon. Turn right into picnic area before/adj to river bridge. Designated parking in car park adj to riverside picnic area, signed.

ℹ Parking adj to riverside picnic area, an ideal spot to take your chair for a walk to enjoy some riverside views. Likely to be more peaceful than 7 . Inspected 2014.

CHARLIEU

| 9 | I7 | 42190 | | N46°09.624' E004°10.665' |

🚐 7 🛢 None; See 7

➡ Rue de Chantermerle. Follow sp 'Complex Sportif' and 'Camping' through town onto Rue de Chantermerle. Go straight on and designated parking is on right before Gendarmerie, signed.

ℹ Parking adj to boules club in residential area. Historic town centre with Benedictine abbey and small town and tourist commerce 400m. Inspected 2014.

ST DENIS DE CABANNE

| 10 | I7 | 42750 | | N46°10.313' E004°12.628' |

🚐 7 🛢 None; See 7

➡ D48. Turn off D4 at traffic lights onto D48, sp 'Mars'. Turn right into large car park, not signed.

ℹ Parking near school on outskirts of town. Local commerce 200m. Inspected 2014.

BELMONT DE LA LOIRE

| 11 | I7 | 42670 | | N46°09.936' E004°20.787' |

🚐 20 at P les Arcade; 2 at Service Point 🛢 Custom; 2 Cont elec points

➡ Place de l'Eglise. From west follow D4, sp 'Chauffailles', and turn left at the D31/D4 roundabout, signed. For Service Point turn left to the church, signed. Service Point against church. For parking turn right and drive past Les Arcades and the TO, parking on right: N46°10.041' E004°20.672'.

ℹ Parking in large car park 200m from TO. Benedictine abbey in town surrounded by some local commerce. Reinspected 2014.

COURS LA VILLE

| 12 | I7 | 69470 | | N46°06.243' E004°19.400' |

🚐 10 🛢 Custom

➡ Chemin de la Rivière. From south follow D308 around north side of town, sp 'Chauffailles'. After passing the Intermarché on left, turn right, signed, and drive past sports ground. Follow road downhill and Aire on left, signed. Lift barrier to enter.

ℹ Aire in a residential area adj to Ambulance taxi station and tennis club. Stream adj. Hardstanding near entrance, grass parking further back. Reinspected 2014.

ST HILAIRE SOUS CHARLIEU

| 13 | I7 | 42190 | | N46°06.632' E004°11.298' |

🚐 2 👕 None; See 15

➤ Exit Pouilly sous Charlieu on D35, sp 'St Hilaire' and 'Boyer'. Follow D35, sp 'Boyer', then turn onto D49, sp 'Boyer'. Turn right into lane, sp 'Le Grand Couvert Architecture Rurale'. Designated parking in car park 50m to right, signed.

ⓘ Parking adj to barn visitor attraction, for free entry press button. Enter €2 into slot and the exhibit comes to life. Bread oven being built. Rural views from parking. Inspected 2014.

NOAILLY

| 14 | I7 | 42640 | | N46°08.173' E004°00.678' |

🚐 2 👕 None; See 15

➤ From St Germain Lespinasse approach Noailly on D4. Turn left in town centre, sp 'Ecole' and signed. Follow road for 400m then turn left, sp 'Parking' and signed. Parking on left.

ⓘ Designated parking in small car park adj to park. Inspected 2014.

ST HAON LE CHATEL

| 15 | I7 | 42370 | | N46°03.830' E003°54.777' |

🚐 3 👕 Custom

➤ D39. Turn off D8, sp 'St Haon le Châtel'. Follow road to left, signed, and in 400m follow road to left again, sp 'St Croix' and signed. Aire 100m on right, signed.

ⓘ Peaceful Aire on edge of historic town. Petite Village of Character 200m uphill. Inspected 2014.

RENAISON

| 16 | I7 | 42370 | | N46°02.863' E003°55.276' |

🚐 8 👕 Custom

➤ Rue des Rivières. Approach Renaison on D9 from Roanne. Follow D9 into centre, then turn left in central square, signed. Follow road downhill for 400m then turn right, signed. Aire 400m on left, signed.

ⓘ Pleasant, peaceful shaded Aire by small river and weir at edge of town. Grass and gravel parking available. Small town commerce 600m. Inspected 2014.

ST ANDRE D'APCHON

| 17 | I7 | 42370 | | N46°02.040' E003°55.625' |

🚐 3 👕 Custom

➤ La Prébande. Turn off D8 at roundabout into St André d'Apchon. Turn right, sp 'Eglise' and signed. Follow road to end, then turn left, sp 'Eglise' and signed. Follow road to right at church and Aire 400m on right, signed.

ⓘ Aire located on outskirts of village with views of Côte Roannaise grapes. Local commerce 250m. Church has interesting tiled roof. Reinspected 2014.

ARCON

| 18 | I8 | 42370 | | N46°00.557' E003°53.294' |

🚐 6 👕 Custom; Nice WC

➤ D51. From St André d'Apchon follow D51 to Arçon. Aire on right adj to road 100m from church, signed.

ⓘ Really pleasant rural community Aire with space for 3 motorhomes next to Service Point and 2 more spaces with panoramic views on terrace above. Walking routes adj. Inspected 2014.

LES NOES

| 19 | I7 | 42370 | | N46°02.459' E003°51.105' |

🚐 10 🍴 Custom

➡ D47. From Renaison on D9 turn left onto D47, sp 'Les Noes'. Follow D47 to Les Noës and Aire on left at start of village, approx 6.3km.

ⓘ Pleasant rural village Aire near a large reservoir. Peaceful location to get away from it all; nice walk around reservoir. Local commerce 100m. Inspected 2014.

VILLEREST ★

| 20 | I8 | 42300 | | N45°59.189' E004°02.578' |

🚐 20; €6/night Apr-Oct; +€0.25pp tax; Collected; Free Nov-Mar 🍴 Custom; At toilet block; Inc; Apr-Oct; Flot Bleu Pacific; €4 (2 x €2); Nov-Mar

➡ D18. Exit D53 onto D18, sp 'Villerest'. At roundabout turn right, sp 'Lac de Villerest'. Follow road for approx 1km and Aire is on right overlooking lake, signed.

ⓘ Terraced Aire overlooking large leisure lake near the Gorges de la Loire. Leisure lake has numerous tourist commerce, swimming beach and water slides. Updated 2016.

ROANNE ★

| 21 | I7 | 42300 | | N46°02.267' E004°04.969' |

🚐 10; €6/night; Collected; Max 6 days 🍴 Flot Bleu Euro; CC; €2.10; Elec 1 Token/12hrs

➡ Allée de l'Amiral Merveilleux Du Vignaux. From D53/D207/D482 roundabout in centre near river bridge turn off, sp 'Maison du Port'. Turn right and cross canal on bridge, sp 'Capitainerie'. Follow road to right and Aire is 200m past Capitainerie, signed.

ⓘ Landscaped Aire; lovely outlook over canal basin and boats. Nicely laid out; plenty of space; grass between large level bays. Canal adj, boat hire avail. Large town commerce 450m. Inspected 2014.

AMPLEPUIS

| 22 | I8 | 69550 | | N45°58.180' E004°19.896' |

🚐 10 🍴 Custom; Water below ground under covers by barrier

➡ Rue Paul de la Goutte. From south on D8 exit at D8/D10/D165 roundabout, sp 'Centre Ville'. Turn 1st left, sp 'Salle des Sports Daniel Pierrefeu'. Entrance to Aire 180m on left, signed. Drive down slope and follow road behind building. Service Point on right against building, adj to basketball court, signed.

ⓘ Aire adj to municipal sports building, only likely to be busy during events. Small town commerce 300m. Reinspected 2016.

LES SAUVAGES

| 23 | I8 | 69170 | | N45°55.238' E004°22.627' |

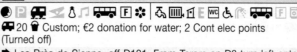

🚐 20 🍴 Custom; €2 donation for water; 2 Cont elec points (Turned off)

➡ Les Près de Sienne, off D121. From Tarare on D8 turn left onto D121, signed. Fork left, avoiding village centre and staying on D121. Follow road for 600m, then turn right at village boundary sign towards play area, signed. Service Point up 1st turning on left, signed.

ⓘ Peaceful Aire with ample parking; space likely and can accommodate any unit configuration. Parking by weigh bridge has views. Local commerce 200m. Reinspected 2016.

JOUX

| 24 | I8 | 69170 | | N45°53.302' E004°22.553' |

🚐 10; At lake 🍴 Custom

➡ D79. From east on N7 turn left onto D79, sp 'Joux'. Aire on left in 1.3km at start of village, sp 'Salle des Fêtes' and signed. For parking exit Aire to right and take 1st right, sp 'P Aire de Repos'. Follow lane along lake for 400m to parking on right: N45°53.427' E004°22.944'.

ⓘ Service Point at bottom of very sloping car park. Some level parking adj to village hall could be used if no event on. Lakeside parking is level and offers shaded parking with view of lake obscured by deciduous foliage. Picnic area with BBQ adj. Reinspected 2016.

Photo: Aire de Repos — Aire de Repos

PONTCHARRA SUR TURDINE
`25` | I8 | 69490 | N45°52.452' E004°29.491'

4 Custom; Tap behind WC; Cont WC

➡ Place Albert Schweitzer, off D33. From Tarare turn off N7 at roundabout, sp 'Pontcharra s/ T'. Follow road to town, then at traffic lights turn right onto D27, sp 'St Forgeux' and signed. Turn immediately left onto D33, sp 'St Romain' and signed, and turn left into car park at La Poste. Service Point adj to La Poste, signed.

ℹ Impractical Aire in small car park with 5.5m bays and no overhang. Benches and children's play area adj. Dog toilet adj. Reinspected 2016.

ST FORGEUX
`26` | I8 | 69490 | N45°51.458' E004°28.601'

10 Custom; 2 unmetered CEE elec points

➡ From N7 turn onto D31 at roundabout on edge of Pontcharra sur Turdine, sp 'St Forgeux'. In 1.2km turn onto D27, sp 'St Forgeux'. In St Forgeux turn sharp left (tight turn) onto D632, signed. Follow road downhill, then turn left at bottom into Aire, signed.

ℹ Popular Aire adj to sports facilities on edge of pretty, well kept village. Views across field to village on hillside; uphill access. Reinspected 2016.

VIOLAY
`27` | I8 | 42780 | N45°51.153' E004°21.306'

3 Custom; 3 Cont elec points (Not working)

➡ Place Giroud. Turn off D1 opp D49 turning to Villechenève, signed. Turn left into car park, the Aire is located at the far end.

ℹ Adj to panoramic view, but obstructed by conifers. Local commerce 100m, adj to D1. Inspected 2012.

ST JUST EN CHEVALET
`28` | I8 | 42430 | N45°54.846' E003°50.851'

15 in car park on D1/D53 junction Urba Flux; Elec €2; Water free

➡ D1. From Champoly follow D53 through town. At the end of the road turn left onto D1, sp 'Roanne'. Service Point immediately on right, signed.

ℹ Service Point and parking in centre adj to small town commerce. The parking is unlevel and used as local HGV parking at weekends, suggest `29` instead. Inspected 2014.

CHAMPOLY
`29` | I8 | 42430 | N45°51.346' E003°49.940'

20 Euro Relais Junior; €2

➡ Salle des Fêtes, off D24. From Noirétable on D53 turn off D53, sp 'Champoly'. As approach town turn right, sp 'Salle de Fêtes' and signed. Follow road and Service Point on left, signed. 3.5t parking adj to Service Point and large car park around Salle des Fêtes.

ℹ Aire at Salle des Fêtes in a peaceful location overlooking countryside. 300m from centre with local commerce. Inspected 2014.

Photo: Rod Poxon

SAINT MARCEL D'URFE
`30` | I8 | 42430 | N45°52.404' E003°53.015'

5 Euro Relais Mini; 4 CEE elec points in car park (Not working); 1 Cont elec point adj to sink and BBQ

➡ D24. From St Germain Leval turn off D1 onto D24, sp 'St Marcel d'Urfé'. Follow D24 to St Marcel d'Urfé, passing village boundary and following road to left. Then turn right, signed. Service Point on left before tennis courts, signed.

ℹ Pleasant Aire adj to municipal facilities which inc a BBQ and covered sink with Cont elec point. Large pond adj, no swimming. Local commerce 200m. Inspected 2016.

NOIRETABLE

| 31 | I8 | 42440 | | N45°48.369' E003°46.126' |

🖿 6 🛢 Flot Bleu Pacific; Token (FB); €3; Flot Bleu Elec; 1 Token/4hrs; 4 CEE elec points

➡ Rue du Plan d'Eau. Turn off D1089 onto D110, sp 'La Côte en Couzan', 'Plan d'Eau' and signed. Follow road for 800m then turn right into car park, sp 'Plan d'Eau' and signed. Follow road through car park and to left to Aire.

ℹ Landscaped Aire at small leisure lake, no view. Lake has swimming beach, popular fishing and lots of green space. Town commerce and gambling casino 1km. Inspected 2014.

CHALMAZEL

| 32 | D4 | 42920 | | N45°42.183' E003°51.184' |

🖿 8 🛢 Flot Bleu Pacific; Token; €2; 1 Token/4hrs; 4 CEE elec points

➡ Off D6. Exit Chalmazel on D6, sp 'Boën'. Turn right, sp 'Salle Polyvalente' and follow the road between the sports field and the cemetery. After passing the cemetery turn left into Aire.

ℹ Alt 841m. Pleasant landscaped Aire. 1st bays have view of château; bays furthest from entry may be difficult for longer vehicles, drive-in, back-out may be necessary. Narrow road up to village; quite steep 150m walk. Inspected 2016.

CHALMAZEL STATION

| 33 | I8 | 42920 | SKI | N45°40.658' E003°49.539' |

🖿 20; €12/24hrs 🛢 Custom; Inside barrier; 6 16amp Cont elec points

➡ D6.3. Follow D6 through Chalmazel. 3km south of Chalmazel turn left onto D6.3, sp 'Sauvain' and 'Station de Ski'. In 1.6km turn right, sp 'Station de Ski'. Aire on left as arrive at ski resort, signed. Enter through barrier.

ℹ Alt 1117m. Aire adj to small ski resort. Ski lift open for walkers/mountain bikers in summer; lots of trails in the area. Small resort commerce adj. www.loire.fr/jcms Inspected 2016.

BOEN SUR LIGNON

| 34 | J8 | 42130 | | N45°44.641' E004°00.142' |

🖿 100 🛢 Custom

➡ Blvd Louis Moisieux. From east on D1089 go straight over roundabout with D8, then turn left, sp 'Centre de Secours' and signed. Turn left after passing Hopital Local, sp 'Centre de secours' and signed. Aire in large car park on left, signed.

ℹ Aire located in large gravel car park, can accommodate any unit configuration and space likely. Adj to park with woodland walks. Town commerce and Château Boën 200m, open daily Mar-Nov €4.50pp. www.chateaumuseeboen.fr Inspected 2016.

PANISSIERES

| 35 | I8 | 42360 | | N45°47.292' E004°20.634' |

🖿 7; €6.20/night inc elec; Collected 🛢 Custom; 7 10amp Cont elec points

➡ Allée des Acacias. From north on D60 turn left on east side of town, sp 'Ferme Seigne'. Follow road for 400m and turn left again, sp 'Ferme Seigne'. Turn right, sp 'Relais Camping-Car'. Aire on right adj to building, signed.

ℹ There is an additional €3.20pp charge to use the toilet block with showers and laundry. Local commerce 600m. Inspected 2012.

MONTROTTIER

| 36 | I8 | 69770 | | N45°47.535' E004°27.786' |

🖿 5; Grass and hardstanding parking 🛢 Custom

➡ Chemin du Plan du Rieu. From north turn off D7 onto D24, sp 'Montrottier'. Turn left, signed, then 1st right. Service Point on right in 150m, signed: N45°47.676' E004°27.867'. From Service Point return to D24 and turn left. Take 2nd right, sp 'Aire de repos camping-car'. Follow road downhill to the sports facilities.

ℹ Aire in pleasant medieval town. Service Point on outskirts and accessible by any unit. Parking narrow on approach, turning subject to car park congestion; unsuitable for big unit configurations. Pleasant parking adj to open access green space and overlooking fishing pond. Inspected 2016.

BIBOST
| 37 | I8 | 69690 | | N45°47.699' E004°33.085' |

🚐5 🚰 Urba Flux; Customised; WC emptying under left flap in gravel; 2 16amp CEE elec points in Service Point (Open flap)

➡ D91. Turn off D389 onto D91, sp 'Bibost'. As enter village take 1st turning on left down slope to sports facilities, signed.

ℹ Pleasant stop in a small peaceful car park on outskirts of village. Village hall and limited sports facilities adj, some open access. WC locked at time of inspection. Local commerce 500m. Reinspected 2016.

MESSIMY
| 38 | J8 | 69510 | | N45°41.862' E004°40.656' |

🚐3 🚰 Custom; Push top of tap

➡ D75. From north on D311 turn left at roundabout, sp 'Parc d'Activities des Lats' and signed. Follow road straight on, then round to right. Service Point on left, signed: N45°42.098' E004°41.536'. For parking, go straight over roundabout staying on D311, sp 'Thurins'. Turn right onto D75, sp 'Messimy - Le Bourg' and signed. Turn right in 650m, sp 'Parking des Randonneurs' and signed. Designated parking on left.

ℹ Designated parking in car park 250m from local commerce, footpath adj. Various cycle and walking routes depart from here. Poss to park at Service Point in industrial estate. Inspected 2016.

ST LAURENT DE CHAMOUSSET
| 39 | I8 | 69930 | | N45°44.450' E004°27.774' |

🚐3; Max 48hrs; 7m bays 🚰 Custom; Push top of tap; Cont WC

➡ Places des Roches, D4. From east turn off D389 at roundabout onto D101, sp 'St Laurent de C'. In 4.7km go straight over roundabout onto D4, sp 'Tarare'. Follow D4 through town, then turn left, signed. Aire immediately on left, signed.

ℹ Designated parking opp Service Point. 250m from small town commerce. Inspected 2016.

ST GENIS L'ARGENTIERE
| 40 | I8 | 69610 | | N45°42.567' E004°29.180' |

🚐2; 9m bays; Gravel parking; Difficult access 🚰 Custom; Honesty box; Difficult access; Cont WC

➡ D25. Turn off D489 onto D25, sp 'St Genis l'Argentière'. Turn right off D25 into sports facilities, sp 'P' and signed. Service Point immediately on right. Designated motorhome parking at end of car park, signed.

ℹ 2 designated gravel bays with rural views on edge of sports facilities. Difficult access. Village with local commerce 500m. Inspected 2016.

CHAMBOST LONGESSAIGNE
| 41 | I8 | 69770 | | N45°46.354' E004°21.990' |

🚐2 🚰 Custom

➡ D101. Exit village on D101, sp 'Pannisières' and signed. Turn left, signed, 400m before 3.5m height restricted bridge. Aire on left, signed.

ℹ Aire located on edge of village adj to recycling point. Local commerce 200m. Inspected 2012.

VERRIERES EN FOREZ
| 42 | I8 | 42600 | | N45°34.251' E003°59.882' |

🚐5 🚰 Flot Bleu Pacific; Token (FB); Flot Bleu Elec; 1 Token/4hrs; 4 CEE elec points

➡ D44. North of village turn off D496 onto D44, sp 'Verrières en Forez' and signed. Follow D44 to village centre, then turn left by war memorial, sp 'Parking'. Aire 40m on left, directly behind church.

ℹ Alt 816m. Landscaped Aire on edge of small village with local commerce 150m. Inspected 2016.

MAROLS | 43 | I8 | 42560 | 🏃 | N45°28.662' E004°02.358'

🚐 10; Max 48hrs ⛺ Custom; 4 CEE elec points; Cont WC

➡ C2. Turn off D5 in village, signed. Follow road to square, then turn right past TO. Turn left, sp 'P', and follow road. Turn 2nd left, sp 'Stade' and signed. Aire 200m on left, signed, opp sports facilities.

ℹ Alt 874m. Aire at open access sports facilities with views over the valley. Visit the small, historic village, 600m, for 5 mins of fun; known as 'Artists Village' with various temporary and permanent exhibitions throughout. TO in main square. Inspected 2016.

GPS Co-ordinates for SatNav

The GPS Co-ordinates published in this guide were taken onsite by our inspectors. We consider them a valuable and unique asset and at the time of publishing have decided not to publish them as electronic files for use on navigation devices. You have permission to type in the co-ordinates of an Aire you intend to visit but not to store or share them. For the security of our copyright:

- **Do not compile them into lists**

- **Do not publish, share or reproduce them anywhere in any format**

ST SYMPHORIEN SUR COISE | 45 | I8 | 69590 | 🏛 | N45°38.026' E004°27.532'

🚐 5 ⛺ Custom; Token; 1 Cont elec point; All in/adj to WC

➡ D4. In town follow sp 'Lyon' to navigate one-way system onto D4 northbound. Aire in car park adj to D4, signed.

ℹ Aire located in popular local car park. D4 is a busy and noisy road during day. Pleasant town centre with town commerce 300m. Tokens from tabac/Mairie. Reinspected 2016.

ST MARTIN EN HAUT - Larajasse | 46 | I8 | 69850 | | N45°38.535' E004°32.111'

🚐 5; Grass and gravel parking ⛺ Custom; 3 taps: 1 by urinal, 1 under sign in ground with hose (WC rinse), 1 by door

➡ Off D311. Exit St Martin en Haut on D311 towards St Symphorien sur Coise. In 2.4km turn left off D311, then left into lane, sp 'Village Vacances l'Oree du Bois' and signed. Follow road 650m downhill, across stream, up the other side, then to left. Aire on left, signed.

ℹ Peaceful Aire in rural location adj to vacation village with café and pay per day trout and carp fishing lake. Voie Verte cycle route/walks adj. Reinspected 2016.

LUZINAY | 47 | J8 | 38200 | | N45°35.306' E004°57.200'

🚐 4 ⛺ Tap only

➡ Rue des Allobroges. Turn of D36, sp 'Luzinay - Centre'. Follow road through village and the Aire is in the central car park behind the weigh bridge, signed.

ℹ Designated parking in small village adj to well maintained green space and picnic area. Space likely. Inspected 2016.

ST GEORGES D'ESPERANCHE | 48 | J8 | 38790 | | N45°33.348' E005°04.504'

🚐 10 ⛺ Custom

➡ Chemin des Picarnus. From D75 exit roundabout onto D53, sp 'St Georges d'E. Centre'. Follow D53 4km into town, then follow sp 'St Georges Centre' over 2 roundabouts. At end of road follow signs through car park to Aire. Narrow access and 3.5t weight restriction on Aire.

ℹ Popular Aire with 5 spaces; poss to back onto/overhang grass. Green space adj. Small town commerce 150m. Reinspected 2016.

ST JEAN DE BOURNAY | 49 | J8 | 38440 | N45°30.060' E005°08.300'

🚐 50; No parking Mon 5am-2.30pm (Market) 🔧 Custom; Lift circular cover for drive over drain and circular cover by tap for WC disposal

➡ Rue Joseph Chavrier. From south follow D518, sp 'Vienne'. Turn right in front of Intermarché and drive through store car park past entrance and up 9t weight restricted hill. Turn right, then immediately left, signed. Turn right into car park and Service Point immediately on right, signed. All other routes are narrow and 3.5t weight restricted.

ℹ Parking in large car park just 200m from town centre. Supermarket 200m. Reinspected 2016.

VIENNE | 50 | J8 | 38200 | N45°32.320' E004°52.352'

🚐 6 🔧 Custom

➡ N7. From north on A7/E15 exit at Junction 9, sp 'Vienne'. Follow dual carriageway along the Rhône for 1.8km. At traffic lights turn left, sp 'St Symphorien'. Go under bridge and turn left at roundabout, sp 'St Symphorien' and signed. After 2 sets of traffic lights turn right into car park, signed. Take 3rd row on left to Aire.

ℹ Town commerce and bank adj, but Vienne centre 1.5km. Market in car park Fri noon-8pm. River Rhône nearby, access restricted by dual carriageway. Reinspected 2016.

REVENTIN VAUGRIS | 51 | J8 | 38121 | N45°28.094' E004°50.541'

🚐 4 🔧 Custom; At WC; No drive over drain; Tap not threaded

➡ Rue Mouret. Turn off N7 at roundabout onto D131, sp 'Reventin' and signed. In 450m turn left, sp 'Reventin' and signed. In the village turn left at end of road, signed, then turn right, signed. Aire on left adj to WC, signed.

ℹ Dead quiet Aire on edge of village; space likely. Village centre with local commerce 150m. Inspected 2016.

EYZIN PINET | 52 | J8 | 38780 | N45°28.481' E004°59.984'

🚐 8; Max 48hrs 🔧 Custom

➡ Rue du Stade, off D38. Turn off D502 onto D38, sp 'Eyzin-Pinet'. Follow D38 into village and the Aire is on the left, signed.

ℹ Pleasant, well located Aire adj to green space, but only 150m from village centre with local commerce. Inspected 2012.

VILLE SOUS ANJOU | 53 | J8 | 38150 | N45°21.759' E004°51.705'

🚐 5 🔧 Euro Relais Box; 1 CEE elec point

➡ Rue Emile Romanet. Approach from south on D131. At roundabout with gate houses turn right, sp 'Ville s/s Anjou - Centre' and signed. Turn right before church, then turn into the 3rd car park on left to Aire, signed.

ℹ Aire in long, narrow car park with longest bays at far end adj to playground. Poss for large motorhomes only when car park empty. Small rural village adj. Inspected 2016.

ST PRIM | 54 | J8 | 38370 | N45°26.665' E004°47.619'

🚐 3 🔧 Custom; Tap and WC emptying to right of drive over drain by disabled parking bay; Lift stainless steel cover; WC in lower level

➡ Rue du Village. Turn off N7 onto D37, sp 'St Prim'. Follow road uphill, then turn right onto D37, sp 'St Prim' and signed. In St Prim follow road to left, signed, then turn right in front of church into car park, sp 'P'. Drive up slope beside church to Aire. Drive over drain on left, parking to right on gravel.

ℹ Aire in centrally located car park in small village. Access around Aire/car park not possible for large vehicles particularly during school drop off/pick up. Local commerce 100m. Inspected 2016.

☑ Submit updates
• Amendments
• New Aires
• Not changed

Visit www.all-the-aires.co.uk/submissions.shtml
to upload your updates and photos.

! △ ⚠ ☼ 🏛 🏢 ⛲ 🍴 🎿 ⛵ 🚜 🏭
🌐 P 🚐 ⛵ 🛢 🎵 🚌 F ✿
♿ 🏛 🔼 E WC ♿ 🐾 🚌 F 🔲
SP 🌳 🛝 🧗 💧 🚶 🚲 🛶 🪂

Take at least 5 digital
photos showing
• Signs
• Service Point
• Parking
• Overview
• Amenities

FONTANES

| 56 | I8 | 42140 | | N45°32.808' E004°26.408' | SP 🌳 🛝 🧗 📷 🚶 🚲 🛶 🪂 |

🌐 P 🚐 ⛵ 🛢 🎵 🚌 F ✿ | ♿ 🏛 🔼 E WC ♿ 🐾 🚌 F 🔲
🚐 3 ⛽ Custom

➡ Hameau de Chantemerle. Approach Fontanes from south on D3. Turn left as enter village down a steep slope, signed. Follow road and Aire is on right, signed.

ℹ Aire adj to sports facilities in a peaceful rural village. History info panel and walking panel adj. Local shop selling regional produce 200m uphill. Reinspected 2013.

ST JEAN BONNEFONDS

| 57 | I8 | 42650 | 🏛 | N45°27.243' E004°26.821' | SP 🌳 🛝 🧗 📷 🚶 🚲 🛶 🪂 |

🌐 P 🚐 ⛵ 🛢 🎵 🚌 F ✿ | ♿ 🏛 🔼 E WC ♿ 🐾 🚌 F 🔲
🚐 Poss, but extremely unlevel ⛽ Euro Relais Mini; Token (ER)

➡ Off D32. From village centre follow D32, sp 'St Chamond'. Turn left as exit village into car park, signed. This is a steep and sharp turn that is unsuitable for vehicles that are underpowered or have low overhangs. Service Point at far side of car park, signed.

ℹ The parking angle is about 8 per cent so this is really just a Service Point which is difficult to access. Inspected 2012.

ST VICTOR SUR LOIRE ✳

| 58 | I8 | 42230 | ⚓ | N45°26.900' E004°15.387' | SP 🌳 🧗 🚶 🚲 🛶 🪂 |

🌐 P 🚐 ⛵ 🛢 🎵 🚌 F ✿ | ♿ 🏛 🔼 E WC ♿ 🐾 🚌 F 🔲
🚐 9; Max 72hrs; Landscaped bays ⛽ Flot Bleu Pacific; Free; Flot Bleu Elec; Token; €2.80; 1 Token/4hrs

➡ Lieu-Dit St Victor sur Loire. From St Etienne on D201 follow sp 'St Victor sur Loire'. At St Victor sur Loire follow sp 'P Base Nautique'. As approach the marina turn left, signed. Aire 50m on right.

ℹ Very popular Aire overlooking leisure lake. Medieval village adj. Updated 2016.

CHAMBLES

| 59 | I8 | 42170 | | N45°26.541' E004°14.338' | SP 🌳 🛝 🧗 📷 🚶 🚲 🛶 🪂 |

🌐 P 🚐 ⛵ 🛢 🎵 🚌 F ✿ | ♿ 🏛 🔼 E WC ♿ 🐾 🚌 F 🔲
🚐 3; 7m bays ⛽ Flot Bleu Pacific; Token (FB); Flot Bleu Elec; 1 Token/4hrs; 4 CEE elec points; Cont WC 50m, up steps

➡ Chemin de la Pive. Turn off D108 in Chambles. Aire in 200m in car park, signed.

ℹ Small, unlevel, landscaped Aire only suitable for small motorhomes. Bus stop adj. WC and tap at far end of car park. Village offers 5 mins of fun wandering and has tourist commerce. Inspected 2016.

ST BONNET LE CHATEAU

| 60 | I8 | 42380 | 🏢 | N45°25.587' E004°03.822' | SP 🌳 🛝 🧗 📷 🚶 🚲 🛶 🪂 |

🌐 P 🚐 ⛵ 🛢 🎵 🚌 F ✿ | ♿ 🏛 🔼 E WC ♿ 🐾 🚌 F 🔲
🚐 20 ⛽ Aire Services 7010

➡ Blvd du Haut Forez. Enter village on D498, then at north end of village turn off, sp 'Estivareilles'. Follow road to left, sp 'Estivareilles'. Turn left into 2nd fuel station entrance, then go immediately right into Aire, signed.

ℹ Alt 865m. Aire in large parking area adj to boules club and main town bypass; suffers road noise. Aire overlooked by 600-year-old gothic collegiate church, 650m. Inspected 2016.

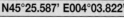

PLANFOY

61 | **I8** | **42660** | N45°22.467' E004°26.945'

🚐 10; Max 48hrs 🚰 Flot Bleu Pacific and Flot Bleu Elec x2; Token; €2.50; 1 Token/6hrs elec; 8 CEE elec points

➡ Chemin de la Ramée, off D1082. From Planfoy head south on D1082, sp 'Annonay'. 250m past the town boundary turn left, sp 'Le Vignolet', 'Stade' and signed (very small). Aire 200m uphill on left.

ℹ Alt 1019m. Popular, landscaped Aire in a peaceful location on edge of village. Overflow parking poss at adj picnic area. Signed walks, inc walk to lake. Old Service Point at adj stade has working tap and drain. Reinspected 2016.

LE BESSAT

62 | **I8** | **42660** | N45°22.117' E004°31.668'

🚐 6; Other undesignated parking 🚰 Flot Bleu Pacific; Token; €2.50; Flot Bleu Elec; 1 Token/4hrs; 4 CEE elec points

➡ Croix de Chaubouret, near D2/D8 junction. Turn off D8 at Croix de Chaubouret onto D2, sp 'La Valla en Gier'. Aire on left in 50m, signed.

ℹ Alt 1201m. Ski centre opp. In national park with walking trails. In a sheltered spot without views. Inspected 2012.

VANOSC

63 | **I9** | **07690** | N45°13.680' E004°33.622'

🚐 10 🚰 Custom; 16amp CEE elec (Turned off)

➡ D570. From Villevocance on D121 turn onto D570, sp 'Vanosc'. Follow sp 'Vanosc' for 2.5km. Turn right at entry to Vanosc by recycling bins, signed. Stay right and Service Point on left.

ℹ Pleasant Aire on edge of village adj to community hall (on upper terrace). 7 hedged hardstanding bays, additional parking and grass parking avail. Musée du Car, old bus museum, adj behind industrial buildings, signed: N45°13.684' E004°33.673'; open 3-6.30pm Wed-Sun. Inspected 2016.

BOULIEU LES ANNONAY

64 | **J8** | **07100** | N45°16.168' E004°40.188'

🚐 6; Other undesignated parking in area 🚰 Custom; Donation

➡ Chemin du Lavoir. Turn off D820 into Rue du Musard (3.5t restricted), opp D342 turning to St Clair. Take 1st left at 1914-1918 war memorial, sp 'Aire de Camping-cars'. Follow right fork, signed, then go round bend and turn right, signed. At end of road turn left into Aire.

ℹ Popular, pleasant, peaceful Aire with 6 hedged bays in an unrestricted car park. Adj to park with boules court, picnic benches and play area. Charming medieval centre 400m with local commerce. Reinspected 2016.

ST DESIRAT

65 | **J8** | **07340** | N45°15.891' E004°47.854'

🚐 10; Max 1 night 🚰 Aire Services 6000 and Aire Services Elec x2; Token (3/3); 1 Token/1hr elec; 8 CEE elec points; 1 Token free from wine cave, additional €2

➡ D291. At Champagne boundary turn off D86 onto D291, sp 'St Désirat' and 'Maison des Vins'. Cross railway track and Aire on right at wine cave under Rochevine sign on hillside, signed. May also be poss to park at Musée de l'Alambic, 1.3km: N45°15.515' E004°47.546'.

ℹ Aire in large car park at wine cave. Large shop with a big selection of local wine; open daily 9am-6.30pm, closed noon-2pm Mon-Fri. Musée de l'Alambic fruit distillery, 900m, worth a visit; see directions. www.cave-saint-desirat.com Reinspected 2016.

BEAUSEMBLANT

66 | **J8** | **26240** | N45°13.085' E004°49.980'

🚐 6; Max 48hrs 🚰 Custom

➡ Rue du 11 November 1918. Turn off N7 onto D122 at roundabout near La Croix des Mailles, sp 'Beausemblant'. Follow D122 for 2.3km to village and turn right at the car park, signed. Aire to the rear of the car park, signed.

ℹ Pleasant landscaped Aire just minutes from N7. Local commerce adj. Reinspected 2013.

HAUTERIVES

| 67 | J8 | 26390 | | N45°15.301' E005°01.849' | SP |

🚐 30; €6.80/24hrs 🚰 Custom; Inside barrier; €3/3hrs; Cont WC

➡ Off D187. Exit town to south on D538, sp 'Romans'. After passing Intermarché supermarket, but before town boundary, turn left onto D187, sp 'Complexe Sportif' and signed. Turn left by sports facilities, signed. Enter through barrier.

ℹ Popular Aire with large, gravel parking area adj to park and stream, no view. Palais Idéal 250m, very unique building that is worth a visit; open daily €6.50pp. www.facteurcheval.com Lafuma factory shop 13km in Anneyron (outdoor equipment specialists); open 7 days/week. Self-service laundry 650m at Intermarché. Reinspected 2016.

ST DONAT SUR L'HERBASSE

| 68 | J9 | 26260 | | N45°07.107' E004°58.980' | SP |

🚐 Poss; 2 unrestricted car parks 🚰 Custom; Tap on building, drain opp, lift cover to right of sign

➡ D574. Follow D67 to St Donat sur l'Herbasse. In town follow sp 'Charmes' past commerce. At roundabout turn right onto D574, sp 'P Place du 8 Mai 1945'. Turn left staying on D574, sp 'St Bardoux'. Service Point on left adj to Rugby Club Donatien, signed.

ℹ Service Point at sports facilities. Park either adj to boules court opp Service Point or in P Place du 8 Mai 1945, passed en route, market here Sat am. Town commerce 500m. Inspected 2016.

ST ROMAIN D'AY

| 69 | J9 | 07290 | | N45°09.855' E004°39.788' | SP |

🚐 4 designated bays; Max 7m 🚰 Flot Bleu Pacific; Token (FB); Flot Bleu Elec; 1 Token/4hrs

➡ D6. Turn off D578a onto D6, sp 'St Romain d'Ay'. Follow D6 to St Romain d'Ay, then turn left, sp 'Halle Marché' and signed. Aire immediately on left.

ℹ Small Aire adj to park, covered community space and public WC. Church has carillon and plays music on the hour. Local commerce 200m. Reinspected 2016.

HAVE YOU VISITED AN AIRE?

GPS co-ordinates in this guide are protected by copyright law

Visit www.all-the-aires.co.uk/submissions.shtml to upload your updates and photos.

ℹ Submit updates
• Amendments
• New Aires
• Not changed

Take at least 5 digital photos showing
• Signs
• Service Point
• Parking
• Overview
• Amenities

ARDOIX

| 71 | J9 | 07290 | | N45°11.322' E004°44.217' | SP |

🚐 3; Large motorhomes must reverse for overhang 🚰 Euro Relais Junior; Token (ER)

➡ Place du Grand Champ, D221. From Sarras follow sp 'Ardoix' onto D221, then a further 6.5km to village. As enter village turn left at the roundabout, signed. Aire on left, signed.

ℹ 3 landscaped hedged bays on edge of village offering rural views. Small park adj. Local commerce 300m. Reinspected 2016.

ANDANCE

| 72 | J9 | 07340 | | N45°14.418' E004°48.014' | |

🚐 2 🚰 None; WC 50m, at park; See 73

➡ Rue des Tours. In Andance turn off D86 into car park, sp 'P50' and 'SPAR'. Follow road 50m, past SPAR, to river and turn left. 2 designated spaces on right adj to river, signed. Other routes poss and preferred by GPS, but narrow.

ℹ 2 designated bays adj to and overlooking Rhone river. Mooring for large barge adj that will affect view if in use. Local commerce 50m opp park with WCs and play area. Inspected 2016.

GERVANS

`73` J9 26600 N45°06.546' E004°49.831'

3 at school; 5 at cemetery; Max 24hrs ♔ Custom; Donation

▶ Rue de l'École. From N7 turn onto D258, sp 'Gervans Village' and signed. Follow signs through village; narrow, but passable. Best parking 200m past Service Point, next to cemetery: N45°06.614' E004°49.700'.

ℹ Service Point and 1st parking area next to school. 2nd parking is pleasant and has valley views. Reinspected 2013.

LALOUVESC

`74` I9 07520 N45°07.176' E004°32.035'

3; Max 9m ♔ Euro Relais Junior; Token (ER); May-Sept

▶ D532. From Annonay on D578a enter Lalouvesc and turn right at end of road onto D532, sp 'Le Puy'. In 100m turn right, sp 'Camping' and signed. Service Point in 50m on right adj to WC: N45°07.277' E004°32.036'. For parking follow one-way road past Service Point back to D532 and turn left. Turn right in 50m opp Vival, sp 'P 120'. Follow road and designated parking on left, signed.

ℹ Alt 1088m. Peaceful designated parking overlooking park with playground and WC. Small town commerce 100m. Market Thurs 6am-1pm in car park by Service Point. Inspected 2016.

ST FELICIEN

`75` I9 07410 N45°05.078' E004°37.718'

6; Also see `76` ♔ Euro Relais Junior; €2

▶ Place de Québec. From south on D234 turn right just past Gendarmerie into Rue de la Pré Lacour, signed. Aire 30m on right behind Gendarmerie.

ℹ Aire in small underused car park with recycling bins. Village centre with local commerce 300m uphill. Reinspected 2016.

ARLEBOSC

`76` J9 07410 N45°02.204' E004°39.145'

15 ♔ Custom; WC down steps/slope turn right

▶ Place du Marché, off D578. From north on D578 turn right at village boundary, sp 'Place du Marché', 'Poste', 'Mairie' and signed. Service Point at old weighbridge, signed.

ℹ Pleasant Aire located in large car park with plenty of parking; space likely and can take any unit configuration. Pretty village with local commerce adj. Reinspected 2016.

COLOMBIER LE VIEUX

`77` J9 07410 N45°03.967' E004°41.641'

7; Grass and gravel parking; Also see `76` ♔ Custom

▶ D234. From east on D234 turn right just before church, signed. Service Point is immediately behind the church.

ℹ Hell's bells - every 15 mins all night! Small rural village with some other parking roadside, but away from church. Inspected 2014.

TOURNON SUR RHONE

`78` J9 07300 N45°04.403' E004°49.291'

10; €5/24hrs; Collected ♔ Euro Relais Junior

▶ Chemin de Labeaume, off D86. From south follow D86, sp 'Annonay'. Turn off D86 as exit town to north, sp 'P 240 Places' and signed. Aire at far side of car park, signed. Overflow parking: N45°03.829' E004°50.599'. Turn off D86 at river bridge roundabout onto 3.5t restricted road, sp 'Maison Pour Tous' and signed. Follow road along river and turn 1st right, signed. Parking in 1st car park on left, not signed.

ℹ Aire in corner of car park north of town adj to derelict industrial building. Reinspected 2014.

ST AGREVE
| 79 | I9 | 07320 | 🏛 | N45°00.618' E004°23.599' |

🚐 10 📍 Aire Services Plastic; Token (3/3); €2.50

➡ D120/Ave des Cevennes. From Lamastre on D533, go straight over roundabout onto D120a, sp 'Le Puy'. Turn 1st right, sp 'P Centre Ville'. Turn left, sp 'P'. Aire in car park on right, signed.

ℹ Alt 1061m. Aire in large car park tucked away behind the town centre. The town is agricultural and remote. Market Mon. Inspected 2014.

COLUMBIER LE JEUNE
| 80 | J9 | 07270 | | N45°00.676' E004°42.088' |

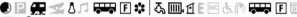

🚐 3 📍 Euro Relais Mini

➡ D209. Service Point located in village square/parking just off D209. Parking at tennis court: N45°00.677' E004°41.958' also adj to D209 as exit village towards Le Crestet.

ℹ Rural village with local commerce inc convenience store. Inspected 2012.

LAMASTRE
| 81 | I9 | 07270 | ⚓ | N44°59.221' E004°34.783' |

🚐 50 (Summer); 10 (Winter); Max 48hrs; No parking Wed/Sat 6am-1pm (Market) 📍 Raclet; Token; Euro Relais; Token/CC; €2.50
➡ Place Pradon. Approach on D534 from Tournon sur Rhône. After passing tourist train on right turn right, sp 'P Pradon' and 'Aire Pique Nique'. Follow road into large car park, Service Point is on the right. For summer parking continue through car park into additional parking, sp 'P 500' and signed: N44°59.242' E004°34.710'.
ℹ Aire located in large pleasant car park with parking on grass or gravel. Shallow crayfish river adj with slipway/access. Adj tourist train runs through the Gorges du Doux. http://trainardeche.fr Town commerce 150m. Reinspected 2016.

ST ROMAIN DE LERPS
| 82 | J9 | 07130 | | N44°58.785' E004°47.771' |

🚐 4; Park adj to road as terraced parking has narrow exit 📍 Euro Relais Junior; Token (2/1)

➡ D287. Adj to D287 at village boundary by rock terraced parking, signed.

ℹ Rural village with historic building. Parking poss but no designated bays. Inspected 2012.

CORNAS
| 83 | J9 | 07130 | 🏛 | N44°57.609' E004°50.840' |

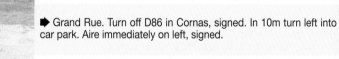

🚐 3 📍 Euro Relais Mini

➡ Grand Rue. Turn off D86 in Cornas, signed. In 10m turn left into car park. Aire immediately on left, signed.

ℹ Very convenient for D86, therefore some road noise. Walks on old roads through vines to rear of Aire. Updated 2015.

ROMANS SUR ISERE
| 84 | J9 | 26100 | 🏢 | N45°02.728' E005°03.531' |

🚐 4; Max 48hrs 📍 None

➡ Parking Gambetta P3, D532/Avenue Gambetta. Follow sp 'Marques Avenue', designated parking opp Marques Avenue building in centre of road.

ℹ Designated parking in popular car park with narrow exit. Main road either side of car park, cars may be parked in designated parking. Secondary school adj. Marques Avenue is an outlet centre with 70 shops open 10am-7pm Mon-Sat. Inspected 2014.

VERNOUX EN VIVARAIS
85 J9 07240 🏛 N44°54.149' E004°38.977'

🚐 4; Max 48hrs; 9m bays; Grass parking 🚰 Euro Relais Junior; Token (ER); €2

➡ D14. Enter town from north on D14. Turn left, sp 'Camping Municipal', then turn 1st left beside recycling bins. The Aire is on the right adj to D14 outside Camping Bois de Prat, signed.

ℹ Aire adj to pleasant municipal campsite. Parking is on grass in hedged bays just before campsite barrier. Small town commerce 500m. Reinspected 2016.

PRIVAS
86 J9 07000 🏛 N44°43.874' E004°35.585'

🚐 20 🚰 Urba Flux

➡ Route des Mines. Exit town on D7, sp 'Villeneuve-de-burg' and signed. Turn left by city wall, signed. Follow road through car park. Aire at bottom of hill, signed.

ℹ Aire in a very large gravel area with a remote/undesirable feel. Town 450m uphill. Inspected 2014.

LACHAMP RAPHAEL
87 I9 73130 N44°48.648' E004°17.317'

🚐 6 🚰 Aire Services Plastic; €2

➡ D122. From west on D122 Aire is on right at entrance to village, signed.

ℹ In beautiful area, a short distance from Gerbier de Jonc and Mt Mezenc. Local commerce in village. Visited 2013.

Info/photos: Alan Hoida

LE LAC D'ISSARLES
88 I9 07470 N44°49.183' E004°03.700'

🚐 15; €10.80/24hrs inc elec; Collected 🚰 Custom; 24 unmetered elec points; Shower in WC

➡ Le Village. Turn off N102 onto D110 at La Fayette, sp 'Coucouron'. In 5.2km turn left onto D16, sp 'Coucouron'. In 14km take 1st exit at roundabout onto D116, sp 'Le Lac d'Issarlès'. In 850m turn right down slope, signed. Aire on left at 2nd bend.

ℹ Alt 991m. Popular, open Aire in lake resort town. Local and tourist commerce 50m. Lake, no views, with swimming beach and pedalo hire, 500m. Reinspected 2016.

LA PALISSE
89 I9 07510 N44°46.667' E004°06.211'

🚐 6; €12/night; + €0.50 tax; Pay at barrier 🚰 Euro Relais Junior; 1 unmetered CEE and 4 6amp elec points; Inside barrier

➡ D160. From St Cirgues en Montagne take D160 north, sp 'Le Lac d'Issarlès'. Follow road for 3.4km. Once lake is visible the Aire is on the right, signed. Enter through PARKNIGHT barrier.

ℹ Alt 1032m. Small roadside commercial Aire overlooking La Palisse leisure lake. No shade. WC by Service Point. Lake 100m downhill. Inspected 2016.

Villerest

THUEYTS

91 | I9 | 07330 | N44°40.330' E004°13.208'

🚐 10; Max 24hrs 🚰 Aire Services 3000; €2

➡ Chemin de la Condamine. Turn off N102 in town, when signed, into Chemin de la Condamine, sp 'Belvedere'. Follow road for 350m, bends round to right. Aire at end at sports facilities.

ℹ Popular Aire adj to open access sports facilities with exercise circuit. Shaded and open parking. Village 500m with local commerce. Reinspected 2016.

MEYRAS

92 | I9 | 07380 | N44°40.768' E004°16.113'

🚐 20; €4/night Apr-Nov; Collected; Free Dec-Mar; Max 48hrs 🚰 Aire Services Plastic; €4; Slow water tap by sports building

➡ Chemin des Diligences, off D26. From N102 turn onto D26, sp 'Meyras' and signed. After 1.4km turn left, sp 'Meyras' and signed. Aire on right in 180m by stadium, signed.

ℹ Peaceful Aire with shaded and open parking adj to open access sports field. Village of Character, 200m, is pleasant for a wander and has local commerce and TO. Reinspected 2016.

CHOMERAC

93 | J9 | 07210 | N44°42.422' E004°39.483'

🚐 20 🚰 Custom

➡ Allée Réne Cassin. Approach on D2 from Privas. Turn off D2 onto D2c, sp 'Chomerac' and signed. Turn 2nd left into Rue de l'Europe, signed, then 1st right into Allée Réne Cassin, signed. Service Point on right adj to WC. Parking further on.

ℹ Large open parking that can accommodate any unit configuration. Boules court and open access sports field adj. Inspected 2016.

LALEVADE D'ARDECHE

94 | I9 | 07380 | N44°39.045' E004°19.428'

🚐 12 🚰 None

➡ Rue des Écoles. Turn off N102 in town to the Intermarché supermarket. Designated parking along left edge of Intermarché car park opp car wash, signed.

ℹ Designated parking at supermarket 150m from small town commerce. Self-service laundry adj, €8/18kg. River access 100m right out of car park. Convenient night halt. Inspected 2016.

NOTRE DAME DES NEIGES

95 | I9 | 07590 | N44°36.009' E003°56.168'

🚐 30; Max 48hrs 🚰 None; Cont WC adj to scout building; See **96**

➡ Lieu-dit Notre Dame des Neiges. In Bastide-Puylaurent follow D906 east, sp 'N.D. des Neiges'. At roundabout turn onto D4, sp 'N.D des Neiges'. In 1.3km turn left onto D4a, sp 'Abbaye de N.D. des Neiges'. In 700m go straight on alongside abbey, signed. Designated parking at far end, signed.

ℹ Alt 1076m. Popular designated parking in tranquil, tree-lined car park with picnic area; can accommodate any unit configuration. Car park owned by adj Trappist abbey, which offers overnight accommodation for hikers, pilgrims and scouts. Abbey not open to public, but church is. www.notredamedesneiges.com Inspected 2016.

LA BASTIDE

96 | I9 | 48250 | N44°35.479' E003°54.327'

🚐 4 🚰 Euro Relais Junior; €2

➡ Place de l'Église. In La Bastide turn off D906 onto D6, sp 'Mende'. Turn immediately left and drive beside church towards TO, sp 'Stade'. Aire on right between church and TO.

ℹ Alt 1016m. Aire in centre of village with local commerce and TO. Pleasant riverside picnic area downhill. Two lengthy walks pass through: Old pilgrimage of Régordane from Le Puy-en-Velay to St-Gilles and route of Robert Louis Stevenson from Le Monastier-sur-Gazeille to St-Jean-du-Gard. WiFi password available from TO. Inspected 2016.

GPS co-ordinates in this guide are protected by copyright law

Visit www.all-the-aires.co.uk/submissions.shtml
to upload your updates and photos.

Take at least 5 digital
photos showing
• Signs
• Service Point
• Parking
• Overview
• Amenities

| LARGENTIERE | 98 | I9 | 07110 | | N44°32.295' E004°17.502' |

🚐 5; Level parking adj to Service Point 🚽 Aire Services 3000; Adj to WC

➡ D5. Turn off D104 at roundabout onto D5, sp 'Largentière'. Follow D5 for 3.8km. 200m after 3.9m height restricted bridge turn left into car park adj to Carrefour Contact supermarket. Follow road to right and Service Point on left, signed.

☑ Aire in large, open municipal car park adj to main route. Supermarket and local commerce adj inc very good regional products shop. Reinspected 2016.

| VINEZAC | 99 | I9 | 07110 | | N44°32.363' E004°19.496' |

🚐 5; See info 🚽 Euro Relais Junior; €2

➡ Place du 19 Mars 1962, off D423. From D104 turn onto D423, sp 'Vinezac'. After 1.8km turn left, sp 'Mairie' and 'Stade'. Parking on right. Service Point in lower car park. Turn left before war memorial, then immediately right, sp 'Boul'. Go downhill and to right, signed. Service Point on right.

☑ Service Point in lower car park adj to graveyard; some parking opp. Top car park by Mairie has pleasant views and is landscaped with 5m bays, but some have large overhang. Nice 12-13th century church 120m. Reinspected 2016.

| ST PAUL LE JEUNE | 100 | I10 | 07460 | | N44°20.369' E004°09.199' |

🚐 10; Max 48hrs 🚽 Flot Bleu Océane; Token

➡ D901. Turn off D901 in town centre, signed. Service Point to right, parking to left in area set back from main route: N44°20.395' E004°09.194'.

☑ Pleasant well located Aire with parking set away from the main road but in the town centre. Small town commerce adj. Inspected 2014.

| BANNE | 101 | I10 | 07460 | T | N44°21.917' E004°09.417' |

🚐 10 🚽 Euro Relais Junior; Token (2/1); €3

➡ Parking at church, off D251. Turn off D901 north of St Paul le Jeune onto D251 (restricted to 8m length), sp 'Banne'. Follow road uphill for 3km. Turn right at church, then immediately right again, signed. Aire at base of church.

☑ Aire located at base of church, Hell's bells, on edge of village with panoramic views. Banne, adj, is a Petite Village of Character with a ruined fortification. Small market at church Monday am. Inspected 2014.

| LES VANS | 102 | I10 | 07140 | | N44°24.375' E004°08.224' |

🚐 20; 6pm-9.30am only; Max 1 night 🚽 None

➡ Chemin du Champvert. Enter town on D104a, then turn left at roundabout, sp 'Alès'. Follow road straight over next roundabout. At next roundabout turn left into centre commercial car park. Designated parking on right, signed.

☑ Designated parking in retail area which includes Carrefour supermarket. Only allowed to park in evening and for 1 night. Inspected 2016.

RUOMS
103 | I10 | 07120 | ▲ | N44°25.530' E004°19.915' | SP

🚐 15; €10.80/night Oct-Apr; €12/night May-Sept; +€1.60 tax; CC
🚰 Aire Services Plastic; 15 10amp CEE elec points; Inside barrier

▶ Adj Camping La Grand' Terre. Turn off D111 close to Ardèche river bridge, sp 'Camping La Grand' Terre'. Follow road to right and Aire on left before campsite barrier, signed. Enter through PARKNIGHT barrier.

ℹ️ Popular, landscaped commercial Aire 400m from Ardèche river. Public leisure space adj inc outdoor gym. Campsite adj, but can only use public facilities. Area popular with all nationalities and very busy in peak season. Inspected 2016.

ST ALBAN AURIOLLES
104 | I10 | 07120 | 🏛 | N44°25.628' E004°18.059' | SP

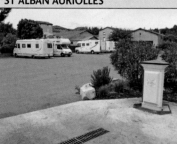

🚐 20 🚰 Euro Relais Junior; Token (ER); €3; 2 unmetered Cont elec points on wall

▶ Rue Marius Perbost, off D208. From D104 turn onto D208 on southern edge of Maison-Neuve village. After 7.3km, in St Alban Auriolles, turn left into Rue Marius Perbost, signed. Aire on left in 60m at rear of 'Foyer Rural'.

ℹ️ Aire in large car park 100m from small town commerce. Market Monday am. North of Gorges de l'Ardèche. Updated 2015.

VALLON PONT D'ARC
105 | I10 | 07150 | 🛶 | N44°24.291' E004°23.839' | SP

🚐 30; €6/24hrs; CC; Pay at Service Point 🚰 Euro Relais Tall; CC

▶ Chemin du Chastelas, off D390. From south on D290 turn onto D390 at roundabout, sp 'Centre Ville'. After 750m turn right into Chemin du Chastelas, signed. Aire on right in 80m, signed.

ℹ️ Aire 700m from Ardèche river and canoe hire. Tourist commerce 350m. Town located on D290 at start/end of Gorges de l'Ardèche. Reinspected 2014.

ORGNAC L'AVEN
106 | I10 | 07150 | T | N44°18.247' E004°25.964' | SP

🚐 5 🚰 Custom; Tap unsuitable for hose attachment

▶ D217. Turn off D901 onto D174, sp 'Orgnac l'Aven'. Follow sp 'Orgnac l'Aven'; D174 becomes D217. As enter town turn right adj to roadside parking, signed. In 10m at end of hedge turn left into Aire.

ℹ️ Pleasant Aire located in a small village. Boules court adj. Small town commerce 100m. Grotto and prehistory museum a 2km walk/cycle: N44°19.093' E004°24.757'. Inspected 2014.

ST REMEZE
107 | I10 | 07700 | 🏭 | N44°23.739' E004°30.375' | SP

🚐 6; Max 48hrs 🚰 Custom; Mar-Nov

▶ Les Chais du Vivarais, D362. Enter St Remèze on D4. In village turn onto D362 at roundabout, sp 'Larnas' and signed. Aire on left at edge of village at Cave Co-operative, signed.

ℹ️ Aire in Cave Co-operative parking, no purchase necessary. 450m walk to village with local commerce. D4 leads to Gorges de l'Ardèche. Updated 2015.

VILLENEUVE DE BERG
108 | I9 | 07170 | 🏃 | N44°33.750' E004°30.232' | SP

🚐 13 🚰 Custom; WC disposal on top

▶ Rue de la Gendarmerie. From Montelimar in east turn off N102 onto D902 at roundabout, sp 'Villeneuve de Berg'. 200m after passing the boundary sign turn right, sp 'Gendarmerie' and signed. At end of road turn left behind Gendarmerie. Turn right at cemetery, signed. Follow road to Aire behind sports facilities.

ℹ️ Popular Aire that can accommodate any unit configuration. Bays to left have panoramic countryside views. Bays to right overlook sports facilities. Town commerce 500m. Inspected 2016.

ALBA LA ROMAINE

| 109 | I9 | 07400 | T | N44°33.195' E004°35.832' |

30; €4/night; Collected — Euro Relais Junior

➤ Turn off D107 onto D263, sp 'Alba la Romaine'. Turn off D263, sp 'P Obligataire' and signed. Aire in the large village car park.

ℹ Aire located in the obligatory car park adj to Beau Village. Village is a labyrinth of streets built of chequered black basalt and white limestone with a ruined château and remains of Roman city. Tourist and small town commerce 200m. Updated 2015.

AUBIGNAS ✶

| 110 | J9 | 07400 | | N44°35.236' E004°37.899' |

10; €3 minimum donation — Euro Relais Mini

➤ D363. From N102 turn onto D363, sp 'Aubignas'. After 550m turn left to stay on D363. Stay on D363 following sp 'Aubignas' and signed. Then take sharp left before village into Aire, signed. Service Point behind small building.

ℹ Peaceful Aire in car park with panoramic views of village and countryside, but can be windy. Fortified village 300m. Updated 2016.

LE TEIL

| 111 | J9 | 07400 | | N44°33.079' E004°41.370' |

10; Max 72hrs — Custom

➤ Allée Paul Avon, off N102. Exit Le Teil to east on N102, sp 'Montelimar'. Just before river bridge turn right, signed. At Stop junction go straight on. Then in 50m turn left into what looks like the car park for Restaurant des Allées. Aire behind and to the left of the restaurant.

ℹ Small Aire in former municipal campsite adj to river Rhône, no view due to flood protection bank. Some road noise, but only 550m from town commerce. Reinspected 2016.

MONTELIMAR

| 112 | J9 | 26200 | | N44°33.907' E004°45.407' |

30; Max 48hrs; Grass parking — Urba Flux Tall

➤ Chemin du Bois de Laud. In town follow sp 'Valance', then 'Aire de Camping-Car'. Follow signs past E.Leclerc supermarket and fuel station, then continue uphill. Turn right, sp 'Aire de Camping-Car'. Aire down slope.

ℹ Pleasant Aire. Supermarket 200m. Walled city and town centre with small town commerce 600m. Updated 2016.

VIVIERS

| 113 | J9 | 07220 | T | N44°28.929' E004°40.765' |

26; €6.50/night; Collected; Apr-Oct; Max 7 nights — Custom; Apr-Oct; Cold water showers; 26 unmetered elec points

➤ Chemin du Valpeyrouse, in former campsite. Follow D86 through town towards Aubenas, signed. Turn left off D86, sp 'Centre Culturel' and signed. Aire on left in 350m, signed. Hedges restrict access, large motorhomes can only fit on bays nearest entrance or in entrance car park.

ℹ Former municipal campsite with 26 hedged bays, toilet block with cold water showers/sinks. Town commerce and tourist attractions 800m. Day parking adj to TO: N44°28.802' E004°41.537'. Reinspected 2014.

LARNAS

| 114 | I10 | 07220 | | N44°26.929' E004°35.874' |

5 — Euro Relais Junior

➤ D262. The Aire is behind the Mairie on left as enter village from St Remeze. DO NOT take D262 from St Montan to Larnas, as St Montan bans motorhomes due to narrow single file centre.

ℹ Aire in village parking area with pleasant view over vines. Car park also recycling point and municipal store. TO adj. Interesting church 100m. Inspected 2014.

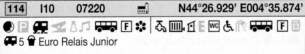

DONZERE
115   J10   26290   N44°26.452' E004°43.132'

🚐 20 🛒 Custom; No drive over drain

➡ N7. Exit N7 at roundabout onto D541, sp 'Donzere' and 'Aire de Repos'. Turn immediately right, sp 'Aire de Repos'. Follow caravan symbol to right for Service Point, signed.

ℹ Very noisy roadside lay-by adj to busy N7. Popular with motorhomers, but this is a busy route so use extra security. Reinspected 2016.

BOURG ST ANDEOL
116   J10   07700   N44°22.527' E004°38.620'

🚐 7 🛒 Aire Services 3000; 2 unmetered CEE elec points

➡ Chemin de la Barrière. Approach from Vallon Pont d'Arc in west. Turn left, sp 'P Gare Gratuit' and 'Parking Gratuit 151 places'. Drive past LIDL and the train station and Aire on left, signed.

ℹ In car park with no designated motorhome parking and only suitable parking closest to railway line. Train track and old warehouse adj. LIDL 100m, town square with commerce leading to medieval centre 300m. Gorges de l'Ardèche 10km. Inspected 2016.

CLANSAYES
117   J10   26130   N44°22.161' E004°47.807'

🚐 40; €10/night (Until 11am) inc service; Collected 🛒 Custom; 5amp elec €4

➡ Aire de Toronne. From St Paul-Trois-Châteaux on D133 turn onto D571, sp 'Clansayes'. Aire on right, signed.

ℹ Commercial Aire in a nice peaceful spot. Swimming pool, €4pp, showers and BBQ on site. Rural views. Updated 2017.

ST PAUL TROIS CHATEAUX
118   J10   26130   N44°20.832' E004°46.225'

🚐 20; Max 24hrs; 5m car bay plus overhang; Max 9m 🛒 Custom

➡ Parking Chausy, Lieu-Dit le Courreau. Turn off D59 at roundabout, sp 'P Chausy 120 places' and 'Stade Municipal'. Pass football pitch, then turn 1st left and then left again into car park. Service Point at far end of car park, signed.

ℹ Popular car park and parking with best overhang adj to pleasant green park. Car park oversubscribed Tues am, market adj. TO and police adj, historic centre 150m. Reinspected 2016.

ROCHEGUDE
119   J10   26790   N44°14.828' E004°49.819'

🚐 5; Max 6m 🛒 Euro Relais Mini

➡ D817. Turn off D8 at roundabout, signed. Turn left onto D817 in village centre, sp 'Lagarde-Paréol'. Aire immediately on right.

ℹ Small roadside Service Point and parking area under trees. Medieval town dominated by château. Reinspected 2016.

SUZE LA ROUSSE
120   J10   26790   N44°17.385' E004°50.887'

🚐 1; See info 🛒 Custom

➡ Impasse de la Zone Artisanale. Exit town on D94, sp 'Nyons'. At edge of village turn left onto D251, sp 'Bouchet'. In 200m turn right, signed. Service Point immediately on right.

ℹ 1 narrow space adj to Service Point. Overnight parking at Cave Co-operative on D94 towards Bollène is ideal for visiting impressive fortified town dominated by château: N44°17.283' E004°50.276'. Reinspected 2016.

Cave Co-operative

ST RESTITUT

121 | J10 | 26130 | N44°19.877' E004°47.455'

5 Custom

➡ Off D859. Turn off D59 onto D859 at roundabout, sp 'St Restitut'. After passing village boundary sign on left, turn right at roundabout, sp 'Centre Ville', then immediately left into car park, signed. Service Point at far end of car park.

ℹ Aire on far side of car park; only likely to be busy weekends and holidays. Local commerce and hilltop village adj. Large caves open to public, follow sp 'Caves Cathèdrale'. Reinspected 2016.

Banne

VISAN

123 | J10 | 84820 | N44°20.905' E004°58.228'

20; Max 48hrs Custom; Elec €3; 28 unmetered elec points; Pay at shop

➡ Domaine des Lauribert. Turn off D976, sp 'Domaine des Lauribert' and signed. Follow lane through vines for 1.2km, then turn right, sp 'Domaine des Lauribert' and signed. Aire on right, signed.

ℹ Aire on 3 terraces, shade on one. Daily 6.30pm wine tasting, no obligation to buy. Good views of vineyards and hills. www.lauribert.com Visited 2016.

Info/Photos: Ken & Jean Fowler

MARSANNE

124 | J9 | 26740 | N44°38.762' E004°52.317'

7; Max 48hrs Custom

➡ D57. Exit village to north on D57, sp 'Mirmande'. Aire on right before village boundary sign, signed.

ℹ Small Aire with some reinforced grass parking on edge of village opp school and adj to Aire Naturelle campsite. Can be busy at school drop off/pick up times; used by families for adj play area and exercise trail. Historic centre with ruined castle and local commerce 100m. Reinspected 2016.

SAOU

125 | J9 | 26400 | N44°38.769' E005°03.649'

6; Max 24hrs; Max 9m Custom; WC opp

➡ D538. Turn off D538, sp 'Parking Obligatoire'. Aire on right before height barrier, signed. Long motorhomes subject to other parked motorhomes.

ℹ Small, landscaped Aire on edge of old town with quaint narrow streets. 2500-acre Forest of Saou perched on adj clifftop. 12km long, but just 2km wide; only one road in and out. Inspected 2016.

PUY ST MARTIN

126 | J9 | 26450 | N44°37.624' E004°58.507'

20; €3/day; Honesty box; Max 48hrs; Grass parking Custom; €3; Honesty box; Cont WC by Mairie

➡ Impasse de Fleurs. Turn off D6 in village onto D107, sp 'Manas', 'Mairie' and signed. Turn left at crossroads into Rue de Lavoir, signed. Turn right, signed, then left into Aire.

ℹ Popular, pleasant Aire at former municipal campsite turned motorhome Aire. Village with local commerce and supermarket 100m. Reinspected 2016.

CHAROLS
| 127 | J9 | 26450 | | N44°35.498' E004°57.259' | SP |

🚐 10; 3 long bays closest to Service Point 🔧 Custom; 1 CEE elec point (Not working)

➡ Place Carrovolis, adj to D128. At roundabout turn off D9 onto D128, sp 'Pont du Barret'. In 10m turn right into the adj car park. Aire is at the far end of the car park.

ℹ Aire in car park; popular with motorhomers on hot days as partially shaded by deciduous trees. Small park adj. Convenience store adj, additional local commerce 100m. Reinspected 2016.

GRANE
| 128 | J9 | 26400 | | N44°45.338' E004°52.061' | SP |

🚐 10; €2pp/night; Free 1st night for France Passion; Collected; Grass parking 🔧 None; Water €1

➡ Domaine Distaise, off D104. From Loriol sur Drôme on D104 travel towards Crest/Grane for 3km. The private Aire is on the left down long drive, signed.

ℹ Private Aire at fruit and pig farm that also has gîtes. Parking to front on grass, some distant road noise. Fruit, meat, bread and meals avail. Owner's dogs roam free. Updated 2016.

CREST
| 129 | J9 | 26400 | | N44°43.554' E005°01.241' | SP |

🚐 25; €5/24hrs; €7/24hrs inc service; Collected 🔧 Aire Services 3000; CC; €5

➡ D538. From west on D104 turn left at traffic lights onto D538, sp 'Centre Ville'. After 600m take 1st exit at roundabout into car park. Long motorhome spaces along right-hand edge of car park, adj to boules club. Service Point across car park. Car park has 3.5t weight restriction.

ℹ Aire in popular town car park. Historic town on river Drôme with steep cobbled lanes. Laundrette 400m in Rue Général Berlier. WiFi avail. Reinspected 2016.

SAILLANS
| 130 | J9 | 26340 | | N44°41.729' E005°11.633' | SP |

🚐 30; €3; Max 24hrs; No parking 8pm-6am during periods of flooding 🔧 Aire Services 3000; CC; €5

➡ Gîte Rural. From Crest follow D93 to Saillans. At the roundabout turn left, sp 'Centre Ville' and signed. Turn before town, signed. Follow road for 1km; single track in places.

ℹ Popular Aire adj to river Drôme, no views due to defensive bank. Canoe hire in season. Riverside walk. Small town commerce 300m. Reinspected 2016.

HAVE YOU VISITED AN AIRE?

GPS co-ordinates in this guide are protected by copyright law

Visit www.all-the-aires.co.uk/submissions.shtml
to upload your updates and photos.

ℹ Submit updates
• Amendments
• New Aires
• Not changed

Take at least 5 digital photos showing
• Signs
• Service Point
• Parking
• Overview
• Amenities

MONTBRISON SUR LEZ
| 132 | J10 | 26770 | | N44°25.669' E005°01.466' | SP |

🚐 Poss at Service Point; 6 at Mairie 🔧 Euro Relais Mini; Token (2/1); €2; Water tap in entrance; 1 Cont elec point on building; At Mairie: 4 unmetered CEE elec points; Water tap in hedge near fountain

➡ Hameau de Crochamp. Turn off D538 south of Montbrison, sp 'Stade'. Follow road to left and Aire on left in 600m at sports field, signed. Additional parking in centre: N44°26.187' E005°01.052'. From Service Point return to D538 and turn left. In 1km turn left onto D24, signed. Parking on right at Mairie, signed.

ℹ Open, rural Aire adj to open access sports field. Lavender field adj, wine grown opp. Space likely. Additional parking in small pleasant hamlet adj to Mairie and local commerce. Reinspected 2016.

NOVEZAN
133 | J10 | 26110 | ⛺ | N44°24.468' E005°04.777'

🚐 8; €7/night inc service and showers; Pets and extra people at additional charges 🔧 Custom; €4; Report to reception; Apr-Sept

▶ Les Barroux. Turn off D538, sp 'Camping Les Terrasses Provençales'. Follow road uphill 300m. Aire on left outside Camping Les Terraces Provençales, signed.

ℹ Landscaped, open, designated Aire outside remote seasonal campsite. www.lesterrassesprovencales.com Inspected 2016.

NYONS
134 | J10 | 26110 | 🏃 | N44°21.489' E005°08.315'

🚐 15; €2/30 mins; €10/24hrs; CC; Max 48hrs 🔧 Flot Bleu Pacific (Green); Inside barrier

▶ Promenade de la Digue. Turn off at D538/D94 roundabout, sp 'Nyons' and 3.5t weight restricted. Cross river bridge and turn left at roundabout, signed. In 220m turn right, signed. Enter through Flot Bleu Park barrier.

ℹ Popular Aire adj to busy outdoor swimming pool. Limited dappled shade. River across road. Market Thurs; no parking on access road all day. Town commerce 300m. Reinspected 2016.

MIRABEL AUX BARONNIES
135 | J10 | 26110 | 🏛 | (A) N44°25.669' E005°01.466'

🚐 (A) 8; (B) 10; Donation; Max 48hrs 🔧 (A) Custom; (B) None

▶ (A) Chemin de Grottes. Turn off D538 opp D160 turning, sp 'Vieux Village'. After 200m turn left and Aire is immediately ahead, signed. (B) N44°18.863' E005°05.785': Turn off D538 onto D160, sp 'Villedieu'. Turn 1st right and drive past play area to parking on right, signed.

ℹ (A) Popular landscaped Aire part shaded by deciduous trees. On edge of small village in wine producing area, lots of wine tasting opportunities. Adj bells noisy during day, silent at night. (B) Additional parking adj to picnic and children's play area. Town 200m. Reinspected 2016.

(A)

(B)

MONTBRUN LES BAINS
136 | J10 | 26570 | 🏨 | N44°10.343' E005°26.304'

🚐 15 🔧 Flot Bleu Pacific; €2

▶ Lioron. Service Point near town centre on D542 to right of U Express store entrance: N44°10.445' E005°26.441'. For parking, exit store to right. In 350m turn right onto D189, sp 'Ferrassieres' and signed. In 350m turn right, signed. In 300m turn right, signed, then in 100m turn left; do not cross 2t weight restricted bridge. Aire 350m on right, signed.

ℹ Peaceful designated parking in pleasant lay-by with rural views just 300m from town across historic bridge. Option of open or shaded parking. Pleasant historic town also has thermal water. Inspected 2016.

DIE
137 | J9 | 26150 | 🏨 | N44°45.060' E005°22.391'

🚐 20; €5/24hrs Oct-Apr; €9/24hrs May-Sept; Collected 🔧 Custom

▶ Car park 'Aire de Meyrosse' on D238. From south on D93 take 2nd exit at roundabout onto D238. After 600m turn right into car park. Aire straight ahead. Service Point adj to toilet block in main car park.

ℹ Busy on Wed/Sat am (market). TO and historic town with local commerce adj. Reinspected 2016.

CHICHILIANNE
138 | J9 | 38930 | R | N44°48.734' E005°34.499'

🚐 15; Grass parking 🔧 Aire Services Plastic; Token; €3

▶ D7b. Turn off D1075 onto D7, sp 'Chichilianne'. Follow road for 3.5km, then turn right onto D7b, sp 'Les Oches' and 'Chichilianne'. Drive through Les Oches and Aire on right as enter Chichilianne, signed.

ℹ Alt 986m. Popular parking with mountain views; grass parking between trees or in the open. Charming village adj, tourist commerce and boulangerie 50m. Inspected 2016.

TREFFORT

139 K9 38650 ⚓ N44°54.434' E005°40.281' `SP` 🌳 ⛺ 🚶 📷 🧍 🚴 🎣 ⛵

🚐 130; 1st hr free; €10/24hrs; CC/€; Pay at machine near Service Point
🚰 Euro Relais Junior; Inside barrier; 2 unmetered CEE elec points

➡ Le Lac. From north follow D110b towards Treffort, sp 'Treffort' and 'Le Lac'. Go past the turning to Treffort onto D110g, sp 'Le Lac'. In 1.7km turn left, sp 'Base Touristique' and signed. Follow road to barriered car park. After barrier follow road straight on past cafés and Service Point on left: N44°54.342' E005°40.305'.

ℹ Aire at leisure lake, parking is lakeside but trees obscure view. Green space and picnic tables adj. Tourist commerce. Multiple boating options and walking, inc suspension bridges. www.lac-monteynard.com Inspected 2016.

GRESSE EN VERCORS

140 J9 38650 SKI 🎿 N44°53.506' E005°32.850' `SP` 🌳 ⛺ 🏃 📷 🧍 🚴 🤸 🎿

🚐 5; Max 24hrs 🚰 Custom 500m; No tap

➡ D8d. In Gresse en Vercors centre turn off D8a onto D8d, sp 'Station'. Turn left at roundabout, sp 'Station'. Service Point in 1km opp commerce: N44°53.638' E005°32.976'. Parking 500m, past ski lifts, at end of road turn around, signed.

ℹ Alt 1243m. Small Aire at small ski resort with views of slopes. Tourist/ski commerce 150m. Ski lifts adj, including chair and drag. Signed walks from Aire. Market Mon in village. Inspected 2016.

VASSIEUX EN VERCORS

Photo: Carol Weaver

Photo: Jean & Ken Fowler

141 J9 26420 🏛 N44°53.857' E005°22.210' `SP` 🌳 ⛺ 🏃 📷 🧍 🚴 🎣 ⛵

🚐 30 🚰 Custom; €3; Pay at La Poste

➡ D76. From Die follow D518 for 21km over very scenic Col de Rousset (winding road with hairpins but wide enough). Fork left onto D76 and follow road for 8km. Aire on right in very large, open area just north of village.

ℹ Alt 1040m. On plateau with excellent views of mountains. Nice village with local commerce 300m. Memorial de Resistance 800m. Updated 2016.

LA CHAPELLE EN VERCORS

Info/Photos: Colin Simcox

142 J9 26420 🏛 N44°58.110' E005°24.999' `SP` 🌳 ⛺ 🏃 📷 🧍 🚴 🤸 🎿

🚐 5; Max 24hrs 🚰 Flot Bleu Océane; Token (FB); €3

➡ Rue de la Salle des Fêtes. Turn off D518 in centre, sp 'WC publics'. Turn left after passing church, opp Hôtel de Ville, then immediately turn right. Turn 1st right and Aire on right behind Hôtel de Ville, signed.

ℹ Aire in thriving town with open air swimming pool, open in the summer. Small town commerce 100m. Good walking in surrounding area. Visited 2016.

CORRENCON EN VERCORS

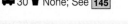

143 J9 38250 SKI N45°01.273' E005°31.719' `SP` 🌳 ⛺ 🏃 📷 🧍 🚴 🤸 🎿

🚐 30 🚰 None; See **145**

➡ D215. From Corrençon en Vercors follow sp 'Le Clos de la Balme'. Parking allowed at Clos de la Balme, which is the parking at the end of the road, not signed.

ℹ Alt 1228m. Unrestricted parking at ski lifts. In summer the parking is unattractive, but space likely and can take any unit configuration. Pony/miniature horse rides and small resort commerce at base of 2 chairlifts, 400m. Inspected 2016.

VILLARD DE LANS

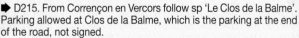

144 J9 38250 SKI N45°04.000' E005°33.346' `SP` 🌳 ⛺ 🏃 📷 🧍 🚴 🤸 🎿

🚐 20; Max 48hrs; See info 🚰 Water tap by rock

➡ Chemin des Bartavelles. From Lans en Vercors on D531 go to right onto D215, sp 'Villard - Cote 2000' and 'P Camping-Cars'; other motorhome sign is for campsite. At roundabout turn left onto D215a, sp 'Villard Cote 2000' and 'P Camping-Cars'. At next roundabout turn left back onto D215, sp 'Villard Centre'. Follow road uphill, then turn right, sp 'Office du Tourisme' and signed. Aire 300m on right behind rock, signed.

ℹ Alt 1026m. Designated parking on edge of winter sports resort. Helicopter landing area adj. Toboggan run nearby. Also poss to park in P3 at Côte 2000 ski station: N45°02.846' E005°33.411'. Alt 1139m; near ski lifts and cable car. Inspected 2016.

ST JEAN EN ROYANS
145 J9 26190 N45°01.200' E005°17.425'

🚐 6 🛒 Custom

➡ Place du Saut de l'Ane, Rue de la Gare. As approach from north on D76 go straight over roundabout, signed. In 650m turn right into Rue de la Gare. Aire 150m on left, signed.

ℹ️ Open, tranquil Aire away from the main roads, but just 100m from small town commerce. Supermarket 400m downhill. Reinspected 2016.

ST MARCELLIN
146 J9 38160 N45°09.282' E005°19.073'

🚐 15; Popular town parking adj 🛒 Custom; Cont WC

➡ P Champ de Mars. Enter town from east on D1092. At roundabout turn onto D518, sp 'St Vérand'. Go straight on at 1st traffic lights, then in 100m turn right into parking, sp 'P Champ de Mars'. For Service Point carry on straight and turn right at 2nd traffic lights. Service Point 150m on right by recycling bins at corner of square, signed: N45°09.316' E005°19.160'.

ℹ️ Aire adj to multiple parking options in town centre. Small town commerce adj. Market in square Sat 5am-2pm. Germanic maypole in town. Miniature statue of liberty in Roybon, 17km. Reinspected 2016.

ST ANTOINE L'ABBAYE
147 J8 38160 T N45°10.387' E005°13.070'

🚐 12 🛒 Urba Flux Tall; €2; Cont WC

➡ Rue des Terreaux, off D27. In centre of village turn off D27 into Rue des Terreaux, sp 'P'. Turn 1st left into large gravel car park; Service Point on left.

ℹ️ Aire in large car park with parking on several terraces, offering open or shaded parking. Lovely ancient Beau Village with abbey adj. Several walks around area; TO has leaflet. Inspected 2016.

SASSENAGE
148 J9 38360 N45°12.810' E005°40.129'

🚐 8 grass bays; 9 hardstanding; Max 48hrs; Max 3.5t 🛒 Depagne Mini

➡ Rue Pierre de Coubertin. From north on D1532 follow sp 'Gendarmerie' and signed. Follow road past gendarmerie and around to right, then at roundabout turn left, signed. Turn left at Stop junction, signed. Follow road past lake and to right. Service Point immediately on right, parking on left, signed.

ℹ️ Popular Aire surrounded by municipal sports facilities and leisure lake, no views. Designated cycle paths adj. Laundrette and small town commerce by gendarmerie 900m. Château de Sassenage in town open 1st Sunday of month at 10.30am, €10pp. www.chateau-de-sassenage.com. Inspected 2016.

LANS EN VERCORS
149 J9 38250 SKI N45°07.456' E005°35.465'

🚐 20 🛒 Custom; Very slow water

➡ Route de St Donat. Turn off D531 at roundabout onto D106, sp 'Lans en Vercors' and 'Domaine Skiable'. Drive through the village, then on the other side turn right, sp 'Massif de l'Aigle' and signed. Aire is in the large car park at the base of the ski lifts, signed.

ℹ️ Alt 1000m. Aire in large open car park at base of small drag lift. Seasonal café adj. Ski activity in winter, parasailing and walking in summer. Local resort commerce 400m. Pleasant drive through gorges to Engins. Inspected 2016.

PONT EN ROYANS
150 J9 38680 N45°03.790' E005°20.173'

🚐 €5/night inc elec; Collected; Apr-Oct 🛒 Custom

➡ La Plage. Turn off D518 by sports field, opp cemetery, sp 'Camping Municipal'. Aire 130m at former municipal campsite, signed. D531 is a stunning drive; can be narrow and 3.5m height restriction in places.

ℹ️ Former campsite turned Aire on the bank of the river Bourne; walk 800m along the quay to the town's famous suspended houses. TO 600m. Beautiful Gorge of the Bourne 16km. Good walking in surrounding area. Visited 2016.

Info/Photos: Colin Simcox

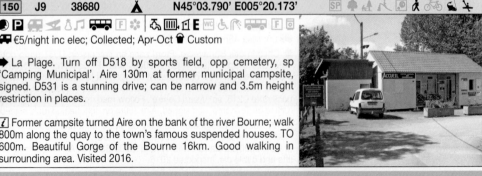

ALPE DU GRAND SERRE
151 K9 38350 SKI N45°01.719' E005°51.433'

🚐 12; €5/night; + €0.55pp tax; Collected 🚽 Custom (Under construction); 12 10amp CEE elec points

➡ D114. Adj to D114 on right as exit village towards Grenoble. Aire in car park adj to tennis courts. WC/shower by radio mast, parking at rear backing onto grass. Easier approach from La Valette in south. From D1091 there are steep hairpin bends that take you up/down 1000m in altitude, 2nd gear hill.

ℹ Alt 1363m. Aire on edge of small ski resort with resort commerce. Parking backs onto open access sports facilities. Children's play area adj. Car park being renovated with new Service Point being added at time of inspection. Inspected 2016.

CORPS
152 K9 38970 🏛 **(A) N44°49.096' E005°56.963'**

🚐 **(A)** 10; **(B)** 5 🚽 **(A)** Tap on stone wall, under foliage; **(B)** None

➡ 2 parking areas: **(A)** Rue St Eloy. Follow N85 through Corps. Opp Hotel le Napoleon turn onto D212c, sp 'Tennis' and signed. Follow road uphill and parking on left, which is virtually a hairpin bend, signed. **(B)** N44°49.088' E005°56.718': Rue de la Fontaine. Turn off N85 onto D357, sp 'Super Dévoluy'. Turn left into car park, signed. Easier to access than **(A)**.

ℹ Alt 961m. **(A)** Designated parking in sloping car park overlooking town. Walks from car park. **(B)** Level car park, also bus and HGV parking, with BBQ area. Small town commerce 300m downhill from **(A)** or uphill from **(B)**. Town on Route Napoleon. Inspected 2016.

(A)
(B)

LES DEUX ALPES
153 K9 38860 SKI N45°01.433' E006°07.287'

🚐 40; €8/24hrs; €12 inc CEE elec (compulsory Dec-Apr); Pay at machine; Max 7 days 🚽 Urba Flux Tall; Outside Aire, adj to WC

➡ Parking de la Passerelle, D213. Turn off D1091 onto D213 by dam, sp 'Les Deux Alpes'. Follow D213 uphill following sp 'Les Deux Alpes'. Aire on left after bridge just before entering resort, signed.

ℹ Alt 1592m. Popular commercial Aire on outskirts of ski resort. Ski and tourist commerce 500m uphill. Ice skating rink, ski lifts and glacial skiing open all year; free shuttle bus in summer. Area very popular with skiers, snowboarders and mountain bikers. Inspected 2016.

HAVE YOU VISITED AN AIRE?
GPS co-ordinates in this guide are protected by copyright law

Visit www.all-the-aires.co.uk/submissions.shtml
to upload your updates and photos.

ℹ Submit updates
- Amendments
- New Aires
- Not changed

Take at least 5 digital photos showing
- Signs
- Service Point
- Parking
- Overview
- Amenities

AURIS EN OISANS
155 K9 38142 SKI N45°03.110' E006°04.708'

🚐 20; €5/day; Collected 🚽 Euro Relais Junior; €2; 7 CEE elec points; 2 or 3 points share 1 16amp fuse, for battery charging only

➡ Residence la Meije. Turn off D1091 at Le Freney d'Oisans onto D211a, sp 'Auris en Oisans'. Follow D211a uphill for 8.3km following sp 'Auris en Oisans Station', then turn onto D211e. At Auris en Oisans station veer left, then follow road downhill to left. Aire 400m on right, signed.

ℹ Alt 1586m. Pleasant asphalt Aire on edge of small ski resort; amazing views across mountain valley. Can be exposed in bad weather. Resort commerce 600m. Various indoor and outdoor resort activities avail, especially in school holidays. www.auris-en-oisans.fr Inspected 2016.

ALLEMONT
156 K9 38114 ⚓ N45°07.888' E006°02.499'

🚐 3; Plus additional parking 🚽 Aire Services 3000; Token (3/3)

➡ Chemin des Grand Champs. In Rochetaillée turn off D1091 onto D526, sp 'Allemont'. Follow D526 past Allemont and up hairpin bends of dam. At 2nd hairpin bend turn left along dam edge, sp 'Base Nautique' and signed. GPS taken here. Turn 1st left into car park. 3 motorhome bays in entrance and Service Point at far end. Actual GPS: N45°07.984' E006°02.566'.

ℹ Aire in sloping car park adj to reservoir, partial views through deciduous trees. Footpath by Service Point to small leisure facilities inc boat hire, no swimming. Local commerce 150m uphill. Level parking opp side of dam: N45°07.696' E006°02.749'. Inspected 2016.

ALPE D'HUEZ | 157 | K9 | 38750 | SKI | N45°05.236' E006°04.773'

🚐 75; €10/day; + €0.83 tax; CC; Pay at machine; Max 4 days
🏠 Raclet x2; Inside barrier; WC adj to barrier

➡ Chemin de Fond Morelle. From D1091 turn onto D211 and follow road uphill for 10.8km, sp 'Alpe d'Huez'. Fork right onto the compulsory motorhome route, sp 'Itinéraire Obligatoire' and signed. At the top turn right, signed. Follow road around car park and under chairlift, then turn right again, signed. Follow road and Aire through barrier, signed.

ℹ Alt 1860m. Large popular commercial Aire with panoramic mountain views. Can be exposed in poor weather. Ski lifts and resort 250m, with access to large number of pistes. Golf course adj. Popular with walkers and cyclists in summer. Reinspected 2016.

VAUJANY | 158 | K9 | 38114 | SKI | N45°09.410' E006°04.803'

🚐 8; Max 9m 🏠 Euro Relais Mini; Free; Elec; Token; WC at cable car

➡ Rue des Combes. From D526 turn onto D43a, sp 'Vaujany'. Follow road 4.8km uphill to Vaujany. In Vaujany turn right, sp 'Pôle Sports Loisirs'. Follow road downhill past cable car station, then turn right. Aire on right, signed.

ℹ Alt 1194m. Popular landscaped Aire at base of cable car overlooking Cascade de la Fare waterfall. Lift to village and 2 separate cable cars connecting large ski area, noisy when running. Café adj, local and resort commerce in village, 300m. Reinspected 2016.

LE CHEYLAS | 159 | K8 | 38570 | | N45°22.305' E005°59.409'

🚐 10 🏠 Custom; Water very slow; All elec points turned off; Cont WC; Apr-Oct

➡ D523. From north on D523 drive through traffic lights adj to commerce, then turn immediately right at next set of traffic lights, signed. Service Point to right adj to WC.

ℹ Aire opp local commerce, accessible via underpass, adj to busy, noisy main road. Large car park suitable for any unit configuration, also used by HGVs. Very convenient night halt. Inspected 2016.

COMBE DE L'OURS STATION | 160 | K8 | 73670 | SKI | N45°21.467' E005°49.967'

🚐 50 🏠 None; See 161

➡ La Combe de l'Ours chairlift. From Grenoble follow D512 north, sp 'Parc Naturel Régional de la Chartreuse'. Continue on D512 for 28.3km, then turn right, sp 'Télésiège Combe de l'Ours'. Follow road uphill and parking on left before chairlift, not signed.

ℹ Large open parking area adj to 6 person ski lift with seasonal (weekend in summer) snack bar, mountain bike/ski depart and bike wash (token). Deserted in summer, may feel isolated and likely to be alone. Inspected 2016.

ST PIERRE DE CHARTREUSE | 161 | K8 | 38380 | SKI | N45°20.578' E005°48.743'

🚐 9; Max 9m 🏠 Euro Relais Mini; Token (ER); WC at church, 50m

➡ Parking du Couzon. Turn off D520b onto D512, sp 'St Pierre de Chartreuse'. Then turn off D512 by church, sp 'Plan du Ville', 'P du Couzon' and signed. Turn left past the church and the Aire is on the left past the pharmacy, sp 'P du Couzon' and signed.

ℹ Alt 878m. Tucked away Aire, but adj to small town commerce and only a few hundred metres from main route. Small ski resort with supporting commerce; ski lift 300m. Inspected 2016.

ST HUGUES DE CHARTREUSE | 162 | K8 | 38380 | SKI | N45°19.029' E005°48.207'

🚐 15 🏠 None; See 161

➡ Parking du Cret des Égaux, D57b. From St Pierre de Chartreuse take D512, sp 'St Hughes des Chartreuse'. Turn left onto D57b, sp 'St Hughes des Chartreuse' and 'Les Égaux'. Follow D57b through the small village of St Hughes des Chartreuse, then uphill, sp 'Les Égaux'. Parking on left before drag lift, sp 'P'.

ℹ Alt 950m. Small rural car park with lovely 360° views. Signed walking paths for summer, short drag lift, cross country skiing and snow shoe walking in winter. Reinspected 2016.

ST HILAIRE DU TOUVET

| 163 | K8 | 38660 | | N45°18.152' E005°52.821' |

🚐5; Additional unrestricted parking in centre adj to TO 🛒 Custom; Showers €2.50 at adj campsite

▶ Chemin du Bec Margain. From Le Touvet follow sp 'St Hilaire du Touvet' on D29, then onto D30. Drive through village on D30, passing the TO and local commerce. Turn off in front of tennis courts, sp 'Terrain du Foot' and signed. Service Point on right at far end adj to tennis courts.

ℹ️ Alt 1017m. Aire adj to sports facilities and municipal campsite with café and open access washing machines. Village has local commerce, TO (with parking: N45°18.632' E005°53.259') and convenience store. Winter sports include cross country skiing and snow shoe walks. Inspected 2016.

VIRIEU SUR BOURBRE

| 164 | K8 | 38730 | | N45°28.898' E005°28.669' |

🚐4 🛒 Custom

▶ Rue du May. Turn off D73 in village centre onto D17, sp 'Le Pin' and signed. Aire on left as exit village opp boundary sign, signed.

ℹ️ Parking in shady dell adj to water-wheel and grassy, terraced picnic area. Lake de Paladru further up D17. Village centre 450m. Market Fri pm. Updated 2014.

LA BATIE MONTGASCON

| 165 | J8 | 38110 | | N45°34.704' E005°31.709' |

🚐10; Max 48hrs; See info 🛒 Custom; Donation

▶ Rue des Tisserands. From La Tour du Pin (west) follow D1516 into town, then turn right onto D145, sp 'St André le Gaz'. Service Point on right adj to Musée du Tisserand, signed; day parking only at museum. Best parking at cemetery: N45°34.723' E005°31.858'. Turn right from Service Point, then 1st left, sp 'Cimetière'. Parking 150m; most level parking adj to dead end road.

ℹ️ Service Point adj to textile museum. Level parking at D1516/D91 junction in centre is adj to local commerce but suffers road noise: N45°34.853' E005°31.707'. Parking at stadium is impractical, but peaceful and 750m from centre: N45°34.511' E005°31.845'. Reinspected 2016.

Cemetery

AIX LES BAINS

| 166 | K8 | 73100 | | N45°41.797' E005°53.339' |

🚐64; €13/24hrs; CC 🛒 Euro Relais Junior; 52 6amp elec points; All inside barrier

▶ Rue des Goélands. From north on D991 turn right at roundabout onto D991d. Turn 1st left into Blvd Garibaldi, then right at 2nd roundabout. At end of road turn left. Go straight over roundabout, then turn 1st left, signed. Enter through PARKNIGHT barrier.

ℹ️ Commercial Aire at former municipal campsite. Pretty, bustling lakeside resort town with tourist commerce and facilities. Beach 500m. Visited 2016.

Info/Photos: David Hayward

CHAMBERY

| 167 | K8 | 73000 | | N45°33.772' E005°55.982' |

🚐5; Max 6m 🛒 Depagne Mini; Mar-Oct

▶ Espace Sportif Delphine et Jonathan. Exit N201 at Junction 18 following sp 'Chambéry'. Go under bridge and fork left, sp 'Lyon' and 'Valence'. Go straight over the roundabout, sp 'Parkings'. Turn left at next roundabout into sports centre and Aire is at end.

ℹ️ Aire in small car park adj to sports centre, most parking occupied by local vehicles. Very limited parking, arrive early. Historic town centre 400m; go straight over roundabout, turn left and keep walking. Reinspected 2016.

LE BOURGET DU LAC

| 168 | K8 | 73370 | | N45°39.195' E005°51.772' |

🚐20 hardstanding; 10 grass; €6.20/24hrs Oct-Mar; €9.50/24hrs Apr-May; €12.50/24hrs Jun-Sept; CC; Max 4 days Jun-Sept; Max 7 days Oct-May 🛒 Custom; Inside barrier; €2.10

▶ Blvd Ernest Coudurier, outside Camping L'Île aux Cygnes. From south on D1504 follow sp 'Bourget du Lac', then 'Lac'. Turn right off D1504 onto D14, sp 'Lac'. Turn right, sp 'Camping', then 1st right, signed. Follow road straight on, signed. Enter Aire via Urba Flux barrier adj to campsite entrance, signed.

ℹ️ Landscaped commercial Aire outside campsite. Lake nearby, but no views. Use of WC, showers, laundry and private beach. www.lebourgetdulac.fr Reinspected 2016.

LE REVARD
169 K8 73100 SKI N45°41.042' E005°58.738'

🚐5; 5m car bays, some overhang poss 🚰 Euro Relais Junior; CC; €2

➡ Boucle de Bellevue. Turn off D913 onto D913a, sp 'Le Revard'. Follow road around resort and Service Point on left opp P1, signed.

ℹ Alt 1538m. Service Point adj to car park in small resort. Go to P2 for walkways and viewpoints over Aix-les-Bains. No suitable motorhome parking, although poss to park here low season. Poss to walk old cog railway line from here to Aix-les-Bains. Inspected 2016.

LESCHERAINES
170 K8 73340 ⛺ N45°42.245' E006°06.675'

🚐10; €4/day; Collected; Max 48hrs; 8m bays 🚰 Euro Relais Mini; Token (ER)

➡ Base de Loisirs. Turn off D911 onto D912, sp 'Lescheraines'. Drive through Lescheraines, then turn left, sp 'Base de Loisirs'. Follow road to leisure lake and Aire on right before campsite, signed.

ℹ Peaceful, pleasant Aire before campsite at recreation area and leisure lake. 5 landscaped bays that could fit 2 motorhomes, so park expecting to share. Inspected 2016.

LA FECLAZ
171 K8 73230 SKI N45°38.515' E005°59.016'

🚐40; €4.30/night; Pay at TO 🚰 Raclet; Token (ER); WC at building opp

➡ D206a. From D912 turn onto D913, sp 'La Féclaz'. In 2.9km at entrance to village turn left, sp 'P Camping Cars'. Follow road and Aire on right in 550m, signed.

ℹ Alt 1200m. Aire adj to small ski/walking resort with cross country skiing and button ski lift, 100m. Very peaceful in summer. TO and resort centre with local commerce and chairlift 350m: N45°38.722' E005°58.976'. Reinspected 2016.

AILLON LE JEUNE
172 K8 73340 SKI N45°36.557' E006°06.265'

🚐10 🚰 Custom; Press down on red part of tap

➡ D32a. Turn off D206 onto D32a in Aillon le Jeune by the Mairie and church, sp 'Aillon le Jeune - Station'. Follow road for 2km, around left-hand bend and then straight across roundabout, signed. Aire on right, signed.

ℹ Alt 946m. Aire located in small ski resort with resort commerce; drag lift adj, chairlift 150m. Part of Bauges Nature Park, an ideal place for a walk/cycle in summer. The Charter House, former Carthusian monastery, now a museum. www.parcdesbauges.com www.esf-les-aillons.fr Inspected 2016.

AIGUEBELLE
173 K8 73220 🚆 N45°32.586' E006°18.374'

🚐10 🚰 Custom; Empty WC by lifting round cover by Service Point or down drive over drain

➡ Rue de la Gare. From south on D1006 turn right at 1st traffic lights as enter town, sp 'Gare SNCF'. Follow road to Aire in car park on right, adj to train station, signed.

ℹ Aire in car park by train station. Pleasant grass parking allowed on adj green, signed. Other parking can be busy with HGVs, especially market day, Tues, when best to arrive after 2pm. Railway noise at night. Small town commerce 100m. Reinspected 2016.

BOURGNEUF
174 K8 73390 🚆 N45°33.165' E006°12.653'

🚐10 🚰 Flot Bleu Océane; 2 x €1

➡ D925. At D925/D204 roundabout turn right into village. Take 1st left turning, sp 'Restaurant Pizzeria' and signed. Follow road in front of pizzeria and Aire is in large open area behind boulangerie.

ℹ Peaceful, pleasant Aire on edge of village with lovely views of mountains across fields. Local commerce adj. Reinspected 2016.

LA ROCHETTE

| 175 | K8 | 73110 | | N45°27.155' E006°06.185' | SP |

🚐 30 🔧 Euro Relais Junior

➡ D925. Exit D925 at roundabout with D202 into roadside lay-by, passing under 3.2m height barrier. Parking to left, Service Point to right behind WC: N45°27.130' E006°06.063'.

ℹ Popular, pleasant lakeside Aire. Main route adj; suffers constant road noise. Enjoyable walk around pleasant park and lake. Always busy due to convenient, easy access and suitability for all unit configurations under 3.2m high. Unrestricted parking opp popular with HGVs. Inspected 2016.

GPS Co-ordinates for SatNav

The GPS Co-ordinates published in this guide were taken onsite by our inspectors. We consider them a valuable and unique asset and at the time of publishing have decided not to publish them as electronic files for use on navigation devices. You have permission to type in the co-ordinates of an Aire you intend to visit but not to store or share them. For the security of our copyright:

- **Do not compile them into lists**

- **Do not publish, share or reproduce them anywhere in any format**

ALLEVARD

| 177 | K8 | 38580 | | N45°23.304' E006°04.262' | SP |

🚐 10; Max 24hrs 🔧 Custom; Drive over drain inc lift cover for fixed WC tank emptying

➡ La Côte du David. From south turn off D525 at roundabout, sp 'Establissement Thermal' and signed. Turn right, signed, and follow road downhill. At bottom turn right to Service Point, signed. From north follow signs through town.

ℹ Aire in disused area next to fire station. Town has thermal spa resort complete with all resort commerce, 150m, which includes thermal baths and a casino. Suitable for any unit configuration. Reservoir walk 600m. Inspected 2016.

LA CHAMBRE

| 178 | K8 | 73130 | | N45°21.784' E006°17.858' | SP |

🚐 9; Max 72hrs 🔧 Flot Bleu Pacific; Token; €2; 3 CEE/4 Cont elec points, adj to parking

➡ D76. Exit La Chambre on D76 to north. Turn right into Aire after crossing river bridge, sp 'Centre Sportif et Culturel' and signed.

ℹ Landscaped sloping parking on the edge of town. Tokens from adj hotel, which has a bar/restaurant, or cheese co-operative, which has a small shop. Small town commerce 200m; market Tues. Inspected 2016.

ST JEAN DE MAURIENNE

| 179 | K8 | 73300 | | N45°16.766' E006°20.826' | SP |

🚐 10; Max 48hrs 🔧 Flot Bleu Euro; CC; €2

➡ Place du Champ de Foire, D906. From south on D1006 turn left onto D77 at traffic lights, sp 'St Jean de Mne'. At 1st roundabout turn right and cross bridge. In 650m turn right, sp 'Chambery'. Go straight over next roundabout, sp 'Centre de Secours', and Aire in car park on left. Service Point to rear of lower car park.

ℹ Popular Aire in town centre car park. Parking adj to Service Point is sheltered from most town noise. Overflow parking in adj unrestricted car park. Town commerce 150m. Reinspected 2016

VALLOIRE LES VERNEYS

| 180 | K8 | 73450 | SKI | N45°08.655' E006°25.187' | SP |

🚐 28; €9.40/24hrs May-Nov; €13/24hrs Dec-Apr 🔧 Euro Relais Junior; 28 16amp CEE elec points; All inside barrier

➡ D902/Route du Galibier. From St Michel de Maurienne follow D902 through Valloire to Les Verneys and drive through Les Verneys. Aire is on left just past chairlift, adj to D902. Enter through PARKNIGHT barrier.

ℹ Alt 1573m. Landscaped commercial Aire between main road, some road noise, and small river. Chairlift 100m. Local commerce adj, larger resort commerce at Valloire. Inspected 2016.

LES MENUIRES

| 181 | K8 | 73440 | SKI | N45°19.525' E006°32.035' |

🚐 74; €5/12hrs; €10/24hrs; CC 🛢 Flot Bleu Euro; Outside barrier; €2; Flot Bleu Elec; €2/4hrs

➡ From Moûtiers on N90 exit at Junction 40 onto D117, sp 'Les Menuires'. Follow D117 for 26km, then turn right at roundabout to stay on D117, sp 'Val Thorens' and signed. In 1.5km turn left, sp 'Flot Bleu'. Follow road uphill to Aire. Service Point on left, parking on right. Enter through Flot Bleu barrier.

ℹ Alt 1736m. Large commercial Aire popular during ski season, deserted in summer. There is an additional pay Service Point inside barrier. In the 3 valleys ski area, ticket office and lift to village nearby. Reinspected 2016.

BESSANS

| 182 | L8 | 73480 | SKI | N45°18.536' E006°58.589' |

🚐 7 🛢 Euro Relais Tall; €2

➡ Aux Gardes. From Lanslebourg-Mont-Cenis on D902 turn left onto D902a, sp 'Bessans' and 'Espace Loisirs'. For parking turn immediately left, sp 'Les Lacs'. Grass parking on left or follow road to parking on left. For Service Point follow road to Bessans, then turn right before village, signed. Service Point 150m on left: N45°19.070' E6°59.350'.

ℹ Alt 1710m. Service Point in small village with local commerce and co-operative cheese makers. Grass and gravel parking poss by leisure lake with lifeguards in season, no dogs. Parking also poss at ski depart points off D902 and at Beau Village Bonneval-sur-Arc. Inspected 2016.

TIGNES

| 183 | L8 | 73320 | SKI | N45°27.485' E006°53.904' |

🚐 30; €7/night; Collected 🛢 Urba Flux Tall; Adj to WC

➡ D87a. Turn off D902 onto D87a at top of Lac du Chevril, sp 'Tignes'. Drive across dam, then go straight over roundabout to stay on D87a, sp 'Tignes - Le Lac'. Follow road for 6km, driving around lake and following sp 'Val Claret' through tunnel. At next roundabout turn right and enter bus parking.

ℹ Alt 2110m. Car park at small ski resort adj to golf course. Pleasant leisure lake for fishing, boating and BBQs 700m. Resort commerce 500m. Ski lifts 200m past tennis courts. Some lifts operating in summer for walkers and mountain bikers. Inspected 2016.

VAL D'ISERE

| 184 | L8 | 73150 | SKI | N45°27.307' E006°58.194' |

🚐 20; €9/night; Collected; Max 3 days; Grass parking 🛢 Custom

➡ D902. Take D902 from Bourg-St-Maurice (north) and Aire is on right adj to D902 in Val d'Isère, signed.

ℹ Alt 1804m. Aire adj to main route between 2 gondolas in popular ski resort. Resort commerce adj. D902 over Col de l'Isère is an exhilarating drive, but there are limited barriers and long drops. Surrounding mountains range from 1785m to 3456m high. www.valdisere.com Inspected 2016.

Photo: Rob Beggs

LE PRAZ COURCHEVEL

| 185 | K8 | 73120 | SKI | N45°25.831' E006°37.485' |

🚐 20 🛢 Flot Bleu Pacific (Green); €3

➡ D91a. On D91a pass through Le Praz towards Courchevel. Turn left, sp 'Parking Jean Blanc'. Aire on left in Parking Jean Blanc just after bend leaving village.

ℹ Alt 1285m. Expansive, level car park deserted in summer, busy in winter. Mountain views and views across to ski jumps. Small resort commerce 250m, inc cable car both seasons, lake with water ski drag in summer, ski jumping and ski lifts linking to Mirabelle in winter. Reinspected 2016.

LA PLAGNE VILLAGES ⭐

| 186 | L8 | 73210 | SKI | N45°30.318' E006°41.337' |

🚐 39; €20/night inc service and elec; CC; Max 15 days 🛢 Custom; Inside barrier; 30 10amp CEE elec points

➡ Follow D221 up numerous hairpin bends following sp 'La Plagne', then 'Plagne Villages'. In La Plagne turn left at roundabout on D223, sp 'Plagne Villages' and 'P Caravaneige'. Follow road for 1.5km into La Plagne Villages. Pass top station of small triple gondola on left and continue straight on, sp 'Parking'. Aire at rear of car park, signed. Enter through barrier.

ℹ Alt 2084m. Landscaped commercial Aire underneath chairlift and adj to slopes; can literally ski from your motorhome. Ticket office, resort commerce and triple gondola 250m. Skiing ideal for intermediates with links to Les Arcs. WiFi avail. Reinspected 2016.

LA LECHERE

187 | K8 | 73260 | N45°31.180' E006°29.057'

SP

🚐 12; €3/day; Collected; See info for free parking 🚰 Flot Bleu Fontaine

➡ Parking 3, Village 92, Thermal Spa Complex. From south exit N90 at Junction 37, sp 'La Léchère'. Turn left at T-Junction onto D990. Follow road under N90, then turn left, sp 'Doucy'. Go straight over roundabout into car park of thermal baths. Pass Mairie on left, then turn left into designated parking, signed, or right to Service Point.

ℹ Aire at thermal spa with restaurant, café, and bar onsite. Riverside walks. Also poss to park for free at Base de Loisirs de Morel: N45°30.621' E006°29.540'; unlevel parking by swimming pool. Pleasant walk back to village and thermal spa from here. Reinspected 2016.

LES ARCS

188 | L8 | 73700 | SKI | N45°35.795' E006°47.520'

SP

🚐 30; Max 7 days; Max 3.5t 🚰 None

➡ D119, Arc 1600. From Bourg St Maurice on D1090 turn onto D119, sp 'Les Arcs'. Follow road for 13.7km. Go over roundabout, sp 'Arc 1600'. Parking on left in 600m.

ℹ Alt 1540m. Unrestricted resort parking allowing 7-day parking. Road noise from main resort road. Free ski bus to slopes. Popular campsite 'Le Versoyen' at Bourg St Maurice, passed en route. http://en.lesarcs.com Reinspected 2016.

LA ROSIERE

189 | L8 | 73700 | SKI | N45°37.482' E006°51.369'

SP

🚐 20; Max 15 days; Max 8m; Max 3.5t; Winter only 🚰 Flot Bleu Pacific; Token; €10

➡ D1090. Follow D1090 north out of Bourg St Maurice. Aire signed on left just before village, behind Sapeurs Pompiers (fire station).

ℹ Alt 1850m. Winter only Aire, opens mid Dec; Service Point closed and parking used as a municipal yard in summer. Nice family resort with sunny south-facing slopes. Links to Italian resort La Thuile. Ski info: www.larosiere.net. Reinspected 2016.

BEAUFORT

190 | K8 | 73270 | N45°43.183' E006°34.029'

SP

🚐 7 🚰 Flot Bleu Fontaine

➡ D925/Avenue des Sports. From Albertville follow sp 'Beaufort' on D925 for 19km. Aire at start of village on left in cross country skiing depart car park, adj to Centre de Secours.

ℹ D925/Avenue des Sports. From Albertville follow sp 'Beaufort' on D925 for 19km. Aire at start of village on left in cross country skiing depart car park, adj to Centre de Secours.

LES SAISIES 1

191 | K8 | 73620 | SKI | N45°45.749' E006°32.024'

SP

🚐 100; €7.50/24hrs; Pay at machine 🚰 Flot Bleu Pacific; By WC; €2; No drive over drain

➡ D218b. From Flumet in north follow D218b for 14.5km, sp 'Les Saisies'. Follow road uphill, then at 1st roundabout in Col de Saisies turn left into Aire, signed.

ℹ Alt 1650m. Aire in large car park on edge of resort. Chairlift 200m, resort commerce 400m. Popular family ski resort with Olympic Nordic ski course. www.aed-montagne.com Reinspected 2016.

LES SAISIES 2

192 | K8 | 73620 | SKI | N45°44.826' E006°32.123'

SP

🚐 50; €16/night inc 16amp CEE elec; CC 🚰 Custom; Inside barrier; Flot Bleu Standard Plus; Opp entrance; €2

➡ D123. Follow D218b through Les Saisies towards Beaufort. As exit resort turn right onto D123, sp 'Bisanne 1500'. Follow D123 uphill for 1.7km, sp 'Quartier de la Fôret'. Aire on right at bend in road, opp Flot Bleu (see info), signed. Enter through barrier. Signed from Les Saisies. Advise approaching from Les Saisies, not Villard sur Doron.

ℹ Alt 1672m. Winter caravaneige (winter sports campsite) operating as summer Aire. Flot Bleu in lay-bay opp entrance. Resort of Les Saisies 2km downhill. Inspected 2016.

ALBERTVILLE - CONFLANS

193 K8 73200 T N45°40.443' E006°23.828'

🚐 6; Max 24hrs 🛒 Flot Bleu Pacific

➡ D105. From Beaufort on D925 follow sp 'Albertville'. In Albertville turn left at traffic lights onto D105, sp 'Cité de Conflans' and signed. Follow road uphill and Aire in car park on right, signed. From other directions follow sp 'Cité de Conflans'.

ℹ Aire in car park with open and shaded parking adj to the small, walled medieval city of Conflans, 200m up steps and hill (less steep route through adj park). Albertville town commerce 500m downhill and across river. www.albertville.fr Reinspected 2016.

FAVERGES

194 K8 74210 N45°44.969' E006°17.159'

🚐 25 🛒 Custom

➡ D2508/Route d'Annecy. From Annecy turn off D1508 at roundabout, sp 'Faverges - Centre' and signed. Aire on right in 1.3km just before Carrefour supermarket, signed.

ℹ Popular Aire adj to main route, some road noise during day. Pleasant views of adj rocky hills. Adj to supermarket with laundry. Plenty of cycle paths to explore area. Waterfall and caves at nearby Seythenex; pay, open Apr-Sept 10am-5pm. www.cascade-seythenex.fr Reinspected 2016.

UGINE

195 K8 73400 N45°44.791' E006°25.034'

🚐 17; Market Wed am 🛒 Flot Bleu Euro; CC; €2.50; Showers in WC, 8am-8pm (Summer)/8am-5pm (Winter)

➡ D1508. From west on D1508 turn right into service road immediately after 1st roundabout, signed. Parking in bays on right, Service Point adj to TO.

ℹ Aire adj to main route, suffers road noise. WC with showers in adj old railway station building, now TO. Supermarket opp. Pleasant park across railway line with cycle path to Annecy and Albertville; access via railway underpass. TO has town walks around architecture and steel works photographs. www.ugine-tourisme.com Reinspected 2016.

DOUSSARD

196 K8 74210 (A) N45°46.994' E006°13.453'

🚐 (A) 10; Max 24hrs; (B) 30; 5 Jul-2 Sept; Max 24hrs; Max 7.5m 🛒 None; See **197**

➡ D281. Turn off D1508 onto D281, sp 'Doussard'. (A) Parking immediately on left, sp 'P 24hrs'. (B) N45°46.555' E006°13.457': Follow D281 into Doussard. Turn left into Rue de la Poste, sp 'Poste', then turn 1st left into Place du Pre de Port, sp 'Groupe Scolaire' and signed.

ℹ (A) Roadside parking adj to pleasant grassy picnic area. Parking shaded in morning. Lake Annecy recreation beach 1.4km, no views. (B) Parking in large car park for school, not needed in summer. Shaded and open parking. Local commerce 300m. Inspected 2016.

LATHUILE

197 K8 74210 N45°47.688' E006°12.476'

🚐 40; €8/night (Low season); €10/night (High season); Inc 2amp CEE elec; Collected 🛒 Custom; €2 if not staying; Honesty box

➡ Route de la Porte. From Annecy on D1508 turn right before turning to Lathuile, signed. Follow road to left, signed, and under bridge for cycle path. Aire on left in 400m, signed. Drivers of motorhomes over 8m or 4t must visit reception before parking.

ℹ Grass parking at popular, peaceful and pleasant commercial Aire 700m from Lake Annecy, no view. Designated cycle path to Annecy 400m. Access to lake 250m from end of road. Ideal place to enjoy a holiday. Inspected 2016.

THUY

198 K8 74230 N45°53.666' E006°18.376'

🚐 6; Max 48hrs 🛒 None; See **197**

➡ Rue des Vernaies. Turn off D909 at roundabout, sp 'Lac du Thuy'. Designated parking 70m on left, signed.

ℹ Designated gravel parking overlooking trout fishing lake with mountain views. Local fishing licence required; no swimming. Pleasant picnic area and walk around pond. Distant road noise from D909. Inspected 2016.

THONES
`199` K8 74230 N45°52.838' E006°19.259' SP

🚐 6; Max 48hrs 🚰 Flot Bleu Pacific; 2 x €1

➡ Route de Paradis. At D909/D12 roundabout north of town turn onto D12, sp 'Office du Tourisme'. Turn 1st right, sp 'Office du Tourisme', then follow road across river/storm drain bridge and turn left, signed. Parking area 200m on left, signed; 3.5t weight restriction. For Service Point drive past Aire, then turn right at roundabout, sp 'Gendarmerie'. Service Point on left just past Gendarmerie: N45°53.071' E006°19.058'.

ℹ Designated parking at end of car park; trees offer some shade. Pleasant resort nestled between hills. Small town commerce, TO and LIDL 400m. Inspected 2016.

COMBLOUX
`200` K8 74920 N45°53.927' E006°37.978' SP

🚐 7 🚰 None; See `201`

➡ Route du Bouchet. From Megève on D1212 enter Combloux, then turn left at roundabout, sp 'Domain Skiable'. Follow sp 'Domain Skiable' uphill for 550m, then turn right, sp 'Téléski' and signed. Aire in car park on right in 600m, signed.

ℹ Peaceful designated parking in rural hamlet adj to small park. Views of Mont Blanc from some bays and park. Drag ski lift 100m. Inspected 2016.

ST GERVAIS LES BAINS
`201` L8 74170 SKI N45°53.265' E006°42.774' SP

🚐 30 🚰 Raclet; Token (ER); €2

➡ Impasse de la Cascade, off D909. From Combloux follow D909, sp 'St Gervais'. At D909/D902 roundabout go straight over to stay on D909, sp 'Les Contamines'. Cross bridge, then turn right by boulangerie, sp 'Patinoire' and 'P 100 places'. Drive straight on into car park behind Patinoire (skating rink).

ℹ Alt 818m. Aire in large car park unpopular with motorists. Bins are emptied every morning, park as far away from these as possible! Ski gondola 200m. Pleasant Victorian resort with tourist commerce 400m. Reinspected 2016.

LES HOUCHES - Chamonix
`202` L8 74130 SKI N45°53.562' E006°46.018' SP

🚐 22; €15/24hrs inc 10amp CEE elec, WiFi and service; CC; Apr-Nov; See info 🚰 Custom; Outside barrier; CC; €5; 10amp CEE elec

➡ Route du Pont. From Sallanches on A40/N205 in west exit at Junction 27, sp 'Les Houches - Centre'. At roundabout turn left onto D243. Follow road for 550m, then turn left into Rue du Pont, before village boundary, signed. Follow lane uphill to Aire on right, signed. Enter through Urba Flux barrier, Service Point just after entrance, signed.

ℹ Alt 1016m. Summer-only, landscaped commercial Aire in foothills of Mont Blanc. www.campingcarmontblanc.com Out of season, or for a short halt, exit N205 at Junction 25 and follow sp 'Aire de la Fontaine': N45°54.942' E006°46.017'. Inspected 2016.

CHAMONIX MONT BLANC
`203` L7 74400 SKI N45°54.951' E006°52.171' SP

🚐 100; 1st hr free; Hourly or €12.50/24hrs inc service; CC/€ 🚰 Custom; Inside barrier

➡ Parking Grépon, off D1506. Turn off D1506 at roundabout, sp 'P+R Grépon' and 'Aiguille du Midi'. Aire in far corner of parking for the gondola to Aiguille du Midi. Barriered entry, pay upon exit.

ℹ Cable car to Aiguille du Midi, 300m, also has WC. Free bus to town centre at cable car. Reinspected 2016.

CHAMONIX
`204` L7 74400 SKI N45°55.705' E006°52.624' SP

🚐 15; Poss for large motorhomes on right 🚰 None; See `203`

➡ D1506. Follow D1506 through Chamonix Mont Blanc, sp 'Martigny'. Parking adj to D1506, sp 'P 24hrs'.

ℹ Alt 1035m. Popular roadside parking suffering road and train noise. Only 400m from the happening resort area of Chamonix Mont Blanc. Another overnight option is `203`. Inspected 2016.

PLAINE JOUX

`205` `L7` `74480` N45°57.033' E006°44.353'

🚐 20; €10/night inc token and showers; Collected 🚰 Flot Bleu Pacific; Token (FB)/1 x €2; 16amp elec for winter visitors

▶ D43/Route de Plaine-Joux. From Chamonix on N205 exit at Junction 22 at Le Fayet and follow D43 north 12km through Plateau-d'Assy to Plaine-Joux. Aire on both sides of road in large parking area before restaurants and paragliding centre. 8 spaces to left by Service Point, 8 spaces adj to grass to right, further grass parking beyond, all signed.

ℹ Alt 1360m. 3 areas with fantastic views of Mont Blanc, subject to weather. Local resort commerce adj. Ideal place if you fancy throwing yourself off a mountain attached only to a kite, otherwise known as paragliding, or if you enjoy watching people who do. Limited downhill skiing in winter. Reinspected 2016.

SALLANCHES

`206` `K7` `74700` N45°55.920' E006°38.026'

🚐 3; Max 24hrs; 7m bays + 2m overhang 🚰 Flot Bleu Pacific; 2 x €1; Inspection cover to left behind Service Point

▶ Parking de Charousse, D1205. From Cluses follow D1205 south, sp 'Chamonix'. At roundabout follow sp 'Sallanches' staying on D1205. Drive through Sallanches and the Aire is after the commerce on the right, signed.

ℹ Convenient overnight parking adj to main route through. Town commerce 200m. Ideal place to restock before heading up the mountains. FIAT Professional towards Passy. Inspected 2016.

FLAINE

`207` `L7` `74300` SKI N46°00.274' E006°41.345'

Les Carroz d'Araches

🚐 30; €2/12hrs; €5/24hrs; Pay at machine 🚰 WC 50m; Do not empty cassette in WC; See info

▶ From Cluses take D1205 south and turn onto D6, sp 'Les Carroz D'Arâches'. Follow D6, then D106 for 24.8km to Flaine (wide road with hairpin bends). Aire in car park P1, sp 'P Camping Cars'.

ℹ Alt 1582m. Designated parking at ski station used to store snow ploughs and other items in summer. Poss to service at Les Carroz d'Araches: N46°01.517' E006°38.632' on way up/down but Service Point is in throws of closing; only WC emptying poss and overnight parking banned. Reinspected 2016.

LE CHINAILLON

`208` `K7` `74450` SKI N45°58.534' E006°27.641'

🚐 10; Max 48hrs 🚰 Custom

▶ Lieu-Dit Le Chinaillon, off D4. From Le Grand Bornand follow D4, sp 'Le Chinaillon'. At Le Chinaillon take 1st right and follow road past Service Point and ski lifts to designated parking at end, signed. Service Point and WC 300m from parking at Le Chatalet ski lift: N45°58.426' E006°27.437'.

ℹ Alt 1288m. Parking on peaceful edge of small ski resort with tourist commerce. 2 chairlifts, 300m. Ski bus stop adj. Reinspected 2016.

LE GRAND BORNAND

`209` `K8` `74450` SKI N45°56.485' E006°26.178'

🚐 10; Max 48hrs 🚰 None; WC 100m

▶ Route de la Broderie. Drive east through town, sp 'Col des Annes'. Turn right onto bridge over stream, sp 'L'Envers de Villeneuve'. Aire on left in 100m, sp 'Le Pessey' and signed.

ℹ Alt 922m. Designated motorhome parking area 400m from pleasant ski resort with tourist commerce. Ski bus in season. Motorhomes banned from all other car parks. Reinspected 2016.

MONT SAXONNEX

`210` `K7` `74130` N46°03.206' E006°29.058'

🚐 7; At Service Point or church 🚰 Custom

▶ Route de l'Église. Take D4 from Cluses, sp 'Le Reposoir'. Turn right off D4 onto D268, sp 'Mont-Saxonnex'. Follow road uphill. After 4.5km, at top of hill, turn right after boulangerie, sp 'Office du Tourisme' and signed. Service Point 150m on right, parking opp or at church: N46°03.296' E006°28.990'.

ℹ Alt 991m. Service Point and level, sheltered parking adj to sports facilities. Further parking with excellent views by church. Pleasant hilltop village with local commerce and TO. Inspected 2016.

LE REPOSOIR
211 | K7 | 74950 | N46°00.598' E006°32.172'

🚐 8 🏠 Custom; 4 CEE elec points; Self-cleaning WC

➡ D204. From roundabout on D1205 in Cluses turn onto D4, sp 'Le Reposoir'. Follow road for 11km. Turn left onto D204 in Le Reposoir between church and Mairie. Aire on right in 200m, signed.

ℹ Alt 980m. Pleasant Aire at base of nursery drag lift. Local commerce 150m. Monastère Chartreuse du Reposoir nearby, founded in 1151 AD. Reinspected 2016.

CLUSES
212 | K7 | 74300 | N46°04.145' E006°33.620'

🚐 5; No parking Thurs noon-8pm (Market) 🏠 Flot Bleu Euro; CC; €2/20 mins

➡ Rue Joseph Depoisier. From Taninges follow D902, sp 'Cluses'. As enter Cluses turn right at roundabout onto D902b, sp 'Thyez'. Go straight on at traffic lights, then turn left at road split. Go under overpass, then turn 1st right into Rue Jean Mermoz. Follow road to end, signed. Service Point to right of WC, signed; best parking opp Service Point, sp 'P'.

ℹ Service Point adj to riverside car park, no views. Car park is unrestricted, but many bays only 5m and permanent market markings are confusing. Pleasant riverside park adj with outdoor gym, cycle path and play area. Town commerce adj. Inspected 2016.

SIXT FER A CHEVAL
213 | L7 | 74740 | N46°03.399' E006°46.783'

🚐 30 🏠 Euro Relais Junior; Free; Euro Relais Mini Elec; Token (ER); €4/12hrs; 4 CEE elec points

➡ D907. From Samoëns on D907 follow sp 'Sixt Fer à Cheval' and 'Cirque du Fer à Cheval'. Pass straight on through village, sp 'Cirque du Fer à Cheval' and signed. Aire on right next to river just after village boundary sign.

ℹ Alt 767m. Popular Aire adj to, and with views of, river with paddle depart point. Located in a pleasant scenic valley setting 300m from Beau Village with tourist commerce, inc rafting and TO. Cirque du Fer à Cheval 5.5km further up road. Reinspected 2016.

SAMOENS
214 | L7 | 74340 | SKI | N46°04.366' E006°41.948'

🚐 30 🏠 Flot Bleu Pacific; €6

➡ D254. Exit Samoëns on D4, passing Camping Le Giffre. Cross river bridge and take fork to left onto D254, sp 'Vercland'. Continue for 1.7km to Vercland. In Vercland turn right when road bends left, sp 'La Foge' and signed. Follow road under chairlift building, 3.6m height restriction. Service Point on right, signed. For parking continue past Service Point to end of car park, signed.

ℹ Alt 827m. Aire currently being renovated. Located in small village with only a bar/restaurant and chairlift. Samoëns has lots of unrestricted parking in summer which is worth looking for, most car parks are height barriered in winter. Reinspected 2016.

LES GETS
215 | K7 | 74260 | SKI | N46°08.983' E006°39.501'

🚐 30; €17/night mid Dec-mid Apr; Free mid Apr-mid Dec; Collected; Long stay discounts; Max 7 days 🏠 Flot Bleu Euro; CC; €2; No drive over drain; Additional emptying point at parking

➡ Parking Perrières, off D902. Approaching from Cluses turn off D902 at roundabout at entrance to village, sp 'Perrières'. Service Point to left, parking to right at bottom of chairlift, signed.

ℹ Alt 1120m. Level Aire adj to ski lift at bottom of ski slope; separated from car park. 800m from lively ski resort with lifts open ski season/Jul-Aug. Pleasant in summer, popular with mountain bikers and walkers. Popular in winter (early arrival essential). www.lesgets.com Reinspected 2016.

LE PRAZ DE LYS - La Savolière
216 | K7 | 74440 | SKI | N46°08.497' E006°36.278'

🚐 100; 1hr free for service; €10/24hrs Dec-Apr/mid Jun-mid Sept; Free May-mid Jun/mid Sept-Nov; CC; Long stay discounts 🏠 Flot Bleu and Flot Bleu Elec; Token; €2; 1 Token/4hrs elec (Max 12hrs); 32 16amp CEE points

➡ Chemin Rural dit de la Savolière. From Les Gets or Taninges on D902 turn onto D307/308, sp 'Praz de Lys'. In 5.5km at top of hill turn left, signed. Follow road and enter through Flot Bleu barrier. Col de Ramaz closed in winter.

ℹ Alt 1424m. Terraced Aire offering mountain views, peaceful in summer. Hotel/restaurant and ski bus stop on main road. 1km level walk/cycle to small town/resort commerce. 3 2km-chairlifts and one drag lift offering good local skiing. Road popular with road cyclists in summer. Reinspected 2016.

SOMMAND | 217 | K7 | 74440 | SKI | N46°09.681' E006°33.293'

🚐 8 opp pond; 10 at base of ski lifts 🚰 Flot Bleu Pacific; €2; No drive over drain

➡ D308. From Taninges take D907 west. At roundabout in Mieussy turn right onto D308. Follow road for 10.5km. Space for 8 motorhomes opp pond on right: N46°09.620' E006°33.027'. Or take right-hand fork just past pond into large parking area at base of ski lifts. For Service Point turn right 200m before fork: N46°09.539' E006°32.959'.

ℹ Alt 1413m. Aire in pretty ski village with peaceful, pleasant feel in summer. Good downhill and Nordic skiing. Resort commerce in ski season; very quiet in low season, but lovely mountain walks and an ideal spot to watch cyclists slog up the hill. Reinspected 2016.

CHATEL 1 | 218 | L7 | 74390 | SKI | N46°15.447' E006°49.773'

🚐 12; €6/noon-noon; €10/noon-noon inc service; Collected/pay at campsite 🚰 Flot Bleu Pacific; Token (FB)/€; €6; Flot Bleu Elec; 1 x €2/1hr; 8 CEE elec points; See campsite for overnight elec

➡ Route des Freinets. From Abondance follow D22 towards Châtel. Before Châtel turn right off D22 at roundabout onto D230, sp 'Linga' and 'Pré la Joux'. Follow road through Le Clos du Tour, then at end of road turn left and immediately left again, sp 'Camping l'Oustalet'. Aire in 300m on right, opp Camping l'Oustalet, signed.

ℹ Very small Aire offering parallel parking on grass. May be more pleasant to stay at campsite. Rural ski resort/summer walking. Tourist commerce 200m, ski lift 400m. Access to Portes de Soleil ski area and poss to ski to Switzerland. Reinspected 2016.

CHATEL 2 | 219 | L7 | 74390 | SKI | N46°14.091' E006°47.457'

🚐 15; €6.20/night; Buy ticket at machine 🚰 Custom; Token/CC; €6.30/150L water or 6hrs elec; 8 CEE elec points on 2 bollards at parking; Token/€

➡ D228a. From Abondance follow D22 towards Châtel. Before Châtel turn right onto D230 at roundabout, sp 'Linge' and 'Prés la Joux'. Follow road through Le Clos du Tour, then at end of road turn right, sp 'Linge'. Service Point and token machine 3.5km on left, signed: N46°14.319' E006°47.593'. Parking 350m further on left, signed.

ℹ Alt 1200m. Max 6hrs in Service Point car park and no parking 7pm-8am. 15 designated bays 350m further up D228a towards chairlift. Landscaped Aire on outskirts of ski resort. Ski lift 500m. http://info.chatel.com Inspected 2016.

LA CHAPPELLE D'ABONDANCE | 220 | L7 | 74360 | SKI | N46°17.521' E006°46.998'

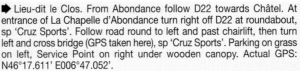

🚐 30 🚰 Urba Flux Tall; CC; WC at ski lift

➡ Lieu-dit le Clos. From Abondance follow D22 towards Châtel. At entrance of La Chapelle d'Abondance turn right off D22 at roundabout, sp 'Cruz Sports'. Follow road round to left and past chairlift, then turn left and cross bridge (GPS taken here), sp 'Cruz Sports'. Parking on grass on left, Service Point on right under wooden canopy. Actual GPS: N46°17.611' E006°47.052'.

ℹ Alt 900m. Best summer stopover in valley. Pleasant grass parking with mountain views adj to small stream. Pleasant grassy area with wooden canopies and BBQ/wood oven, but only 100m from local and tourist commerce. In winter ski lift 200m. Inspected 2016.

ABONDANCE | 221 | K7 | 74360 | SKI | N46°16.813' E006°42.923'

🚐 100 🚰 Flot Bleu Euro; CC; €2.50; Square inspection cover

➡ D22. In Bioge turn off D902 onto D22, sp 'Abondance'. Follow D22 15.5km to Abondance, then at the roundabout turn right, sp 'Centre Village' and signed. Aire immediately on right in large car park. Service Point adj to tennis courts, signed.

ℹ Alt 913m. Large, open gravel car park on edge of winter sports resort with mountain views. High ropes course and tennis courts adj. Poss to lift cover even if Service Point inoperable. Inspected 2016.

HABERE POCHE | 222 | K7 | 74140 | SKI | N46°14.909' E006°28.351'

🚐 20 🚰 Euro Relais Mini; 4 20amp elec points; Seasonal WC opp, at TO

➡ D12. Aire in car park in centre adj to D12/D22 junction, not signed. Service Point by fire station. Parking also allowed at base of chairlift in P Bois Noir: N46°14.693' E006°28.274'. Exit Aire to right on D12 and turn 1st left, sp 'P'. Parking in 1st car park on left.

ℹ Alt 947m. Central car park in small ski resort with 3 ski lifts. Hell's bells in Service Point car park. Local and ski commerce adj. Poss to park in large, level car park at Les Moises Foyer de Ski Fond, cross country departure: N46°16.105' E006°27.881'; 3km on D12, sp 'Thonon'. All ski lift parking peaceful in summer. Inspected 2016.

ANTHY SUR LEMAN
223 | K7 | 74200 | N46°21.534' E006°25.303'

🚐 5; Max 48hrs; Max 7m 🚽 Custom

▶ Rue du Lac. From Douvaine turn off D1005 at roundabout, sp 'Anthy s/ Léman'. Go straight across roundabout and through retail park. At next roundabout turn left onto D33, sp 'Anthy s/ Léman'. Follow road for 1.4km, then turn right into Rue du Lac, signed. Aire on right before lake, signed.

ℹ️ Popular, oversubscribed Aire with inadequate parking just 100m from Lac Léman (Lake Geneva). 5 bays, but 2 inaccessible without careful manoeuvring by other motorhomers. Aire also used to access car park through 1.9m height barrier. Inspected 2016.

ANTHY SUR LEMAN - Corzent
224 | K7 | 74200 | N46°21.783' E006°26.504'

🚐 3; Max 48hrs; Max 7m 🚽 None; See **223**

▶ Rue de la Plage. Turn off D33 onto C3, sp 'Corzent Le Lac'. At roundabout go straight over into narrow road with cycle path, signed. Follow road along lake edge and parking on right, signed. Be aware, the one-way system is narrow in places.

ℹ️ Popular designated parking at recreation beach adj to Lac Léman (Lake Geneva). Parking oversubscribed on hot days and holidays when space unlikely. Parking only allowed in designated bays, but if you get a space it is perfect if you like a splash in the water. Restaurant adj. Inspected 2016.

EXCENEVEX/YVOIRE
225 | K7 | 74140 | T | (A) N46°21.394' E006°21.099'

🚐 (A) 5; Free; Max 5t; (B) 30; Pay per hr; Max 24hrs 🚽 None

▶ 2 parking options off D25. Excenevex: (A) Turn off D25 at roundabout onto D225, sp 'Massongy'. Turn immediately right into car park, signed by bins. Yvoire: (B) N46°22.075' E006°19.485': Turn off D25 at roundabout into Chemin de Feycler. Turn immediately left and enter car park via barrier.

ℹ️ (A) Parking in small, level car park adj to D25 just 300m from Lac Léman (Lake Geneva). Poss to walk/cycle to (B) from here. (B) Seasonal sloping grass parking in barriered pay car park on outskirts of lakeside Beau Village, 350m. Inspected 2016.

(A) | (B)

ST PIERRE EN FAUCIGNY
226 | K7 | 74800 | N46°03.555' E006°22.506'

🚐 4; Max 48hrs 🚽 Custom; 2 unmetered CEE elec points

▶ D208/Ave de la Gare. On D1203 turn onto D12 at large roundabout crossing river, sp 'Le Grand Bornand'. Turn right in 1.5km, immediately before railway track, signed. Drive past train station, then turn left into station car park. Drive through car park to Aire at end, signed.

ℹ️ Aire adj to main road and train line with crossing bell, but trains are electric and don't run at night. Shade from trees in afternoon. Small town commerce adj. Inspected 2016.

LA ROCHE SUR FORON
227 | K7 | 74800 | N46°03.846' E006°18.780'

🚐 20; Max 48hrs 🚽 Euro Relais Junior

▶ Parking du Canada, D27. From north on D2 follow sp 'La Roche sur Foron'. At roundabout turn left, sp 'Centre' and signed. Follow road straight on, then at T-junction turn right, sp 'St Sixt', 'P Canada' and signed. At roundabout turn left onto D27, sp 'St Sixt' and signed. In 150m turn left, sp 'P Canada' and signed. Follow road downhill and to right to Aire. Not suitable for large motorhomes and has very steep, narrow access.

ℹ️ Aire in peaceful car park adj to stream. Pleasant town with commerce and 13th century historic quarter 200m via footpath. Riverside walk. Space likely as difficult access restricts visitors. Reinspected 2016.

ANNECY
228 | K8 | 74000 | N45°53.437' E006°08.341'

🚐 10; Max 24hrs; Max 8m 🚽 Custom; Also see **282**, may be easier to access

▶ Chemin de Colmyr. Turn off D1508 1km south of Annecy, sp 'Chapelle de Colmyr' and signed. In 60m turn right, signed. Aire on left. 3.5t weight restriction on access road.

ℹ️ Very popular, small, landscaped Aire 60m from lake; arrive early. Large lake with cycle and footpaths to lovely resort town. Swimming beach 150m, lifeguarded in season. Reinspected 2016.

LA BALME DE SILLINGY
229 | K7 | 74330 | N45°58.294' E006°01.869'

🚐 25; €6/24hrs; Collected; Apr-Nov; Max 48hrs 🛎 Custom

➡ D1508. From Annecy follow D1508 towards Bellegarde for 7km. After passing lake turn left, sp 'Crématorium' and signed. Follow road past car park, then turn left into Aire, signed.

ℹ Aire by small leisure lake, no view; popular on hot days and holidays. Parking entirely shaded in afternoon. Fishing lake, picnic area, park and café adj. Reinspected 2016.

THOIRY
230 | K7 | 01710 | N46°14.209' E005°59.282'

🚐 1; See info 🛎 Custom

➡ Chemin du Pont de Gremaz. In Thoiry turn off D89 main route into Chemin du Pont de Gremaz. Follow this road downhill and the Service Point is 600m on the left, signed. Not signed through Thoiry.

ℹ Roadside Service Point adj to pleasant picnic area with footpath and steps to small stream. 1 bay adj to Service Point, but this is also a padlocked gate into picnic area. Parking in picnic area poss at times. Inspected 2016.

MIJOUX
231 | K7 | 01410 | SKI | N46°22.155' E006°00.133'

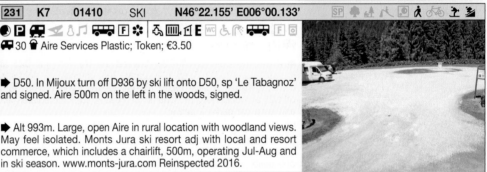

🚐 30 🛎 Aire Services Plastic; Token; €3.50

➡ D50. In Mijoux turn off D936 by ski lift onto D50, sp 'Le Tabagnoz' and signed. Aire 500m on the left in the woods, signed.

➡ Alt 993m. Large, open Aire in rural location with woodland views. May feel isolated. Monts Jura ski resort adj with local and resort commerce, which includes a chairlift, 500m, operating Jul-Aug and in ski season. www.monts-jura.com Reinspected 2016.

CHEZERY FORENS
232 | K7 | 01410 | N46°12.936' E005°51.797'

🚐 20; Grass parking; Max 1 night 🛎 Aire Services Plastic; Token; €2

➡ D991. Between Mijoux and Bellegarde on D991 near junction with D14. Turn off D991 at village boundary sign, sp 'Camping Chezery Le Valserine'. Aire in large field outside campsite.

ℹ Large open grass parking behind municipal campsite. Village with local commerce inc fromagerie 500m. Visited 2015.

Info/Photos: Alistair & Helen MacFadyen

LELEX
233 | K7 | 01410 | SKI | N46°18.022' E005°56.042'

🚐 8; Max 7 days 🛎 Aire Services 3000; May-Oct: Water €2/10 mins, Elec €4/24hrs; Nov-Apr: Water €5/10mins, Elec €8/24hrs; CC; 3 16amp CEE elec points

➡ Chemin de Frenet. Turn off D991 in the village by the bus stop and just before/after hotel bar, signed. Follow road downhill and the Aire is on the left before the tennis courts, signed.

ℹ Alt 845m. Peaceful Aire with designated parking surrounded by pleasant green space. 3 bays to right of Service Point for motorhomes using elec; 5 bays against tennis courts without elec. Village is small winter sports resort; ski lift to Monts Jura, 900m. Inspected 2016.

BELLEYDOUX
234 | K7 | 01130 | N46°15.331' E005°46.793'

🚐 7; See info 🛎 Flot Bleu Pacific; Token (FB); €2/20 mins

➡ D33. Adj to recycling area on right as exit village towards St Claude, signed.

ℹ Alt 873m. Aire adj to municipal store and recycling area. Some level parking near Service Point; parking opp is unlevel, but very suitable. Walking and cross country skiing routes detailed on notice board. Rural village in foothills of the Alps, limited local commerce. Limited parking at cross country depart, 500m. Reinspected 2016.

NANTUA
235 | J7 | 01130 | (A) N46°09.288' E005°35.815'

(A) 13; (B) 50; €7.50/night; Collected (A) 13; (B) 50; Both €7.50/night; Collected

▶ D74, adj to lake. From Montréal la Cluse follow D1084 along lake edge, sp 'Nantua'. At end of lake, before war memorial, turn right, sp 'Aire de Pique Nique'. Motorhomes allowed in lakeside car park immediately on right (B) N46°09.438' E005°36.197'. For Service Point and (A) continue along lake. At next roundabout turn right, sp 'Aire de Pique Nique' and signed. Service Point on left in 50m: N46°09.260' E005°35.827'. (A) 100m on right, signed.

ℹ️ (A) Landscaped bays between road and lake, partial views. Daytime trains only on adj track. (B) Lakeside car park with space for 50+ motorhomes subject to parked cars. Adj leisure lake popular on hot days and holidays; swimming (cold) and boat hire poss. Tourist commerce adj, LIDL 150m. Reinspected 2016.

IZERNORE
236 | J7 | 01580 | N46°13.116' E005°33.000'

10; Max 48hrs Custom

▶ Impasse des Cyclamens, Rue de l'Oignon. From Nantua follow D1084, sp 'Bourg en B', then D979, sp 'Izernore'. At roundabout turn onto D18, sp 'Izernore'. In 4.6km turn left at roundabout, sp 'Groupe Scolaire' and signed. Follow road to Aire on right, signed.

ℹ️ Pleasant, open Aire with countryside views to the foothills of the Alps. Ideal retreat if Nantua **235** is busy. Can take any unit configuration. Bins emptied Mon 7am. Inspected 2016.

CHANAY
237 | K7 | 01420 | N46°00.307' E005°46.966'

3 Aire Services 3000; CC; €3

▶ Route de Bocconod. Approach from north on D991, a pleasant and easy drive. In Chanay drive past the commerce and Mairie on right, then turn right into Route du Bocconod, sp 'Pompiers' and signed. Follow road for 140m and the Aire is on left, signed.

ℹ️ Peaceful Aire in car park on edge of village adj to fire station and open access sports field/park, dogs must be kept on lead. Local commerce on main route, 300m. Inspected 2016.

SEYSSEL
238 | K7 | 01420 | N45°57.092' E005°50.010'

7 Custom

▶ Rue François Broisin. Approach Seyssel from south on D992, then turn left before river bridge onto D991, sp 'Seyssel'. Turn 1st right, sp 'Aqualoisirs' and signed. Follow road to right along river. Pass under bridge and Aire is immediately on left.

ℹ️ Aire in small parking area adj to Rhône river and leisure lake, no view. Some noise from adj road bridge. Riverside parking with views allowed mid Sept-May. Leisure lake with water ski line and picnic area 150m. Inspected 2016.

SERRIERES EN CHAUTAGNE
239 | K8 | 73310 | N45°52.761' E005°50.547'

17; Max 72hrs Flot Bleu Fontaine; WCs adj

▶ Place Jules Verne. Turn off D991 in village centre by local commerce, signed. Service Point immediately on left adj to public WC. Parking 150m past lake on left, signed.

ℹ️ Popular, landscaped open Aire adj to swimming lake, partial views from some bays. Local commerce 150m. Inspected 2016.

BELLEY
240 | K8 | 01300 | N45°45.345' E005°40.691'

14 Urba Flux; 2 x €1

▶ D41. Follow sp 'St Germain les P' through town onto D41. Aire on right adj to D41 as exit town, signed.

ℹ️ Pleasant Aire adj to sports facilities. Children's play area and green space adj. Town commerce and centre, 400m, has large market Sat am. Reinspected 2016.

CREMIEU
`241` J8 38460 T N45°43.521' E005°14.801'

🚐 5; 5m bays 🚽 Custom; Cont WC at Mairie, 70m

▶ Place du Monument, Rue du 19 Mars 1962. Approach from west on D24. Turn left before town, sp 'Gendarmerie', then immediately left again, sp 'Gendarmerie'. Aire immediately on left, signed. DO NOT follow GPS through town!

ℹ️ Inadequate parking as bays are only designed for cars, other unrestricted parking adj. Interesting fortified medieval town adj with small town and tourist commerce. Town holds annual medieval festival in September. Inspected 2016.

BALAN
`242` J8 01360 N45°50.098' E005°05.754'

🚐 20; Outside of school hrs only 🚽 Custom

▶ Place du Longevent. Turn off D84b, main route through village, sp 'Salle Polyvalente'. Turn 1st right, signed. Drive through car park and Service Point is at rear, signed.

ℹ️ Aire at rear of school, ideal to use at weekends and during school holidays. Access is banned on the following days/times: Mon/Tues/Thurs/Fri 8.15-8.30am, 11.20-11.40am, 1.15-1.30pm, 4.20-4.40pm. Inspected 2016.

JONS
`243` J8 69330 N45°48.106' E005°05.023'

🚐 8 🚽 Euro Relais Box; 1 CEE elec point

▶ Chemin des Meules. Turn off D55 at roundabout, signed. Aire 50m on right, signed. Difficult, narrow entrance.

ℹ️ Aire offering shaded and open gravel parking adj to small village. Green space adj. Local commerce 50m beyond roundabout. Inspected 2016.

MEXIMIEUX
`244` J8 01800 N45°53.959' E005°11.598'

🚐 30 🚽 Euro Relais Box; Token (ER); €2

▶ Rue des Stades. Turn off D1084 at roundabout, sp 'ZI les Verchères' and 'Complexe Sportif'. Turn left in 220m and the Aire is on the right, signed.

ℹ️ Aire in large open car park suitable for any unit configuration; space likely. Noise from adj main road and railway. ALDI adj, town commerce 300m. Nearby Pérouges is a Beau Village and has medieval centre; 1.7km uphill walk as no motorhome parking. Inspected 2016.

BOURG EN BRESSE 1
`245` J7 01000 ⛺ N46°12.531' E005°14.416'

🚐 20; Max 48hrs; See info 🚽 Euro Relais Box

▶ Allée du Centre Nautique. From north on D1083 turn left at traffic lights, sp 'Carre d'Eau'. Follow road straight on and Service Point is to the right of the campsite entrance, signed.

ℹ️ Service Point in large municipal car park outside campsite entrance, campsite now closed. Swimming pool complex adj and cycle paths to town. Ideal if `246` full or unavailable. Also parking for 20 motorhomes at E.Leclerc supermarket on outskirts, 3.5t weight restriction: N46°13.218' E005°14.610'. Inspected 2016.

E.Leclerc

BOURG EN BRESSE 2
`246` J7 01000 T N46°11.906' E005°14.297'

🚐 5; 10m bays, some overhang 🚽 None; WC 150m; See `245`

▶ Blvd de Brou. From north on D1083 turn left at traffic lights onto D1075, sp 'Brou'. Continue south on D1075, then turn off, sp 'Monastère Royal de Brou'. Designated parking in one-way car park immediately on left, signed; must enter at far end.

ℹ️ Designated parking under lime trees. Although only 5 designated bays, the rest of the car park is unrestricted. Tourist commerce and WC 150m. Royal monastery 100m across park; open daily, €7.50pp. www.monastere-de-brou.fr Inspected 2016.

ST ANDRE SUR VIEUX JONC

247 J7 01960 N46°09.165' E005°09.115' SP

🚐 5; €5/night; Collected 🚽 Custom

▶ Impasse des Lys. From Bourg en Bresse head south on D1083. At roundabout turn right onto D117, then 1st left onto D67a, sp 'St Andre-s-Vieux-Jonc'. After 3.8km turn left, signed. At roundabout take 2nd exit into Chemin du Stade, signed. Aire in 240m after road bends to left, signed.

ℹ️ Peaceful Aire in well maintained lawned area in residential location adj to open access sports field. Parking in designated bays only; charges may apply to service at certain times of year. Local commerce 500m. Reinspected 2016.

ILLIAT

248 J7 01140 N46°11.100' E004°53.281' SP

🚐 4; Hedged bays 🚽 Custom

▶ Chemin du Bois Cholon. Follow D933 through St Didier sur Chalaron, sp 'Pont de Veyle'. At small war memorial turn right onto D66a, sp 'Illiat'. Follow road for 5km, then 300m after passing Illiat boundary sign turn right, signed. Service Point immediately on right at WC: N46°11.229' E004°53.206'. Follow road past fishing pond to designated parking on left, signed.

ℹ️ Designated parking adj to fishing ponds, no view. Popular fishing spot at weekends. Local commerce 300m. Inspected 2016.

CHATILLON SUR CHALARONNE

249 J7 01400 N46°07.157' E004°57.605' SP

🚐 Poss; See info 🚽 Custom

▶ Ave de la Poste. Approach from south on D2. Turn right, sp 'Salle Montpensier', 'P Gratuite' and 'La Poste'. Turn 1st left opp La Poste into car park, sp 'Salle Montpensier'. Service Point is on the left, signed.

ℹ️ Service Point in car park adj to local commerce. Town commerce 200m. Car park has no designated motorhome space and is marked with 5m bays, but parking should be poss outside busy periods. Inspected 2016.

THOISSEY

250 J7 01140 N46°10.190' E004°48.134' SP

🚐 7 🚽 None; See **254**

▶ Rue de l'Arquebuse. Turn off D7 in centre of town, sp 'P Arquebuse' and signed. Follow road for 200m, past parking and fire station, and designated parking is at end, signed.

ℹ️ Peaceful designated parking adj to allotments, apartments, park and stables/riding school. Small town commerce 250m, market Sun am. Ideal place to stock up before visiting one of the remote Aires, like Illiat **248**. Inspected 2016.

TREVOUX

251 J8 01600 N45°56.423' E004°46.018' SP

🚐 14; €5/night; Pay at campsite 🚽 None

▶ Chemin du Camping. From D933 exit roundabout by river, sp 'Camping'. Parking on right, signed.

ℹ️ Aire controlled by municipal campsite. Unrestricted day parking near river, 200m. Reinspected 2016.

JULIENAS

252 J7 69840 N46°14.141' E004°42.441' SP

🚐 5; 6m bays; See info 🚽 Euro Relais Mini

▶ Route de la Prat. From N79/A6 (Junction 29) roundabout follow sp 'Juliénas' onto D169. Follow D169 9.8km to Juliénas, where it becomes D17e. Go straight over roundabout, sp 'La Prat' and signed. Follow narrow road downhill for 200m and Aire on right, signed.

ℹ️ Peaceful Aire overlooking fields and beaujolais vines. Designated parking on curve and requires parallel parking, though Aire only likely to be busy during beaujolais festivities in Nov. 2km discovery walking trail from village. Market Mon am. Local commerce 200m. Inspected 2016.

SALLES ARBUISSONNAS EN BEAUJOLAIS | 253 | J7 | 69460 | N46°02.461' E004°38.173'

8 Depagne; WC emptying down wastewater drain; WC at parking

➡ Parking du Breuil. In St Étienne des Oullières turn off D43 onto D19, sp 'Salles Arbuissonnas'. Follow D19 for 3.4km. After passing under old railway bridge the Service Point is immediately on right, signed: N46°02.644' E004°38.241'. For parking pass Service Point on D19 and turn 1st right. Turn 1st right again and immediately right into car park, sp 'Parking du Breuil'.

ℹ Pleasant parking with green space overlooking beaujolais vines on hills. Impressive monastic priory with Romanesque cloister adj; open Wed-Sun 2-5pm all year, 10am-12.30 Apr-Oct, €4.50pp. Local commerce 150m. Inspected 2016.

BELLEVILLE | 254 | J7 | 69220 | N46°06.392' E004°45.253'

6; Max 48hrs; 11m bays + 3m overhang Custom

➡ Rue du Vivier. Exit A6/E15 at Junction 30, sp 'Belleville'. At roundabout go straight over, signed. At next roundabout turn right, signed. Turn right before next roundabout, signed. Aire at end of road on left, signed.

ℹ Marked parking under deciduous trees 200m from small town commerce and McDonald's. In Beaujolais wine region, signed driving tour from town. Ideal night halt just off A6/E15 toll motorway and D306/N6 primary route. Reinspected 2016.

BEAUJEU | 255 | I7 | 69430 | R | N46°09.747' E004°34.420'

5 Euro Relais Mini; Token (ER)

➡ Rue du Stade. Exit Beaujeu to west on D337 towards Les Dépôts. Turn off at the village boundary sign, sp 'Le Stade' and signed. Turn 1st left, signed. Aire at sports facilities at bottom of hill. Well signed through town.

ℹ Aire adj to municipal sports facilities with plenty of unmarked parking. On edge of town full of French charm; historic capital of Beaujolais region. Wine tasting and woodland walks adj. Small town commerce 600m. Inspected 2016.

QUINCIE EN BEAUJOLAIS | 256 | J7 | 69430 | N46°07.194' E004°37.143'

4 at Cave Co-operative; 7 adj to Service Point Custom; WC closed 10pm-6am

➡ D9. From Belleville follow D337, sp 'Beaujeu'. Turn off D337 onto D9 opp large dice, sp 'Quincié en B'. Designated parking in Cave Co-operative car park on left, signed. For Service Point and additional parking follow D9 straight on for 200m, then turn into car park on right, signed: N46°07.234' E004°36.973'.

ℹ Aire in pleasant beaujolais wine producing village. Cave Co-operative has shop open to public. Local commerce 150m from Service Point. Explore region by foot via 4km wine growing path starting in town square. Inspected 2016.

ST ETIENNE LA VARENNE | 257 | J8 | 69460 | N46°04.620' E004°37.794'

5; On other side of church Custom; 1 2amp CEE elec point; WC at Mairie

➡ Place de la Mairie. At roundabout south of Odenas turn off D43 onto D62, sp 'St Étienne la Varenne'. Follow road for 2km, then at top of hill turn into St Etienne la Varenne, sp 'Mairie - Ecole'. Turn left before church, signed, and Service Point to rear of church, signed.

ℹ Aire in centre of pleasant hilltop village in beaujolais wine region. Caveau Communal and local commerce opp. Inspected 2016.

VILLEFRANCHE SUR SAONE | 258 | J8 | 69400 | N45°58.367' E004°45.082'

103; €12/night inc 10amp elec; CC Euro Relais Junior; Inside barrier

➡ Route de Riottier. Exit A6 at Junction 31.2 and turn right at roundabout, sp 'Plan d'Eau'. Follow sp 'Plan d'Eau' straight on, then turn right, sp 'Camping'. Turn right into the campsite, signed. Enter through PARKNIGHT barrier.

ℹ Large commercial Aire occupying campsite adj to River Saône. Reinforced grass parking under deciduous trees. Campsite and facilities block open May-Sept, operates as Aire the rest of year. Adj riverside park and beach are very pleasant. Inspected 2016.

All of the listings in this section are Service Points without designated parking. The majority are located either at supermarkets or outside campsites.

Height barriers are rare at supermarkets and overnight parking should be possible. Always park considerately. Supermarket Service Points often lack a waste water drain.

Most campsites are municipally owned. Parking outside may be possible when campsites are closed. Acquiring tokens in rural locations may be difficult or impossible, especially in low season.

Remember to be a responsible tourist whenever offsite parking.

L'ARBRESLE | 259 | I8 | 69210 | N45°49.373' E004°36.338'

🚰 ▥ ⛽ E WC ♿ ☂ 🚌 F 🔄
☂ Custom

➡ Place des 3 Communes. Exit town to south on D389, sp 'Clermont FD'. At roundabout exit, sp 'Éveux'. Take 1st right and then 1st exit at roundabout and the Service Point is adj to recycling bins. Reinspected 2016.

CHAUSSAN | 260 | I8 | 69440 | N45°38.037' E004°38.279'

🚰 ▥ ⛽ E WC ♿ ☂ 🚌 F
☂ Custom (Dysfunctional); Tap on side of building

➡ D34. In Mornant turn onto D34, sp 'Chaussan'. In Chaussan turn left at roundabout, signed. Inspected 2012.

MORNANT | 261 | J8 | 69440 | N45°36.935' E004°40.254'

🚰 ▥ ⛽ E WC ♿ ☂ 🚌 F 🔄
☂ Euro Relais Junior; 2 unmetered CEE elec points

➡ Rue Boiron, adj to D30. Outside municipal campsite, signed. Reinspected 2016.

ST GALMIER | 262 | I8 | 42330 | N45°35.573' E004°20.157'

🚰 ▥ ⛽ E WC ♿ ☂ 🚌 F 🔄
☂ Aire Services Plastic; €1

➡ Route de la Thiéry. Turn off D12 onto D6, sp 'Chevrières' and 'Camping'. In 650m turn left, sp 'Camping' and signed. Go straight across roundabout onto 3.5t weight restricted road. Drive past campsite and Service Point on right, signed. Turn around point 200m past Service Point. Inspected 2016.

ST PRIEST EN JAREZ | 263 | I8 | 42270 | N45°28.721' E004°21.522'

🚰 ▥ ⛽ E WC ♿ ☂ 🚌 F 🔄
☂ Flot Bleu Euro; CC; €2

➡ At fuel station, off N82. From south on A72 exit at Junction 10 and turn right onto N82, sp 'St Priest en Jarez'. Aire at the fuel station of the Casino supermarket, signed. Inspected 2012.

ST ETIENNE DE ST GEOIRS | 264 | J8 | 38590 | N45°21.219' E005°20.097'

🚰 ▥ ⛽ E WC ♿ ☂ 🚌 F 🔄
☂ Flot Bleu Standard Plus; €2

➡ Chemin de la Pierre, adj to D154d. Exit St Étienne de St Geoirs towards Grenoble-Isère Airport on D519c, then D154d. Take 2nd exit at retail park roundabout, then turn immediately right into 3.5t weight restricted road. Service Point on left at end of car park before fuel station, signed. Inspected 2012.

ST VICTOR | 265 | J9 | 07410 | N45°06.631' E004°40.641'

🚰 ▥ ⛽ E WC ♿ ☂ 🚌 F 🔄
☂ Euro Relais Mini; Token (ER); No drive over drain

➡ Les Bessons. From St Félicien drive through St Victor on D532. After town turn left on bend by tennis court, sp 'Camping' and signed. Follow road up through holiday huts towards campsite and Service Point on left before campsite. Inspected 2016.

LE CHEYLARD | 266 | I9 | 07160 | N44°54.722' E004°26.451'

🚰 ▥ ⛽ E WC ♿ ☂ 🚌 F 🔄
☂ Euro Relais Junior; €2

➡ D120, at Super U. From Le Cheylard, take D120 east towards Beauvene. At roundabout turn left to Super U. Service Point in own bay at rear of fuel station and adj to Vulco tyres. Updated 2012.

Photo: Keith & Sue Lawrence

PORTES LES VALENCE | 267 | J9 | 26800 | N44°50.993' E004°52.153'

🚰 ▥ ⛽ E WC ♿ ☂ 🚌 F 🔄
☂ Custom

➡ D7, at Intermarché. Just off D7 as enter town from south, signed. Service Point in 24hr fuel station, signed. Reinspected 2014.

CREST | 268 | J9 | 26400 | N44°44.297' E005°00.285'

🚰 ▥ ⛽ E WC ♿ ☂ 🚌 F 🔄
☂ Flot Bleu Euro; CC; €2/20 mins

➡ Adj to D538/D93 roundabout, at fuel station of Casino supermarket. Signed. Reinspected 2016.

LA VOULTE SUR RHONE | 269 | J9 | 07800 | N44°48.447' E004°47.550'

🚰 ▥ ⛽ E WC ♿ ☂ 🚌 F 🔄
☂ Euro Relais Junior; Token (2/1)

➡ D86, ZI Quai Jean Jaurès at Intermarché supermarket. Service Point just past fuel station at rear of supermarket car park. Inspected 2013.

ST DIDIER SOUS AUBENAS 270 — I9 07200 N44°36.683' E004°24.550'

🚰 📖 🔁 E WC ♿ 🛗 🚌 F ⊡

Flot Bleu Pacific; Token; €2

➡ N102, at Casino supermarket. From south on N102 Casino supermarket is on left-hand side of road in commercial area just before the roundabout north of town. Flot Bleu to right of fuel station. Inspected 2014.

VILLENEUVE DE BERG 271 — I9 07170 N44°34.310' E004°30.703'

🚰 📖 🔁 E WC ♿ 🛗 🚌 F ⊡

Euro Relais Mini; Token; No drive over drain

➡ Off N102. Turn off N102 at the D902/N102 roundabout into the Intermarché supermarket. Service Point at the back of the fuel station. Inspected 2014.

LES CROTTES/ST THOME 272 — J9 97220 N44°30.045' E004°38.052'

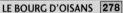

🚰 📖 🔁 E WC ♿ 🛗 🚌 F ⊡

Raclet; Unmetered CEE elec (Not working)

➡ D107. Adj to D107 just before entrance to Les Crottes from Viviers. Signed. Reinspected 2014.

PIERRELATTE 273 — J10 26700 N44°22.588' E004°42.194'

🚰 📖 🔁 E WC ♿ 🛗 🚌 F ⊡

Euro Relais Junior; Token (ER)

➡ Rue Antoine de St Exupéry. Turn off D458 at roundabout onto D358, sp 'Pierrelatte'. Follow road to roundabout above train track and take the 2nd exit onto D13, sp 'Mairie'. Turn right, and right again and the Service Point is on the right. Inspected 2014.

GRIGNAN 274 — J10 26230 N44°25.198' E004°53.624'

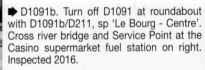

🚰 📖 🔁 E WC ♿ 🛗 🚌 F ⊡

Euro Relais Mini; Token (ER); No drive over drain

➡ D541, at Intermarché supermarket. Exit Grignan on D4, then D541 towards Donzère. 600m after town boundary, turn left into the Intermarché supermarket. The Aire is behind the supermarket, signed. Updated 2014.

DIEULEFIT 275 — J9 26220 N44°31.215' E005°03.364'

🚰 📖 🔁 E WC ♿ 🛗 🚌 F ⊡

Euro Relais Mini; €2; Token (ER)

➡ Supermarket and self-service laundry adj. D538 has lavender/honey/wine producers/sellers offering motorhome parking. Reinspected 2016.

DIE 276 — J9 26150 N44°45.033' E005°21.983'

🚰 📖 🔁 E WC ♿ 🛗 🚌 F ⊡

Flot Bleu Océane; Token; €3; May-Sept

➡ Lieu-Dit Largner. From south on D93 take 2nd exit at roundabout onto D238. After 1km turn left at traffic lights, sp 'Camping Municipal' and signed. Follow sp 'Camping Municipal' to Camping Municipal de Justin. Service Point outside campsite. Reinspected 2016.

SUSVILLE 277 — K9 38350 N44°55.487' E005°46.965'

🚰 📖 🔁 E WC ♿ 🛗 🚌 F ⊡

Flot Bleu Euro; CC; €2; Inspection cover

➡ N85. Service Point at the Casino supermarket fuel station adj to N85. Accessible off roundabout by service road. Reinspected 2016.

LE BOURG D'OISANS 278 — K9 38520 N45°03.418' E006°02.077'

🚰 📖 🔁 E WC ♿ 🛗 🚌 F ⊡

Flot Bleu Euro; CC; €2

➡ D1091b. Turn off D1091 at roundabout with D1091b/D211, sp 'Le Bourg - Centre'. Cross river bridge and Service Point at the Casino supermarket fuel station on right. Inspected 2016.

LE PONT DE BEAUVOISIN 279 — J8 73330 N45°31.726' E005°41.438'

🚰 📖 🔁 E WC ♿ 🛗 🚌 F ⊡

Flot Bleu Euro; CC; €2

➡ D1006, at the Super U. Exit Le Pont de Beauvoisin towards Les Échelles. In the retail park turn left at the roundabout, then immediately right into the Hyper U. The Service Point is immediately on the right. Reinspected 2016.

AUSSOIS 280 — L8 73500 N45°13.467' E006°44.756'

🚰 📖 🔁 E WC ♿ 🛗 🚌 F ⊡

Euro Relais Junior; €2

➡ Impasse du Loup. From Lanslebourg-Mont-Cenis turn off D1006 onto D83, sp 'Aussois'. Follow D83 8.7km to Aussois, then continue through village. Before leaving village turn left, sp 'Camping Municipal'. Turn left, immediately right, then right again, all sp 'Camping'. Drive past the sports facilities and Service Point on left outside municipal campsite. Inspected 2016.

LANSLEBOURG MONT CENIS 281 — L8 73480 N45°17.066' E006°52.290'

🚰 📖 🔁 E WC ♿ 🛗 🚌 F ⊡

Euro Relais Junior; 1 x €2

➡ D1006. From west on D1006 the Service Point is in a lay-by on right as you enter village at 'Lanslebourg' town sign. Reinspected 2016.

ANNECY LE VIEUX 282 K8 74940 N45°54.433' E006°09.117'

🛁 ⊞ 🚽 E WC ♿ 🚿 👣 🚌 F ▣

🍶 Custom

➡ Rue Centrale. From Thrones in east follow D909, sp 'Le Lac' and 'Annecy'. Follow road along lake edge, then turn left at 1st roundabout, sp 'Annecy', and right at next roundabout, signed. Service Point 350m on left. Reinspected 2016.

DEMI QUARTIER 283 K8 74120 N45°52.289' E006°37.848'

🛁 ⊞ 🚽 E WC ♿ 🚿 👣 🚌 F ▣

🍶 Flot Bleu Euro; CC; €2

➡ D1212, at Casino supermarket. Service Point adj to fuel station, signed. Inspected 2016.

PASSY 284 K8 18140 N45°55.141' E006°42.263'

🛁 ⊞ 🚽 E WC ♿ 🚿 👣 🚌 F ▣

🍶 Flot Bleu Pacific; Token; €2

➡ D39. Turn off D39 into Super U supermarket. Service Point near car wash. Inspected 2016.

SAMOENS 285 L7 74340 N46°04.626' E006°43.154'

🛁 ⊞ 🚽 E WC ♿ 🚿 👣 🚌 F ▣

🍶 Flot Bleu Euro; CC; €6

➡ D4, outside Camping le Giffre. From Taninges turn right off D907, sp 'Camping le Griffe'. Follow road straight on. After road bends to left, Service Point on left, signed. From Service Point, turn right at roundabout and cross river. Unrestricted parking on right adj to river: N46°04.567' E006°43.057'. Reinspected 2016.

LOISIN 286 K7 74140 N46°16.117' E006°19.002'

🛁 ⊞ 🚽 E WC ♿ 🚿 👣 🚌 F ▣

🍶 Aire Services Plastic; Token; €2

➡ Turn off the D1206/D35 roundabout sp 'Centre Commercial'. The Service Point is in the Super U fuel station. Inspected 2016.

CHANAZ 287 K8 73310 N45°48.683' E005°47.343'

🛁 ⊞ 🚽 E WC ♿ 🚿 👣 🚌 F ▣

🍶 Aire Services 3000; Token (3/3)

➡ Chemin de Cavettaz. Turn off D921 north of Chanaz, sp 'Camping'. Follow sp 'Camping' and the Service Point is in 650m outside the campsite entrance. Inspected 2016.

MONTALIEU VERCIEU 288 J8 38390 N45°49.662' E005°25.292'

🛁 ⊞ 🚽 E WC ♿ 🚿 👣 🚌 **F** ▣

🍶 Depagne

➡ D52f. Turn off D1075, main route through town, at roundabout following sp 'Vallee Bleue'. At next roundabout turn left, sp 'Camping' and signed; or turn right into large unrestricted car park. Turn right to campsite entrance, then left at roundabout. Service Point at end of car park, signed. Inspected 2016.

PONT D'AIN 289 J7 01160 N46°02.423' E005°20.531'

🛁 ⊞ 🚽 E WC ♿ 🚿 👣 🚌 F ▣

🍶 Flot Bleu Pacific; 2 x €1

➡ D1084. Exit town on D1075, sp 'Genève'. At roundabout turn left onto D1084, sp 'Genève'. Turn left at next roundabout into Super U. Service Point adj to fuel station. Inspected 2016.

PONT DU VAUX - ST BENIGNE 291 J7 01190 N46°26.220' E004°57.161'

🛁 ⊞ 🚽 E WC ♿ 🚿 👣 🚌 F ▣

🍶 Euro Relais Junior; Token (ER); €2

➡ D2/Rue de l'Hôpital. From Pont de Vaux take D2 towards St Trivier de Courtes. After 950m turn right at the roundabout. The Aire is at the ATAC supermarket on the right adj to D2. Service Point adj to fuel station. Reinspected 2016.

Photo: Geoff Myatt

LOGIS-NEUF (CONFRANÇON) 292 J7 01310 N46°15.328' E005°03.561'

🛁 ⊞ 🚽 E WC ♿ 🚿 👣 🚌 F ▣

🍶 Euro Relais Junior; €2

➡ D1079. From Bourg en-Bresse follow D1079, sp 'Mâcon'. After entering Logis-Neuf turn left onto D45, sp 'Vandeins'. Turn 1st left into Casino supermarket. Service Point adj to fuel station. Inspected 2016.

SANDRANS 293 J7 01400 N46°03.707' E004°58.347'

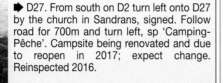

🛁 ⊞ 🚽 E WC ♿ 🚿 👣 🚌 F ▣

🍶 Raclet; Token (2/1); €3

➡ D27. From south on D2 turn left onto D27 by the church in Sandrans, signed. Follow road for 700m and turn left, sp 'Camping-Pêche'. Campsite being renovated and due to reopen in 2017; expect change. Reinspected 2016.

GPS Co-ordinates for SatNav

The GPS Co-ordinates published in this guide were taken onsite by our inspectors. We consider them a valuable and unique asset and at the time of publishing have decided not to publish them as electronic files for use on navigation devices. You have permission to type in the co-ordinates of an Aire you intend to visit but not to store or share them. For the security of our copyright:

- **Do not compile them into lists**

- **Do not publish, share or reproduce them anywhere in any format**

Vicarious Shop

A75 Aire de l'Aubrac

A89 Limagne

MOTORWAY SERVICE POINTS

Do not park overnight at motorway service stations and rest areas!

French motorway service and rest areas often allocate parking with car and caravan signs. The parking areas may look nice, however motorhomes, caravans, trucks and vans are frequently broken into at motorway rest areas. Often the occupants are asleep during the burglary; surely a situation you would not want to be in. The following motorway service areas all have a motorhome/coach Service Point. We have observed that they are often broken, full of rubbish or obstructed by parked trucks. Vicarious Media recommends that you never park overnight at motorway services and rest areas and maintain vigilance at all times when using them.

Town	Map ref.	Grid ref.	GPS	Aire name and location
ATLANTIC				
SAUGON	A	D9	N45°11.364' W000°29.392'	Aire de Saugon Est. A10/E5 northbound between Junctions 39a and 38.
SAUGON	A	D9	N45°11.330' W000°29.550'	Aire de Saugon Ouest. A10/E5 southbound between Junctions 38 and 39a.
SAINT ANDRE DE CUBZAC	B	E9	N44°58.849' W000°25.793'	Aire de l'Estalot. A10/E5 southbound between Junctions 39a and 41.
BORDEAUX	C	E9	N44°38.853' W000°26.160'	Aire des Landes. A62/E72 northbound between Junctions 2 and 1.1.
BORDEAUX	C	E9	N44°38.659' W000°26.279'	Aire des Landes. A62/E72 southeast between Junctions 1.1 and 2.
AGEN	D	E10	N44°11.978' E000°30.367'	Aire d'Agen-Porte d'Aquitane. A62/E72 between Junctions 7 and 6. Accessible both sides.
LIPOSTHEY	E	D10	N44°21.614' W000°51.067'	Les Porte des Landes. A63 between Junction 17 and 18. Exit to Aire de Les Porte des Landes. Accessible both sides.
LESPERON	F	D10	N43°56.216' W001°05.400'	Aire de l'Océan Est. A63/E70 northbound between Junctions 12 and 13.
LESPERON	F	D10	N43°56.195' W001°05.593'	Aire de l'Océan Ouest. A63/E70 southbound between Junctions 13 and 12.
BAYONNE	G	C11	N43°25.390' W001°35.963'	Aire de Bidart. A63/E80 southwest between Junctions 4 and 3.
BAYONNE	G	C11	N43°25.306' W001°35.813'	Aire de Bidart. A63/E80 northeast between Junctions 3 and 4.
PAU	H	D11	N43°25.262' W000°35.911'	Aire de Lacq-Audejos. A64/E80 southeast between Junctions 8 and 9.
LIMOUSIN & AUVERGNE				
ST SULPICE LES FEUILLES	A	F7	N46°18.833' E001°25.223'	Aire de Boismandé Est. A20/E9 northbound between Junctions 22 and 21.
ST SULPICE LES FEUILLES	A	F7	N46°18.765' E001°25.052'	Aire de Boismandé Ouest. A20/E9 southbound between Junctions 21 and 22.
MERLINES	B	G8	N45°37.355' E002°27.375'	Aire de la Haute Corrèze. A89 between Junctions 24 and 25. Accessible both sides.
LORLANGES	C	H8	N45°20.122' E003°16.338'	Aire de La Fayette. A75/E11 at Junction 21. Accessible both sides.
ST FLOUR	D	H9	N45°01.910' E003°08.095'	Aire de Service du Cantal. D909. Exit A75/E11 at Junction 29. Accessible both sides.
A89 LIMAGNE	E	H8	N45°51.004' E003°24.412'	Aire de Limagne, A89 near Junction 28. Accessible both sides.

MOTORWAY SERVICE POINTS

Town	Map ref.	Grid ref.	GPS	Aire name and location
MEDITERRANEAN				
LA LOZERE	A	H9	N44°52.177' E003°14.947'	Aire de la Lozère. A75/E11 at Junction 32. Accessible both sides.
AUMONT AUBRAC	B	H9	N44°44.418' E003°17.358'	Aire de l'Aubrac. A75/E11 southbound at Junction 35. Service Point at Simply supermarket.
AUMONT AUBRAC	B	H9	N44°44.709' E003°17.294'	Aire de l'Aubrac. A75 between Junction 34 and 35. Accessible both sides.
LE CAYLAR	C	H10	N43°51.896' E003°18.714'	Aire du Caylar. A75/E11 at Junction 49. Accessible both sides.
CAPENDU	D	G11	N43°10.590' E002°32.584'	Aire des Corbières. A61/E80 eastbound between Junctions 24 and 25.
CAPENDU	D	G11	N43°10.736' E002°32.541'	Aire des Corbières. A61/E80 westbound between Junctions 25 and 24.
BANYULS DELS ASPRES	E	H12	N42°34.797' E002°50.785'	Aire du Village Catalan. A9/E15 between Junctions 42 and 43. Second Service Point: N42°34.767' E002°50.767'. Accessible both sides.
CAVES	F	H12	N42°56.993' E002°58.346'	Aire de la Palme. A9/E15 northbound between Junctions 40 and 39.
CAVES	F	H12	N42°57.047' E002°58.109'	Aire de la Palme. A9/E15 southbound between Junction 39 and 40.
NARBONNE	G	H11	N43°12.926' E003°05.633'	Aire de Narbonne-Vinassan. A9/E80 northeast between Junctions 37 and 36.
NARBONNE	G	H11	N43°12.866' E003°05.328'	Aire de Narbonne-Vinassan. A9/E80 southbound between Junctions 36 and 37.
BEZIERS	H	H11	N43°21.530' E003°20.795'	Aire de Béziers-Montblanc. A9/E15/E80 northeast between Junctions 36 and 34.
BEZIERS	H	H11	N43°21.609' E003°20.577'	Aire de Béziers-Montblanc. A9/E15/E80 southwest between Junctions 34 and 36.
NIMES	I	I10	N43°52.512' E004°26.888'	Aire de Nîmes-Marguerittes. A9/E15 southwest between Junctions 23 and 24.
CARTELS	J	H11	N43°41.512' E003°21.278'	Sortie 54. A75 Junction 54, Le Bosc. Accessible both sides.
FABREGUES	K	I11	N43°32.879' E003°47.733'	Aire de Montpellier-Fabrègues. A7/E80/E714 southwest between Junction 32 and 33.
LANCON PROVENCE	L	J11	N43°35.325' E005°11.543'	Aire de Lançon de Provence. A7/E80/E714 southbound between Junctions 27 and 28.
LANCON PROVENCE	L	J11	N43°35.405' E005°11.510'	Aire de Lançon de Provence. A7/E80/E714 northbound between Junctions 28 and 27.
ROUSSET	M	K11	N43°28.079' E005°39.375'	Aire de Rousset. A8/E80 eastbound between Junctions 34 and 33.
ROUSSET	M	K11	N43°28.305' E005°38.637'	Aire de l'Arc. A8/E80 westbound between Junctions 33 and 32.
BRIGNOLES	N	K11	N43°25.322' E005°59.480'	Aire des Terrasses de Provence. A8/E80 between Junctions 34 and 35. Accessible both sides.
VIDAUBAN	O	K11	N43°24.872' E006°27.256'	Aire de Vidauban Sud. A8/E80 eastbound between Junctions 35 and 36.
MIDI-PYRENEES				
BRIVE-MONTAUBAN	A	F9	N45°01.916' E001°31.483'	Aire de Pech Montat. A20/E9 between Junctions 53 and 54. Accessible both sides.
SEVERAC LE CHATEAU	B	H10	N44°19.839' E003°04.930'	Aire de l'Aveyron. N88. Exit A75/E11 at Junction 42. Accessible both sides.
MONTANS	C	G10	N43°51.786' E001°53.844'	Aire des Issarts. A68 northeast between Junctions 8 and 9.
MONTANS	C	G10	N43°51.120' E001°52.831'	Aire de Sanbatan. A68 southwest between Junctions 9 and 8.
AVIGNONET-LAURAGAIS	D	G11	N43°21.311' E001°48.271'	Aire de Port-Lauragais. A61/E80 between Junctions 20 and 21. Accessible both sides.
CAPENS	E	F11	N43°20.262' E001°14.742'	Aire du Volvestre. A64/E80 westbound between Junctions 28 and 27.
POITOU				
VILLIERS EN PLAINE	A	E7	N46°25.734' W000°30.328'	Aire de la Chateaudrie. A83 eastbound between Junctions 9 and 10.
VILLIERS EN PLAINE	A	E7	N46°25.828' W000°30.241'	Aire de la Chateaudrie. A83 westbound between Junctions 10 and 9.
NIORT	B	E7	N46°17.777' W000°22.770'	Aire du Poitou-Charentes. A10/E5 southbound between Junctions 32 and 33.

Town	Map ref.	Grid ref.	GPS	Aire name and location
SAINT LEGER	C	D8	N45°36.578' W000°35.863'	Aire de St Léger. A10/E5 northbound between Junctions 36 and 35.
SAINT LEGER	C	D8	N45°36.622' W000°36.131'	Aire de St Léger. A10/E5 southbound between Junctions 35 and 36.
BEDENAC	D	E9	N45°10.397' W000°19.956'	Aire de Bedenac. N10/E606 southbound between junctions with D145 and D250.
PAMPROUX	E	E7	N46°27.275' W000°01.036'	Aire de Rouillé-Pamproux. A10/E5 northeast between Junctions 31 and 30.
PAMPROUX	E	E7	N46°27.066' W000°00.956'	Aire de Rouillé-Pamproux. A10/E5 southwest between Junctions 30 and 31.

RHONE-ALPS

Town	Map ref.	Grid ref.	GPS	Aire name and location
DRACE	A	J7	N46°08.649' E004°46.068'	Aire de Dracé. A6/E15 southbound between Junctions 29 and 30.
LES SALLES	B	I8	N45°51.254' E003°48.675'	Aire du Haut Forez. A89/E70 eastbound between Junctions 31 and 32.
NERONDE	C	I8	N45°51.026' E004°13.523'	Aire de la Loire. A89 between Junctions 33 and 34. Accessible both sides.
COMMUNAY	D	J8	N45°35.462' E004°49.946'	Aires de Communay-Nord. A46/E15/E70 southwest, 2.3km after Junction 16.
L'ISLE D'ABEAU	E	J8	N45°36.721' E005°12.552'	Aire de l'Isle-d'Abeau. A43/E70 eastbound between Junctions 6 and 7.
L'ISLE D'ABEAU	E	J8	N45°36.818' E005°12.729'	Aire de l'Isle d'Abeau. A43/E70 westbound between Junctions 7 and 6.
SEYNOD	F	K8	N45°52.607' E006°04.251'	Aire des Fontanelles. A41/E712 southwest between Junctions 16 and 15.1.
PASSY	G	K8	N45°55.304' E006°39.785'	Aire de Passy-Mont Blanc. A40/E25 southbound between Junctions 20 and 21.
CHATEAUNEUF	H	K8	N45°32.829' E006°09.376'	Aire de l'Arclusaz. A43/E70 westbound at Junction 23.
CHATEAUNEUF	H	K8	N45°32.898' E006°09.332'	Aire du Val Gelon. A43/E70 eastbound at Junction 23.
ST RAMBERT D'ALBON	I	J9	N45°16.563' E004°49.754'	Aire de St Rambert d'Albon. A7/E15 northbound between Junctions 13 and 12.
ST RAMBERT D'ALBON	I	J9	N45°16.490' E004°49.576'	Aire de St Rambert d'Albon. A7/E15 southbound between Junctions 12 and 13.
PONT DE L'ISERE	J	J9	N45°01.237' E004°52.615'	Aire de Latitude 45. A7/E15 northbound between Junctions 14 and 13.
PONT DE L'ISERE	J	J9	N45°01.035' E004°52.482'	Aire de Pont-de-l'Isère A7/E15 southbound between Junction 13 and 14.
LA BAUME D'HOSTUN	K	J9	N45°04.500' E005°12.551'	Aire Porte de la Drôme. A49/E713 southwest between Junctions 9 and 8.
LA BAUME D'HOSTUN	K	J9	N45°04.291' E005°12.730'	Aire de Royans-Vercors. A49/E713 northeast between Junctions 8 and 9.
SAULCE SUR RHONE	L	J9	N44°43.178' E004°47.276'	Aire de Saulce. A7/E15 northbound between Junctions 17 and 16.
MONTELIMAR	M	J9	N44°30.779' E004°46.834'	Aire de Montélimar. A7/E15 northbound between Junctions 18 and 17.
MONTELIMAR	M	J9	N44°30.980' E004°46.757'	Aire de Montélimar. A7/E15 southbound between Junctions 17 and 18.

A75 Aire de l'Aubrac

Sortie

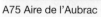

Chatel-Guyon

Uvernet Fours

This list of closed Aires is provided to prevent unnecessary journeys. The Aires have been confirmed closed by inspectors on location. Closed Aires that have no alternative Aire are marked with an **X** on the mapping. Closed Aires are listed in each region, alphabetically by town name. The map reference number from the edition in which they were published is also provided.

Town	Map number and edition	GPS	Year closed
ATLANTIC			
ARES	157 South Ed	N44°46.181' W001°06.707'	2016
ARTOUSTE FABREGES	98 South Ed	N42°52.817' W000°23.917'	2016
BERGERAC	54 3rd Ed	N44°50.760' E000°29.275'	2010
BISCARROSSE	145 4th Ed	N44°24.636' W001°10.065'	2013
BISCARROSSE PLAGE 2	148 4th Ed	N44°26.391' W001°14.883'	2013
BRANTOME 1	228 South Ed	N45°22.700' E000°38.733'	2016
BRANTOME 2	78 3rd Ed	N45°21.416' E000°39.167'	2010
CAVIGNAC 1	93 3rd Ed	N45°05.964' W000°23.279'	2010
DUNE DU PYLA (PILAT)	151 South Ed	N44°35.833' W001°11.900'	2016
GOURETTE 2	95 4th Ed	N42°57.445' W000°19.837'	2013
JAVERLHAC	2 4th Ed	N45°34.060' E000°33.730'	2013
LAC DE VIELLE ST GIRONS	133 South Ed	N43°54.178' W001°18.572'	2016
LALINDE	26 South Ed	N44°50.365' E000°44.585'	2016
LE MOUTCHIC	160 4th Ed	N44°59.934' W001°08.431'	2013
LESCAR 2	90 4th Ed	N43°20.025' W000°25.806'	2013
LESPARRE MEDOC	171 4th Ed	N45°18.769' W000°56.733'	2013
LIMEUIL 1	28 South Ed	N44°52.967' E000°53.383'	2016
MONTIGNAC 1	18 South Ed	N45°03.668' E001°09.548'	2016
MONTALIVET LES BAINS 1	165 South Ed	N45°22.230' W001°08.658'	2016
MONTALIVET LES BAINS 2	166 South Ed	N45°22.120' W001°08.657'	2016
MONTPON MENESTEROL	213 4th Ed	N45°01.253' E000°09.601'	2013
MUSSIDAN	60 3rd Ed	N45°02.508' E000°21.137'	2010
PAU	88 4th Ed	N43°17.951' W000°22.581'	2013
PERIGUEUX 1	74 3rd Ed	N45°10.882' E000°43.357'	2010
POUILLON 2	109 4th Ed	N43°35.639' W001°00.942'	2013
PREIGNAC	176 4th Ed	N44°35.125' W000°17.731'	2013
SOUSTONS	126 4th Ed	N43°44.798' W001°19.291'	2013
ST JULIEN EN BORN	136 4th Ed	N44°04.248' W001°13.814'	2013
LIMOUSIN & AUVERGNE			
AYDAT 1	35 3rd Ed	N45°39.630' E002°58.628'	2010
LE PUY EN VELAY	99 South Ed	N45°02.634' E003°53.574'	2016
PINOLS	101 4th Ed	N45°03.175' E003°24.760'	2014
RIOM ES MONTAGNES	162 South Ed	N45°17.059' E002°39.263'	2016
SALINS	165 4th Ed	N45°11.492' E002°23.617'	2014
MEDITERRANEAN			
AGDE	66 South Ed	N43°17.954' E003°28.259'	2016
AIGUES MORTES	2 105 4th Ed	N43°33.933' E004°11.733'	2013

Town	Map number and edition	GPS	Year closed
ARGELES SUR MER	62 3rd Ed	N42°34.627' E003°02.125'	2010
ARGENS MINERVOIS	52 4th Ed	N43°14.448' E002°45.865'	2013
AVIGNON 1	150 South Ed	N43°57.111' E004°47.621'	2016
BOLQUERE PYRENEES 2000 1	22 4th Ed	N42°30.983' E002°03.533'	2013
BORMES LES MIMOSAS	130 3rd Ed	N43°09.317' E006°20.800'	2010
CAIRANNE	132 4th Ed	N44°13.807' E004°55.721'	2013
CANET EN ROUSILLON	37 South Ed	N42°41.967' E003°01.335'	2016
CARCASSONNE	6 South Ed	N43°12.324' E002°22.362'	2016
CARNON PLAGE 2	94 3rd Ed	N43°33.198' E004°00.590'	2010
DAUPHIN	150 4th Ed	N43°54.034' E005°47.041'	2014
DRAGUIGNAN	53 3rd Ed	N43°31.974' E006°26.976'	2010
FONTCOUVERTE	131 3rd Ed	N45°46.242' W000°32.491'	2008
FONTIES D'AUDE	37 3rd Ed	N43°11.154' E002°27.154'	2012
FREJUS 1	140 3rd Ed	N43°25.238' E006°44.550'	2010
FREJUS 2	141 3rd Ed	N43°25.458' E006°44.264'	2010
HYERES 'LE MEROU'	178 4th Ed	N43°06.550' E006°10.893'	2014
LA BOUILLADISSE	165 4th Ed	N43°23.386' E005°35.912'	2014
LA MOTTE 1	48 3rd Ed	N43°29.457' E006°32.081'	2010
LA REDORTE	95 3rd Ed	N43°14.912' E002°39.520'	2010
LA SEYNE SUR MER	173 4th Ed	N43°06.795' E005°51.469'	2014
LE BARCARES 3	40 South Ed	N42°47.350' E003°02.033'	2016
LE BARCARES 6	43 4th Ed	N42°47.200' E003°02.283'	2013
LE LAVANDOU	4 3rd Ed	N43°07.458' E006°21.456'	2010
LES ARCS	192 South Ed	N43°27.292' E006°28.644'	2016
LODEVE	79 4th Ed	N43°44.017' E003°19.083'	2013
MARSEILLAN PLAGE	39 3rd Ed	N43°18.999' E003°32.715'	2010
NEVACHE	236 South Ed	N45°01.004' E006°38.177'	2016
PELVOUX	200 3rd Ed	N44°52.133' E006°29.100'	2010
PEZENS	5 South Ed	N43°15.329' E002°15.813'	2016
PONT DU FOSSE 1	5 3rd Ed	N44°40.075' E006°13.870'	2010
PORT DE BROSSOLETTE	57 4th Ed	N43°10.281' E003°10.846'	2013
PORT ST LOUIS DU RHONE 1	110 4th Ed	N43°23.006' E004°48.439'	2014
PUICHERIC	17 3rd Ed	N43°13.628' E002°37.618'	2010
ROUTIER	7 South Ed	N43°06.492' E002°07.391'	2016
SABLET	134 4th Ed	N44°11.598' E004°59.695'	2013
SETE BEACH 2	3rd Ed	N43°22.964' E003°38.458'	2010
SIX FOURS LES PLAGES 2	172 4th Ed	N43°04.760' E005°48.587'	2014
ST GILLES	110 3rd Ed	N43°40.337' E004°26.020'	2010
ST MICHEL L'OBSERVATOIRE	147 4th Ed	N43°54.938' E005°42.982'	2014
ST TROPEZ 1	186 4th Ed	N43°16.180' E006°38.054'	2014
STE CECILE LES VIGNES	131 4th Ed	N44°15.078' E004°53.409'	2013
STE MAXIME 2	194 4th Ed	N43°18.474' E006°37.992'	2014
STE MAXIMIN LA STE BAUME	170 South Ed	N43°27.420' E005°51.196'	2016
TREBES	98 3rd Ed	N43°12.539' E002°26.798'	2010
UVERNET FOURS	212 South Ed	N44°22.091' E006°37.668'	2016
MIDI-PYRENEES			
AUZAT	134 4th Ed	N42°45.867' E001°28.833'	2013
BAGNAC SUR CELE	19 4th Ed	N44°40.082' E002°09.475'	2014
CASTELSARRASIN	41 3rd Ed	N44°02.279' E001°06.835'	2012
CASTRES	87 3rd Ed	N43°37.225' E002°15.203'	2012
CUQ LES VIELMUR	62 3rd Ed	N43°38.464' E002°05.846'	2010
GOURDON 1	92 3rd Ed	N44°44.948' E001°22.535'	2010
LISLE SUR TARN	77 3rd Ed	N43°51.708' E001°49.122'	2012
LOURDES 2	161 4th Ed	N43°05.296' W000°03.161'	2014
MARCIAC	164 3rd Ed	N43°31.571' E000°09.759'	2010
MILLAU 1	83 4th Ed	N44°05.695' E003°04.944'	2014
NAUSSAC	24 South Ed	N44°31.293' E002°04.774'	2016
NOGARO	172 South Ed	N43°45.871' W000°01.995'	2016
PINSAC	5 4th Ed	N44°51.293' E001°30.719'	2014
RISCLE	169 South Ed	N43°39.697' W000°04.737'	2016

CLOSED AIRES

Town	Map number and edition	GPS	Year closed
SERRES SUR ARGET	130 South Ed	N42°58.150' E001°31.133'	2016
SOULOM	156 South Ed	N42°57.350' W000°04.364'	2016
TOULOUSE	203 South Ed	N43°35.236' E001°29.442'	2016
POITOU			
AVAILLES LIMOUZINE	61 3rd Ed	N46°07.385' E000°39.626'	2010
AYTRE (ANGOULINS)	106 South Ed	N46°06.778' W001°07.381'	2016
BAIGNES STE RADEGONDE	102 4th Ed	N45°23.045' W000°13.776'	2013
BOURG CHARENTE 1	107 4th Ed	N45°40.427' W000°13.461'	2014
BOURG CHARENTE 2	108 4th Ed	N45°40.344' W000°13.677'	2014
BOYARDVILLE	157 4th Ed	N45°58.140' W001°14.268'	2014
CHATELAILLON PLAGE 1	109 South Ed	N46°03.768' W001°05.476'	2016
CHATELAILLON PLAGE 2	159 4th Ed	N46°04.351' W001°05.162'	2014
CHATELAILLON PLAGE 3	160 4th Ed	N46°04.635' W001°05.253'	2014
CHATELAILLON PLAGE 3	111 South Ed	N46°04.611' W001°05.317'	2016
CONFOLENS 1	79 3rd Ed	N46°00.768' E000°40.047'	2010
DISSAY	44 3rd Ed	N46°42.750' E000°24.810'	2010
FOURAS 1	165 4th Ed	N45°58.894' W001°05.210'	2014
JARNAC	191 South Ed	N45°40.598' W000°10.390'	2016
LA PALMYRE 2	69 3rd Ed	N45°41.432' W001°10.610'	2010
LA TREMBLADE	142 4th Ed	N45°45.986' W001°08.343'	2014
LE CHATEAU D'OLERON 1	111 3rd Ed	N45°53.303' W001°12.298'	2010
LES MATHES 1	42 3rd Ed	N45°43.063' W001°08.870'	2010
MERIGNAC	64 3rd Ed	N45°41.687' W000°05.141'	2010
MONTLIEU LA GARDE	169 South Ed	N45°14.919' W000°15.071'	2016
PORT DES BARQUES 2	136 3rd Ed	N45°56.950' W001°05.733'	2010
PORT LES MINIMES	62 3rd Ed	N46°08.533' W001°10.277'	2010
ROCHEFORT 1	39 3rd Ed	N45°56.597' W000°57.518'	2010
RONCE LES BAINS	92 3rd Ed	N45°47.582' W001°09.010'	2010
SAINTES	120 4th Ed	N45°45.300' W000°37.711'	2014
SECONDIGNY	32 3rd Ed	N46°36.274' W000°24.979'	2010
ST GENIS DE SAINTONGE	123 4th Ed	N45°28.785' W000°34.108'	2014
ST GERMAIN DE MARENCENNES 1	116 South Ed	N46°04.632' W000°47.247'	2016
ST JEAN D'ANGELY 1	59 3rd Ed	N45°56.960' W000°32.178'	2010
ST YRIEIX	26 3rd Ed	N45°41.160' E000°08.857'	2010
RHONE-ALPS			
AIGUEBLANCHE	50 3rd Ed	N45°30.169' E006°30.068'	2010
AIX LES BAINS	95 3rd Ed	N45°42.180' E005°53.186'	2010
AIX LES BAINS	200 South Ed	N45°42.309' E005°53.281'	2016
BELLEGARDE SUR VALSERINE	147 South Ed	N46°06.420' E005°49.900'	2016
BOURG ST MAURICE	180 South Ed	N45°36.210' E006°45.960'	2016
CHALLES LES EAUX	137 South Ed	N45°32.900' E005°59.262'	2016
CHATILLON EN DIOIS	81 3rd Ed	N44°40.952' E005°26.873'	2010
COURCHEVEL LA TANIA	184 South Ed	N45°25.895' E006°36.030'	2016
DONZERE (MARKET)	2 3rd Ed	N44°26.600' E004°42.598'	2010
LES BORELS - Casteljau	87 South Ed	N44°23.974' E004°12.808'	2016
LES CARROZ D'ARACHES	164 South Ed	N46°01.517' E006°38.632'	2016
LES ROCHES DE CONDRIEU	48 South Ed	N45°27.239' E004°46.094'	2016
MORZINE	106 3rd Ed	N46°10.456' E006°42.623'	2010
ST CIRGUES EN MONTAGNE	77 3rd Ed	N44°45.351' E004°05.706'	2010
ST DONAT SUR L'HERBASSE	67 4th Ed	N45°07.122' E004°58.301'	2014
ST GENIS POUILLY	148 South Ed	N46°15.816' E006°01.814'	2016
ST JUST	94 4th Ed	N44°18.097' E004°36.350'	2014
ST PAUL DE VARAX	71 3rd Ed	N46°05.953' E005°07.761'	2010
ST PIERRE DE CHARTREUSE 1	87 3rd Ed	N45°20.477' E005°49.059'	2010
ST SORLIN EN VALLOIRE	54 4th Ed	N45°17.417' E004°57.250'	2014
ST TRIVIER DE COURTES	202 South Ed	N46°27.540' E005°04.838'	2016
TOURNON SUR RHONE 1	28 3rd Ed	N45°04.230' E004°49.716'	2010
VALLOIRE	187 South Ed	N45°10.135' E006°25.761'	2016
VILLARS LES DOMBES	43 3rd Ed	N45°59.572' E005°01.548'	2012

LPG-GPL cup adaptor.

LPG-GPL cup hand gun.

316 LPG fuel stations are listed here. GPL, as it is named in France, is available at most motorway service stations and the cup shaped connector is standard across France.

TOWN	GPS	DIRECTIONS
ATLANTIC		
AGEN	N44°10.708' E000°38.004'	Géant. D17/Ave de Lacapelette. 3km south of town.
AIRE SUR L'ADOUR	N43°43.342' W000°15.874'	Total. D824/Ave de Bordeaux. 2km north of town.
ARCACHON	N44°39.141' W001°08.819'	Avia. D650/Blvd Mestrezat. 150m north of 157. 2.5km east of town.
BAYONNE	N43°30.290' W001°26.721'	E.Leclerc. Adj to D817/D107 roundabout. Northeast of town. Access not ideal for motorhomes over 8m.
BAYONNE	N43°29.543' W001°27.541'	Total. Ave du Marechal Juin. 750m west of A64 Junction 6. 1.3km east of town.
BERGERAC	N44°50.100' E000°26.867'	E.Leclerc. Adj to D936/D936e1 roundabout. 3.4km southwest of town.
BERGERAC	N44°51.017' E000°29.575'	Total. N21/Blvd Chanzy. 800m east of town.
BERGERAC	N44°49.950' E000°29.800'	Total. N21/Route d'Agen. 2.6km south of town.
A63 BIDART (North)	N43°25.306' W001°35.813'	Total. Aire de Bidart. A63/E80 northbound between Junctions 4 and 3.
A63 BIDART (South)	N43°25.390' W001°35.963'	Total. Aire de Bidart. A63/E80 southbound between Junctions 3 and 4.
BIGANOS	N44°38.183' W000°57.583'	Auchan. D3e13. 1.25km south of town. LPG pump under 2.95m high canopy.
BILLIERE	N43°18.349' W000°24.186'	Total. D817/Blvd Charles de Gaulle. 700m northwest of town.
BISCARROSSE	N44°23.417' W001°09.650'	Super U. D652/Ave du Maréchal Lyautey. 500m south of town.
BIZANOS	N43°18.214' W000°19.374'	Total Access. D817/Route de Tarbes. 3km northeast of town.
BORDEAUX	N44°52.971' W000°33.796'	Auchan. Blvd Aliénor d'Aquitaine. 250m south of A630/E5 Junction 4.
A630 GRADIGNAN - BORDEAUX (East)	N44°47.172' W000°35.689'	Agip. Aire de Thouars Nord. A630/E70 eastbound between Junctions 17 and 16.
A630 GRADIGNAN - BORDEAUX (West)	N44°47.155' W000°35.734'	Agip. Aire de Thouars Nord. A630/E70 westbound between Junctions 16 and 17.
BOULAZAC	N45°11.138' E000°46.488'	Intermarché. D5/Ave Marcel Paul. 850m east of roundabout junction with N221. 800m north of town.
CASTELJALOUX	N44°19.167' E000°05.600'	Intermarché. Rue Pierre Dufiet, off D933. 775m northeast of town.
A63 CESTAS (East)	N44°44.544' W000°42.435'	Total. Aire de Bordeaux-Cestas. A63/E70 eastbound between Junctions 24 and 25.
A63 CESTAS (West)	N44°44.752' W000°42.200'	Total. Aire de Bordeaux-Cestas. A63/E70 westbound between Junctions 25 and 24.
DAX	N43°43.032' W001°03.072'	Total. D129/Route Georges Chaulet. 1km north of town.
DAX	N43°44.467' W001°01.000'	Total. Route de Carrère, off D824 roundabout. Take exit for C6/Le Hort.
EYSINES	N44°53.545' W000°40.058'	Total Access. D2215/Ave du Médoc. 1.7km west of town.
FUMEL	N44°29.500' E000°58.183'	Intermarché. Ave de Ladhuie, 150m northeast of roundabout junction with D710. 660m south of town.

LPG-GPL

TOWN	GPS	DIRECTIONS
GUJAN MESTRAS	N44°37.001' W001°04.447'	Super U. D650e3/Ave de Césarée, 250m north of roundabout junction with A660. 2km south of town.
LA TESTE DE BUCH	N44°38.793' W001°09.437'	Elf. Adj to D1250/D1251 roundabout. 1.8km north of town.
A64 LACQ-AUDEJOS (East)	N43°25.300' W000°35.900'	Agip. Aire de Lacq-Audéjos. A64/E80 eastbound between Junctions 8 and 9.
LANGON	N44°33.126' W000°15.893'	TTotal. Adj to D116/D8 roundabout. 1km north of A62/E72 Junction 3. 1.5km west of town
LANGON	N44°32.509' W000°15.298'	E.Leclerc. D932e2, at roundabout. 830m east of A62/E72 Junction 3. 1.6km southwest of town.
LESPARRE MEDOC	N45°18.083' W000°56.043'	Total. D1215/Route de Bordeaux. 300m south of roundabout junction with D203.
LIBOURNE	N44°53.864' W000°12.524'	Total. D670/Ave du Général de Gaulle, 500m southeast of junction with D1089. 3.25km southeast of town.
LORMONT (North)	N44°52.412' W000°30.375'	Total. N230/E70 northbound between Junctions 26 and 27.
MARMANDE	N44°30.316' E000°09.032'	Total. D813/Ave Jean Jaurès. 1km northwest of town.
MARMANDE	N44°29.333' E000°10.817'	Carrefour. D813/Ave Hubert Ruffe. 2km southeast of town.
MARSAC SUR L'ISLE	N45°11.650' E000°39.583'	Auchan. D710e/Ave Louis Suder. 1.1km north of town.
MERIGNAC	N44°49.659' W000°40.264'	Total Access. Rue Gutenberg, at roundabout junction with D106. 2.25km southwest of town.
MERIGNAC	N44°50.516' W000°39.866'	Total. Ave de l'Yser. 600m southwest of town.
A630 MERIGNAC (North)	N44°51.003' W000°40.031'	Total. A630/E5 northbound between Junctions 10 and 9.
MONTPON-MENESTEROL	N45°00.367' E000°08.550'	Intermarché. Adj to D6089/D9 roundabout. 1.6km west of town.
MUSSIDAN	N45°02.467' E000°21.100'	Super U. D6089. 1km northwest of town.
OLORON STE MARIE	N43°11.432' W000°37.041'	Total. D936/Ave Charles Mourieu, 160m south of roundabout junction with D6. 1km west of town.
ORTHEZ	N43°29.114' W000°45.923'	Total. D817/Ave Francis Jammes. 750m east of town.
ORTHEZ	N43°29.367' W000°47.800'	E.Leclerc. D817/Route de Bayonne. 1.8km west of town.
PAU	N43°18.417' W000°22.583'	Avia. D834/Ave Jean Mermoz. 1.4km north of town.
PAU	N43°19.118' W000°22.722'	Total. D834/Ave Jean Mermoz. 2.7km north of town.
LE LUY - PAU	N43°21.600' W000°23.017'	Intermarché. D834 roundabout. Take the exit for D716. 7km north of Pau.
LONS - PAU	N43°19.767' W000°22.850'	Géant. Ave du Perlic. 370m east of roundabout junction with D834. 4km north of town.
PERIGUEUX	N45°11.849' E000°42.019'	Total. D939/Route Pierre Sémard. 2km northwest of town
PERIGUEUX	N45°11.417' E000°44.150'	Total. D6021/Ave Michel Grandou. 1.3km northeast of town.
PESSAC	N44°46.865' W000°38.980'	Total. Ave de Haut Lévèque. 500m northwest of A63/E70 Junction 26a (southbound) or 26 (northbound). 3km southwest of town.
PONT DU CASSE	N44°13.606' E000°40.317'	Total. D656/Ave Le Cahors. 950m southwest of town.
SARLAT LA CANEDA	N44°52.697' E001°13.015'	Avia. D704/Rue du Lot. 1.4km south of town.
A63 SAUGNAC ET MURET	N44°21.719' W000°51.072'	Total. Aire de Muret. A63/E5 southbound between Junctions 17 and 18.
A10 ST ANDRE DE CUBZAC	N44°58.724' W000°25.881'	Total. Aire de l'Estalot. A10/E5 southbound between Junctions 40a and 41.
ST ASTIER	N45°08.702' E000°31.424'	E.Leclerc. D3/Blvd Mal de Lattre de Tassigny. 300m west of town.
A89 ST LAURENT SUR MANOIRE	N45°09.021' E000°47.919'	Total. Aire du Manoire. A89/E70 at Junction 16. Accessible both sides.
A62 ST MICHEL DE RIEUFRET (South)	N44°38.795' W000°26.255'	Total. Aire des Landes. A62/E72 southbound between Junctions 1.1 and 2.
ST-PIERRE-DU-MONT	N43°52.586' W000°30.370'	Total. Ave de St-Sever. 1.8km southeast of town.
ST SEVER	N43°46.400' W000°34.033'	Intermarché. D933. 1.65km north of town.
ST VINCENT DE PAUL	N43°44.451' W001°01.047'	Total. Route de Carrere. 150m north of junction with D824. 1km west of town.
ST VINCENT DE TYROSSE	N43°40.000' W001°17.183'	E.Leclerc. D810/Route de Bordeaux. 1.6km east of town.
PINEUILH - STE FOY LA GRANDE	N44°50.483' E000°14.633'	E.Leclerc. D936E6/Route de Bergerac. 2km northeast of town.
TARTAS	N43°50.600' W000°45.650'	Elan. D824/Aire de Champigny. 4km east of town. Accessible both sides.
TERRASSON-LAVILLEDIEU	N45°07.708' E001°19.043'	Total. D6809. 1km east of town.

TOWN	GPS	DIRECTIONS
TONNEINS	N44°24.012' E000°17.906'	E.Leclerc. D813/Ave Pierre Mendés France. 1.25km north of town.
TRESSES-MELAC	N44°50.416' W000°29.626'	Elf. D936/Ave de Branne. 2.5km west of town
VILLENEUVE SUR LOT	N44°24.242' E000°41.278'	Total. D911/Route de Bordeaux. 1.6km west of town.

LIMOUSIN & AUVERGNE

TOWN	GPS	DIRECTIONS
BELLERIVE SUR ALLIER	N46°07.059' E003°24.670'	Total. D2209/Ave de la République. 600m east of town.
BRIVE LA GAILLARDE	N45°09.885' E001°30.649'	Total. D1089/Ave Ribot. 1km northwest of town.
BRIVE LA GAILLARDE	N45°10.129' E001°33.640'	Géant. D1089/Ave Marie et Pierre Curie. 2.5km east of town.
A71 CHAMPS	N46°03.508' E003°06.748'	Total. Aire des Volcans d'Auvergne. A71/E11 between Junctions 12 and 13. Accessible both sides.
CLERMONT-FERRAND	N45°47.350' E003°07.070'	Total. D2009/Blvd Amboise Bruguière. 1.5km northeast of town.
CLERMONT-FERRAND	N45°48.839' E003°06.545'	Auchan. D2009/Blvd Étienne Clémentel. 4.3km north of town.
GUERET	N46°10.621' E001°53.899'	Intermarché. D4/Le Verger, 100m south of N145/E62 Junction 47. 2.2km east of town.
LAGUENNE	N45°14.740' E001°46.407'	Auchan. D1120/Ave de Coulaud. 650m north of town.
LE PUY EN VALEY	N45°02.827' E003°53.583'	Total. N88/Blvd Maréchal Joffre. 900m northeast of town.
A20 MASSERET	N45°32.489' E001°30.506'	Total. Aire de Porte de Corrèze. A20/E9 between Junctions 42 and 43. Accessible both sides.
MAURIAC	N45°12.945' E002°20.331'	Carrefour. D681/Rue du Commandant Gabon. 250m southeast of town.
MAURIAC	N45°12.865' E002°20.801'	Carrefour. D922/Route d'Aurillac southbound. 1km southeast of town.
MAURS	N44°42.538' E002°11.763'	Total. N122/Route de Bagnac. 300m southwest of town.
MONLUCON	N46°20.288' E002°34.041'	Auchan. D745/Ave des Martyrs. 2.6km west of town. 3.5m height restriction.
MONTMARAULT	N46°19.413' E002°57.855'	Heep. D2371/Route de Moulins. 1km northeast of town.
PARSAC	N46°11.865' E002°11.130'	Total. Aire de Parsac. N145/E62. 1.5km east of town. Accessible both sides.
RIOM	N45°52.707' E003°06.992'	Carrefour. Adj to D6/D6a crossroads. 1.7km south of town.
ST JUNIEN	N45°53.839' E000°55.215'	Carrefour. Ave Nelson Mandela, adj to D941 roundabout. 1km northeast of town.
ST POURCAIN SUR SIOULE	N46°17.687' E003°17.695'	Total. D2009/Route de Gannat. 1km south of town.
THIERS	N45°50.546' E003°30.879'	Pireyre & Pascal. D2089/Ave du Général de Gaulle. 2.5km southwest of town.
USSEL	N45°32.592' E002°17.843'	E.Leclerc. D157. 1.4km west of town.
BELLERIVE SUR ALLIER - VICHY	N46°07.055' E003°24.683'	Total. D2209/Ave de Vichy. 700m east of town.
YZEURE - MOULINS	N46°33.273' E003°20.191'	Total. D707/Route de Lyon. 1km south of town.

MEDITERRANEAN

TOWN	GPS	DIRECTIONS
AIMARGUES	N43°41.752' E004°12.051'	Elf. D6313/Route de la Petite Camargue. 1.5km north of town.
AIX EN PROVENCE	N43°31.704' E005°25.957'	Total. D64/Route de Galice. 500m west of town.
AIX EN PROVENCE	N43°30.957' E005°27.980'	Total Access. Ave Henri Mauriat, 350m north of A8/E80 Junction 31. 1km southeast of town.
AIX EN PROVENCE	N43°29.049' E005°23.000'	Total Access. D59/Rue Victor Baltard, 2.5km northwest of A51/E712 Junction 3.
APT	N43°52.990' E005°22.870'	Total. D900/Ave de Lançon. 1.5km northwest of town.
ARLES	N43°40.212' E004°37.282'	Total. D35/Ave Bachaga Said Boualem. 1km southwest of town.
ARLES	N43°39.109' E004°40.148'	Total. Aires des Cantarelles. N113/E80 southbound between Junctions 7 and 8.
AUBAGNE	N43°17.557' E005°35.606'	Auchan. Chemin des Bonnes Nouvelles. 1km west of town.
AVIGNON	N43°55.928' E004°46.980'	Elf. Rocade Charles de Gaulle. 1.5km southwest of town.
BEZIERS	N43°19.896' E003°14.875'	Total Access. Ave de la Devèze. 1.5km southeast of town.
BEZIERS	N43°21.260' E003°13.756'	Elf. Ave du Docteur Jean Marie Fabre. 1.5km northeast of town.
BOUC-BEL-AIR (North)	N43°26.022' E005°23.728'	Esso. Aire de Chabauds. A51/E712 northbound between Junctions 2 and 3.
BOUC-BEL-AIR (South)	N43°26.509' E005°23.731'	Total. Aire de la Champouse. A51/E712 southbound between Junctions 3 and 2.
BRIANCON	N44°54.234' E006°37.739'	Total Access. N94/Ave du Dauphiné. 500m northwest of town.
CANNES	N43°33.309' E007°00.339'	Total. Blvd du Riou. 500m northwest of town.
CANNES LA BOCCA	N43°33.056' E006°57.461'	E.Leclerc. Chemin de la Bastide Rouge. Adj to roundabout junction with D6007. 1km west of town.

LPG-GPL

TOWN	GPS	DIRECTIONS
CARCASSONNE	N43°12.431' E002°20.140'	Total. D118/Route de Limoux. 500m west of town.
CAVAILLON	N43°49.854' E005°03.270'	Total. D973/Ave de Cheval Blanc. 1.3km south of town.
CHATEAU ARNOUX ST AUBAN	N44°05.172' E006°00.494'	Total. D4096/Ave Jean Moulin. 500m south of town.
CHATEAUREDON	N44°01.015' E006°12.733'	Elan. N85/l'Hubac et St Jean. 350m north of town.
PORT COGOLIN	N43°15.823' E006°34.653'	Total. Adj to D98a/D559 junction. 400m south of town.
A9 COURSAN (North)	N43°12.961' E003°05.536'	Total. Aire de Narbonne-Vinassan. A9/E15 northbound between Junctions 37 and 36.
A9 COURSAN (South)	N43°12.829' E003°05.390'	Total. Aire de Narbonne-Vinassan. A9/E15 southbound between Junctions 36 and 37.
DIGNE LES BAINS	N44°05.379' E006°14.229'	Intermarché. D19/Ave du 8 Mai 1945. 300m south of town.
FOS SUR MER	N43°25.664' E004°57.947'	Elf. N568 northbound. 1km southeast of town.
FOS SUR MER	N43°28.274' E004°54.490'	Elf. N568. 4.8km northwest of town. Accessible both sides.
FREJUS	N43°26.121' E006°43.489'	Total. DN7/Ave de Verdun. 1km northwest of town.
FUVEAU	N43°27.948' E005°36.384'	Total. D6 southeast. 4km northeast of town.
GAP	N44°32.479' E006°03.471'	Total. N85/Ave de Provence. 1.5km southwest of town.
A55 GIGNAC LA NERTHE (East)	N43°23.458' E005°15.500'	Agip. Aire de Rebuty. A55 eastbound between Junctions 7 and 6.
A55 GIGNAC LA NERTHE (West)	N43°23.537' E005°15.419'	Total. Aire de Gignac-La-Nerthe. A55 westbound between Junctions 6 and 7.
A57 LA GARDE (South)	N43°08.987' E006°02.050'	Total. Aire de la Chaberte. A57 southbound between Junctions 6 and 5.
A7 LANCON DE PROVENCE (North)	N43°35.377' E005°11.235'	Total. Aire de Lançon de Provence. A7/E80/E714 northbound between Junctions 28 and 27.
A7 LANCON DE PROVENCE (South)	N43°35.377' E005°11.596'	Total. Aire de Lançon de Provence. A7/E80/E714 southbound between Junctions 27 and 28.
A75 LE CAYLAR	N43°51.858' E003°18.727'	Total. Aire de Service à 75. A75/E11 at Junction 49. Accessible both sides.
LE LUC	N43°22.883' E006°18.250'	E.Leclerc. D97. 1.6km southwest of town.
LE PONTET	N43°58.619' E004°51.469'	Total. D907/Route de Lyon. 1km north of town.
LES PENNES-MIRABEAU	N43°24.558' E005°19.264'	Elf. D368. 0.5km east of town.
LODEVE	N43°43.516' E003°19.380'	Super U. D609. 1.6km south of town.
MANOSQUE	N43°49.347' E005°47.262'	Total. D4096/Ave Frédéric Mistral. 1.5km southwest of town.
MANOSQUE	N43°50.267' E005°48.300'	E.Leclerc. D4096/Blvd du Maréchal Juin. 1.25km northeast of town.
MANOSQUE	N43°51.017' E005°49.417'	Auchan. D4096/Route de Volx. 3km northeast of town.
A9 MARGUERITTES (North)	N43°52.094' E004°26.342'	BP. Aire de Nîmes-Marguerittes. A9/E15 northbound between Junctions 24 and 23.
A9 MARGUERITTES (South)	N43°52.502' E004°26.918'	Total. Aire de Nîmes-Marguerittes. A9/E15 southbound between Junctions 23 and 24.
MARIGNANE	N43°26.587' E005°13.439'	Total. Aéroport Marseilles Provence, 130m southwest of D20d/D20 roundabout. 1.5km north of town.
MARSEILLE	N43°17.165' E005°25.649'	Total. D2/359 Blvd Mireille Lauze. 2.5km east of town.
MARSEILLE	N43°20.969' E005°20.558'	Elf. D5/Chemin du Littoral. 3.5km north of town.
MARSEILLE	N43°19.433' E005°27.199'	Elf. D4/Ave Frédéric Mistral. 4km northeast of town.
MARSEILLE	N43°19.659' E005°21.958'	Total. Route de Lyon. 2km north of town.
MARSEILLE	N43°18.227' E005°24.062'	Elf. Blvd Françoise Duparc. 2.5km east of town.
A50 MARSEILLE (East)	N43°17.518' E005°27.211'	Total. Aire de la Pomme. A50 eastbound between Junctions 3 and 4.
MARVEJOLS	N44°33.791' E003°17.520'	Total. D809/Ave Theophile Roussel. 1km north of town.
MAUGUIO	N43°37.085' E003°59.312'	Total. D24/Route de Montpellier. 1.5km west of town.
MONTPELLIER	N43°38.095' E003°49.375'	Total. Ave de l'Europe. 3km northwest of town.
MONTPELLIER	N43°35.712' E003°50.889'	Total Access. D65/Ave de Vanières. 3.2km southwest of town.
A8 MOUGINS (North)	N43°35.377' E007°02.122'	Total. Aire de Bréguières Sud. A8 northbound between Junctions 42 and 44.
A8 MOUGINS (South)	N43°35.522' E007°02.167'	Total. Aire de Bréguières Nord. A8 southbound between Junctions 44 and 42.

TOWN	GPS	DIRECTIONS
NARBONNE	N43°10.468' E002°59.552'	Total. Ave Général Leclerc. 1.4km southwest of town.
NICE	N43°39.818' E007°12.108'	Total. Blvd Léon Morate at Aéroport de Nice Côte d'Azur. 3km southwest of town.
NICE	N43°40.179' E007°12.994'	BP. Blvd René Cassin. 2.5km southwest of town.
NICE	N43°42.412' E007°17.544'	Total. Blvd de l'Armée des Alpes. 1.5km east of town.
NIMES	N43°48.609' E004°19.744'	Total. N113/Route de Montpellier. 2km southwest of town.
NIMES	N43°49.304' E004°19.761'	Elf. N106/Blvd Pasteur Marc Boegner. 1.5km southwest of town.
PERPIGNAN	N42°40.673' E002°53.451'	Total. Ave d'Espagne. 1km south of town.
PERPIGNAN	N42°40.089' E002°53.004'	Auchan. D900/Route de Perthus. 2.4km southwest of town.
PERTUIS	N43°40.844' E005°30.028'	Carrefour. D956/Route d'Aix. 1.5km south of town.
A8 PUGET-SUR-ARGENS (North)	N43°27.995' E006°40.323'	Total. Aire du Canaver. A8/E80 northbound between Junctions 37 and 36.
QUISSAC	N43°54.850' E003°59.717'	Vulco. D999/Ave de l'Aigoual. 400m north of town.
ONET LE CHATEAU	N44°22.170' E002°35.412'	Total. D988/Route d'Espalion. 1km north of town.
ROQUEFORT LES CORBIERES	N42°59.367' E002°58.339'	Total. D6009/Cambouisset. 1.5km east of town.
RUOMS	N44°26.563' E004°20.936'	Super U. Chaussy, 120m east of D579/D557 roundabout. 1.2km south of town.
SALON DE PROVENCE	N43°37.961' E005°05.890'	Total. Blvd du Roi René. 800m south of town.
SALON DE PROVENCE	N43°37.150' E005°05.766'	Total. D538/Ave de la Patrouille de France. 2.3km south of town.
ST MAXIMIN LA STE BAUME	N43°26.836' E005°51.739'	Total. DN7/Route de Nice. 500m south of town.
TOULON	N43°07.027' E005°56.454'	Total. Ave Édouard le Bellegou. 500m southeast of town.
TOULON	N43°07.387' E005°56.279'	Total. N97/Ave Georges Clemenceau. 500m east of town.
VAISON LA ROMAINE	N44°14.525' E005°04.831'	Total. Ave Victor Hugo. 450m east of town.
VENCE	N43°42.908' E007°07.022'	Total. Adj to M236/M2 roundabout. 1km south of town.
A9 VILLETELLE (North)	N43°42.742' E004°07.886'	Total. Aire d'Ambrussum. A9/E15 northbound between Junctions 27 and 26.
A9 VILLETELLE (South)	N43°42.971' E004°08.050'	Total. Aire d'Ambrussum. A9/E15 southbound between Junctions 26 and 27.
VITROLLES	N43°25.252' E005°16.113'	Total. D113. 5km south of town.

MIDI-PYRENEES

TOWN	GPS	DIRECTIONS
ALBI	N43°55.167' E002°07.900'	Total. D988/Ave François Verdier. Southwest of town.
ALBI	N43°55.110' E002°06.435'	E.Leclerc. N88/Rue des Portes d'Albi, 800m west of N88 Junction 14. 3.2km west of town.
AUCH	N43°39.883' E000°35.500'	E.Leclerc. Rue Paul Valery, 600m west of N124/N21 junction. 2km north of town.
AUSSILLON-MAZAMET	N43°30.535' E002°21.680'	Elan. N112/Blvd du Thoré. 1km north of town.
AUTERIVE	N43°21.792' E001°27.470'	Carrefour. D820/Route de Toulouse. 1.9km northwest of town.
BAGNERES DE BIGORRE	N43°04.850' E000°08.350'	Total. D935/Ave de la Mongie. 1.9km north of town.
BALMA	N43°36.580' E001°29.570'	Total Access. D50/Ave de Toulouse. 750m northwest of town.
BALMA	N43°35.369' E001°30.837'	Total. D826/Route de Castres. 2.2km southeast of town.
BESSIERES	N43°47.882' E001°36.743'	Super U. D630/Ave de Castres. 500m east of town.
BLAGNAC	N43°38.282' E001°23.416'	Total Access. D2/Route de Grenade. 570m northwest of town.
BLAGNAC	N43°38.480' E001°22.483'	Elf. D902/Voie Lactée northbound between Junctions 902.1 and 902.2. 1km west of town.
BLAYE LES MINES	N44°01.617' E002°09.333'	Super U. D73/N2088/Ave d'Albi, at crossroads. 1.9km east of town.
CAHORS	N44°25.467' E001°26.433'	Total. D820/Route de Toulouse. 2.5km south of town.
A61 CARCASSONNE (North)	N43°21.165' E001°48.587'	Total. Aire de Port Lauragais. A61 northbound between Junctions 21 and 20.
A61 CARCASSONNE (South)	N43°21.193' E001°48.386'	Total. Aire de Port Lauragais. A61 southbound between Junctions 20 and 21.
CASTELSARRASIN	N44°02.584' E001°06.294'	Total. D813/Ave du Maréchal Leclerc. 400m north of town.
CASTELSARRASIN	N44°03.850' E001°05.833'	E.Leclerc. D813/Route de Moissac. 3km north of town.
CASTRES	N43°37.033' E002°14.650'	Avia. D89/Ave de Roquecourbe. 1.2km north of town.
CAZAUBON	N43°56.050' W000°03.800'	Elan. D626/Blvd des Pyrénées. 600m east of town.

LPG-GPL

TOWN	GPS	DIRECTIONS
CAZERES	N43°12.650' E001°05.050'	Carrefour. D6/Ave Pasteur. 650m north of town.
A64 CLARAC	N43°06.625' E000°36.820'	Total. Aire des Comminges. A64 between Junctions 17 and 18. Accessible both sides.
CONDOM	N43°57.083' E000°22.267'	Total. D930. 700m south of town.
A61 DONNEVILLE (North)	N43°29.133' E001°32.976'	Carrefour. Aires de Toulouse-Nord. A61 northbound between Junctions 19.1 and 19.
A61 DONNEVILLE (South)	N43°29.026' E001°32.942'	Carrefour. Aires de Toulouse-Sud. A61 southbound between Junctions 19 and 19.1.
ESTANCARBON	N43°06.764' E000°47.271'	Total. D817. 500m north of town.
FIGEAC	N44°36.667' E002°01.667'	Esso. Adj to D840/D2/D19 roundabout. 500m northwest of town.
FOIX	N42°56.883' E001°37.550'	Total. D117, 300m east of N20/E9 Junction 11. 2.5km southeast of town.
FONBEAUZARD	N43°40.672' E001°25.403'	Total. D4/Route de Fronton. 1km west of town.
GOURDON	N44°43.243' E001°22.103'	Elan. D673/Route du Fumel. 2km southwest of town.
LALOUBERE	N43°12.616' E000°04.385'	Géant. D935/Route du Maréchal Foch. 2.5km south of town.
LAVAUR	N43°41.762' E001°48.968'	Agip. D87/D112. 500m south of town.
LAVELANET	N42°55.455' E001°50.275'	Super U. Rue des Pyrénées, adj to roundabout junction with D117. 1.9km southwest of town.
LECTOURE	N43°54.983' E000°37.683'	Elan. N21. 1.9km south of town.
LOMBEZ	N43°28.233' E000°55.367'	Intermarché. Ave du Docteur Raynaud. 1km southeast of town.
LOURDES	N43°05.835' W000°02.295'	Total. Blvd du Lapacca. 800m northeast of town.
A20 MONTALZAT	N44°13.966' E001°31.689'	Total. Aire du Bois de Dourre. A20/E9 between Junctions 59 and 58. Accessible both sides.
MONTAUBAN	N44°00.267' E001°20.478'	Total. N2020/Route de Toulouse. 500m southwest of town.
OLEMPS	N44°19.517' E002°33.467'	Super U. D212, adj to roundabout junction with D888. 3km south of town.
PAVIE	N43°37.000' E000°34.517'	Total. N21/Route de Tarbes. 1.4km west of town.
PORTET SUR GARONNE	N43°31.492' E001°24.021'	Total Access. D120/Route d'Espagne. 400m south of town. Elf station 180m south on opposite side also has LPG: N43°31.475' E001°23.941'.
POUZAC	N43°04.857' E000°08.365'	Total. D935/Ave de la Mongie. Southeast of town.
REVEL	N43°27.823' E002°00.417'	Elan. D622/Ave de Castres. 600m north of town.
RIEUMES	N43°24.817' E001°06.950'	Carrefour. D28/Route de Samatan. 200m north of town.
SAIX	N43°35.309' E002°11.123'	Auchan. Rue Albert Calmettes, adj to roundabout junction with N216. 750m north of town.
SEBAZAC CONCOURES	N44°23.633' E002°36.167'	E.Leclerc. Ave Joël Pilon, 500m from roundabout junction with D988. 1.3km south of town.
ST AFFRIQUE	N43°57.483' E002°52.217'	Super U. D999. 1.4km west of town.
ST ALBAN	N43°41.015' E001°25.232'	Elf. D4/Route de Fronton. 500m southeast of town.
TARBES	N43°14.374' E000°03.632'	Total. Adj to D935a/D935b roundabout. 1.5km northwest of town.
TOULOUSE	N43°39.480' E001°25.175'	Total. D820/Ave des États Unis. 3.5km north of town.
TOULOUSE	N43°35.292' E001°25.411'	Total. Blvd Déodat de Séverac. 2.3km southwest of town.
TOULOUSE	N43°37.894' E001°28.966'	Auchan. Chemin de Gabardie, 250m north of D112/D64d roundabout junction. 1.5km northeast of town.
TOULOUSE	N43°34.856' E001°23.735'	Total Access. Route St Simon. 2km west of town.
A620 TOULOUSE (North)	N43°36.032' E001°23.904'	Total. A620 northbound at Junction 28.
A620 TOULOUSE (South)	N43°35.658' E001°23.836'	Total. A620 southbound at Junction 28.
VENERQUE	N43°25.700' E001°26.733'	Intermarché. Adj to D19/D35 roundabout. 500m south of town.
VIC EN BIGORRE	N43°23.086' E000°03.062'	Intermarché. D6. 300m south of town.
VILLEFRANCHE DE ROUERGUE	N44°21.550' E001°59.182'	Elan. D911. 100m east of D1/D926 roundabout junction. 3.8km west of town.

POITOU

TOWN	GPS	DIRECTIONS
BARBEZIEUX ST HILAIRE	N45°27.678' W000°08.545'	Total. Adj to D731/D5 roundabout. 1.5km southeast of town.
CHASSENEUIL DU POITOU	N46°37.875' E000°21.421'	Total. D910/Route de Paris. 2.5km south of town.
GEMOZAC	N45°34.549' W000°40.658'	Super U. Adj to D732/D6 roundabout. 850m north of town.

TOWN	GPS	DIRECTIONS
LA ROCHELLE	N46°09.405' W001°07.185'	Total. Ave Jean Paul Sartre. 2.3km east of town.
MONTMORILLON	N46°25.135' E000°51.270'	E.Leclerc. D727. 1.3km west of town.
NAINTRE	N46°45.234' E000°29.042'	Q8. D910. 1km south of town.
NAINTRE	N46°45.406' E000°29.083'	Intermarché. Ave du Cerisier Noir, 150m from D23/D910 roundabout. 1km south of town.
NEUVILLE DE POITOU	N46°41.079' E000°15.277'	Total. D62. 600m east of town.
NIORT	N46°18.994' W000°28.369'	Total. D811/Ave de la Rochelle. 1km south of town.
NIORT	N46°20.428' W000°23.708'	Elf. D611/Route de Paris. 5.6km east of town.
A10 NIORT (North)	N46°17.835' W000°22.297'	Total. Aire du Poitou-Charentes. A10/E5 northbound between Junctions 32 and 33.
A10 NIORT (South)	N46°17.729' W000°22.807'	Total. Aire du Poitou-Charentes. A10/E5 southbound between Junctions 33 and 32.
A10 PAMPROUX (North)	N46°27.089' W000°01.107'	Shell. Aire de Rouillé-Pamproux. A10/E5 northbound between Junctions 31 and 30.
A10 PAMPROUX (South)	N46°27.177' W000°01.043'	Total. Aire de Rouillé-Pamproux. A10/E5 southbound between Junctions 30 and 31.
POITIERS	N46°36.252' E000°19.944'	Total. D910/Rocade Ouest. 2.7km north of town.
PUILBOREAU	N46°10.601' W001°06.219'	Total. Aire de Puilboreau. N11/E601/E3 northbound. 1.2km south of town.
ROYAN	N45°37.907' W000°59.524'	E.Leclerc. N150/Ave du 4éme Zouave. 3.9km east of town.
RUFFEC	N46°01.260' E000°11.386'	E.Leclerc. D736/Chemin des Meuiers. 1.2km southwest of town.
SAINTES	N45°42.183' W000°37.466'	Total. D137/Route de Bordeaux. 4.6km south of town.
SAINTES	N45°45.384' W000°39.100'	Carrefour. D128/Blvd de Vladimir. 2km northwest of town.
ST GENIS DE SAINTONGE	N45°29.371' W000°33.951'	Total. D137/Ave de Saintes. 900m north of town.
ST JEAN D'ANGELY	N45°56.667' W000°30.333'	E.Leclerc. Rue France III, 270m south of D218 roundabout junction. 1km east of town.
ST MAIXENT L'ECOLE	N46°24.438' W000°13.537'	E.Leclerc. D8, 220m west of D611 roundabout junction. 1.7km southwest of town.
TONNAY CHARENTE	N45°57.010' W000°55.599'	Total. D137. 3km east of town.
VILLEGATS	N46°00.060' E000°12.036'	Shell. Aire de l'Eglantier. N10 northbound. 1km north of town.

RHONE-ALPS

TOWN	GPS	DIRECTIONS
ALBERTVILLE	N45°39.664' E006°22.991'	Total. N90 northbound at Junction 29. 1.8km south of town.
ALBY SUR CHERAN	N45°49.128' E006°00.261'	Total. D1201/Route d'Aix les Bains eastbound. 1.3km west of town.
A7 ALLAN (North)	N44°30.781' E004°46.888'	Shell. Aire de Montélimar. A7/E15 northbound between Junctions 18 and 17.
A7 ALLAN (South)	N44°30.889' E004°46.787'	Total. Aire de Montélimar. A7/E15 southbound between Junctions 17 and 18.
ANNECY	N45°54.558' E006°07.063'	Total. D1501/Blvd de la Rocade. 1.4km northeast of town.
BOURG DE PEAGE	N45°02.196' E005°03.242'	Total. D2532n/Blvd Alpes Provence. 900m south of town.
BOURG EN BRESSE	N46°11.328' E005°14.625'	Total. D1075/Ave du Maréchal Juin. 2.5km southeast of town.
BOURGOIN-JALLIEU	N45°35.675' E005°16.323'	Total. Rue de l'Etissey. 300m south of town.
BRON	N45°44.340' E004°54.298'	Total Access. D383/Blvd Périphérique Laurent Bonnevay northbound. 750m northwest of town.
CALUIRE	N45°48.287' E004°51.556'	Auchan. D48e. 1.6km northeast of town.
A40 CEIGNES (North)	N46°06.893' E005°29.434'	Total. Aire de Ceignes Cerdon. A40/E21 northbound between Junction 8 and A42/E611 interchange.
A40 CEYZERIAT (North)	N46°12.159' E005°17.768'	Total. Aire de Bourg Jasseron. A40/E62/E21 northbound between Junctions 7 and 6.
A40 CEYZERIAT (South)	N46°12.177' E005°17.665'	Shell. Aire de Bourg Teyssonge. A40/E62/E21 southbound between Junctions 6 and 7.
CHAMBERY	N45°35.584' E005°53.800'	Total Access. N201/E712 northbound at Junction 14.
CLUSES	N46°03.687' E006°33.776'	Total. Ave de la République. 1.4km west of town.
A46 COMMUNAY (North)	N45°35.356' E004°49.529'	Total. Aire de Communay-Nord. A46/E15/E70 northbound at Junction 17.
A46 COMMUNAY (South)	N45°35.458' E004°49.686'	Total. Aire de Communay-Sud. A46/E15/E70 southbound at Junction 17.
A6 DARDILLY (North)	N45°48.477' E004°46.161'	Total. Aire de Paisy. A6 northbound between Junctions 34 and 33.1.
A6 DARDILLY (South)	N45°49.230' E004°45.969'	Auchan. Aire de Dardilly. A6 southbound between Junctions 33.1 and 34.
A6 DRACE (North)	N46°08.048' E004°45.998'	Avia. Aire de Taponas. A6/E15 northbound between Junctions 30 and 29.

LPG-GPL

TOWN	GPS	DIRECTIONS
A6 DRACE (South)	N46°08.612' E004°46.056'	Total. Aire de Docteuracé. A6/E15 southbound between Junctions 29 and 30.
EYBENS	N45°09.117' E005°44.391'	Total. N87/E712 northbound between Junctions 6 and 5.
FEURS	N45°44.579' E004°12.447'	Total. D1089/Bigny. 1.1km west of town.
FEYZIN	N45°40.486' E004°50.908'	Elf. D312, 500m south of A7 Junction 6.
L'ALBENC	N45°13.177' E005°26.127'	Total. D1092/Route de Grenoble. 700m south of town.
A43 L'ISLE D'ABEAU (North)	N45°36.803' E005°12.797'	Total. Aire de l'Isle d'Abeau. A43/E70/E711 northbound between Junctions 7 and 6.
A43 L'ISLE D'ABEAU (South)	N45°36.749' E005°12.555'	Esso. Aire de l'Isle d'Abeau. A43/E70/E711 southbound between Junctions 6 and 7.
LA BATHIE	N45°36.733' E006°27.008'	Elan. Aire de Langon. N90 southbound at Junction 34. Accessible from both sides.
LA MOTTE SERVOLEX	N45°36.628' E005°53.194'	Total Access. N201 southbound between Junctions 14 and 13.
LA RAVOIRE	N45°34.119' E005°57.777'	Total. D1006/Ave de Chambéry. 1.3km north of town.
LES HOUCHES	N45°53.901' E006°48.725'	Total. N205/Route Blanche southbound at Junction 28.
A89 LES SALLES (North)	N45°51.279' E003°48.568'	Shell. Aire du Haut-Forez. A89/E70 northbound between Junctions 32 and 31.
A89 LES SALLES (South)	N45°51.366' E003°48.860'	Total. Aire du Haut-Forez. A89/E70 southbound between Junctions 31 and 32.
LORIOL SUR DROME	N44°45.640' E004°50.282'	Intermarché. Allée de la Serpentine, 125m south of N7/D104 roundabout. 1.6km northeast of town.
LYON	N45°44.099' E004°50.361'	Total. Rue de Gerland. 3.2km south of town.
MACON	N46°17.107' E004°48.470'	Total. D906/Route de Lyon. 2.9km south of town.
MONTELIMAR	N44°33.317' E004°44.250'	Casino. D540. 1km west of town.
MONTELIMAR	N44°31.970' E004°44.776'	Carrefour. D540a/Route de Marseille. 2.6km south of town.
MONTELIMAR	N44°31.135' E004°44.708'	Total Access. N7. 4km south of town.
OYONNAX	N46°15.029' E005°38.487'	Total. Cours de Verdun. 1.4km southwest of town.
PIERRE BENITE	N45°41.834' E004°49.492'	Total. D15/Blvd de l'Europe. 670m south of town.
PONT DE CLAIX	N45°08.308' E005°42.165'	Total. D1075, at junction with D269. 1.7km north of town.
A7 PORTES LES VALENCE (North)	N44°51.937' E004°51.991'	Total. Aire de Portes Lés Valence. A7/E15 northbound between Junctions 16 and 15.
A7 PORTES LES VALENCE (South)	N44°52.034' E004°51.873'	Shell. Aire de Portes Lés Valence. A7/E15 southbound between Junctions 15 and 16.
ST GENIS LAVAL	N45°40.728' E004°47.529'	Auchan. A450 at Junction 6b. 1.4km south of town.
ST PRIEST	N45°42.425' E004°59.210'	Total Access. D306/Route de Grenoble. 3.3km northeast of town.
SALLANCHES	N45°56.686' E006°37.798'	Total Access. D1205/Ave de Geneve. 800m north of town.
A7 SEREZIN DU RHONE (North)	N45°37.787' E004°49.077'	Total. Aire de Sérézin du Rhône. A7 northbound between Junctions 8 and 7.
A7 SOLAIZE (South)	N45°39.138' E004°50.208'	Elf. Aire de Solaize. A7 southbound between Junctions 6 and 7.
ST ETIENNE	N45°26.529' E004°24.579'	Total Access. N488/100 Rue de la Montat. 1.7km east of town.
ST ETIENNE	N45°27.909' E004°22.670'	Total Access. Ave de Verdun. 3km north of town.
ST JEAN DE BOURNAY	N45°29.933' E005°08.250'	Intermarché. Lotissement du Stade, off D518. 500m south of town.
A7 ST RAMBERT (North)	N45°16.542' E004°49.752'	BP. Aire de St Rambert d'Albon. A7/E15 northbound between Junctions 13 and 12.
A7 ST RAMBERT (South)	N45°16.681' E004°49.508'	Total. Aire de St Rambert d'Albon. A7/E15 southbound between Junctions 12 and 13.
ST VALLIER	N45°11.700' E004°48.855'	Total. N7/Ave de Québec. 2km north of town.
VALENCE	N44°56.572' E004°51.571'	Avia. D533/Ave Gross Umstadt. 2.75km northwest of town.
VALENCE	N44°56.412' E004°54.491'	Total Access. Blvd Gustave André. 1.5km east of town.
VALENCE	N44°55.188' E004°52.675'	Total Access. D2007n/Ave de Provence. 1.8km southwest of town.
VILLARS	N45°28.557' E004°20.661'	Auchan. D201, 500m south of A72/E70 Junction 10. 1.1km north of town.
VOIRON	N45°21.515' E005°35.537'	Total. D592/Ave du Docteur Valois. 500m south of town.
A48 VOREPPE (North)	N45°16.686' E005°37.456'	Total. Aire de Voreppe. A48/E713 northbound at Junction 12.
A48 VOREPPE (South)	N45°16.635' E005°37.363'	Agip. Aire de l'Ile Rose. A48/E713 southbound at Junction 12.

INDEX

M

INDEX

INDEX

The French Aires situation is constantly changing and customer feedback has proven vital in keeping the guide up to date. Photographs are essential because they provide the supporting evidence we need to confirm that your submissions are accurate. The truth is that Submissions without photos are like reading a book in the dark. Filling in a submission form onsite is best practice because you are unlikely to remember everything, however it is essential that you record GPS coordinates onsite. The best way to keep an accurate record is with your digital camera by following this photographic checklist.

Take photos of the:

- Parking area from several angles
- Surrounding area from several angles
- Service Point showing all working parts/sides
- Close-up of the payment slot to identify token or payment type.
- Close-up of the electricity points and trip-switches to identify plug type and amperage
- Designation signs and information boards, including close-ups of text.
- Also take GPS coordinates onsite

Please name photos by the town name, region, and the person's name to be credited if they are published.

You can submit your text and digital photos online at www.All-the-Aires.co.uk/submissions.shtml. We cannot process printed photos, but they are still useful as record shots.
If you have lots of submissions and photos burn them to disk and post them to:
Vicarious Media, Unit 1, North Close Business Centre, Folkestone, CT20 3UH.

Considerable thanks go to the Aire Heads who have provided photographs and information about the Aires they have visited. Some of the Aire Heads are listed below:

Alan Potter, Carol Weaver, Chris and Angela Irving, Chris Partington, David Hayward, Alistair MacFadyen, Jean and Ken Fowler, Pete and Niki Warnes, Patricia and Geoff Houghton, Geoffrey Hyde Fynn, M A Godfrey, Kevin and Gwyneth Holley, R Allen, Harold Meads, Andrew Shribman, Alan Kirk, Alastair Hibbert, Alison Standring, Anita Norman, Ann Beck, Brenda and Maurice Cope, T Ball, Bob Palt, Ann Bowers, Chris Foreman, Robert Cooper, Colin Salter, Darren Cooke, Dave Wybrow, Deb Cox, Derek Smith, John Dunn, Elizabeth O'Leary, Frank Butler, Andy Braunston, Gwyneth and Bill Scott, Graham Baldock, Glenys Swatman, Richard Hall, Ian and Janet Wallace, Ian Coull, Ian Lones, Ian Mathison, John Knox, John Ridd, John Reynold, Karen Farmer, Keith Taylor, Kim Ivory, Lee Hart, Elizabeth Cook, Margaret Dean and Dixie, Anna Mills, Mervyn Kettle, Michael and Julie Rollison, Mick Bartle, Mike Crampton, Martin and Joanne Rennie, Maureen and David Abbott, Hans Modder, Paul Prebble, Paula Lasse, Pauline and Robert Hardy, Penny Reynolds, Peter Swann, Peter Skynner, Phil Wilde, Mul Mullarkey, Phil and Julie Hutchins, Jean Dew, Robert Brown, Robert Horan, Jenny Jones, Richard Mantle, Rodney Martin, Sue James, Martin Newey, Martin Grimes, Colin Simcox, Sarah Jamieson, Peter Skynner, Simon Piron, Steve Howard, Sue Procter, Sue Cartlidge, Sue Procter, Trevor Mace, M Ward, Roy and Wendy Manning, Colin Simcox, Carol Pardy, Fatima Rosales Naya, Linda and Mike Reading.

Please use this form to update Aires information in this guide. If the Aire is already listed, complete only the sections where changes apply. Please write in capital letters and circle appropriate symbols.

Town/Village:

Region:

Road name/number:

Date Visited:

Surroundings:

⚓ Coastal	🌲 Rural	🚜 Farm	SKI Ski resort	⛵ Marina
🏛 Residential	🏭 Village	🏃 Park	☼ Day parking	! Warning
🏢 Urban	⛴ Riverside or lakeside	⛺ Campsite	T Tourism	R Recommended

Please circle 1 or more symbols as appropriate

Page Number: Postcode – if known:

🚐 Number of Spaces:

Time limit: Cost:

Parking symbols:

🌐 Overnight parking possible	🚐 Hard surface	🚌 Large motorhomes
P Designated motorhome parking	⛵ Sloping	F Free of charge
	🔦 Illuminated	❀ Open all year
	🎵 Noisy	

Please circle 1 or more symbols as appropriate

🪣 Service Point type: Cost:

Payment/Token type:

Sanitation symbols:

🚰 Water	E Electric hook up	🚿 Showers
▥ Grey water disposal	WC Toilets	F Free of charge
⌷ Toilet disposal	♿ Disabled toilet	🚿 Showers

Please circle 1 or more symbols as appropriate

Leisure Information Symbols:

SP Shaded parking	🎱 Boules	🦆 Bird watching
🌳 Green space suitable for dogs/children	🚶 Walking - path or trail	⛷ Ski downhill
🎋 Picnic tables/benches	🚴 Marked cycle route	⛷ Ski cross country
🧗 Children's play area	🎣 Fishing	
	🚣 Boating (unmotorised)	

Please circle 1 or more symbols as appropriate

Please turn over

AIRE/LPG SUBMISSION FORM

Directions - Brief, specific directions to Aire/LPG:

GPS Coordinates:

Information - Brief description of location and amenities:

Name and email or address - so information can be credited:

Your feedback is vital to keep this guide up to date. Fill in this form whilst you are at the Aire. Please name photos with the town name, region, and the name you want credited if they are published. Please submit your text and digital photos online at **www.All-the-Aires.co.uk/submissions.shtml** or post your completed forms and CDs of photos to **Vicarious Media, Unit 1, North Close Business Centre, Folkestone, CT20 3UH.** You can print off more forms at **www.All-the-Aires.co.uk**

Please include at least five photos showing the parking area in different directions and close-ups of any signs. Photograph the service point showing working parts, and the token slot, so that we may identify the token type, don't forget the grey drain. Submissions without photos are like reading a book in the dark. We cannot process printed photos, but they are still useful as record shots.

Thank you very much for your time.

By supplying details and photographs you are giving unrestricted publication and reproduction rights to Vicarious Media.

Please use this form to update Aires information in this guide. If the Aire is already listed, complete only the sections where changes apply. Please write in capital letters and circle appropriate symbols.

Town/Village:

Region:

Road name/number:

Date Visited:

Surroundings:

Coastal	Rural	Farm	SKI Ski resort	Marina
Residential	Village	Park	Day parking	! Warning
Urban	Riverside or lakeside	Campsite	T Tourism	R Recommended

Please circle 1 or more symbols as appropriate

Page Number: Postcode – if known:

Number of Spaces:

Time limit: Cost:

Parking symbols:

Overnight parking possible	Hard surface	Large motorhomes
Designated motorhome parking	Sloping	F Free of charge
P	Illuminated	Open all year
	Noisy	

Please circle 1 or more symbols as appropriate

Service Point type: Cost:

Payment/Token type:

Sanitation symbols:

Water	E Electric hook up	Showers
Grey water disposal	WC Toilets	F Free of charge
Toilet disposal	Disabled toilet	Showers

Please circle 1 or more symbols as appropriate

Leisure Information Symbols:

SP Shaded parking	Boules	Bird watching
Green space suitable for dogs/children	Walking - path or trail	Ski downhill
Picnic tables/benches	Marked cycle route	Ski cross country
Children's play area	Fishing	
	Boating (unmotorised)	

Please circle 1 or more symbols as appropriate

Please turn over

AIRE/LPG SUBMISSION FORM

Directions - Brief, specific directions to Aire/LPG:

....

....

....

....

GPS Coordinates:

....

Information - Brief description of location and amenities:

....

....

....

....

Name and email or address - so information can be credited:

....

....

....

....

Your feedback is vital to keep this guide up to date. Fill in this form whilst you are at the Aire. Please name photos with the town name, region, and the name you want credited if they are published. Please submit your text and digital photos online at **www.All-the-Aires.co.uk/submissions.shtml** or post your completed forms and CDs of photos to **Vicarious Media, Unit 1, North Close Business Centre, Folkestone, CT20 3UH.** You can print off more forms at **www.All-the-Aires.co.uk**

Please include at least five photos showing the parking area in different directions and close-ups of any signs. Photograph the service point showing working parts, and the token slot, so that we may identify the token type, don't forget the grey drain. Submissions without photos are like reading a book in the dark. We cannot process printed photos, but they are still useful as record shots.

Thank you very much for your time.

By supplying details and photographs you are giving unrestricted publication and reproduction rights to Vicarious Media.

Please use this form to update Aires information in this guide. If the Aire is already listed, complete only the sections where changes apply. Please write in capital letters and circle appropriate symbols.

Town/Village:

Region:

Road name/number:

Date Visited:

Surroundings:

⚓ Coastal	🌳 Rural	🚜 Farm	SKI Ski resort	⛵ Marina
🏛 Residential	🏭 Village	🏃 Park	☀ Day parking	! Warning
🏢 Urban	🚣 Riverside or lakeside	⛺ Campsite	T Tourism	R Recommended

Please circle 1 or more symbols as appropriate

Page Number: Postcode – if known:

🚐 Number of Spaces:

Time limit: Cost:

Parking symbols:

◑ Overnight parking possible	🚐 Hard surface	🚌 Large motorhomes
P Designated motorhome parking	⬒ Sloping	F Free of charge
	⚱ Illuminated	✿ Open all year
	♫ Noisy	

Please circle 1 or more symbols as appropriate

🪣 Service Point type: Cost:

Payment/Token type:

Sanitation symbols:

🚰 Water	E Electric hook up	⚲ Showers
🛢 Grey water disposal	WC Toilets	F Free of charge
🚽 Toilet disposal	♿ Disabled toilet	▣ Showers

Please circle 1 or more symbols as appropriate

Leisure Information Symbols:

SP Shaded parking	⊡ Boules	🦆 Bird watching
🌳 Green space suitable for dogs/children	🚶 Walking - path or trail	⛷ Ski downhill
🏕 Picnic tables/benches	🚲 Marked cycle route	🎿 Ski cross country
🧗 Children's play area	🎣 Fishing	
	🚣 Boating (unmotorised)	

Please circle 1 or more symbols as appropriate

Please turn over

AIRE/LPG SUBMISSION FORM

Directions - Brief, specific directions to Aire/LPG:

....

....

....

....

....

GPS Coordinates:

....

Information - Brief description of location and amenities:

....

....

....

....

....

Name and email or address - so information can be credited:

....

....

....

....

Your feedback is vital to keep this guide up to date. Fill in this form whilst you are at the Aire. Please name photos with the town name, region, and the name you want credited if they are published. Please submit your text and digital photos online at **www.All-the-Aires.co.uk/submissions.shtml** or post your completed forms and CDs of photos to **Vicarious Media, Unit 1, North Close Business Centre, Folkestone, CT20 3UH.** You can print off more forms at **www.All-the-Aires.co.uk**

Please include at least five photos showing the parking area in different directions and close-ups of any signs. Photograph the service point showing working parts, and the token slot, so that we may identify the token type, don't forget the grey drain. Submissions without photos are like reading a book in the dark. We cannot process printed photos, but they are still useful as record shots.

Thank you very much for your time.

By supplying details and photographs you are giving unrestricted publication and reproduction rights to Vicarious Media.

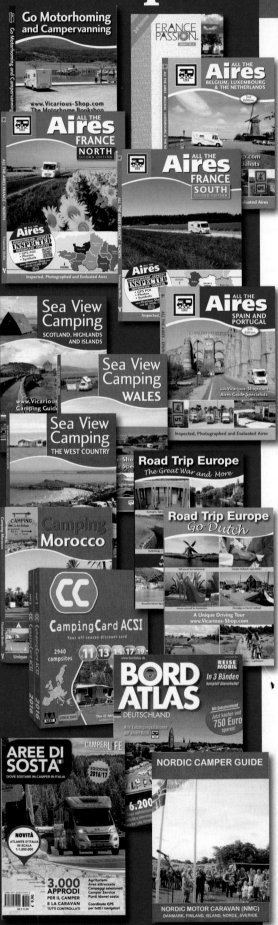

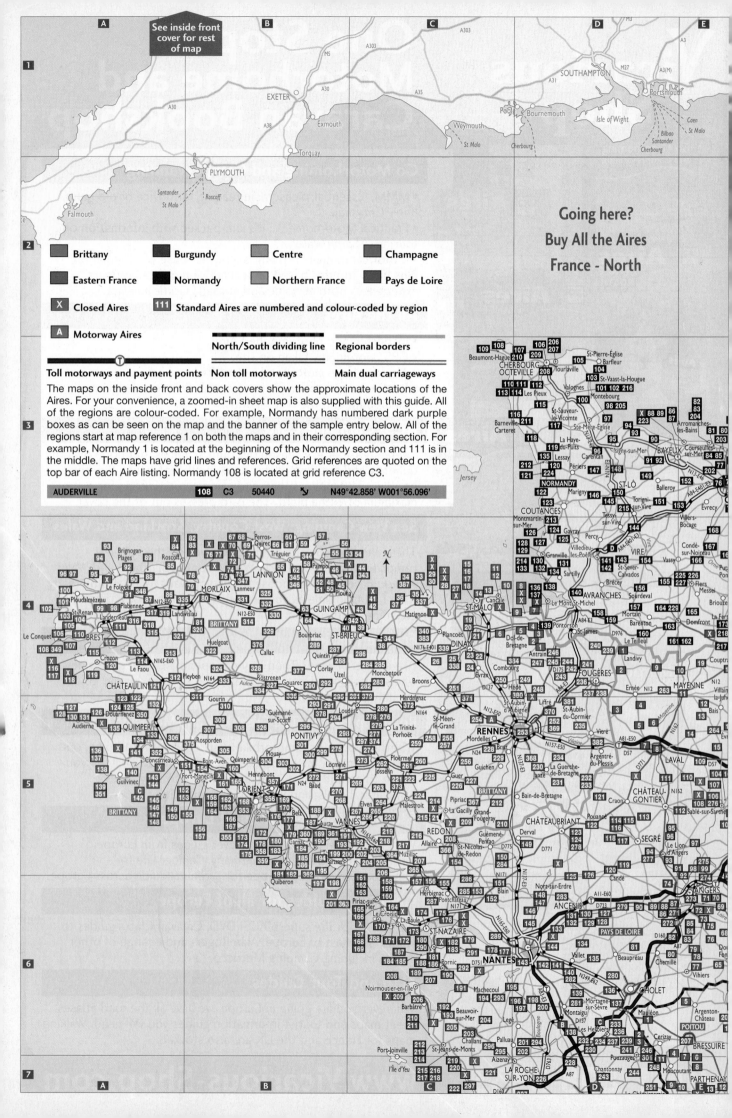

See inside front cover for rest of map

Going here?
Buy All the Aires
France - North

Brittany · Burgundy · Centre · Champagne · Eastern France · Normandy · Northern France · Pays de Loire

X Closed Aires

111 Standard Aires are numbered and colour-coded by region

A Motorway Aires

North/South dividing line · Regional borders

Toll motorways and payment points · Non toll motorways · Main dual carriageways

The maps on the inside front and back covers show the approximate locations of the Aires. For your convenience, a zoomed-in sheet map is also supplied with this guide. All of the regions are colour-coded. For example, Normandy has numbered dark purple boxes as can be seen on the map and the banner of the sample entry below. All of the regions start at map reference 1 on both the maps and in their corresponding section. For example, Normandy 1 is located at the beginning of the Normandy section and 111 is in the middle. The maps have grid lines and references. Grid references are quoted on the top bar of each Aire listing. Normandy 108 is located at grid reference C3.

| AUDERVILLE | 108 | C3 | 50440 | ⚓ | N49°42.858' W001°56.096' |